Global Operations and Logistics

♦♦♦

Text and Cases

Global Operations and Logistics

◆ ◆ ◆

Text and Cases

Philippe-Pierre Dornier

École Supérieure des Sciences Economiques et Commerciales
Groupe ESSEC
France

Ricardo Ernst

Georgetown University
School of Business
USA

Michel Fender

École des Ponts
France

Panos Kouvelis

Washington University
Olin School of Business
USA

JOHN WILEY & SONS, INC.

New York   Chichester   Brisbane   Toronto   Singapore   Weinheim

Photo Insets: Courtesy Bose Corporation
Background: © Intek Imagineering/Master file

ACQUISITIONS EDITOR	Beth L. Golub
MARKETING MANAGER	Leslie Hines
PRODUCTION EDITOR	Kelly Tavares
TEXT DESIGNER	Nancy Fields
COVER DESIGNER	Laura Boucher
ILLUSTRATION COORDINATOR	Anna Melhorn

This book was set in Times Roman by Carlisle Communications and printed and bound by Hamilton Press. The cover was printed by Lehigh Press.

This book is printed on acid-free paper.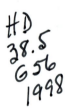

The paper in this book was manufactured by a mill whose forest management programs include sustained yield harvesting of its timberlands. Sustained yield harvesting principles ensure that the numbers of trees cut each year does not exceed the amount of new growth.

0-471-12036-7

Printed in the United States of America

10 9 8 7 6 5 4 3 2

About the Authors

◆ ◆ ◆

Philippe-Pierre Dornier has a master's degree in Engineering from École des Mines, an ESSEC degree (Graduate School MBA), and a PhD from École des Mines de Paris. He is currently a Professor in Logistics and Production at ESSEC. He was in charge of the postgraduate programs from 1992 to 1995. In 1993, Professor Dornier created the Institute des Hautes Études Logistiques (IHEL) which is sponsored by companies like, France Télécom, La Poste, Andersen Consulting, DHL, Tailleur Industrie, CAT, Fret SNCF. Professor Dornier has been and currently is involved in several studies: logistics impacts of the Chunnel, how to manage the interface between logistics and marketing, military logistics in France, how to manage third party logistics, and a comparative study in the field of spare parts distribution. He is the editor of the Cahier de l'IHEL.

He was Associate Dean of the Master's in Management and Engineering Logistics from 1989 to 1996. Today, he is in charge of the Executive Program at ESSEC and is Scientific Director of IHEL. He has consulted with numerous companies including France Télécom, Michelin, Rexel, Seita and is associated with the logistics group work of the French army. His activities as consultant have allowed Professor Dornier to work on logistics strategy and on physical distribution organization at the French, the European and the worldwide scale. He is currently a managing partner of Newton-Vaurial and Co. He is also author and co-author of two books on logistics.

Ricardo Ernst is an Associate Professor of Operations Management at the Georgetown University School of Business. He holds a Civil Engineering degree from the Universidad Católica Andrés Bello and an MBA from the Instituto de Estudios Superiores de Administración, both in Venezuela. He received an MA degree and his PhD in Operations Management from the Wharton School, University of Pennsylvania. He is currently the co-director of the Global Logistics Research Program at Georgetown University School of Business. Through this program, he has worked with Black & Decker, Xerox, and Ryder Dedicated Logistics among others.

He spent his sabbatical year 1993–94 in France as a Visiting Professor in the Department of Logistics and Production at the École Supérieure des Sciences Économiques et Commerciales (ESSEC), and as a Visiting Professor in the Department of Industrial Management and Logistics at the Institute de Haute Études Commerciales (Groupe HEC). In both institutions he did research and taught courses in the area global logistics. One of the projects he worked on was done in collaboration with the French train company SNCF, which evaluated the logistics impact of opening the channel tunnel in Europe. His research interests include strategic analysis of logistics systems (supplier-manufacturing-distribution linkages) at both macro (strategic positioning of logistics, marketing/manufacturing interfaces) and micro level (models and methods for inventory control, inventory classification procedures).

He has consulted with several national and international firms, including General Motors, CASE Corporation, Fairchild Industries, and Fritz Companies. His contributions have appeared in several journals, including *Management Science, Interfaces, European Journal of Operational Research, Transportation Science, IIE Transactions, Naval Research Logistics, Journal of Operations Management, Journal of the Operational Research Society, International Journal of Operations and Production Management.* Dr. Ernst is a member of INFORMS, Council of Logistics Management, POMS, and APICS, and is in the Editorial Review Board of *Production and Operations Management* and *the Journal of Global Information Management.* He is a frequent speaker in international conferences and executive seminars.

Michel Fender received his degree in Agronomy Engineering from the *Institut National Agronomique Paris-Grignon.* He has an MBA from *HEC-ISA* and a Ph.D. from *Ecole Nationale des Ponts et Chaussees.* He is currently Professor of Global Logistics and Vice-President of the Master's in International Business at *Ecole Nationale des Ponts et Chaussees, the MBA des Ponts* in France. Through this program he teaches logistics and manufacturing strategy not only in France, but in Argentina, the United Kingdom, India, Japan, and several Carribean nations as well. His research focuses on logistics cooperation in supply chains.

While at ESSEC Business School, Professor Fender was director of the Master's in Purchasing Management Program from 1993 to 1996 and director of the Master's in Management and Engineering Logistics from 1996 to 1997. He collaborated in the creation of the IHEL (*Institut des Hautes Etudes Logistiques*). Professor Fender frequently teaches logistics and general management in various executive programs. He is an experienced consultant, working in fields ranging from the automotive components, food, and pharmaceutical industries to the French Army.

Panos Kouvelis is currently a Professor of Operations and Manufacturing Management at the Olin School of Business at Washington University in St. Louis. He received his PhD in Industrial Engineering and Engineering Management at Stanford University, MBA and MS in Industrial and Systems Engineering at the University of Southern California, and a diploma in Mechanical Engineering at the National Technical University of Athens. He has previously taught at the Fuqua School of Business, Duke University and the Management Department of the University of Texas at Austin. He teaches courses in Global Operations and Logistics, Operations Strategy and Operations Management. He has received numerous teaching awards and has been frequently mentioned as a top operations management professor in surveys of top MBA programs by *Business Week.* He often teaches in executive management programs and offers short customized courses to interested companies. He currently teaches in the Executive Master's in Manufacturing Management at The Olin School of Business.

He is an accomplished and prolific researcher, ranked in the top ten operations management researchers in terms of research productivity and quality (recent survey *in Journal of Operations Management*). His research interests include global supply chain management, manufacturing strategy, the study of marketing/manufacturing interfaces, project management, scheduling of operations, process reengineering and layout design. He has published over forty articles *in Management Science, Operations Research, Naval Research Logistics, IIE Transactions, Production and Operations Management, Journal of Operations Management, European Journal of Operations Research, Operations Research Letters, Journal of Operational Research Society* and other high quality academic journals. He also frequently contributes chapters in edited books on global supply chain management and optimization issues. He currently serves as Department Editor of *Project Selection, Coordination and Management of IIE Transactions,* as associate editor of *Supply Chain Management Issues of Management Science,* and is on the editorial review board of *POMS* and *MSOM.* In the past he edited special issues for *the Journal of Global Optimization* and the *Journal of Intelligent Manufacturing.* His book on Robust Discrete Optimization was published in 1997 by Kluwer. He has consulted with IBM, Dell Computers, Hanes, Duke Hospital and Reckitt & Colman on supply chain, operations scheduling and manufacturing system design issues.

Preface

◆ ◆ ◆

Background

One of the authors was invited to spend his sabbatical year in France in 1993, where among other things, he was supposed to teach "Logistics in the U.S." It was a very interesting proposition, since the expectation was to teach the French students what American companies are doing in the area of logistics. After discussing with the French the content of the potential syllabus, we discovered we were not speaking the same language (i.e., in addition to the French-English complication). The first conflict was with definitions; the American definition of logistics was basically limited to include transportation, warehouse management, and inventory control. All the notions about integration of marketing and manufacturing, sourcing alternatives, and supply chain management, were parts of operations. In Europe, logistics also covers the role of the American operations. That is when the concept of putting our ideas together in the form of a book was born. We agreed that there is no such thing as American operations and European logistics. We also discovered that there was an urgent need to consolidate our experiences and define what we called global operations and logistics. We spent many hours debating what would be a coherent way to deliver the message to our audience, i.e., a global individual. The result is this book which offers, we believe, not only the opportunity of comparing what is happening in Europe relative to the U.S. and vice versa, but also to compare the perspectives taken by the two geographically separated worlds.

The French team had a very interesting set of cases that were new and refreshing because they illustrated situations that, even though familiar in the underlying generality of the operations and logistics problem, they were very specific to the realities of Europe. The American team had a set of cases that were also new because of the novelty of the issues discussed. The combination resulted in a refreshing set of cases that go beyond the typical cases currently available for studying operations and logistics.

Potential Courses

The world is becoming more and more a global marketplace. Geographical boundaries are disappearing and the expectation is that managers must be prepared to face the realities of this new challenge. That is why new courses with a global and/or an international orientation are now being introduced in many business schools. This book is useful for any course that covers global and/or international operations and/or logistics. Based on our description above, we have established throughout the book the importance of linking the two concepts of operations and logistics to address the fundamental issue of managing flows of products, services, and information.

The book takes a very strategic view of the operations and logistics problem. Even though we are aware of the importance of linking analytical skills with strategic thinking, it would be very difficult to cover both in detail. In addition, the complexities of the global environment are still developing. At this point, there is an urgent need for developing frameworks that would help in the thinking process. We do, however, offer specific guidelines that would guide the interested reader in the direction of finding more analytical material. The instructor's manual presents in detail how to break down the different sections to cover different topics. One of the most important features of the book is that you don't need to follow it in a linear form (i.e., from Chapters 1 to 12) to get the message. Different alternatives are possible to cover a full semester, as well as short elective courses. As described below, we introduce a generic syllabus for the entire book and many alternatives. Samples of our current syllabus will also be provided.

Organization of the Book

Obviously, there are many different approaches that could be taken to understand the complexities of the issues involved in managing and coping with the global environment of business. One of the main features of the book is that it allows the reader to decide what chapters are relevant to the topic he or she is addressing. In that sense, we have maintained a flow that goes from Global Operations and Logistics *Strategies* in Part I, to the Global Operations and Logistics *Planning* in Part II, and finally the *Management* of Global Operations and Logistics in Part III. The rationale for this flow in presentation is the following: companies first decide how to evaluate the potential strategies available for managing the overall logistics system available. This involves understanding the possible options and deciding where and what to do in aggregate terms. Once the strategy is defined, the next step is planning how to use that system just designed through the strategy. Simply, it involves using the available facilities and players in a more efficient way. No new decisions about increasing capacity or finding new locations is made since those decisions were made at the strategic level. The main output of this step is to plan how to use the logistics system. Finally, once that the plan is made, the next step is to execute and manage to make sure that the plan was the correct one, and at the same time, collect feedback for the next iteration of strategic thinking.

In Part I we introduce the general framework for understanding the issues related to global operations and logistics. We start with motivation about the importance and salience of the topics that are illustrated with figures from different countries. We also talk about the evolution of global flows, logistics as a source of service for managing global flows, the impact of external forces on the definition of an appropriate strategy for globalization, and some basic principles of designing the global operations network. Chapters 2 to 4 go into the details of developing strategies for the global operations and marketing issues. We introduce a definition of competitive priorities and the implications of their linkage with the current financial indicators. We also discuss the strategy process formulations with an operations and logistics orientation. In Chapter 3 we introduce a conceptual framework and the driving forces behind the global operations process. Chapter 4 discusses in detail the available marketing strategies in the context of our global operations and logistics framework, such as global versus local marketing and the meaning of the global product. The cases come from a variety of places including Europe, Asia and America.

In Part II Chapter 5 begins with a discussion of the issues related to the inbound logistics operation, such as managing multiple suppliers and deciding about outsourcing. We offer a detailed framework for analyzing what should be outsourced and which vendors are more suitable partners. Chapter 6 gets into the other side of the logistics system which we call outbound logistics. Issues about centralization and decentralization of the distribution function are discussed in detail, including the current utilization of logistics providers or third party logistics. In Chapter 7 we discuss the problems of demand volatility, information distortion and the bullwhip effect in supply chains. We also address the problem of going from a domestic to a global supply chain and the issue of vertical integration in supply chains.

Chapter 8 deals with the problem of global logistics design for global operations. We discuss how to configure a global logistics network as a function of the level of outsourcing and postponement in satisfying the final demand. A framework is introduced to explain the different orientations that facilities might have according to the market, the product, or the technology process they want to use. Finally, issues of capacity expansion and new product allocation to existing network of facilities is discussed and illustrated with examples.

Chapter 9 discusses one of the most current topics in global operations and logistics: risk management in global operations. We spend a significant part of the chapter explaining the concept of operating exposure as it is affected by the exchange rate risk, which is one of the most underestimated factors in analyzing global markets. We discuss the mix of financial and operational hedging as an innovative strategy for benefiting the corporation over the long run in relation to sourcing strategies. Specific price strategies for exporting firms and detailed micro and macro strategies are defined and illustrated with examples. Each chapter in Part II of the book has cases to illustrate and discuss the different points presented.

Part III deals with the effective management of global operations and logistics. We start in Chapter 10 with the critical issue of information management. Specific emphasis is given to the definition of a truly global information system with its required capabilities and limitations. Chapter 11 gets into performance measurement and evaluation in global operations. We elaborate on the appropriate metrics to be used when dealing with a global network in order to capture the required integrated nature of the process. In this chapter we also discuss how to measure the performance and value added by logistics providers. Finally, Chapter 12 discusses the organizational structures for global logistics excellence. Given the required interrelations among multiple companies, we explore in detail the organizational implications of sectorial logistics cooperation. We conclude by discussing the difficulties of accomplishing efficiency on the geographically dispersed organizations. Cases in Part III of the book highlight the points mentioned, including international service operations and the evaluation of performance for various facilities in global networks.

Each of the chapters within the sections covers specific topics that are illustrated with multiple cases. We didn't want to limit the cases to illustrate a specific situation. In fact, most chapters have more than one case that illustrates the approach used in a specific context. The cases should be used for illustration purposes. There is no case that can cover all situations. We are very aware of that through our teaching experience, and that is why we strongly believe that the text portion of the book will be instrumental in broadening the situations illustrated by the cases into more generic situations.

We present the material in the order described, but we are confident that the material can be used in many different orders. Then for example, to cover the new ideas related to supply chain management and the relationship with operational hedging (a very current topic), Chapters 7 and 9 would be very relevant. To discuss the issues of new product development and the interaction with the logistics infrastructure, Chapters 3 and 8 address them directly. Obviously, Chapters 1 and 2 are basic, since they introduce the basic framework for understanding the overall complexity of the global operations and logistics problem.

Instructor's Manual

The four of us have taught courses related to global operations and logistics. The instructor's manual will cover in detail how to use this book through a syllabus designed to cover each chapter. This general syllabus presents how to use the entire book, including the reading per session and the suggested cases to be used. In each session, we provide suggested cases and an additional case for those occasions where the instructor wants a longer session on a topic or for offering variety. A detailed teaching note that describes the content, message and best pedagogical approach for each case. We will also illustrate, through the general syllabus, how to develop shorter courses to emphasize particular topics. Samples of our current syllabus will also be included.

Our philosophy, as we said before, is that there is not a single case that is capable of illustrating or covering all the issues. Therefore, for each of the potential sessions to be covered, we provide some of the lecture material that we have used in our current classes. Then for example, in Chapter 4 we offer as supporting material, some lectures on choice of international entry mode and countertrade in international operations. We also include materials on the *maquiladora* effect before and after NAFTA, how the volatile exchange rates can put operations at risk, internationalization of services, etc. This material is provided as samples of the overheads we currently use.

We also plan to offer a yearly seminar where faculty willing to participate will learn how to teach global operations and logistics. In the seminar, we will provide a life delivery of some of the cases, plus details about what is covered in the book.

◆ ACKNOWLEDGMENTS

This book is the result of a close collaboration of four faculty members from different academic institutions and different geographical areas. Given the topic of the book, we should be masters of managing the operations and logistics of such a global project. We are indebted to technology (e-mail, fax and phone) for allowing communication and exchanges of information to be made easier. The most challenging problem has been the language barrier; as many of us know, people write and communicate easier in their native language, especially if that is still your main language.

This book is the result of our joint efforts, the writing proceeded in both French (the "French team" and English (the "American team"). What a challenge! Operations and logistics is an easy task relative to developing a manuscript that would have a consistent style and flow of ideas. In that sense, we are profoundly indebted to Lisa Harrington and Joan Kalkut. Lisa for accepting to help with the editing of a project where she could not see the scope and still continue with it. Joan, for her endless patience, incredible organization skills, and willingness to even consult a French dictionary to make sure all the words made sense. She really helped by continuously asking the right questions about content, message and presentation.

Special thanks go to Drhuva Banerjee, who significantly helped develop the material presented in Chapters 5 and 8. Many of the ideas presented were discussed during his tenure at ESSEC and while working with one of the authors.

We want to thank all the students in the different schools where we have taught this material (ESSEC, Duke University, Georgetown University, HEC, Washington University in St. Louis, WHU in Germany, IML in Switzerland) for bearing with us through the development of these ideas and for the positive reaction and helpful feedback we have tried to incorporate into our thinking.

One of the salient advantages of the book is the close relationship with real problems. This book is about problems faced by real companies and not merely theoretical constructs. Many of the topics covered in the book have been studied through discussions with companies associated within the IHEL (Institute for High Studies in Logistics) at ESSEC. Particularly, we would like to acknowledge the founding members of IHEL: DHL, La Poste, France Telecom, Tailleur Industrie, CAT, Andersen Consulting, Fret SNCF and the ESSEC Group.

The discovery of many concepts was stimulated by discussions with Michelin. We participated in the restructuring of its logistics evolution in Europe and throughout the world. More particularly, we would like to acknowledge Gilles Deraison, Worldwide Logistics Manager of Michelin, Gerard Serre, Logistics Manager of Yoplait, Gerard Aube, Logistics Manager of La Scad, Didier Warkol, Logistics Manager of Metro, Frederic Lecomte of Essilor, and Jean-Dominique Bosq, ICI US Logistics Manager.

We also want to acknowledge the contribution of Fritz Companies for the opportunity of exploring in detail the issues faced by a truly global logistics provider. In particular, Lynn A. Fritz whose vision and understanding of the global operations and logistics issues brought a reality check to many of the frameworks in the book.

Georgetown University School of Business has been a particularly supportive institution. Through the Program for the Study of Global Logistics that one of the authors co-directs, we had the opportunity to discover and develop important ideas. In particular, both member companies and people including Black & Decker, Xerox, and Ryder Dedicated Logistics, Ken Homa, John Clendenin, Peter Peck, and Terry Goodwin have contributed in a special manner.

We are grateful to the reviewers of this text, Fred Raafat, San Diego State University, Marilyn Helms, University of Tennessee at Chattanooga, and Kaylan Singhal, University of Baltimore for their insightful comments and constructive criticisms.

The Wiley team was also very helpful. Our editor Beth Golub believed in the project from the very beginning and helped through the process of ups and downs to make sure that we stayed the course and within the planned timetable. Kelly Tavares and the production team have been extremely helpful by guiding us through the process in a very organized and timely manner.

We would like to thank our families in a very special manner. The problem with four authors is that listing all family members (including pets) would require another book. We sincerely thank our families for all they have done to make this book possible.

Doubtless, we are forgetting many people that one way or another helped with the project. In particular, our colleagues in the different universities, but as with the family problem, four authors are in itself too many colleagues. We apologize to them in writing and promise to tell the world who they are. Finally, thanks to the world for being *Global*!

Contents

◆ ◆ ◆

Introduction to Global Operations and Logistics

◆ ◆ ◆

Business today is set in a global environment. This global environment is forcing companies, regardless of their location or primary market base, to consider the rest of the world in their competitive strategy analysis. Firms cannot isolate themselves from or ignore external factors such as economic trends, competitive situations, or technology innovation in other countries if some of their competitors are competing or are located in those countries. Nowadays, it is not uncommon for a company to develop a new product in the United States, manufacture it in Asia, and sell it in Europe.

Until recently, many firms focused their attention on marketing, finance, and production functions. Such an attitude is justified to a certain degree, because if a firm cannot produce and sell its products, little else matters. However, this approach fails to recognize the importance of the *activities that must occur between* points and times of production (supply) and points and times of purchase of the product (demand). These are the *operations* and *logistics activities*. They affect the efficiency and effectiveness of both marketing and production. They affect the nature and timing of a company's cash flows, and finally, they affect the firm's profitability.

Today's global environment is characterized by substantial wage–rate differentials, expanding foreign markets, high-speed information links, and improved transportation. As a result, efficiency barriers of time and space between countries are breaking down. Operations and logistics functions necessarily must adopt a global dimension. In fact, global operations and logistics are responses to the increasing integration of international markets as firms try to remain competitive.

The emphasis of this book is on corporations that source, produce, distribute, and market in multiple nations and compete in a *global* arena. The management of operations and logistics in these global firms differs from that in their domestic counterparts along several key dimensions. First, global firms must be able to identify and analyze factors that differ across nations that influence the effectiveness of the *operations* function. These include worker productivity, process adaptability, governmental concerns, transportation availability, culture, and so on. In addition, because of the distances involved, transportation and distribution are of greater significance, so the *logistics* function's efficiency has greater impact on the firm's profitability. Finally, these geographically dispersed sets of facilities and markets must be integrated and managed to enhance the strategy of the business unit. In this context, the logistics function, because of its integrating role, attains strategic importance.

This book addresses the differences between local and global operations. It emphasizes the need for cross-functional decision making in order to meet the managerial challenges of

1

the twenty-first century inherent in managing across national boundaries. The book presents recent data on the operations and logistics of global firms and illustrates themes with case studies from countries in different continents including North and South America, Europe, Asia, and Africa. The collaborative effort of four authors from geographically dispersed universities offers the opportunity to combine ideas, knowledge and perspectives from different environments.

The book is written from the perspective of the director of operations and/or logistics, vice-president of operations and/or logistics, or other senior level managers with primary responsibility for the production and distribution of manufactured products. It delves into the notion that sourcing, manufacturing, and distribution are of primary importance in the formulation of business and corporate strategy. We look at the strategic decisions within operations and logistics as they impact the ability of the firm to achieve its selected overall strategies. Chapters cover global manufacturing strategies, including development and implementation; global operations planning, including global sourcing and logistics; logistics issues for exporters and importers; international facility location; and global operations and logistics management, including organizing multiplants, offshore operations, and performance evaluation. By analyzing actual cases, problems, and examples set in "foreign" countries or involving firms competing in global markets, the book exposes readers to the critical issues of global operations and logistics.

◆ GLOBAL OPERATIONS AND LOGISTICS DEFINED

The trend toward an integrated world economy and global competitive arena is forcing companies to develop strategies for designing products for a global market and maximizing the firm's resources in producing them. Planning and operating in the global arena requires new management skills—for example, developing a truly global network of warehouses, distribution centers, and consolidation points; optimizing multiple transport service types; and designing information and communication systems that integrate the supply chain.

Companies also must foster appropriate managerial skills to assess problems and opportunities derived from sourcing internationally. Fluctuating exchange rates, risky inflationary conditions in many countries, hidden costs of international sourcing (e.g., unreliable supply and infrastructure networks), inventory positioning trade-offs, differences in operations effectiveness and efficiency among global vendors—all of these factors generate risk and uncertainty that must be managed. As a knowledge area, global operations and logistics attempts to teach the concepts and skills needed to address this management challenge.

Global operations is the process of planning, implementing, and controlling the flow and storage of raw materials, in-process inventory, finished goods, and related information from point of origin to point of consumption for the purposes of satisfying global customer requirements while efficiently using the firm's global resources.

Logistics is the management of flows between marketing, and production. The functionally oriented approach to organization structure arbitrarily separates a firm's activities into a limited number of organizational divisions. The logistics process cuts across all functional areas, thus creating important interfaces. Managing the activities of one function alone can produce suboptimal performance. It subordinates broader company goals to the goals of the individual function. To manage the interface activities effectively, some mechanism for encouraging cooperation among the functions must be established. It is the premise of this book that the global operations and logistics functions should play a preeminent role in managing these interfaces.

Just as companies ignore external factors and competition at their own peril, companies cannot isolate the decision process of the different functional areas when trying to design and manage product/service processes across functional areas. Every organization has to be analyzed as a system in which the different functional areas (e.g., marketing, operations, finance) and the different members (e.g., suppliers, manufacturers, retailers, customers, competition and governmental parties) are all interrelated. This book analyzes the global environment and the decision situations faced by a firm operating in it from this *systems* perspective.

◆ OBJECTIVES OF THE BOOK

The objective of this book is to enable readers to do the following:

1. Develop an understanding of the state of the art of strategic management thinking as it applies to firms with global operations and logistics functions.
2. Develop a capacity for analyzing operations and logistics problems on a functional, business, and company-wide basis.
3. Develop an awareness of the organizational structures used in operations and logistics, and their strengths and weaknesses.
4. Develop an understanding of the key criteria utilized in multinational location site selection, global facilities configurations, and international sourcing networks' development.
5. Become acquainted with the realities of operating different types of production/distribution firms.
6. Consider a range of general management issues for handling individual operations and logistics decisions with a strategic point of view.
7. Gain an appreciation of the complexities associated with implementing changes in functional, business, and corporate strategies, and discuss approaches to handling such complexities within a global operations and logistics framework.

◆ HOW THE BOOK IS ORGANIZED

Global Operations and Logistics is organized into three main parts, described as follows.

Part I: Global Operations and Logistics Strategy

Part I covers chapters 1 to 4. We start the book with a chapter on the importance of global operations management and logistics. This chapter emphasizes the recent trends toward globalization of the operations and logistics functions, and explores the scope and character of international competition. It also discusses the differences between domestic and global operations, and looks at different ways to organize international production and distribution.

In Part I, we also introduce the main framework of analysis on which the book is based (illustrated in Figure 1). Four main external elements affect the development of the global operations and logistics process—market, competition, level of technology, and government regulation—all defined in detail in chapter 1. The global operations and logistics process will be defined as a three-step sequence: strategy, planning, and managing. We also define in detail all the activities involved in the global operations and logistics process of multinational corporations.

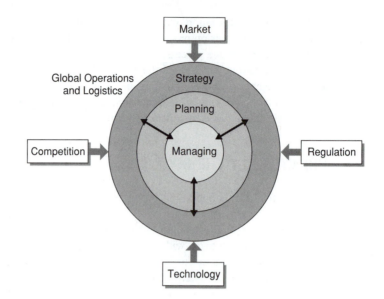

Figure 1   Global Operations and Logistics Process

Chapters 2 to 4 examine alternative strategies for competing in the global marketplace. The operations and logistics strategy is the sum of a number of separate decisions. These chapters outline potential implications of competing on product innovation, fast response, excellent customer service, and cost leadership for the structure of a company's logistics network. They also look at the decisions required to support the different strategies in each of the decision categories of the global operations and logistics strategy framework. Among the most innovative and contemporary topics addressed are the advantages of developing manufacturing facilities abroad, as well as the characteristics of products to be allocated to offshore facilities.

Part I also discusses the advantages and disadvantages of following a local versus a global approach to markets. It raises considerations of scale economies in international capacity expansion strategies and in logistics network development. The cases address issues of offshore manufacturing strategies, the relative merits of centralization versus decentralization in marketing, manufacturing, and purchasing, and of global capacity expansion and supply chain structure options.

Part II: Global Operations and Logistics Planning

Part II, chapters 5 to 9, discusses global purchasing and procurement policies and distribution planning and control systems, with particular emphasis on problems and opportunities derived from sourcing internationally. It looks at strategies for locating facilities in an international context, taking into account the challenges of dealing with multiple suppliers and the strategic decision of outsource.

Part II examines the entire global supply chain from suppliers to end users. It includes the interface between centralized and decentralized production and distribution networks. After dealing with the sourcing function, we focus on the distribution function by analyzing global distribution strategies and different types of supply chains, ranging from vertically integrated chains to those consisting of third-party logistics contractors, i.e., outsourcing the logistics function.

Finally, Part II addresses how global political, economic, social and government regulation issues differ from such issues in a domestic situation, and how they impact global operations and logistics. It discusses in detail the important complicating factors a firm needs to consider in assessing its operating exposure to real exchange rate shocks. It highlights the role of the supplier in the global operations context and the sourcing and distribution initiatives of successful global companies. The extensive number of cases included in Part II illustrate and discuss all the ideas presented in detail.

Part III: Effective Management of Global Operations and Logistics

Part III, chapters 10 to 12, examines the structure and coordination of international manufacturing, and distribution networks, and analyzes the management challenges inherent in their effective operation. Network centralization, *local presence* decisions, and various sourcing and distribution patterns are discussed, as are the coordination issues that arise in an international supply network. Critical to the way a sourcing and a logistics network functions is the use of information, experience and management planning, and control systems in controlling customer service. Part III topics include: vertical supplier relations, horizontal relations among different-country subsidiaries of a multinational corporation, customer service measurement, and traditional inventory–transportation service trade-offs in global distribution. Managing relationships within the global supply chain network so as to create value and eliminate waste is also emphasized. This section identifies productive opportunities for mutual benefits between customers and suppliers. It also discusses the problems of balancing global perspectives with local preferences.

Finally, the authors discuss work-force management and development in multinational companies, prevailing organizational structures in global logistics networks and typical forms of managerial control in global operations organizations. The case studies cited in this section point out issues in designing multiplant networks, evaluating the role and the performance of the various facilities in such networks, and coordinating manufacturing activities.

◆ ◆ ◆

Global Operations
and Logistics Strategies

Chapters 1 – 4

In the first part of this text, we examine alternative operations and logistics strategies for competing in the global marketplace. Consider the operations and logistics strategy as the combination of decision categories that go from the purchasing decisions to the definition of the network structure and the logistics organization to support it. We outline the most important decision categories that form the operations and logistics strategy, together with the main decision issues that fall within each category. We examine the implications of corporate competition (product innovation, fast response, excellent customer service, cost leadership) for the structure of your logistics network, along with the nature of decisions that support the different strategies in each of the decision categories of the global logistics strategy framework. We take a look at innovative and contemporary issues, such as the advantages of developing manufacturing facilities abroad and the characteristics of products allocated to offshore facilities. We compare local and global approaches to markets, presenting the advantages and disadvantages of each, and raise considerations of scale economies in international capacity expansion strategies and logistics network development. The cases in Part I address issues of offshore manufacturing strategies, relative merits of centralized or decentralized marketing/manufacturing/purchasing in an international organization, and global capacity expansion and supply chain structure options. ◆

Chapter 1

Global Operations and Logistics: Evolution and Design

◆ ◆ ◆

This chapter addresses the following key concepts:

◆ *The evolution of global flows*

◆ *Logistics as a source of service for managing global flows across the supply chain*

◆ *The impact of external factors on global flows*

◆ *Designing and managing appropriate flow paths*

◆ *Basic principles of global operations and logistics*

◆ FORCES OF GLOBALIZATION

Logistics and operations have never before played such an important role in business organizations. Changes in customers' expectations or geographical locations continually transform the nature of markets, and, in turn, generate constraints that modify the flows of goods within companies. Technological breakthroughs and emerging markets open up new ways of reorganizing, adapting, and optimizing the flow of raw materials, semifinished goods, products, spare parts, and recycled materials.

Traditionally, logistics and operations developed within geographical areas, and they were controlled by one functional area (i.e., marketing or production). The management of physical flows was defined by this restricted geographical area, and by a focus on meeting the needs of the controlling function.

Today, new pressures are defining the approaches and frameworks used by companies. These pressures include inventory duplication, physical incompatibility of logistics infra-structures, and the limited capacity of individual reaction to overall changes in the supply chain. The new approaches are significantly different from those that determined the old activities related to the physical flows. Conceptual and managerial tools now being applied to physical distribution management provide interesting solutions. These tools reflect a new vision for global operations/logistics.

Three main forces are at the root of this evolution:

1. The integration of internal functions—including physical distribution management, marketing, manufacturing, etc.—across the corporation
2. The increasing cooperation among the logistics and operations areas of the different members in the supply chain (sectorial integration)
3. The search for improved geographical integration, which goes beyond the traditional areas of economic activities to encompass the entire world as a source of customers, knowledge, technology, raw materials, and so on.

As you can see, a *global* approach clearly encompasses more than just geographical boundaries. This book will look at a new managerial approach to gaining competitive advantage through better understanding of global relationships.

Increasing product supply and improving product life-cycle management can only come about through interfunctional cooperation. Those who work in marketing, research and development, production, and purchasing acknowledge that thinking in terms of logistics and operations management allows them to better recognize conflicts or bottlenecks in the implementation of ideas. Managers in these areas, therefore, have begun to seek management tools that promote a better interface between traditional manufacturing/marketing and logistics. Designing and introducing new products, withdrawing products from the market, launching sales promotions, defining after-sales policy, and setting service performance levels are just some of the potential areas of cooperation between logistics and other functional areas of the company. We will explore such opportunities in later chapters.

Given the considerable potential for evolution and the significant impact operations and logistics managers have within the organization, such managers are critical to a company's success in penetrating new markets, realizing higher service levels, and the like around the globe. Consequently, logistics and operations management must be assessed and implemented in a new global context.

◆ OPERATIONS AND LOGISTICS: APPLICATION AND OBJECTIVES

Before continuing, we need to revisit the terms *operations* and *logistics*. In the introduction we define *operations* to include any physical process that accepts inputs and uses resources to transform those inputs into valuable outputs. More specifically, operations is the process of planning, implementing, and controlling the efficient, cost-effective physical and information flows for material, from point of origin to point of consumption, to meet customer needs.

Logistics is the management of flows between business functions. Today's definition of logistics encompasses a much broader range of *flows* than in the past. Traditionally, companies included only simple inbound raw material or outbound finished product flows in their definition of logistics. Today, however, this definition has expanded to include all forms of product and information movement, described as follows.

Global Flows in a Business Organization

In order to satisfy the demands of its markets, a business organization must structure the products or services it offers according to some or all of the following physical flows:

- Raw materials from the original source stocking point through delivery, to the customer

- Semi-finished goods out of proprietary manufacturing facilities, or suppliers' factories or warehouses
- Machine tools and machines from one manufacturing facility to another
- Finished products between plants, the company's own warehouses, customers' warehouses, or warehouses belonging to logistics service companies
- Consumables and spare parts from warehouses to repair technicians' vehicles, or to customers' premises where products are installed
- Goods and parts to be repaired from customers' premises to repair and renovation facilities
- Supporting equipment for sales, such as display stands, advertising boards, literature, and so on from companies to appropriate agent
- Empty packaging returned from delivery points to loading points
- Sold products or components returned from delivery points to their initial point of warehousing or manufacture (reverse flow)
- Used/consumed products to be recycled, retrofitted, reused or disposed of (reverse flow)

These myriad flows, which are the basis of operations' and logistics' activities, have taken on greater significance today. They cover greater geographical area than before, and include new types of flows such as reverse logistics (for recycling, for example).

In Figure 1–1, we define the main families of operations/logistics flows. Two criteria characterize these families: the direction of the flow and the flow relationships involved.

Direction of the Flow

From the outset, investment in logistics has focused mainly on the flows from companies to markets. Growing concerns for protecting the environment and conserving resources have spawned the need to manage reverse flows—from markets back to the company. The emphasis here is on reusing, repackaging, renovating, or disposing of used articles.

Increased competition and the desire to please customers has also generated a significant flow of return products. Companies offer sales incentives that include taking back overstock/unsold goods. (The Renault automobile corporation's spare-parts facility located in Cergy-Pontoise, France, reports that for every five trucks of goods sent out, one truckload of overstock comes back.) Other firms offer thirty-day trial periods with money-back guarantees. These and other sales techniques create significant return flows—on the order of 20 percent of total sales for some firms.

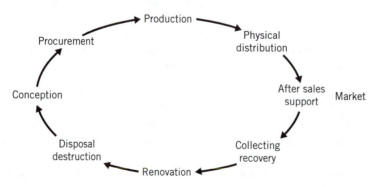

Figure 1–1   Operations and Logistics Flows

Flow Relationships

When discussing flows, direction of the flow is not the only important dimension. We are also concerned about the entities involved in managing these flows.

Direct and reverse flows occur between the internal structures of the organization (either managed by the organization itself or by a logistics provider company), or between the inside structure and one from outside—for example, a customer or a supplier. A company's products and their performance may even involve the flow between two outside entities, such as the relationships between a wholesaler and a retailer. All the related information flows that concern the creation and management of overall activities and considerations of logistics and operations must be associated with these physical flows. In Figure 1–2 we represent the connection between direct and reverse flows in the logistics chain.

Logistics: A Source of Service

Logistics—the management of flows—is first and foremost a provider of service. Whether the company deals with consumer goods or industrial products, the expectation of the logistics function in terms of a provision of service is the same. The type of service provided, however, is likely to be different.

In the consumer goods sector, for example, the key criteria sought for logistics include short delivery time, delivery reliability, no inventory shortage, and quality transport. In industrial markets, the criteria include spare parts support, accessible technicians, and reliable maintenance.

The total logistics service package is the result of a logical sequencing of interim steps. At each step, an intermediate provision of service occurs that contributes, ultimately, to the final result. In after-sales service, for example, the total parts delivery time (when parts are not sourced directly from a warehouse) comprises the sum of the intermediate procurement delivery times of the different transit entities involved. In a make-to-order process, the delivery period is the result of all the periods generated by the stages of procurement, production and distribution. In all cases, the aggregated delivery times must remain compatible with the delivery deadline agreed upon by the marketing department.

	Internal logistics	External logistics
Direct flows	• interplants • plant/warehouse	• with suppliers (supply of materials and components) • with customers (products, spare parts, promotional and advertising materials)
Reverse flows	• warehouse/warehouse	• with suppliers (packaging, repairs) • with manufacturers (elimination, recycling) • with customers (overstocks, repairs)

Figure 1–2   Different Types of Flows

Given this fact, it is logical that effective coordination between all parties involved in operations and logistics enables the service proposed to the customer. The quality of the relationships between different functions and parties, therefore, determines the overall performance of the logistics function.

As with any production activity, logistics requires production tools (warehouses, order preparation procedures, trucks and so on) whose optimization must guarantee the lowest production cost possible. This means that a production process must be created in terms of flow management to fit the corporation's cost objective.

Logistics and operations management are involved in two basic types of activities: flow design relative to the product and process, and management of physical process (planning and control).

From a process management viewpoint, *satisfying customer demand* is the overriding process that directs all activities. This process involves transforming inputs to customer-valued outputs, and directing the flow of goods to and from the firm to the customer. Put more simply, customer demand fulfillment involves both inbound or manufacturing processes, and outbound or distribution activities. The specific mix of activities that make up operations and logistics varies from firm to firm, depending on a company's particular organizational structure and the importance of individual activities to its operations.

◆ FLOW MANAGEMENT

We now focus on the primary environmental factors that affect the design and management of a logistics system. We start by defining the impact that these environmental or external factors impose on companies. We then describe the design stages that companies undertake in response to these factors, and conclude with a description of the elements involved in the flow management.

Impact of Environmental Factors on Flow Management

Business environments change constantly. Logistics managers, therefore, regularly must implement significant modifications to the logistics systems they manage, and do so on a quick-response basis. Four forces drive business-environment change: the market, competition, technological evolution, and government regulation (Figure 1–3). These four factors cause companies to adjust their logistics strategies and tactics continually.

The Market

Markets change under the influence of products, customer requirements, logistics service expectations, geographical location shifts, and the like. The consumer goods sector, for instance, has experienced huge change as a result of product proliferation, shortened product life cycles, and the growing internationalization of markets. All three trends require constant adaptation of the logistics response. This is explored in detail in chapters 4 and 6.

Competition

Competition spurs companies to modify their logistics supply chains on an ongoing basis. This is particularly true in cases where product differentiation is difficult by means of price, technology, or innovation. Logistics and operations management may well be a means of differentiation for a particular company.

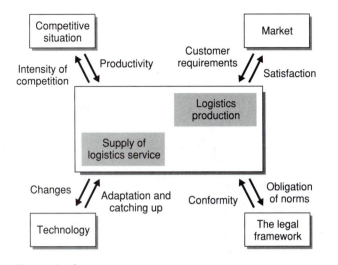

Figure 1-3   How Its Environment Affects Logistics

Technology

Technology offers new resources frequently. This is true in the area of logistics as well as in other areas of the company. Technology changes affect logistics in the form of manufacturing innovations that allow for more efficient means of changing the product mix. Information technology, in particular, has transformed the way in which operations management and logistics function. One particular example is the use of bar codes and electronic data interchange (EDI) to enhance not only the speed but also the accuracy of information.

Government Regulations

Government regulations frequently have a significant impact on logistics activities. For example, environmental regulations in Europe require manufacturers to take back product packaging materials from customers. These regulations have spawned entire logistics networks centered around managing reverse flows of waste packaging.

It is interesting to note that environmental forces affecting the flow management occur outside the organization. Market, competition, technology, and government regulation are forces that affect the company no matter what. Companies react to these external forces in different ways, and those companies that are proactive are in a better position to benefit from these forces—that is, use them to competitive advantage. In the following section, we describe the required steps for companies to proactively design an appropriate flow management system.

Designing the Flow Management System

There are five main stages involved in setting up an effective flow management system (Figure 1-4).

Stage 1: Logistics Considerations in Product Design

Companies must factor logistics considerations into their overall product design. This is the first portion of the logistics design phase. This stage requires studying product

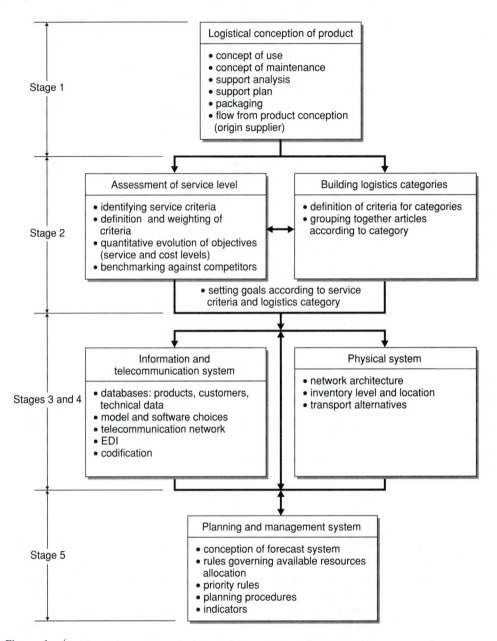

Figure 1-4   The 5 Stages That Go into the Conception of the Flow Management System

characteristics (e.g., shipping characteristics) and its means of production and customer delivery. This analysis takes into account all the features required for efficient movement of the product through the entire flow channel. It also should consider after-sales support issues. The physical product characteristics and design will affect the type and size of spare parts flows, as well as those of repair or renewal components.

Product and logistics flow design also must take into account how and in what conditions the customer will use the product. Such analysis determines strategy by projecting repair and replacement needs. It identifies who will perform the repairs at what location.

The second part of the logistics design phase involves simulating the actual flow generated after product design. With the help of consolidated information originating from the firm's research unit, procurement and production departments, and the channel of distribution, the company can simulate the main flows, including transfers, stocking, and packaging.

The logistics design of the product then lays down the relationship between different functions—that is, between the logistics department and research/development, and between marketing and after-sales. From this collaboration, appropriate management methods and tools should be developed that reflect an interfunctional approach.

Stage 2: Setting Objectives

Stage 2 involves setting the objectives for the flow management. These objectives differ greatly, depending on the market or product. For consumer products some of the objectives include:

- Short delivery times (from the moment the order is made to reception of the product)
- Reliable delivery times
- No shortage of inventory
- Sufficient logistical information associated with the product's distribution
- Capacity to consolidate an order
- Quality of transport

This phase essentially comprises a market study and consequently, comes within the scope of marketing. Its objective is to determine the expectations of the logistics service. It assumes that a strong relationship between the product managers and sales managers exists.

Flow management objectives also are distinguished according to logistics categories—that is, the grouping of products by similar service or handling requirements.

Stage 3: Designing the Information Systems

Information takes on a special dimension in matters pertaining to flow management. Information's prominence in flow management stems from the fact that physical flows are more complex, operations increasingly are spread out among different locations, and there is a growing demand for fast reaction and short delivery times. Traditionally, information related to flows was static in nature, with large databases in one location. Today, conceiving an information system requires that the following issues be addressed:

- Information that has been generated and collected must be able to be transmitted and exploited in real time. Wherever a facility, a warehouse, a means of transport, or a container may be in the world, the flow situation must be able to be traced and reacted upon.
- There must be a capacity for information sharing. As noted, companies collect information from numerous players in the course of moving product through their supply chains. This information must be shared among all the players—both internal and external—so everyone has the latest information of product status. To this end, more and more companies are using electronic data interchange (EDI) and other forms of electronic communication.
- Lastly, the information system must be flexible. Logistics solutions change constantly. Information systems must be able to accommodate this change instantly.

Chapter 10 discusses in more detail the features of these logistics and operations information systems.

Stage 4: Design of a Physical System

The physical system involves the actual organization of the network of facilities that carry products. Each player in this physical system executes a defined role (e.g., consolidator, major distribution center, cross-docking facility). Although we cover the subject of physical system design in greater detail in chapter 6, we highlight several important issues that must be addressed in designing an effective physical flow system:

- The global architecture of the system—that is, number of locations for production and distribution
- The location of logistics hubs and their function in meeting customer requirements
- Inventory policies implemented at each location
- Selection of appropriate transportation

Stage 5: Designing the Management System

Finally, designing the flow management system requires defining the planning and management system used to control and verify that the objectives are accomplished. This system consists of rules and procedures that control the execution of the required steps. More than anything, planning and managing the flow boils down to the capacity to store and communicate information, and to use it to make decisions in real time to verify that the flow is responding appropriately to external factors.

This management system should incorporate two characteristics. It must assist in decision making by indicating the actual flow situation and by enabling managers to diagnose status, problems, and so forth. Second, it must operate at the interface between the objectives and the realities of the physical and information flows. Chapter 11 develops these points in more detail.

Once designed, the logistics system must be operated and managed. These activities can be organized along three axes, as described in Figure 1–5. These axes are:

- Management of *physical* activities
- Management of *information*—data entry and processing
- *Planning and management* of the operations

In the following section, we present the drivers that are forcing companies to take a new approach to managing the flows labeled *operations* and *logistics*.

◆ GLOBAL OPERATIONS AND LOGISTICS: AN INTEGRATED APPROACH TO MANAGING FLOWS

As mentioned earlier, today's global economic environment is causing profound changes in how companies manage their operations and logistics activities. Changes in trade, the spread and modernization of transport infrastructures, and the intensification of competition have elevated the importance of flow management to new levels.

Logistical sub-systems / Operations	Procurement (suppliers)	Manufacturing (plants)	Distribution (depot/ warehouse)	After-sales
Physical	• Preparation for the flow to plant • Packaging • Direct or indirect delivery to plant • Pre-manufacturing	• Inter-workshop flow • Preparation delivery to depot or immediate delivery to customer • Packaging • Delivery	• Storeroom organization • Preparation order • Packaging • Approach transport and final transport • Post-manufacturing	• Installation • Preparation order spare part rechange • Packaging • Delivery
	• Reception • Open-checking • Replace in inventory • Repair	• Reception • Open-checking • Repair	• Reception • Checking returned items • Tests • Put in inventory • Destruction • Checking packaging	• Request/tests • Repair • Dispatch to repair centers
Information	• Data entry, update, database, packaging products, customers, place of delivery • Data entry order • Data entry inventory in and out • Monitoring pre- and post-manufacturing operations • Shipment documents • Data entry and monitoring level of service • Information from key indicators			
Planning and management	• Procurement planning	• Plant planning • Order procurement	• Forecasting • Monitoring of orders • Transport and delivery loop • Order procurement	• Forecasting • Monitoring orders spare-parts • Delivery planning • Order procurement
	Analysis key indicators			

Figure 1–5   Operations in a Logistics Management System

Intensification of Trade

The success encountered by the most advanced economies in the world can be attributed to their ability to conquer new markets, especially those beyond their own borders. Historically, this phenomenon tends to repeat itself. Since World War II, however, and especially since 1970, a new phenomenon has appeared. Those countries whose economies have prospered most significantly have been forced to internationalize not only their trade, but also their procurement processes and production facilities.

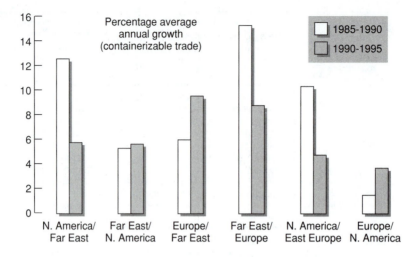

Figure 1–6   Percentage Growth for Trade between Main Trading Areas
Source: TBS/DRI World Trade Service, 1991

From 1985 to 1990, trade between the three largest economic areas in the world—North America, Europe, and Southeast Asia—enjoyed very high rates of annual growth. In 1994, world trade grew by 9 percent in volume and 12 percent in value. For the first time, trade in goods exceeded the $4,000 billion mark (see Figure 1–6). Trade with Southeast Asia went up by an average of 15 percent, with highs of more than 10 percent in the cases of China and Singapore, and of 20 percent for Malaysia, Thailand, and South Korea.

The explanation for the dynamism of the economies of Southeast Asia lies in the fact that this part of the world has enjoyed and will continue to enjoy the highest growth rate. Such has been the growth of trade in the economies of Southeast Asia that their share of overall trade will go up from less than 20 percent in 1990 to almost 33 percent in the year 2010.

Along with the growing internationalization of trade, we are witnessing increased harmonization and rationalization of markets in large areas of the world. Indeed, in order to stimulate growth and orchestrate this rationalization, countries have begun creating integrated economic areas. The most significant of these areas include the European Economic Community (EEC) and its extension to additional European countries and the North American Free Trade Agreement (NAFTA), set up in 1994 by the the United States, Mexico, and Canada.

To this list of economic areas must be added APEC, which brings together all the Pacific countries, and SEATO, which binds Australia, New Zealand, Japan, Hong Kong, South Korea, New Guinea, and Chile. SEATO makes up 44 percent of the world's population and nearly half of its wealth (Figure 1–7). MERCOSUR is the new addition in South America and was formed by Argentina, Brazil, Paraguay, and Uruguay.

New Characteristics of Flows

Economic development is changing the characteristics of global logistics flows—their intensity, physical requirements, and the like. Concerning flows, two trends stand out in the context of globalization. The first trend is the intensification of traffic, which is straining infrastructure capacity in many areas. The second is the rapid growth of return flows caused

		EEC	APEC	NAFTA
Population	1995	361 Million	335 Million	371 Million
	Forecast in 2010	383 Million	439 Million	493 Million
Geography	Surface area (1000 km^2)	3,600	3,059	21,338
Economy	Hourly salary cost	55 FF	5 FF	50 FF
	GDP (billion francs)	22,475	3,564	34,000
	Rate of growth	3.1%	6.5%	5%

Figure 1–7   The World's Main Economic Areas

by the growing awareness of ecological matters, more aggressive sales techniques, and even by the imbalance between flows at an international level.

Today, infrastructure capacity overloads affect virtually every transportation mode—air, motor, rail, water—throughout parts of the world. In Europe, for example, congestion, bottlenecks, and lack of road-system capacity cause longer delivery times and reduced transport reliability. They generate extra costs linked to lower quality of service, delayed goods movements, breaks in production, lower productivity in vehicle use, higher energy costs, and lost man-hours. In France, such losses totaled 17 billion francs in 1993, and are estimated to rise to 275 billion francs by 2010.

This phenomenon forces corporations to modify their logistics organization and invent fresh solutions—that is, alternative means of transport, new sites for warehouses, or reallocation of inventory. More specifically, companies may change their operating approach in any of the following three ways in response to infrastructure problems:

- Increase procurement areas by implementing international sourcing policies
- Pursue wider geographical spread and greater mobility of production facilities, or
- Implement worldwide distribution for markets.

Basic Principles of Global Operations

Operations and logistics management is forced to adapt to the competitive and strategic environment. The logistics system formed by all the members in the global supply chain faces pressures to integrate its activities. This integration takes different approaches, depending on how the environmental factors affect the particular companies involved.

We divide the integration into three types: geographical, functional, and sectorial. These three types form the basis for our *global operations/logistics framework*. Companies must set up specific management and organization methods to make these three types of integration possible. Taken as a whole, they make up what we call global operations and logistics (Figure 1–8).

Geographical Integration

The first type of integration—geographical—refers to the fact that geographical boundaries are losing their importance. Companies view their network of worldwide facilities as a

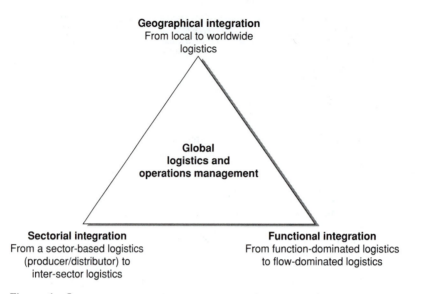

Figure 1—8   The Three Poles That Make up Global Logistics and Operations Management

single entity. Implementing worldwide sourcing, establishing production sites on each continent, and selling in multiple markets all imply the existence of an operations and logistics approach designed with more than national considerations in mind.

In Europe, geographical integration has been occurring at a rapid pace since January 1, 1993. At that time, customs duties between European Economic Community countries were abolished. This elimination of borders caused companies to rethink their physical flow structures for Europe as a whole. The usual practice of setting up sales subsidiaries in each country and creating country-specific logistics support and production systems was no longer appropriate.

This same type of integrated organization is emerging around the world. Firms no longer view production as country-specific, but rather, see it on a global scale. This is made possible through full geographic integration of logistics and operations. It is possible for a company to make or buy some components in one country, have them delivered to another country for final assembly, and finally, move them to yet another country for sale.

Geographical integration becomes possible not only because of data processing and communication technologies, but also thanks to excellent worldwide new means of transport. Express delivery services such as Federal Express, DHL, UPS, and TNT, with their planes, hubs, systems of collection, tracking, and final delivery, allow companies to send articles long distances, in the shortest time possible, and at low cost compared to the cost of carrying inventory.

Functional Integration

The responsibilities of operations management and logistics are no longer limited to coordinating the physical flows relating to production, distribution, or after-sales service. They are expanding to include such functions as research, development, and marketing in the design and management of flows. This functional integration improves flow management considerably.

When setting up projects for developing new models, automobile manufacturers such as Renault in Europe have two teams working together: one from the R & D department and the other from the logistics group. The teams' assignment is to simulate the flows required in the procurement and manufacturing stages according to the elements prepared by the research unit. The logistics department, for instance, can affect the automobile design stage by recommending modifications in order to create savings in logistics.

Sectorial Integration

In traditional supply chains, suppliers, manufacturers, distributors, and customers each work to optimize their own logistics and operations. They act individually, concerned only with their part of the flow system. As a result, they inadvertently create problems and inefficiencies for other players in the channel—all of which add cost to the total system. Leading firms, realizing this situation, are beginning to extend their view beyond their corporate boundaries and work cooperatively with all channel parties in an effort to optimize the entire system. We call this cross-boundary cooperation Sectorial Integration.

In the field of consumer goods, ECR (Efficient Consumer Response) has been one of the first successful attempts at sectorial integration. Producers and distributors (retailers) have jointly defined areas of cooperation, and have developed solutions that are derived from the supply perspective, rather than driven by the products themselves. There is a change in orientation. For the producer, selling the product to a distributor is not the ultimate objective. Rather, the distributor is the channel through which the producer reaches the final customer. It is in the best interest of both parties—producer and distributor—to cooperate in order to satisfy the end customer. The following are some results of such cooperation:

- Optimization of flows of goods
- Efficient new product launches
- An adequate fit between product range and demand
- Effective coordination of promotions and negotiations

The three types of integration—geographic, functional and sectorial—are the key drivers we use for explaining the framework for a new global operations/logistics approach. By understanding the particular implications in each case, companies can define how better to prepare for the environmental forces they encounter and so gain competitive advantage. The framework, and the linkages to the overall strategy formulation, are the topic for the next chapter.

◆ A NEW APPROACH

In this chapter we introduced some of the environmental elements forcing companies to adopt a new approach to understanding the challenges of the global economy. The global economy, and therefore the existence of global flows, is an accepted reality. More and more companies are extending their operations worldwide.

There are three main questions companies need to address in approaching globalization in a proactive manner:

1. What are the forces shaping the global economy?
2. What are the consequences of globalization?
3. How can we take advantage of the dynamic process?

The primary message about these global environmental factors is that they are external to the companies. Companies either react to the changes or are left completely out of the game.

Consequences of these changes include new competitive pressures (i.e., service is becoming more important than cost savings), sophistication of customers, and product life cycle compression, for example.

After defining the different types of flows, we have looked at some of the issues firms face when trying to design and manage the appropriate flow from raw material acquisition to final customer satisfaction. By presenting the three types of integration (geographic, functional and sectorial), we explain how companies can make the best of their supply chain.

The trend toward globalization is generating a new approach to operations and logistics. First, from a cost minimization approach, operations/logistics is now perceived as a service provider. Earlier we showed how more and more companies see operations and logistics as a source of services that must be incorporated in the overall definition of objectives.

Secondly, operations and logistics have evolved from simply moving products through the supply chain to being information providers. Developments in technology allow greater access to information for planning and management purposes.

Finally, companies are moving away from vertical integration, where all operations and logistics issues were handled from an internal orientation, to external integration, which connects all members of the supply chain. Geographic, functional, and sectorial integration are the foundation for the framework used in this book. Ensuing chapters elaborate on the ideas introduced in this chapter.

DISCUSSION QUESTIONS

1. Define the terms *operations* and *logistics*.
   Which of the two terms is broader in terms of the potential activities it encompasses?

2. What are the three main forms of integration necessitated under a *global approach* to operations and logistics activities?

3. What are the different types of physical flows encountered in logistics activities? Give examples from specific manufacturing and service environments.

4. What are the five main stages involved in setting up an effective flow management system?

5. Define the term *geographical integration*. What does geographical integration require in order for a firm to achieve it?

6. Define the term *functional integration*. Why is it important? How can it be achieved by firms?

7. Define the term *sectorial integration*. Give an example of an industrial practice that can be characterized as achieving sectorial integration.

REFERENCES

Bowersox, D. J., and D. J. Closs. 1986. *Logistical management* 3d ed. New York: Macmillan Publishing Co. Inc.

Braithwaite, A., and M. Christopher. 1991. Managing the global pipeline. *International Journal of Logistics Management* 2 (2).

Cooper, J. C. 1993. Logistics strategies for global businesses. *International Journal of Physical Distribution and Logistics Management* 23 (4): 12–23.

Copacino, W. C., and F. F. Britt. 1991. Perspectives on global logistics. *International Journal of Logistics Management* 2 (1): 35–41.

Christopher, M. 1990. Delivery quality service. *New York: Free Press,* 226.

Christopher, M., and A. Payne. 1991. Relationships marketing: bringing quality, customer service and marketing together. Oxford: Butterworth Heinemann.

Coyle, J. J., and E. J. Bardi. 1988. The management of business logistics 3d ed. St Paul: West Publishing.

Fawcett, S. E., and L. M. Birou. 1992. Exploring the logistics interface between global and JIT sourcing. *International Journal of Physical Distribution and Logistics Management* 22 (1).

Johnson, J. C., and D. F. Wood. 1986. Contemporary physical distribution and logistics. New York: Macmillan.

Roberts, J. 1990. Formulating and implementing global logistics strategy. *The International Journal of Logistics Management* 1(2).

Stern, L. W., and A. I. El-Ansary. 1992. *Marketing channels*. New York: Prentice-Hall.

Vickery, S. K. 1989. International sourcing: Implications for just-in-time manufacturing. *Production and Inventory Management* 30(3): 66–72.

Zeithaul, V., and N. Parasuraman. 1990. Delivery quality service. *New York: Free Press.*

◆ CASE 1–1: Centrum Co. ◆

Richard Stern, a Georgetown MBA student, was appointed a summer intern in the Logistics Department of Centrum Co., in May 1995.

Centrum was a company that manufactured and sold in the United States electrical components for the auto industry. The company did not run international operations and therefore lacked global logistics expertise. Its ownership was closely held by the Gates family. Centrum had $40 million in revenues in 1994, up from $35 million the year before. In December 1994, the company decided to move its headquarters to a bigger facility in Reston, Virginia.

Amid all these changes and developments, the CEO and founder, Jonathan Gates, decided to buy an Interlubcke wall unit to furnish the lobby of the new corporate headquarters.

The logistics manager decided then to give Stern what he thought was a reasonably easy first assignment. He wanted the new intern to analyze the buy and shipment of the wall unit for the new CEO's office.

Interlubcke is one of the most fashionable furniture makers in the world. It is based in Prague, the Czech Republic. During the communist years the company was the exclusive source of quality furniture for the Eastern European leaders. During the early 1990s, after its privatization, the firm started marketing to the West its distinctive style now commonly called *Interlubkish* in the arts world. Some of its pre-capitalist creations were recently displayed at the Metropolitan Museum of Modern Art. Each piece of furniture was custom made. The buyer had to select one of 190 designs and provide the required measures when placing the order. Jonathan Gates discovered an Interlubcke ATURA wall unit in an upscale furniture store during a

business trip to Paris, France, and wanted that specific design.

Richard Stern called Interlubcke and the company informed him that it did not deal directly with American customers. Instead, the Czech firm referred him to their American representative, Palm Beach Design in Miami, Florida. Mr. Bill Ziegler, from Palm Beach Design, sent Stern their offer. The wall unit would cost $52,323 delivered at Centrum's door. Since the wall unit would arrive in unassembled modules, they offered an on-site assembly fee of 5% of the unit price. They estimated a two-month delivery limit after the day Centrum placed the order. Detailed information on this offer is included in Exhibit 1.

Stern also contacted the French furniture store, Heggard et Cie. Miss Jacqueline Du Pre from Heggard sent him a fax with the price and the delivery alternatives that could be selected. The wall unit cost would start from FR. 125,000 (exchange rate: $1 = 4.95FR) and would depend on the shipping alternative that Centrum would choose. Delivery time ranged between 45 and 70 days. The detailed information of this offer can be found in Exhibits 2, 3 and 4.

Mr. Gates, the eccentric CEO, expected to have the wall unit installed within three months, ready for the new headquarters' inauguration party. Although at the beginning this wall unit project looked trivial, Richard Stern realized that it should be analyzed carefully.

With all the available information, Stern was requested to write a one- or two-page memo including the following points:

1. What alternative do you recommend?
2. What elements have you considered in your decision?
3. Is there any additional information you would need to ask the supplier before closing the deal?
4. What logistics aspects do you think are key for the successful conclusion of this operation?

Mariano de Beer prepared this case under the supervision of Professor Ricardo Ernst, Georgetown University, School of Business, as the basis for class discussion rather than to illustrate either effective or ineffective handling of an administrative situation. Copyright © 1997 by Georgetown University, Washington, DC 20057, USA.

PALM BEACH DESIGN

222 Rodeo Rd.
Miami, FL 333399

Bill Ziegler
Manager
Corporate Accounts

August 30, 1995

Mr. Richard Stern
Logistics Intern
Centrum Co.

Dear Mr. Stern:

Thank you for your interest in the ATURA Wall Unit, from Interlubcke. Based on the measurements that you kindly provided, we are attaching the prices and conditions of this offer. We are confident you will be soon a member of the select group of people with Interlubcke furniture in America.

Manufacturer: Interlubcke, Czech Republic

Item: Wall Unit

Design: ATURA

Measurements: 222.6 cm L × 259.2 cm H

Special Features: Extra 60 cm tablettes

Price: $52,323

Terms: Payable within one week of order confirmation

Delivery: In Centrum Co., Reston, VA. Estimated within 2 months after order confirmation.

The Interlubcke wall unit will be custom-made according to your measurements. All furniture transactions include our exclusive Palm Beach Service Guaranteed®.

The Palm Beach Service Guaranteed® includes:

1. Delivery to your home or office by our own truck fleet.

2. On-site assembly of the Interlubcke unit for just a 5 percent extra charge.

3. Delivery within three months of the order confirmation or your money back!

4. Free one-year subscription to the Interlubcke newsletter.

As exclusive representatives of Interlubcke in the United States, we are delighted to offer the full Original Interlubcke Collection®. Call us for a free catalogue!

If you decide to buy this magnificent Interlubcke unit, please call us toll-free at 1-800-123-4567.

Sincerely,

Bill Ziegler

Bill Ziegler

Manager
Corporate Accounts

PS: Don't miss the opportunity to buy our new German Deco lamps specially designed to match the Interlubcke wall units!

Exhibit 1

HEGGARD ET CIE.
Boutique Celestins
18 Quai des Capuchines
75000 Paris

August 30, 1995

Centrum Co.
Etats Unis

Monsieur Stern:

Regarding inquiry of the Interlubcke ATURA Wall unit, these are the alternatives that you have to purchase it from us:

Item: Interlubcke Wall Unit

Design: ATURA

Specifications: 222.6 cm L × 259.2 cm H, 60 cm tablettes

Packaging: The wall unit will be delivered in modules to be assembled. Assembly is easy and instructions will be provided.

Alternatives:

1. FOB† Le Havre

Cost at Le Havre Harbour: Fr. 125,000

Payment: In full when placing the order.

Delivery: From Paris approximately 45 days from order reception.

For your convenience, please find attached a letter from Encore Transport, that has managed in the past some of our shipments to the United States.

2. CIF† Baltimore

Cost at Baltimore Harbour: Fr. 160,000

Payment: In full when placing the order.

Delivery: In Baltimore in approximately 70 days from order reception.

I look forward to hearing from you in the near future.

Jacqueline Du Pre

Sales Manager

Exhibit 2

Encore Transport M.T.S
FAX TRANSMISSION

DE/FROM:	ENCORE TRANSPORT	DOMINIQUE AUDIOPHILE
A/TO:	HEGGARD ET CIE	JACQUELINE DU PRE
DATE:	27/8/95	FAX REF.: DB.98789

Madamme:

Answering your maritime freight price quotation inquire regarding the following merchandise:

- 448 kg. 1862 m3 of furniture, price Fr. 125,000
- Goods not intended for reselling in the USA

Please find below our offer:

1. Freight in France

-Freight to Le Havre with handling	1580FRF
-Maritime Freight: Le Havre/Baltimore	1170USD
-Insurance	2500FRF

2. Freight in the USA

-Import charges	1125USD
-Transfer Freight	145USD
-Internal Taxes	135USD
-Other Taxes	345USD
-Customs: Duties	2700USD
-THC	700USD
-Freight to Reston, VA	1180USD

Freight services in the U.S. will be handled by our correspondent in Baltimore: Brusaw and Son.

Payments should be made by your customer directly to us seven working days prior to the shipment.

The USA section of our offer stands also for an eventual CIF order.

We stay at your service for any other inquiry.

Sincerely,

Dominique Audiophile

Exhibit 3

Brusaw and Son
Customs Brokers-Foreign Freight Forwarders-JATA Agents
Baltimore Harbor, Maryland

FAX MESSAGE
TO: RICHARD STERN
CENTRUM CO.
FROM: JOHN BRUSAW
DATE: 8/30/95

Dear Mr. Stern:

We have been contacted by our correspondent in France regarding a shipment from Le Havre with

destination Reston, VA.

We would like to inform you that additional local charges that must be paid to us are approximately:

Foreign Charges:	$1096
Transfer of Documents:	$450
Brusaw and Son Handling:	$750
Inland freight:	$1150
Warehouse Charges:	$100
Storage:	$120

If you decide to hire our services, to expedite the process we will require two documents as soon

as possible:

1. A copy of Customs Form 3299, which we need you to complete

2. A copy of the commercial invoice, for which we will need you to send us a translation from French.

Please note that it normally takes 2 or 3 days to secure release from the time we get the paperwork.

If you have any questions, please call us at 410-003-0909.

Yours truly,

John Brusaw

Exhibit 4

◆   CASE 1 – 2: Bull Group   ◆

In June of 1990, Monsieur Fillet was named Director of Logistics of the Bull Group in order to reconsider the group's global organization after its latest acquisition, in 1989, of Zenith Data Systems (ZDS). He has operational responsibility over the logistics of Bull SA and supervises, moreover, functionally, all global logistics (cf. Appendix 1). Returning to the Group in 1988, Monsieur Fillet has since this period experienced a difficult situation for global information systems, which prompts him to quickly undertake the necessary considerations for his department. He aims his objectives at a reduction of operating costs and at an improvement in the quality of service.

Monsieur Fillet therefore decides to conduct a study that will allow him to consider the adaptation of the logistics to the targeted objectives. He hopes, at the outcome of this study, to be able to propose an ensemble of recommendations, as well as one or several scenarios for the evolution of the logistical system. These results will be outlined in front of the GEC (Group Executive Committee), which is composed of all the general directors of Zenith Data Systems, Bull SA and Bull International SA, and the directors of the following departments:

> marketing, finance, legal and fiscal, strategy and planning, product line.

Each general director has a responsibility on the global level. For example, the general director of Bull SA (France) is in charge of all aspects pertaining to the industrial or logistical sector for CMB (Bull Business Machines).

The global policy regarding product lines and marketing is established for the entire corporate structure. On the other hand, everything pertaining to operations is decided by each company within the group.

1. History of the Bull Group

Bull's history begins during the 1960s within the framework of the "assessment plan" launched by General de Gaulle, in order to allow France to gain its independence in the realm of information systems equipment. During this period, the notion of profitability was therefore not paramount. Strategic aims in the realm of the national economy prevailed and, bearing in mind the backlog over certain countries, the investment promised to be lengthy and substantial. Not being acquainted with the details of the group's evolution, Monsieur Fillet obtained from the com-

munications department important dates and the major periods of change in structure that had occurred periodically over the life of the group.

It is in 1919 that the Norwegian engineer Frédrik Rosing Bull registers his first patent for an adder-sorter statistical machine that utilized perforated cards.

The French company H.W. Egli Bull is created in Paris in 1931 to manufacture Bull machines. It is on this date that the first "tabulator," Bull T30, equipped with a printer, becomes available. In 1933, H.W. Egli Bull becomes Bull Business Machines (CMB), thanks to a "syndicate of users" anxious to create a European industry.

In 1951, CMB puts the GAMMA 3 on the market, one of the first electronic calculators in the world that inaugurates scientific computation.

The technological innovations come one after the other, and in 1962, CMB puts out a compact computer. Meanwhile, Honeywell and Nippon Electric Corporation (NEC), who will not delay to intervene in Bull's history, sign a long-term agreement that allows NEC access to Honeywell's products and technologies.

In 1964, General Electric Corporation acquires a controlling interest in Bull (66%), and therefore the most significant European manufacturer of computers becomes second worldwide. Bull changes its name to Bull General Electric, and CMB becomes a holding company with 34%.

The French assessment plan is launched in 1966 at the same time of the creation of the International Information Systems Company (CII) through a merger of CEA (CGE/CSF) SEA (Schneider) and ANALAC (CSF). Bull General Electric releases during this same period the GAMMA 55, the first office computer.

In 1970, Honeywell Inc. acquires a controlling interest in the information systems activities of General Electric. Bull General Electric becomes Honeywell-Bull. CIT-Transac is created at the heart of the CGE Group (General Electric Company).

In 1976, Honeywell Bull merges with the large-scale information systems activities of CII to create CII-Honeywell-Bull, controlled by the French government (53%) and Honeywell (47%). The mini-information systems activities of CII and Télémécanique-Electrique are regrouped into a new company, SEMS, entrusted to the Thomson Group, another nationalized group. CII-Honeywell-Bull is reinforced by the takeover of SEMS and Transac in 1983, and takes the name Bull, while the French government acquires a controlling interest in it (97%). Honeywell-Bull Inc. is created in 1987 by Bull (42.5%), Honeywell (42.5%) and NEC (15%) from Honeywell Information Systems.

By Philippe-Pierre Dornier and Michel Fender, Professors at l'ESSEC, March 1992. Revised May 1994.

In 1988, CMB takes control of Honeywell Bull Inc. with 61% of the capital. The Group then ranks 9th worldwide. Bull puts the Bull DPS 9000 on the market, the most powerful administration server in the world.

In 1989, Honeywell Bull becomes Bull HN Information Systems, Inc. CMB's capital participation in Bull HN increases to 69.4%, that of Honeywell decreasing to 15.6% and that of NEC remaining unchanged at 15%. CMB acquires Zenith Data Systems, the information systems division of Zenith Electronics Corporation, which strengthens the group's global dimension and increases its business figures to 41.2 billion francs.

In 1990, Honeywell is no longer the partner of Bull HN, a decision made within the framework of a recentralization of activities of the American group. But Zenith Data Systems' anticipated development in the American market erodes rapidly. In effect, the majority of public contracts and notably the American military have pulled out as a result of Zenith's change in nationality. Nevertheless, in 1989, the Bull group positions itself among the large worldwide manufacturers of information systems equipment.

2. Bull Products and the Information Systems Market

From Proprietary Systems to Configured Products

Traditionally, information systems activity involved so-called "proprietary" products. Each manufacturer produced its niche in the market by a game of incompatibility, and each provision came at a high price to the client. Today, with the appearance of compatibles and Asian assemblers, so-called "standardized" products represent a majority segment of the market. These products cover the lines of micro-computers (DOS 052, MAC), printers or workstations (UNIX). They affect, in the smallest capacity, large systems that only benefit from a pseudo-standard (IBM).

The notion of a proprietary product has evolved toward that of a "configured" product; that is to say that a certain number of elements of the information processing system (motherboard, software, etc.) remain dedicated to the clients.

The Bull Group's strategy henceforth consists of producing "global solutions" and no longer simply equipment. Thus, the strategy of Bull's proposal consists of producing integrated systems that provide at the core a large system of the type DPS 7000, DPS 8000 and DPS 9000, assuring database administration, overall security, communications networks allowing a connection between this large system, and the central servers distributed throughout the departments of the client's business, which then serve the workstations and end-users' computers. Bull is present throughout all of the different levels of this proposal by directly associating the performance and security offered by the traditional large systems GCOS 7 and 8 and the wealth of systems operating under UNIX.

The ensemble of this proposal responds to 3 strategically essential criteria relative to systems:

1. The systems are distributed: the global architecture is flexible and is capable of responding to centralized or decentralized demands and to follow client's evolution.
2. The systems are open: the solutions are based on international standards, which guarantees the perenniality of the client's investment.
3. The systems are integrated by communications networks.

Such an offer encompasses the totality of the implementation of an information system: configuration, delivery, installation. It is therefore necessary to deliver the software, the documentation, configured products, and standard products at the same time. The sale is accomplished through direct and indirect sales, but implies a synchronization of delivery, comprising a central system, workstations, printers, documentation and software made to order.

The "Time to Market"

The information systems sector is highly competitive and evolving, characterized by a significant technological dimension. The company that succeeds in such a market is the company that is able to develop and apply successful product and production process technologies, allowing them in effect to acquire an experienced operation as quickly as possible, which will guarantee a segment of the growing market within a high volume market. Additionally, the evolving technological variable and the emergence of new client needs involve rigorous mastery of the cycle of technological life and the marketing of products and services. Every launch of a new product or product line is the object of an announcement. A delay in the announced release date can give rise to questions concerning the project's profitability and especially cause the company to lose market points to the competition which will only be recovered with great difficulty. The ability to manage research and development for multiple product lines to integrate marketing and production functions for the involved divisions constitutes a real key factor for success allowing the company to be on time to market with a product that has a short life span. Bull, like the other manufacturers, therefore integrates into its strategy this dimension of the "time to market."

Distribution Channels

From 1988 to 1989, distribution was characterized by an increase in indirect sales, which increased from 10% to 21% of the total business figures, whereas direct sales experienced a decrease. During the same period, the sale of standard systems increased from 18% to 21% of equipment business figures, whereas proprietary systems experienced a decrease. This is a major evolution for an information systems manufacturer such as Bull. The increased portion of systems sold via an intermediary introduced a double danger relative to the appearance of distribution networks threatening to compete with the manufacturer and the commercial contact that it has with the clients.

Figure 1 allows one to visualize the distribution of business figures in 1989 by product type, by type of revenue, by area of activity, and by geographical area.

The business of replacement parts (which lie within the responsibility of commercial management and within miscellaneous provisions) is not to be called into question. In effect, Monsieur Fillet has become aware of a report that proves the profitability of these departments. In light of this information and being that they comprise one of the continuous services that the organization offers, Monsieur Fillet therefore decides not to devote himself to the activities of replacement parts and miscellaneous provisions, at least initially.

3. Bull's Structural and Logistical Functions

Monsieur Fillet establishes for his study the different centers that are involved in the group's logistics.

Production Centers

More than 8000 people are directly employed in 10 production centers around the world: in Boston and St. Joseph in the United States, in Contagem in Brazil, in Bangalore in India, and in Sydney in Australia.

At the heart of the European Economic Community, six factories are producing: Caluso in Italy, Barcelona in Spain, and France, including the industrial ensemble in Angers, which regroups the factories at Joué-lès-Tours (JLT), Villeneuve d'Ascq (VDA) and Belfort.

Table 1 shows the type of production by production site. If the production of the factories in Sydney, Contagem, and Bangalore are destined for local sales, the subsets manufactured in Barcelona are then distributed in Europe.

The production of Belfort, Angers/JLT, and Boston has a global distribution. Those of St. Joseph also, with the exception of Europe and the Middle East. Only the subsets and kits manufactured by St. Joseph are destined for Europe.

The production of VDA is destined uniquely for Europe. As for that of Caluso, the printers are distributed globally and the GCOS 6 are distributed to Europe (VDA + Angers).

Without providing precise information about the volume of their production, it is possible to classify the sites in relation to the magnitude of their production:

1	Angers/JLT
2	Boston
3	St. Joseph
4	VDA
5	Belfort
5 tie	Caluso

The group's international dimension is also a reality in terms of their presence in various markets, for if in 1985 the percentage of business figures realized outside of France was 36%, in 1989 the percentage reached 70%.

Logistics Centers

They are involved as much with physical distribution operations as with supply operations. They cover various different functions, which can be: transit (customs clearing), bulking/unbulking, administration, order processing, shipment and invoicing, stocking, supply of finished products, packaging and, eventually, post-manufacturing.

The principal logistics centers are located in Boston, which constitutes the logistical antenna for the United States, in Roissy (France) near the Charles de Gaulle international airport for import/export operations, in Croissy-Beaubourg, near Marne la Vallée (France) for provisions (General Administration Circulation France-DGDF), in FACI-St-Ouen (Invoicing of International Business) and in Angers, International Delivery Center (CIL).

In France we must add the center in Paris North II, near Roissy, which regroups Bull's global replacement parts inventory but which does not enter into this study.

Finally, the European subsidiaries are equipped with local distribution centers located in:

Finland	Helsinki
Sweden	Stockholm
Norway	Oslo
Denmark	Copenhagen
Belgium/Lux.	Brussels
Holland	Amsterdam
Germany	Cologne
Austria	Vienna
Switzerland	Zurich
UK	London
Italy	Milan
Greece	Athens
Spain and Portugal (cluster)	Madrid

The administration of international trade (supplies, production or distribution) is carried out with the heart of the Bull group by LCI (Logistics of International Commerce) re-

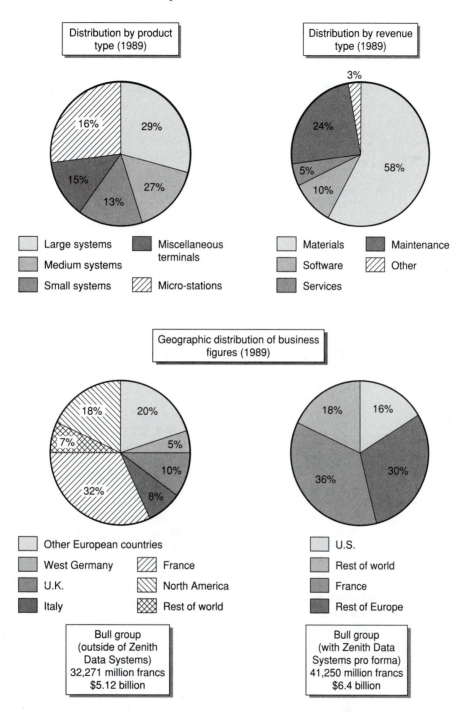

Figure 1   Geographic Distribution of Business Figures (1989)

Table 1

	GCOS4	GCOS6	GCOS7	GCOS8	UNIX	MICRO	peripherals
			Type of Production by Production Site.				
CALUSO (Italy)	*	*			*		*
ANGERS/JLT (France)			*		*		
VDA (France)					*	*	
BELFORT (France)							*
BANGALORE (India)			*				
CONTAGEM (Brazil)			*				
ST. JOSEPH (USA)						*	
BOSTON (USA)		*		*	*		
SYDNEY (Australia)						*	
BARCELONA (Spain)	SUB-SETS						

porting to Monsieur Filler and covering the following domains:

> customs
> transports
> the data processing system necessary to these activities

The LCI is therefore in direct relation to the transit center in Roissy (CTR), import and export invoicing and administrative operations profiting subsidiaries, and direct clients of the Commercial Oversees Network (CRO) in St Ouen near Paris.

Imports of United States and South East Asian origin are essentially components and subsets.

During the time in which Monsieur Fillet engages his study, a single European community is still not a reality. Nevertheless, it is evident that the actions to take must take into account the notion of European business development.

Certain logistics sites are already destined to play a more specific role:

FACI-St-Ouen	invoicing
Roissy, Angers, PNII	bulking, unbulking
Croissy-Beaubourg, and	eventually
Marne la Vallée	post-manufacturing
Boston	customs administration

There is no stocking in Roissy, which serves uniquely as a platform and there is no bulking/unbulking at Marne la Vallée.

Finally, the industrial and logistics sites of the Bull Group in Europe can have very different functions, often depending upon their historic origin.

Table 2 identifies the principal characteristics of Bull's European sites as a function of commercial brands, types of products manufactured by an industrial site or distributed by a logistics center and finally, the functions that they fulfill.

Commercial Distribution of Bull Products

There exists several commercial distribution networks:

> the network France + oversees (RCO)
> the Bull Europe network (West + East)
> the Zenith micro Europe indirect sales network

It is also necessary to distinguish the direct clients, called large accounts, from the network of resellers. In France in general, the large accounts regroup large administrations such as DGI (General Administration of Taxes), SNCF, EDF or large companies, Alcatel, Thomson, insurance companies, or banks.

Resellers deal with the distribution of products to smaller size clients.

For wide distribution products, the reliability of four-month forecasts is only 20% to 30% and the review cycle of these products is 6 weeks at this time. The development of the logistics plan should allow for an improvement in the reliability of the forecasts.

The client's order follows an administrative circuit punctuated by procedures that engage the client, the service of commercial administration, supply planning and production (see Figure 2). The order is accompanied by a requested delivery date that is in the majority of cases delayed in order to consult the availability of the product, either real or provisional, and calculated based on the production plan. The lag time takes the form of a delay in the confirmation of the order, which is 5 days on the average for Bull and 0 to 2 days for the competition. This lag time should not be so large that it impinges upon the delivery date requested by the client. The delay for delivery for a product in stock is 4 to 6 days for Bull and an average of 2 days for the competition. The gap between the actual delivery date and the accepted delivery date measures the respect of Bull's commitment to the client.

Table 2

	Commercial Brands		Types of Products Manufactured by the Site		Function Fulfilled by the Site	
Production Sites and Logistics Centers	Bull	Zenith	Conf. P.	WDP	Production	Logistics
Angers/Joué les Tours	*		*	*	*	*
Croissy-Beaubourg à Marne la Vallée	*	*		*		*
Genevilliers		*		*		*
Seclin		*				*
Roissy	*					*
FACI-St-Ouen	*					*
Incarville	*					*
Villeneuve d'Ascq	*			*	*	
Caluso	*		*	*	*	*

Distribution Network of Bull Group in Europe

Conf. P. = Configured products
WDP = wide distribution products

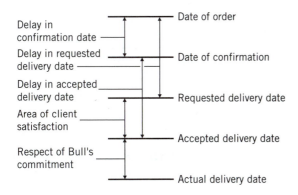

Figure 2   Administrative Circuit

Orders fulfilled from inventory imply a readjustment of the needs that are estimated and integrated into the production plans of the factories, which launches a cycle of supply orders.

A good mastery of delivery delays is not without relation to the level of inventory, which for Bull is only 3.6 times per year, whereas it is 8 times per year for the competition.

If sales to large accounts is done by direct sales, one of the marketing objectives is to develop indirect sales (VI), which increase from 40% to 70% of the business figures over the next five years. In effect, the market has evolved in recent years as a result of technological pressures.

Bull should therefore intensify its network of resellers, for it is easier to reach a large number of individual clients via their intermediary, rather than seek to contact them directly.

Additionally, it is necessary to produce a high volume of sales, for the markup for wide distribution products is small, on the order of 5 to 6%.

4. The Quality of Services

The services provided around the sale of hardware products plays an important role in the client's final satisfaction. Numerous surveys conducted yearly allow large information systems companies to position themselves in relation to each other. The Datapro survey, one of the most respected, indicates that since 1985 there has been a continuous improvement in the quality of service that Bull offers its clients. Nevertheless, the services produced specifically by the company's logistics activity still show a significant deficiency against the competition. Moreover, clients' service expectations in the domain of wide distribution products in particular, continue to evolve and to become more demanding (see Table 3).

The "benchmark" objectives represent the criteria of the information systems market in the year of 1992. The level of dues corresponds to the number of deliveries not accomplished by the requested date. The level is expressed in absolute value and not as a percentage of total deliveries, for an order for a Wide Distribution Product (WDP) not delivered on time must be considered as lost.

Finally, in matters concerning inventory levels, the figures show furthermore that the volume of inventory is 3 times higher than that of the competition. Monsieur Fillet's predecessor left behind a small study which indicates the inventory retention costs.

The costs increase by 35% per year of which:

24% are for financial expenses, of which
   costs for physical storage   12%
   finance charges   12%
6% are due to price erosions
5% are due to product obsolescence

Table 3

	Benchmark	Bull (89/90)	1991	1992
WDP Task Force Objectives				
Respect promised delivery date	99%	40–50%	70%	95%
Order processing	7 days	30–60 days	10 days	5 days
Finished products as % of business figures	13–15%	30%	20%	16%
Amount due	—	15.000	10.000	5.000

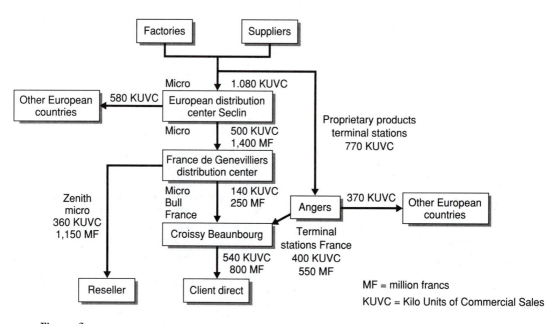

Figure 3   Physical Flow: France

5. Quantitative Logistical Data

To back up his reflections, Monsieur Fillet also makes use of data relative to the flow of volume and to the operating costs for the logistics sites in France.

Figures 3 and 4 represent the flow of supply and distribution of finished products, first on the level of France, and then on the European level. These diagrams permit one to position the role of Bull's various operational entities and to valorize the volume of this flow in KUVC, that is to say, in kilo units of commercial sales (1 UVC corresponds to one catalogue product) and in monetary value (MF).

The European center in Seclin plays a central role in draining the supply flow of components, of semi-finished products originating from the group's factories and third party suppliers. These products are distributed among the national distribution centers according to the commercial brand, the direct or indirect nature of the sales, and the destination of the product, either configured or standardized.

The logistic for distribution of wide distribution products utilizes the resources operating within the geographic sites of Roissy, Seclin and Angers, all of whose logistical missions have been detailed elsewhere in the report. These resources are measured in personnel, administrative and physical, in handling and stocking material, and in warehouse, office and packaging areas (Table 4). The logistic equally utilizes averages principally associated with production sites (UPF: Unit of Production and Fabrication; UOP: Unit of Scheduling and Planning).

Sales forecasts, which have been realized, allow us to size the necessary logistical resources to put into place Forecasts of ZDS Europe base 100 in 1990, 225 in 1994, according to a pattern of consistent increase and of which one-third are destined for the French market (in KUVC).

As can be understood by the preceding material, logistical resources between configured products and wide distribution products are not dedicated, but for the most part,

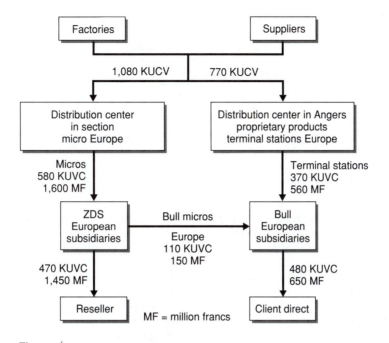

Figure 4 Physical Flow: Europe

Table 4

| | | | | Seclin | | UPF | |
	Trading Accounts for: 1991 Physical Indicators—Wide Distribution Products						
	Actual 91	Roissy PGD	Angers CIL	ZDS Europe	ZDS France	DGDF	UOP
Bull Staff							
Administrative	86	3	4	33	9	28	9
Support	13	—	16	−3	—	—	—
Store	7	6	1	—	—	—	—
Total	106	9	21	30	9	28	9
FLOW (KUVC)							
Micro	2,020	300	—	1,080	500	140	—
TX/Stations	1,370	200	770	—	—	400	—
Total	3,390	500	770	1,080	500	540	0
AREA (Warehouses, offices, workshops) (m2)							
Tools							
Easements							
Total	25,000	900	5,650	10,800	—	7,500	150

Table 5

Forecasts of Bull SA (in KUVC)					
	1990	*1991*	*1992*	*1993*	*1994*
Terminals and peripherals	—	122	135	—	—
Q 400, workstations	—	15	12	—	—
Total	137	147	—	154	162
KUVC Equivalent	—	770	800	840	880
Of which France (%)	—	52	52	—	—
Others (%) Essentially Europe	—	48	48	—	—

shared. Such is the case with the International Logistics Center in Angers, which operates for three large families of products (proprietary products, configured products and wide distribution products).

Furthermore, the origin of purchases of configured products is diverse both inside and outside the group. Afterward, the shipment of these products involves the commercial network in France and the international networks.

In addition to the preceding information, that which concerns principally the logistical functions of bulking and unbulking, stocking, handling and order preparation, transport, supply and shipping costs on the international level represent significant costs. To apprehend the level of these expenses, Monsieur Fillet has the idea to draw up a global map charting the logistical flow in terms of the principal European countries and to reconcile them with actual transport expenditures (cf. Appendices 2 and 3).

To satisfy the demand, and as it has been explained, Bull SA imports from outside European countries components and finished products of primarily North American, Japanese, and South East Asian origin (cf. Appendix 4). The

measure of economic performance for the means of transport employed (aerial or maritime for intercontinental) is evaluated in francs/kg and is computed on the value in francs/kg of the imported component or finished product. Monsieur Fillet has in his possession a statistical study of the imports of United States origin (cf. Appendix 5).

The first step of Monsieur Fillet's strategy has consisted in assembling an ensemble of quantitative data (costs and volumes) and qualitative data (organization and logistical structure, level of service, characteristics of the information systems market) on the logistical mission over which he has direct operational responsibility for France.

You are asked to assist Monsieur Fillet with the reorganization plan, on the level of the development of industrial and logistics sites as well as on the level of the distribution of logistical functions among these sites. The essential difficulty of the problem resides in the necessarily global approach, which must be implemented, associating the flow of imports and exports, in the end obtaining a feasible optimization of the logistical costs generated by the study of the level of service that the market desires.

Appendix 1
Structure of the Bull Group in 1989

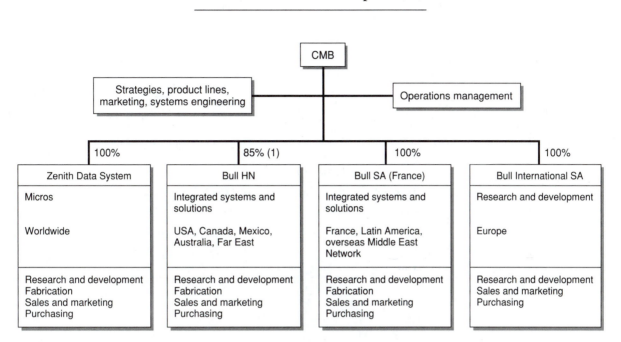

Appendix 2
1990
Worldwide Traffic
European Traffic Flows

Import and Export	Cost	Gross weight (tons)
FRANCE ITALY	302 K$	857 T
ITALY FRANCE	326 K$	970 T
UK ITALY	227 K$	171 T
ITALY UK	70 K$	68 T
FRANCE UK	156 K$	138 T
UK FRANCE	110 K$	212 T
TOTAL	1191 K$	2416 T

Appendix 3
European Shipments and Cost 1990

Country	Gross weight (tons)	%	Cost (million francs)	%	Price/kg
West Germany	784 T	28%	1.2 MF	20%	1.47
Italy	987 T	35%	1.4 MF	24%	1.46
Ireland	417 T	15%	1.9 MF	33%	4.62
Great Britain	231 T	8%	0.7 MF	11%	2.92
Switzerland	176 T	6%	0.2 MF	3%	0.97
Netherlands	69 T	3%	0.1 MF	3%	2.37
Other	146 T	5%	0.4 MF	6%	2.40
TOTAL	2810 T	100%	5.9 MF	100%	2.10

Appendix 4
Import Flow of Bull S.A. in 1990

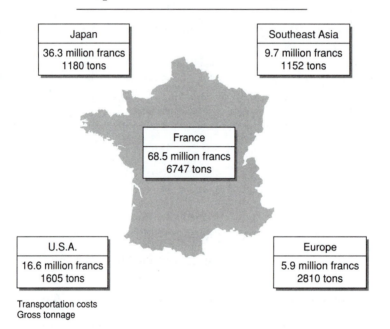

Japan
36.3 million francs
1180 tons

Southeast Asia
9.7 million francs
1152 tons

France
68.5 million francs
6747 tons

U.S.A.
16.6 million francs
1605 tons

Europe
5.9 million francs
2810 tons

Transportation costs
Gross tonnage

Appendix 5
Transportation Cost Originating in the USA

Year	Gross Weight (tons)	Cost (million francs)	Price per Kilo
1988	1.298 T	14.2 MF	10.97
1989	1.056 T	14.3 MF	13.62
1990	1.605 T	16.6 MF	10.31

- Does not include imports directly from Seclin
  - Air   82 T
  - Maritime 345 T
  - Total   427 T

C h a p t e r   2

The Strategic Framework

◆ ◆ ◆

This chapter addresses the following key concepts:

◆ *The historical perspective of operations/logistics role*

◆ *The strategic framework for tackling new challenges*

◆ *A definition of competitive priorities and the implications of their linkage with logistics*

◆ *Strategy process formulation with an operations/logistics orientation.*

As we have shown in chapter 1, global operations and logistics focus on the management of flows—from raw materials procurement to finished product delivery to the customer. The management of these flows represents huge financial outlays for companies worldwide. In the United States, for instance, logistics costs represent up to 25 cents of every dollar of goods sold. In 1994 the world market spent £2.5 trillion on logistics-related activities, according to the *Financial Times*. In 1994, *Fortune* magazine reported that American companies spent U.S. $670 billion (10.5 percent of the gross domestic product) to wrap, bundle, load, unload, sort, reload, and transport goods. By 1999, worldwide logistics expenditures are expected to rise to nearly U.S. $2.1 trillion by 1999 (approximately 16 percent of worldwide gross national product).

Relentless optimization of manufacturing in the last two decades, and the application of new managerial approaches such as just-in-time (JIT), total quality management (TQM), and flexible manufacturing systems (FMS) have significantly improved performance. However, they also have fueled an increase in both the volume and complexity of logistic activities. In today's business environment, products must move from more international origins to more scattered market destinations, faster and more efficiently.

Management of global operations and logistics is thus a major challenge for companies— and a major opportunity. Management has all but exhausted cost reduction opportunities in manufacturing. Not so in logistics, where such opportunities still abound. This reality makes improving logistics as important to corporate strategy as improving manufacturing and marketing.

The challenges of global operations and logistics demand new answers. Researchers continue to create new managerial models based on the application of concepts like delocalization, modularization, delayed differentiation, and postponement. *Delocalization* refers to the practice of adding value to a product at different locations closer to the customer. *Modularization* refers to the practice of assembling a complete product using different modules purchased from different sources (e.g., computers). Modularization necessitates a change in product design to accommodate this process. *Delayed differentiation* and *postponement* refer to the customization of orders after demand has been identified and recorded (e.g., labeling product at the last minute).

Practitioners, for their part, are creating new organizational units and experimenting with applying these models to real-life operations. For example, a 1994 survey by The Conference Board (a New York-based economic research/education group) showed that many companies were consolidating all their logistics functions in various regions (e.g., Europe) into one organizational unit headed by a newly appointed senior director. Another study by the University of Maryland in 1995 found that there is a shift in approach where best practice companies are beginning to consolidate logistics functions at headquarters rather than keeping their logistics systems decentralized.

◆ STRATEGIC ROLE OF OPERATIONS AND LOGISTICS

The trend toward an integrated world economy and global competitive arena is forcing companies to design products for a global market, and to rationalize their production processes so as to maximize corporate resources. Companies must coordinate their functional activities within a coherent strategy that addresses the global nature of their business.

Unfortunately, when it comes to corporate strategy, most operations/logistics functions remain relegated to traditional reactive/tactical roles. Top management views operations and logistics as tactical in nature, designs strategy without their input, and relegates them to a cost-minimizing role. There are several reasons for this outdated management attitude, including:

• The functional dominance of certain areas in the formulation of corporate strategy
• A short-term view of operations/logistics' contributions
• A belief that operations and logistics are technical specialties and not strategic business functions

Functional Dominance in the Formulation of Corporate Strategy

Historically, top management has viewed finance and marketing as the primary keys to corporate success. These functions exercise tremendous and, at times, excessive influence on the formulation of corporate strategy. Top executives seemingly prefer to focus on activities that connect to the external environment, rather than those—like operations and logistics—that deal with internal activities. This attitude perpetuates the pattern of functional dominance established by finance and marketing.

As a result, operations and logistics managers typically have not been included in the formulation of strategy. They have been left to deal with the consequences of strategies that fail to take logistics and operations into account, and so have been placed in the untenable position of complaining about something over which they had little or no input or control. This situation tends to reinforce the perception that operations and logistics managers are short-term, detail-driven individuals who lack a global perspective, and are therefore poorly suited to participate in strategic vision development.

Short-Term View of Operations/Logistics' Contributions

Typically, top management views the operations/logistics function as a firefighting unit that constantly faces and resolves crises. Operations and logistics managers are evaluated and rewarded on their performance on short-term numbers (quarterly inventories, adherence to monthly schedules, weekly yield rates, etc.) and are offered little incentive to focus on long-term performance goals. Instead of participating in the decision process for an overall integration, operations/logistics is used as the entity that executes once decisions have been made.

Operations and Logistics as Technical Specialties, Not Strategic Functions

Operations and logistics frequently are viewed as technical functions, staffed by specialists having the skill and experience to resolve detailed technical problems during the implementation phase of strategies. This view has been fueled by the fact that operations and logistics managers have frequently failed to explain their functions clearly and effectively, in terms that top management understood. Practitioners have used specialized jargon and terminology that was unfamiliar to higher management. Marketing and financial executives, on the other hand, have always been able to explain their activities and their relevance in a straightforward manner, with understandable business language.

More and more, operations/logistics is becoming the critical facilitator for integrating the overall strategies developed by companies. When marketing decides to implement any of the decisions relating to the famous four Ps (product, place, promotions, price), operations/logistics is there not to correct the strategic decisions for a particular promotion, for example, but to coordinate the actual execution. By integrating operations and logistics in the decision process, companies can gain a competitive advantage by rationalizing the resources required for accomplishing this task. Marketing understands customer needs, but operations/logistics is responsible for delivering to the final customer.

As another example, when manufacturing decides to follow a policy of producing according to seasonality (e.g., large runs for Christmas), as opposed to a steady "level" production run, operations and logistics are there not to change the manufacturing strategy, but to coordinate the actual implementation.

Leading companies supercede tradition and view operations and logistics as the source for competitive advantage. They adopt a new approach that does more than optimize the specific, separate linkages along the supply chain. Rather, it takes an overall view of the system required to accomplish a global optimization. Operations/logistics is becoming the critical facilitator for integrating this *systems* approach to managing a global enterprise.

In the context of this leading-edge "systems" view of global business, the remainder of this chapter discusses a strategic framework and process for using operations and logistics as a source of competitive advantage. The idea is to present a new approach for understanding the overall process of linking the flow of goods and services to their final destination by rationalizing the use of resources.

◆ THE STRATEGIC FRAMEWORK

For simplicity in analysis, the logistics system can be divided into two segments: inbound and outbound logistics. Inbound logistics involves providing all the materials and goods

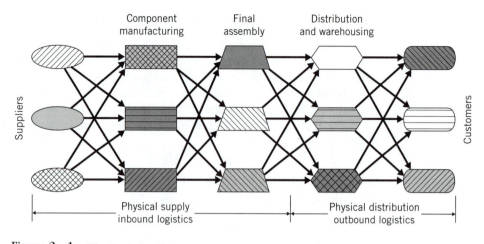

Figure 2−1   The Logistics System

required for making the products; outbound logistics encompasses how the manufactured products move from final assembly through distribution and warehousing to the hands of the customers (see Figure 2–1).

Companies cannot isolate the inbound from the outbound segments because it is the overall flow that results in the satisfaction of final customers. However, by dividing the logistics system into inbound and outbound, we can characterize the different trade-offs. These trade-offs cannot be analyzed in isolation but must be viewed in the context of the organization's overall performance objectives.

The Three Dimensions of Global Operations and Logistics

To facilitate this trade-off analysis, we look at the existing operations/logistics system through our global logistics framework (outlined in chapter 1). The framework serves as a tool to optimize and manage material flows. It has three dimensions: functional, sectorial, and geographic (see Figure 2–2).

The *functional dimension* highlights the cross-functional nature of logistics. Most organizations are segmented into discrete activity areas—e.g., marketing, finance, manufacturing. The logistics process cuts across all functional areas, and so enables the creation of important interfaces. These interfaces must be managed collectively. Companies must avoid assigning managerial predominance over these interfaces to one functional area. Doing so serves only to sub-optimize overall performance toward corporate goals. Firms must create incentives for cooperation among the functions.

For example, IBM restructured its sales force compensation system to encourage intrafunctional cooperation among sales, marketing, manufacturing, and distribution. Under the new system, the salesperson is compensated based on a certain percentage of the actual sale, as well as on the quality of service provided, as perceived by the customers (i.e., when the product was received). Marketing must check with manufacturing about availability before making commitments to customers. This system eliminated the traditional conflict of salespeople making promises, and then blaming manufacturing for late delivery.

The *sectorial dimension,* or interfirm integration, refers to the efforts by supply chain partners to coordinate and manage their activities as a single, unified entity, rather than as

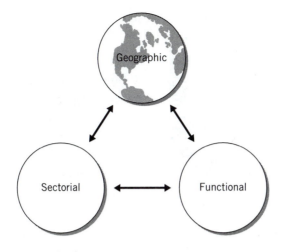

Figure 2-2   Global Logistics Framework

separate entities. The main idea is that industrial markets are formed by suppliers and customers or, more generally, by buyers and sellers. Lasting relationships are beneficial for all parties involved. Successful supply-chain integration requires parties to share knowledge about resources, organization, strategies, and so forth. By sharing this information, companies can optimize the total channel, eliminating redundancies, flow roadblocks, and other inefficiencies that add cost without adding value.

In the supermarket industry, for example, manufacturer Procter & Gamble (P & G) does not view the U.S. supermarket chain Safeway as its final customer. The consumer is the final customer, and Safeway is the system used by P & G to deliver product to the consumer. By coordinating their activities, P & G and Safeway can optimize their mutual supply chain.

A 1992 study by the Food Marketing Institute and Andersen Consulting shows that the average retail price was reduced by more than 10 percent without sacrificing much of the margins for the participants by coordinating activities such as promotions, packaging, and new product introduction, as well as by sharing all the relevant data (see Figure 2-3). Super-markets gain market share by being able to offer lower-priced product; manufacturers have a more efficient operation relative to the competition; the consumer ends up paying less.

Finally, there is the *geographic dimension* of global operations/logistics. Management of global operations and logistics differs from management of domestics operations in several key ways. First, there is the need to identify and analyze factors that differ across nations that influence the effectiveness of these functions. Such factors include worker productivity, process adaptability, governmental regulations and issues, transportation availability, culture, and so on. Second, because of the distances involved in global operations, transportation and distribution are of greater significance. The efficiency and effectiveness of the logistics function has a greater impact on the firm's profitability. Finally, geographically dispersed facilities and markets are much more difficult to manage and serve, respectively.

Relationships Among the Three Dimensions

The overall objective of optimizing any logistics system is to maximize profitability. By looking at the relationship among the three dimensions in the global logistics framework, we

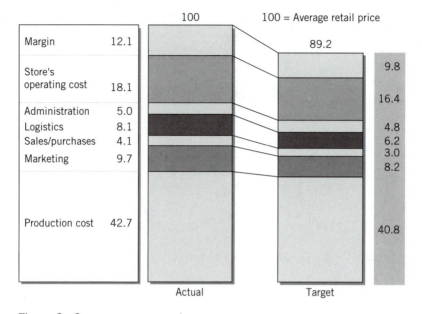

Figure 2–3   Cost Structure in the Supply Chain
Source: Food Marketing Institute and Andersen Consulting (1992)

can identify the best orientation for a given company. We define three basic types of orientations:

- Resource-oriented logistics
- Information-oriented logistics
- User-oriented logistics

Resource-oriented logistics is the management of the different resources (capital, materials, people) required in manufacturing of products to be delivered to the final customers. Resource-oriented logistics focuses on the relationship between the functional and the geographical dimensions. By looking at the world as a supply of resources and a market for customers, we can see how the functional dimension can benefit from the geographical dimension. Companies with a strong marketing emphasis need to balance marketing expenditures with tight control over manufacturing costs. Therefore, they may elect to search in different geographical locations for the manufacturing site that minimizes labor cost. Or, they may want to centralize manufacturing in one location to obtain economies of scale.

The emphasis of the logistics, then, is oriented toward optimizing the use of resources. By the same token, and as we have mentioned before, the market for products is becoming independent of the geographical boundaries. If the market is the world, the company must coordinate the resources of its different functional areas to satisfy the global needs.

Information-oriented logistics concerns the management of information as a source of competitive advantage. More than the flow of products, the logistics system is directly involved with the flow of information (e.g., availability of products, time to deliver, customer needs). Companies that segment their customers into many markets and/or offer a great variety of options for their products are interested in changes in customer tastes and/or technology developments. Information-oriented logistics, then, is related to the relationship between the sectorial dimension and the geographic dimension. Logistics partners, for example, offer the possibility of accessing information in areas not traditionally within the purview of a company. Suppliers may offer information on the latest developments for a component, while the transportation company allows access to new markets (e.g., mail order). Involvement in the geographic dimension is the source of information for changes that may be occurring in a different environment.

User-oriented logistics focuses on the final customer. Supply chain partners collectively can analyze the existing logistics system, identify its bottlenecks, redundancies, and so on, and collaboratively improve it. The main objective is to not only win new customers, but to maintain existing ones. By the same approach, companies in the logistics system can better cooperate to develop technologies because each of the participants can bring their core competence to bear on the matters at hand. By maintaining a user-oriented focus, the logistics system gains flexibility in responding to the needs of customers. The flexibility is realized by the combination of the different companies involved through the right coordination.

All three orientations attempt to rationalize resources in order to maximize profitability. The continuous synergies in resources-oriented logistics, information-oriented logistics, and user-oriented logistics define the dynamic forces of what we refer to as global operations and logistics (Figure 2–4).

It is important to emphasize the dynamic nature of the global business environment. This dynamism compels companies to adopt each of the three orientations with different intensities at different times. Different internal or external forces (e.g., regulations, technology changes, competition) may prompt a company to switch priorities. For example, at a given time, a company may be driven by resources-oriented logistics and focus on optimizing the global manufacturing/production facilities network.

Or, motivated by changes in the structure of competition and existing distribution channels, the company may shift its emphasis to coordinating with members of the logistics system, thereby switching its primary orientation to a user-oriented focus. This does not mean that the resources orientation is not important (the company will still maintain the global network), but rather, that the new changes force the firm to emphasize cooperation with the distribution members of the logistics system.

Companies cannot excel in every dimension all the time. The importance of the different dimension is driven by the dynamic nature of the marketplace. In the following section, we discuss the different competitive priorities that companies may pursue.

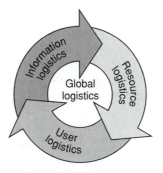

Figure 2–4   Dynamic Forces of Global Logistics

Competitive Priorities

Financial indicators are commonly used for measuring the performance of companies. However, financial measures by themselves paint an incomplete picture of a company's operations. We suggest complementing the traditional financial measures with a set of operational measures that allow for a better understanding of the way in which the logistics system is analyzed. More specifically, we refer to cost, quality, service, and flexibility. Some refinements of the measures are detailed as follows.

Cost

Initial Cost: The cost of acquiring the product that can be raw materials cost for a manufacturing company, or finished goods costs for a distributor firm (relevant for consumer products)

Lifecycle Cost: The cost of acquiring, maintaining and disposing of the product (relevant in industrial markets)

Quality

Design Quality: The features, styling, and other product attributes that enhance fitness for use (relevant in luxury products)

Conformance Quality: Product conformance to set production standards (relevant to all product markets)

Service

Delivery Speed: Ability to produce and deliver the product quickly, with little turnaround time (relevant in time-based competition)

Delivery Reliability: Ability to produce and deliver products within a consistent time frame, according to contractually specified time intervals (relevant to all markets)

Flexibility

New-Product Flexibility: Ability to introduce new products quickly and effectively (relevant in time-based competition)

Customization: Ability to produce a large variety of products that match the needs of a highly segmented market (relevant for mass customization)

Product Mix Flexibility: Ability to efficiently and effectively adjust the production mix in response to product demand fluctuations/cyclicality (relevant for cyclical markets)

Production Ramp-Up Flexibility: Ability to rapidly expand the production process to accommodate rapid mass production (relevant for changing/uncertain markets)

In order to understand how to use the performance criteria, we divide them into two types: winning and qualifying criteria. A *winning criteria* is one that distinguishes a company relative to its competition—customers buy a firm's products because of that specific criteria (e.g., cost for a commodity-type product). A *qualifying criteria* is defined as the minimum level required to participate in the competition (e.g., quality for a commodity-type product).

We believe it is not possible for a company to achieve *winning* status in all four criteria—cost, quality, service, and flexibility—simultaneously. At most, firms may achieve two winning criteria at any given point. Companies, however, may achieve winning status on any combination of criteria—e.g., quality and service.

We also argue that qualifying criteria, while secondary in importance, are never irrelevant. If a company uses service as the winning criteria, cost must still be within a reasonable range in order for the company to compete. When Laura Ashley, a global clothing and furnishings retailer based in the United Kingdom, decided to outsource its entire outbound logistics system, the winning criteria was quality of the products resulting in a high loyalty among the customers. The motivation for outsourcing, however, was distribution cost in the form of inventory, because worldwide stocks had gotten out of control.

Our third premise is that the *selection* of a specific winning criteria—cost, quality, service, or flexibility—is not the primary issue. More important is how a company defines that winning criteria in the context of its logistics system. For example, for high-tech manufacturer Hewlett-Packard's low-end ink jet printer products, quality is a qualifying criteria because most competitors offer similar features. Most printer manufacturers offer similar specifications—e.g., pages per minute, resolution, paper size—so it is difficult to make any of the features a distinguishing factor in quality. It is a qualifying criteria in the sense that if a company does not offer these basic features, it cannot compete. Service might be the winning criteria if defined as availability in stores. However, flexibility might be the criteria if defined as the flexibility of being in different stores at the same time. HP has to analyze (and react) by managing the operations and logistics for the most efficient way of reaching the distribution channels.

Finally, the process of defining competitive priorities is dynamic in time and space. Products move along the product life cycle (PLC) and as they do, the character of their competitiveness changes. By the same token, products in different geographic markets are positioned in different stages of the PLC. Companies need to adjust the logistics system in order to accommodate this dynamic process. As an example, Bose Corporation, a major manufacturer of high-quality audio equipment, first started selling its high-fidelity speakers in specialty stores, but now also sells them through mass discounters such as Price Club. These products have evolved from having quality as their winning strategy to having service as the winning criteria.

In the competitive environment, these four criteria define the performance of different companies. As seen in Figure 2–5, customers exercise buying preferences and define market size. Responding to these preferences, different competitors generate output that emphasizes certain criteria (unique combinations of cost, quality, service, and flexibility). These criteria combinations are perceived by customers as that company's *performance*. Customers buy the "performance" they like best, and in so doing, define market share for each competitor.

Ideally, the particular performance criteria/elements selected by a company in response to customer preferences define the requirements for its operations and logistics system. A company that emphasizes service as a winning criteria will have operations and logistics requirements that are not the same as a company whose winning criteria is quality. In the first case, the service requirements force companies to have a high level of availability for

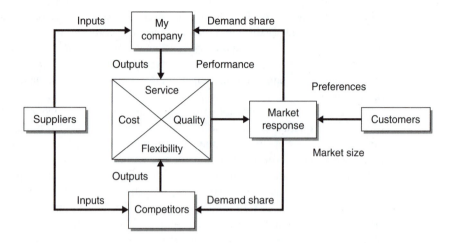

Figure 2–5   A Competitive Framework for Operations and Logistics

their products. If the product is not on the shelf, a sale may be lost. In these cases, customer loyalty is low. This requirement forces the company to manage inventories with high levels of safety stock and emphasize the user-oriented focus to coordinate with the other members of the logistics system.

If a company's winning criteria is quality, on the other hand, customers probably would be willing to wait for the product because they are highly loyal. In such a case, the operations/logistics requirements focus on making sure that quality standards are maintained. This constitutes a resource-oriented focus.

◆ THE CONCEPT OF AN OPERATIONS AND LOGISTICS STRATEGY

What is operations and logistics strategy? The challenge of defining operations and logistics strategy is not straightforward. Some elements of strategy have universal validity and can be applied to any firm, regardless of its nature. Others appear heavily dependent on the firm's structure, culture, and economic environment. We find it useful, therefore, to separate the concept of *strategy* from the process of *strategy formulation*.

Operations and logistics strategy is best viewed as a multidimensional concept that embraces all the critical operations and logistics activities of the firm, providing it with a sense of unity, direction, and purpose. To that end, we propose the following comprehensive definition:

Operations and logistics strategy

- is a coherent, unifying, and integrative pattern of decisions
- determines and reveals the organization's purpose of operations and logistics activities in terms of the firm's long-term objectives, action programs, and resource allocation priorities
- attempts to support or achieve for the firm a long-term, sustainable advantage by responding properly to opportunities and threats in the firm's environment

An operations and logistics strategy must be comprehensive, but at the same time must break down the complex web of decisions into analyzable pieces. A comprehensive operations and logistics strategy is made up of twelve decision categories:

1. structure of facilities networks
2. choice of operations process technology
3. choice of logistics process technology
4. vertical integration of supply chain
5. work force
6. operations planning and control
7. distribution planning and control
8. quality management
9. transportation policy
10. customer service policy
11. organization
12. sourcing

This organizing framework of decision categories is presented in Table 2–1. The collective pattern of decisions in these areas determines the strategic capabilities of the operations and logistics function. Like any other system, the operations and logistics system is able to do certain things well, and other things only with difficulty—if at all. Trade-offs are a fact of business life. Choices must be made, and some goals must be elevated at the expense of others. A consistent pattern of choices that supports the firm's priorities lays out a clear strategic orientation for the firm.

The twelve decision categories can be further classified into two general categories: *structural and infrastructural* decisions. The structural decisions are of an irreversible nature, have long-term impact, and constitute the bricks and mortar of the operations and logistics system. The infrastructural decisions deal with the nonstructural features of the operations and logistics system. They encompass procedures, control systems, and organizational alternatives of the various activities. In general, they are more tactical in nature because they encompass myriad ongoing decisions. They also do not require highly visible capital investments. The classification of the decision categories into structural and infrastructural is depicted in Table 2–1.

Structural Decisions

We now comment on the twelve decision categories. A brief summary of our main points can be seen on Table 2–1. We start with the four decision categories classified at *structural* choices.

Facilities Network

Structuring the network of facilities involves long-term decisions of an irreversible nature. This process addresses such issues as number of plants, their locations and capacities, and the extent and type of focus of the facilities. Facilities may be focused by geography, product group, process type, or stage in the product life cycle. The structuring of the network must go beyond physical flows and include the nature of information flows and supplier/customer relationships of the various facilities in the network.

Table 2–1 *Decision categories in operations and logistics strategy*

OPERATIONS AND LOGISTICS STRATEGY			
Structure		*Infrastructure*	
Major Decision Categories	*Issues/Decisions*	*Major Decision Categories*	*Issues/Decisions*
Facilities Network	Supply chain structure Number of echelons For each echelon • number of facilities • facility size • facility location • facility focus Links between facilities • information flows • sourcing patterns	Work Force	Training/recruiting Payment system Job security
		Operations Planning and Control	Centralization/ decentralization Computerization decision Rules inventory coverage level Location of inventory
Operations Process Technology	Equipment Extent of automation Investment timing	Distribution Planning and Control	Centralization/ decentralization Distribution channel selection
Logistics Process Technology	Storage/transportation technology Extent of information technology		Inventory coverage level Location of inventories
		Quality	Improvement programs Control standards Measurements
Vertical Integration	Extent of integration Direction (forward/backward) Balance of capacity	Transportation Policy	Transportation modes Logistic alliances Subcontracting
		Customer Service Policy	Frequency of delivery Ordering methods Pricing/discounts
		Organization	Structure Reporting Support groups Performance measures
		Sourcing	Purchasing Supplier selection Offshore sourcing

Operations Process Technology

This category involves choosing which processes, among a number of alternatives, will be used to produce particular products. It also encompasses other issues such as the technology flexibility, labor skills requirements, and investment exposure.

Logistics Process Technology

Similarly, this category involves choosing among a number of alternative technologies to perform the various logistics activities. A vast array of technological choices must be made in terms of the firm's investments in transportation equipment and information technologies linking the various facilities in the network, as well as for locating inventories in the logistics pipeline.

Vertical Integration

An important issue of a firm's operations and logistics strategy is the issue of vertical integration. This issue determines the firm's width of internal span of process, and its links and relationships at either end of the process spectrum with suppliers, distributors, and customers. The important issues related to vertical integration involve deciding which of the principal activities should be performed in house, which activities should be outsourced or subcontracted, and what type of subcontracting/suppliers arrangements should exist. Issues related to supplier reliability and impact of integration on product quality and cost are also important.

Infrastructural Decisions

Moving on, *infrastructural* choices comprise eight decision categories.

Work Force

The main issues in work-force management are recruiting, training, evaluation, promotion, and placement of personnel, development of incentive and reward systems, management development, and employee job security and benefits.

Operations Planning and Control

Both aggregate and short-term planning and control issues fall under this category. In aggregate planning, the firm must deal with issues of balancing capacity to variable demand over a planning horizon. In planning materials and production over shorter horizons, the firm must make decisions about appropriate support systems (MRP, JIT). Scheduling and resource control on an hourly or daily basis are other typical tactical decisions.

Distribution Planning and Control

The firm must decide the way in which it will organize and control its distribution system (centralized versus decentralized), choose appropriate distribution channels (retailers, wholesalers, discount stores, etc.) to bring its products to the market, decide on the level of inventory coverage to be provided, manage its inventory systems and decide on how to allocate the inventories of the various items in the product line in plant, regional, or field warehouses. It is also important for the firm to decide on the type of computerized distribution planning system and to find effective ways to implement them.

Quality

Quality management is critical for most global firms. A quality strategy should be based on a well-articulated philosophy fully supported by top management and based on measurable objectives. Major decisions in quality management involve choosing quality improvement programs, allocating resources among them, setting measurable quality targets, allocating quality responsibilities, and developing decision tools and measurement systems for the quality efforts.

Transportation Policy

Setting a transportation policy involves choosing among modes of transportation, deciding on shipment sizes, routing, and scheduling. Transportation decisions are highly interrelated with customer service and inventory policy and location decisions.

Customer Service Policy

The customer service policy broadly includes inventory availability, speed of delivery, order-filling speed, and accuracy. It is strongly linked to inventory and transportation policies. Low levels of service allow centralized inventories at a few locations and the use of less expensive modes of transportation. Exactly the opposite holds true for high customer-service levels.

Organization

A solid organizational infrastructure is essential to support the operations and logistics task. The firm must address how to organize and what layers of management it will use, while also setting operating policies and establishing well-understood lines of authority and responsibility. Developing a corporate culture that reinforces the overall operations and logistics strategy also is crucial.

Sourcing

The firm must decide on the role of purchasing and offshore sourcing in its overall strategy, choose the appropriate organizational form for its purchasing department, deal with make-or-buy decisions for various product components, formulate a supplier relations strategy, and set evaluation guidelines for supplier performance and choice.

◆ THE STRATEGY PROCESS

The concept of strategy and the process of strategy formulation are inseparable in any actual organizational setting. The strategy formulation process has a number of key objectives, including:

- Defining key players and their role in formulating and implementing the strategy
- Deciding on the type and sequence of interactions the key players should have
- Designating the nature, timing, and extent of information flows among key players
- Determining the manner and extent of communication about the strategy formulation process among the various constituencies inside and outside the firm
- Suggesting support tools and methodologies to be used as part of the process

We suggest a simple working framework to support the process of developing an operations and logistics strategy. This framework is depicted in Figure 2–6. It consists of six main activities in corporate planning. These are as follows:

Activity 1:   Setting the firm's mission and objectives
Activity 2:   Developing marketing strategies to meet these objectives

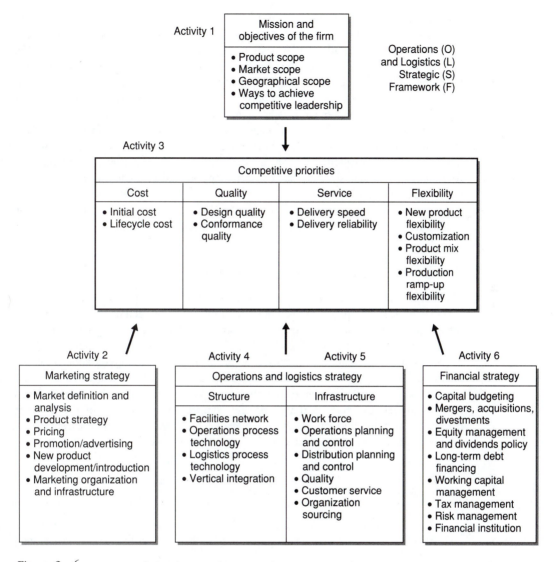

Figure 2−6   Framework for the Development of Operations and Logistics Strategy in Corporate Decisions

Activity 3:   Identifying the firm's competitive priorities for the different product markets

Activity 4:   Making structural choices as part of the development of an *operations and logistics* strategy that supports the previously established competitive priorities

Activity 5:   Developing the needed infrastructure to support the structural choices of the operations and logistics strategy

Activity 6:   Developing financial strategies that support the firm's objectives and competitive priorities

The purpose of this framework is to facilitate the corporate debate in formulating an operations and logistics strategy that successfully supports the competitive priorities in the marketplace. A successful strategy should lead to breakthroughs in terms of products or processes, or at least support the firm's needs better than the operations and logistics functions of key competitors. The formulation process should be viewed as dynamic, flowing smoothly between levels of activities (i.e., iterations between activities 1 and 2, activities 2-5, activities 4-6, etc.), rather than as a static, sequential process. The intention of the framework is to help develop a strategy formulation process that explicitly includes the operations and logistics perspective in the discussion of corporate-level issues. At the same time, the process explicitly recognizes the need for interfunctional communication and coordination. It emphasizes the idea that strategy should be business- and market-driven, rather than functionally driven.

In the following paragraphs, we describe the various activities that constitute the operations and logistics strategy framework (O&LSF) depicted in Figure 2–6.

Defining the Mission and Objectives of the Firm

The mission of the firm is a statement of the current and future expected firm activities. It also makes clear the unique competencies the firm has developed or intends to develop over time to assume a position of competitive leadership and maintain a long-term advantage. The mission statement includes a broad description of the products (product scope), markets (market scope), geographical coverage of the firm's activities (geographical scope), and interpretation of competitive advantages. In Table 2–2, we provide a structure for presenting the mission statement. Observe the emphasis not just on presenting the current scope of the firm's activities, but also on the scope and competitive advantages of the firm within a reasonable planning horizon (three to five years). The specific example in Table 2–2 is the mission statement of an American Bank in Taipei, the capital city of Taiwan.

Table 2–2   *Mission statement of an American Bank in Taipei*

	Current	Future
Product Scope	Provide corporate customers with: • financial services • trade services • foreign exchange investment advisory service • project finance Build products and services that generate fee-based revenue	• Expand product scope through integrated financial service • Continue the development of fee- and commission-based products • Emphasize produce differentiation
Market Scope	Provide products and services to: • Governmental organizations • Private corporations • Financial institutions	• Limit to large customers selected middle market names only • Participate in capital market at home and abroad
Geographical Scope	• Major parts of Taiwan	• Expand geographic boundaries within Taiwan
Competitive Advantage	• Talented people	• Increase efficiency and service expertise • New product development • Active participation in legislative reform

Defining the mission and competitive advantages is essential, as all input during the strategy formulation process must be linked to the objectives of the firm. Coming up with the mission statement gives managers an opportunity to reflect on the current status and priorities of the firm, and to identify weaknesses and opportunities for growth.

Developing Marketing Strategies

Development of marketing strategies requires careful thinking regarding a number of items:

- Market definition and analysis (market segmentation, clear definition of product-market segments)
- Product strategy (product-line design, product variety, bundling of products, branding strategies)
- Pricing (product line pricing, price/quality relationships)
- Promotion and advertising strategies
- New product development and introduction (concept development, prototype development, market feasibility analysis, new product introduction)
- Marketing organization and infrastructure (planning, control, incentives, and information systems to support marketing activities)

Decisions on all of these factors must be made in a way that best supports the firm's mission and objectives.

Setting Competitive Priorities for Various Product Markets

In the first two activities, the firm decides on the markets in which it will compete and on the products it will offer to different market segments. This third activity requires the firm to be explicit about the ways in which its products will compete in the various market segments. Typically, competitive priorities fall into one of the four competitive criteria dimensions discussed earlier. Doubtless, the linkage between the competitive priorities and the relationship with the dimensions of the global logistics framework should be understood to determine which one of the orientations (resource, information, or user) should be followed.

Choosing a Structure for an Operations and Logistics Strategy

This activity requires a consistent pattern of structural decisions in operations and logistics that effectively supports the competitive priorities in the different product markets. The structural decision categories, as elaborated earlier, include the structure of facilities networks, choice of operations process technology, choice of logistics process technology, and vertical integration of the supply chain.

Choosing Infrastructure for an Operations and Logistics Strategy

This activity requires a consistent pattern of infrastructure decisions in operations and logistics that effectively supports the competitive priorities in the different product markets. The infrastructure decision categories are: work force, operations, planning and control, distribution planning and control, quality, transportation policy, customer service policy, organization, and sourcing.

Developing Financial Strategies

One of the main limitations for the implementation of any strategy is financial resources. Certainly, all functional areas compete for resources; development of financial strategies requires careful decision making with respect to the following areas:

- Capital budgeting (defining criteria to be used for investment selection, allocation of capital to different business projects)
- Mergers, acquisitions, and divestment (identifying such opportunities and providing guidelines to evaluate them)
- Equity management and dividends policy (share purchasing, new equity issues and preferred stocks, stock splits and stock consolidation, dividends policies)
- Long-term debt-financing (selecting sources and magnitude of long-term debt, type of interest, maturity conditions, etc.)
- Working capital management (cash and credit management) and pension fund management
- Risk management (hedging strategies), financial organization, and managerial infrastructure (accounting procedures, measures of financial performance, scope of treasury function and required information systems support)

◆ LINKING TO STRATEGY

As this chapter indicates, linking the operations and logistics functions with the corporate strategy of the organization, as well as with the other functional areas, is critical to the long-term success of the firm. Without such a linkage, a corporation cannot achieve a leading position as a truly global enterprise. The global operations and logistics framework outlined in this chapter serves as a basis for structuring such an enterprise. It will be used extensively throughout this book.

DISCUSSION QUESTIONS

1. List several reasons for the typically reactive role of operations and logistics in the formulation of corporate strategy.

2. What are the three main orientations in a logistics system? Give examples of each.

3. Explain the difference between *winning* and *qualifying* criteria in the marketplace for a firm. Provide examples from specific competitive situations. What is the importance of explicitly recognizing winning and qualifying criteria?

4. What are the main decision categories of an operations and logistics strategy? Explain in detail what each involves.

5. What are the main activities that make up the operations and logistics strategic framework? Describe the main issues and choices to be considered in each of these activities.

6. Explain the difference between structural and infrastructural decisions in the formulation of operations and logistics strategy.

REFERENCES

Cooper, J. C. 1993. Logistics strategies for global businesses. *International Journal of Physical Distribution and Logistics Management* 23(4): 12–23.

Czinkota, M. R., and I. A. Ronkainen. 1988. *International marketing.* New York: The Dryden Press.

Fawcett, S. E., and L. M. Birou. 1992. Exploring the logistics interface between global and JIT sourcing. *International Journal of Physical Distribution and Logistics Management* 22(1).

Garvin, D. A. 1992. *Operations strategy: Text and cases.* Englewood Cliffs, N.J.: Prentice-Hall.

Hayes, R. H., S. C. Wheelwright, and K. B. Clark. 1988. *Dynamic manufacturing: Creating the learning organization.* New York: The Free Press.

Hax, A., and N. S. Majluf. 1991. *The strategy concept and process: A pragmatic approach.* Englewood Cliffs, N.J.: Prentice-Hall.

Hill, T. 1989. *Manufacturing strategy: Text and cases.* Homewood, Ill.: Richard D. Irwin Inc.

◆ CASE 2-1: Michelin ◆

The executive committee of Michelin Europe is meeting to discuss the main orientation to give to its logistics development plan for the next five years. The committee is made up of the group's European managing director, sales director, production director, flow planning director (DOE/PR), distribution logistics director (DOE/GD) and, lastly, the integrated sales network director. They all hold responsibilities at the European level.

Europe is one of the four geographical areas out of which Michelin runs its manufacturing and sales operations, the others being North America, Asia, and the rest of the world, which includes Africa, South America, and Australia. Europe covers seventeen countries, which have different types of sales entities. There are manufacturing facilities in five of the countries only. They are France, The United Kingdom, Germany, Spain, and Italy.

The managing director recalls the three objectives that he has decided concerning the logistics development plan for the year 2000. With the sales manager's agreement, he stresses the utmost importance of maintaining a high service level as a competitive advantage and he asks the sales manager to present the guiding principles of sales strategy and the types of tire distribution channels chosen in Europe.

To begin with, the sales manager reminds the other committee members that it is important to make the distinction between two sorts of markets; original equipment (OE) destined for automakers and replacement tires (RT). On the former market the key factors are the following:

- Automakers have European production and sales strategies. Their production planning is done on a European basis, even though parts procurement is dealt with at the level of local entities. The special feature of the tire business is that one brand of tire can be replaced by another. Automakers reach annual market share agreements, which entails intermittent procurement. Moreover, production facilities tend to change a great deal and which implies changing production procurement sources.
- The tire manufacturer delivers tires or mounted tires; that is to say, the tire already mounted on the wheel. A trend toward mounted tires has been recently noticed.
- The automakers can be divided into two categories. They are either manufacturers or automobile importers, the latter accounting for a marginal share of this market.
- In the fields of sales and technology tire makers give preference to their relationships with automakers for strategic purposes. The choice of brand when replacing a tire is strongly influenced by the type of tire mounted in the first place.

The sales problem in the other tire market is vastly different. Customer demand varies depending on customer type, and sales distribution channels tend to be particular to each country.

Michelin's strategic and sales position on this market is:

- Maintain customer independence and a low level of market concentration. The manufacturer seeks extensive distribution as opposed to some competitors, who give preference to selective distribution.
- Develop a real image of technical expertise as regards tires, particularly in the field of tires for heavy trucks.

By Philippe-Pierre Dornier and Michel Fender, Professor at L'Essec, May 1997.

This argument makes sense in relation to the preceding objective described in that both approaches strive to prevent the market from being dominated by big distributors. Achieving this second objective means that the tire maker must invest in training for dealers to make them competent technically and able to provide quality service to their customers.

Michelin's customer groups and their main characteristics for replacement tires are as follows;

Specialized dealers. Specialist tire dealers for whom selling tires accounts for all or a major part of their business. They sell the whole range of categories and all brands. They are either independent dealers or belong to a chain, whether controlled by a tire manufacturer or not. They sell to end users, garages, or dealers. They are, therefore, retailers or small, local wholesalers. It is important to differentiate between several sub-categories in this first category:

• Dealers controlled by manufacturers
• Independent dealers who are not controlled by manufacturers
• Multiple dealers not controlled by manufacturers
• Dealers who are basically wholesalers

Garages, automobile dealers and service stations. Repairs and gas rather than tires are their main business. Nevertheless, the share of tire sales in their overall business is growing.

Franchised, multispecialist dealers. Their business revolves around automobile parts. They are automobile parts dealers and quick replacement centers located close to large shopping malls and big supermarkets.

Two-wheel vehicle dealers. These specialize in two-wheel vehicles. It's an extremely atomized distribution market to begin with, and then becomes heavily concentrated.

Other tire manufacturers sell directly to point-of-sale distribution, hypermarkets, and gas stations. All these flows are known as sell-in. Sell-in enables the manufacturer to identify the proportion of customers he sells replacement products to. However, sell-in does not give a true reflection of replacement tire sales to the end user. In fact, many European or national specialized dealers sell to wholesalers who, themselves, sell on to dealers, garages, specialized dealers, hypermarkets and gas stations plying local or regional markets. These flows between first-line dealers, who do business directly with the manufacturer, and second-line dealers are called sell-out. They are the firms which reach the end user. Sell-out helps understand the interplay between manufacturers and end users.

The situation between the countries as far as the relative importance of the different channels used is rather different.

So when France and the United Kingdom are compared, for example, the manufacturer-controlled sales network share is twice as big in the UK than in France, and the opposite is true for automobile makers. Accounting for such differences in order to break down service levels according to customer type will be seen later on.

Analyzing quantitative data for the French market for private automobiles enables us to set forth the following points:

• The sales network controlled by manufacturers tends to progressively increase its market share to the detriment of the other distribution channels, accounting for only 19% of sell-in for private automobiles.
• Franchised dealers are improving market penetration, while still remaining the least successful means of distributions with 8.3%.
• There has been a gradual concentration of delivery points, which have lost 5,000 delivery points in the past three years, to 18%.

The same analysis of the private automobile market in the UK gives the following results, which contrast with those in France.

• The sales network controlled by the manufacturer seems to be losing some ground.
• Wholesalers and independent dealers, who have doubled their share, have benefited from this drop.

These trends in the private automobile market are the same as those noticed in heavy truck and van markets. Controlled sales networks are more numerous in the former market compared to the latter.

Next the sales manager gives the findings of a logistics maturity study of sales distribution channels. These findings are as follows:

• Manufacturers ignore the logistics behavior of its customers. It is understood in a sales sense rather than in a logistics one. The first step is to have the products listed and then push flows in order to take up selling space.
• General sales terms do not take into account logistics parameter inducements such as delivery volumes or periods. This is true for two basic reasons.

1. This approach would mean that manufacturers would have to provide a higher quality of service, which they would be incapable of doing themselves. Difficult economic circumstances would ensue.
2. Such an approach would give preference to big customers, which would go against the manufacturer's sales strategy, whose objective is to continue having a myriad of customers with small volume order.

As far as the levels of service sought by customers are concerned, the sales manager points out that they should be understood according to two types of activity:

- OE service levels
- RT service levels

Knowledge of OE service levels is not really very accurate. However, with regard to the manufacturer's practice of systematically giving preference to OE deliveries over RT deliveries, performance must be excellent. Automakers' expectations may be summarized as:

- Post-manufacturing or mounting
- Maximum product availability products
- Possibility of synchronous flows
- Delivery from advance inventory

On the RT market Michelin's sales teams have noticed the following expectations:

1. Customer-supplier contact

- Proximity of supplier for goods pick-up off the shelf
- Opening hours adapted to the customers' opinion times, such as Saturday morning
- Efficient, suitable communication means; telephone, free telephone number, fax, free fax number, answering machines and EDI
- Limited ringing before answering phone
- Quality of physical and telephone reception
  - Speaker identifies himself, recognizes customer, speaks the same language
  - Prolonged, personalized and confidential relations with contact according to territory or distribution channel
- Professionalism of manufacturer's interlocutor
  - Product knowledge, product and service availability, customer's characteristics
  - Quality, reliability, and speed of information, answers and delivery time commitments
  - Anticipation of customer's needs
  - Dealing with specific or exceptional customer demands
- The quality of relations and value adding by all interlocutors who come into contact with the customer, supplier's and service provider's personnel

2. Logistics order processing

- Invoicing:
  - Frequency, grouping according to customer account, made out for each point of sale
  - Clearness and accuracy of documents
  - Print-out and storage medium
  - Efficient information system

- Accuracy and reliability of the information; inventory, payment terms, conditions of sales, customer characteristics
- Deferred order management
- Processing confidentiality

3. Physical order processing

- Meeting customer demand, required delivery time, pace of delivery, exceptional order processing
- Regularity of deliveries
- Compliance with and reliability of orders
- Identification of delivered products
- Quality of carriers; clean equipment, personnel, image, contact, knowledge of customer, discretion
- Physical processing meets customers' logistics approach
- Customer inventory at suppliers'
- Demand for recently manufactured articles

4. After-sales service

- Claims processing; setting up consumer service
- Error processing; orders, invoicing, transportation
- Return of unsold articles

5. Other services

- Collection of casings
- Collection of waste

The European sales manager goes on to explain that faced with such a great number of different situations regarding service level, which is made even more complicated by the characteristics of the products, elaborating logistics families becomes necessary as illustrated in Table 1. It was deemed wise to begin by distinguishing, country by country, between product categories according to sales volume (ABC classification) and to set this criterion against the order profile in

Table 1

Axis of Typological Classification of Tire Products

| | | | RT market | |
	Class	OE Market	Large SDs	Other SDs
Category				
Private automobiles	A	M4	M3	M2
Private automobiles	B	M4	M2	M1
Private automobiles	C	—	M1	M1
Vans	—	M3	M2	M1
Motorcycles	A	M2	M1	M1
Agricultural vehicles	—	M2	M1	M1
Wheels	—	M4	M1	M3
Casing returns	—	—	M2	M1

terms of order quantities (four classes, numbered M1 through M4, M4 denoting the highest volume, were used). This led to big specialist dealers (SD) standing out and the others (based on annual turnover).

The second stage amounted to taking into account the delivery speed by distinguishing four delivery times:

- a: urgent, within 24 hours
- b: urgent replenishment within 48 hours
- c: less urgent restocking within three days
- d: 2 weeks

The results appear in Table 2.

Table 2

Delivery Times Taken Into Account.

| | | | RT market | |
	Class	OE Market	Large SDs	Other SDs
Category				
Private automobiles	A	a	c	b
Private automobiles	B	a	c	a
Private automobiles	C	—	a	a
Vans	—	a	b	c
Motorcycles	A	a	c	c
Agricultural vehicles	—	b	c	c
Wheels	—	—	c	–
Casing returns	—	—	d	d

Desired service levels in terms of delivery times allow a deeper understanding of the question. Five delivery times were identified:

- Off the shelf collection, i.e., the customer collects the articles from the tiremakers' manufacturing facility
- In a matter of a few hours, or same-day delivery
- D+1, that is to say, the order is sent in on day D and delivery takes place the following day
- Weekly, i.e., delivery is the week following the order
- Beginning of the month M+1 where the order is sent in during month M and the customer wants delivery to be made the following month, usually in the first days.

The European managing director thanks the sales manager for his presentation, which helps to clarify the group's sales objectives, which really serve as a set of requirements for the efficient logistics organization in terms both of the production of the service and logistics costs. In particular, service levels to offer customers appear to be extremely varied, a point which will obviously make for great complexity in setting up supply chains. The chief executive then stresses the importance of imagining logistics systems that are simple and above all flexible, especially when confronted with likely market changes and the manufacturer's market position. Indeed the second problem he would like to find solutions for is the lack of coordination between the two main logistics actors who are involved in producing the service. Therefore, before deciding on the information system and on information flow procedures it is essential to have an organization which will allow the group:

- To meet the firm's overall targets (constant improvement of customer service, cost cutting and increased responsibility for the different people involved)
- To include in its working, answers to the system's current shortcomings and undesirable effects
- To make sure that the information system does not become a brake on the firm's progress and that the system permits efficient management of reliable information through an integrated communication network

The two main actors in the logistics process are DOE/PR responsible for planning the three main final production stages, manufacturing, vulcanizing and marking the tires and DOE/GD in charge of getting orders ready, shipping and delivery to customers' points of sale (logistics and distribution). The planning manager, DOE/PR, and distribution manager, DOE/GD take it in turn to speak and analyze the present situation, underlining any dysfunctioning, which has come to light. The planning manager speaks first to explain the way the logistics process works and its six principal functions:

Forecasting. Estimates for future orders are made by a forecaster in each sales office, one in each country. He may specialize in one of the markets (OE or RT) and reports, in some cases, to the office's OE, RT or OE and RT sales manager, or in other cases to the logistics manager (the DOE/GD's correspondent in each country). The estimates are drawn up to the market customer code on a monthly basis, for the following eighteen months. Forecasting, in terms of overall volumes, gets worse when dimension forecasts rather than global forecasts are made. Information goes back and forth between sales forecasts and sales targets (drawn up from marketing information). The sales department signs the forecasts prepared by the forecaster. The aggregate figure coming from the different sales offices is prepared by the DOE/PR, which adds no value to the process but merely gives an interpretation. The impact on logistics of erroneous sales forecasts are not well understood by the sales management (manager and sales manager). A comparison is made between forecasting and allocation demand or AD (for details about allocation demand see the next paragraph) to check that inventory available from AD does not exceed targets.

The efficiency of the forecasting chain is rather mediocre. Differences between forecasts and actual results are between 20% and 40%, depending on item code and by country. The difference for overall volume may reach 20%.

Allocation demand function (DA).   This function is fulfilled once a month looking forward to four months, the first month the planning is done more definitively by the supply manager working in the office. The objective is to supply the offices with future sales using demand allocation figures. The supply manager reports to the logistics manager. He may send in other signed ADs throughout the month. In order to assess his demand the supply manager relies on both forecast sales figures and inventory for sales, sets the rules for inventory levels by item code within a framework of inventory levels laid down by DOE/GD and issues the allocation demand. This is approved by DOE/PR, which regulates and arbitrates at a first level. This stage ends with an approved allocation demand (AAD). The aim of this first stage is to manage the undesirable effects of shortages by taking into account production capacity, on the one hand, and overall inventory levels on the other. The supply manager, in fact, tends to overestimate his needs in his desire to anticipate shortages. Three or four years ago total ADs were between 30% and 40% higher than total overall inventory. The initial aim of AAD was to validate the AD in relation to available capacity of instant production. Depending on the country and on the moment of the time, an AD may correspond to a need to replenish inventory or sales for the following month. Information is not necessarily channeled back to the supply manager after the AAD stage has been completed, except there is a big difference between an allocation demand and the AAD. The calculation of the difference is carried out automatically and is based on sales offices' forecasts and safety delivery times.

The result of this procedure is that the supply manager is responsible for the analysis of initial theoretical dimensioning of inventory. Future modifications are the result of load/capacity balance decisions or due to the stated will to diminish inventory. No supply manager function at the European level exists.

Planning function.   A calculation of net production needs by product (NPNP) per item is carried out in the first place at the overall continental level, then broken down by plant and technical category at the DOE/PR level. Factors taken into account here are the AAD, available manufacturing inventory and objectives of manufacturing inventory from overall inventory objectives. A framework for management

one year ahead per manufacturing country has been set up. It is adhered to as often as possible given the above allocation although events that crop up have to be taken into account, too. Among other things, net production needs affect the manufacturing performances for each country and for each geographical location, which in turn have a bearing on distribution performances. Manufacturing and distribution planning functions (MDP) at country level are informed of the breakdown of overall net production needs for each country and each plant. NPNP defines workloads plant by plant on a monthly basis and MDP draws up the load plan and the Master Production Schedule for each plant on a weekly basis. MDP and the plant decide upon weekly scheduling together. The breakdown on a weekly basis is not an engagement as such. MDP is the sole engagement. At the plant daily scheduling is drawn up over a four-week period, which must stick to the plan with a given leeway of 5% either side of the target. MDP monitors this. Converting manufacturing engagements into products available takes into account customized tires and breaks down production by specification while allowing for questions of quality and transport times by the vulcanizing department. Production available for distribution (PAFD) equals total inventory entries and the spare products from the previous month (which may be made up of products actually available and forecast ones).

Allocation function.   There exist algorithms that allocate production to distribution to be managed by sales office. They seek to answer the three following questions:

• Who are finished products to be allocated to?
• Where are they to be picked up?
• How many finished products are involved?

When shortages occur, they are spread out over the sales offices in such a way as to affect inventory coverage proportionally. The second question is answered in two stages. In the first one allocation takes place on a country basis. In the second stage spare products are allocated according to optimization of transportation costs, the cost of residual inventory and the regularity of supplying. Allocation feeds sales available and opens up credit for transportation scheduling which checks that total current shipments and shipment requirements are lower or equal to allocation.

Inventory management function.   Inventory building through the production system is the outcome of two sets of opposite seasonal factors—sales demand and capacity and the production tool adapting insufficiently well to short- and medium-term production runs. (The production tool is not capable of allowing for dimensional diversity at precisely the right moment quickly nor well enough). The sales organization has its part to play in inventory building as well in that it is the source of uncertainty in sales forecasts and initiating campaigns which reinforce the seasonal phenomenon. It has to be added that sales demand does not make itself known once a month and, what is more, the sales office cannot be sure at what moment in the month it will be delivered. Products are withdrawn according to delivery requirements, which leads to precocious geographical allocations and causes some places to hold too much inventory while others hold too little. The supply manager is not aware of delivery times or the location of products or product allocation carried out by the central program when the AD is made.

Distribution function.   Order management, the responsibility of the plant, has adopted the basic principle of giving priority to OE over RT and never to cause the automobile manufacturers to be in a position of inventory shortage. Items that have short production runs are dealt with through inventory at the European level, and imports have been grouped together into regional distribution centers (DC) and factory warehouses (FW) (physical distribution of products). In some countries distribution centers are aware to a degree of each others' inventory positions, which means that it is possible to send a missing item from one center to another in case of need. The delivery department's tasks are to take delivery of articles from the marking department, imports, shipment direct automobile manufacturers, advance inventory and distribution centers and exports. The department constantly seeks to optimize transportation by taking into account smoothing of the stores' activities and the storage capacity of customers, even though it cannot control customers' delivery reception times.

Local computerized logistic information systems (on the scale of the country) check whether delivery calls from sales offices and distribution centers are valid by monitoring ready inventory forecasts. An inventory call is characterized by a level of quality, a maximum delivery deadline, a minimum one, a desired deadline, and a quantity. Every week, the national system is fed with delivery calls in the shape of forecast entries based on the consolidated weekly Master Production Plan.

As a conclusion to the presentation, the planning director makes one or two observations concerning organization, which he believes should be studied in detail after the process has been formalized. He points out that decision making is spread out and that processes from one country to another vary enormously (without any link between manufacturing and sales) and by type of function (forecasting, supply, etc.) while the corresponding functions have not been set up at the European level. Decision processes are organized at different stages of the monitoring system either from local (sales offices or plant) to central (DOE/ PR), or vice versa, with information loops of monitoring or

adjustment to be added. Production scheduling occurs at three levels in the organization structure (DOE/PR/PFD at the plant level) and their degrees of reactivity are not the same. Moreover, three schedules drawn up by separate entities, vulcanization, marking and shipment, overlap. No synchronization of information exists between the three systems, and as a result the number of actors increases and the dilution of responsibility is greater. In each country, distribution has a national and European responsibility.

The planning director brings his presentation to an end by asking several questions that the European development plan must take into consideration. The questions are:

- What role should the final allocation demand play?
- Can delivery requirements be done away by allowing physical flows to be managed on a basis of push flows governed by a delivery schedule dictated by the logistics function rather than on that of pull flows determined by delivery calls?
- What is the required minimum amount of information that has to be sent to the sales organization at each stage of the process?

The European physical distribution director is then invited to speak. His responsibility for flows begins when articles leave the shipping department at the plants and ends when they are delivered to point of sale on the customers' premises. Planning and distribution responsibilities make up a major part of his task.

He starts by recalling that in 1995 Michelin had a network of 69 manufacturing facilities worldwide. Twenty-two were located in France, 20 in other European countries, 19 in North America, 2 in Africa, 4 in Asia, and 2 in South America. From the beginning of the eighties, Michelin took the decision to specialize its European production facilities. After having specialized its workshops into product categories (private automobiles, heavy goods vehicles), production management began to concentrate manufacturing of a given product at the national level and at the level of a group of countries in one main manufacturing entity. In spite of the growth in the number of items and therefore of the number of products manufactured in the same plant, most products have had a decrease in the number of European sites at which they are manufactured, usually one or two sites. This trend has been reinforced because automobile manufacturers themselves have, at the same time, demanded that the origin of products for original equipment be limited so that they may check the production site before deliveries begin.

The consequences of this specialization of production on the scale of several European countries enjoying production means are measured in flows exchanged between countries. These cross-border flows are necessary in order to recreate locally the product range required to satisfy market demands (sales). It is clear that all these incoming flows are not only down to the specialization of production entities. They are also linked to the structural imbalance that exists between production sites located nationally and national consumption demand. However, an analysis limited to European flows only shows that in terms of production capacity, with the exception of Italy, all countries could be self-sufficient. Table 3 gives the self-sufficiency coefficient of European countries with manufacturing sites. The coefficient represents, for a given country, the ratio between the total capacity for the European market country by country. The capacity is calculated as the sum of products sold to other European countries out of that country's own production plus the country's consumption.

Table 3

Self-Sufficiency Coefficient for European Production Countries					
Country	France	UK	Spain	Italy	Germany
Self-sufficiency coefficient	1.09	0.93	1.11	0.77	1

Table 4 gives the weighting that import flows for each of the Michelin European production countries represent. It can be noticed that even countries like France or Spain, which have the greatest number of production sites and the highest capacity (self-sufficiency coefficient of 1.09 and 1.11, respectively), have a surplus when compared to their respective national demand. Imports from facilities based in other European countries were, in 1994, 36% of sales in tons for France and 43% for Spain.

Table 4

European Import Flows for All Product Categories (1994 flows)					
Country	France	UK	Spain	Italy	Germany
Imports in tons	36%	46%	43%	61%	52%

Overall, 45.3% of all sales in Europe come from import flows. The proportions when all product categories are taken into consideration may be very different from those for a given product category. Thus, where private automobile replacement tires are considered, the import flow figures are as follows:

- 67% for the UK
- 48% for Spain
- 40% for Germany

A concrete illustration of cross-border flows between countries with specialized production sites the origins of flows by country may be given in percentages for any given country as illustrated in table 5.

Each country makes between a little more than a third (Italy) and a little less than two-thirds (France) of its own needs. The rest comes mainly from France and Germany and in similar proportions, from Italy, Spain, and the UK.

The initial position of the physical distribution structure requires that a distinction be made between the market made up vehicle manufacturers and the replacement market. The main entities that exist at the present moment are: Factory Warehouses (FW) located on the production sites or near production sites, distribution centers (DC) and advance inventory (AV).

The current logistics function in these entities and their characteristics are as follows:

Factory warehouses (FW)
- Storage areas dedicated to production pushed products
- Concentration of imported flows and storage
- Handling of large-volume shipments
- More frequent recourse to subcontracting for reasons of flexibility
- Export
- Supplying distribution centers
- Supplying fitting centers
- Direct delivery to OE

Distribution centers (DC)
- Proximity storage
- Delivery to customer
- Sales function (ordering)
- Handling of casings (heavy vehicle tires for retreading)

Advance inventory (AV)
- Dedicated to the OE market
- Located in the plants, the general store, on a carrier's site (the carrier consolidates a maker's order with different manufacturers or even in a DC)
- Local storage areas
- Synchronous delivery flows

OE tire distribution to automakers may be done in one of two ways: either by delivering directly from the production site or from advanced inventories located near the customer's plants.

Automakers could force tire manufacturers to set up multibrand advanced inventories. This overall plan is not applicable in the UK where dedicated distribution centers, forerunners of advanced inventories, deliver to automakers.

Table 5

			Cross-Flows by Origin and Destination			
Origins	France	UK	Spain	Italy	Germany	Total
Destinations						
France	**64%**	11%	9%	9%	7%	100%
UK	28%	**48%**	8%	8%	8%	100%
Spain	22%	9%	**57%**	7%	5%	100%
Italy	31%	11%	9%	**39%**	10%	100%
Germany	23%	10%	8%	5%	**54%**	100%

As far as the replacement market is concerned (RT), the present logic governing distribution is that of the local distribution system. The DC represents a compulsory channel for the RT customer. The choice of range is managed locally in harmony with market analyses gotten by centralized services. As for distribution in France, two delivery modes exist:

- Proximity zone (PZ): an area of a delivery zone in a DC that enjoys two deliveries a day, deliveries that are carried out using the center's own means in terms of vehicles and personnel, by *locatiers* or messenger services.
- Shipment zone (SZ): The remaining part of the delivery zone in a DC, which is delivered once a day by truck rental firms or hauliers.

When a shortage is noticed in a DC, it is the closest regional DC leader that helps out. Such deliveries go under the name of regional deliveries ex SZ. Ex regional deliveries are also imaginable, and they account for several percentage points in the overall picture. Total emergency deliveries amount to 20% of products ordered.

Some product categories are not included in this overall plan. They are:

- Two-wheel vehicles (concentrated in 4 DCs in France)
- Civil engineering, which is concentrated in 2 DCs in France because of the low volumes involved and the difficulty of maintenance
- Inventories of C products managed by a central European site due to their low demand and weak seasonal nature

The trend of the manufacturers' physical distribution structure over the last few years has led to distribution being concentrated through reducing the number of storage centers of the distribution center type (DC). The trend has meant that most manufacturers have seen their strategic position weakened vis-à-vis their small customers, who are a key development axis in the face of the danger that organized distributions represent.

As a matter of fact, the geographical distance of customers from the main storage sites, which is the result of such changes, means:

- Customers no longer pick up their deliveries at the sites.
- There are no longer multiple deliveries in the same day.
- The DCs' commercial role has been taken over by specialized dealers.

In spite of the concentration trend we have just mentioned, the multiplicity of delivery points (direct customers or DCs) has led to the frequency of deliveries being reduced, this so as to keep down transportation costs. The consequence has been an increase in supply uncertainty.

Moreover, repositioning DC storage by specializing the DCs by category and in some sizes runs the risk of worsening the service quality and thereby increasing the costs of delivery services in and outside of the region.

Lastly, it is important to note that the optimization of production means and the ensuing specialization of production sites engenders an increase in import flows, the added costs of which are largely compensated for by the gains in manufacturing costs.

This evolution must not make us lose sight of the search to reduce shortages and the factoring in of maintenance costs, which include order preparations, which will tend to diminish in logistics distribution sites because of the palletization of products. The pallet thus, becomes, the shipment unit for a given item.

Dominant in the search for a solution is the necessary concern for the optimization of both downstream flows (final distribution) and upstream flows (import flows). The distribution structure must also be capable of handling different types of flows.

A set of logistics functions needs to be set up in order to make the product available to the customer. The Physical Distribution Director shows figure 1, which presents the different alternative plans designed according to the allocation and localization of these logistics functions on the different sites (PU: Production unit, LD: logistics department or post manufacturing operations carried out). These plans may be used as a basis for discussion to define the appropriate organization of the supply chain in OE and RT markets.

Transportation organization varies from one country to another. Thus, in France, transportation is carried out by the manufacturer itself, truck rental firms in the proximity zone, and by messengers (there are 200 at national level, on average four per DC) for the shipment zone. Prices are negotiated at local level and submitted to centralized level for authorization. In Great Britain local messenger services are relied upon. They are managed from centralized level. Although in the past the factory warehouse services were responsible for the plant and the distribution center of the sales organization, today the negotiation function for transportation has been brought together at country level for supplying distribution centers and outgoing flows from DCs to customers.

The physical distribution structure and the organization of logistics monitoring including sales forecasts, production and distribution scheduling, are at the service of Michelin Europe's sales strategy. Developing its own sales network makes up part of this sales objective. Michelin's sales network is made up of retail outlets, which specialize in tire sales. They carry mostly Michelin products and references and also competitors' products. At this juncture the European chief executive wonders how it is possible to use, to maximum effect, the logistics synergy that exists between the logistics structures and systems of the tire manufacturer and its sales network, without running the risk of discriminatory sales policies and cannibalization in its very own markets. Each big manufacturer has had its own sales network for a very long time. The war between rival manufacturers, therefore, is over sales networks and the battle is over one key factor, price.

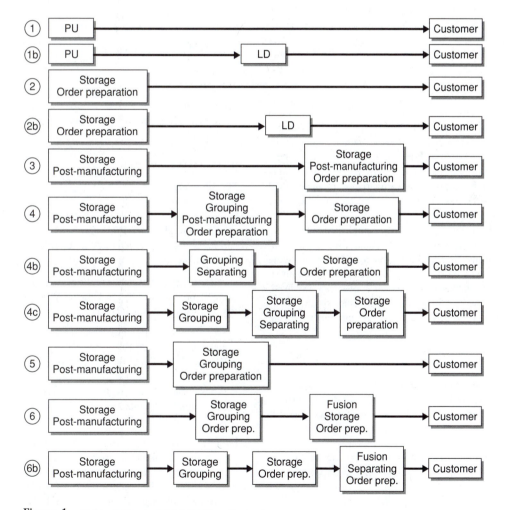

Figure 1 Typical Physical Distribution Scenarios

The European integrated distribution network director speaks. First, he recalls that the European structure of the Michelin network offers a complete range of brands including competitors' brands. The network's name is Euromaster and operates in eight countries: Germany, Austria, Spain, Finland, France, The Netherlands, Great Britain and Sweden. The network owes its expansion to external growth. Its main mission consists of dealing in tire products and some automobile equipment products, such as batteries, shock absorbers, exhaust pipes and brake shoes. Over 50% of business is accounted for by Michelin brand products, and the manufacturer sells a large share of its production using this integrated network.

The network's main mission is to continue to secure for Michelin a direct distribution channel to the market; i.e., the end user in order to fight against the danger that the phenomenon of concentration represents. In such a context the sales network sets out to maximize sales of the manufacturer's tires, to send information concerning the market back upstream and to obtain accurate assessment of sell-out while, at the same time, ensuring a high level of profitability.

The job of the sales network as far as tires are concerned may be broken down into three parts. The general public, selling tires to the end user; professional, oriented to the maintenance of European fleets (programmed actions), which depend on the development of 24-hour emergency services; and, lastly, dealers, wholesalers as opposed to the retailers. The sales network's strong points are wide national coverage in the main countries where it is present, its strong professional reputation, and its presence in the fleet vehicle market. The evolution of channels of distribution is characterized by the growing importance of specialized dealers in heavy vehicle tires to offset the growth of the consumer market.

If the tire manufacturer is to accomplish business success for its sales network in each country, it is required to adapt its needs to the local situation. However, some elements seem to stand out and show that there are common characteristics between all the major countries involved. The basic elements contained in any logistics specifications for the network should take into account the following needs:

Service quality

- Equality in the handling of business by the manufacturer for the whole network and its customers; in particular, respecting delivery times for each country.
- In cases where the sales need is the most important issue, if it is a question of replacing one available product for one that is out of stock, the sales office should call on its own means in order to obtain the missing product.
- Information about product availability at the manufacturer's on request.

Logistics costs

- Concerning this question, it must be said that the expectations of the sales network were not clearly explained since the logistics costs of supply were not visible as they were included in the product's purchasing price. However, it is obvious that the network, through its higher awareness of logistics supply costs, is in a better position to renegotiate its procurement prices.

Logistics organization

- The network would like to give preference, above all, to its main occupation, which is to sell. As a consequence its requirements, concerning logistics solutions are, that they do not take up resources in the local sales offices or at the central level.

A preliminary analytical study has made it possible to define the manufacturer's sales network's main logistics characteristics and the current methods that the manufacturer's sales network uses to handle flows. This study has been carried out from a dual standpoint; the network's and the manufacturer's. The characteristics have been grouped together under the following headings:

Sales forecasts

For the sales network:
- Information concerning seasonality not taken into consideration
- Sales targets not updated in a formal fashion, but monitored constantly

For the manufacturer:
- No specific handling of the network's flows, especially the calculation of the forecast risk
- The central logistics function plans forecasts without including current inventory in the network in its calculations

According to the network director, including the sales forecast process within the logistics process requires that the following questions be answered:

- Should the network make sales forecasts, and in a general manner, who should be responsible for the forecast?
- How detailed should this forecast be (time scale, item etc.)?
- Whose task should it be to approve the forecast?
- What should the objective of the forecast be? Selling-in or selling-out?

Order management. In most of the countries involved no system of sales forecasts made by the sales network and communicated to the manufacturer actually exists. This could be done at the regional level, but not by point of sale. An office in the network may make up to eight orders in a day, which may make up one or two daily deliveries. This system means that there are eight order preparation forms at the manufacturer's. Consequently the total number of deliveries for a given office in the network is about 2.8 deliveries a day, even though average inventory is high.

Not so long ago, at a time when national consumption of tires was not highly seasonal, (i.e., + or − 5% compared to the average figure for Great Britain), sell-out included peaks depending on the campaign cycles. Nowadays, as far as the sales network in Great Britain is concerned, inventory management at points of sale is done from predetermined regional inventory and the inventory's maintenance responsibility lies in the hands of the people at that point of sale.

The sales network director described in detail the ordering system that is in operation in France. There exists available information per item. Included in this information is an indication of weekly average consumption which provides a calculation of a threshold, depending on the product's life cycle, for smoothing (i.e., 80% for cumulated data n − 2, and 20% for the data from the previous week n − 1): Supply (n) = V(n − 1)*0.8 + V(n − 2)*0.2.

This approach appears to be risky because it does not take into account local promotion campaigns or products that are nearing the end of their life cycles for which extra promotional efforts are made. It is rather ideally suited to an item management plan of the A type rather than the C type.

- The logistics manager also has the opportunity to use a manual threshold.
- In fact, inventory is also managed visually, in at least 30% of cases. Inventory management is of the physical type and not the logical type. On top of all this there is the fact that no account is taken of working process ordering.
- Orders are telephoned in, which allows for immediate feedback about the product's availability at the manufacturer's.

Inventory management. Calculated at about 50 days, the high inventory levels are explained by three factors. First, logistics managers are not particularly used to managing their own inventory. Second, the number of items in inventory is particularly high as there are 2,000 tire products and 5,000 products overall. Finally, the terms of sale that the manufacturer offers during promotional campaigns which tend to stimulate bulk buying. The questions raised in this consideration are:

- Should inventory management be left up to the offices?
- Who takes decisions as to product allocation between sales offices in case of shortage?

This inventory mainly concerns A type items while for other item types restocking is done on a just-in-time basis. Such a logic can be explained by the will demonstrated by the people at point of sale to benefit from price reductions related to bulk purchases. To reach the threshold required for such reductions, from the point of view of risk management, it is preferable for them to order items that have a high turnover rate.

The inventory, then, looks like an inventory of listed items embracing a logic of daily replenishing. With two to four tires for each product category, the total number of tires in inventory come to 1,200. Moreover, there is valid doubt, at this stage, about the quality of computerized inventory management for entries and withdrawals: 30% of the sales offices check inventory three or four times a week, 30% once or twice a week and the remaining 40% once a year when inventory taking is carried out.

Analysis of the breakdown of the sales network's inventory reveals that the main product categories make up 81% of sales turnover, yet account for only 64 percent of total inventory value. Figure 2, which shows inventory volume and sales volume for a sample of brands offered in sales offices, highlights some anomalies in comparison to a

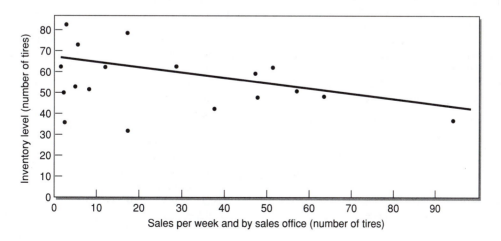

Figure 2   Modelization of Product Coverage for Products in the Sales Network

linear regression (modelized coverage, where each dot in the sample corresponds to a make of tire in one country).

Deliveries.   The main elements noticed are the following:

- The manufacturer's order preparation method, which was on a continuous call basis in the stores, lets the sales logistics manager infer that no logistics supply formalized by the manufacturer exists or that logistics is dedicated to serving his customer.
- Emergency deliveries of unavailable products are made between different points of sale.
- Inventory is not updated harmoniously in the sales offices. The difference is between one hour and one to two days, sometimes days in terms of delivery times.
- The sales network receives statistics from suppliers who devise and communicate the information.
- The sales network's competitors on the British market are delivered every day. This method is possible for the Michelin network besides the three weekly deliveries. The new organization of deliveries to network points of sale has resulted in a reduction in the frequency of daily deliveries from 3.5 to 2.4.

The European sales network director goes into one or two details to do with the supply chains' logistics organization that rival sales networks use or that are similar in design to the one that Michelin has set up. A study of some of these sales networks reveals that three strategies are pursued:

- Logistics completely integrated upstream. In other words, from the manufacturing stage all the way down to the moment the end user enters into possession of the product. Automobile makers, who consider the sales network as one brand, fall into this category.
- Logistics integrated according to product line. This is achieved through using a distribution platform run by the network's central procurement department. Specialized dealers organized into integrated business give preference to this type of setup.
- Logistics organizations which are left up to the suppliers. The supplier's service becomes, in such cases, a criterion of choice. This group includes multi-specialty dealers whose core business is carried out with vehicle equipment manufacturers.

The two criteria that determine a sales network's logistics strategy are the following:

- The type of product. The general logic is chosen in accordance with the products to be handled. Shock absorbers are never handled by a sales network's platform but accessory products, that are to be found on sale in stores, are solely supplied through these platforms. Tires are usually distributed by the manufacturers.
- The type of sales network. Here, three types stand out.
  - Automobile sales networks, which represent one make of automobile. This is a captive sales network as far as the major share of supplies is concerned.
  - Specialist sales networks, which do their business in clearly defined product lines. The high volume they deal in for shock absorbers and exhaust pipes, for instance, enables them to purchase directly from suppliers.
  - Auto center sales networks. This type of sales network, characterized by multiproducts, and multi-brands, comes up against the problems of the many suppliers they have to deal with, small orders per center and per manufacturer. These sales networks use the services of a logistics platform or a wholesaler for all products with a small turnover.

The logistics strategies and structures of equipment manufacturers' suppliers can be analyzed according to three basic criteria:

- The way they have set up their manufacturing facilities; i.e., whether they have chosen a single or several sites.
- Their logistics organization, which depends on the volume of business for each country, for each region. The minimum volume of business has to generate a big enough flow to fill one truck per week and per manufacturing site.
- The sales strategy they have adopted on the subjects of product range, pricing policy and geographical coverage in Europe.

An analysis of the main suppliers present in the tire manufacturer's sales network reveals wide-ranging logistics approaches on the part of the producers. The logistics strategies discovered may be arranged into three categories:

- Integrated logistics or controlled logistics all the way down to the end user. Market leaders come into this category—e.g., Michelin, Goodyear, Dunlop. For the firms in this group logistics makes up a key part of their strategy.
- Makers who do not dominate their logistics operations but who, on the contrary, undergo them. Members of this group choose to use means which are adapted to volumes. The category is made up of second-tier tire manufacturers like Uniroyal and Pirelli.
- Logistics operations which are not integrated at all. Their approach is to entrust operations to such middlemen as specialized purchasing platforms or

wholesale distributors. In this category are to be found third-tier manufacturers and equipment makers such as Bendix and Valeo.

The European sales network director puts forward an outline of the future sales network logistics plan, which could serve as a reliable basis for the final version. He reminds his audience of the thinking that has governed the sales network's logistics operations up until the present date. It relies on the notion that, within the context of a general logistics approach geared to reducing costs and maximizing profitability, the natural tendency has been to look to the procurement function to come up with the required solutions. This tends to translate into practices such as supplying sales offices by whole truckloads. He warns that such a move would run the risk of entering into conflict with the logistics organizations that tire manufacturers have developed. He feels, thus, that it is relevant to think carefully about the type of future logistics structure that is required for the sales network.

He goes on to say that the important questions that need to be answered in the logistics development plan are:

• What benefit is there for a sales outlet to have a supply platform?

• Who are the potential suppliers for the platform?
• What is the sales network's logistics operating procedure for each country?
• What are the logistics operating procedures used by competitors?
• Is setting up a logistics operation at the European level a viable solution?

The group's European managing director begins by thanking each colleague for his contribution and then goes on to suggest that a working party be formed for each one of the three subjects deemed to be lines of investigation likely to lend substance to the future European logistics development plan for the five years to come.

1. Logical process of flow monitoring.
2. Physical organization of the supply chain.
3. Logistics synergy with the integrated sales network.

The subjects should be dealt with simultaneously and in an interactive fashion, since the results of the work on the first subject will be the constraints and opportunities of the following two, which depend on each other and are interrelated.

◆ CASE 2–2: El Remache C.A. ◆

"I don't know what's wrong with the customers," says Ernesto Sordo, sales manager of ERCA's Industrial Division for the last twenty years. *"In the past, the salesmen ("vendedores") were able to meet the quotas with no problem. Of course, there were minor delays, but everything could be arranged in the next visit. The new vendedores ask too many details!"*

It is 8:00 A.M. and the sales force is ready to go and visit customers. Virgilio Rodriguez, assistant manager of El Remache C.A. (ERCA) Industrial Division, is eager to follow his action plan for the day. After all, he has just joined the company, and wants to demonstrate his capabili-

This case was prepared by Professor Ricardo Ernst, Georgetown University, School of Business, and Matteo Recagni with the collaboration of Christoph von Reiche as basis for class discussion rather than to illustrate an effective or ineffective handling of an administrative situation. Most numbers and names have been disguised. Copyright © 1997 by Georgetown University, Washington DC 20057, USA. All rights reserved.

ties. However, he is getting used to the idea that salesmen do not receive adequate information about their clients.

The Company

Dirk Gutschleg founded *El Remache C.A.* in 1948. Coming from Germany right after the war, he took with him to Mexico a very entrepreneurial view. He thought that fasteners, nuts and bolts were little—but important—parts needed in many items, from shoes to pants, from engines to transformers.

At the beginning, he faced typical immigrants' problems such as language barriers and cultural misunderstandings. He found that employees tended to be unreliable and to operate behind his back. Because of this, he demanded that all of the company information pass through him. As time went by, business flourished, and Mr. Gutschleg gradually adopted a more passive role. Although knowledgeable about every ERCA's major detail, he had to delegate formal authority to his son, Markus Gutschleg, and to the current general manager, Rafael Marquez.

Currently, Mr. Gutschleg, Sr., foresees the aggregate performance of the four-company holding that includes ERCA. His son joined the company five years ago, after three years of experience with *Procter & Gamble* in Mexico. Rafael Marquez, instead, achieved his current status after working for years at El Remache's shop floor.

Like his predecessor, Mr. Marquez centralizes every piece of information. He reserves the right to approve any major decision, and says, "We share only the information that is necessary. In Mexico, you never know when a worker is going to leave you and go to the competition."

The top managers' familiarity with this system does not make Mr. Gutschleg, Sr., less worried about the future. Nowadays, employees tend to demand more information and participation in the decisional processes. In this sense, Markus Gutschleg is trying to implement the ideas learned at Procter & Gamble.

All things considered, ERCA's managers find it more difficult to run the business, even if it has been very profitable over the years. Dark clouds—among them, the incoming North American Free Trade Agreement (NAFTA)—are threatening ERCA's nearly monopolistic role in Mexico's marketplace.

Customers and Products

ERCA divides its clients, according to the volume of their purchases, into three categories: A, B, and C. Since most products are commodities—and clients can easily buy them somewhere else—customer service is an important aspect of the business, in terms of both responsiveness and product quality.

Product availability, delivery date, quotation process, and solving-problem capability greatly affect the firm's profile in the marketplace. Despite this, at ERCA a simple order quotation can require a couple of weeks, and the overall responding process takes longer. In contrast, the competition offers quicker delivery times and sometimes better prices, although for lower quality segments (ERCA enjoys the quality leadership among Mexican fastener manufacturers).

Delays on promised delivery times represent a serious problem. Even standard products are often unavailable. To make things worse, vendedores make false promises of immediate product availability. However, Javier Gonzalez—product manager of the Industrial Division for the last fifteen years—stresses that "not all clients are unsatisfied with the service we offer. We have been in this industry for a long time and customers know our reputation."

For special articles, ERCA's lead times range from four to six weeks, versus the competitors' three to four weeks. ERCA delivers standard articles in one day and not-in-stock articles in fifteen days. Regarding new special products, an order quotation takes up to two weeks. Similar problems affect sample deliveries. For example, a client asked for some samples and received them five weeks later.

"Many problems have to do with the attention that each sales representative gives to his major clients. If he, in conjunction with the client, is able to plan ahead (two-three months), delivery problems become very rare," says Enrique Jardia, Production Manager. Mr. Jardia has been with the company for over thirty years. Originally a machine's assistant at the mill center, he has had the opportunity to see, from that particular angle, the evolution of the company.

Sales personnel compensation includes a base salary and, in most cases, a sales-based commission. Vendedores' base salary starts at 700,000 old pesos plus a 1.75% commission for delivery products ($1 = 3,000 old pesos).

Customers often find that a typical order may require filling out up to nineteen forms. Three secretaries receive customer calls, and they cannot usually reach the vendedores who are usually out visiting clients. Therefore, the secretaries only take orders, listen to complaints and, for requests of technical assistance, try to reach some technical staff members.

Although Mr. Gutschleg Jr. personally possesses a historical perspective of the company's performance, ERCA does not have a formal forecast system. Given the numerous products sold, including many custom orders, managers find it difficult to monitor available historical data and foresee future sales.

Competition

In Mexico, El Remache enjoys the market leadership in its field. However, two main competition forces threaten its position. On one hand, many small Mexican companies aim to gain market share. Often founded by former ERCA employees, these companies focus on high-quantity production of few, selected products and do not have access to international purchasing of high-quality raw material. On the other hand, new potential U.S. competitors are approaching Mexico's market. This process escalated after the less protectionist policy adopted by the Mexican government in 1992, as a move toward NAFTA.

The U.S. competitors are both in the high-volume/low-cost and specialized/high-cost niches. The low-cost U.S. competitors sell at $3.30 per thousand units sold, versus ERCA's $6.60. The high-cost U.S. competitors sell at a much higher price ($14 per thousand units sold). However, the threat of competition works both ways: Mexican companies now find it more profitable than before to sell into the North American market.

Production Process

ERCA manufactures fasteners from three different raw materials. The fasteners also vary in size, color, and similar features. The different steps of the fastener manufacturing process depend upon the type of product needed.

Materia Prima (raw material)

The raw material inventory consists of eighteen different diameters of steel and four different diameters of tin wire. In addition, ERCA has in stock aluminum, whereas it orders copper only when needed. ERCA receives raw material deliveries twice a month, and uses up to 62 tons of it per month. Deliveries from the U.K. and Japan take up to twelve weeks, compared to six weeks from the U.S. Nevertheless, ERCA currently prefers to buy from the Japanese, who are offering better prices as a response to temporary protectionist measures taken by the U.S. government against them.

Mexican raw material's alternative sources, although low in cost, suffer from low quality and unreliable delivery capability.

Primer Proceso (first process)

To manufacture fasteners, ERCA uses forty machines that deliver the rivets by performing only one production step. Each of these machines can produce only one fastener size at a given time, and can be reset to a different diameter if needed. The machine supervisors on the production floor decide upon job execution schedules. They give higher priority to urgent orders and try to minimize the machines' setup times.

Cafeteras (coffee makers)

The cafeteras—which look like coffee makers—represent an old and outdated production line, still maintained because dedicated to specific articles that would be hard to manufacture in other ways. The cafeteras are bulky, but also highly flexible. New machines to substitute the cafeteras would cost more and generate longer production times, because of tooling requirements. Since many fashion articles require rapid deliveries of the cafeteras' manufactures, these machines maintain a fundamental role within ERCA.

Lavadoras (washing machines)

After the primer proceso, the products—at that point covered with oil—must pass through the washing stations. Successive operations—such as quality control or second processes—require clean products and have to be interrupted if a dirty item reaches them. Unfortunately, these interruptions occur fairly often, and, in addition, only two workers on a single shift currently operate the lavadoras.

Currently, about three tons of work-in-progress (WIP) are waiting in front of the washing stations. Although the latter should take only ten minutes to wash a single 90 Kg box, in reality they end up processing each day much less than the expected 4320 Kg.

Revision (quality control)

All of the products must pass through quality control. A white paper order, inserted within the box, indicates that the control personnel took only visual samples from the box. Conversely, a red paper order shows that the inspection covered all of the products in the box (this procedure applies only to high value items for important customers). Finally, urgent orders require an additional orange paper. Currently, the revision's WIP is approximately one equivalent working day.

Segundos Procesos (second processes)

The product achieves its final shape at the end of the second processes, which are also responsible for most of the defectives. These final processes include: (1) Barrenado y Roscado (boring and threading), (2) Roto Finish (deburring, tumbling), (3) Ranuradoras and Roladoras (guiding, bending, and squeezing), and (4) Galvanoplastia (plating).

In the first process the machines further refine the fasteners. Currently, barrenado y roscado shows a four to five equivalent working day WIP.

Not all of the fasteners require the second process, but only the ones whose heads need polishing before entering the galvanoplastia.

The third process suffers from four major problems. First, it would require more qualified personnel. Second, its requirement variability would benefit from a higher volume. Third, any one of the machines, in turns, breaks down. Finally, the process does not have a proper balance among its different capacities. These problems lead to a Ranuradoras and Roladoras' WIP of six weeks, and make this operation one of the major bottlenecks of the whole manufacturing process.

For almost 90% of the products, plating represents the last step. Currently, it works twenty-four hours a day, in two shifts, with two weeks of WIP. In addition, ERCA has to subcontract part of the work. After the plating, operators have the products washed once again and subjected to a final quality control.

Order Processing

ERCA sells its products through two distribution channels: a small internal shop—the *tiendita*—and ERCA's sales representatives. Small customers go to ERCA's plant, whereas important customers are visited by ERCA's vendedores. The tiendita sells only in-stock, standard products. The customers come, ask for a specific article, or bring a sample of it. The clerk checks whether the article belongs to

ERCA's standard inventory and, in the affirmative case, consults the stock manager. The latter verifies whether any other client has already reserved that particular item, and, in the negative case, the clerk completes the transaction with the clients. In addition, if the clerk does not find an article in ERCA's standard inventory, he knows enough about the product to suggest an alternative article currently in stock.

Apparently complex, this procedure actually permits ERCA to reduce the number of sale steps, because its personnel does not have to exchange paperwork. In addition, personal selling—centered on the expertise of the clerk Antonio Reyes—allows ERCA to conserve a stronger link with the client. Mr. Reyes spends 10–15 minutes with each client. By using sample measurement tools and measurement conversion tables, Mr. Reyes helps the customer and personalizes the selling process. The customer receives the right fastener, in a short time.

Opposite characteristics portray ERCA sales representatives' effort. The vendedores visit the clients, hope to generate orders, and in the process offer very little assistance to the customers, who most of the time already know what they want. In addition, there are no sales policies or incentives to emphasize the sale of standard over special articles. Sometimes vendedores visit clients because they happened to drive close to the customers' sites, and have to stay outside ERCA's offices until 4:00 P.M. anyway.

The unwritten requirement that vendedores must visit clients for at least six hours a day creates paradoxical situations. Vendedores kill extra time waiting in Mexico City's traffic jam, rather than offer a better use of themselves back at the plant. They visit customers of categories A and B up to four times a month.

In addition, vendedores often approach their job in a disorganized way. For instance, they generally do not schedule their daily visits to the client's representatives (compradores). This bad habit results in undesired waits and missed meetings. The customers' assignments to different vendedores do not follow logical patterns, and several salesmen may end up serving the same area of Mexico City.

Since they do not carry an updated price list, each time the vendedores have to recalculate price estimates in front of their clients. The absence of a price list derives from a poor connection between ERCA's sales and manufacturing personnel. Another negative factor—the absence of a forecast system—prevents ERCA from predicting future demand. This drawback forces ERCA to increase prices every six months of some percentage—say, 5 to 10%—regardless of the actual behavior of the company in the marketplace.

Aware of this procedure, ERCA's big customers simply pre-order fasteners in quantities sufficient to cover their future six-month needs. Since ERCA cannot deliver this bulk of products quickly, the customers end up receiving the fasteners approximately when needed, but at a discounted price.

Technically, the order processing takes an average of one week. The vendedores give immediately a price estimate, but cannot furnish a reliable delivery date. As mentioned before, even if they do, they end up often misleading the clients. Therefore, they cannot require the clients to sign the orders, and when ERCA finally delivers the fasteners, the clients can return the packages with no penalty. This practice creates relatively big stocks of undelivered orders, not to mention its fostering mutual mistrust between ERCA and clients.

Delivery System

ERCA's delivery system exemplifies the nature of the main criticisms to the firm. Exhibit 1 shows the Pareto diagram of the problems experienced in ERCA's daily deliveries (entregas) of products, in May–June 1992:

- Lack of time ("falta de tiempo") on the part of the truck drivers represented the number one reason for delivery problems, and accounted for 41% of the missing deliveries.
- "No es material solicitado" (11%): the customer claimed not having requested the material. Since customers do not sign the original order, they can refuse the delivery without incurring any penalties.
- "No quiso recibir cliente" (11%): at delivery, nobody was waiting for the truck because it arrived on the wrong day.
- "No hubo cheque" (10%): at delivery, the client did not have the check to pay for the delivery. In ERCA's business, firms do not commonly use accounts receivable.
- "Pedido duplicado" (7%): duplicated order (i.e., ERCA had already delivered that particular order to that client).
- "Descompuso camioneta" (5%): the truck broke down.
- "No encontro direccion" (3%): the truck driver could not find the right address.
- "Faltan datos en factura" (3%): ERCA's administration did not properly fill out the invoice.
- "Horario comida cliente" (2%): the truck driver arrived during lunch time; in ERCA's business, companies do not receive products all day long.
- "No hay pedido" (2%): at delivery, both the client and the truck driver realize that the former never requested that particular order.

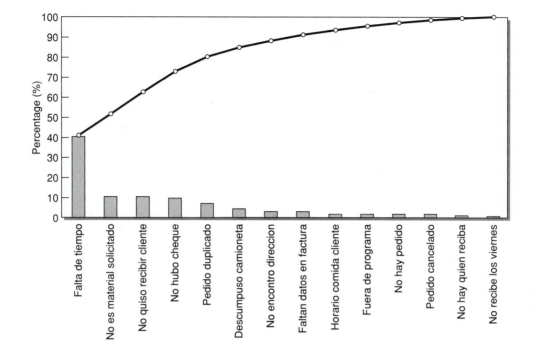

Exhibit 1   Diagrama de Pareto Problema en las Entregas Diarias Mayo-Junio 1992

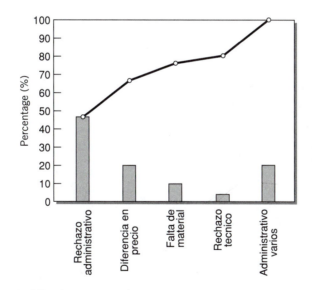

Exhibit 2   Diagrama de Pareto Notas de Credito Mayo-Junio 1992

- *"Pedido cancelado"* (1.5%): canceled order.
- *"No hay quien reciba"* (1%): at delivery, nobody was waiting for the truck, even if the latter came on the right day.

- *"No recibe los viernes"* (0.5%): The truck driver tried to deliver on Fridays to companies that do not receive products on such a day.

The lack of coordination between vendedores and delivery personnel is shown in Exhibit 2. In this case, the diagram shows the reasons for rejected products in the form of credit notes. In the first place, with 46%, one finds the administrative refusal (*rechazo administrativo*), which represents the sum of all the effects considered in Exhibit 1. Other reasons include:

- *Diferencia en precio* (20%): difference in price with respect to the original order
- *Falta de material* (10%): lack of raw material
- *Rechazo tecnico* (4%): technical problems, such as wrong tolerances
- *Administrativo varios* (20%): general administrative problems

The Future

Mr. Gutschleg, Sr., is concerned about the future. ERCA will soon face NAFTA. This situation is not like the one he faced in 1948. Times have changed, and the company has enjoyed many good years.

He realized that being young and aggressive, the new salesmen, often find themselves trapped in a system that excessively limits their responsibilities and therefore penalizes their possibility to grow. The old management maintains a vertical information and decision-making structure that leaves little space to salesmen's entrepreneurship. This results in a general lack of coordination between marketing—geared toward new perspectives—and operation—still anchored to the old ones. *The existing system has worked for many years. How can we change now?*

The Globalization of Operations Strategies

◆ ◆ ◆

Chapter 3 will discuss the following key concepts:

◆ *A conceptual framework with the four driving forces behind the globalization process*

◆ *Global market forces*

◆ *Technological forces*

◆ *Global cost forces*

◆ *Political and macroeconomic forces*

◆ *Current and future challenges*

◆ INTRODUCTION

The last fifteen years have witnessed the evolution of a new global manufacturing environment. The vast majority of manufacturers now have some form of global presence—through exports, strategic alliances, joint ventures, or as part of a committed strategy to sell in foreign markets or locate production plants abroad. Previously, large multinational corporations dominated the international marketplace, which domestic firms generally ignored. Today, however, most companies realize that it is essential to be aware of and participate in international markets. The main goal of this chapter is to examine the factors and forces that are driving the increasing globalization of operations activities.

In this book, firms that have majority ownership in either foreign sales organization/ distribution networks or production plants are defined as *multinational*. Multinational firms have extended their organizations and operations to more than one country. They also may be global in the sense that they have a borderless corporate culture, and they tailor their production and markets to local needs. All other firms are considered *domestic,* even if they export or engage in some form of international alliance, such as joint ventures or license agreements.

Globalization Is Increasing

Trends among U.S. manufacturers illustrate the growing size and importance of global operations:

- About one-fifth of the output of U.S. firms is produced abroad.
- U.S. companies hold more foreign asset stocks than any other nation, currently standing at more than $500 billion, and growing at about 7 percent a year. The rate of return of these assets is generally good—over $50 billion a year—and most of the profit is reinvested in the foreign affiliates.
- One quarter of all U.S. imports and exports are between foreign affiliates and the parent U.S. companies. The major share of these intrafirm flows involve transfer of manufactured goods.
- By the early 1990s, U.S. multinational firms accounted for 53 percent of the total number of firms and 89 percent of the worldwide sales of all companies in The Conference Board database.
- More than half of U.S. companies increased the number of countries in which they reported operating from the late 1980s through the early 1990s. The number of firms operating in ten or more countries rose most quickly, to well over 20 percent of the expansionary group.
- Manufacturing assets held by multinational enterprises in foreign countries are substantial and rapidly increasing.

Two factors underlie the dramatic rise of globalization. First, global reach is important to a firm's survival. Among U.S. manufacturers in the 1980s, multinational companies were 50 percent more likely to survive under the same corporate identity than strictly domestic companies. Second, multinational firms are more profitable and grow faster. Among twenty major U.S. manufacturing industries, multinational firms grew faster than domestics in nineteen of the cases and were more profitable in seventeen cases.

Given this environment, the goal of this chapter is to understand the development of successful global operations strategies. These strategies achieve business objectives through a dynamic process of leveraging and managing manufacturing, logistics, and research and development (R & D) activities.

◆ A CONCEPTUAL FRAMEWORK: THE FOUR DRIVING FORCES OF THE GLOBALIZATION PROCESS

The conceptual framework that follows classifies the major factors and driving forces behind the globalization process. Each of these factors affects different industries, even different products, to varying degrees. Even though generalizations are impossible, and "recipes" undesirable in strategy development, the framework will allow an operations manager to structure his or her thinking process in understanding changes in the global environment, prioritizing the importance of various factors, and developing strategic alternatives.

The outline of the conceptual framework appears in Figure 3–1. The factors shaping the global environment and driving the development of global operations strategies of multinational firms fall into four categories: global market forces, technological forces, global cost forces, and political and macroeconomic forces.

Figure 3–1 The Four Forces of Globalization of Operations Framework (or Four Forces Framework (FFF)).

Global Market Forces

Manufacturers cannot afford to ignore the tremendous growth potential of foreign markets. First, they need to attack competitors abroad to develop a competitive balance and protect domestic market share. They also may need to acquire market knowledge in markets other than the home county, to respond quickly to customer orders, and customize products for various local markets. For many products and industries, penetration of global markets depends on having global facilities and/or distribution and supply networks to respond to customer demand in all the relevant competitive dimensions of cost, quality, service, and flexibility.

Technological Forces

In recent years, transportation and communication costs have fallen dramatically, and international operating activities have become much easier to organize. At the same time, the sources of creation and dissemination of knowledge have globalized. Competitive success depends more and more on how quickly and effectively a firm incorporates new product and process technology into the design and production of its products. This need for speed has prompted companies to locate more production and R & D facilities abroad, closer to the suppliers of advanced technological knowledge in component production or of crucial process equipment. Companies have formed joint ventures to share technological knowledge in exchange for market presence. They have located R & D facilities in countries with the most cost-effective technological resources and necessary scientific infrastructure.

Global Cost Forces

The comparative cost advantage of some countries in various inputs to the manufacturing process—from raw materials to labor—has always driven the expansion of multinational operations to new "lower cost" paradises. But as technology diminishes the importance of various cost components (e.g., direct labor cost), while accentuating the magnitude of others (e.g., capital costs), the expansion and location of the various firm activities start to be driven by new categories of total costs (e.g., taxes and total quality costs) and company–local government economic relationships (e.g., government subsidies). As the order-winners in the product markets shift away from production–cost considerations toward quality, delivery speed, and customization, factors such as transportation, telecommunications, and supplier infrastructure assume increasing importance in determining the location of production activities.

Political and Macroeconomic Forces

The international economic and political environment can be best characterized as turbulent and increasingly complex. A variety of political and macroeconomic factors—exchange rate volatility, regional trade agreements, open markets, and managed trade, for example—continuously shape the global manufacturing environment. Increasing global trade during the 1980s meant that any company operating in more than one major currency had a powerful reason to invest abroad to try to match the currencies of its costs to the currencies of its revenues. Such matching reduced the risk of losses due solely to currency movements. Additionally, multigovernment initiatives to open markets and managed trade, such as Europe 1992 and the North American Free Trade Agreement (NAFTA), are dramatically changing corporate plans. Companies are hurrying to rationalize facility and logistics networks to meet the new market requirements of these regulations.

The next four sections discuss each of these forces in more detail and describe firms' successful strategies for dealing with them. The remaining discussion moves beyond classification of the driving factors for the globalization of operations to a structured conceptual approach to be used in shaping a global operations strategy. The goal is to move from this skeleton of the conceptual framework to the fully developed framework, which appears in Figure 3–2.

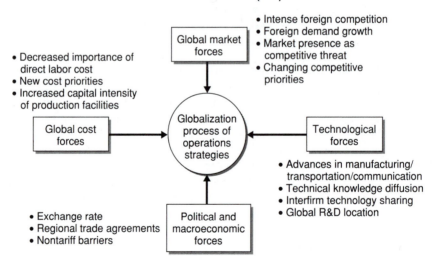

Figure 3–2   Detailed Exposition of the Four Forces Framework (FFF)

◆ GLOBAL MARKET FORCES

The nature of global market forces, how they contribute to the globalization of operations activities, and the strategies manufacturers pursue in response to them, are characterized by five main themes.

Intensified Foreign Competition in Local Markets

Among U.S. manufacturers, penetration of foreign goods in consumer goods markets doubled during the last decade (from 7 percent in 1980 to around 14 percent in the early 1990s). The numbers were even more exaggerated in capital goods markets, where penetration rose from about 14 percent to over 40 percent during the same period. Clearly, foreign competition has intensified in virtually every industry and affects all companies.

As a result, even small- or medium-sized firms that have never marketed or produced products abroad need to understand developments in the global environment. The openness of most international markets today allows foreign firms to compete directly with domestic firms in previously protected local markets. These competitors frequently are large multinationals with integrated global operations. They are adept practitioners of world-class manufacturing and logistics standards, which forces many small- and medium-sized firms to upgrade their operations, to keep abreast of product and process innovations, and to adopt the latest in just-in-time and total quality management techniques. In many cases, small- and medium-sized firms must even consider expanding into international operations—either through exporting, outsourcing some production, or entering into alliances and licensing agreements with foreign partners.

Growth in Foreign Demand

When asked where growth for his or her firm lies, most operations executives typically point to foreign market demand. Why? In 1970, the U.S. market accounted for approximately 40 percent of the world's market demand for the typical bundle of products economists consider. Today, it accounts for less than 30 percent. The U.S. market has not shrunk in absolute terms. Rather, the world market has grown disproportionately, and most of the growth is coming from developing country markets. It therefore makes sense for operations executives to target those markets for future growth potential.

Growth in foreign-market demand necessitates the development of a global network of factories, as well as an expanded sales and distribution network. If *economies of scale* are important in an industry, the global network probably will consist of a few centralized production facilities in countries that offer comparative advantages in the critical production process inputs (i.e., labor, resources). The multinational firm then uses its global economies of scale to attack local markets.

If *customization and fast response* drive the industry, and economies of scale are less important, then the resulting global network will contain multiple facilities, each dedicated to serving a specific local or regional market.

Having the opportunity to operate in, and meet the demand of global markets complicates the production planning task of the global operations manager. It requires attention to complicating factors such as currency movements and coordination of dispersed production facilities. On the other hand, operating on a global scale allows more efficient utilization of resources and a more stable production plan. Companies can take advantage of regionally different demand fluctuations to smooth production.

Global Market Presence as a Competitive Threat

Global presence can be used as a defensive tool to stop aggressive moves by foreign competitors toward penetrating a firm's home market. For example, in the ready-to-eat cereal market, the U.S.-based Kellogg company and its large European competitor Nestlé have large market share in their home markets, but limited presence in their competitor's home market. The two companies maintain a gentleman's agreement of nonaggressive penetration of each other's home markets following unsuccessful past efforts and heavy revenue bleeding from subsequent retaliations. In general, a company that is unable to retaliate against aggressive foreign competitors attempting to penetrate its home market is in a vulnerable competitive position.

Changing Competitive Priorities in Product Markets

For many years, the dominant theory in international production was based on the concept of an *international product life cycle*. Under this theory, a company introduced a product in one or several developed-country markets. When the product entered the decline stage of its life cycle in these markets, the company simply began shipping it to developing-country markets. This strategy regenerated or extended the product's total life cycle by sequentially cultivating markets that lagged behind in customer needs and knowledge on the latest product and process technology developments.

Unfortunately, few industries remain today in which this theory still applies. Product markets, particularly in technologically intensive industries, are changing rapidly. Product life cycles are shrinking as customers demand new products faster. In addition, the advances in communication and transportation technology give customers around the world immediate access to the latest in available products and technologies. Thus, manufacturers hoping to capture global demand must introduce their new products simultaneously to all major markets. Furthermore, the integration of product design and development of related manufacturing processes have become the key success factors in many high-technology industries, where fast product introduction and extensive customization determine market success. As a result, companies must maintain production facilities, pilot production plants, engineering resources, and even R & D facilities all over the world. Apple Computer, for example, has built a global manufacturing and engineering infrastructure with facilities in California, Ireland, and Singapore. This network allows Apple to introduce new products simultaneously in the American, European, and Asian markets.

Presence in State-of-the-Art Markets

In certain industries, particularly hypercompetitive high-technology segments, certain country markets demand state-of-the-art products to meet their consumer needs. For these industries and product markets, customer preferences drive the next generation of product and process innovations. Firms that intend to remain product/process leaders in these state-of-the-art markets must set up production, and in some cases, product development facilities there. Examples of state-of-the-art markets are:

- Japan: Semiconductor process equipment, consumer electronics and machine tools
- Germany: Machine tools
- United States: Aerospace, computers, software

Companies use the state-of-the-art markets as learning grounds for product development and effective production management, and then transfer this knowledge to their other production facilities worldwide. This rationale explains why Mercedes-Benz decided recently to locate a huge manufacturing plant in Vance, Alabama. The company recognizes that the United States is the state-of-the-art market for sport utility vehicles. It plans to produce those vehicles at the Vance plant and introduce them worldwide by 1997.

◆ TECHNOLOGICAL FORCES

Technological forces have shaped the global operations strategies of multinationals in four ways: technological advancements and effective mass customization in global markets; diffusion of technological knowledge and global location; technology sharing and interfirm collaborations; global location of R & D facilities.

Technological Advancements and Effective Mass Customization in Global Markets

If the first major trend of the last decade among U.S. manufacturers was globalization, the second was *fewness*. Fewness characterizes markets that have a limited number of producers. The concept is not new, but it is a strategic quality firms should seek by segmenting existing markets or creating new product niches from scratch.

The average number of all competitors in specific industry segments dropped by 45 percent in the last decade, according to The Conference Board manufacturing database. *Fewness* generally is associated with increasing profitability. A firm that achieves market leadership, and has few competitors in its market segment, is likely to be more profitable than one that typically has many competitors or small market share.

How are firms able to pursue fewness and simultaneous profitability in the global marketplace? The answer is fairly straightforward, and relies on exploiting a unique synergy of global market forces and recent technological advancements in manufacturing and logistics. Fewness is the result, in part, of two forces: diversity among products and uniformity across national markets. Product diversity has increased as products have grown more complex and differentiated and as product life cycles have shortened. At the same time, national markets have become increasingly similar, especially in the industrial countries, and particularly for intermediate goods. Companies have been able to expand their global market presence and simultaneously realize economies of scale, as a result of more flexible manufacturing and distribution methods and better communications and transportation technologies.

Diffusion of Technological Knowledge and Global Location

Advanced technological/production knowledge is no longer the preserve of large American or European multinationals. For instance, the share of the U.S. market for high-technology goods supplied by imports from foreign-based companies rose from a negligible 5 percent to more than 20 percent within the last decade. Moreover, the sources of such imports expanded beyond Europe to include Japan and the newly industrialized countries of Hong Kong, Singapore, South Korea, and Taiwan.

In response to this diffusion of technological capability, multinational firms need to improve their ability to tap multiple sources of technology located in various countries. They also must be able to absorb quickly, and commercialize effectively, new technologies that, in many cases, were invented outside the firm—thus overcoming the destructive and pervasive "not-invented-here" attitude and resulting inertia.

The need to have access to critical technological components for their products forces firms to develop close relationships with dominant foreign suppliers in certain product/ technology areas. Supplier involvement in new product design efforts becomes critically important, thereby causing some companies to locate production facilities close to their suppliers. Two examples of dominant suppliers are Canon and Fanuc, many of whose industrial customers have located close to their plants. Canon leads in global production of motors for fax machines and laser printers, with more than 80 percent of the world market. Fanuc controls more than 70 percent of the world market for machine-tool controllers.

The alternative to dependence on dominant foreign suppliers is a *deep-pocket* investment strategy of developing component production capabilities in-house. This strategy is not only expensive but also risky, especially if the required know-how lies outside the firm's core capabilities. However, some firms pursue it, with IBM's manufacturing of engines for its own laser printers being one such example.

Another clear trend is for companies to locate production facilities close to foreign suppliers of critical process equipment because of the sophisticated nature of this equipment, the devastating effect of prolonged breakdowns or production slowdowns, and the need for process technology know-how in the accelerated cycle of new product–manufacturing process development. In a high-technology environment, for instance, buying process equipment long-distance is not usually a viable solution. For example, both IBM and Xerox recently decided to produce their next generation of video displays in Japan, which has the best process capability for this technology. A large U.S. paper company has built operations in Europe, not only to penetrate the European market, but also to gain fast and easy access to process developments emerging from the major European equipment suppliers, as well as from smaller European competitors. These smaller paper firms are open to licensing agreements for their process innovations, an attractive alternative for U.S. firms.

Technology Sharing and Interfirm Collaborations

In many cases, the main motivation behind interfirm collaborative agreements such as joint ventures, participation in international consortia, technology licensing, and a variety of other alternatives, is the need to gain access to technological developments. In the partnership between Texas Instruments (TI) and Hitachi, two of the world's top-ten chip-makers, the firms began collaborating in 1988 with the intent of sharing basic technologies. As the joint venture succeeded, however, TI and Hitachi decided to capitalize on their success by expanding the agreement to include manufacturing as well. The two partners have now built a joint facility in Richardson, Texas, in order to create the next generation of Dynamic Random Access Memory (DRAM) chips.

The main motivation of joint ventures in the steel industry between U.S. and Japanese firms (for example, LTV and Sumitomo, Inland Steel and Nippon Steel, National Steel and Marubeni) was the desire of the U.S. firms to gain access to advanced process technology, combined with the need for financial backing from Japanese producers. In return, the Japanese obtained broader access to the U.S. market and a production base to supply the American plants of Japanese automakers.

The well-known joint ventures in the auto industry between U.S. and Japanese firms (GM-Toyota, Chrysler-Mitsubishi, Ford-Mazda) followed a similar pattern. U.S. firms needed to obtain first-hand knowledge of Japanese production methods and accelerated product development cycles, while the Japanese producers were seeking ways to overcome U.S. trade barriers and gain access to the vast American auto market.

Global Location of R & D Facilities

As competitive priorities in global products markets shift more toward product customization and fast new product development, firms are realizing the importance of co-location of manufacturing and product design facilities abroad. In certain product categories, such as

Application Specific Integrated Circuits (ASICs), this was the main motivation for establishing design centers in foreign countries. Other industries such as pharmaceuticals and consumer electronics also have taken this approach.

The availability of low-cost, high-quality engineers in some developing countries has been a major factor contributing to the location of R & D facilities abroad. Taiwan has been a primary location for firms looking for highly trained mechanical and electrical engineers; India is a rich source of software engineering talent. Access to creative and highly trained technical workers also seems to be the main motivation behind the recent overseas expansion of Japanese R & D.

As different, more demanding technical standards are increasingly set both by customers and regulators, companies are forced to locate design and R & D facilities in foreign countries to support their global manufacturing and marketing networks. Firms that keep up with developing demands and changing standards in many national markets are more likely to be at the forefront of innovation. Additionally, they may be able to influence the development of new industrial standards (for example, a firm with operations in Europe can influence industrial standards set by the European Community), and thus gain an advantage over firms just exporting to that market.

◆ GLOBAL COST FORCES

Without question, the cost of production inputs affects the global location of activities. However, a drastic shift in cost priorities is occurring away from direct labor cost and toward new cost categories such as poor quality and product design costs. In fact, cost priorities have become much more dynamic, and, as a result, are reshaping global manufacturing strategies more frequently. In this section we discuss the three factors that have influenced this evolution.

Diminishing Importance of Direct Labor Cost in Offshore Sourcing Strategies

Sourcing from foreign suppliers can be a legitimate tactic for staying even with or gaining advantage over the competition. The 1970s and 1980s witnessed an explosive growth of offshore sourcing by multinationals, driven by an obsessive search for the lowest labor costs. This strategy was particularly popular with U.S. manufacturing firms that perceived offshore sourcing as the only alternative to the aggressive invasion of their local markets by low-priced, high-quality imports. In some cases, this approach was the correct one. In the assembly of electronic devices, for example, the typical decision involves choosing between setting up highly automated, very expensive assembly technologies or opting for an offshore sourcing arrangement. The right answer depends on the product and the characteristics of its market. For products with very short model lives, for example, low labor cost locations may be preferable to automation to minimize capital investment.

In many other cases, however, choosing offshore sourcing arrangements was an incorrect decision, based on a misunderstanding of the firm's cost structure. Companies misunderstand their cost structures for a variety of reasons. In many cases, manufacturing managers overstate the importance of direct labor cost because it is the easiest to quantify and the most readily apparent cost element. For many years, standard accounting practices seriously inflated the importance of direct labor costs. Overhead cost allocations were typically based on direct labor costs, thus prompting companies to allocate a large percentage of fixed costs, many of them unaffected by the location decision, to products with slightly higher direct labor cost components. This form of overhead cost allocation cast offshore sourcing as the panacea for reducing overhead expenses, particularly for companies in mature or declining markets. After pursuing such offshore sourcing, many companies were unpleasantly surprised to find that offshore sourcing can lead to fragmented production processes, fewer but less productive facilities, and, in many cases, higher total overhead.

Recent advancements in technology and production methods (e.g., implementation of just-in-time manufacturing methods and set-up time reduction) have reduced direct labor cost to less than 15 percent of total production costs for most manufacturing industries. In high technology industries it is often less than 5 percent. These facts make an offshore sourcing strategy obsolete in many cases. It is irrational to allow the cost category that represents the smallest percentage in overall product costs to drive the location of operations activities.

Many companies have aggressively pursued offshore sourcing as the backbone of their manufacturing strategy. The choice of offshore locations is typically based purely on labor cost considerations. But the comparative advantages of countries with respect to low wages change over time, affected by shifts in exchange rates and in labor demands. Korea and Taiwan were cheap labor wage countries in the 1970s and Thailand in the early 1980s, but China became the favorite offshore sourcing ground of the late 1980s and early 1990s.

The continuous pursuit of the lowest labor cost forces companies to shift operations from one country to another, thus giving rise to the appropriately named *island hopping strategy*. However, the labor cost savings of such a strategy in many cases can be easily consumed by the increased capital, logistical, and operating start-up costs in a new country. Many firms have found that the hidden costs of island hopping strategies are hard to estimate when making the decision to pursue the strategy. Shoe manufacturer Nike learned this lesson the hard way with start-up problems at a new production facility in China in the early 1980s. Hidden costs can include additional training due to lack of skilled workers, high quality costs due to poor workmanship and a lack of quality culture among workers, increased lead-times and associated inventory costs due to poor transportation and communication infrastructure, and unexpected logistics complications due to multilevel and bureaucratic government structures.

Emergence of New Cost Priorities in the Location of Global Operating Activities

New competitive priorities in manufacturing industries—that is product and process conformance quality, delivery reliability and speed, customization, and responsiveness to customers—have forced companies to reprioritize the cost factors that drive their global operations strategies. The total quality management (TQM) revolution brought with it a focus on total quality costs, rather than just direct labor costs. Companies realized that early activities such as product design and worker training substantially impact production costs. They began to emphasize prevention rather than inspection. In addition, they quantified the costs of poor design, low input quality, and poor workmanship by calculating internal and external failure costs. All these realizations placed access to skilled workers and quality suppliers high on the priority list for firms competing on quality. Similarly, just-in-time (JIT) manufacturing methods, which companies widely adopted for the management of mass production systems, emphasized the importance of frequent deliveries by nearby suppliers.

Obviously, successful implementation of such techniques requires the presence of an adequate supplier infrastructure in the location chosen for manufacturing facilities. Lack of worker skills, inadequate transportation and communication infrastructure, and low-quality supply typically prove extremely disruptive for the implementation of any modern production management methods. They also can easily lead to deterioration of productivity standards. These considerations explain why most U.S. companies have chosen to make their overseas manufacturing investments in developed economies (more than 60 percent in developed countries).

Increasing Capital Intensity of Production Facilities

A number of high-technology industries have experienced dramatic growth in the capital intensity of production facilities. A state-of-the-art semiconductor factory, for instance, costs close to half a billion dollars. When R & D costs are included, the cost of production facilities for a new generation of electronic products can easily exceed $1 billion. Similarly huge numbers apply for the development and production of new drugs in the pharmaceutical industry. Such high costs drive firms to adopt an economies-of-scale strategy that concentrates production in a single location—typically in a developed country that has the required labor and supplier infrastructure. They then achieve high capacity utilization of the capital-intensive facility by aggressively pursuing the global market.

Sometimes in capital-intensive industries, competing manufacturers find it beneficial to enter joint venture agreements in order to share capital costs and associated risks. In the semiconductor industry, Texas Instruments and Hitachi, Motorola and Toshiba, and IBM and Siemens share production facilities for sixteen-megabyte DRAM chips. Such partnerships in fast-changing industries tend to be successful, freeing up needed resources for product development.

The location of capital-intensive production processes is strongly influenced by the availability of local government subsidies, in terms of reduced interest rates, favorable price breaks for price-controlled industries, tax holidays or low tax rates, and cost sharing on plants and equipment. In some cases, countries offer deals for special access to raw materials, local financing, grants, employee training programs, and priority access to foreign exchange. Firms searching for foreign assembly or production locations often negotiate directly with the government the terms of investment.

Taxation factors can dominate the location decisions of capital-intensive industries, such as pharmaceuticals and semiconductors. These industries have a significant presence in low-tax countries. Tax benefits have driven pharmaceutical companies to locate in Puerto Rico and Ireland, for instance.

◆ POLITICAL AND MACROECONOMIC FORCES

Political and macroeconomic forces have always shaped global operations strategies, but never more so than they do today. This section provides examples of such forces that have shaped the strategies of multinational companies.

Exchange Rate Fluctuations and the Value of Operating Flexibility in Global Manufacturing and Sourcing Networks

Getting hit with unexpected or unreasonable currency devaluations in the foreign countries in which they operate is a nightmare for global operations managers. Managing exposure to changes in *nominal* and *real* exchange rates (these terms will be defined in detail in chapter 9) is a task the global operations manager must master.

A wide array of financial mechanisms are available for hedging against currency fluctuations, but, as we point out in chapter 9, they are most effective for short-term variations. It is important for the global operations manager to recognize and respond to the wide-ranging strategic problems and opportunities that long-term currency shifts present. Since disequilibrium in exchange rates may last for several months or even years, the firm should strive to maximize its operational flexibility by diversifying production geographically and effectively using global sourcing networks. As a firm's local currency moves out of equilibrium, the company should be in a position to shift its production to those facilities or suppliers that, by virtue of their location, can produce the product or provide input at the lowest cost in the local currency. Firms that have global facility networks or established relationships with vendors in a variety of countries can implement such a strategy most effectively.

If the economics are favorable, the firm may even go so far as to establish a supplier in a foreign country where one does not yet exist. For example, if the local currency is chronically undervalued, it is to the firm's advantage to shift most of its sourcing to local vendors. In any case, the firm may still want to source a limited amount of its inputs from less favorable suppliers in other countries if it feels that maintaining an ongoing relationship may help in the future when strategies need to be reversed.

The need to exploit operational flexibility can play a determining role in the location of the firm's activities. Partial concentration of production and sourcing activities allows companies to respond effectively to exchange rate movements and bargain effectively with suppliers, labor unions, and host governments.

Building operational flexibility is a challenging and sometimes costly proposition, however. It requires establishing a global facility and sourcing network with excess production capacity, if economically feasible. It also requires developing a global product line with a high degree of cross-country standardization; designing and implementing production/supplier switching strategies; and creating incentive systems for managers that reward good decisions in this area.

Becton Dickinson has built a global manufacturing network for its disposable syringe business, with production facilities in the United States, Ireland, Mexico, and Brazil. When the Mexican peso was devalued, the company quickly shifted its production to the Mexican plant, thereby gaining a cost advantage over its competitors' U.S. factories.

Emergence of Regional Trade Agreements and Their Impact on the Structuring of Global Manufacturing and Logistics Networks

The emergence of trading blocks in Europe (Europe 1992), North America (NAFTA), and the Pacific Rim has serious implications for the way firms will structure or rationalize their global manufacturing/sourcing networks. For example, the single European market influences companies' operations strategies as follows:

- Reduction (or elimination) of customs and noncustoms barriers leads to significant economies of scale, as manufacturers gain access to a market of over 350 million people.
- Standardization of security norms and regulations across Europe allows firms to increase standardization of components, subassemblies, and final products. This, in turn, makes available a wider variety of products for the consumer.

- A single European market allows manufacturers to consolidate small plants previously built to serve individual national markets into European-scale facilities.
- The fear of trade protectionism in Europe will motivate strong investments by American and Japanese multinationals in production facilities there.
- In an effort to rationalize manufacturing, distribution, and after-sales service networks across Europe, many companies will pursue mergers and acquisitions of related companies in various European countries. In the absence of such opportunities, they will seek alliances and joint ventures.

These trends are clearly apparent in many industries. For instance, before 1992, 3M's European plants turned out different versions of the same product for the various European countries. Today, 3M manufacturing plants produce goods for all of Europe and, in the process, realize significant cost savings. Similarly, Philips, Thomson, Electrolux, and Ford are in the process of creating pan-European networks of factories (producing both components and finished goods). Other examples of this trend include the following.

- The Philips television factory located in Brugge, Belgium, uses tubes supplied from a factory in Germany, transistors from France, plastics from Italy, and electronic components from a different factory in Belgium.
- IBM assembles its personal computers, PS2, in Greenock, Scotland. The plant buys electronic parts from a plant in Bordeaux, France; circuit boards from an IBM plant in Milan, Italy; and electronic components such as memory chips from other locations in France and Germany.

On a pan-European basis, implementing the strategic changes required for a rationalized factory and distribution network can be painful, and firms can make mistakes. One company shut down its plant in Italy to centralize production in Holland, but kept its Italian sales company intact. Strategically, this appeared to be a sound business decision. But the company made the mistake of penalizing the Italian sales firm for the loss of the Italian factory by costing the sourcing of the Italian marketplace from the Holland plant. The Italian sales company, not surprisingly, started local sourcing outside the company.

With regard to NAFTA, about 7,000 individual tariffs, duties and nontariff barriers to trade will be eliminated over the next ten to fifteen years. This creates the world's largest trading block, comprising a total market of $6 trillion and 360 million people in Canada, Mexico, and the United States. Although NAFTA is more trade-oriented than production-oriented, the easier access to a larger market and greater freedom for sourcing opens up multiple new opportunities for multinational firms. Naturally, these opportunities will significantly impact the development of their operations strategies.

The most important implications of NAFTA for operations strategies are the following:

- The need for rationalization of North American facility and logistics networks among most multinationals. For example, American multinationals must reexamine the role of their *maquiladora* factories within their facility network. The main rationale behind the *maquiladora* strategy was that components from an American manufacturer could be shipped tariff-free to a sister plant in Mexico for assembly and subsequently exported back to the U.S. plant for completion or sale. Tariffs applied only to the value-added portion of the production process, which was provided by cheaper Mexican labor. NAFTA, by allowing for nearly borderless production and free trade, makes this reasoning invalid. The strategic role of *maquiladoras* will fade away.

• Stringent North American content requirements will force European and Japanese firms to invest heavily in the development of North American–based production facilities and supplier networks. Within eight years, for example, NAFTA will require all new automobiles to contain 62.5 percent North American content to qualify for preferential tariff treatment. NAFTA's 62.5 percent regional content requirement is far more restrictive than Mexico's national content requirement of 36 percent. As a result, many European manufacturers—e.g., Volkswagen, BMW, Mercedes—have expanded their North American supply base.

Effects of Trade Protection Mechanisms on Global Operations Strategies

The two broad types of barriers to international trade are tariff and nontariff barriers. *Tariff barriers* are types of direct price protection and are imposed as taxes (duties) on imported goods. They are assessed either as a percentage of the value of the imported good or as a flat tax. The General Agreement on Tariffs and Trade (GATT) has been very successful in drastically reducing the tariffs for most industrial goods traded among developed countries, thereby significantly contributing to the expansion of operations globally. The last round of world trade negotiations concluded in December 1993. Implementation of the tariff-reduction agreements from these negotiations will generate an estimated $235 billion in additional global income each year.

In the last four decades, with the success of GATT, tariff barriers have become less important as a form of trade protection than *nontariff barriers,* or forms of indirect, nonprice protection of exports and imports. The most common form of nontariff barrier is the *quota*—a quantitative restriction on the volume of imports. Textile quotas imposed by industrialized countries against textile imports from developing countries are a good example of a nontariff barrier. Another iteration of quotas is the *voluntary export restraint* (VER), whereby the exporting country is gently warned to restrain its exports to the importing country "voluntarily." The use of voluntary export restraints on Japanese automakers effectively imposed a quota on U.S. imports of Japanese cars. Japanese firms responded by (a) upgrading the mix of cars exported to the United States in order to maximize revenue per unit sold, and (b) increasing their investment in U.S. production facilities.

The 1970s and 1980s also saw the increasing application of another form of nontariff barrier—*trigger price mechanisms* (i.e., establishment of a minimum price for sales by an exporter from a foreign country), particularly by the United States and the European Union. The U.S. government used trigger price mechanisms in both semiconductors and steel as a way to eliminate dumping by foreign manufacturers. Unfortunately, in these cases the trigger price mechanisms misfired. They caused the exporters' prices to increase in the United States, thus generating additional profits for low-cost foreign producers. These profits enabled the companies to make greater investments in technologies that reduce production costs and further expand manufacturing facilities in North America.

Governments also use other forms of nontariff barriers, including local content requirements, technical standards and health regulations, and procurement policies.

As discussed under NAFTA, *local content requirements* are designed to promote import substitution by specifying that a certain portion of the value added must be produced inside the country. For example, both Texas Instruments and Intel built semiconductor facilities in Europe (Italy and Ireland, respectively) in response to increases in the amount of semiconductor processing required by local content rules in Europe. Similarly, the European

Union has established strict local content rules (with specific time tables) for Japanese car manufacturers in Europe.

Response to local content requirements has been an important factor in the globalization of operations strategies. In some cases, local content requirements may preclude penetration of a specific market. The firm may deem the sales potential in the market too small to justify a manufacturing investment, or may view the local supplier base as inadequate to fulfill quality specifications. In other cases, market presence may be essential to tap sales potential or to gain access to specific resources, but the local content rules force decisions on the amount and form of manufacturing investment that are suboptimal from the firm's perspective.

Technical standards and health regulations relate to matters such as consumer safety, health, the environment, labeling, packaging, and quality standards. The United States, for instance, prohibits imports of many types of agricultural products on such grounds; Japan refused to import U.S. skis for a number of years on grounds that Japanese snow was different from U.S. snow. The Philips manufacturing plant in Brugge, Belgium, used to employ seventy engineers just to adjust the seven different types of television sets rolling off the assembly lines to meet widely differing reception and technical standards throughout the European Community. These adjustments cost Philips about $20 million a year; different electrical plugs alone accounted for an amazing $2 million annually.

Governments also adopt *procurement policies* that favor domestic producers. For instance, the U.S. government has "Buy American" regulations to give U.S. producers up to 50 percent price advantage on Defense Department contracts.

Fortunately, thanks to harmonization of standards and regulations in the EC, these situations are changing rapidly today, and operating across borders is becoming much easier.

◆ CURRENT AND FUTURE CHALLENGES

Global competition has become a powerful driving force behind manufacturing investment, operations, and strategic decisions. Globalization has forced rapid change on companies historically immune to foreign competition. Arguably, the pace of change has left many companies unprepared. Accustomed to serving domestic customers and fighting well-known competitors, many firms are finding it difficult to adapt to new competition.

The challenges of globalizing operations strategies differ among companies. For some, expanding the firm's global presence and gaining market access is the dominant driver of their international investment decisions. Others search for the next low-wage country for their labor-intensive operations. Many are involved in the difficult effort of rationalizing their global production and logistics networks or the search for cost-effective access to technological resources and engineering talent.

One of the most difficult challenges global operations managers face is to integrate their extended international activities into a coordinated global system that meets the firm's competitive needs. Many American multinationals face this challenge, and they must deal with the fact that, in the past, they expanded their operations internationally simply by replicating their domestic networks.

Restructuring operations networks, which are rife with overcapacity and duplicated processes, is another difficult challenge.

Emerging multinationals, on the other hand, must expand their global presence. Operations managers must decide what production strategies to use to supply foreign markets, where to locate production sites, and whether to consider joint ventures and other strategic alliances as alternatives in expanding their operations. Small and medium firms are facing the challenges of building international infrastructure with limited resources. In many cases, as suppliers of large multinationals, these smaller companies are forced to follow their big global customers in their international expansion, particularly as JIT supplying systems continue to expand. Sometimes, supplier firms pursue closer links with their big customers to take advantage of the larger firms' resources and global experiences; in other cases, supplier firms form joint ventures with local suppliers in the foreign country in which their global customer operates in order to provide continuity of supply and maintain quality standards.

As information in The Conference Board's U.S. manufacturing database indicates, the following lessons learned should influence the development of operations strategies in the future:

- **The globalization of operations strategies pays.** Global presence is important for long-term survival, and firms that pursue global strategies are overwhelmingly the superior performers in terms of both growth and profitability.
- **Pursuing "fewness" pays.** Typically, fewness is achieved through successful segmentation of global markets, and it often relies on product diversity in the product line and increased standardization across national markets. Pursuing this strategy is important, because it allows the firm to respond in a profitable way to the customization needs of various local markets.
- **Global location of R & D pays.** Globally distributed R & D pays off because it allows access to multiple sources of technological knowledge and accelerates the diffusion of learning and the creation of the learning production organization. It is cost-effective through access to less expensive, but high-quality engineering talent. It also can minimize capital exposure through joint ventures or strategic alliances.
- **Globalization is a gradual process, not a one-time event.** The development of successful global operations strategies requires careful consideration of the dynamic nature of the forces that shape the global competitive environment and careful allocation of the firm's resources in meeting long-term competitive goals. Successful companies do not go everywhere at once. They select markets and production locations. Preferred markets are those that are growing quickly, setting new technological and quality standards, and that suit the firm's overall business strategy.

DISCUSSION QUESTIONS

1. Explain the difference between "multinational" and "domestic" firms. Provide examples for each.

2. What are the four driving forces of the globalization process?

3. What are the main trends in the globalization of markets that shape the formulation of operations strategies?

4. Why do small- or medium-sized firms that have never marketed or produced products abroad need to understand developments in global markets?

5. What are the implications of increased emphasis on customization and quick customer response for the structuring of global operations and logistics networks?

6. How can global market presence be used as a competitive threat? Provide examples.

7. What are some of the deficiencies in applying the international product life cycle theory in global markets today?

8. What are state-of-the-art markets? What is their importance in the structuring of global operations and logistics networks?

9. How are firms able to pursue *fewness* and simultaneous profitability in the marketplace?

10. What are the implications of the diffusion of technological knowledge for the development of global operations networks?

11. What has been the main motivation behind collaborative agreements between American and Japanese firms in the auto industry?

12. Why do firms globalize the location of R & D facilities?

13. What are the implications of the diminishing importance of direct labor costs for offshore sourcing strategies?

14. What is an *island hopping* strategy? What are the hidden costs behind such a strategy?

15. What are the effects of increasing capital intensity of production facilities on the structuring of global operations and logistics networks?

16. What are some of the important political and macroeconomic forces shaping global operations strategies?

17. How can operating flexibility in a global production network be used to hedge against exchange rate fluctuations?

18. How do recently formulated regional trade agreements impact the structuring of global manufacturing and logistics networks?

19. Name several types of nontariff barriers that governments use for trade protection reasons. How do firms adjust their global operations strategies in response to them?

REFERENCES

Bartlett, C. A., and S. Ghoshal 1989. *Managing across borders: The transnational solution.* Boston: Harvard Business School Press.

De Meyer, A. 1991. New manufacturing strategies: Taking advantage of uniform standards and alternative technologies. In S. G. Makridakis and associates, *Single market europe.* San Francisco, Calif.: Jossey-Bass Inc.

Kehoe, P. J. 1990. The internationalization of U.S. manufacturing. Washington, D.C.: National Academy Press.

Porter, M. E. 1986. Changing patterns of international competition. *California Management Review* 28 (2); 9−40.

Prahalad, C. K., and Y. L. Doz 1987. *The multinational mission: Balancing local demands and global vision.* New York: Free Press.

Taylor, C. R. 1991. Global presence and competitiveness of U.S. manufacturers. Report Number 977, The Conference Board, New York.

Vernon, R., and L. T. Wells, Jr. 1986. *Manager in the international economy.* Englewood Cliffs, N.J.: Prentice-Hall.

Yip, G. S. 1992. *Total global strategy.* Englewood Cliffs, N.J.: Prentice−Hall.

◆ CASE 3−1: Renault Mexico ◆

Mr. LECLERE-BESSONET, Director of the Management of North American Territories of the state-run corporation Renault, stated at the beginning of 1982:

"After committing ourselves to Renault's development in the United States, and now that our collaboration with AMS has reached its peak, we need to consolidate our position on the North American continent by applying our policy of industrial development prepared over the last five years to Mexico."

Renault in the United States

Renault, the leading French manufacturer with 35% market share internally and 13% market share in Europe, projecting global sales of 2.2 million vehicles in the coming years,

has decided, under the direction of its two successive presidents, B. VERNIER-PALLIEZ and B. HANON, to attempt a new conquest of the North-American market (6 million vehicles a year), avoiding the errors committed at the time of the terrible experience of La Dauphine in the 1960s. Since then, the market has become more demanding, requiring sophisticated engine components: the catalytic converter, the automatic transmission, anti-pollution devices pushing manufacturers to increase the size of the cylinders to a minimum of 1,500 cubic centimeters.

Thus, the state-run corporation acquired a 46% share of America's fourth largest automotive manufacturer, AMC, in 1979.

Its goal is to capture 3 to 4% of the U.S. market, with the aid of three product lines:

• Renault products imported from France (approximately 36,000 vehicles in 1982)

By Philippe-Pierre DORNIER and Emmanuel DOULAS; Rev. 10/93.

- AMC products derived from Renault (180,000 vehicles with the brand name Alliance in 1982) manufactured in Kenosha (AMC)
- Jeep products, a subsidiary of AMC, located in Toledo

Adaptation of French Models

If the production of Jeep's factory is that of a purely American product, production at the Kenosha plant is an adaptation of the French model to American regulations. For the first time, the R9 found itself renamed "Alliance" and soon the R11 will become the "Encore," the two products having been strongly Americanized (anti-shock, anti-pollution, safety standards). To succeed at capturing the American market, Renault needed a "European" automobile manufactured by Americans.

This adaptation of the French model to American standards has introduced the problem of supplying the factory with parts.

Technical Composition of a Motor Vehicle

A vehicle can be considered to be formed of four ensembles offering a more or less large degree of homogeneity:

- the motor-propulsion group (engine & transmission)
- the chassis and mechanical elements
- the body
- the equipment

The distribution of value of the final vehicle's different groups of parts, excluding labor, is generally as shown in Table 1. Labor costs for the final assembly represent 8% of the total value of the vehicle.

Outfits of a very hereogenetic quality are generally outsourced. The chassis and the body already represent more specific ensembles, and Renault has the means and the equipment to produce them in large quantity in France. The production of these agents, strengthened by the capabilities of the AMC plant, can be relatively flexible at the heart of the workshops to supply all of Renault's automotive factories, both in France and abroad.

The motor-propulsion group, by far the most specific, requires for its assembly specialized production units. The most important of these is Cléon in France, the only

assembly plant to manufacture the "C" engine (1,400 cubic cm cast iron) from its conception more than 15 years ago to a current rate of 3,700 engines per day, as well as the new 1,700/2,000 cubic cm cast iron, the "F" engine, for which global demand is estimated at 3,200 motors per day beginning in 1988. These two motors are manufactured in proportions such that today the Cléon plant can export 6% of "F" motors to Renault's foreign subsidiaries. The "C" motor equips the R5, R9, R18, Fuego, and the "F" the R11. But the modular design of many of the vehicles allow the adaptation of the "C" or the "F" engine to any model in the series. The maximum production capacity of the "F" engine for Cléon is 2,200 engines per day.

Supply of the Mexican Factory in Sahagun

The Mexican factory in Sahagun is supplied following the CKD model (Completely Knock Down). The process applied to the Renault 18 assembled in Sahagun is as follows: The CKD of Renault's Grand-Couronne factory in France (Seine Maritime) consolidates and stocks all the parts necessary for the assembly of the models manufactured in factories abroad. Thus, for a given model, here the R18, the Grand-Couronne plant gathers the parts by lots of 50 or 100. The lots are then packed. The technique requires the utilization of packaging specific to each lot and they are placed in a wood crate. This type of packaging represents in materials and labor costs, approximately 16% of the cost of the parts that it contains. Shipments are made in lots of 40 to 80 crates and made almost exclusively by boat. Transport costs represent 10% of the cost of the parts. The assembly plant therefore receives only assembly kits by 50 or 100 of which it must guarantee the administration which represents .2% of the costs of the parts. The principal problems are therefore concentrated in the Grand-Couronne plant, which in effect only receives vehicle orders from the foreign assembly plants. Its operating costs, somewhat variable, are 8.5% of the cost of the forwarded parts. Financial and commercial controls are organized at the state-run corporation's head office: its cost is .04% (parts cost) to which .6% data processing expenses must be added.

The Renaults 9 and 11 are going to represent in the end the only production of the Mexican factory in Sahagun. The manufacture of other models there will be stopped from now until 1984. The projects of the plan to fabricate R9s and R11s allow one to estimate the cost of the parts assembled in Sahagun as a function of their origin:

Origin Kenosha (sheet iron and various equipment):	11,500 Fr
Origin France (mechanicals and various equipment):	6,500 Fr
The average cost of an equipped engine destination Sahagun:	5,000 Fr

Table 1

Distribution of Worth

Chassis and Mechanicals	Body	Equipment	Motor-Propulsion Group
34%	20%	28%	18%

The largest portion of shipments is made by the maritime route with a gain of 4% in relation to traditional packaging. But here the system requires a more significant recourse by plane against emergency repairs to avoid the shutdown of the assembly lines in the case of a break in supply. Approximately 3% of the total weight of the parts are transported by plane and 20% of these shipments are treated as urgent. An additional warehouse should have been conceived in Sahagun. Operating costs and the annual costs associated with it represent 1,600,000 Fr per year. The Mexican factory should have equally admitted to a more significant management of its production (cost: 1% of the cost of the imported parts) and implemented more sophisticated data processing (1% of the cost of the imported parts + 800,000 Fr/year). Administrative expenses at the firm's headquarters represent .2% of the cost of the parts to which it must add 1.2% for data processing fees.

Supply of the North American Factories

When a North American buyer places an order for a particular vehicle, that vehicle is generally not already built, rather, the client waits no more than 15 days from the date of the order to receive it. Otherwise the client will, in the best of cases, change dealers, or will even change brands altogether.

Vehicle production has therefore developed out of this assumption: deliver client orders from week A to the manufacturer, buy the parts, produce the vehicles, and deliver them to the client in week A + 2. . . .

In order to meet the parts supply demands of the American Motors factories, and to adapt to the standards applied to the suppliers of large American manufacturers, standards defined by AIAG (the American equivalent to the union of automotive workers in France), Renault has had to adapt to a very different system to which European automotive manufacturers are not accustomed. In 1982 Renault became, in effect, a simple supplier of AMC. The American affiliate thus passes on to its headquarters weekly orders for parts like any other of its local suppliers. This system has allowed Grand-Couronne's suppliers to receive contained and reusable containers for which the price is generally included in the purchase price of the part. The factory's activities are all the more simplified (cost: 4.5% value of parts in variable cost).

These containers have the advantage of being directly usable on the assembly line. The only supplementary costs are inherent in the packaging of specific returnable containers, when necessary, and then in their placement in the maritime container.

The investment in reusable containers represents approximately 10% of the cost of the shipped parts, amortized over 5 years.

Renault in Mexico

Since 1960, Renault has positioned itself in Mexico essentially under the name of Renault of Mexico (RdM). It was controlled 40% by the French state-run corporation and 60% by the Mexican government up until 1980.

Afterwards, the Mexican government abandoned the automotive industry to private groups and Renault was from that point forward 100% owner of its Mexican subsidiaries. In its Sahagun factory (Hidalgo province), RdM produces R5s, R12s and R18s, delivered in CKD. This production is destined exclusively for the local market, of which RdM claims approximately 12%.

But the Mexican market, after having been possessed of one of the strongest growth rates worldwide, is in a full recession. After having recorded 571,000 vehicles in 1981, the market attained a painful 250,000 in 1982 and remained at this level for several years.

Nevertheless, Mexico remains a promising market for automotive manufacturers since a population of 80 million (of which 42% are less than 15 years of age) experiences an accelerated growth rate (2.6% per year).

The country possesses much potential wealth, which is only beginning to be exploited. A lax administration today slows development, leaving the country facing serious financial difficulties. Thus, finance charges in Mexico are 36% per year, whereas in France and in the United States, rates are at 10%. With a 38% market share, Volkswagen is the leader in Mexico, followed by Datsun, Chrysler and Ford, each with a 10% market share.

During this time, the dollar is at 8.00 Fr/$.

"Automotive" Manufacturers in Mexico

To reach the goals set by the automobile law and the various relative ordinances, manufacturers must estimate, firm by firm, their productions and their sales so as to balance their annual foreign currency budgets. The requirement for local integration is calculated using the price of the equivalent model in the country of origin (article 5 of the automotive law, see appendix 1).

One must not spend, in foreign currency, at one time, more than 50% of:

Dealer price × 0.85 of the French factory sale price of the equivalent vehicle (the remaining 15% represents the manufacturer's markup);

For example, for a R9 or R11 with a dealer price of 45,300 Fr, the cost of the parts imported from France cannot exceed:

$$0.85 \times 45,300 \text{ Fr} \times 0.5 = 19,250 \text{ Fr}$$

Faced with this obligation, every automotive manufacturer maintains a markup on the purchase of local parts in relation to the French price when the rate of integration is greater than 35%.

Faced with the obligation of national integration, the markups that it can generate and the advantage of foreign currencies, a large portion of automotive manufacturers have invested in Mexico:

1. To be able to manufacture local components without significant markup, which is what would have been the case with the local manufacturers.
2. To export products which bring in enough of the foreign currency necessary for the purchase of parts from their origin (at least 50% of the value calculated according to the previous formula).

Regarding the choice of an automotive manufacturer to manufacture locally, Renault must determine the dimensions of the future plant, taking into account, for example, the global demand for engines or body parts, but also these requirements in a foreign currency. These requirements should meet importation at the completion of collections CKD necessary to Renault's Mexican market.

In the case of a local production of engines, the former would be 75% integrated locally and its average sale price at Kenosha is estimated at 4,500 Fr in 1984 (a portion of small equipment would be installed in the United States) from which point the factory would have completed its "rise in industrial rate."

The Choice of the Localization of the Factory in Mexico

To determine its geographical implementation in Mexico, Renault must take several factors into account (refer to appendix 2 for a geographical location of cities).

1. The majority of its production will be in Kenosha, Wisconsin, United States, with the surplus destined for Renault's Mexican plant located 90 km from Mexico City, in Sahagun.
2. It is not possible, taking into account Mexican laws, to install oneself less than 100 km from either the North American border or the Atlantic coast: seven sites are selected (reduced finally to four sites).
3. Mexico's immediate surroundings have a traditionally strong union presence, which has often inconvenienced the Renault administration (the *escalafon* principle: promotion by seniority by all usual channels is confused).
4. Certain Mexican provinces are ready to favor Renault with certain "incentives" (land gifts, exemption from local taxes, etc.).

Modes of Transport

A. Delays

Forwarding to and from the destination (be it Vera Cruz or Tampico in Mexico, be it Houston or Charleston in the United States) can be carried out either by truck (approximately 2 days) or by train, for which the average delay is 25 days.

The liaison Mexico-Kenosha AMC can be envisioned in three forms, as shown in Table 2.

Table 2

Mexico-Kenosha Liason			
	Truck Only	*Rail Only*	*Piggy Back[1]*
Factory => border	1.5 to 2.5 days	5 to 25 days	2 to 3 days
Customs	0.5 days	2 days	2 days
Customs => Kenosha	4 days	8 days	6 days
Total	6 to 7 days	15 to 35 days	10 to 11 days

[1]Piggy Back: trucks and trailers for the Mexican portion of the trip, the trailers are forwarded on special wagons for the American portion of the trip.

B. Costs and Distances

The table of distances between the principal reserved places is given in appendix 3, the two border crossing points between Mexico and the United States are Laredo and Eagle Pass.

Ground Transport: Mexico and the USA

It is possible to utilize two drivers in the same truck to reduce the delays by 2. The cost for an additional driver is $400 per day. A driver covers approximately 500 km per day. Table 3 summarizes the ground transport by truck and train.

Maritime and Aerial Transport

Maritime transport is feasible either in its traditional form or by container. The latter is of two types, the 20' and the 40'. The first can be filled to 18 tons and the second to 24 tons. But volume restrictions are such that the containers are filled to 75% to 80% of their capacity by weight by assembled modules, and to 95% by elementary components. American legislation dictates that only one 20' be loaded on each truck, whereas truckers do not hesitate to put two on in Mexico.

The characteristics of maritime transport are presented in appendix 4. The average cost of a kilo of mechanical automotive parts was estimated in 1992 at 45.00 Fr per kilo, body parts at 15 F/Kg and equipment at 55F/Kg.

Table 3

	Ground Transport: Mexico and USA	
	Container 20' or 40'	*Cases*
Loading of truck or freight car (including administrative costs)	$100 per container	$7.5/ton
Truck mileage costs USA and Mexico	$70/100km by flatbed able to hold 1–2 containers according to total weight	$5/ton/100km
Rail mileage costs in Mexico	$20/km per container	$1.5/ton/100km
Rail mileage costs in USA	$40/100km per container	$3/ton/100km

Aerial transport is envisioned either by bulking or by parcel service. Information relative to these types of transport is outlined in appendix 5. The transfer of the bill of lading between France and Mexico requires 45 days delay.

Customs Restrictions

Customs regulations in Mexico require that every imported vehicle is subject to a 300% tax. Vehicles manufactured locally that do not satisfy minimum levels of national integration (see Article 5 in Appendix 1), are considered as imported vehicles.

Customs duties on imported parts have been fixed at approximately 12% of the part's value.

Renault Corporation has experience with these customs restrictions with its American subsidiary. It decided to place its Kenosha factory in a "customs control operation." The cost of such an operation (customs procedures on the factory's premises) is about $300,000. One must take into account "various administrative costs" at an annual sum of $100,000.

To guide your discussion of this case, the following questions are proposed for your consideration:

- What are Renault's strengths and weaknesses with regard to the strategy of international market growth which the company is pursuing?
- What are the arguments that favor the installation of a new Renault factory in Mexico?
- What type of product and in what quantity must be fabricated? What location appears to be the most judicious?
- What system of logistical distribution (transport, stockage, customs procedures, seems to you the best adapted to respond to commercial objectives and to regulations restrictions?
- What is the interest in placing a factory under customs control (or under a simplified system)?
- What is the best way to organize and manage the flow of information necessary to manufacturers, financiers, retailers, those in charge of transports, customs?

Appendix 1
Excerpts from the Law Relating to the Rationalization of the Automotive Industry

The degrees of the vehicles' national integration will be evaluated by model, based on the cost-part formula.

For those vehicles that will not abide by the minimal standards for integration, importation taxes equivalent to those of imported vehicles must be paid, except if the Secretary, under advice from the Commission, has allowed a temporary decrease in integration because businesses are being seriously hurt, but for reasons not directly attributable to it.

Article 11

Terminal manufacture companies are not allowed to manufacture components produced by the separate parts industry, with the exception of those parts that they already produce or that are authorized by the Secretary. If the company cannot meet with the law's requirements, the Secretary, under advice from the Commission, can authorize that the separate parts industries manufacture additional automotive components to those already produced, when it constitutes an additional benefit for the country's economy and for the development of national industry; the latter understanding to strive to meet international production standards, and designates the major portion of its production for exportation, and to respect any other conditions set by the Secretary.

Chapter III Budget of Foreign Currency

Article 14

Terminal manufacture companies must produce the net foreign currency revenues necessary to their importations and payments abroad. The foreign currency budget determined for each company by the Secretary, taking into account the Commission's recommendations, must be balanced a minimum of yearly for each model.

Article 15

To calculate the foreign currency produced, the Secretary will consider the sum total of net foreign currency revenues resulting from vehicle exportation, tools and automotive components, as well as the exterior capital designated to augment the social capital of the companies, and the external finances in foreign currency allocated for the acquisition of machines and production equipment.

Article 17

To calculate the outflow of foreign currencies, importation totals and exterior payments made by terminal manufacture companies will be taken into account, as well as increase of importations of separate parts industries necessary to the production or automotive components destined for vehicle assembly and for original equipment repairs.

Considering

That for several years, the federal government has pursued a policy encouraging the development and integration of the automotive and separate parts industries, which has allowed the structuring of a significant industrial framework constituting a first-rate source of employment.

That to consolidate the obtained results, as a function of current national and international estimates, and the new objectives of industrial policy and external commerce, set out in the National Plan for Development, it is necessary to rationalize the automotive industry such that it most effectively contributes to the national objectives and priorities.

That in order to do so, the automotive industry must no longer constitute a burden for the commercial balance of the country, and in the future must produce the foreign currencies necessary to its operations.

That the vehicles and their components must be manufactured for a profit, with optimum quality and prices competitive with the global market so they may be accessible to the national consumer, and in particular, those high value-added vehicles, exported.

That to attain the objectives of a balance of payment and of competitiveness, it is necessary to affect those structural modifications within the industry which will rationalize the production of components, and produce, in a general fashion, the benefits offered by peak economies.

Article 5

Vehicles must display the following minimum levels of national integration:

Degree of Integration
Model Year

Vehicle	1984	1985	1986	1987 Forward
Utility Vehicles	50%	50%	55%	60%
Light and Commercial	65%	70%	70%	70%
Mid-size and heavy-weight utility	65%	70%	75%	80%
Road Tractors	70%	90%	90%	90%
Full-size Buses	70%	90%	90%	90%

Appendix 2
Map of the United States/Mexico

Appendix 3
Table of Distances (in km)

	Chihuahua	*Monterrey*	*San Luis Potosi*	*Torreon*	*Kenosha*
EAGLE PASS	750	400	950	550	2500
LAREDO	850	350	800	600	2500
SAHAGUN	1600	1000	500	1050	3600
VERA CRUZ	1900	1000	800	1300	
TAMPICO	1400	600	400	900	
HOUSTON	1400	900	1300	1300	
CHARLESTON	3500	3000	3400	3200	

Houston → Galveston = 100 km

1 driver: 500 km/day

Appendix 4
Logistical Maritime Costs
(tariffs per container are in $)

	Tariffs			Frequency		Delays		Remarks
	20'	40'	Trad.	Contain.	Trad.	Transp.	Customs	
LE HAVRE/ VERA CRUZ	1500	2200	300/T	3/mo.	2/mo.	19 days	8 days	With the traditional method, the gap between 2 boats can be up to one month
LE HAVRE/ TAMPICO	1350	2000	270/T	3/mo.	2/mo.	21 days	8 days	
LE HAVRE/ HOUSTON (conference)	1650	2400	330/T	3/mo.		24 days	3 days (at Laredo)	
LE HAVRE/ GALVESTON (off conference)	1650	2400		1/wk.		11 days	3 days (at Laredo)	For 500 or more, 2 drivers can be used to divide the time in half
LE HAVRE/ CHARLESTON	1650	2400		1/wk.		9 days	3 days (at Laredo)	To speed unloading, organizational costs are approximately 2000.

Appendix 5
Logistical Aerial Costs
(tariffs for aerial transport are in FF)

	Tariff	Frequency	Delays		Remarks
	Traditional	Traditional	Transp.	Customs	
Paris/Mexico Bulking	15.20F/kilo	1/week	1 day	3 days (at airport)	Bulking is done Monday-Friday for Saturday shipment
Paris/Mexico Parcel Service					
0–45 kg	53.30/kg	1/day		3 days	The three-day customs delay can be reduced to one day through exceptional means
46–100kg	41.05/kg	"		"	
101–200kg	20.90/kg	"		"	
201–500kg	18.30/kg	"		"	
501–1000kg	15.15/kg	"		°	
1T–2T	15.15/kg	"		"	

◆ CASE 3-2: Pizza Hut Moscow ◆

"Pizzastroika" was the term coined to commemorate the September 1990 opening of the two Pizza Hut restaurants in Moscow. The opening was the culmination of five years of negotiation, planning, and training involving Pepsico and its joint-venture partner Mosrestoranservise, the restaurant-operating division of the city of Moscow.

In May 1991, after nine months of operation, the Pizza Hut restaurants were averaging 20,000 customers each week. One of the restaurants was capable of producing 5,000 pizzas each day and had the distinction of being the largest pizza kitchen in the world. Lines of people were always waiting to gain entrance, and although many problems had arisen, the joint venture had generated more sales than anyone had predicted.

Andy Rafalat, regional director of Pizza Hut's operation's in Eastern Europe and the Soviet Union, had managed the Moscow venture from its inception. Rafalat, 39, was faced in May 1991 with a difficult decision. During initial negotiations with the city of Moscow, Pizza Hut had agreed to transfer management of the joint venture over to the Russians eventually. Were the Russians prepared to take the helm?

History of Pizza Hut

On June 15, 1958, Dan and Frank Carney, two college students from Wichita, Kansas, opened the first Pizza Hut restaurant. It was a sterling success. By the following

February, the Carney brothers had opened two more restaurants and had begun to develop plans for the first franchised outlet. The chain grew rapidly: 43 restaurants opened by 1963, and 296 by 1968. Pizza Hut went public in 1969 and in 1977 was acquired by Pepsico, Inc. In 1971 Pizza Hut had become the largest restaurant chain in the world in both sales and number of restaurants. Sales reached $1 billion in 1981 and $13 billion in 1988. In 1990 Pizza Hut, still headquartered in Wichita, had over 7,000 units and 125,000 employees worldwide.

Pizza Hut restaurants usually displayed a distinctive free-standing design and characteristic red roof. Until 1985 all Pizza Hut restaurants were full-service, eat-in/carryout, family-style operations seating about 60 to 90 customers and normally open from 11 a.m. to midnight. In 1985 Pizza Hut began opening delivery-only units to meet rising competition from such pizza delivery restaurants as Domino's.[1]

History of Russian Joint Ventures

In January 1987 the Presidium of the USSR Supreme Soviet authorized the establishment of joint ventures between Western companies and Soviet entities such as factories and government organizations. President Mikhail Gorbachev envisioned that this joint cooperation would satisfy Soviet requirements for certain industrial products, raw materials, and foodstuffs; attract foreign technology, management experience, material, and financial resources; and develop the export base of the country.[2]

When the law was first introduced, a foreign partner was entitled to a maximum of 49% ownership in a venture.[3] The decree required that all joint ventures be self-supporting and established a two-year tax holiday, after which profits would be taxed at 30%. No limitations existed on the number of partners or composition of the joint venture's capital structure. Foreign companies were not allowed to "repatriate" their profits, that is, they could not convert ruble earnings into hard currency. Therefore, Western partners often attempted to formulate strategies through which

[1]Kaufmann, Patrick J., Pizza Hut, Inc., Harvard Business School case, 1987.

[2]Jeffrey M. Hertzfeld, "Joint Ventures: Saving the Soviets from Perestroika," Harvard Business Review, January-February 1991, p. 85.

[3]In 1991, there was no ceiling on foreign ownership of joint ventures—in effect, joint enterprises could be 99% foreign-owned. In addition, President Gorbachev authorized the establishment of 100% foreign-owned companies in the Soviet Union.

the joint ventures would generate more hard currency than they used.

History of the Pizza Hut Joint Venture

During 1987, Anatoly Dobrynin, then Soviet Ambassador to the United States, and Donald Kendall, the chairman of Pepsico, discussed the possibility of opening a Pizza Hut in Moscow. Pepsico had been doing business in the Soviet Union since 1972, when it signed an agreement to provide Pepsi-Cola concentrate in exchange for Stolichnaya vodka. Dobrynin and Kendall, believing that the time was right for introducing a restaurant business, decided that the Pizza Hut operation would be a component of a $3 billion commercial countertrade pact between Pepsico and the Soviet Union.

The pact involved the creation of 26 new Pepsi plants in the Soviet Union; Pepsico retained exclusive rights to the sale of Russian vodka in the United States. The deal also included the construction by the Soviets of ten commercial-shipping vessels that would be sold or leased. Foreign-exchange credits generated for the Soviets from the sale and lease of the ships would be partly used as investment in the Pizza Hut restaurants.[4] Kendall commented at the signing of the deal:

This latest agreement further strengthens a highly success-ful and long-standing trade relationship between Pepsico and the Soviet Union. Equally important, as trade between nations expands, so does the level of understanding and cooperation among those nations' citizens. This agreement reflects increasingly closer ties between the US, the Soviet Union, and other Western interests, and the expressed optimism for a shared future. It expands even further the positive collaborations which can help bring the two super-powers and their people closer towards the universally shared goal of world peace.[5]

Altruism and improved relations were not the only reasons for the trade agreement. Business rationale was also strong. The Pizza Hut joint venture was viewed by some as a symbolic "toe in the water," for both Pizza Hut and Western businesses planning to start joint ventures. Recent political changes suggested that the East European market would soon open to capitalist operations. Eastern Europe was the largest untapped base of consumers in the world and according to Rafalat the thinking at the time was that Pepsico's experience with both Soviet consumers and long-standing trade relations with an East European government

would provide the company with considerable leverage and a strong "calling card" in this emerging market.[6]

The decision to begin USSR operations in Moscow was a reasoned one. Moscow, with a resident population of 9 million, was one of the largest cities in the world.

Pizza Hut would be a 49% partner in the joint venture and was required by the terms of the pact to source the majority of its food requirements locally, to engage in the transfer of both financial and technological expertise, and to train a Russian management team for eventual on-site management. The technology transfer included manage-ment and distribution training and training on the state-of-the-art equipment to be used in the restaurant.

Many business analysts believed that the joint venture had symbolic importance to the future of business in the Soviet Union. Kendall waxed philosophic: "We are not, however, just bringing pizza to Moscow. Nor are we just helping to satisfy the local Soviet appetite for consumer goods. We're helping to meet the changing needs of the Soviet economy."[7]

Culture Clash

Managing this joint venture was not an easy task. Many times the problem was just getting each side to understand what the other wanted. Many of the Pizza Hut team's preconceived notions about doing business didn't apply. Rafalat commented:

Don Kendall gets the request and passes it down on our side. We can't be sure it is always passed down on the Russian side. The first people we met here were construc-tion people. They simply wanted to build a pretty restau-rant. We said, our job is not about buildings, it's about a system of management. It all dragged on and on, and after 18 months we were told there was no real interest in developing Pizza Huts at all. They had no concept of the difference between a small Vietnamese restaurateur and a multinational chain. We had to work out a book of rules. That took time. The words we were using had totally different meaning to these guys.[8]

This communication problem was the largest barrier in the early days. Interpreters seemed unable to help. For instance, the Soviet staff protested operations running 365 days a year. They believed, given a need to close for

---

[4]*"Pepsi Will Be Bartered for Ships and Vodka in Deal with the Soviets,"* The New York Times, *April 9, 1990, p. A1.*

[5]*"Pepsico Signs Largest-Ever Commercial Trade Pact with the Soviet Union,"* PR Newswire, *April 9, 1990.*

[6]*Abdo, Geneive, "Pizza Hut Opens its First Restaurants in Mos-cow,"* Reuters, *September 11, 1990.*

[7]*Pizza Hut News release,* Pizza Hut Opens First Two Restaurants in Moscow, *September 11, 1990.*

[8]*Peel, Quentin, "Pizza Hut Gives Food for Thought to Soviets,"* Financial Times, *September 21, 1990, p. 18.*

"hygiene days," that it was impossible. Pizza Hut had to explain the concept of cleaning as a part of routine, daily business operations.

During these times, Mosrestoranservise provided as much assistance as it could. Assistance was limited, however, because of the difficulties and changing environment in Moscow at the time.

Construction of the Restaurants

Senior Pizza Hut managers wanted to have two restaurants in Moscow located in high-traffic areas. They finally signed contracts to build restaurants at 12 Gorky Street, near Pushkin Park and only minutes from the Kremlin, and at 17 Kutozovsky Prospekt, one of Moscow's busiest streets. Taylor Woodrow International was chosen to manage the construction of the Pizza Hut restaurants using design and construction standards similar to those found in the West.

Taylor Woodrow, based in England, assembled an international team to construct the restaurants. Some 100 laborers including skilled craftsmen from Britain, Italy, Sweden, Portugal, Poland and Russia worked at the two sites. In the demonstration of how to accomplish individual tasks, the spoken and written word often took second place to sign language. The work encountered supply problems, as Taylor Woodrow, divisional director, Ian Greenwood, pointed out: "We had no local builders' merchants on hand, even for basic things like nuts and bolts, so we had to import just about everything in the way of tools and equipment—even down to screwdrivers." As a result, costs of production were three to four times higher than they would have been in Western Europe.[9]

Finding and Creating Supply Sources

Pizza Hut managers soon found that the establishment of internal supply sources would be a significant challenge. Although McDonald's had created an entire food-production facility to supply its restaurant, Pizza Hut decided to source 70% of all supplies from existing local suppliers within the Soviet Union (see Exhibit 1), in order to help them improve their quality and standards. Rafalat believed that this approach would ensure the long-term viability of the operation and provide benefits to the growing class of Soviet entrepreneurs. "We are not food producers," he explained. "Our expertise is in restaurants. Where possible, we're happy to share know-how and technology that enables the Soviets to make what we need, sell it to us at a profit, and also meet local market needs."

At the same time, however, Rafalat realized that Moscow's long and extreme winters would make internal sourcing especially challenging. The city often experienced shortages during the winter months, and some Muscovites were known to survive entirely on pickled vegetables. Moreover, Rafalat could not expect to purchase supplies from the warmer, southern republics of the country, which were refusing to send supplies to Moscow because of the escalating political and ethnic tensions.

Pizza Hut faced other supply problems. Cheese, one of the main components of pizza, was common in the Soviet Union, but not mozzarella cheese, which, was unavailable. Rafalat visited numerous cheese-processing plants around the country but with little success;

We couldn't find anybody even interested in supplying us. Finally, we found one in Motensk, 300 kilometres from Moscow, somebody who had been touched by Western thinking. He was happy to give it a try. We would provide the equipment and expertise, he would make the cheese.

Pizza Hut flew the Russian to England to see how the cheese was made and brought cheese-making experts to his plant to provide training on the modern process and equipment. Nevertheless, the mozzarella produced was unacceptable, because the domestic milk did not contain enough butterfat. Cheese had to be imported until a sufficient number of cows could be raised on a strict diet of Western grain.

The search for a supplier for meat toppings also met with no success. Both quality and reliability were missing from every meat plant Rafalat visited. Finally, Pizza Hut's Swedish meat supplier agreed to set up its own joint venture with a partner in Moscow and guaranteed that Pizza Hut would receive the lion's share of its output. Unfortunately, the plant would not be ready for at least another year, so another key ingredient had to be imported.

Pizza Hut also needed to find a way to transport supplies to the restaurants. Because refrigerated trucks were virtually nonexistent in the Soviet Union, Pizza Hut had no choice but to import two trucks to form its own distribution system. The trucks were painted with the distinctive Pizza Hut logo so that they might also serve as a traveling advertisement for the joint venture.[10]

Market Research

In many ways, the Moscow restaurants were an experiment. Because of the novelty value of the Pizza Hut product, typical marketing-research methods and tools were useless for establishing market size and taste preferences. Pizza

---

[9] *"Taylor Woodrow Creates a Slice of Western Living for Muscovites,"* Origin Universal News Services Limited, *September 10, 1990.*

[10] Reuters, *September 11, 1990.*

Hut managers observed, however, as McDonald's opened a restaurant in the city's Pushkin Square in January, customers in the thousands lining up to taste Western-style fast food. They believed the same novelty value would play a strong role in bringing Russians into Pizza Hut restaurants. Pizza, however, was not an unknown food in the Soviet Union; it had been served by Italian and Canadian joint-venture restaurants. It was even prepared by some Russians at home. In addition, a traveling pizza truck offered customers individual slices of pizza. These pizza foods were of varying quality and taste; thus the Soviet consumer had come to view products termed Pizza as having a varying quality.

Pizza Hut scheduled bake-offs to allow Muscovites to sample and compare its product with others. The company received rave reviews. Rafalat believed the Soviet consumers were easily able to discern quality and would communicate their findings quickly through word of mouth.

Pizza Hut would also be different because it would offer both fast- and full-service meals. Rafalat thought that a dinner at Pizza Hut could be viewed as a trip to an expensive restaurant, while McDonald's would still offer only fast-food. Rafalat wanted to combine speed with service and offer Soviet consumers something entirely new: quick table service geared for the entire family. "The market is not consumer driven at all," Rafalat said, "... there is a real lack of consumer choice. Pizza Hut will immediately be ranked as a four- or five-star restaurant in the city."

Pizza Hut decided to offer a menu comparable to that found in Western Pizza Huts—with Pepsi soft drinks, a newly brewed Soviet bottled beer, and wines from Hungary and the Soviet Union. They also developed a "Moscow Pizza" with a salmon-based topping designed to fit with the fish-heavy Soviet diet. (See Exhibit 2.)

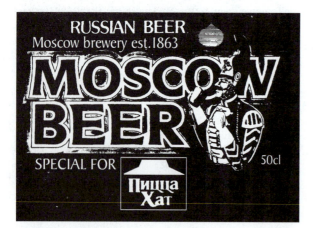

Pricing, the Ruble, and Hard Currency

The restaurants would also differ from other Moscow restaurants in that customers would be able to purchase pizza in either rubles or hard currency. The Gorky Street restaurant would have a walk-up window for ruble customers and a full-service restaurant for hard-currency customers. The restaurant at 17 Kutozovsky Prospekt would actually be two separate full-service restaurants. Both ruble- and hard-currency customers would receive full service, but they would never interact with each other.

Rafalat had attempted to determine who would visit each type of restaurant based on customer's incomes. The average monthly income for a Soviet citizen at the time was 250 rubles. Recently, however, a burgeoning middle class of entrepreneurs had found a higher standard of living than the government employees. Rafalat believed that this middle class enjoyed an average monthly salary of approximately 2,000 rubles. He hoped to serve these entrepreneurs in the ruble restaurants. He also thought that Westerners and black marketeers would visit the hard-currency restaurant. His initial estimates were that the foreign customers would be 40% Americans and 30% Japanese with Germans, Australians, and British making up the balance.

Ongoing changes in the currency exchange rate complicated pricing decisions for the restaurants. At the time the joint venture was being negotiated, the official government rate was 1.6 dollars per ruble, although most people believed that the ruble was worth far less. It was against the law for Soviets to hold hard currency, which over the years had led to the creation of a black market. In the late 1980s, many Soviets were illegally purchasing hard currency on the black market at a rate of approximately 10 rubles per dollar. By the time the Pizza Hut restaurants were ready to open, Soviet President Gorbachev had acknowledged that the ruble had been artificially propped up and he had introduced a mixed exchange rate. He set an official rate of 2 rubles per dollar and a tourist rate of 6 rubles per dollar. At the same time, however, because the poor quality of Soviet goods had been recognized around the world, the black-market rate had fallen to nearly 30 rubles per dollar.[11] This trend suggested that the Soviet government still had a long way to go before reaching an equilibrium between its fixed exchange rate and the free market rate established by the black market.

After studying these fluctuations in the exchange rate, and attempting to set reasonable prices for restaurants' food, Rafalat decided that the restaurants would offer identical menus, but that the prices would differ. Prices in

---

[11] "Soviet Banks to Set Market Rate for 'Tourist Ruble'," Reuters, November 29, 1991.

the ruble restaurants would be roughly comparable to those found in some of the better full-service Soviet restaurants. Prices in the hard-currency restaurants would be similar to those found in Pizza Hut restaurants in the United States. For instance, a large pepperoni pizza in the ruble restaurant would cost 18.20 rubles, while it would cost $6.90 in a hard-currency establishment. At the tourist exchange rate in September 1990 (6 rubles per dollar), an American student would pay more than twice as much money to eat in the hard-currency restaurant as he/she would pay to eat in one of the ruble restaurants.

Why then would an American choose to pay in dollars? The answer was simple: Pizza Hut planned to maintain a standing line of at least 30 minutes in front of the full-service ruble restaurant. Therefore, foreigners would be paying extra for the quick service. (The long line was also intended to serve as a testament to the value of the Pizza Hut product.) The mixed-pricing decision was key to Rafalat's strategy: Pizza Hut would gain a source of hard currency, which was important because foreign companies could not repatriate ruble profits, and be able to hedge the extreme exchange-rate risk.

Human Resources

The requirement that the management of the joint venture would eventually be 100-percent Soviet made the hiring of management personnel a critical task. "Our experience is that, to make joint ventures work, you have to give the local management team the responsibility for running the business," Rafalat said. "I will be called the deputy general manager. I will be like the coach, training the people around me, not taking an active part in the business."[12] This Pizza Hut strategy differed widely from that of the McDonald's joint venture.

In addition to the legal requirement, another rationale for emphasizing Soviet management of the joint venture was the sometimes contradictory Soviet view of Westerners, particularly Americans. Westerners were loved because of the economic and technical assistance they could provide but hated because of the elite status their knowledge and finances afforded them.

Rafalat decided that the best way to find managers was to visit restaurants in Moscow. At one particular establishment, he noted that the staff smiled (a rarity in Moscow) and that the interior was clean. When Rafalat and representatives from Mosrestoranservise spoke with the manager, Alexander H. Antoniadi, they found that he also knew his sales and profit figures. Highly impressed, they offered him the job of general director of the Pizza Hut restaurants. He accepted.

Antoniado, 46, had managed five different restaurants in the Moscow system, including one full-service restaurant,

two fast-food restaurants, and a bakery. Born in Georgia and of Greek descent, he was one of few Soviets who had visited the West. He considered his exposure to Western management practices and service levels a significant factor in his past (and potential future) success. "You can't compare Western and Soviet restaurants," Antoniadi said. "You [Westerners] are used to taste, quality, and far higher worker discipline. Moscow restaurants employ people who are not used to Western service standards."

After Antoniadi was named general director, Pizza Hut still needed two on-site managers for the restaurants. They approached Alexander Youdin and Boris Paiken, both 36, who ran a Georgia-style fast-food cafe called the Pancake, after its famous main dish as a joint venture. Both were known for their commitment to quality and their democratic form of management. Initially, Paiken resisted leaving his joint venture, because he believed Pizza Hut would not allow Soviets to manage the operations. He called them "stables," meaning that he thought Russians, like livestock, would provide little more than physical assistance. After lengthy discussions with Pizza Hut managers, however, he joined the team.

Pizza Hut also needed a financial specialist. Olga Ignatova, 27, was a former member of the Moscow Finance and Planning Department. Rafalat and members of the Pizza Hut team were so impressed with her work during the initial phases of the joint venture that they offered her the opportunity to come aboard as a member of the staff.

Valery Ginsberg, who held a doctorate in steel and alloys from the Moscow Institute, was hired as director of technical services. Ginsberg had initially been hired by Taylor Woodrow International during the construction phase. His knowledge and exacting work ethic earned him an offer to join the management of the joint venture.

The entire management staff was flown out of the country to train in a Pizza Hut restaurant in the United Kingdom. The goal was to establish an understanding of the Pizza Hut philosophy, not necessarily standard procedures. "We wanted people to understand both systems," Rafalat said.

We told them to take a look at the UK system, and then decide how it could best work in Moscow. Taking people out for training meant they would come back totally different people. Telling them the same thing here had no meaning. It was only when they went to London and saw our restaurants working that the penny really dropped.

Hiring and Training Staff

In hiring staff for the joint venture, Pizza Hut found it had an extremely strong group of applicants from which to choose. In an attempt to hire 300 kitchen and wait staff, Rafalat placed an advertisement in the Moscow Communist Youth daily newspaper. The text of the advertisement read:

---

[12]Peel, Financial Times, *September 21, 1990.*

Joint Soviet-American venture invites you to test yourself in a new job. You will gain great experience in the Pizza Hut system of restaurants, developed in 55 countries. We invite young people, 18-25 years old, who are ready to work with enthusiasm. If you meet our needs, we will be glad to speak with you.

The small advertisement elicited 3,500 responses. The applicant pool was the most qualified one Pizza Hut management had ever encountered.

The two basic requirements were that applicants speak at least one foreign language and have some experience working in restaurant joint ventures. Many applicants had college degrees, while some had masters and doctorates. Another characteristic Pizza Hut deemed important in hiring was that an applicant have as little experience as possible working in government-owned establishments. Rafalat believed that individuals became accustomed to a low-productivity work ethic in typical Soviet enterprises, because in general, such enterprises were characterized by lax discipline and almost total job security.

Many of the applicants were former staff of the McDonald's joint venture. Two reasons were cited for their leaving McDonald's: (1) they viewed Pizza Hut's full-service restaurant as being a prestige environment in which to work and (2) McDonald's management had hired so many to staff their restaurant that individuals were actually referred to by numbers, not by their names.

Three hundred people were eventually hired to staff the two restaurants, three times the number for a Western Pizza Hut with comparable output. Rafalat believed that the oversize staff was necessary because of the expected low productivity and unique Soviet employment laws that gave workers two days on, two days off. "As for finding the right people, we had to turn our personnel rules upside down," Rafalat said. "All the good English speakers are academics, so that was no good. Instead, we chose people who were as near to street-wise as possible."

The staff that was eventually hired could only be termed eclectic. For instance, the 16 cashiers all had banking diplomas, many of the members of the wait staff were young mothers with little or no academic training, while some of the kitchen staff held doctorates in engineering. Although many employees were extremely academically advanced, their experience with Western service levels and productivity standards was limited.

A staff of trainers from Britain, Australia, Belgium, Canada, Egypt, and the United States flew into Moscow two months prior to the openings. Their goal was to establish an understanding of and commitment to service unseen in the Soviet Union at that time. One of the ways Pizza Hut attempted to create that understanding was to establish standards of performance relative to each person's job. These standards involved both actual job activities and general work-place attitudes and demeanor.

Rafalat believed that an understanding among workers of a "democratic" work-environment would also be needed. "Unfortunately, a part of the Soviet mentality is to maintain the minimum of your potential. This is a consequence of the autocratic management system. Many think that you can forget about standards." For this reason, he created the first standards incentive program in the Soviet Union. The system was unique in that employees were given full incentive payments to start, but amounts were debited as employees failed to meet standards. For example, each worker contracted to work 173 hours per month and would receive a salary of 600 rubles. If an individual were tardy or failed to show up for work, an established amount of his or her monthly salary would be subtracted. If a waitperson failed to smile or deliver food on time, she or he would have an amount subtracted from salary.

Waiting tables presented unique problems and required equally unique solutions. Waiters and waitresses in Pizza Huts would be allowed to receive tips, although tipping was an unfamiliar practice to Soviet consumers. Customers would have to be educated about both the practice of tipping and the amounts appropriate to various service levels.

The restaurants were to have two separate, wait staffs. The ruble restaurant was viewed as the training department for waitpersons; the more experienced and efficient staff would work in the hard-currency restaurant. Because holding hard-currency was illegal for Soviet citizens tips received by waiters/waitresses in the hard-currency restaurants would be held by management in an account. The staff would be given a catalogue (covering many goods that could not be found in the Soviet Union) from which they could then choose items. Management would use funds from their accounts to purchase the goods on the staff's behalf.

Opening

Despite the many hurdles faced by Rafalat and the joint venture, the two restaurants opened as scheduled in September 1990. The opening was as much an event as any international summit. VIPs from Pepsico and Pizza Hut, Soviet and United States government officials, and the international press were all on hand. Kendall and U.S. Secretary of Commerce Peter Mosbacher, and former Soviet Ambassador to the United States Anatoly Dobrynin—all sat down with Rafalat to sample the first pizzas to come from one of the world's largest pizza kitchens. (The capacity was twice that of a normal Pizza Hut restaurant.) The training team serenaded the trainees with a song specially written for the occasion.[13] (See Exhibit 3)

Lines of customers formed on the first regular business day, but they were not as long as those seen during the launch of the McDonald's restaurant. About 100 people waited for the doors to open that morning. Some expressed a desire to be among the first in the Soviet Union to try Pizza Hut. Others gave more pragmatic reasons: "I ate pizza recently in New York, and I wanted to have a taste," said one young woman. "I came today because in a few months it's likely to be like McDonald's, where some of the ingredients, like tomatoes and lettuce, are always missing."[14]

The First Several Months of Operation

As business continued, Rafalat, Antoniadi, and the management staff found that the skill most necessary in managing operations was flexibility. The only thing they could count on was the unanticipated:

Only a few days after opening, the regional government temporarily closed both restaurants ostensibly for not having a sanitation permit. In reality, however, the closures resulted from a power struggle between the radical Moscow City Council and the conservative District Council. The incident left Rafalat wondering what the country's worsening political situation would mean for the two restaurants and for any expansion plans. But one thing he knew for sure: He would need to cover his bases with all levels of the Soviet government; federal, republic, and local.[15]

Another problem that presented itself not long after the opening was an increase in the prices of supplies. The Soviet government raised prices on basic foodstuffs by an average 300%. Soviet wages rose, but only by about 20%, making Pizza Hut prices less accessible to ruble customers. This problem was compounded by Pizza Hut's decision to raise prices by 40% to make up for the increased cost of supplies.

On the positive side, Pizza Hut found new sources for supplies. When supplies from the government were unavailable, black marketeers proved to be quite ingenious at locating new sources. The Soviet government had recently allowed private farmers to grow and sell excess crops. Once, during the middle of the winter, a private farmer showed up at one of the restaurants' back door with a truck full of tomatoes. Whenever Pizza Hut used these sources,

---

[13] "Pizzastroika," pp. 1-4. Coincidentally, the Moscow restaurants were opened the day after an opening in Beijing. The Beijing opening was viewed as one of the first steps in renewing Western business interests in China following the Tiananmen Square protests and subsequent supporters of democracy crackdown.

[14] Ibid.

[15] "Wanna Make a Deal in Moscow?" Fortune, October 22, 1990, p. 13.

however, the prices were considerably higher than government goods.

Employee turnover was low in the Pizza Hut restaurants relative to other joint ventures such as McDonald's. "Low," however, in the Soviet Union still meant hiring one new person each day. If that rate continued, the entire staff would turn over in a year's time. The turnover made ongoing training a necessity and resulted in sizable lost productivity. Moreover, the ongoing training did not yield the same results as seen with the original staff. New employees did not have the same level of respect for standards or the same level of enthusiasm regarding working at Pizza Hut. Thus, overall quality and service levels began to fall.

The establishment of a team ethic among employees was one of the goals of the managers, but employees believed that their management had made little progress toward this end. "McDonald's does team building," a kitchen staff member said. "They took all of their employees on a cruise. They also took them to dinner and they gave them a Christmas and New Year's party. They have a soccer team that is composed of former Olympic athletes; we do too. Perhaps our management could arrange a game in one of the Moscow city stadiums."

Moreover, other factors began to cause tension between the ruble and hard-currency staffs. Different service requirements and the greater level of gratuity compensation in the hard-currency restaurant created resentment among the ruble staff. Staff turnover in the hard-currency restaurant was also low, which opened up a few slots for the many ruble waitpersons who wanted to move up. On the other hand, while the hard-currency waiters and waitresses were receiving larger tips, the catalogue from which they could order goods was strangely absent. They began to wonder when they would be able to make use of the tips they were saving in their accounts. One waitress said, "I get a receipt for the tips that I turn in. I have been saving these receipts, but I still haven't been able to use them. The catalogue? I have no idea when it will arrive or what is in it."

The standards incentive program created by Rafalat had been successful in rewarding workers who maintained standards, but it did not penalize those who did substandard work, nor did it award exceptional service. Compensation could not fall below a floor of 300 rubles. Because this salary level provided an income that was greater than that of the average Soviet, many found little reason to maintain standards. Absenteeism, particularly among the kitchen staff, became a daily problem. Employees who worked overtime to cover absenteeism received no benefit from their additional work.

Not only did many employees work overtime, but they also were often required to do jobs that they were not hired to perform. They became proficient at all functions within the kitchen operation, but again, they received no incentive for their contributions. Employees who maintained standards felt cheated not only by their peers, but also by a management staff that did not recognize their efforts.

Even without absenteeism, the shift arrangement created stress for many employees. Employees were scheduled 12 hours a day, 2 days on, 2 days off. Soviet managers believe this schedule was necessary to give employees time to stand in line for food and other supplies. The employees, on the other hand, believed they would prefer a Western-style 8-hour, 5-day schedule. Schedules were a source of frequent discussion, and the policy had been changed at least four times since the restaurants opened. Rafalat had been told by Soviet managers that the employees voted on the scheduling policy. Employees said that management simply handed it down.

The long hours caused problems in the personal lives of the wait staff. Some 80% of the wait staff were married, and 60% had children. The long hours caused many to feel that they were being negligent regarding their parental responsibilities. Furthermore, many did not complete their shifts until after midnight, which prevented them from leaving in time to use Moscow's subways. Many had to use taxis, which were quite expensive. Commutes were long, and some employees traveled as much as 90 minutes one way each day.

Communication between management and staff was limited. Many employees believed that, when they voiced their concerns, these opinions were not welcomed and fell on deaf ears. "There is a difference between words and deeds," a cook said. "They never take our claims seriously. In fact, we don't even know if they receive them. If you can substantiate your suggestions, then and only then can things change." Another said:

Many people would like to see a union. However, it is very difficult to organize one. This is because of the philosophy in this country. Unions that support a specific group of workers really don't exist. The government controlled our working conditions until now. They were supposed to act in our interest. Many feel that, if they voice their complaints, they could lose their jobs. They are not happy about voicing their complaints.

Despite their expressed dissatisfaction, most staff believed that they would suggest seeking employment at Pizza Hut to others. One waitress summed up the feelings of the staff: "The work here is much more exciting and pays much better than anything you might be doing while working for the state, though it has not proven to be what we dreamed capitalism would be like."

Conclusion

Andy Rafalat smiled and looked from the dining room at the line of customers reaching around the block. His "toe in the water" was being called a success. It had exceeded expectations in sales and profitability. (See Exhibit 4.)

Rafalat knew there were critical problems: employee turnover was high, quality was diminishing, and employee discontent was rising. Soon the Russian managers would take over total management of the operation. Would they be able to turnaround the growing problems? What could he do to better prepare them for the management transfer?

On a different level of worry were the rumors of growing discontent with the Gorbachev government. If Gorbachev's reform policies fell out of favor, what would be the result for the Pizza Hut joint venture?

Exhibit 1

PIZZA HUT MOSCOW
Weekly Food Requirements Purchased Locally

French bread	8,000 loaves
Garlic puree	320 lbs.
Flour	8,800 lbs.
Mushrooms	680 lbs.
Onions	6,640 lbs.
Tomatoes	5,000 lbs.
Cucumber	5,000 lbs.
Carrots	5,000 lbs.
White cabbage	2,600 lbs.
Beetroot	5,000 lbs.
Pickles	5,000 lbs.
Ice cream	2,000 lbs.
Pepsi syrup	264 gallons
Beer	1,000 bottles

Exhibit 2

PIZZA HUT MOSCOW
Full-Service Menu

Добро пожаловать в Пицца Хат!

Закуски

Чесночные гренки

Салат-бар

Пан пицца и Тонкая и хрустящая™ пицца

Фирменные блюда – "ПИЦЦА"

	Малая (15 см)	Средняя (27 см)	Большая (33 см)
Маргарита	6.20	10.00	14.00
Пепперони	7.85	13.00	18.20
Вегетарианская	8.40	14.00	19.60
Гавайская	8.70	14.50	20.30
Московская морская "Москва"	9.50	16.00	22.40
Европейская	9.80	16.50	23.10
Мясной пир	10.05	17.00	23.80
Суприм	10.30	17.50	24.50
Супер Суприм	11.15	19.00	26.60

Напитки

Безалкогольные напитки	Малый (330 мл)	Кувшин
Пепси	1.20	4.80
Диет Пепси	1.20	4.80
Фиеста или Танец	1.20	4.80

Пиво	
Пиво местного производства	3.50

Вино	
Красное или белое вино: в бутылках	20.00
в разлив	4.00

Горячие напитки	
Чай	1.00
Кофе	1.50

Десерты

Мороженое	4.50
Мороженое Сандей	6.50
Яблочный пирог	4.00

Пицца для дома

Exhibit 2 *Continued*

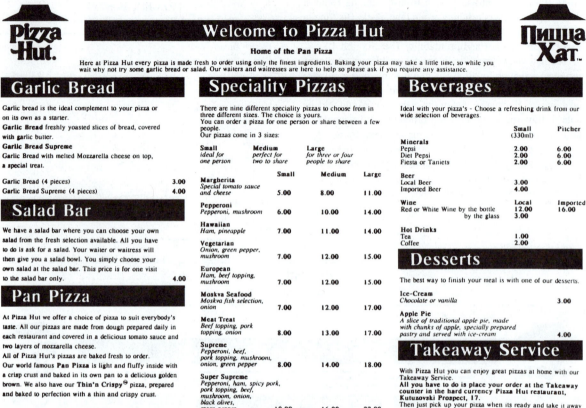

Welcome to Pizza Hut
Home of the Pan Pizza

Here at Pizza Hut every pizza is made fresh to order using only the finest ingredients. Baking your pizza may take a little time, so while you wait why not try some garlic bread or salad. Our waiters and waitresses are here to help so please ask if you require any assistance.

Garlic Bread

Garlic bread is the ideal complement to your pizza or on its own as a starter.
Garlic Bread freshly yoasted slices of bread, covered with garlic butter.
Garlic Bread Supreme
Garlic Bread with melted Mozzarella cheese on top, a special treat.

Garlic Bread (4 pieces)	3.00
Garlic Bread Supreme (4 pieces)	4.00

Salad Bar

We have a salad bar where you can choose your own salad from the fresh selection available. All you have to do is ask for a salad. Your waiter or waitress will then give you a salad bowl. You simply choose your own salad at the salad bar. This price is for one visit to the salad bar only.   4.00

Pan Pizza

At Pizza Hut we offer a choice of pizza to suit everybody's taste. All our pizzas are made from dough prepared daily in each restaurant and covered in a delicious tomato sauce and two layers of mozzarella cheese.
All of Pizza Hut's pizzas are baked fresh to order.
Our world famous **Pan Pizza** is light and fluffy inside with a crisp crust and baked in its own pan to a delicious golden brown. We also have our **Thin'n Crispy**® pizza, prepared and baked to perfection with a thin and crispy crust.

Speciality Pizzas

There are nine different speciality pizzas to choose from in three different sizes. The choice is yours.
You can order a pizza for one person or share between a few people.
Our pizzas come in 3 sizes:

Small ideal for one person   **Medium** perfect for two to share   **Large** for three or four people to share

	Small	Medium	Large
Margherita *Special tomato sauce and cheese*	5.00	8.00	11.00
Pepperoni *Pepperoni, mushroom*	6.00	10.00	14.00
Hawaiian *Ham, pineapple*	7.00	11.00	14.00
Vegetarian *Onion, green pepper, mushroom*	7.00	12.00	15.00
European *Ham, beef topping, mushroom*	7.00	12.00	15.00
Moskva Seafood *Moskva fish selection, onion*	7.00	12.00	17.00
Meat Treat *Beef topping, pork topping, onion*	8.00	13.00	17.00
Supreme *Pepperoni, beef, pork topping, mushroom, onion, green pepper*	8.00	14.00	18.00
Super Supreme *Pepperoni, ham, spicy pork, pork topping, beef, mushroom, onion, black olives, green pepper*	10.00	16.00	22.00

Beverages

Ideal with your pizza's - Choose a refreshing drink from our wide selection of beverages.

	Small (330ml)	Pitcher
Minerals		
Pepsi	2.00	6.00
Diet Pepsi	2.00	6.00
Fiesta or Taniets	2.00	6.00
Beer		
Local Beer	3.00	
Imported Beer	4.00	
Wine	Local	Imported
Red or White Wine by the bottle	12.00	16.00
by the glass	3.00	
Hot Drinks		
Tea	1.00	
Coffee	2.00	

Desserts

The best way to finish your meal is with one of our desserts.

Ice-Cream *Chocolate or vanilla*   3.00

Apple Pie *A slice of traditional apple pie, made with chunks of apple, specially prepared pastry and served with ice-cream*   4.00

Takeaway Service

With Pizza Hut you can enjoy great pizzas at home with our Takeaway Service.
All you have to do is place your order at the Takeaway counter in the hard currency Pizza Hut restaurant, Kutuzovski Prospect, 17.
Then just pick up your pizza when its ready and take it away

The prices on this menu are for US Dollars, payment can also be made in Pounds Sterling, Deutschmarks or Finnish Marks.
We also accept the following credit cards: American Express, Diners Club, Mastercard, Visa and J.C.B.

Exhibit 3

PIZZA HUT MOSCOW
Serenade for the New Trainees

With a song in their hearts

THE training team launched their trainees into action with a specially devised song, set to the melody of 'Those Were The Days' ...

Once upon a time there were two brothers
Frank and Daniel Carney were their names
They lived in Wichita which is in Kansas
And they started up the biggest pizza chain

They named it Pizza Hut
They named it Pizza Hut
It grew and grew all over this great land
It grew so wide and far
Into the USSR
At Pizza Hut you know you've got it made

The training team was captained by a Belgian
She sent for reinforcement global wide
From around the world the Training Team were comin'

With an assistant called Ivan by her side

They came from Canada and America
Egyptians too were not left out of the crew
There were some Brits and Welsh
They needed someone else
So they threw in an Aussie too

Now all of you take heed to what we tell you
The future of success is in your hands
So remember all the things that we have taught you
And you'll make the greatest pizzas in the land

You all are Pizza Hut
You all are Pizza Hut
The way you smile
They'll come from near and far
You've all worked very hard
You're held in high regard
You are the pride of the USSR!

Exhibit 4

PIZZA HUT MOSCOW
Pizzastroika

Pizza Hut. NEWSROUND   PEPSICO FOOD SERVICE INTERNATIONAL

NEWS FROM THE EURAFME REGION   NOVEMBER 1990

Pizzastroika!

Openings are culmination of five years' effort

RUSSIA'S first two Pizza Huts surged into Moscow in September with the world's media proclaiming Pizzastroika!

The two restaurants - one in Gorky Street, close to the Kremlin and the other in the residential centre of Kutozovski Prospekt, are the culmination of five years negotiation, planning and training and a tribute to the sound US/USSR PepsiCo relationship of more than 16 years.

Care

For the population of Moscow, Pizza Hut, with its emphasis on customer care, service and hospitality for all the family, represents a new Russian revolution. The restaurant set-up is a joint venture, with installation and training 100 per cent Pizza Hut and the management team totally Soviet.

Fifteen Pizza Hut trainers from Britain, Australia, Belgium, Canada, Egypt and the US worked in Moscow for eight weeks sharing new concepts of service and standards with the 300-strong Moscovite team.

But the menu for the new restaurants salutes the Russian appetite with a special fish-topping pizza, borscht soup and pickled cabbage.

Opening

The grand opening of the new restaurants saw a host of VIP's, including dignitaries from Moscow City council, PepsiCo, Whitbread, Pizza Hut and PFSI around the world as well as key suppliers.

An early problem caused by a local regulation saw both Huts closed for a few days. Happily, this was soon sorted out, and they are now pulling in around 20,000 customers a week.

A key aim of the project is to continually develop local sources of food supplies for these restaurants.

Expertise

As part of its investment, Pizza Hut gave government sectors and cooperatives financial and technological expertise for the production of food and beverage needs.

There will be on-going management and distribution training and consultation on state-of-the-art

Пицца Хат.

Above, Red Square at night; left, the Russian Pizza Hut logo

equipment for the production and process of mozzerella cheese, meat and other foodstuffs.

Said regional operations executive Andy Rafalat: " We must ensure consistency of our food supply without becoming food manufacturers . Developing local food supplies is also our important contribution to the continued

● Continued on Page 2

PFSI becomes Pizza Hut Worldwide

IN a major reorganisation of the business, PepsiCo has announced that PFSI is to form parts of two new companies - Pizza Hut Worldwide and PFS Worldwide Distribution.

From January 1st 1991 this new company will include the international franchised company-owned and joint venture Pizza Hut operation, currently the responsibility of PFSI.

Steve Reinemund is to be president and chief executive officer of the new company which will operate from the current headquarters in Wichita, Kansas.

Also from January 1st Gill Butler will become chief executive officer of PFS Worldwide Distribution - an area pinpointed as significant for future development. Details of the re-organisation will be finalised over the coming months

* Changes to Eurafme team and PepsiCo moves - see page 5.

◆ Case 3 – 3: Guangzhou Machine Tool ◆

Introduction

Liu Ming returned to his office after hosting a group of American visitors on a tour through the Guangzhou Machine Tool factory. As factory director, he had been able to answer most of their questions honestly and with some depth. The questions were similar to those he had asked at least one hundred times before; but many of the answers still eluded him. He decided to stay late that evening and spend some uninterrupted time reflecting on the questions. Before he rushed off to his next appointment, he made an abbreviated list of topics he knew he had to address. These he scribbled quickly on a piece of paper. It read: quality, productivity, small competitors, central government controls, markets, social services, and survival.

The Chinese Economy and Guangzhou

Since economic reform in 1978, China's real GNP has grown by an average of 9% per year. Except for the brief setback in 1989 because of the Tiananmen Square incident, the Chinese economy has been bustling with life. In the first eight months of 1992, China's real GNP grew at an annualized rate of 14%. In contrast to the former Soviet Russia, which is barely able to feed its people, China has $40 billion in foreign-exchange reserves. Chinese shops are crammed with goods and customers.

Guangzhou (formerly known as Canton) is the capital of Guangdong Province and is only 75 miles from Hong Kong. Its geographical proximity to Hong Kong and its "Special Economic Zone" status has made Guangzhou the richest city in China. While the real GNP growth of the rest of the nation averages 9% per year, the ten-year average growth of Guangdong Province is more than 12 percent. In the past three years, the average growth rate in Guangdong has been 24%. Some have suggested that this is a faster growth rate than any region has experienced in the history of the world.

The majority of Hong Kong residents have their roots in Guangdong Province. It is apparent to even the casual observer that residents of both Guangzhou and Hong Kong are driven by money, and both have the resourcefulness of beating the rules. For instance, a Guangzhou businessman bought 300 turkeys and listed them as "Texas chickens," because the regulations did not include turkey. A Hong Kong businessman recently brought sausage skins into China as "machine tools," because that was the only category that recognized "casings" (*Financial Post*, November 25, 1991).

However, only the private sector of the Chinese economy seems to be enjoying the boom. State-run factories, especially larger ones, are clamoring for more autonomy in managing their operations. Factory managers claim that there is too much interference from government departments. Unless they have full operational autonomy, they say, state-run factories will be unable to compete in the market economy. Recently, authorities *have* given increasing autonomy to factory managers. For instance, managers can withhold a portion of their output from the state's allocation network for sale through market channels. Exhibit 1 contains data about the Chinese economy for 1990.

"State-run enterprise" is a shorthand term for the Chinese designator "enterprise under the ownership of all the people." These were

- established and maintained with central government investment
- overseen by central government authorities or their local representatives
- included in central government plans that (1) specified allocations of funds and materials that the firm would receive from government sources and (2) set output targets for goods to be delivered to the state.

Collectives are owned by the workers rather than by "all the people."

Of the state-run enterprises and collectives, some are large and centralized, such as steel manufacturers. Some are owned by a town, county, or other administrative unit. (The units of administration are, in increasing order of size: village, town (small towns, usually in rural areas), county, city, province. Note that "city" is larger than "county," unlike the U.S.) "Township" implies ownership; "town"

Exhibit 1

China in 1990	
7.97 million enterprises	23,851
6.17 million are private; almost all have 1-2 employees	1,295
104,000 are state-run	13,008
1,685,000 are collectives	8,510
(The Chinese currency is yuan (¥) or RMB.)	

implies a unit of administration. "Above township" is a term that specifies public ownership of enterprises by units of administration including, and larger than, towns. The following statistics describe "above township" enterprises; i.e., state run or collectives, owned by towns or larger units.

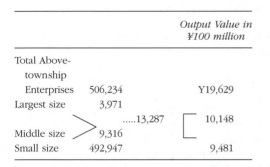

		Output Value in ¥100 million
Total Above-township Enterprises	506,234	Y19,629
Largest size	3,971	
		……13,287
Middle size	9,316	10,148
Small size	492,947	9,481

Less than 5% of above-township enterprises have joint ventures or co-management with other firms (Chinese or foreign).

Company Background

The Gunangzhou Machine Tool factory (GMT) is part of the Guangzhou Machine Tool & Tool Industry Corporation, a large state-run enterprise in Guangzhou which controls several factories in the Guangzhou region. The Guangzhou Machine Tool factory was built in 1938 to produce common lathes.[1]

GMT produces three main products that are defined by the dimensions of the workpiece. Series I processes parts less than 320 mm in diameter and 750-1000 mm in length. Series II processes parts less than 400 mm in diameter, and 1000-2000 mm in length. Series III processes parts less than 460 mm in diameter and 750-1000 mm in length. GMT also produces basic numerically controlled (NC) lathes that process parts 320–460 mm in diameter. These NC lathes are controlled by tape rather than by computer—that is, they are not computer numerically controlled (CNC). Series I–III products were mostly designed in the early 1970s.[2]

---

[1]A metal cutting lathe is a tool that rapidly turns a piece of metal, known as the workpiece. A stationary cutting tool, when applied to the workpiece, removes small amount of metal. Repeatedly moving the cutting tool along the spinning workpiece, produces a part of the desired (round) dimensions. Common lathes are also known as universal lathes.

[2]Some outsiders feel that the machines resemble those designed in the late 1950s. This view is supported by the fact that much of Chinese industry slowed down (at best) during the Great Leap Forward (1958-1961). A period of stability reigned until the onset of the Cultural Revolution (1966-1976), at which time practically the entire country stalled. Designs produced in the early 1970s often had to be based on the latest available technology which may have been 1958 vintage.

The three product lines are supplemented by a number of smaller machine tools, as well as some machines of much older design. Therefore, although the three products dominate output, the factory actually produces a wide variety of products. This variety is compounded by the fact that GMT will customize products according to customer desires. The basic designs, and many of the parts, are standardized, however. Most customization is performed to comply with local laws and customs. For instance, American customers want left-hand handles, although the original design is for a right-hand handle. When exporting to France, GMT installs emergency brakes to comply with French safety laws. Singapore requires special color codes.

Aware that top machine tool manfacturers in Japan, Europe and the U.S. introduce new products up to twice a year, GMT factory management constantly pursues new product development. At this writing, GMT is designing several new products, with an emphasis on more sophisticated NC lathes, including CNC equipment. GMT has some CNC tools at the prototype production stage, but problems with reliability of the NC products indicate that it will be some time before CNC tools are ready for sale. The main method of new product design is reverse engineering Japanese and German machines.

Pricing reflects the relatively low cost of manufacturing in China. Machines sell for RMB 20,000 to RMB 100,000,[3] depending on the series and the degree of customization. Many developed nations have stopped production of low cost (and relatively low tolerance) machine tools. Some newly industrialized places, such as Taiwan, produce competing products, but Liu Ming felt strongly that GMT's products were not only less expensive, but of higher quality. In addition, GMT's ability to customize equipment generates sales. The primary competition is from other Chinese machine tool manufacturers—especially new, small firms that are not burdened by the regulations imposed on state-run enterprises.

In addition, Liu Ming was not sure whether there would be a long-term market for these lathes. While he felt that there would be limited demand for high precision machine tools, he was not sure of the market for his relatively low precision tools. CNC equipment was coming down in price and was clearly of higher quality. GMT's segment of the machine tool market in China was nearing the saturation point, so that exports were picking up a larger share of sales. In each of the last two years, 50–60% of output was for export. GMT began exporting in the 1970s as a government-sponsored method of bringing foreign currency into China. In fact, the government subsidized the factory in its export efforts until 1990, when the government

---

[3]$1 = RMB 6.3.

decided that GMT was self-sufficient. (GMT is the largest machine tool exporter in China.) When the subsidies ended, the factory gained the right to use a portion of the foreign currency it earned.

GMT markets products at exhibitions in countries in which it sells. These include Malaysia, Singapore, Thailand, some European countries, and even the United States. In addition, GMT is represented at a large annual business convention in Guangzhou.

GMT has been looking for foreign capital investment recently. It now has a cooperative venture with a company in Hong Kong which borrows money from the China Bank in Hong Kong in order to buy equipment from foreign machine tool manufacturers. The factory recently bought a West German machining center for $600,000 and a three-year-old East German milling machine for $200,000, both for the purpose of fabricating parts—not for reverse engineering. The machining center has a 160-tool automatic tool changer, and is used for high tolerance parts. Recently factory management decided to purchase machine tools valued at $3 million in order to promote technology transfer, hopefully adding value to GMT's lathes.

Production

The GMT factory is arranged according to a process layout. Different shops fabricate, assemble, test, paint and package products. In the fabrication areas, the shop again is arranged by process. Milling equipment is assigned to one area; lathes, drills, grinding machines, and so on, each are assigned to separate areas. There are about 550 machines in the factory, 300 of which are lathes.

Raw materials are simple. To make a machine tool, the factory uses castings of metal, a motor, and other electrical parts. The motor and other electrical parts are purchased from vendors who have provided reasonably good delivery and quality performance. It is not unlikely, however, that at least one vendor will be late—causing a slowdown of the assembly shop.[4] Castings were previously done on site, but problems with pollution control caused GMT to move the foundry 70 kilometers away. Castings are cut to size and shape by machine tools. The (roughly) 1,200 parts are then assembled in the assembly shop, tested, painted and packaged in respective shops.[5] Nearly all the machine tools in

the factory are Chinese. The machining process varies widely, depending on the part. Some parts require only a few steps and therefore a short time for fabrication. Others require up to two months of time and thirty steps. Steps include milling, drilling, routing, and heat treating. GMT uses relatively small batch sizes in order to keep WIP under control. (For instance, main axles have a batch size of 160.) Set-up and run times also vary widely by part. Because of variations in parts, set-up time can take as much as three or four days of the two-month flow time. These variations arise in part because of slightly different designs or from customization.

The time from receiving an order to delivery is usually about three months, including the foundry. Customers who place rush orders can expect a one-month lead time if they are willing to pay a premium. Factory management prefers not to expedite delivery, however. The factory does hold some finished goods inventory. When demand is high, finished goods inventory will be as low as ten machines; during slack periods, inventory could reach 200 to 300 machines. In periods of high demand, Liu Ming felt, rapid delivery would increase sales. GMT is able to make and hold components that are common among different machines, substantially reducing lead time. These components are also used for repair parts.

Production planning is the responsibility of the Vice-Director of Operations.[6] His decisions on quantity and timing are based on actual orders received and sales forecasts. Due to market volatility, his proposals are thoroughly examined in meetings with the Director and the three other Vice-Directors. Production decisions are made by month, one month in advance. The quantities are not adjusted after these decisions are made. If the factory meets the quota before the end of the month, workers take paid time off. GMT found that using the one-month time buckets created quality problems, since workers rushed to get things done at the very end of the month. To avoid assembly downtime and quality problems, they now use a 30-30-40 system; that is, GMT does 30% of the month's assembly from the first to the tenth of a given month; 30 percent from the eleventh to the twentieth; and 40% from the twenty-first to the end of the month. Separating the month into three increments helps to keep things in control. At times, however, the fabrication workshops do not provide the assembly shop with components on schedule, and hence assembly must slow down.

---

[4]It is the factory's responsibility to maintain good working relationships with its suppliers. The central government stopped central planning for the factory in 1978. As long as the factory pays State taxes (that is, taxes to the central government), it is pretty much left on its own for daily operational issues. Therefore, GMT can choose its suppliers and work with them for maintaining delivery and quality performance.

[5]Of the 1,200 parts, some are elaborate—such as the main axle; and some are simple—such as screws.

[6]This person reports to the factory director and is peer with Vice Directors of Marketing, Technology, and Administration. The factory director reports to the Communist Party Secretary, who is the most powerful figure in the factory. Recently this position has been eroded by economic reform, but the Party secretary still has considerable clout.

On the factory floor work groups report to a work group leader, who reports to a supervisor of the work shop. The supervisor reports to the Vice-Director of Operations. In addition to supervisory responsibility, work group leaders perform tasks as members of these work groups. Work groups receive specific work schedules from the supervisor of the work shop based on the Vice-Director of Operations' production plan.

At full capacity, GTM can produce 4,000 machine tools a year. Current production is between 3,000 and 3,800 tools per year. Employees currently work a six-day week, eight hours a day. The majority of the factory operates on two shifts, although the heat-treat area works in the third shift, due to electricity supply. Heat—treat requires a significant amount of energy, and with power plants encouraging customers to level the peak demand by working at night, GMT gets better rates for doing so.

Human Resources

The factory employs 2,600 people. Line workers have been trained at the junior or senior high school levels. Most technical staff members are college educated, although a few have degrees from polytechnic schools. Administrators and managers come mostly from polytechnic schools.

There are twelve pay scales, ranging from a low salary of 55 RMB (roughly $9) per month to 220 RMB ($35) a month. In general, there are three parts to the pay of a worker in China: the salary, the bonus and the allowance. Salaries for large state-run enterprises (such as GMT) are fixed by the central government. These may vary by region for line workers. (By contrast, township enterprises and other small firms have more flexibility, and therefore may have lower labor costs.) The bonus is based on the profitability of the factory and can be as high as 100% of the salary. The allowance includes low rent housing, schooling for children, worker training, medical care and so on. Liu Ming reflected, "We cannot continue to provide housing for our employees. We are not a housing company. We cannot continue to run a kindergarten when we have to compete with township companies. Housing and kindergartens are community responsibilities, not factory responsibilities. They do not even help us attract workers. Since we are in the fertile Guangdong region, farmers are quite wealthy compared to people who work in other enterprises. Machine tool manufacturing is heavy, dirty and loud. Workers prefer farming and light industry. We use bonuses in addition to the allowance to attract workers, since they want more than housing and other social services. They are looking for pay, good working conditions, and so on. It is a slight advantage to have free medical care for workers and their families; but it does not seem to be enough."

The average age of factory employees is around 40. Piecework is used as an incentive wherever possible. Promotion is generally from within. A person is promoted based on recommendations of colleagues and supervisors, with the final decision made by factory management. In the past, most people stayed with the company for their entire career. Today, however, GMT is developing a contract system whereby a worker will sign a contract to stay at the factory for three to five years. In this way, they hope to hold on to workers long enough to amortize training and hiring costs.

The government is encouraging modernization. It realizes that automation will displace some workers, but full employment seems to be secondary when weighed against the goals of the four modernizations (modernization of industry, agriculture, national defense, and science and technology). In order to cope with the potential unemployment problems, the government allows state employees to quit their jobs and set up small businesses of their own. In the bustling Chinese economy, there are millions of such small businesses employing five people or fewer.

Reflections

Liu Ming reflected on his twenty-two years at GMT. Things had changed radically in that time. He thought of GMT's import/export license and the benefits it provided. Customers can now fax their orders to GMT, even from overseas. Joint ventures are now a possibility and an appealing one. Joint ventures pay no tax for three years and then have a lower tax rate than the large state-run enterprises.

As Liu Ming looked at the abbreviated list of questions, he decided to fill it out before addressing each one. Even as he wrote, however, he knew that the answers—if there were any—were interdependent.

- How could GMT improve the quality of their products? What did "quality" mean, anyway?
- How could he improve productivity in the factory?
- What was he to do about new and smaller competitors who were not burdened with providing social services for their employees?
- If the government would not give him even more freedom, what measures could he pursue to improve responsiveness and competitiveness?
- What if the government eased central controls?
- What new markets could he pursue?
- What if the government allowed him to take a very creative approach—even restructuring the firm?

Chapter 4

Global Marketing Strategies

◆ ◆ ◆

This chapter will address the following points:

◆ *Marketing as it relates to changing global customer behavior*

◆ *Global versus local marketing*

◆ *Integration of logistics and operations to produce a global product*

◆ *Efficient consumer response*

The challenge for companies today is not whether to go global, but how to tailor global marketing strategies to fit a variety of environments and consumer behaviors. This chapter provides a structural approach to help managers think about how they should set up the different areas of the marketing function as the business shifts to a global approach. It also includes examples of companies that have tackled the implementation challenges of global marketing, including facing changing consumer behavior. As these examples will illustrate, the success of global marketing strategies depends significantly on the presence of integrated logistics systems and well-developed global operations strategies.

◆ CHANGING CONSUMER BEHAVIOR

The basic marketing mix decisions consist of four separate, but interconnected, functions. These are the four Ps of marketing—product, price, promotion, and placement. Companies satisfy consumer needs by developing and manufacturing the goods desired in a market; by educating potential clientele regarding the existence and qualities of those products; by balancing product cost between quality and prices; and by ensuring that adequate volumes of products are distributed to sales outlets in a timely fashion.

Developing successful marketing strategies is complex enough, even at the domestic level. As might be expected, globalization significantly increases the complexity of these tasks, and every function of the marketing mix may require modification in order to do business in the global environment.

For example:

- Foreign markets not only are physically removed; they also differ culturally.
- Specific cost structures in the foreign market may dictate special pricing.

114

- Distribution channels found in the domestic environment may be unavailable in the foreign market.
- Portions of the product may have to be modified to meet local needs.
- Promotional methods may need to be adjusted to local media.

In addition to the pressures of globalization, recent changes in customer behavior have shaken up the four pillars of marketing strategy. These changes have caused manufacturers, wholesalers, and retailers to adapt their strategies and organization structure in order to meet new expectations. Key consumer changes include individualism, time-based competition, environmentalism, and global products.

Individualism

Consumers emphasize their own needs and expectations. This has not always been the case. At other times in history (e.g., during World War I and World War II), and in other cultures (e.g., some Asian cultures), the desires of individuals have taken a back seat to the needs of society at large. In recent years, however, backed by a growing awareness that many Western societies are accepting and/or encouraging such an attitude, consumers have openly demanded that individual desires be satisfied in all aspects of life. From a business standpoint, this trend means the era of standard products is over, and the era of extreme product customization is at hand.

This new era has several consequences for business entities:

- Previously homogeneous market segments must be divided into thinner subsets to account for emerging individual needs.
- An explosion in the number of products offered places new pressures on product branding.
- A drop in individual product turnover means that the same level of stock of a product remains on the shelf for a longer time.
- The validity of the ABC product classification—classifying products as fast movers (As), moderate movers (Bs), and slow movers (Cs) based on their level of sales—is reduced. In the past, the few fast movers typically accounted for a disproportionate amount of sales (i.e., 20 percent of the product will be fast movers and will account for 60 percent of sales). The moderate and slow movers were the majority of products but made a less than 40 percent contribution to the firm's sales. As a result of increased market segmentation and widespread customization, however, more products are now moving into categories B and C in terms of individual sales levels. The overall contribution of products in category B and C has grown substantially, while the few fast movers actually experience declining sales levels. While before, items in A category received most of the firm's attention, now it becomes a competitive necessity to focus on B and C items.

As any student of forecasting knows, forecasting aggregate demand for a group of products is easier than forecasting for individual products. The reason is that variance of aggregate demand, mostly due to a risk-pooling effect, is lower than the sum of variances of the individual product demands. Something similar occurs in forecasting demand for a large class of customized products. The standard product represents aggregate demand of previously homogeneous segments, while customized products are the individual products of the newly created subaggregates of this segment.

Time-Based Competition

Time has become a major determinant of success for companies. Firms that get their product to market faster—through all the phases of design, production, and distribution—gain competitive advantage. In fact, more firms are adopting a time-based competitive strategy.

This trend has a number of consequences. For example, the fresh products market (more products with expiration dates, short shelf lives) has grown tremendously. This requires logistics and operations management to be organized to provide just-in-time supply and delivery. Also, manufacturing processes must be restructured to accelerate new product introduction—getting the product to the final point of sale faster.

Environmentalism

Environmental awareness is growing around the world, spurred by a combination of new government regulations and burgeoning public concern. This trend has a number of consequences:

- *Green* products, with little or no packaging, have proliferated. This lack of packaging significantly impacts the logistics and materials management associated with these products.
- A growing requirement to recover packaging at point-of-sale (reverse flow) necessitates a reverse logistics infrastructure.
- Transportation must be viewed from an environmental impact perspective—factoring environmental impact into inventory location/site selection and transportation tradeoff analyses.

Global Products

Our approach to developing global marketing strategies goes back to the basic premises of this book—the need to embrace the three forms of integration: functional, sectorial, and geographical. Whatever line of business is being studied, new fundamental rules confront the resulting operation.

As a result of *geographical* integration, for example, we see the development of a market approach that embraces global as well as local marketing. Global marketing inevitably is dependent on building global linkages and the operations management to accompany them. As a result of *sectorial* integration, manufacturers and distributors, whose main concerns are to provide the best service for the end user, are collaborating.

As a result of *functional* integration of logistics and operations, we see the satisfaction of the vast and emerging consumer whims through carefully thought-out global products (designed in a way that allows each customization to occur later). Global service solutions are also developed, with costs estimated for the whole length of the products' life cycles. Managers must pay particular attention to service and cost factors that are linked with logistics and operations management and physical distribution and/or logistical support.

◆ GEOGRAPHICAL INTEGRATION: GLOBAL VERSUS LOCAL MARKETING

Global marketing must address all aspects of changing consumer behavior. Global marketing entails operating simultaneously in different environments, coordinating international activities, and learning from the experiences gained in one country to make marketing decisions in other countries. Developing a global marketing strategy that successfully responds to consumer pressures means embracing the three forms of integration advocated in this book—functional, sectorial, and geographical. It also means incorporating both a global and a local marketing approach. These two approaches may appear contradictory at first glance, but are, in fact, complementary. The type of product or market will determine the particular make-up of an approach.

Global Marketing

Global marketing is driven by three business development trends:

- A global consumer base offers more buyers with the same needs.
- Consumers are prepared to give up specific requirements in order to obtain a better deal—for example, better quality at a lower price.
- Companies are more aggressive in pursuing economies of scale in both manufacturing and marketing.

To the first point, global marketing assumes that across the globe there are consumers with identical needs. Global marketing's task is to identify these global consumer groups and put together product offerings that appeal to them. These product offerings are not country-specific and, as such, are more standardized. Companies such as Coca-Cola, Bennetton, and Mercedes-Benz have adopted global marketing strategies. Thus, for example, although Coca-Cola has had to create many different formulas to meet individual tastes (diet, caffeine-free, etc.), worldwide, more people than ever are deciding that Coca-Cola is a product they like.

Implementing a global marketing strategy is considerably easier today than it was just five years ago. New marketing tools and technologies have helped companies reach new markets and track sales in those markets more effectively—thereby creating worldwide product availability. These marketing tools/technologies include:

- Databases built up by electronic point-of-sale data collection
- Media developments such as satellite TV
- Advertising agencies setting up worldwide networks
- Product standardization

Product standardization has obvious advantages for a firm, affecting brand name, product characteristics, methods of distribution (e.g., role of distributors), packaging, sales techniques, and basic advertising messages. However, implementing a global marketing strategy requires major changes in business organizations. Companies must set up logistics and operations management capabilities in the different geographical locations. These capabilities must be consistently effective, regardless of the location. For instance, a company can only offer a fast, reliable parts distribution service throughout Europe if the service provided is the same at all locations. International transport firms are becoming more adept at providing such consistently reliable service around the world.

Local Marketing

For all those who argue in favor of global marketing and product standardization, an equal number tout the benefits of localized marketing—micro-segmentation of customers and products, or even customized products. With a localized marketing focus, products take on a national, regional, or even personal character. More and more countries have seen a noticeable increase in the heterogeneous nature of demand. As already noted, consumers today appreciate supply's adapting to their personal requirements.

A localized marketing approach to international business adds significant complexity to a global logistics system. Market segments multiply, and companies must have the infrastructure to reach and serve the customers in these segments around the world.

Few find global marketing appropriate to their business, given the number of factors that slow down, or even hinder, any shift to this approach. Despite the creation of more integrated trade areas, identical customer requirements are far from reality. Local cultural particularities demand specific product adaptation. Thus, most companies must adopt the localized marketing approach for most of their global business. Other issues also complicate a global approach, including disparate customer expectations; differences in markets' structure and potential (customs duties and regulations, while relaxed in the large trading areas, still diminish the apparent potential of some markets); and a gap between promotional tools and consumers' sensitivity to product promotion. These impediments mean that, at best, global marketing is adapted to suit the reality of the local situation. More often, it is discarded and a local marketing approach is adopted. The combination of global and local generates a set of requirements that we define glocal logistics and is discussed in detail in Chapter 12.

◆ FUNCTIONAL INTEGRATION OF LOGISTICS AND OPERATIONS: THE GLOBAL PRODUCT

Product/Service Expectations

Customer satisfaction is at the heart of customer loyalty. Satisfaction results when a company or product meets a whole array of customer expectations, such as product availability, delivery reliability, support, and quality. For example, in the automobile market, the expectations of most customers are not limited to the actual vehicle. Rather, expectations may encompass issues such as durability (the quest for a vehicle that will run for 100,000 miles), safety, and ease of maintenance. Consequently, the customer purchases more than just the bare product. He or she also buys its availability during its life cycle. The customer/vehicle user must be able to go to any dealer in the network and have the vehicle repaired in the shortest time possible. The service network, therefore, must be big enough and sufficiently capable to respond quickly to such demands.

In food distribution, supermarkets seek to increase the turnover of shelf space and optimize sales turnover and yearly margin per meter of shelf space. Thus, any product advertised for sale by the supermarket must be found on the shelves. If the product is not available, supermarkets experience turnover and margin losses. Supermarket suppliers, therefore, must be able to guarantee reliable product supply to meet the supermarkets' advertised commitments. Vendors need a reliable logistics system to deliver these products as promised.

In this era of time competition and mass customization, different aspects of logistics contribute to meeting customer expectations. Logistics helps to plan a range of services that differentiates the original unbranded product (see Figure 4–1). If competing companies have equivalent technology and product performance, logistics can help one firm differentiate itself by adapting to customers in a way that keeps costs down and improves service.

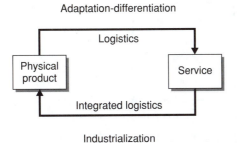

Adaptation-differentiation

Figure 4–1   Differentiation through Logistics and Industrialization of Logistics

Logistics cannot keep costs down if it operates only in a reactive mode, however. In order to realize maximum cost reductions, logistics must be considered from the start—from the product conception stage.

Before developing logistics and operations strategies, the firm must know what customers want in terms of service. To this end, the company should conduct a service quality study. The conception of systems, their purpose, and the management methods set up must be driven by customer expectations for service.

A service quality study should:

- Identify and define service components
- Prioritize service components by customer need
- Define the quantitative measures for each component
- Position the firm for each of these criteria compared to its competitors

Naturally, study findings will reflect the diversity of customers' expectations with regard to service. Companies will thus find it useful to group customers into homogeneous service segments and identify logistics responses for each grouping.

Interactions between Marketing, Operations Management, and Logistics

If the marketing and logistics departments develop simultaneous engineering methods for the different components of products (i.e., contribute to the product/service design by simultaneously developing the product/service aspects under their respective control and continuously sharing information and using feedback), in all likelihood, the suitability of the products will improve and manufacturing costs will decrease (Figure 4–2).

Cooperation between marketing and logistics affects both the conception stage of the product and its management during the stages of growth, maturity, decline, and definitive withdrawal from the market. Thus, both activity areas should be involved from the time of product conception. By being involved at the earliest stage in a product's life cycle, logistics and operations can design an optimum flow system. This system should take into account:

- The physical characteristics of the product—such as size, volume, weight, or fragility—that affect flow management
- The product's modularity (i.e., the product is a collection of smaller sub-products/modules, many of them independently designed) and its suitability for pre- and post-manufacturing

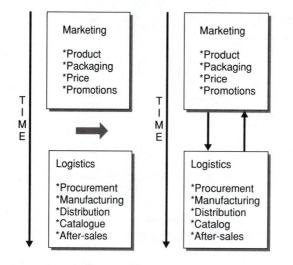

Figure 4–2   Simultaneous Development of Marketing and Logistics

- Product packaging—both consumer and secondary—and any special needs for logistics
- The system used to track product throughout the flow channel

Early and exhaustive logistics involvement is important regardless of the predicted life cycle of a product. Long-lived products can be sustained with a thoughtfully designed logistics system. Short-lived products absolutely depend on a logistic system for rapid deployment and sales ramp-up.

◆ SECTORIAL INTEGRATION: MANUFACTURER/DISTRIBUTOR

The need to maximize customer satisfaction at the lowest cost requires that all those in the logistics chain adopt a new cooperation. Virtually unheard of a decade ago, logistics alliances are now spreading as a way of lowering distribution and storage operating costs. For many manufacturers and distributors, these ventures offer opportunities to dramatically improve the quality of customer service. The typical agreement involves a provider of customized logistics services and a producer of goods that jointly engineer and launch a system to speed goods to customers.

Companies with successful logistics partnerships recognize that this activity is a critical part of a global marketing strategy. Traditionally, product, promotion, and price have been the key competitive ingredients, with time and place competencies taking a back seat. In global marketing, however, the focus is changing. The companies forming logistics alliances are seeking to exploit their logistical competencies and use this superiority to gain and keep customer loyalty.

Undertaking a global marketing approach on the sectorial level requires strategic reflection about three fundamental questions:

- What will the partners' strategic position be at the end of the alliance?
- Why would the prospective partner agree to an alliance?
- Which of the partner's weaknesses would the alliance improve?

Other practical questions to address include:

- What resources are the partners willing to contribute to the relationship?
- How will conflicts and problems be resolved?
- What assessment method will be used to evaluate the workings of the partnership and its results?
- How will performance results be shared?
- What are the provisions for renegotiating or dissolving the partnership?

Cooperation on the level of strategic partnerships creates a paradox. Companies elect to give up independence and autonomy in order to strengthen an area of expertise. In so doing, they develop a common action aimed at an individual goal. Cooperation requires that specific behaviors be adopted (posture) rather than a strategic approach. The goals of cooperation seem to be:

- Addressing uncertainty in various business variables (e.g., demand, price, costs, supply)
- Maintaining management oversight and control over the service provider
- Achieving goals that are only accessible through the combined efforts of several organizations
- Solving problems or seizing opportunities

In the strategic partnership approach, producers and distributors are working out different ways of integrating activities. These companies put logistics and operations management at the heart of their thinking.

◆ EFFICIENT CONSUMER RESPONSE (ECR)

A supply chain links all production and distribution activities, from raw materials procurement, to manufacturing, to final delivery to the consumer. The frequency and speed of communication through the chain has a significant effect on inventory levels, efficiencies, costs, and lead times. Many initiatives, programs, and systems have been developed recently to speed up this flow of information. These electronic communication systems between manufacturer and distributor have a number of names: electronic data interchange (EDI), quick response (QR), and efficient consumer response (ECR). We elaborate on one—ECR—as an effective approach to achieving sectorial integration between manufacturers and distribution, which contributes to the success of an integrated global marketing/distribution/operations strategy.

The ECR project was launched in the United States in 1992 by the Food Marketing Institute, and conducted by Kurt Salmon Associates. The supermarket industry adopted it as a business strategy in which distributors, suppliers, and grocers worked together to bring products to consumers. Estimates suggest that the potential savings for the industry total more than $30 billion.

ECR's main objective is to rationalize the distribution chain in order to increase the value to consumers (see Figure 4–3).

In the dry grocery segment, estimates predicted that industry-wide adoption of ECR could cut supply-chain inventory from 104 days to 61 days and cut consumer prices by an average of 10.8 percent.

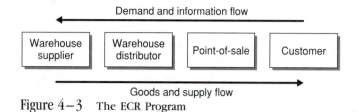

Figure 4-3   The ECR Program

Figure 4–4 shows the four areas in which companies needed to cooperate to achieve these goals:

- Product flow optimization (see chapter 6)
- Promotions and terms of sale
- Product mix
- New product introduction incorporating logistics and product life cycle issues

The main prerequisites for the proper implementation of an ECR project are:

- Developing EDI (see chapter 10)
- Setting up special partnerships
- Elaborating indicators and performance assessment measures (see chapter 11)
- Putting together multi-functional teams (see chapter 12)
- Involving top management

The following conditions will guarantee the success of ECR:

- Never losing sight of the goal: customer satisfaction
- Getting the project piloted by the managing director
- Adopting a positive win–win attitude and rejecting the win–lose attitude
- Measuring the contribution of data processing to the process (EDI, reordering systems, etc.)
- Setting up the means to measure real performance and controlling progress achieved
- Taking into account as realistically as possible competitors' strong points

Without ECR, manufacturers push products onto the market by offering lower prices on large quantities. Several times a year, the manufacturer offers the grocer a low price on a large quantity of product. This is known as *forward buying*. The manufacturer then works with the distributor to offer coupons and incentives to entice the customer to buy the product during the promotion. Products not sold during the promotion are stored in inventory.

ECR focuses on the customers' actual demand, and uses that information to drive the system. Customers pull goods through the store and through the pipeline by their purchases, enabling less inventory throughout the system.

Other approaches have been adopted, particularly in Europe, such as the SRC (Supplier Retailer Collaboration), which was a study carried out by the Coca-Cola Retailing Research Group that included eleven cases of cooperation. The study organized five debate-style seminars, based on the analysis of 127 questionnaire responses, with attendees from 175 business organizations in five European cities. According to study results, the potential total gains expected from the SRC in Europe were between 2.3 percent and 3.4 percent of sales volume at retail price, about three or four times lower than expected gains in the American ECR approach. In the European study, roughly 60 percent of the gains would go to distributors and about 40 percent to manufacturers.

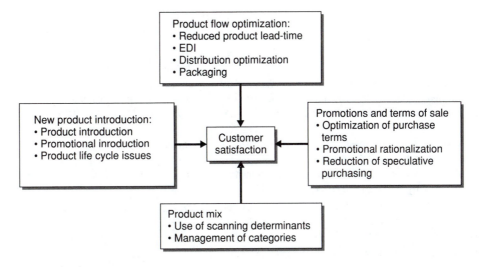

Figure 4–4   Potential Areas of Cooperation in ECR

◆ THE NEED FOR A GLOBAL MARKETING APPROACH

The basic marketing functions of the four Ps—product, price, promotion, and place—are similar for both domestic and global marketing. Because of the differences in cultural, legal, and political environments, however, global marketing becomes much more complex. This complexity is further accentuated by evolving consumer needs.

Changing consumer behavior has important consequences for logistics and operations management: faster product renewal, increased availability, shorter delivery times, higher levels of customization, and extreme levels of functionality.

In this chapter, we have advocated developing a global marketing approach that carefully accounts for the important interfaces with logistics and operating strategy issues. Going back to the premises of our introductory chapter, the firm needs to assess its needs for:

- Geographical integration in choosing between global and local strategy
- Functional integration in achieving the development of the global product and finding ways to customize it as late as possible in the value chain
- Sectorial integration in achieving the timely and cost-efficient product delivery to the demanding consumer via coordinated electronic information flows

DISCUSSION QUESTIONS

1. What are the important trends in consumer behavior to consider when formulating global marketing strategies?

2. Provide examples and clearly define the difference between *global* and *local* marketing.

3. What are the important interfaces between marketing, and operations and logistics strategies during globalization of a firm's activities?

4. What is Efficient Consumer Response (ECR)? What are its main objectives?

5. What activities should a firm pursue in order to implement ECR?

REFERENCES

Angelmar, R. 1988. Conflicts in channels of distribution. INSEAD, Fontainebleau, 1988.

Bensaou, M. 1993. Interorganizational cooperation: The role of information technology: An empirical study of U.S. and Japanese supplier relations. Working Paper INSEAD, 1994.

Bensaou, M., and N. Venkartraman. 1995. Vertical relationships and the role of information technology: An empirical study of U.S. and Japanese supplier relationships in the auto industry. Working Paper INSEAD, 1995.

Christopher, M. 1983. Creating effective policies for customer service. *International Journal of Physical Distribution and Materials Management* 13 (2): 3–24.

Dornier, Ph.P. 1991. Plein Flux sur l'entreprise. Paris, Nathan.

Douglas, S. P., and Y. Wind. 1987. The myth of globalisation. *Columbia Journal of World Business*. Winter: 19–29.

Johnson, J. C., and D. F. Wood. 1993. Contemporary logistics. New York: Macmillan.

Kurt Salmon Associates. 1993. Efficient consumer response: Enhancing consumer value in the grocery industry.

Washington, DC: The Research Department of the Food Marketing Institute.

Lecomte, F., Dornier, Ph. P., and T. Poirier. 1995. Marketing et logistique: Pour un nouveau contrat de coopration. Cahier de l'IHEL n_2, ESSEC, Cergy-Pontoise.

Levitt, T. 1983. The globalisation of markets. *Harvard Business Review* (May–June): 92–102.

Link, G. 1988. Global advertising: An update. *The Journal of Consumer Marketing* (Spring): 69–74.

Ohmae, K. 1989. Managing in a borderless world. *Harvard Business Review* (May–June): 67 (3): 152–61.

Quelch, J., and E. Hoff. 1986. Customizing global marketing. *Harvard Business Review* (May–June): 67 (3): 59–68.

Raffe, H., and R. T. Kreutzer. 1989. Organizational dimensions of global marketing. *European Journal of Marketing* 23 (5).

Segal-Horn, S., and H. Davison. 1992. Global markets, the global consumer and international retailing. *Journal of Global Marketing* 5 (3): 31–61.

Williamson, O. 1985. The economic institutions of capitalism. New York: Free Press.

◆ Case 4–1: Talk to Me: Expansion in the Russian Telecommunications Market ◆

It is 4:30 eastern standard time on June 21, 1995, and three of the senior executives responsible for international business development are debating the decision of whether or not to submit a Letter of Intent to the Russian government for participation in the 50/50 project. They are currently trying to contact Natasha Marianova, their Russian correspondent in Moscow, to advise her of their final decision. In fifteen minutes she is required to submit the company's proposal to the Ministry of Communications; otherwise the opportunity will be foregone.

This case was prepared by the Fuqua MBA students Manuel Angulo, Diego Ondarts, Elvira Puentes and Sara Wood under the supervision of Professor Panagiotis (Panos) Kouvelis as the basis for class discussion rather than to illustrate either effective or ineffective handling of an administrative situation.

Proposal Background

Three months ago the Russian Ministry of Communications approached Talk to Me Inc. (TTM) with the opportunity to participate in the highly visible 50/50 project. This project acquired the name 50/50 because it intends to result in 20 million new subscribers' lines by:

- connecting 50 Russian cities
- establishing 50 long-distance transit switches
- laying 50 thousand kilometers of long-distance digital lines
- manufacturing 50% of all equipment in Russia
- funding 50% from Russian sources[1]

This project is not attempting to modernize systems already in place, but will develop an entirely new telecommunications network. This network will utilize digital as opposed to analog technology, thus requiring state-of-the-art equip-

---

[1]*Russian Telecommunications, Thomas L. Shillinglaw, 1995.*

ment. The result will be an extremely high-quality telecommunication system that will rival those currently in operation in large Western cities.

This project is expected to span ten years (10) with an estimated budget of $40 billion. The plan's success hinges on the ability of Western companies to generate the necessary finance. Due to this fact, companies need to critically assess the associated risk. A Ministry announcement, further impeding the raising of capital, stated that the project has been recently revised to include the installation of 20 million local lines. This is problematic because investing in local lines, unlike investing in long-distance networking, consumes 90% of all capital yet generates only 10% of profits.[2]

Russians will retain control of the jointly founded company and the joint-stock company would get a license to operate the new network for at least 50 years.

Local Russian telephone companies are aggressively pursuing their own expansion projects, which may seriously hinder this last massive centrally planned planning project. For example, US West, an aggressive U.S. company in Russia, signed a joint venture deal with Rossvyazing, the local phone company in Rostov, and Rostelcom, Russia's long-distance company, to provide long-distance digital switching equipment, cellular phone service, cable television, and other services to Moscow.[3]

The 50/50 project is extremely ambitious, even by Western standards, and if it meets its objectives will tremendously improve the current telecommunications capability within Russia.[4]

The Ministry has also approached numerous other American telecommunications companies, for example AT&T and US West, as well as large European organizations, such as Deutsche Telekom and France Telecom; therefore the competition for becoming a major partner is very fierce. Proposals need to be submitted by June 21, 1995, in order to be considered as a candidate for participation in this project that will help privatize Russia's telecommunication infrastructure.

World Market

There are many markets opening for telecommunication companies to invest in around the world. The world economy is increasingly becoming one based on free and continuous flow of information, and the result has been vastly more integrated and efficient markets. The developing countries are recognizing that a modern telecommunications infrastructure is necessary for growth and for attracting foreign investment.

In 1990 there were 36 countries with existing and possible private sector involvement.[5] The other side of the coin is that there are many companies competing for a share of these markets, and many companies are strong in more than one region. Most of these investments will not be profitable for a long time due to the amount of investment needed, but these mostly large international companies are willing to forgo immediate earnings for future cash flows.

Company Background

Talk to Me was founded, as we know it today, in the early 1960s, and became a major player in the telecommunication industry after the breakup of AT&T in 1984. The company is publicly held with more than 50,000 employees, and has nearly two decades of global experience.

The company is known for its ability to be first to the market; for example, in 1975 they launched the first U.S. public data network, which is now the largest in the world. TTM also pioneered the concept of Virtual Private Networks (VPN) and has more VPNs in service than any other carrier.

In 1977, when GTE established the first successful application of fiber-optic communication, TTM was quick to follow, and a year later completed a 100% digital, fiber-optic network in America. This network spans 23,000 miles and is one of the largest in the world. TTM has now become synonymous with fiber optics, which is the leading transmission technology for voice, data, and videoconferencing services.

TTM is one of America's preeminent long distance carriers and currently has 9.2% of the U.S. long-distance market. This market is becoming increasingly competitive. Since 1984 prices have fallen over 60%.[6]

Long-distance carriers, including TTM, are moving into wireless in order to broaden their product offerings. Demand for wireless is growing faster than any other segment within the telecommunications industry and therefore offers an opportunity to grow in the domestic market.

In fact, TTM recently acquired Centel Corp, which made them the ninth largest cellular operator in the United States, serving approximately 392,000 subscribers. TTM's nationally recognized brand has been a powerful force in developing this market so successfully. Market penetration increased 59% over the last year to 5.4% of the population with access to the company's services.

[2]Wall Street Journal, *December 21, 1993, p. 4.*

[3]New York Times, *May 10, 1994, p. 1.*

[4]*Eastern European & Former Soviet Telecom Report, January 1, 1995. Section 1, Vol. 6.*

[5]*Privatizing Telecommunication Systems. William W. Ambrose, Paul R. Hennemeyer and Jean-Paul Chapon. International Finance Corporation. 1990.*

[6]*Standard & Poors, Industry Surveys, June 2, 1994.*

TTM is also concentrating its efforts in the United States on expanding into the $95 billion local communications market. TTM is dedicated to providing this market a package of products, including voice, video, data, and wireless. To this end, joint ventures have been planned with three of America's largest cable TV companies.

The company ended 1994 with net operating revenues of $12.66 billion, which represented an 11% increase over the previous year. Earnings increased 25%.

Due to the growing competition and saturation of the U.S. telecommunications industry, TTM is seeking to expand its international network.

International Division

TTM has been active on the international front since 1989 and has therefore been able to offer communications support to its large U.S.-based corporate clients during their global expansion. TTM now connects more than 280 countries and locations through direct dial services, which is the world's largest global data network. The company also has one of the largest global teleconferencing and e-mail networks. TTM has an interest in more than 35 cable systems internationally, which includes some of the world's major cable systems.

TTM recognizes the need to provide their customers with a global communication system that can provide information around the globe in a quick and accessible manner.

To do this successfully, they have pursued the following:

- Digital connectivity around the world for superior efficiency, quality, and reliability
- One-stop shopping options to simplify setting up and maintaining communications internationally
- 24-hour customer service, including local support in countries around the globe with access to both English and non-English speaking operators
- Compliance with international standards
- Comprehensive portfolio of voice, data, video, facsimile, and videoconferencing services
- Connectivity to practically anywhere in the world
- Building strategic partnerships with international organizations to combine technological and market strengths. These alliances allow TTM to offer global services, with benefits that attract multinational organizations by providing a single dialing plan internationally.

Chairperson Sara Sanders is committed to this international growth through the expansion of TTM's strategic alliances and global network facilities.

TTM's Current Presence in Russia

In 1990, TTM entered into a Joint Venture with the Russian Ministry of Communications (MOC). The MOC is one of two government organizations participating in telecommunications joint ventures; the other organization is Rostelcom. TTM, at that time, was the only U.S. company to offer switched data communication services, including electronic mail, in Russia.

In 1992, the joint venture established the first public data network via the TTM network and provided connections to more than 100 countries around the world. Today, the company has representation in every major Russian city as well as cities within the CIS and enjoys 65% of the data network market share.[7] In order to keep competitors such as AT&T out of the market, TTM is aggressively expanding its network and recently signed an agreement with the Moscow Interbank Currency Exchange. The company is also working hard to attract non-Russian customers, offering the services in Russia as part of the customer's overall discount plan.

The Russian Environment[8]

During 1994, Mr. Yeltsin made concessions to many regions that have been demanding the status of autonomous ethnic republics, thus granting extra leeway in their relations with Moscow. This, however, is not to be interpreted as destabilizing. *Effective regional autonomy* is a vital condition for successful reform and the growth of a market economy within the federation.

However, the *start of the Chechnya war at the end of 1994* has pushed Russia close to disaster and exposed weaknesses within the government. As a result, Mr. Yeltsin's authority and image have suffered. The prime minister, Viktor Chernomyrdin, is consolidating his position for the 1996 presidential elections as well as pursuing *relatively tough monetary and fiscal policies.*

Russia has focused attention on its *international position,* after recovering from a period of extreme weakness and disorientation in the wake of the fall of the USSR. Russia's recent joining of NATO's Partnership for Peace illustrates this point. Russia has also made an agreement on a partnership with the United States to lead to a free-trade zone by the year 2000. A decision concerning the creation of a free-trade zone is to be reached in 1998.

---

[7]*Eastern European & Former Soviet Telecom Report, January 1, 1995.*

[8]*The Russian Country Report. The Economic Intelligence Unit 1st quarter 1995.*

Economic Policy

Since mid-1993 there has been a **gradual tightening of monetary and fiscal policy.** The Russian prime minister, Mr. Chernomyrdin, considers a strong ruble a fundamental condition for economic recovery and the integrity of the Russian Federation.

However, **Russia** has **special characteristics** that make it different to other communist countries: its size, a much longer period of communist rule, and the heritage of the Soviet military-industrial complex. These characteristics imply the need for a targeted industrial policy that addresses specific social issues and is capable of differentiating industries with no future from those which merit support.

Mr. Yeltsin announced his intention to **accelerate economic reforms** with a series of decrees. He has started with **decrees** on tightening up of tax collection, a reduction in taxation on business (profit tax is to be reduced by 10–20%), the elimination of licenses and quotas for exports, including oil and gas, and the regulation and liberalization of the banking sector and advertising.

- The liberalization of trade had been accompanied by moves to tighten customs controls.
- Another decree offered a three-year tax holiday for foreign investors in Russia's manufacturing sector.
- The privatization program succeeded in transferring 75% of GDP to the private sector by the end of 1994.

Economic Indicators

The Russian economy, in its lowest point since the beginning of *perestroika,* seems to show some signs of recovery:

- Expected progress in the control of inflation: at present, the monthly rates are 17.8%, i.e., the annual rate is 558%. Reduction of the monthly rates to below 5% is considered possible. The interest rate has been raised to fight inflation.
- Shifts in the composition of GDP (share of services rising from 38.5% to 50% and share of industry falling from 49% to 43%).
- GDP fell by 15% in 1994. In 1995 a fall of about 2% is expected, followed by a growth of 3% in 1996.
- Investment also fell by 24% compared to 1993.
- Due to tighter monetary conditions, inter-enterprise payment arrears have worsened.
- The ruble continues its steady decline, but it has become internally convertible.
- Agricultural output declines.
- Gross Foreign Debt has increased to $89 billion.

Social Aspects

Social aspects also need to be examined when considering investing in Russia. The country suffers civil unrest, and high crime indexes, and business is under the influence and control of the "Mafia." There is also an anti-foreign sentiment surfacing as a result of the Russian's fierce national pride. Finally, unemployment has been rising (13.5% of total labor force = 10 million people).

Telecommunications

The changes launched by *perestroika* in 1987 have achieved limited success in the telecommunications industry. The system is obsolete: it provides only 14 telephones to every 100 people, which is approximately 25 phones per 100 households[9] (1/5 the U.S. rate). Copper cables laid in czarist times are still in use, with nicks and corrosion, and 200,000 villages have no phones. The service in the two main cities, Moscow and St. Petersburg, is, at best, archaic. Obtaining a dial tone can be a triumph of will. Calls are often not completed, abruptly cut off, plagued with static and other "mysterious noises," and there are years of delay for installation of a phone line. In the rest of the country the service, if it exists, is much worse.

The country, until recently, has not been linked by any communication network. Russia, previously, had placed very limited priority on developing telecommunications. The main reasons for this were:

1. Stringent restrictions that had been placed upon Western exports to USSR under COCOM. This limited the types of technology accessible to the USSR.
2. There was an absence of regulatory policies.
3. High capital cost was beyond the reach of the government.
4. Controlling information flow through the country was a priority for the government.

Russia has been a land of promises—all promise, in fact, and little bankable business. Foreign investment has increased, but huge uncertainties regarding these investments remain.

In September 1993, Presidential Decree 1466 banned any new regulation on inbound investment and stated that any new legislative act that causes "material damage" to foreign firms or joint ventures will not apply to enterprises established before such acts come into force. However, this minimal security clause has not been adhered to in practice:

---

[9]*Ibid.*

for example, the value-added tax law implemented in December 1993 may have serious implications regarding the transfer of capital to Russia.

Despite this uncertainty, 12,000 foreign companies have established a presence in Russia. The prevailing sentiment is that "You better get in now so that you are there when Russia finally gets on its feet." However, many of them are just skeleton firms with sales facilities, and only 10% are in operation.

The telecommunications industry has been more effective, perhaps due to the general consensus that an upgraded communication system is a prerequisite for any serious attempt of development, within a country that comprises eleven time zones. The number of phones has increased by 500,000 units in the last two years. Improvements in long distance services and the new openness of the Russian economy have raised the international telecommunications calls up to 4.5 billion minutes, a 36-fold increase from two years ago. Now, more than 600 private companies (Russian and foreign) are operating in the Russian telecom sector.

Massive increases in investment, however, are needed to reach the minimum Western standards. 50/50, the world's biggest telephone-engineering venture, is the ambitious plan expected to fill the gap over the next decade.

Suppliers

Most of the local suppliers are former state-owned companies not familiar with Western industrial practices. They are still more politically oriented than market or economic oriented. Their equipment is outdated, and thus products are unable to meet Western technical standards. However, the industry is characterized by good professional and engineering standards and low wages continue to exist.

Competition

Each region is trying to improve the telecommunications situation they are in. A number of contracts have been signed with the West to provide modern telecommunications systems. The contracts have been in diverse areas: fiber optic cable, local telephone networks, cellular telephones, satellite communications. Russians like American products, but the equipment has to be modified to convert it to the European standard that they adopted.[10]

The main competitive threats in Russia are some of the large European telecommunication companies such as Deutsche Telekom and France Telecom and some U.S.

---

[10]Ibid.

players, AT&T, US West and some smaller organizations. Most of these companies are concentrating their efforts on improving and expanding the system in Moscow and St. Petersburg and are entering into joint ventures with individual Russian partners on these localized projects. However, as competition and lack of profitable opportunities dry up in the large cities, companies are moving into the more rural regions. A recent example is AT&T's $200 million, 4-year joint venture with Rostelcom, Moscow Local Telephone Network, and Telmos to expand Moscow's local and domestic long distance service for residents and businesses, and improve the city's international service. This project will handle the local and long-distance needs of 1 million subscribers and will add 400,000 new subscribers to the current service.

Joint Ventures in Russia

Establishing a joint venture in Russia requires an understanding of Russian joint venture laws and the associated bureaucracy. The most suitable form of foreign investment in Russia is the closed joint-stock company. Shares of such a company are issued and distributed amongst its founders. A disadvantage of this arrangement is that funds cannot be raised on the local equity market but can be raised through new share issues. There is a lengthy registration process involved with JV's that requires various documents to be notarized and submitted to the relevant government ministries. Group management is required.

Acquisition of an Existing Firm

The only other way to establish a presence in Russia, currently, is to partly acquire an existing firm. This has been recently achieved by Philip Morris and Credit Suisse. In most cases, the company has to obtain prior approval from the Ministry of Finance before the acquisition can go forward. A further barrier is the unstable exchange rate, which hinders the process of asset valuation.

The Russian Proposal

Diego Escobar, the Director of International Operations, had his serious doubts about the proposal. However, he recognizes the 50/50 project represents a significant opportunity for TTM. This is the most highly visible telecommunications project currently being undertaken in Russia and is being pursued by many Western companies. It would enable TTM to work with both Rostelcom and the MOC and obtain shares in the most significant of Russia telecommunication infrastructure projects.

Share allocation will be determined by each party's contribution, such as cash contributions, technology transfer, cable systems, etc., all of which will be required for the project's development.

However, as with previous business dealings in Russia, there are some concerns. Although, the Russian Communication Ministry oversees the telecom infrastructure, it deals only with matters relating to standards, frequencies, and licenses. Two other Ministries, the Committee of Defense and the Ministry of Science, also have an active participation in the overseeing of Russia's telecommunication system. This lack of a central decision making authority creates ambiguity in the legislation and licensing policies, resulting in a very short-term approach to investment.

Financing for this project could be obtained from one of the many consortiums currently financing business development in Russia. Some of the more well known are:

OPIC: This organization has been active in Russia and CIS since the insurrection and has invested over $2.6 billion to support U.S. investment.

European Bank for Reconstruction and Development: This organization offers advice, loans, equity investments, and debt guarantees to countries committed to multiparty democracy and pluralism.[11]

World Bank: This bank is the largest source of financial assistance to developing countries to stimulate economical growth.

Export-Import Bank: This is an independent U.S. government agency that supports U.S. exports through various financing methods.

Decision Analysis

TTM's current exposure in Russia is $300 million. It is anticipated that the cost of the investment in the 50/50 project will be $5 billion. Russia's current economic and political instability makes further investment tenuous. In addition, there are many other challenges to doing business in Russia such as:

- Lack of a legal infrastructure
- Shortage of local financing
- Lack of technical standards
- Government favoritism
- Continued restrictions on communication technology transfer to Russia by the U.S. government

---

[11]*Members Guide to Financing Sources for Russia, US/Russia Business Council, February 1995.*

The committee is divided between aggressively pursuing Russian business development and waiting for the June 1996 presidential elections and further legislation concerning tax and foreign investment to be passed.

Boris Yeftushenko, TTM's Russian expert in New York is standing by waiting to translate any last-minute details to TTM's submission to the 50/50 project.

Bibliography

Ambrose, William W., Paul R. Hennemeyer, and Jean-Paul Chapon. "Privatizing Telecommunication Systems." *International Finance Corporation,* 1990.

AT&T Annual Report, 1994

Bloomberg Business News. "Company News; $40 Billion Project for Russian Telephones Begun." *The New York Times,* October 8, 1994.

Eastern European & Former Soviet Telecom Report, Section 1, Vol. 6, January 1, 1995.

Hudson, R. L. "Industry focus, phone project may be Russia's new window to West; Some fear $40 billion modernization may be just another five-year plan." *The Wall Street Journal,* December 21, 1993.

Hudson, R. L. "Technology and Health: U.S. West to become partner in a firm. Russia is forming for Phone Network." *The Wall Street Journal,* March 31, 1994.

Hudson, R. L. "Three phone firms begin planning for Russian job." *The Wall Street Journal,* October 7, 1994.

"Industry Surveys." *Standard & Poors,* June 2, 1994.

"Members Guide to Financing Sources for Russia," *US/Russia Business Council,* February 1995.

Reuters, "Company news, upgrade planned for Russian phone network," January 20, 1994.

"The Russian Country Report," *The Economic Intelligence Unit,* 1st quarter 1995.

"Russian deal for Airtouch," *The New York Times,* December 30, 1994.

Shillinglaw, Thomas L. *Russian Telecommunications,* 1995.

Sprint Annual Report, 1994

Sprint Information.

Stevenson, R. W. "Russia seeks help to fix its phones." *The New York Times,* October 5, 1994.

"U.S. West in Russian venture," *The Wall Street Journal,* October 19, 1993.

The Wall Street Journal, page 4, December 21, 1993.

◆ Case 4–2: Zamech Ltd. ◆

ABB-Zamech Ltd. (Zamech) is one of the 1,300 companies that form the international conglomerate, ABB. Zamech employs 3,200 people in the small town of Elblag, in Northern Poland. It became part of ABB as the result of an historic joint venture (JV) agreement signed in 1990. Now, after 5 years of restructuring, Zamech is finally considered to be a "normal" company in the vast ABB system. The core business of Zamech is the design, construction, and maintenance of large turbines used in power generation. Pawel Olechnowicz, the CEO of Zamech, has recently learned that Westinghouse and General Electric have established sales offices in Warsaw and that they are lobbying the very plants and utilities that were the exclusive customers of Zamech for almost 50 years. The key questions for Zamech today are: now that the world's largest players have entered into the battle for market share in Poland, can Zamech continue to thrive; and what exactly is Zamech's role in ABB's struggle for market supremacy?

Zamech before JV

To understand the history of Zamech one must keep in mind the recent history of the town that contains it. Elblag is one of the oldest small towns of the southern Baltic sea shore with a history going back to the 13th century when it was occupied by the Teutonic Knights. More recently it was occupied by Prussians for roughly 175 years prior to the end of World War II. The history of "modern" industry in Elblag can be traced to Ferdinand Schichau who opened a machine factory in 1837 and manufactured his first steam engines in 1840. Subsequently a shipyard was built at his factory and the town became a center of ship building in the 1870s. Schichau's plant was manufacturing various kinds of heavy machines including locomotives and employed a few thousand workers. After the First World War, Elblag was incorporated into the Eastern Prussia Province and was on the periphery of the German state.

Research Associate Chester G. Chambers prepared this case under the joint direction of Professors Simon Johnson and Panos Kouvelis of Duke University, and David Young of INSEAD. It is intended to be a basis for class discussion rather than to illustrate either effective or ineffective handling of an administrative situation.

When Hitler came into power, Germany started to develop its armed forces and Elblag's industry was shifted to military production. The population grew from 60,000 at the start of the twentieth century to about 140,000 by the middle of the Second World War. In the final period of the war, the town was used as a fortress. In January of 1945 fighting aimed at conquering the city began and the mostly German inhabitants of Elblag were scattered both East and West. The broken English of a book telling the town's history states,

Long-term fights resulted in huge destruction. Historical center of Elblag was destroyed to the largest extent. The town became a large debris. The Old Town was destroyed almost in 90 per cent. . . . The machines which preserved were taken away by Russians.

A few weeks after the end of the war, the first Polish settlers started to come to Elblag. In August 1945 a Polish administration took over the area. They soon rebuilt most of Zamech and used it to repair various industrial equipment including steam turbines which were to become Zamech's core business. In the late 1940s the foundry, which was still located at the site, was used to supply castings for industries all over Poland. In the fifties the company started its career as a major manufacturer of steam turbines.

When Elblag became a Polish city again, very slow reconstruction of its historical center began and is still underway. Of course all of Poland was dominated by Communism after the end of World War II and Zamech had had Communist governments as its only customers for roughly 50 years. Zamech was the only supplier of turbines to the power generation industry in Poland for most of that period. It also had a significant presence in three other areas: production of large gears, production of cast items for the shipbuilding industry such as anchors and propellers, and production of all the spare parts used in turbine operations. Exhibit 1 is a description of the core business of Zamech just before the joint venture and at present.

During the Communist regime, the dominant theme in Zamech's development was vertical integration. Zamech housed everything from a foundry where it processed its raw materials to a workshop producing nuts and bolts. One motivation for this was that the supplier network was so unreliable that it took just as long to get parts and supplies from external sources as it took to make them yourself. The structure of the company also reflected the structure of the

Exhibit 1

Zamech Products in 1988 and 1995

1988

Power Generation   Zamech was the sole supplier of large coal-fired turbine technology to the entire Polish electric distribution system. Zamech also made smaller turbines for use on ships, mines, large factories, and other large users of electricity without access to the electricity generated in Poland's power plants.

Marine Items and Gears   Zamech produced gears that were used in systems that transfer large power streams. These gears were used mainly for transmission of drives for electric power generators, large water pumps, marine propulsion, open mine belt conveyors, rolling mills, and open coal mine excavators. In the marine area Zamech manufactured fixed pitch propellers and shafts as well as anchors and rudders for ships.

Foundry   Zamech used both induction and arc-type electric furnaces for melting metals. This was a "full service" foundry. Its output included carbon steel and alloy steel castings for turbines, cast iron castings for industrial uses, and bronze and brass castings for marine use. Products ranged from very small items to turbine castings and propellers up to 8 meters in diameter.

1995

Power Generation BAU   In addition to the core business of turbine manufacturing, Zamech added a Power Service BAU. This unit monitors the technical condition, quality, efficiency, and environmental influence of equipment used by utilities. The first director of this service was brought in from Zurich. After the business was established, its control was passed to a Polish manager with a long history with Zamech. License agreements with ABB enable Zamech to use technology and designs not available in 1988. Zamech is now positioned to apply an expanded technology base to plant upgrades, modernization and construction. Zamech has been designated as ABB's center for retrofit and modernization of the 120 MW and 200 MW turbines throughout Europe. Zamech has also become the leading manufacturer for the GT8 gas-powered turbines. A total of 10 have been delivered by the end of 1994. They are in use in the United States, Libya, Finland, and Greece. Historically there has been no market for these types of turbines in Poland.

Marine and Gears BAU   Zamech has expanded this business to include modernization and retrofit services for transmissions which have been in use for long periods. Zamech has also added controllable pitch propellers to its product line. These are propellers that have blades whose pitch can be adjusted by remote control. This greatly increases the blades' efficiency and the ship's stability. Zamech is Poland's only manufacturer of these systems. Zamech also continues to make stoppers and chain releasers for the shipyard industry as well as complete rudder blades.

Foundry BAU   Zamech uses both induction and arc-type electric furnaces for melting metals. They specialize in carbon steel, alloy steel, nodular cast iron, bronze, and brass. Production is centered on steam and gas turbine components for the Power Generation BAU. The foundry continues to make some large elements for the Marine and Gears BAU, including both fixed and variable pitch propellers, and steel components for ships.

District Heating BAU   Zamech makes pre-insulated pipe sections with complete fixtures and accessories. Zamech offers full service including design, training, supplies, fittings and operational maintenance. Zamech is participating in roughly 60% of all ongoing district heating projects.

---

political system. All functions were completely centralized and the company was organized along functional lines. According to one manager

We were extremely centralized here. We had one manufacturing plant for everything, with one manufacturing director in charge. Every product was designed in one central design office: turbines, ship's propellers, gearboxes. In [a single] process office, they prepared production sheets for marine products and turbines. We had central purchasing. We had huge overheads. It was a stupid way of doing things.[1]

The supplier system had another highly noticeable effect. According to another Zamech manager, "Zamech had to take raw materials in huge bulk simply to ensure supply. [We placed] minimum deliveries of 10 tons of a raw material, even when we needed only 200 kg."[2]

However, the dominant characteristics of the old firm were all shaped by the fact that all of COMECOM (the bloc of Communist countries) was an "economy of shortage." For large items, power plants made requests to the central government. It was the government that made decisions on which orders would be filled in a given year. Some plants had been requesting the same items for five years. Customers gladly accepted any product delivered because they had waited so long to get it.

---

[1]Tony Jackson, "The Challenges Facing ABB's Engineering Ventures in the Former Communist Bloc," *Financial Times*, April 16, 1993.

[2]*Ibid.*

The Fall of Communism

The now world-famous union of workers known as Solidarity was a major factor in the changing landscape of Poland. Solidarity was born in 1980 in Gdansk, Poland, which is about 35 miles west of Elblag. Its leader, Lech Walesa, led numerous national and regional strikes, with the central issues being working conditions and wages. However, the history of Polish resistance to Communism is much older than Solidarity. Significant protests took place in 1956 and 1970. A shrine stands in central Elblag today in memory of those who were killed during these actions. Solidarity is thought to be a major factor in the disintegration of Communism in Poland, but some people in Poland give most of the credit to the United States in general and Ronald Reagan's policies of the eighties in particular.

As Communism fell, the customer base for Zamech's products disappeared. The economy was disintegrating. Zamech stood with a very high inventory, high receivables, and high liabilities. It became almost impossible to get credit. By 1989 roughly 60% of receivables were more than 60 days overdue. This created an intense cash flow problem and made Zamech unable to pay its suppliers. The government stopped subsidizing exports, and the COMECOM market disappeared almost overnight. In this atmosphere Zamech was quickly going bankrupt. Zamech could not buy new equipment because it had no money, so its capital stock was deteriorating. For the previous decade, schools had been inadequately funded and the quality of its graduates was steadily dropping. These conditions caused a growing gap in quality and productivity between Zamech and the companies of the West.

In the old system the managing director was elected by the workers council and approved by the central government. Late in 1988 the workers council in effect "fired" the managing director and held an election for a new one. There was a year-long campaign for the position before Pawel Olechnowicz was finally selected. He was installed in early 1990. The council also decided to seek an outside company to become a partner or to take over operations. They initiated this process in 1988, even before clearly defined procedures were established in Poland to do so. This outside partner had to be well financed and have the necessary access to markets and expertise to modernize the operations. Zamech approached GE, Westinghouse, Mitsubishi, and ABB with ideas about the formation of a Joint Venture (JV). Only ABB had any interest and when Communism completely collapsed in 1989 negotiations kicked into high gear.

Why a JV with Zamech?

At the time of the formation of this joint venture, Zamech had several features that made it attractive. First, there was a fairly high level of technical competence. Zamech had over 1500 engineers and was the only local supplier of turbines for power generation and other functions. The old system and the culture of Poland meant that people had a tendency to grow up, work, and retire, in the same area. The result was that the average worker at Zamech had 18 years of experience. Even though the talent pool was and still is small, the longevity of service meant that Zamech had accumulated a large technical staff and a great deal of experience in the work force.

There was a genuine feeling of attachment to the company. The Poles were very hesitant Communists. Very little loyalty was directed to the government. It was much more often directed to the company. In the old system Zamech also had a social function. The company provided many social services such as a hotel where employees could stay at affordable rates, access to resorts for manager's vacations and the like. Everyone at Zamech felt that it was one of the best companies in Poland before the JV was even considered.

A second attribute of Zamech was its foundry. Generally, when Western investors come into an undeveloped country there is a problem developing a network of reliable suppliers. In turbine manufacturing the most basic supply is steel and the first step in the production process is casting the large parts. Zamech could control the quality of these items internally and could have reliable delivery of them relatively easily.

Zamech also had an attractive location. This is significant in two distinct ways. First, turbines are extremely heavy items and the transportation system in Eastern Europe leaves much to be desired; therefore being close to the end user is a decided advantage. Second, the location in Eastern Europe results in very low labor cost. At the time of the JV, the average salary of the unionized workers (not the Engineers) was roughly 40 cents/hour.

The idea had a great deal of employee support. The workers council initiated the process and selected the man that they thought could lead the JV. They decided that they would fully support the JV as long as he were left in charge. For this reason Olechnowicz had a much longer "honeymoon" than anyone else would have had. He was only elected days before the deal went through, so ABB got the full benefit of this "grace period."

On the other hand, there were also several major drawbacks to the idea. The most significant problem was obvious. This was Poland and that meant dealing with the Polish economy and government. By 1989 the currency was very unstable, inflation was very high (reaching nearly 100% per year), the future was incredibly uncertain, the infrastructure was poor, the Communist constitution was still in effect, the sole customer for turbines was a government that was essentially bankrupt, and no one could predict how long it would take for the situation to stabilize.

The technical skill of the company was quite good by Polish standards, but not by ABB's. There was basically no computerization of either production or financial control. There were no environmental controls, and the foundry was so filled with dust that you could hardly see from one end to the other. There was relatively little automation, and there were no plans for its development. It was clear that many receivables on the books would never be paid even though liabilities were equally high. Many of the social services provided by Zamech could not be profitable on their own.

While it is clearly advantageous to be close to the power plants, the town of Elblag is very small, it has no airport, a highly unreliable phone service, and it is a relatively a long way from major centers like Warsaw and Krakow. Although it was only about 35 miles from Gdansk, this was also the birthplace of Solidarity and most Western companies think strong unions mean it is hard to make major changes, especially with respect to the size of the work force and social functions. Although the work force was bloated considering the low levels of incoming orders, no layoffs had occurred in Poland in almost 50 years. From a socio-logical standpoint, the Poles were intensely proud of the accomplishments and culture of Poland. No Western country had a major investment presence there and many believed that it Zamech was viewed as a foreign company, it would be doomed.

Pawel Olechnowicz

Here was the personification of both the pros and cons of Zamech as a candidate for a joint venture. Pawel Olech-nowicz joined Zamech as a metallurgist in 1976 after gradu-ating with a master's degree in that field. He has been with Zamech since his graduation and was the manager of the foundry since 1980. He sought out some Western style man-agement education on his own, taking courses in Gdansk in accounting, marketing, psychology, and organizational be-havior. He is extremely forceful, charismatic, and bold. As manager of the foundry he was quite popular. He represented the workers on regional level workers councils and was known throughout Zamech. On the other hand, the foundry is in some ways the most "low tech" aspect of Zamech. Olechnowicz had absolutely no experience in a capitalist system and no experience managing anything approaching the size of Zamech. The official language of ABB is English, and Olechnowicz did not understand a word of it. There were also many people at Zamech with far more experience with the company. Ironically, this was one of the things that attracted the workers council to him.

In some ways he is the proverbial restless soul. In his words, "I hate the stable position." He has initiated signifi-cant changes in the organizational structure every year and says that he often pushes for change more rapidly than ABB seems to want. He is extremely authoritative and says about firing people who cannot manage change, "I have no problem firing these people. Many people find it difficult, but for me it has never been a problem." Part of his approach for changing Zamech was to appoint managers to restructure a department or function. If they failed to do this to his satisfaction, they were dismissed.

He had a honeymoon period of a couple of years, which was very useful because, as he states it, "it is very hard to show where things are going to people who have no concept of what a profitable company is supposed to be, it just looks like more work." When asked about the changes at Zamech he states, "It was not a dramatic change. It was a revolution." He also states, "ABB brought options, and vision but not in detail. ABB gave Zamech inspiration, motivation and freedom to change in ways that we felt would be profitable."

Who Is ABB?

Asea of Sweden and Brown Boveri of Switzerland merged in 1988. Both companies had a major presence in their home markets but were considered marginal players on the global stage. Percy Barnevik was selected as the new CEO. After seven years Asea Brown Boveri (ABB) has become one of the major players on the global stage in the areas of power generation, power distribution, industrial systems (including robotics), and transportation. Barnevik is one of the most famous leaders in the business world and accord-ing to a *Financial Times* survey, ABB has been the most respected company in all of Europe for the past two years.[3] The arrival of ABB as a world class player on a global scale may be the most talked about business story of the decade. Three major issues stand out in this emergence: restructur-ing, acquisitions, and consolidation. The restructuring of the organization is the most cited. Before the merger, the head office of Brown Boveri had 4,000 people in Baden, Switzerland, while ASEA had 2,000 people in Vasteras, Sweden. Currently, the head office of ABB contains 150 people.[4] Barnevik likes to call his operation, "multidomes-tic." He has created a "master matrix" whereby in one dimension ABB is a global network where Business Area Unit (BAU) managers answer to a chief for that area worldwide. In the other dimension each company must answer to a country manager deeply concerned with the home market of that country. ABB now has 210,000 employees divided into 1,300 companies and almost 5,000

[3] *"Europe's Most Respected Companies,"* Financial Times, *Septem-ber 19, 1995.*

[4] *Kets de Vries, and F.R. Marnfred, "Making a Giant Dance,"* Across the Board, *October 1994.*

profit centers (BAUs) located in 140 countries.[5] A typical profit center has 150 people with never more than five people between the CEO and the shop floor. The fundamental premise behind this decentralization is that every person at ABB should feel that the customer is in charge, and that if the distance between a manager and the end customer is small, that manager will always directly feel the pressure of the customer's needs. According to Barnevik, ABB purposely went overboard in its move toward decentralization. Everyone had to become comfortable with the notion of major changes on a regular basis.

ABB was one of the first major Western investors to come into eastern Europe and now has over 50 companies in this area with over a dozen businesses in Poland. In the past five years the company has been involved in more than 100 acquisitions and joint ventures that have added some 100,000 employees to its payroll. After an intense, five-year period of decentralization some consolidation has begun. Barnevik believes that about 300 of ABB's 1,300 organizations must be either merged with other units or sold.

The financial results are quite impressive. During the first half of 1995 orders received were up 16% (in US $) to $17.97 billion.[6] Revenues increased 17% to $15.3 billion. Operating earnings climbed to $1.4 billion, an increase of 14%, and operating margin reached 9%. Income before taxes rose by 32% and net income increased 41%. On the other hand, some critics have serious doubts about the long-term health of ABB with Barnevik in command. His global design means that he and his top executive group of eight people have a staggering responsibility. Barnevik has stated,

What I have tried to do is to recreate small-company dynamism through having 5,000 profit centers and 1,300 legal entitles. I have also made an effort to reduce the layers. I am fully aware, however, of the pros and cons of doing so. Fewer layers mean bigger spans of control and fewer jobs to which one can be promoted.

Obviously, making our kind of organization work is a lot more demanding. You can mess it up easily. If you have poor business-area managers who don't understand the system, it may become clogged. Decisions will be pushed upward. It is important that within this matrix you give a clear mandate to the various people in the system. People must have a well defined role.[7]

JV Agreement

There were three major and immediate results of the joint venture agreement. First, Olechnowicz was retained as CEO of Zamech. This was not at all the standard policy of ABB. Typically, a manager would be brought in from a similar business in another country to start up the operations. After some measure of stability was established, then a local manager would be put in place. ABB is renowned for its intense computer integration and leveraging of information technology. Olechnowicz had no experience in this area. Zamech had almost 6,000 employees at this point and Olechnowicz had never managed anything larger than the foundry. On the other hand, the unique situation with the selection by the workers council meant that there would probably have been protests if anyone tried to oust Olechnowicz at this point. His retention was one of the few conditions that the workers council insisted upon. A second result was the creation of Elzam. The Polish government created this new entity, which encompassed all of Zamech and its ancillary services. The joint venture only involved the subset of Elzam's operations that ABB wanted. These operations were purchased from Elzam, along with the name Zamech, which was well known in Poland. Some equipment was purchased outright from Elzam, while some, along with the land, was leased. Services that ABB did not want were left with Elzam, as were many managers. These services included cleaning, a section of the foundry, a hotel, and manufacturing plants for small items like nuts and bolts. After the JV was formed, many other services were later shifted to Elzam, and this accounts for the major fall in the work force size. The dropping of these unproductive businesses meant that the average productivity of the remaining work force went up significantly.[8]

The workers council was agreeable with this for several key reasons. First, no one was fired; this was the primary concern of the council as well as the leadership of Solidarity. Second, they were assured that no wages would be reduced even though the company was losing money. In fact, one of the first actions of ABB was to simplify the wage scale and more than double the hourly wage for the most common laborers. Their wages rose from 40 cents/hour to roughly $1.10/hour. Third, it was believed that the JV was the only way to save Zamech. Finally, the fact that unemployment quickly rose from 0 to over 25% in the town of Elblag must be taken into account.

The joint venture was structured as a purchase of 76% of the company by ABB for a cash price of $5 million. The remaining 24% was held by the Polish government with

---

[5]Kets de Vries, and F.R. Marnfred, "Making a Giant Dance," Across the Board, *October 1994.*

[6]All costs are in US dollars unless otherwise noted.

[7]Kets de Vries, and F.R. Marnfred, "Making a Giant Dance," Across the Board, *October 1994.*

[8]Profit in thousands of U.S. dollars per employee from 1990 to 1995 were $500, $1,700, $2,830, $4,500, and $5,200, respectively.

the understanding that 5% was property of the workers council. The workers have yet to receive any of this 5%. The purchase price actually showed up as a cash inflow to Zamech and served to stem cash flow problems. ABB also acquired the work-in-process and raw material inventories, existing contracts, and orders. Finally, within the articles of formation for the new company was the declaration that Zamech was to become a producer of a gas-powered turbine sold by ABB known at the GT8. Exhibit 2 shows the series of events involved in the formation of this venture.

What Has Been Done?

Since the establishment of ABB Zamech Ltd, the organization has undergone a complete revolution. The organizational structure has changed each year. Organizational charts from January 1990, May 1990, and May 1995 are shown in Exhibits 3, 4, and 5. The developing organizational chart shows a clear move away from organizing the company simply by function to a more product-focused structure. It also shows the general philosophy of ABB in the formation of small Business Area Units (BAUs) and the addition of new businesses. ABB has an organization called "Power Ventures" that exists to help move new acquisitions to the stage of being just a "normal" ABB operation. The CEO of Zamech actually reported to the head of Power Ventures for the first few years. Some members of Power Ventures lived in Poland for the first year while others visited on a weekly basis.

The activities dominating 1990 included the spinoff of many businesses to Elzam. According to the CFO, Zamech

sometimes went overboard with this concept. Some operations were placed into Elzam even though Zamech still bought the service and was the only customer for that operation. New organizational charts were developed and many "advisors" from Power Ventures were on the scene daily. A sales organization was created and staffed by employees that had already established long-term relationships with the power plant managers. They promoted the idea of utility overhauls and major repairs since the market for new turbines was very weak. They also sold the idea of "retrofitting" old systems to improve efficiency and service life instead of building entirely new ones. A lot of capital reduction took place as it was left to or given to Elzam. Some machines were modernized and new equipment was brought in for testing and quality control.

In 1991 Zamech created a District Heating BAU. Throughout Poland, power plants and other sites generate hot water. This water is piped into the neighboring towns and delivered into radiators in apartments and other buildings. Zamech's district heating business sold pipes that were designed and made in other ABB plants. At this stage Zamech was the "middle man" in the transaction, serving as the sales force and delivery manager.

Zamech began to focus its organization by products. A service division for turbines was created, and Marine and Gears was made a separate BAU. The planning department was modernized, and production planning was computerized and updated. Production delays and schedule deviations were recorded and studied. A more sophisticated MRP (Material Requirements Planning) system was introduced based on ABB standards. Power services branch offices

Exhibit 2

			Significant Events in the Creation of ABB Zamech Ltd
1-4	Mar	1989	First meeting at Zamech initiates negotiations to form a joint venture.
4	Apr	1989	Negotiators from ABB and Zaklady Mechaniczne (Zamech) meet for the first time.
12	Jun	1989	An agreement is signed between ABB and Zamech as to the form of negotiations for establishing a joint venture.
14	Jul	1989	Percy Barnevik, the president of ABB, comes to Poland to meet with government representatives.
17	Jan	1990	Zamech's workers council and other employees' delegates meet and give their consent to the restructuring of Zamech aimed at establishing a joint venture.
20	Feb	1990	Pawel Olechnowicz is appointed as Zamech's general director by Tadeusz Syryczyk, the Minister of Industry.
1	Mar	1990	The workers council gives its consent for the creation of Elzam and the sale of the name Zamech.
14	Mar	1990	The cabinet's Economic Committee, led by Vice-Premier Leszek Balcerowicz, gives its consent for the formation of a joint venture.
2	Apr	1990	Zamech Spolka (Zamech Ltd) is registered.
3	Apr	1990	The first board meeting: Pawel Olechnowicz is appointed chairman of the board and ABB Zamech Ltd's chief executive officer.
1	May	1990	ABB Zamech Ltd takes over and begins operations.

Exhibit 3

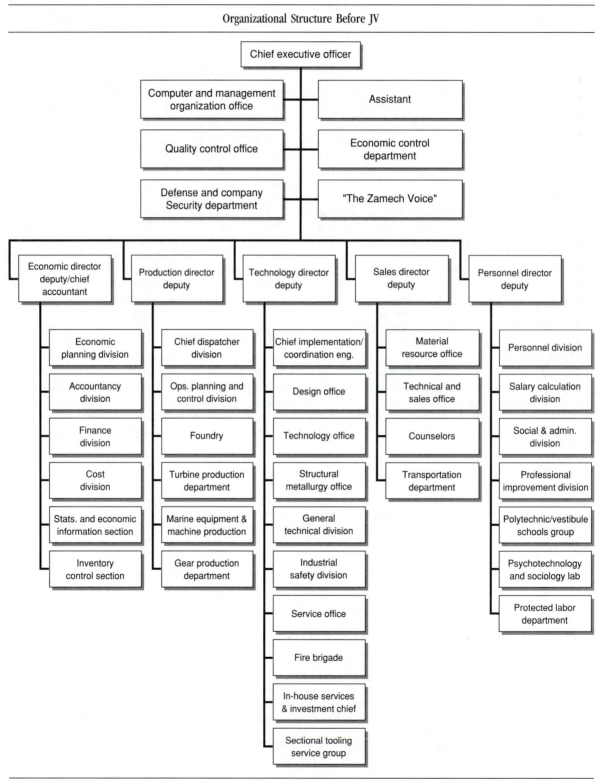

Organizational Structure Before JV

were created. These offices began to sell services to utilities that Zamech had not offered before. These included monitoring, maintenance, and data collection for local power plants. The first GT8 turbine was delivered, generating revenue of $20 million. Its design was brought in from ABB and it was the first gas turbine ever built by Zamech. The GT8 is a relatively small (50 MW) turbine that can be started and shut down quickly, and produces much less pollution than coal-fired models. It is most often used in small power plants, ships, and mining. It has no market in Poland and is purely an export product.

By 1992 the Business Area Unit had become the building block of the organizational structure. Quality of output reached the point where Zamech could become part of ABB's Power Plant Production network. This means that Zamech is able to serve as suppliers to all other ABB companies. Branch sales offices and salesmen got more authority to sell ABB products. These offices could sell a full range of products and negotiate prices from other ABB factories for items not made in Elblag. Zamech created five regional offices around Poland, and two GT8 turbines were delivered.

Full implementation of the BAU structure means that factories account for their revenues as sales to both external customers and other BAUs. Specific buildings were designated as factories for a particular BAU. Thus, each BAU became a profit center with its own production capability. In 1993 a new factory was opened to manufacture the pipes that were used in the District Heating Business. This process is fairly simple. A steel pipe is inserted into a larger plastic sleeve. The gap between the pipe and the sleeve is filled with an insulating foam. The pipe is then tested to ensure that the insulation was installed properly. In 1993 Zamech established a training center where pipe fitters from all around Poland could learn about Zamech pipes and the installation procedures required. Three GT8 turbines were delivered.

Exhibit 4

Organizational Structure, May 1990

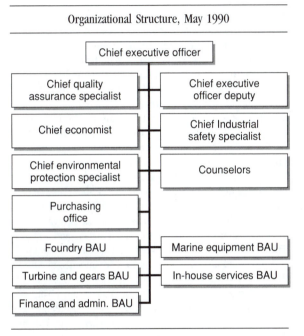

Exhibit 5

Organizational Structure, January 1995

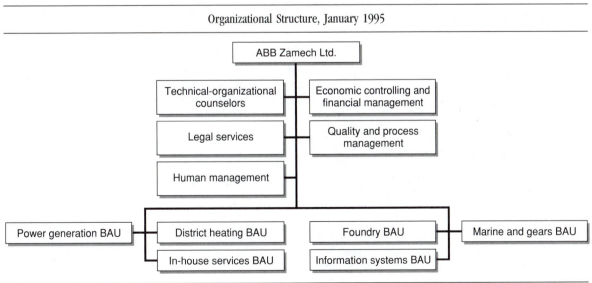

By 1994 the decentralization of production at Zamech was complete. Management's focus at this point was "redirected" toward quality and manufacturing processes. A new factory was opened for the production of large diameter pipes for the District Heating BAU. This plant was located in southern Poland. The extra site provided an additional training facility and cut transportation costs. Zamech began to form teams that could provide Large Project Management (LPM) for its customers. An LPM team has the capabilities to manage large construction projects such as a major overhaul or complete construction of a power station. These teams can acquire products from Zamech, other ABB suppliers, and outside manufacturers, construction companies, and finance companies. Also in 1994, ABB designated Zamech as its center for 120 and 200 MW steam turbine retrofitting and repair. This role will involve Zamech with ABB operations worldwide. In this year Zamech was also designated as the main center for GT8 production and delivered four units.

Wages and Payments

The old pay scale for workers in the plant was based on strictly defined output rates. Anything over that rate generated bonus pay. According to Olechnowicz, it was possible for one worker to make 7 times what another worker made performing the same task. Many workers would turn down promotions because they could make more money performing routine tasks than they would supervising them. The economy of shortage meant that orders were so far behind and demand was so great, that every available body was moved to production. Many items were never inspected, or there was no time for inspections until after assembly. The pay system implied that if the quota on your task was 10 units per hour, it was more lucrative to make 20 of poor quality than to take the time to make 10 of acceptable quality. This was facilitated by the fact that available inspectors were few and far between. Zamech worked for higher quality and had some procedures in place to get it, but the pay scale rewarded increases in volume and finding ways to cut corners.

Three dramatic changes were made to this system. In the old system workers were paid in cash at the end of the month. Everyone knew exactly what everyone else was making. One of the first things that the new venture did was to establish bank accounts for all employees. For many Poles these were the first bank accounts that they had ever had. Now all payments could be made by direct deposit and would not be common knowledge and sources of envy or debate. The next major change was the elimination of the volume bonuses. The scales were simplified and solid hourly wages were established. The average worker in the plant had his wages increased from roughly 40 cents/hour to over $1.10/hour. The third major change was the elimination of other "perks" and "bonuses" that were common

in the old system. Vacation policies were spelled out, and the supervisor's duties and powers were more clearly defined. In the old system it was possible to "reward" good or favored workers with special vacation leave, vacation "bonuses," and resort stays. With the separation of these social functions, their abuse was eliminated.

Training and Education

Training and education are particularly important in the turnaround of Zamech. Exhibit 6 shows the total number of employees receiving some formal training in each year. [Note the numbers may be greater than the total work force due to multiple training programs for some individuals.] In addition to formal educational programs, top management forums occur once a year where the 500 managers meet in a rented local movie theater. Olechnowicz discusses strategy, the CFO discusses financial results and costs, and the quality and process manager presents information about the production processes and products.

Beginning in 1992 all of Zamech's employees were split into groups of 30. These groups attend a six-hour session once each year on one Saturday morning. At these sessions they meet with all of top management to discuss Strategy, Information Systems, Human Resources, Quality, and Finance. These are set up as one-hour sessions with each of the top six executives at Zamech. These sessions are intended to educate the entire company about Zamech's goals and plans, and to hold a discussion of problems and strategies. Zamech has also continued the operation of the company radio station that broadcasts continuously throughout the work areas. This medium is routinely used to provide music and local and national news. It also serves as a forum for managers, labor unions, and other workers' groups to share information or to educate the company about events or changing practices and policies. The broadcasts are heard throughout the entire compound of buildings that make up the site of Zamech.

There is also a semi-annual "discussion of problems" session when the work force splits into groups to discuss leadership, teamwork, management styles and roles, strategy, process improvements and other business-related information. Zamech also performs annual surveys of all work-

Exhibit 6

Participation in Training (Number of Participants)					
Types of Training	1990	1991	1992	1993	1994
Internal training	400	4491	4658	4634	4162
External training	172	456	1143	1400	2016
Total participants	572	4947	5801	6034	6178
Total costs (1,000's)	31	132	148	409	615

ers. The first of these surveys was performed by ODI Consultants. The focus at that time was to get a general feel for the state of the organization and morale of the work force. Since this first effort, more frequent, smaller surveys have been conducted to focus on specific areas that were seen as needing improvement.

ODI was very involved in 1991 and 1992. In addition to the surveying of workers, ODI was contracted to perform two-day training sessions in which every worker was introduced to the concepts of quality awareness. They also helped develop quality action teams and trained about 5% of the work force to be team leaders. Zamech also contracted the services of INSEAD, Gustaw Kaser Training International, ABB Corporate Communications Ltd., Sundridge Park Executive Development, BSI Quality Assurance, and Cicero Languages International as part of its training efforts. Today more than 53% of white-collar workers are university graduates and about 30% speak English. In 1989 white-collar workers accounted for 29% of total staff. Today it is roughly 46%. (See Exhibit 7.) The white collar work force is roughly 1/3 women while the blue collar work force is around 17% women.

Zamech maintains two classrooms for computer-based training for employees and local students selected by Zamech. In fact, Zamech has agreements in place with the local high schools whereby the schools identify potential candidates before their last year of coursework. Zamech then interviews and often hires the student, signs him to a service contract, and helps the students in course selection, provides some exposure to Zamech's operations, and begins

computer literacy training after school. This is done to ensure that the brightest students in Elblag are committed to Zamech before any other companies can attract them. Computers are so rare in Poland that Zamech is about the only supplier of PCs to the schools of Elblag. Zamech gives about 100 old PCs per year to these schools. Exhibit 8 shows the total expenses on information technology (IT) in thousands of U.S. dollars over the past five years. Exhibits 9 and 10 show the number of persons receiving IT-related training and its total cost over the same period.

Computers

At the time of the formation of the joint venture, the entire inventory of computer equipment at Zamech consisted of a single Russian-made ODRA 1305 computer with 24 terminals. This server could handle about 0.3 MIPS (million instructions per second), which is about half of what a Pentium-based PC or Power PC will handle today. After only five years Zamech has been established as the country manager for six LAN's (Local Area Networks) for ABB sites throughout Poland using over 100 KM of fiber optic cable, a thousand work stations, nine Network servers and seven servers for Lotus Notes. Zamech is also the central point in a satellite communications system that links the six LANs into a single WAN (Wide Area Network) and facilitates long distance communications including calls, faxes, electronic mail, and video conferencing. The local servers are connected via satellite to the country server in Elblag and through this location are connected to a global system of all ABB companies.

Exhibit 7

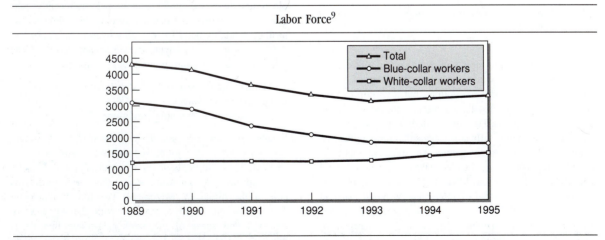

Labor Force[9]

_____

[9]The largest number of workers were moved to Elzam in 1990, but the process continued in 1991, 1992, and 1993. Some attrition also took place.

Exhibit 8[10]

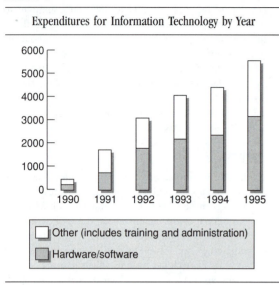

Expenditures for Information Technology by Year

Other (includes training and administration)

Hardware/software

[10]All figures for Exhibits 6 and 8 are in thousands of U.S. dollars.

Exhibit 9

Number of Persons Trained/Year (IT related)

	90	91	92	93	94	95
PC Applications	200	450	835	831	790	1040
TRITON[11]	0	40	150	388	250	200
Lotus Notes	0	0	0	0	40	40
AutoCAD	0	0	10	30	40	20
CAD CATIA[12]	0	0	10	30	30	15

[11]This is the MRP system used in most ABB companies.

[12]This is the document storage and retrieval system that is standard for ABB companies.

The manager of this rapidly growing system is Stanislaw Kurcharski. Zamech was given a very short list of equipment, vendors, and software options, but it was up to Kurcharski to manage its installation, training, maintenance, and day-to-day operations. This role is vitally important because ABB has three major software systems that form a glue that holds its 1300 enterprises together. The most obvious is its common reporting system called ABACUS. This is "hard wired" into a finance and MRP II (Material Requirements Planning) system called TRITON, which was first installed at Zamech in 1991. A whole host of reporting practices, recordkeeping, organization of work, and even organizational structure has been determined by the commitment to the requirements of this system.

Exhibit 10

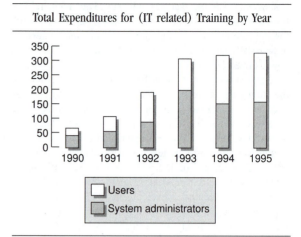

Total Expenditures for (IT related) Training by Year

Users

System administrators

The availability of adequately trained PC users in Poland is quite small. Consequently, the training budget in this area has been huge for the past five years and is expected to stay that way for the foreseeable future. Kurcharski is quick to point out that while ABB offered a great deal of "advice," this system was built by the Poles from the ground up. They feel that it is their creation and they are responsible for it. The pride in the "Polish designed system" is evident as he gives extended tours of the buildings pointing out connections, cables, servers, terminals, etc.

Unions in Zamech

The work force at Zamech is organized into four labor unions. Solidarity is by far the largest, with about 1,300 members. Roughly 140 Zamech employees are members of an engineer's union. There is also a workers' union leftover from the old system that has about 560 members. There recently arose a new union known as Contra, with only 36 members. The head of Solidarity describes the labor relations at Zamech as "stable, we are not too happy, and we are not too mad." The primary focus of Solidarity involves three issues:

1. Maintaining the size of the work force
2. Getting higher wages
3. Improvement of working conditions

Wages have not been raised since the increase six years ago, just after the joint venture was established. A particularly sensitive issue is the fact that the workers never got their 5% share in Zamech that was promised as part of the initial JV agreement. The former managing director moved on to a position with the Ministry of Industry, and some of the workers believe that he is blocking the transfer of 5% ownership that is due them. The workers agreed to participate in a two-hour work stoppage a few years ago in support of Solidarity nationally. However, the workers specify that this action was in support of Solidarity as a national organization and not directed at Zamech in particular.

One of the major changes in moving toward capitalism was the dismantling of the workers council. In the old system the workers council was a partner in all management decisions. Now the only representation is through the trade unions. Consequently the voice of the workers is not the direct influence that it once was. However, in commenting on this change the head of Solidarity states: "It [the workers council] made very important decisions but no one took responsibility. The new system is much better in terms of accountability. When something goes wrong we know who to look at." He also states,

The work has changed because the pay scale has changed. The average responsibility level has increased dramatically. There are fewer workers but the required tasks are the same so the workload has increased and more discipline is needed. Those that left went to work for Elzam so no one lost their jobs. The wages at Elzam are about 70% as much as those at Zamech. The company spends a lot of money on training. Top management selects who will be trained and sets them on a course to be promoted. Solidarity is still focused on things like working conditions, wages, and safety concerns and is not too concerned about training. We don't want to tie management's hands or get too involved in management issues.

Supply Management

Overall, the dollar value of all purchases equals about 54% of Zamech's revenues. In the old system there was a single purchasing department for everything that Zamech needed from paper clips to tons of iron ore to computer technology. While the authority to purchase many routine supplies has been pushed down to the BAU level, there remains a centralized supplier management function. However, the staff involved in this function has been cut from over 100 six years ago, to three or four today. Krzystof Iwko is head of supply management for ABB Zamech and his job is fundamentally different from what it was in the old system. He has been a supply manager for about 15 years and has personal knowledge of all of the major suppliers in Poland and throughout the COMECOM system.

The most noticeable change in the supplier management role is that it is now a global operation. The removal of many restrictions on imports and the ease of capital exchange have opened the door to literally thousands of potential suppliers that Zamech had never dealt with. ABB relies heavily on its information technology to keep track of all of these organizations and products. ABB's focus on IT has produced a powerful computer-based information system that tracks sup-

pliers and contracts all over the world. One of the most obvious results of the "computerization" of Zamech has been the introduction of this supplier tracking system to Zamech.

One result of this ability to shop globally has been a trend away from local sources. Prior to 1989 almost 100% of Zamech's supplies came from within the COMECOM system, and as much as 85% came from within Poland itself. By 1994 Zamech was using suppliers from all over Europe. Based on the dollar values of all supplies, Poland still provides about 43%, Switzerland provides about 36%, and roughly 13% comes from Germany. The rest is brought in from Austria, Denmark, England, France, Italy, the Netherlands, Russia, and Sweden.

Iwko's time over the past few years has been dominated by the development and negotiation of long-term purchasing, or "partnership" agreements. The thinking is that Zamech or ABB as a unit has a much stronger negotiating position than a small BAU. Therefore, Zamech establishes stable agreements and pricing levels that are passed on to the BAU level. Iwko signed four such agreements in 1993, 19 in 1994, and should complete 25 in 1995. These agreements have been focused on the materials considered to have the most "strategic" importance. By the end of 1995, 100% of all of these strategic materials will be handled under such agreements. Under ABB, Zamech has tracked the hours of "extra work" caused by poor quality from suppliers of strategically important items. In the Power Generation BAU this has been cut from an estimated 6,500 hours in 1993 to 4,500 in 1994, and 500 in 1995. Part of the focus of these agreements is that suppliers must guarantee 100% accuracy and inspection prior to delivery. Subsequently, inspection at receiving has been eliminated for these suppliers. This constitutes most of the labor savings mentioned. The impact of these agreements can also be seen in the reduction of delivery times. Some critical parts used by the Power Generation BAU can now be procured in 30 days less time, and the number of suppliers used has dropped by 20%.

From terminals at Zamech, the supply manager has access to information on all of the partnership agreements in place throughout the entire ABB system. Using this data he can shop throughout the world for any commodity needed, with pre-agreed pricing already in place and almost complete confidence in the quality level of that supplier. Using this system, Zamech has shifted most of its supply needs to companies pre-approved by ABB. Iwko has also worked to get Polish firms of sufficient quality involved in the process and has added several Polish firms to this data base.

Quality

The quality and processes manager for ABB Zamech is Ryszard Jaskolski. After graduating from a technical university in Poland, he entered Zamech 21 years ago as a quality controller. He later worked as the production director in the marine department and in the technology office for gear boxes for several years before the JV was established. His mission has been the improvement of Zamech's product quality. This has been improved through a host of factors not the least of which is the improved quality of raw materials. This has cut re-work costs, inspection costs, inventory levels, lead times, and cycle times.

Another major factor in the quality improvement process has been the demands of ABB as a customer. Zamech had been under contract to ABB to provide some items for about 15 years before the JV was established and it was commonly understood that for an ABB job, "special treatment" had to be given. When the JV was started, one of the first things that ABB did was to begin the transfer of technology for the production of a small gas-powered turbine known as the GT8. This was a new product for Zamech and involved a full year of technology transfer and production planning before the first unit was actually produced. ABB demanded a very high level of quality and followed the work very closely. ABB Engineers routinely traveled to Zamech to oversee testing and inspection themselves. Power Ventures provided a Quality "advisor" who remained in Poland for the first year assisting in the development of a quality program and early training. Extensive documentation was provided that defined proper testing procedures, observers' roles, and supervisors' duties. There was very strict enforcement and constant inspection on every aspect of the GT8 production.

Production of the GT8 became a product-centered quality effort.

In 1992 a TQM program was initiated at Zamech, which included quality assurance teams and the development of quality engineers throughout the organization. This personnel was selected in each department and given additional training and information which they then disseminated down the line. All of the quality control (QC)-related personnel meet weekly, monthly, and yearly to look at supplier audits, nonconformance reports, and customer feedback. In 1990 and 1991, Zamech also kept a QC authority at the end of each process to ensure testing and rework as needed. Since 1992 these positions have been gradually eliminated and the QC staff has been reduced. The small group that remains in QC is focused on policy related functions. Today Jaskolski's staff consists of only three people.

Additional factors resulting in quality-level improvements include the updating of equipment at the factory level. However, there has not been a wholesale change of major machinery. Machines are commonly replaced with new ones only after they break down. Much of the investment has been in the acquisition of more modern testing equipment and the replacement of common tools with items of higher quality. Zamech has recently begun the process of instructing and educating Polish customers about quality-related issues. Exhibit 11 gives a breakdown of Zamech's investment spending over the last five years. Actions in the Foundry give a prime example of what has been done to improve quality. The Appendix explains some of these actions in more detail.

Exhibit 11

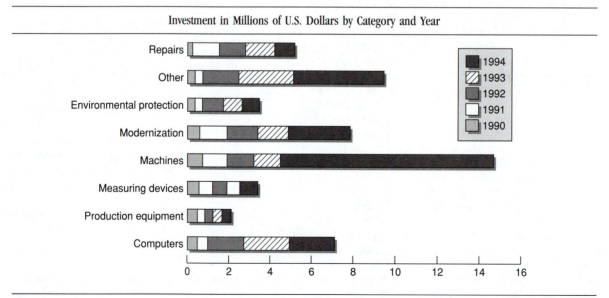

Investment in Millions of U.S. Dollars by Category and Year

Financial Control

Financial control in Zamech prior to 1989 was managed by a single office with a staff of over 100 people. The new structure is consistent with ABB companies all over the world. Accounting data are kept at the BAU level. The only accounting role of the central staff is the consolidation of data from the BAUs to form a single statement about Zamech. On the other hand, the finance function is still highly centralized in that the Finance Office handles all external contacts with banks, insurance brokers, and national ministries. The thinking behind this is that each BAU should benefit from the buying power and negotiating position of ABB and not have to duplicate efforts searching for competitive rates and terms on loans or other agreements.

Each division has a comptroller and its own accounting department. One of the major motivations for the decentralization of accounting functions was to help engineers and other technical people at the BAU level understand the accounting data that they received. In some respects this was a transition approach. ABB brought in new rules and guidelines for accounting and the focus on profit and loss was completely new to most of the organization. It was thought that the data arriving from the accounting function would be quite confusing and often misinterpreted by those not familiar with it. Now that the system has been in place for a few years and the computer technology that supports it has become commonly accepted, the need for these BAU level accountants is largely eliminated, so this function will become smaller and more centralized in the near future.

Current Situation

The joint efforts of Polish managers and ABB's "advisors" have revolutionized life at Zamech. (See the financial results in Exhibits 12 and 13.) A complete restructuring, the introduction of new pay scales, procedures, quality programs, and equipment, the focus on new markets, products, suppliers, and customers have created a radically new player in the Polish markets. However, Pawel Olechnowicz and ABB still face major challenges. What has to be done to take advantage of the momentum for change? What should Zamech's role be in competition for the Polish markets, and how will it help ABB fend off the challenge of Westinghouse and GE? What should this leader who "hates the stable position" do next?

Exhibit 12

Financial Results in Millions of U.S. Dollars					
Description	1990	1991	1992	1993	1994
Orders Received	32.0	97.4	·114.5	165.7	265.1
Sales	42.2	89.8	113.4	133.0	145.4
Net Profit	2.2	6.7	9.7	14.6	16.1
Capital Expenditures	1.8	5.8	7.7	6.9	22.4
Employment (year-end)	4153	3652	3372	3166	3238
Receivables	2.9	11.6	12.7	23.8	33.1
Inventories	18.3	26.3	21.8	14.3	23.1
Advance Payments	0	2.0	1.8	6.6	22.0

Exhibit 13

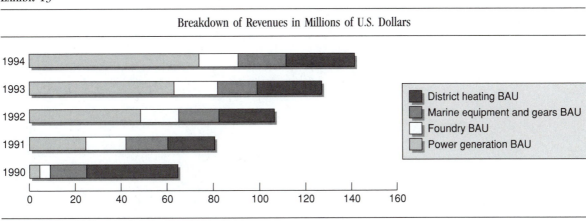

Breakdown of Revenues in Millions of U.S. Dollars

Appendix
Changes in the Foundry

The Zamech Foundry is unique in that it is the only one in the ABB system. The workings of a foundry are essentially the preparation of molds, melting of raw materials, and pouring of castings. As such, the basic technology of the process has not been greatly affected by the joint venture. The foundry was split into two sections as part of the formation of Zamech. One section, which is in a much older building (over 100 years old), was left with Elzam. The other is with ABB and was built in 1971. The Zamech-ABB foundry is basically a "steel" foundry while the section left with Elzam was an iron foundry. The foundry produces about 8,000 tons per year with 5,500 tons of steel, 1,500 tons of copper alloys mostly for ship propellers, and 1,000 tons of iron for the power generation business. Prior to the formation of the joint venture, some workers called the foundry the "hallway to hell." The building is a plain monolithic structure similar to a hangar. Huge cranes drop ore into the furnace and lift out molten steel, copper, and iron which is then poured into molds of anchors, turbine parts, propellers, and other items. After cooling, the molding must be removed and the pieces are ground and polished. The foundry is constantly filled with flying sparks, piles of cooling sand, and the heat of the furnace.

Four major changes have taken place here since 1990. The most expensive change has been the introduction of air-cleaning equipment that has reduced the emissions from the foundry of noxious fumes and dust. De-dusting equipment was first installed in 1993, and dust emissions have been cut by 80–90%. Changes in process design have included the introduction of closed loop water use systems so that water uptake from the neighboring river has been reduced by over 85% while dumping of water back into the river has been virtually eliminated. In addition, the emission of hydrocarbons has been cut by one-seventh and the output of SO_2 and NOX has been cut by over 99% and 33%, respectively. A second major change resulted from the installation of a system whereby the sand used for the castings can be cleaned and reused. This cuts cost because new sand need not be purchased every time a major casting is to be done. It also increases casting quality because the cleaned sand is better than what was originally purchased. Zamech's low labor cost helps to make its foundry a low-cost producer of many items needed by ABB companies, and ABB is taking advantage of it.

The most obvious change is that the foundry is about 30% smaller than it was before 1990. The more focused a foundry is, the easier it is to manage and equip. The castings for turbines are specialty items because of the tightness of specifications, quality of raw materials required, and size and complexities of molds. Not many foundries are capable of doing this type of work, and Zamech hopes to make this work the sole focus of this facility. Although the work on turbine castings is the most technically demanding, it is also the foundry's most value-added product. Zamech expects these orders to grow until they account for all of the foundry's capacity.

PART II

◆ ◆ ◆

Global Operations and Logistics Planning

Chapters 5 – 9

The second part of the text discusses global purchasing and procurement policies, as well as distribution planning and control systems, emphasizing the problems and opportunities derived from internationally sourcing and subcontracting logistics services. Strategies and frameworks for locating facilities are presented within an international context with a thorough analysis of customer service policies appropriate to specific logistics strategies. We present issues such as the degree of centralization in the network, the benefits of "local presence" for customer service in various markets, and the different sourcing and distribution patterns encountered in the global market. In addition, we address how political, economic, social, and government regulation issues differ from those faced domestically, and how these issues subsequently impact the global logistics function. Intriguing planning issues, such as the role of the supplier within a global operations context and the distribution initiatives of successful global companies, are explored. In the examination of issues surrounding planning global operations and logistics, we also look into the logistics and manufacturing concerns of exporting firms, as well as sourcing and location configurations in uncertain environments. We introduce interesting frameworks for combining operational and financial hedging against these uncertainties. The cases in Part 2 address new approaches in outsourcing, such as the idea of using inplants as well as creative alliances with third-party logistics companies. The cases also discuss the specific details of designing a distribution network, combined with the required metrics for accomplishing medium- and long-term objectives. Finally, we present the issue of multinational companies positioning manufacturing in different locations to manage the uncertainties. ◆

Chapter 5

Supplier Network Development

◆ ◆ ◆

In this chapter, we discuss the following points:

◆ *The growing trend toward manufacturing outsourcing*

◆ *The evolving concept of outsourcing*

◆ *A framework for analyzing what should be outsourced and which vendors/providers are most suitable partners*

◆ INTRODUCTION

As discussed in chapter 2, the global operations and logistics system can be divided into inbound and outbound logistics. This chapter explores the issues of developing and managing an effective supplier network.

During the 1980s, many industries radically changed their manufacturing structure as a strategic response to the globalization of markets and consequent increase in competition. As a result, the typical competitive organization in the 1990s is lean and flexible, instead of huge and sturdy, as it was during the 1970s. For many companies, the key to successful restructuring has been to focus on core competencies or strategically important activities and to withdraw from noncore functions. For example, many manufacturers are now outsourcing noncore activities that used to be handled in-house.

As more companies pursue this strategy, the nature of outsourcing has changed tremendously. Not only have the frequency and volume of these transactions increased, but their terms and make-up also have matured. In fact, manufacturing outsourcing has become a strategically important activity for many companies. Consequently, industry must revise its approach to outsourcing decision-making. Instead of focusing only on the traditional quantitative financial aspects of the approach, companies also must consider the "softer" issues of the implications of outsourcing on service.

There is a critical connection between the outsourcing function and the three dimensions of the global operations and logistics framework. The outsourcing function affects the functional dimension because it is directly involved with inbound logistics. The connection with the sectorial dimension is through an evaluation of the possible alternatives available for partnerships. Finally, as geographical boundaries disappear, more suppliers are available, expanding outsourcing options.

This chapter examines this evolved nature of outsourcing. It includes a comparison between the traditional approach (which focuses on price reduction) and the new supplier partnership approach, which closely intertwines suppliers with their customers. In addition, we introduce a framework of analysis to determine which products merit outsourcing by explicitly taking into account their strategic importance to the company. We also analyze the dynamic nature of the outsourcing function over time, as parts and products change throughout the end-product life cycle.

◆ THE EVOLVING CONCEPT OF OUTSOURCING

Today's comprehensive concept of manufacturing outsourcing evolved during the last decade. *Manufacturing outsourcing* refers to the process of determining how and where to procure manufactured goods and raw materials. The practice extends beyond the traditional purchasing concept of buying parts to produce a finished product to a more holistic approach to purchasing.

A common explanation for the changes in outsourcing activities is the phenomenal success of Japanese companies in the world market during the last decade—thanks, in large part, to the superior structure of their manufacturing systems. A unique attribute of this structure is the multiple-layered *supplier pyramid,* discussed later.

The supplier pyramid is the system of supplier tiers required to manufacture an end product. The uppermost tier of the pyramid is the final (end-product) assembly unit that caters to end-user customers. Each tier of the pyramid feeds product/material to the next higher tier. Using this approach, Japanese companies typically produce products with a high content of outsourced materials. As a result, their operational systems are stable, yet agile, flexible, innovative, and efficient in both cost and administration.

The pyramid structure of Japanese industry necessitates a very different approach to supply-chain management for many Western industries. Table 5–1 highlights the contrasts between the traditional Western approach and the newer supplier partnership approach (Japanese model).

As companies around the world attempted to adopt Japanese manufacturing techniques like JIT, they realized that in-plant reorganizations are only part of the program. These techniques demand changes throughout the supply chain. In fact, the effectiveness of streamlining efforts such as JIT depends to a great extent on the quality and nature of linkages along the supply chain—the relationship that organizations share with their supplier companies. Today, effective supply chain management is a potential source of competitive advantage for firms. As a result, Western companies are paying much greater attention to supply chain management and integration.

Table 5–1: *Traditional versus new supplier partnerships*

Traditional Approach	Supplier Partnerships
Primary emphasis on price	Multiple criteria
Short-term contracts	Longer term contracts
Evaluation by bids	Intensive and extensive evaluation
Many suppliers	Fewer selected suppliers
Improvement benefits shared based on relative power	Improvement benefits are shared more equitably
Improvement at discrete time intervals	Continuous improvement is sought
Problems are suppliers' responsibility to correct	Problems are jointly solved
Clear delineation of business responsibility	Quasi-vertical integration
Information is proprietary	Information is shared

The two primary flow elements in a supply chain (or value chain) are *material* and *information.* For *material,* a unidirectional flow across the chain (minimal backtracking) is ideal for efficiency. However, unidirectional flow is not optimal for *information,* which should flow in both directions to ensure effective coordination of activities (e.g., production and delivery schedules) and optimization of assets (e.g., inventory levels) across the value chain.

For example, until recently General Motors (GM) sourced individual components for seats and assembled them in-house; in some cases they bought the complete system as well. Information flow in the chain was more or less unidirectional. The final assembly units designed the entire car and its parts and then passed on the detailed drawings and specifications to the suppliers. The company made minimal effort to understand the capabilities of the suppliers (who were engaged mostly on the basis of price) to deliver the goods per functional specifications and schedules. Now, GM links its systems with those of its suppliers to share information across the channel, improving its planning process and taking better advantage of supplier capabilities.

Reasons for Outsourcing

Many industrial manufacturers are adopting an outsourcing approach, severely curtailing the amount of material they actually manufacture themselves. A classic example is Dell computers, which does not own a manufacturing plant. In 1994, Dell supported $2.9 billion in annual revenues with $60 million of fixed assets. It produced fifty dollars in sales for every dollar invested in plant and equipment. IBM, in contrast, generated about $3.50 for every dollar invested in plant and equipment.

Why do companies decide to outsource elements of their manufacturing? A survey from the Outsourcing Institute in 1995 identified the five top strategic and tactical reasons.

Strategic Reasons

1. Improve business focus
2. Gain access to world-class capabilities
3. Accelerate re-engineering benefits
4. Share risks
5. Free resources for other purposes

Tactical Reasons

1. Reduce or control operating costs
2. Make capital funds available
3. Create cash infusion
4. Compensate for lack of internal resources
5. Improve management of difficult or out-of-control functions

The New Elements of Outsourcing

Competitive forces have prompted a new approach to outsourcing, based on a philosophy of streamlining and smoothing the flow pattern to optimize quality, flexibility, inventory, cost, and response time *globally across the logistics system.* As mentioned before, this outsourcing approach has produced two significant changes. At the industry level, a distinct *hierarchical flow pattern* has evolved, while at the company level, the entire *basis of business relationships* between the buyers and the suppliers has been redefined.

Industry Level Changes: Tierization of Industry and the Supplier Pyramid

The modern approach to outsourcing creates a pyramid-like structure of companies along the value/supply chain. Suppliers are tiered, and the final assembly plant constitutes the top tier; its immediate parts suppliers form the next tier; suppliers to those firms form the third tier, and so on down the line (Figure 5–1). Note that the number of units increases as one goes down the tier levels. For example, basic component manufacturing units are more numerous than first-tier systems in automobile manufacturing.

The widespread use of advanced manufacturing approaches like JIT have enabled organizations to operate with very low levels of inventory. Unfortunately, this makes operations vulnerable to supply disruptions due to factors such as poor quality. These disruptions have much greater consequences for the companies, which no longer carry inventory to buffer lack of production material. Therefore, quality capabilities of vendors are critical in the vendor-manufacturer relationships. Customer and supplier organizations increasingly are working together to upgrade value-adding capabilities across the chain to eliminate potentially costly supply problems.

Time and product variety have also become important competitive priorities. This is driving increased interaction between companies and supplier organizations. Companies have drastically reduced their product design and development times. They also have significantly increased the frequency of the design and development cycle to produce more products more often.

To accommodate these accelerated, more frequent design/development cycles, companies have instituted parallel product development processes in which new products are developed through simultaneous inputs from all relevant functions—manufacturing, marketing, engineering and purchasing. Because many of the constituent parts are outsourced, personnel from appropriate functions in the corresponding supplier organizations also participate in the product development process. One result of this coordinated effort is the trend toward end-manufacturers designing products to reflect their vendors' production capabilities. As

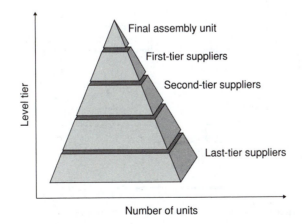

Figure 5–1   The Supplier Pyramid

increased interactions break down the rigid compartmentalizations in the supply/value chain, the boundaries between the tiers grow fuzzy.

Similarly, the trend is moving away from one-time, price-based transactions to mutually profitable, sustainable partnerships that complement each party's competencies. The price of product is no longer the sole, or even primary relationship criterion; other strategically important dimensions like quality and service have become as important.

These developments have redefined the relationships between the customer and supplier organizations. Customer organizations have invested considerable resources in upgrading their suppliers' capabilities. Consequently, the relationships have been developed with a *long-term orientation* to benefit all parties and promote *shared learning* and *economies of scale*. Figure 5–2 depicts these trends.

Company Level Changes: System Purchasing

Organizations are increasingly realizing the inherent advantages of the system-purchasing approach, as compared to an in-house assembly of outside components. We define *system purchasing* as the purchase by the end-manufacturer of completely assembled functional systems that can be directly fitted into the final product. For example, an automobile manufacturer may purchase a dashboard assembly for the car, instead of purchasing the discrete components and assembling the dashboard in-house before fitting it into the car.

This approach is reflected in the recent evolution of the JIT concept to JIT II, which companies such as Bose Corporation have used. In JIT II, a representative employed by the

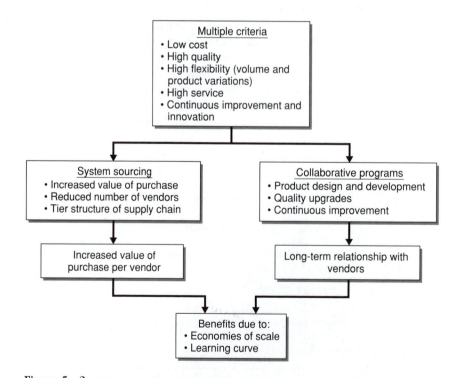

Figure 5–2   Elements affecting the relationship with suppliers. Based on multiple criteria of performance, the trend is toward system sourcing from fewer suppliers that encourages collaborative programs. The overall effect is an increased value of purchase per vendor or supplier and long-term relationships resulting in mutual benefits.

supplier company physically works at the manufacturing firm and is actively involved in manufacturing planning decisions. His or her involvement includes access to data files on other suppliers. These representatives determine manufacturing order quantities and place orders to their company. Naturally, such interdependent relationships require a high level of information sharing and trust, and the manufacturer and supplier become intricately intertwined.

Not all assembly parts are candidates for manufacturing outsourcing. Companies need to evaluate each component item individually and can use the framework presented in the next section to conduct this analysis. The following list summarizes the criteria used by Bose Corporation to assess whether a component is a candidate for outsourcing:

1. A mature, trusting relationship exists with the best supplier in the category.
2. The supplier has a good engineering capability.
3. The volume in the product category exceeds $1 million.
4. The product category involves many transactions, creating a need for an in-plant representative.
5. The technology in the category is not changing at a revolutionary pace.
6. The category does not involve proprietary or core technologies (such as acoustics and electronics).

Black Box Design

In system sourcing, a company delegates part assembly activities to vendors. *Black box design* is a related concept, which involves delegation of design and development activities to suppliers. Thus, in-house value addition is replaced by outsourced value. For example, U.S. and European automakers are increasing their outside purchase of parts from both domestic and foreign sources to maintain quality and value.

Reduced Vendor Base

Because companies are sourcing *assembled* units instead of their components, the number of vendors decreases. This practice is attractive to manufacturers for a number of reasons. First, companies like the convenience of dealing with fewer vendors. Second, Japanese manufacturing approaches in the final assembly plant require high-quality product input. A smaller vendor base facilitates incoming quality assurance. Reducing the number of vendors also allows a company to concentrate its purchasing volume and negotiate better price deals. Finally, a smaller vendor base reduces the cost of vendor selection and certification, which has become quite expensive.

Using this approach, Toyota in the United States employs 340 people to manage 180 direct suppliers, for an output of 3.6 million cars annually. In contrast, General Motors employs 6,000 buyers to manage 1,500 suppliers for an output of 6 million cars annually. Clearly, Toyota reaps many cost savings benefits from consolidating its supplier base.

◆ A FRAMEWORK OF ANALYSIS

When considering manufacturing outsourcing, companies must address a number of strategic questions, including:

- Which products/components should be outsourced?
- What criteria should be used for supplier selection?
- How might these factors change across the life of the main product?

Companies have traditionally analyzed these questions within the make-versus-buy framework. However, this framework is limited, in that it emphasizes only the financial aspects of the decision. Although compatible with the traditional practice of *price-based* purchase decisions, it does not work with newer outsourcing approaches. For example, a simple make-versus-buy framework does not consider issues such as the strategic importance of the part or changing competitive priorities during a product's lifetime.

The Strategic Importance and Criticality Matrix

We propose a framework that broadly categorizes manufacturing parts to determine whether they should be produced in-house or by an outside vendor. The framework depicted in Figure 5–3 and labelled The *Strategic Importance and Criticality Matrix* (SIC Matrix) has two dimensions: the strategic value of the part itself and the criticality of the part to the final product.

The *strategic value* of a part reflects the stand-alone criticality of that part in the market. Some parts, such as print cartridges for laser printers, have this value in the marketplace. Others, such as the plastic case for a Bose radio, have little stand-alone strategic value because the case serves no purpose on its own. Some of the broad indicators of *strategic value* include technological complexity of the part, proprietary nature of the relevant technology, and where the part fits into the product's life cycle.

The *criticality of the part to the final product* is a second important dimension in outsourcing decision-making. This reflects the contribution (or indispensability) of the part to the functional performance of the parent product, irrespective of the strategic importance of the part. The broad indicators of this factor include the percentage value of the part to the final product and the extent to which the quality and reliability level of the final product depends on the part.

In the four categories mentioned in Figure 5–3 (novelty, proprietary, commodity, utility), the *proprietary products* correspond to the concept of core product proposed by Prahalad and Hamel (1990). Such products physically embody the core competencies of the company and constitute the heart and soul of all its products. An obvious example is the engine in

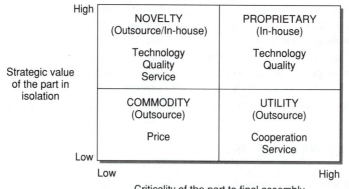

Figure 5–3   Framework to decide what type of parts to outsource. Based on the strategic stand-alone value of the part and the level of criticality of the part for assembly of the final product, we can determine to outsource or produce in-house.

automobiles, one component that automaker Honda, for example, would never outsource to suppliers. Acoustic components in a Bose speaker provide the competitive advantage for the company and that is why in-house production is required.

Another example is oil-field equipment and enclosures for electronic measuring and test instruments. With these two product types, the quality of the buyer's product is significantly impacted by the supplier's product, implying high criticality of the parts to the end product. For instance, a malfunction in oil-field equipment could lead to large losses.

In contrast, *commodities* constitute a class of products involving low (or very standardized and commonly available) technology and having minimal contribution to the principal functional aspects of the end product. The screws used in the manufacture of computers fall into this category. Such screws are very low-technology items and in no way affect the functional performance of a computer. Numerous suppliers of comparable-quality screws also exist, since the technology to produce these items is mature and diffused.

Novelties are products that require sophisticated (or special/restricted) technology but that are not essential to the functioning of the final (parent) product. One such component is the electronic lock for automobile doors, which are not vital for operating the car but are nice options. These products usually operate in price-insensitive, high-end product-market segments, where reliable functional performance and convenience are of prime importance.

Finally, components belonging to the *utilities* class are very critical to the final product but are based on low or readily available technology. An example is radiator caps in vehicles. While they are a very standardized technology, they are an essential functional component. Thus, they need an effective and efficient distribution process to ensure easy availability.

Dynamic Evolution with the Product Life Cycle

Products frequently move across quadrants in the SIC matrix during their life cycles. Newly developed products or breakthrough innovations generate a strategic edge for firms. Such products fall into the proprietary category. As relevant technology diffuses and new products are developed, old products gradually lose their strategic importance and become utilities (Figure 5–4).

Novelty products are not usually part of a firm's R & D portfolio because of their high resource requirements and low strategic value with respect to the final product. For example, in the automotive sector, electronic components have evolved from novelty to proprietary products. Ford and Toyota in the United States, consequently, have been developing in-house production capacity for these items because they are increasingly important to the design of their automobiles.

The principal reasons for outsourcing, based on an empirical study of managers, include (in order of importance): lower price, better quality, only source, advanced technology, consistent attitude, cooperative delivery, and counter trade requirements. We have reclassified these factors into the following broad categories:

- **Resource capability factors**—technology and quality as relates to a vendor's infrastructure capabilities
- **Service factors**—a consistent, highly cooperative attitude toward service and delivery on the part of the vendor
- **Price factor**—any price advantage offered by a vendor that may be exploited by its customer
- **Environmental factors**—elements beyond the control of companies, such as government regulations that limit a company's choice of vendors

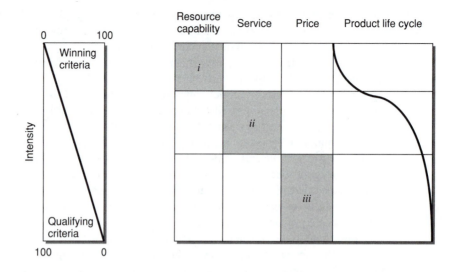

Figure 5–4   Competitive dimension and challenges of the products as they evolve in the product life cycle. For example, at the introductory phase (stage *i*), a product has quality and technology requirements (resource capabilities) while price is the main competitive dimension at the mature level (stage *iii*).

As the final (parent) product evolves along the different stages in its life cycle, its principal competitive requirement changes. In the initial stages, when a new product is launched, it requires design and development of a host of component parts and relevant processes. This is the phase of close collaboration between the company and its principal suppliers in developing their resource capabilities. The product also requires continuous fine tuning (of parameters like quality) and debugging. Thus, *resource* (technology and quality) *capability* forms the main criteria of vendor selection during a product's early life.

During the subsequent growth phase, time to market and ability to meet the escalating demand are the principal competitive requirements. During this phase, delivery reliability and vendors' ability to meet increasing volume requirements are critical. These are the *service* factors used in vendor selection.

During the mature phase of a product, price is generally the main competitive pressure. This stage usually offers the full advantages of economies of scale and the learning curve. Vendors must be cost-efficient and support the *price*-based competitive environment of the final product by providing cost-competitive parts supply.

Outsourcing priorities change over time depending on the product's stage of development and maturity. A product's introductory phase requires very strong quality and technology capabilities in the manufacturing set-up. Thus, the manufacturing set-up should be geared toward exploiting vendor resource capabilities with regard to design and technological bugs, quality, and other initial problems. With time, the manufacturing set-up standardizes, and these concerns dissipate.

During the subsequent phase of rapid market growth, companies must be able to keep pace with surging demand volumes and continually feed hungry distribution channels. This effort requires effective coordination between vendors and assemblers to streamline high-volume product flow across the chain. Companies cannot exploit growing markets unless they maintain delivery, service, and other logistics support commitments at a very high performance level. Thus, delivery reliability is key during this phase.

Finally, as the maturity phase sets in, price becomes a dominant competitive factor. Consequently, companies must address cost effectiveness issues in their manufacturing set-up.

Our framework does not address the decline phase of a product's life cycle. During the decline phase, in order to retain markets and address specific customer needs, companies introduce a host of derivative product lines. As a parent product line mutates, it gives rise to a host of offspring products, each addressing a specific niche market. However, new manufacturing set-ups to support each of these offspring product lines become economically unfeasible because of the short life span and low cumulative volumes of the offspring products. In order to exploit the existing manufacturing set-up for the multiple product lines, companies must develop manufacturing flexibility.

Environmental factors—government restrictions—are beyond the firm's control and may limit the choice of suppliers. Facing this situation, a company may want to commit resources to develop the product in-house or reconsider its business portfolio.

Finally, competitive priorities evolve with time. However, they do not necessarily evolve from one stage to the next, with old priorities shed in the process. Instead, the process is cumulative, and the old priorities continue to be important qualifying criteria; the evolving new priorities correspond to the winning criteria discussed in chapter 2.

The experience of an automotive component manufacturing unit in India illustrates how companies change according to the framework. The company is a market leader in the country and an important player in the global market. Its main products include specialized fasteners and radiator caps. The radiator cap plant was set up in 1992. Almost 90 percent of its output is exported to General Motors USA. The company committed substantial resources during its initial production phase to ensure total quality and audited machine set-ups and processes to ensure compliance to specifications. It also adopted a policy of 100 percent checking of products.

Today, the company has matured its focus to concentrate on meeting delivery commitments. It maintains an enviable record of 100 percent compliance with delivery commitments—a record that has won it a letter of appreciation from General Motors USA. Although the product is not yet in the maturity phase, the company plans to focus on productivity and cost issues in the future.

◆ SUMMARY

The growing strategic importance of manufacturing outsourcing activities and the changes it creates in the relationship between manufacturers and their suppliers require new approaches for decision making. To assist companies in today's inbound logistics decisions, this chapter has identified current requirements and analyzed inbound logistics according to a new framework. One of the dimensions of the Strategic Importance and Criticality Matrix assesses how critical the part is to the final product. The second framework links the evolution of supplier capabilities for different stages of the final product's life cycle. The next chapter brings a similar focus to outbound logistics.

DISCUSSION QUESTIONS

1. Characterize the differences between *traditional* and *new* approaches in supplier management?

2. What are some of the important *strategic* and *tactical* reasons for outsourcing?

3. What does the term *supplier pyramid* mean? How is the structure of the supplier pyramid affected by recent changes in competitive dimensions of the global environment?

4. List criteria you would use to decide whether a certain component is a candidate for outsourcing rather than in-house manufacturing.

5. What is the Strategic Importance and Criticality Matrix (SIC Matrix)? How can you use this matrix for structuring issues and supporting outsourcing decisions?

6. Describe the evolution of outsourcing priorities and needed supplier capabilities over the product life cycle.

REFERENCES

Davis, E. W. 1992. Global Outsourcing: Have U.S. Managers Thrown the Baby Out with the Water? *Business Horizons,* July–Aug.

Dertouzos, M. L., R. K. Lester, and R. M. Solow and the MIT Commission on Industrial Productivity. 1989. Made in America: Regaining the Productive Edge. Cambridge, Mass.: The MIT Press.

Ernst, R., and K. Ferdows. 1991. Intermediate Manufacturing Decisions in a Global Environment. Working Paper, Georgetown University, School of Business Administration, U.S.A.

Flaherty, T. 1989. International sourcing: Beyond catalog shopping and franchising. In Managing International Manufacturing, ed. K. Ferdows, Elsevier, North Holland.

Hahn, C. K., K. H. Kim, and J. S. Kim. 1986. Costs and competition: Implications for purchasing strategy. *Journal of Purchasing and Materials Management* 22 (3): 2–7.

Hill, T. 1989. Manufacturing strategy: Text and cases. Homewood, Ill.: R. D. Irwin.

Houlihan, J. B. 1987. International supply chain management. In Progress in Logistics, ed. M.Christopher, *International Journal of Physical Distribution and Materials Management* 17 (2): 51–66.

McGrath, M. E., and R. B. Bequillard. 1989. International manufacturing strategies and infrastructural considerations in the electronics industry. In Managing International Manufacturing, ed.: K. Ferdows, Elsevier, North Holland.

McMillan, J. 1990. Managing suppliers: Incentive systems in Japanese and U.S. Industry. *California Management Review* 12 (4): 38–55.

Newman, R. G. 1988. Single source qualification. *Journal of Purchasing and Materials Management* 24 (2): 10–17.

Nueno, P. 1993. The evolution of customer supplier relationships. In the proceedings of the symposium on globalization of operations management. Georgetown University, Washington, D.C., U.S.A.

Porter, M. E. 1986. Competition in global industries. Boston, Mass.: Harvard Business School Press.

Prahalad, C. K., and G. Hamel. 1990. The core competence of the corporation. *Harvard Business Review* (May–June): 79–91.

Stewart, T. A. 1993. Welcome to the Revolution. *Fortune* (December): 32–38.

Stuart, F. I. 1993. Supplier partnerships: Influencing factors and strategic benefits. *International Journal of Purchasing and Materials Management* 29 (4).

Tully, S. 1993. Modular Corporation. *Fortune* (February): 52–56.

Tully, S. 1994. You'll never guess who really makes . . . , *Fortune* (October): 124–28.

Tully, S. 1995. Purchasing's new muscle. *Fortune* (February): 75–83.

Venkatesan, R. 1992. Strategic sourcing: To make or not to make. *Harvard Business Review* (November–December): 98–107.

Wheelwright, S. C., and K. B. Clark 1992. Creating project plans to focus product development. *Harvard Business Review* (March–April): 70–82.

Womack, J. P., D. T. Jones, and D. Roos 1990. The machine that changed the world. New York: Macmillan.

Womack, J. P., and D. T. Jones. 1994. From lean production to lean enterprise. *Harvard Business Review* (March–April): 93–102.

◆ CASE 5–1: Bose Corporation: The JIT II Program (A) ◆

John Argitis, president of G&F Industries, was considering an unusual request he had received from Bose Corporation. G&F produced plastic components for Bose speakers. Bose, one of G&F's biggest accounts, had recently requested that Argitis station a representative full-time at Bose headquarters, completely changing the way in which the two companies worked together. The rep would be paid by G&F but would work, in essence, as a plastics buyer for Bose, placing orders to G&F on Bose letterhead, monitoring materials requirements on the plastic components that G&F supplied to Bose, and becoming involved in manufacturing planning at Bose.

Lance Dixon, director of Purchasing and Logistics for Bose, had conceived the idea and was hoping that the program could start in January of 1991, which was only three months away. However, Dixon knew that Argitis had reservations about adding staff to his small company. And several Bose executives, including Tom Beeson, vice president of Manufacturing at Bose, had expressed concerns. Dixon's plan, if implemented, would provide the G&F representative full access to Bose facilities, personnel, and computer systems, and some Bose managers worried that the company would lose control of its own procurement process. Others wondered whether plastics was an appropriate area for this type of relationship. If Argitis agreed to the idea, there would be many details to attend to before January.

Company History

Bose Corporation was founded in 1964 by Dr. Amar Bose, a professor of Electrical Engineering and Computer Science at the Massachusetts Institute of Technology, where Sherwin Greenblatt was earning a master's degree in electrical engineering. Greenblatt and Bose shared a love of music, but recognized that the high-fidelity (hi-fi) products then

Doctoral Candidate Bruce Isaacson prepared this case under the supervision of Professor Roy Shapiro as the basis for class discussion rather than to illustrate either effective or ineffective handling of an administrative situation. Some information has been disguised to maintain confidentiality. "JIT II," "Direct/Reflecting," "Better Sound Through Research," and "Acoustic Wave" are registered service and/or trade marks of Bose Corporation.

available did not accurately reproduce sound. Greenblatt became Bose Corporation's first employee; the two planned to build a company based on innovations in acoustics and electronics. For three years, virtually all of the company's revenues were earned by developing portable, battery-operated equipment; hi-fi was considered "the hobby side of the business." In 1968, however, Bose Corporation launched the 901® speaker, which incorporated proprietary Direct/Reflecting technology, simulating the feeling of live sound by radiating sound waves to the listener directly and via reflections off walls, ceilings, and floors. This speaker was a huge success, lauded by a growing market of audio enthusiasts. Two years later Bose introduced the 501® speaker, which also had Direct/Reflecting technology but was half the size of the 901 speaker. In 1973, Bose introduced the 301® speaker, which produced true hi-fi sound but could fit on a bookshelf.

During the 1970s, sales of Bose speakers grew rapidly, and Bose executives approached the Delco division of General Motors with a proposal to develop a car stereo that would produce exceptional sound. The Cadillac Seville first offered an option for a Delco-Bose sound system in 1982; by 1990 sound systems were available in cars made by General Motors, Honda, Acura, Audi, and Nissan.

Bose Strategy

In 1990, Bose was privately held, with revenues estimated at $720 million. Amar Bose was chairman of the company, and Sherwin Greenblatt was president. Approximately one-third of the company's sales were in Japan, one-third in Europe, and one-third in the United States. The company's motto was "Better Sound Through Research," and Bose Corporation was widely considered the world's largest manufacturer of component-quality speakers.

The company's mission, to "provide outstanding sound experience to everyone in the whole world," was manifested in three aspects of the company's strategy. First, the company constantly sought new markets around the world and had exceptional perseverance in opening markets. For example, Bose entered Japan in 1970 and weathered substantial losses as it tried to establish the Bose brand name among Japanese consumers. The company received its first order from a Japanese car manufacturer in 1982, and by 1990 was the highest selling manufacturer of component-quality stereo speakers in Japan (as well as in Holland, France, Australia, and other countries). Management at

Bose believed that the desire for good sound was universal, and planned to continue opening new markets around the world.

Second, Bose Corporation sought broader channels of distribution. Originally, Bose speakers were sold exclusively in high-end specialty stores that served audio enthusiasts. Throughout the 1980s, Bose added new channels, including electronics retailers including Lechmere, Circuit City, Sears, and Montgomery Ward. Also, Bose began to sell some products by direct marketing.

Third, the company produced systems as well as components. In the early days, true high-fidelity sound had been available only to consumers willing to invest time, money, and patience in their stereo systems. By 1991, consumers expected hassle-free sound and the market for integrated audio systems and portable audio equipment had grown to be more than twice as large as the market for separate audio components (see Exhibit 1). Analysts expected the trend toward integrated systems to continue, driven by advances such as home theater television, which linked big-screen video with surround-sound audio, or "plug and play" equipment, which required minimal setup by the consumer. In 1989, after 14 years of development, Bose had introduced the Acoustic Wave Music System, an integrated, portable, high-performance music system incorporating speakers, an AM/FM receiver, and a cassette tape deck. The product was oriented towards the high end of the portable audio market.

Manufacturing at Bose

It was well-recognized that speakers were among the most important parts of any audio system—if they were of poor quality, even the best sound systems would not produce high-quality sound. Speakers were judged on their ability to reproduce sound accurately, and sound reproduction depended on speaker design, the quality of materials used in construction, and careful attention to detail in production processes. Speakers were one of the most competitive

segments of the audio business, with dozens of manufacturers in the United States, Europe, and the Far East producing a diverse array of designs and technologies. Three subassemblies were the critical components of all speakers:

- **Transducer:** This part of the speaker produced sound waves when electrical signals from a stereo system caused a magnetic assembly to vibrate inside a paper or plastic voice cone. The traditional speaker had at least two transducers—a "woofer," generating low-frequency bass sounds, and a "tweeter," producing higher-frequency sounds.
- **Electronics:** Bose speakers had come to incorporate increasingly sophisticated electronics, including integrated circuit (IC) boards, that managed amplification and maintained a balance between bass and treble.
- **The cabinet:** As the speaker's exterior, the cabinet had to both direct sound waves from the speaker and be attractive in a home or car. Whether the speaker had a wooden or plastic cabinet, Bose maintained unusually high standards for exterior surfaces on its speakers. As one vendor said, "You can have absolutely no defects, and when I tell you no defects, I'm telling you not a tiny imperfection or a small speck of dirt. Nothing."

Bose headquarters were located 23 miles west of Boston in Framingham, Massachusetts. The company had three manufacturing facilities:

- **Westboro, Massachusetts:** The Westboro plant, located approximately 15 miles west of Framingham, was fully integrated—the plant manufactured printed circuit boards and transducers, and assembled finished speakers using electronics and transducers produced at Westboro as well as parts procured from outside vendors. The Westboro facility was the company's largest and most advanced production facility.

Exhibit 1

Annual Factory Sales of Consumer Electronics in the United States (in millions of dollars)						
	1984	*1985*	*1986*	*1987*	*1988*	*1989*
Audio systems	976	1,372	1,370	1,048	1,225	1,217
Portable audio equipment	1,191	1,140	1,389	1,469	1,547	1,595
Separate audio components	913	1,132	1,358	1,715	1,854	1,871
Autosound equipment*	2,500	2,761	3,135	3,523	3,937	4,125

Source: *Consumer Electronics in Review,* by Electronics Industries Association, Consumer Electronics Group.
*Car stereo equipment

- **Ste-Marie, Quebec:** The Canadian plant produced wooden speaker cabinets, and had world-class woodworking capabilities. Rather than assembling six separate pieces into a cabinet's sides, top, and bottom, Bose speakers used a complex construction which joined two three-sided, U-shaped pieces. This construction improved the sound quality of Bose speakers but required precise tolerances during production. The Ste-Marie plant had made sizable investments in computer-controlled machining centers for woodworking.
- **Carrick-Macross, Ireland:** The Ireland plant assembled finished speakers to support Bose sales in Europe.

Due to the company's rapid growth, two other manufacturing facilities were planned:

- **Hillsdale, Michigan:** The Hillsdale facility would specialize in making speakers for the automotive market, providing quick response to car makers, who were prone to tight schedules with frequent changes and who demanded short lead times.
- **San Luis, Mexico:** A facility was planned in Mexico to produce small, inexpensive "bookshelf" speakers as well as wiring harnesses, transducers, and circuit boards for other Bose plants.

In addition, the increasing success in the Japanese market caused some managers to wonder whether a manufacturing facility would soon become necessary in or near Japan.

Manufacturing Strategy

Tom Beeson saw a natural evolution in the products produced by each Bose plant; initially plants often only produced components only for other plants, but then became increasingly self-sufficient. Over time, plants were expected to expand their range of manufacturing capabilities, integrating forward to produce finished products and backward to produce as many of the components required for those products as possible:

If we were big enough, we'd do everything ourselves. Obviously, there are some areas we'd never integrate into, such as owning the steamships or the trucking lines that transport our speakers. However, if it's fundamental to the quality or performance of Bose products, then we want to control it.

Even when sourcing parts from highly capable vendors, Beeson saw three potential problems:

1. The vendor and Bose each had their own priorities and agendas. Consequently, Beeson believed that vendors usually wanted to provide parts that fit their capabilities and schedules, which were not necessarily the components that Bose needed.

2. A long-term relationship with a vendor producing components for Bose would allow that vendor to acquire whatever specialized capital might be desirable and develop particular expertise in manufacturing those parts. On the other hand, however, Beeson felt that relying on the vendor would preclude Bose from developing that expertise, and delay the process of establishing internal capabilities in manufacturing those parts.

3. Beeson believed that vendors would never understand the company's needs or organization as well as Bose employees, and that, if all the components of cost could be tracked accurately, it would almost always cost more to source a part externally than to make it in-house, as long as the volume was sufficient.

Corporate Procurement

In 1990, Corporate Procurement at Bose purchased materials totalling $300 million. As shown by the organizational chart (see Exhibit 2), Corporate Procurement was headed by Lance Dixon, director of Purchasing and Logistics. Dixon reported to Tom Beeson, vice president for Manufacturing; Dixon's background is described in Exhibit 3.

Corporate Procurement was responsible for locating new vendors and sourcing new parts. Vendors were typically involved early on in new product development efforts. For example, when Bose began to develop the Acoustic Wave Music System, Corporate Procurement contacted vendors of AM/FM tuners to obtain design advice and product specifications. Once tuner specifications were set, Corporate Procurement solicited bids, selected and qualified the best manufacturer (on the basis of quality, delivery, and price), and negotiated contracts specifying a variety of performance characteristics. After close supervision of an initial pilot order, the day-to-day management of purchases against the contract was turned over to the plant-level purchasing departments. According to Wayne Sauer, purchasing manager in Corporate Procurement, purchasing managers at the plants had the authority to change suppliers but,

We do our homework up front, and after screening we usually believe we've chosen the right supplier for them. But, if we haven't chosen right, the vendor isn't going to send them many bad parts and stay a Bose vendor for very long.

In 1990, four types of personnel were typically involved in the procurement process:

Design engineer: Design engineers established the specifications for new items, often in concert with vendor personnel.

Materials planner: Materials planners maintained factory inventories at appropriate levels, primarily by

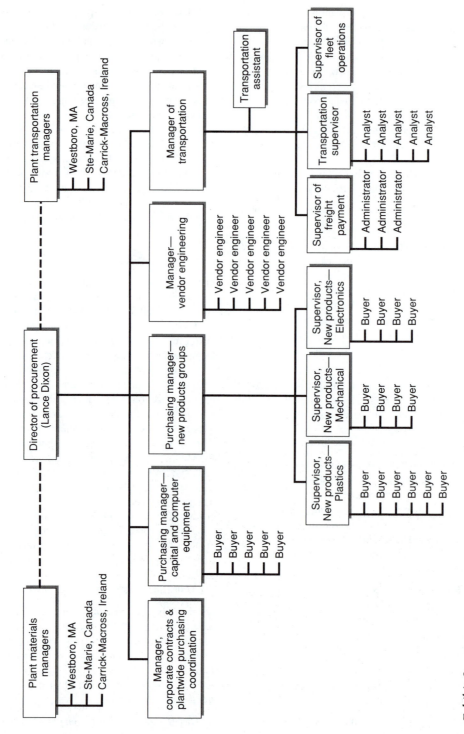

Exhibit 2 Corporate Procurement

Exhibit 3

Dixon's Background

After his discharge from the Marines, Dixon worked in a printing company and then went to Honeywell Corporation, where he managed an engineering support facility that performed printing and photographic lab work. Although Dixon was not in Honeywell's procurement department, he occasionally bought printed materials and noticed that these materials were often procured by people who did not work in Purchasing. As he recalled, "We had fragmentation in dollars, and Purchasing not carrying out its full charter in this area. We know that's done at a lot of companies, but that's not right."

Responding to his suggestion, management put Dixon in charge of centralizing the purchasing of printed materials. Later, when Honeywell bought General Electric's computer division, Dixon established a network of 12 warehouses to provide promotional support for the combined GE/Honeywell sales force. Dixon then was asked by Honeywell's corporate procurement department to help integrate the procurement policies of Honeywell's 14 divisions. Dixon recalled that "I spent three years there helping tie together procurement—a classic corporate procurement job, which I enjoyed."

While in this role, Dixon proposed to change the way nonproduction items were purchased. Honeywell management accepted the proposal and placed Dixon in charge of creating and managing a consolidated function to buy all non-production material for 12 Minneapolis-area Honeywell divisions. Dixon standardized prices with vendors and established consistent procurement practices.

After 14 years at Honeywell, Dixon became director of Purchasing at General Mills' Kenner division. In 1982, Dixon joined the Bose Corporation. In all his procurement assignments, Dixon had sought to establish more uniform procurement policies in all areas of spending activity. As he stated,

In production buying, Purchasing normally carries out the procurement role. However, in non-production buying, for half the companies of the United States the true purchasing department is not the formal procurement department, it's the department heads that have the budget money and take an interest in their lifeblood stuff, which includes items like printing. These department heads are merchandising managers, printshop managers, advertising managers, marketing managers, and sales managers.

---

indicating to the buyers when reorders would be needed. Materials planners worked closely with production planners, who scheduled production in Bose factories.

Buyer: Corporate buyers located items requested by design engineers, placed first-time orders for new items, and made one-time purchases of items such as capital equipment or computers. Plant-level buyers placed orders against contacts negotiated by corporate.

Vendor salesperson: Vendor salespeople visited Bose hoping to obtain orders from buyers, then met with their own manufacturing organizations to ensure that the orders were produced on time and to specifications.

The New Products groups, who monitored the supplier base to find technologies and components, were at the heart of Corporate Procurement. Engineers developing new products relied on them to find components that could meet design, performance, and cost standards. New Products also provided a conduit to incorporate vendor input in products under development.

Each New Products group was responsible for a specific set of commodities. *New Products–Plastics* focused on parts or components made of plastic, *New Products–Electronics* focused on electronics, and *New Products–Mechanical* focused on metal or mechanical items. Each buyer within New Products specialized in one of 37 commodity groups, such as aluminum extrusion, packaging, gaskets, stamping, die castings, or magnets.

The organization of New Products–Mechanical was representative of the New Products groups. Wayne Sauer, a mechanical engineer with experience in metalworking, was manager of New Products–Mechanical. Wayne supervised several buyers, including a mechanical engineer with expertise in manufacturing and mechanical assembly, and an electrical engineer with expertise in computer hardware.

Purchasing at Westboro

Until 1988, no purchasing had been done by the plants; instead, all items had been purchased by Corporate Procurement but delivered to the plants. By 1990, purchasing at Bose Corporation was more decentralized. The plants in Westboro, Canada, and Ireland did their own day-to-day purchasing, typically against contracts negotiated centrally. It was expected that the planned facility in Michigan would also manage its incoming material flow.

Each production line at Westboro had its own operations manager (see Exhibit 4) and support organization (see Exhibit 5). Jim Tabor, plant materials manager, reported formally to Walt Hussey, plant manager, and informally to Lance Dixon. (This was similar to the arrangement at other Bose plants.)

Westboro spent about $140 million per year on items purchased from an active base of about 200 vendors. About

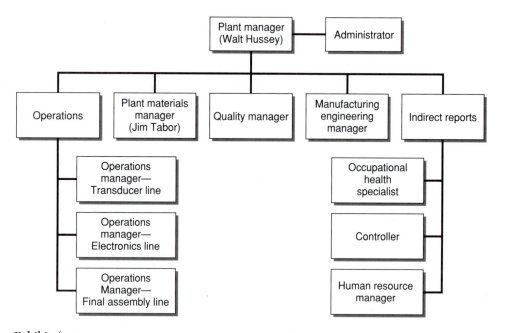

Exhibit 4   Westboro Plant Organization

50% of the plant's purchasing dollars were spent in five categories: electronic components, plastics, printing, corrugated boxes/packaging, and cables/cords. Purchasing was planned in a three-stage cycle:

- **Stage I: Business planning.** The marketing department at Bose Corporation prepared multi-year business plans.
- **Stage II: Aggregate production planning.** Based on the business plan, Westboro prepared a production plan that specified the capacity, tooling, and material volumes that would be needed over the next one to two years.
- **Stage III: Production scheduling.** Based on the aggregate production plan, schedulers at Westboro prepared a detailed "master schedule" outlining requirements for capacity, personnel, and material over the coming 12 months. Production for earlier months was scheduled at a greater level of disaggregation than for later months.

As Westboro materials manager, Jim Tabor coordinated scheduling, purchasing, and inventory. As shown by Exhibit 5, five people reported directly to him: an inventory manager, a warehouse manager, and three materials managers. The inventory manager was responsible for tracking and managing overall inventory levels at Westboro, while the warehouse manager oversaw the operation of the plant warehouse. Each materials manager performed the planning and purchasing to support one production line, and was

assisted by a production control supervisor, a master scheduler, and a purchasing supervisor.

Purchasing supervisors supervised a group of buyers who procured all materials for one production line. Buyers were responsible for managing quality, cost, and delivery. Unlike Corporate Procurement, most buyers at Westboro were not engineers, and instead had come up through the ranks as administrators or expediters. Buyers at Westboro typically started on easier commodities such as hardware or operating supplies, and then moved on to more difficult categories such as plastics and electronics.

Most of a buyer's time at Westboro was taken up by inventory planning which encompassed three activities: deciding what to order, placing new orders with vendors, and adjusting delivery schedules to accelerate or delay delivery on ordered parts. Another 15% of buyers' time was spent on revisions to existing parts; usually this entailed updating documents or ensuring that revised parts met quality levels. The remaining 10% of buyers' time was devoted to renegotiating contracts with existing vendors or, occasionally, switching to new vendors.

Westboro buyers preferred vendors who maintained a secure financial position, were located close to Westboro, could provide fast delivery, maintained consistent production processes (as measured by the use of statistical process control and a quality rating system); and provided good references through Corporate Procurement or other customers. The average lead time on purchase orders placed by

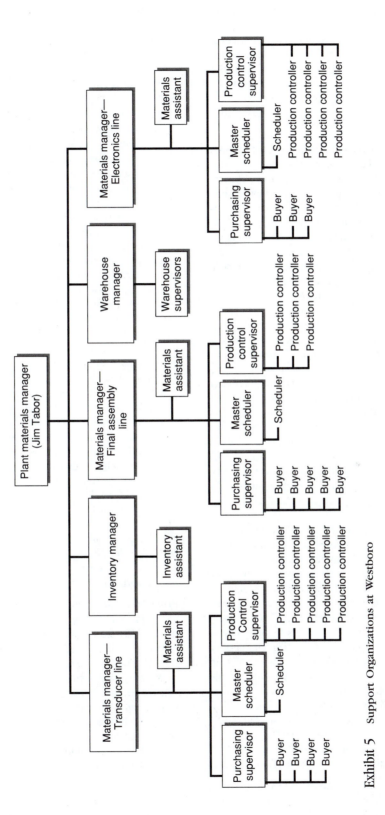

Exhibit 5   Support Organizations at Westboro

163

Bose Corporation was four to six weeks, but one-third of all purchase orders had less than 10 days' lead time. About 35% of all orders were changed within 30 days after placement.

The Evolution of JIT II

In the early 1980s, shortly after he had been hired by Bose, Lance Dixon requested that Corporate Procurement's budget be increased significantly to add more experienced buyers, upgrade the department's information systems, and develop global sourcing programs. Dixon promised a one-year payback on the funds requested, but his request was turned down because company resources were focused on efforts in Japan. As the company grew, Dixon found that every year he needed more people in procurement, and every year at budget time he fought with management over staffing levels.

Dixon and Joe Giordano, vice president for Finance, developed an alternative solution: put purchasing into "profit center mode." Wherever Dixon could drive expenses below standard costs, he would be allowed to reinvest half the savings back into the department's budget. If Dixon did not generate any savings, Corporate Procurement would maintain a level budget. As Dixon said, "I can get the people I need to do the job and not add anything to the payroll."

Dixon also instituted a program to pay cash incentives to buyers. Any time a buyer saved the company money on purchased items, the buyer received a cash reward, typically $100 to $300. This arrangement was patterned after incentive programs commonly found in sales departments. Awards were given for keeping monthly expenditures under standard cost, for unique ideas that led to cost savings, and for other exceptional efforts.

In 1990, Dixon proposed to change the relationship between Bose and certain vendors under a program he called "JIT II." Under JIT II, a vendor representative (the "rep") would replace the vendor salesperson, the Bose buyer, and the Bose materials planner and would be authorized to decide what, when, and how much to order for a particular range of products or services. Reps would determine order quantities, placing orders to their companies to supply Bose without Bose carrying unnecessary inventory. Reps would also provide engineering expertise in their commodity area and help solve problems on the production floor, much as a Bose buyer would. The reps would be stationed full-time at a Bose facility and would be empowered to use the Bose computer systems, but would be hired, evaluated, and paid by the vendor.

Dixon had recommended the commodity areas of plastics and printing as initial candidates for the JIT II program.

Plastics In 1991, Bose Corporation expected to spend close to $14 million on purchases of plastic components. Producing plastics to meet Bose quality standards required considerable experience and skill. Bose used 10 vendors for plastics; the top five vendors received 60% of the dollar volume. Dixon had recommended G&F Industries to be a JIT II vendor in plastics.

G&F's headquarters and plant were located in Sturbridge, Massachusetts, about 40 miles west of Bose headquarters. The company employed about 60 people and had total annual revenues of $12 million. Of G&F's 50 active customers, Bose was the largest account, providing about $2.1 million in annual revenues. The plastic components sold to Bose typically generated a 10% before-tax profit margin. G&F was owned by John Argitis, who served as president and CEO. Argitis had 15 years' experience molding plastic parts at American Optical; in 1978 he moved to G&F as vice president, and in 1986 he purchased the company.

G&F specialized in the production of injection-molded plastic parts. In injection molding, pellets of plastic resin were heated to a liquid state; the liquid was then injected into a mold where it solidified in the shape of the mold's interior. A typical injection molding machine cost up to $200,000; molds cost $75,000–$150,000. Molds were made to produce a part of a specific size and shape, although minor alterations were possible. Molds were typically paid for and owned by the customer.

On any particular job, set-up costs for injection molding could often be greater than the cost of machine operation. Set-up times averaged four hours to change resin colors (keeping the same resin material), six hours to change molds, and 17 hours to change molds, colors, and resin material. The set-ups were performed by highly-skilled technicians who were supervised by plastics engineers; after set-up, machine operation required less skill.

Even if G&F became the JIT II vendor for plastics, it was not clear that G&F would supply all the Bose plants. The facilities planned in Michigan and Mexico would use considerable volumes of plastics, particularly in speaker enclosures for Michigan. The two facilities could either source locally, or use parts that were purchased by Corporate Procurement but shipped directly to the plants.

Printed materials Printed materials included items such as instruction booklets, warranty cards, and promotional materials. In 1990, each Bose department sourced its own printed materials, with 12 vendors supplying printed materials to Bose Corporation. Dixon was concerned that the current decentralized arrangement allowed vendors to charge each manager a different price according to that manager's price sensitivity, and wished to establish United Printing as a JIT II vendor. United received only 12% of the company's overall printing business in 1990, so this would necessitate centralizing the procurement of printed materials. Dixon was concerned that the individual departments might object:

In terms of human relations, the consumer of printing has traditionally insisted that "I run an advertising department or merchandising department and I buy my own printing. Purchasing isn't going to tell me who to buy from." I expect we'll settle that down, and then a department manager will change and we have to go back to war for the next six months. The basic conflict is not with the JIT II program—the basic conflict is the fact that Purchasing's interested enough to want to buy printing.

The Management of JIT II

Neither Beeson nor Dixon was sure that vendors would be interested in participating in JIT II. A qualified rep might cost the vendor $80,000 per year (fully loaded). Dixon and Beeson planned to approach United after they knew whether G&F would participate.

Even if G&F did agree to participate, several issues remained to be resolved. Dixon felt that vendor representatives should be treated, in every respect, as Bose employees—to be listed in Bose telephone directories and have access to all Bose facilities, people, and computer systems. However, several Bose managers had voiced concerns about this arrangement. Some buyers felt that certain information, such as quantities and prices of parts bought from other vendors, should remain confidential—at least to provide an advantage during negotiations.

In the past, vendor representatives had typically worn badges that identified them as vendors, and were permitted

access only to approved locations within Bose facilities. Dixon proposed changing this policy; he advocated that the reps for JIT II vendors be issued badges just like Bose employees and be free to come and go as they chose.

There was also debate about how to ensure that vendors supplied goods at fair prices over the course of the relationship. Dixon felt that the company's previous purchases in a given category provided experience to evaluate vendor prices, but others argued that inflation or changes in raw material prices could quickly render this information obsolete. Finally, although Dixon wished to start the program with G&F and United, formal criteria for determining when and with whom to establish JIT II relationships had not been developed.

Finally, there were questions about how long a JIT II relationship would last in a company growing as rapidly as Bose. As Tom Beeson said,

There's always a conflict between purchasing and manufacturing. Lance wants to buy everything and I want to make everything. However, I don't want vendors assuming responsibility for what we should be doing ourselves. Does the JIT II program facilitate the process of moving into self-control, or does it delay that process?

◆ CASE 5 – 2: Rank Xerox France ◆

Heathrow, 7:30 P.M. The British Midlands flight is on time.

Claude Joigneault is feeling happy. The day spent at Rank Xerox's European headquarters has been successful. The Group's European logistics strategy has been tied up. The Just-in-Time management project has been accepted by the general management. The stakes are high, not only for the Group but also for Rank Xerox's French (RXF) subsidiary.

Claude is the Logistics Director at Rank Xerox France, and is in charge of defining and putting into practice the logistics equipment strategy for France.

The objectives are clear and the current situation and environmental factors are known. So the meeting he has organized the following morning with his project manager, Jerome, should enable him to move ahead on the design of the logistics strategy project methodology for the French subsidiary.

Saint Ouen 8:30 A.M. the following morning.

Claude Recalls the Objectives

1. Conformity of French Strategy and the International Logistics Strategy

The Group has decided to build a European logistics set-up based on a distribution network operating from a European center located in Venray in The Netherlands.

The new fundamental element is the setting-up of a Just-in-Time process between the Group's European subsidiaries to manage information flows, both downward and upward, and also physical flows.

The aim is to achieve the greatest potential flexibility in bringing the stocks to Venray.

2. Improving Customer Satisfaction

The Group's top priority is customer satisfaction.

Detailed analysis shows that a very satisfied customer is a loyal customer who displays blind trust in his supplier. This is an essential point when considering customers' repurchasing decisions of the Group's machines.

3. Cutting Logistics Costs and Machine **Assets**

At European level overall logistics costs come to 12%. Introducing the new strategy should bring this figure down to 8%.

As far as machine assets are concerned, the figure for Europe is 180 days. The aim is to get it down to 80 days. If the objective is reached, huge savings will be made because of the high cost of borrowing money.

Jerome Describes the Current Situation

1. The Distribution Network

The machines are manufactured in three European plants in Mitcheldean, Wales, Neuville-en-Ferrain, close to Lille, France, and Venray, Holland, not far from Dusseldorf, Germany.

Orders from European countries are centralized at European headquarters in Marlow in England. They are then sent to the plants according to a monthly, quarterly, or yearly supply and demand process.

The machines are delivered to each country through each distribution center according to production and/or the level of available stock. Delivery depends on the goodwill of each plant, their goal being to deliver as late as possible in the month.

France uses two warehouses. One is located at Garonor and has a capacity of 11,000 sq. meters where new and repaired machines are stocked. The other one is at Gonesse, has a capacity of 6,300 sq. meters, and is used for returned machines.

The warehouse at Garonor does not have a computerized management system. However, operations are managed through a bar codes system.

Machines are allocated to customers each day at Garonor and are entrusted to ten carriers who provide transport services through 21 regional platforms. The aim is that handling is done on the customers' premises, either by his team or by a subcontractor's team (see transport services, appendix 1). Two carriers provide specialized services, one in common carrier distribution, the other for products called electronic photocopying and printing systems.

The machines are collected by the same teams, the products are prepared on the regional platforms and sent to Gonesse once a month. Machines are sorted into categories depending on different criteria that allow the machines in good condition to be repackaged there and then, to take out parts that cannot be reused, to scrap obsolete products and to send those products that can be reworked back to the plant.

No forward return system has, up until now, been introduced.

Three carriers, along with their subcontractors, deal with 80% of the business.

2. Information Network

Products are sold through two networks. The first one involves direct selling, with a direct sales force approaching public and private major accounts and an indirect sales network comprising 150 Rank Xerox sole agents mainly targeting the mass market.

The direct sales force transmits their details of contracts to the sales secretary, who validate and enter them into a system called SOFIA as they arrive. The agents send in their orders by MINITEL, the French viewdata system, entering the information at their offices via a system called JERI.

Each night all orders are interfaced with the stock machines, in a system called MISTRAL, using a logistics system bearing the name ACCORD.

ACCORD is a recent system featuring functions allowing for the advanced integration of the logistics system with the accounting, invoicing, stock, order follow-up and customer service (after sales) systems.

As soon as a contract is deemed to be ready to install, and given that there is a machine available at Garonor, a preparation request is issued in the morning and the warehousemen can start dealing with the order. A bar code system carries out the complete task of dealing with the order, i.e., machine allocation, batch installation, and accessories for a given contract.

Follow-up of the different stages of the product's progress in the logistics chain is done through the RITA system, a computerized reporting system on MINITEL, reception on platforms, planning and delivery. All Rank Xerox France people involved may call up information about the contract on their screens and see where the contract has got to, ordering, delivery, setting up the machine, etc.

The process for collecting machines is the same, data entry is SOFIA and transmission of collection papers to the corresponding service provider. The information is entered into the same computerized information systems.

No information system links Rank Xerox France to other European sites, not even to headquarters in England.

Electronic information exchange projects in the immediate future are not in vogue. Their implementation can only be envisaged in the long term, given the huge investment they entail.

3. Personnel

At Garonor 49 people are employed in logistics. The break-down is laid out as follows:

Handling (warehouse)	21
Transport and customs	7
Supply demand	14.5
Management, development, secretarial	4.5
Budget and management control	2

At Gonesse 39 people handle returns.

Handling and packaging	11
Repackaging machines	13

Parts repairs and cannibalization	3
(detaching parts for customer service use)	
Production and quality control	4
Administration	
Management and secretarial staff	5

4. Volumes

See Appendix 2. Machine returns amount to roughly half of the whole volume distributed.

5. Costs (in French francs)

Transportation	46,515
Personnel (salaries, taxes on salaries, temporary staff)	20,967
Warehouse costs (including maintenance)	8,209
Information system (share allocated by RXF data processing department)	4,400
Miscellaneous	3,388
TOTAL	83,479

Preliminary studies show potential gains in productivity. One example concerning a single moving operation at Garonor shows a gain of 150 francs. Excluding top of the range products, productivity gains are expected to be 66%.

Return handling costs amount to approximately 175 francs and productivity costs associated with returns are estimated to be 52%.

6. Assets

Stock level calculated in millions of francs and number of days of stock are set out in appendix 3. The results are in line with targets established by the current organization structure.

7. Customer Satisfaction

Results appear in Appendix 4. Achieved levels are satisfactory and correspond to a favorable position compared to other functions in the corporation.

A comparative study taking into account competitors' performances is being carried out and will give an idea of where the service provided should be positioned on the market.

8. Prices

Invoicing by carriers is done each month, and prices are fixed on the basis of product and department (geographical administrative areas in France).

The number of price references is very high indeed, and control is, therefore, long and arduous.

Claude Reviews the Environmental Factors That Must Be Taken into Account in Any Study

1. European Considerations

The JIT strategy has been adopted by the Group. It is based on the following considerations:

- Centralizing stocks in a European center at Venray in The Netherlands. Stocked products are neutral, in relation to allocation of batches for each country.
- An electronic information system supports the strategy. The implementation of a European information network including information exchange between all sites, whether they be plants, distribution, or operational centers. The system will allow for automatic dispatch of order quantities to Venray, to have Venray deliver equipment directly to national central sites, to provide all information needed for reception in the systems of equipment in transit and to make information about the progress of any one operation available instantly.
- Defining a project for machine returns with a view to optimizing re-use of machines (spare parts, re-packaging, and scrap). This strategy includes the environmental protection rules based on the most advanced in Europe, the German *Blue Angle* system.

2. French Considerations

Provide a *faultless service* process including the possibility of customer service differentiation, capacity to deliver products in 48 hours, integration of end-of-month peaks, when 40% of all movements happen in the last three days of the month and continuing to offer services to customers outside the Group.

3. Product Range

Rank Xerox France labeled as *The Document Company* sells a product range made up of the following:

- Products at the very top of the range such as electronic photocopying systems or electronic printing systems, specially customized products made to customer requirement. It is at Mitcheldean and Lille that they are made. Orders come in by electronic mail.

Preparing the systems is a complicated process. They often include several elements that are either assembled beforehand at one of the plants or put together by customer service technicians on the customer's site.

Market expectations concerning delivery are three to four weeks.

- Regular Photocopiers, which come in an entire range going from 12 to 100 copies a minute and weighing between 40 and 300 kilos.

Delivery times are approximately one to three weeks, depending on the importance of the product in the range.

- Commodity products, which cover a great variety of products, small printers, fax machines, personal copiers weighing less than 30 kilos.

Delivery times usually go from two to five days.

Some of these products are provided by suppliers from outside Rank Xerox, mainly from supplier distribution centers located in France. Quantities of these commodity products are naturally high compared to those in the first two categories.

The first category accounts for 1% of all movements, the other two share the rest.

4. Planning

Rank Xerox's experience in implementing new logistics strategies shows that a new project requires a study lasting two months to be carried out. A further month should be dedicated to having it adopted by the different functions and general management and two months for joint labor management instances to give it their go-ahead.

A bidding process takes four months and changing carriers takes another three.

Setting up a JIT process demands about a year's work, and implementing a stock management system takes six months.

Questions

You are Jerome and are in charge of the new strategy project. At the end of the meeting your objective is to present the project, and in particular:

1. The physical and information organizational diagram representing current flows
2. Diagnosis of the current situation
3. Likely developments, given the aims that have been fixed and the European and French orientations
4. The key issues, recommended scenarios, rejected and retained scenarios per logistics category
5. Scheduling and implementation
6. For services sub-contracted outside the firm, draw up the specifications and make a list of both qualitative and quantitative selection criteria
7. Description of the JIT process, short-term information transfer solutions, and your long-range recommendations
8. An analysis of the project's cost/profit ratio
9. The communication and information plans given the economic consequences, the effect on industrial relations and the process of change

Appendix 1
Carrier Services

Product Type	Service Required	
Commodity Product	**Parcel delivery** Unpacked equipment delivered to customer's premises	Customer's company Reception No after-sales service required
Top-range photocopying Electronic photocopying and printing systems	**Delivery to premises** Equipment (except for fax machine) unpacked on customer's premises, ensure that delivery matches customer's order, and in some cases, elements assembled	Customer's office Xerox after-sales Installation by Xerox and customer training by Xerox
Middle-range photocopying	**Start up** Equipment unpacked on customer's premises, elements assembled and product tested	Customer's office Xerox after-sales Customer training by Xerox
Bottom-range photocopying Bottom of the range fax machines	**Installation and demonstration** Equipment unpacked on customer's premises, accessories assembled, machine tested and demonstrated	Customer's office Comment faire vos copies. . . . No after-sales service required

Appendix 2
Volumes Distributed per Regional Platform (Units and Weight)

M = Mitcheldean
V = Venray
L = Lille
H = Hors Groupe

Regional Platforms	Units					Weight (T)				
	M	V	L	H	TOT	M	V	L	H	TOT
PARIS (5)	8712	8895	2211	4577	**24396**	1474	1148	1204	100	**3927**
LYON	1565	1519	315	862	**4262**	248	173	170	19	**610**
CLERM FERRAND	335	313	53	190	**890**	50	32	27	4	**113**
GRENOBLE	676	665	129	368	**1839**	105	77	64	8	**254**
MARSEILLE	1026	984	188	571	**2768**	158	108	99	12	**377**
NICE	666	618	101	380	**1765**	98	61	52	8	**220**
COLMAR	1112	1054	190	634	**2998**	170	109	102	14	**395**
NANCY	499	475	85	279	**1338**	75	51	43	6	**176**
LILLE	1907	1795	298	1078	**5077**	282	184	149	24	**639**
ROUEN	1203	1099	186	697	**3185**	179	105	105	15	**405**
REIMS	269	252	42	152	**715**	40	26	21	3	**90**
NANTES	1396	1320	224	786	**3726**	208	138	112	17	**475**
POITIERS	767	703	112	444	**2026**	112	67	60	10	**250**
ORLEANS	590	563	99	330	**1583**	89	60	50	7	**206**
TOULOUSE	863	799	133	494	**2289**	128	79	71	11	**288**
BORDEAUX	937	852	130	545	**2465**	136	79	70	12	**297**
MONTPELLIER	537	503	79	304	**1423**	78	51	38	7	**174**
TOTAL	23068	22411	4573	12692	**62744**	3630	2549	2437	277	**8894**

Appendix 3
Assets

Type	In Millions of Francs	DOS (Number of days of stock)
Brand new	91.8	15
Renovated	21.6	6
Returns	102.6	31
Loans/Trials	21.6	6
Total	237.6	58

Appendix 4
Customer Satisfaction in percentages
Overall Results in France (from 90-day study)
over the last 9 quarters

Indicator										
Equipment available to meet required time	VS + S	87.4	92.9	87.0	90.4	92.9	96.2	97.6	94.5	90.2
	VS + S + A	95.1	96.5	96.1	96.6	98.4	98.5	99.4	98.1	96.1
Punctuality of delivery	VS + S	85.2	90.1	86.2	89.0	92.8	93.9	95.7	91.3	89.0
	VS + S + A	93.7	94.4	94.0	95.0	97.3	97.4	98.8	93.4	95.9
Equipment matches orders	VS + S	93.8	96.5	94.8	94.2	96.2	97.2	98.2	97.3	96.9
	VS + S + A	97.3	97.6	97.5	97.7	98.6	98.7	99.4	98.7	98.4
Completeness of delivery	VS + S	93.4	96.7	94.7	92.8	96.3	96.5	97.7	96.0	95.8
	VS + S + A	96.9	97.8	97.3	96.9	98.7	98.4	99.5	99.0	98.0
Delivery teams behavior	VS + S	91.0	96.9	93.6	94.3	95.1	96.9	98.2	94.3	95.1
	VS + S + A	97.8	98.7	97.9	98.3	98.0	98.9	99.3	98.0	98.4
Time between delivery and installation	VS + S	87.3	91.4	86.3	89.9	93.0	94.5	95.7	92.5	92.2
	VS + S + A	95.1	95.6	94.7	96.0	97.5	97.6	98.6	97.7	97.1
Installation time	VS + S	89.5	94.3	91.1	91.3	94.2	95.9	96.5	94.7	95.7
	VS + S + A	96.4	96.9	97.3	97.1	98.2	98.0	98.6	98.9	98.9

VS - Very Satisfied   S = Satisfied   A = Acceptable

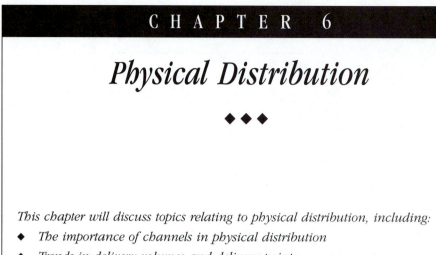

CHAPTER 6

Physical Distribution

◆ ◆ ◆

This chapter will discuss topics relating to physical distribution, including:

◆ *The importance of channels in physical distribution*

◆ *Trends in delivery volumes and delivery points*

◆ *The architecture of a physical distribution network in a global network*

◆ *Third-party logistics firms: evolution and trends*

◆ INTRODUCTION

In the previous chapter we dealt with the dimension of the logistics system that involved inbound logistics—the process of moving raw materials from the initial point of acquisition through to the production process. In this chapter, we discuss the process of moving products from the end of the production line through the distribution cycle, into the hands of the final customers (i.e., physical distribution). Naturally, these two processes and flows (inbound and outbound) cannot be studied independently of one another, as they are integrally linked. Such separation promotes *local* optimization (i.e., optimizing just a segment of the logistics system), as opposed to the desired global optimization that incorporates all the potential linkages that involve the satisfaction of customers. It is only for convenience in this exposition, then, that we separate the inbound from the outbound. Also, outbound logistics presents particular characteristics that deserve analysis in further detail. Outbound logistics has been studied under different functional perspectives previously, with a concentration on the marketing function for its impact on physical distribution.

Marketing literature has identified the importance of including distribution channels in the elaboration of physical distribution networks of finished goods. Indeed, the choice of a distribution channel is fundamental for two reasons:

• The type of channels chosen affects all other variables in the marketing mix, one of which is physical distribution.
• The choice of distribution channels commits the firm for a long period of time.

Hence, it becomes apparent that questions of marketing and channels of physical distribution must be considered simultaneously.

Once the distribution channel is defined, a company must identify the paths that goods should take to best serve the logistics and sales structures. This is the job of defining the physical distribution network. The network is comprised of logistics resources that include warehousing facilities, different means of transportation, and inventory. Warehousing facilities currently can perform many functions that go beyond stocking goods and order preparation—that is, product customization and assembly, and pre- or post-manufacturing. Hewlett-Packard, for example, uses some of its distribution centers to assemble orders for European customers, delaying until the last moment the differentiation (i.e., by postponing) of power supply and instructions.

Regarding different means of transportation, we not only have the option of mixing platforms (i.e., changing from rail to truck or vice versa) but also the expanded alternatives of using new modes such as the channel-tunnel (Chunnel) linking England and France. Through the Chunnel, a company in the south of Italy can transport goods nonstop to northern England. Such new alternatives can require restructuring of the physical distribution in a global scale.

Warehousing and transportation are undergoing major changes as more companies adopt global logistics and operations management systems. The functions linked to the warehouses and the geographical area they cover are constantly being modified. Deregulation and other economic forces have wrought considerable change in the transportation sector, as well. Finally, inventory management has and will continue to be the easiest way of separating the different steps before getting to the customers. The challenge is to optimize the utilization of inventories through the new managerial approaches such as Just-In-Time to rationalize the financial investment that they represent. The distribution network, then, is the outcome of the combination of these factors.

This chapter provides the elements for understanding the relationships between management of flows and channels of distribution. It also looks at trends in warehousing and transportation that affect the architecture or design of a distribution network in the process of globalization. Finally, it will elaborate on the recent trends that we see in the use of logistics providers more commonly known as *third-party logistics* (3PL) firms.

◆ THE IMPORTANCE OF CHANNELS OF DISTRIBUTION IN PHYSICAL DISTRIBUTION

Distribution channels have been the subject of significantly important theoretical developments from different schools of thought. There are mainly three distinguishable approaches: the functional, the consumer utility, and the postponement and speculative model.

The *functional* view of distribution channels relates to the interorganizational models that focus on the mechanisms that regulate relations between organizations. The unit of study may be a given function (marketing, production, or logistics), the channel as a whole, a dyad (couples like producer/distributor or manufacturer/wholesaler), triads (one producer and two competing distributors), or one section of the channel in its relation to its environment. Generally speaking, customers' desires and needs are considered as exogenous variables to which channel members adapt. The functional model attempts to answer two basic question sets:

1. What is the most efficient functional mix (allocation functions between intermediaries)? What is the most efficient combination of functions in economic terms? How should functions be allocated between producer and distributor? For example, should freight and warehousing be entrusted to one sole agent, should

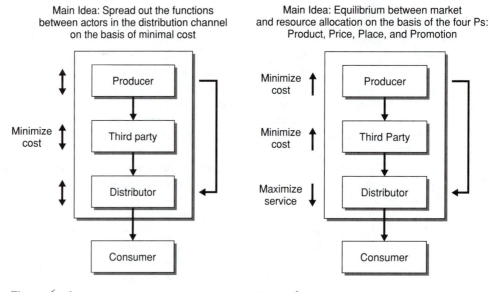

Figure 6–1   Functional Model   Figure 6–2   Consumer Utility

they be taken on by a producer or distributor, within their own structures, or should they be contracted out to a logistics service firm (see Figure 6–1)?

2. What bearing does this functional mix have on the channel's structure in considerations such as number of tiers, number of intermediaries in each tier, and number of channels and intermediaries?

The channel structure depends on the answers to these questions and will assume the following characteristics:

- **Length.** How many intermediaries are there?
- **Width.** Are there one or many intermediaries on a given tier in a defined geographical area? One intermediary constitutes exclusive distribution; several intermediaries create selective distribution. Many intermediaries create intensive distribution.
- **Multiplicity.** How many types of channels are employed to carry the product?

The *consumer utility model* uses notions of marketing mix (Figure 6–2). It emphasizes the role of differentiated marketing functions according to a market segment. These models rely on microeconomic paradigms, the focal point of which is the equilibrium between market and resource allocation.

Marketing management's role is to reach maximum profit objectives by finding the optimal combination of decision-making variables. The analysis is done based on the price, product, promotion, and place variables of marketing.

Finally, the *postponement and speculative model* puts forth an analysis of the intermediary's margin associated with the degree of risk related to speculative gain (see Figure 6–3). Two antagonistic concepts are derived from the model:

Main Idea: Optimize the organization of
the channel by minimizing costs and risks
for producers and distributors.

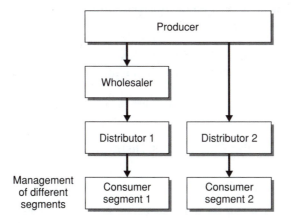

Figure 6–3   Postponement and Speculative Model

- Postponement allows product differentiation to be put off by building up inventory as late as possible—(that is, orders taken at the nondifferentiated, semi-finished inventory stage (e.g., the Hewlett-Packard example described before).
- Speculation involves transforming the product as early as possible in order to achieve economies of scale. Electing to do this involves taking the greatest economic risk.

Regardless of the model used, distribution channels should be analyzed from the perspective of the powerful player—that is, who has the bargaining power for controlling the distribution channel. In that sense, we see an increasing shift toward retailer concentration that limits the access producers might have to the end customers. In any distribution system, retailers represent manufacturers in front of customers. That, by itself, requires a complex set of relationships between players at different levels because the logistics system is not owned by one company but by many different organizations that may have different objectives.

The challenge in this complexity is to find the right set of mechanisms for cooperation, coordination, and control. Then, for example, in the beer industry the bargaining power is in the hands of the producer, because the brand is the powerful element—Anheuser-Busch has more power than wholesalers and retailers because of the pull generated by customers. In the car industry, on the other hand, dealers are very powerful because they hold the key to access to customers, and they understand the preference of a particular region. Market deregulation now allows a particular dealer to carry brands that compete (e.g., a particular dealer could have dealerships of Ford and GM autos at the same time). In fact, the recent trend is toward creation of mega-dealers.

According to a report in the *Economist* (March 4, 1995), distribution channels are facing an interesting process of restructuring. There is a significant trend toward big retailers. For example, in the supermarket industry, the market share of America's top-ten stores in 1987 was approximately 23 percent, while in 1993 the market share was close to 30 percent. In the home improvement industry (e.g., Home Depot) the market share for the top-ten stores went from 15 percent in 1985 to 28 percent in 1993. For toy retailers, in 1987 the top-ten stores had 28 percent of the market share; in 1993, Toys Я Us had by itself close to 25 percent.

The interdependence among players in a channel sets the stage for potential conflict. Some conflicts in channels of distribution may turn out to be beneficial, while others may be disastrous for most of its members. Interdependence means that the results for each firm in a channel of distribution depend on the behavior of the other members. There are several causes of this interdependence:

- Functional specialization of the partners (functional approach)
- Operational interdependence—i.e., each firm needs inputs provided by other channel members
- Ownership of limited resources and power (bargaining power)

Logistics Position in the Channels of Distribution

The Notion of Logistical Families

In any one economic sector, the huge number of possible distribution channels join a host of producers, distributors, wholesalers, sales representatives, and others. This complexity makes it impossible to build a single physical distribution channel. Rather, it is a question of creating differentiated ones in the framework of logistical families.

Logistical families are products grouped together into homogeneous categories. They have in common their satisfaction of identical requirements in terms of flow management.

For each family, a logistical path can be defined, with the simultaneous objective of optimizing the overall flows and those flows associated with the given logistical family. In distribution logistics, the two main segmentation criteria of logistical families usually are delivery time, which is greatly conditioned by the choice of transport mode and inventory position, and order profile. As an example, a particular company might have four logistics families based on the following matrix for orders:

		Low	High
Number of units ordered	High	TYPE 2	TYPE 3
	Low	TYPE 1	TYPE 4

Required delivery time

Putting logistical families into effect in an organization demonstrates a degree of maturity in the management of flows. It translates into a more detailed approach to product distribution, and the establishment of several flow processes, rather than a single process applied to all products.

It is essential to define common or shared diagrams between different channels of distribution in order to minimize the overall logistics economic cost. It is also vital to create a dynamic, multisegment way of looking at channels.

Trends in Delivery Volumes and Delivery Points for Channels of Distribution

Distribution channels are facing an interesting process of restructuring, trending toward consolidation of market power with a handful of mega-retailers. Market trends change the distribution channels and patterns for every firm over time. These changes generate changes in logistics responses as well.

In the following two figures, we present trends observed in Europe. Figure 6–4 shows the evolution of retail sales in France. It is interesting to observe the relative strong growth of hypermarkets sales from 1984 onward, the linear growth for supermarkets, and the unavoidable decline in sales of all other types of retail options.

Figure 6–5 illustrates the changes for a European manufacturer of dry food. Over a six-year period, the figure shows the breakdown of change in sales volumes and the number of deliveries made according to channels of distribution. These channels include the traditional one (small stores), supermarkets, warehouses, and so on. Here, a channel of distribution is taken to mean the type of point-of-sale and the underlying sales structure.

Fluctuations in volume significantly change the number of delivery points. The curve in Figure 6–6 shows that in less than fifteen years, the number of delivery points in France used by a large, international, fresh products importer decreased from 70,000 to 1,000. This change reflects the emergence and phenomenal expansion of deliveries to distributors' warehouses (15 percent in 1980; 85 percent in 1995). Inevitably, it has an impact on producers' physical distribution networks.

In summary, there are two main trends occurring here. Developments in distribution channels have led logistics and operations management to change from a stable environment to one that is in a state of continuous change. This situation has influenced the purpose of logistics and operations management. The solutions devised today to ensure the flow of goods are anything but long-lasting. Companies must create capabilities for just-in-time reconfiguration of goods flows so they can respond to changes in distribution channels on a real-time basis.

Logistics and operations management, as a result, have changed from being designed to exploit a static system to being primarily responsible for dynamically reconfiguring the systems they use. This trend has prompted a modularization of logistical resources, a move that has made reconfiguration much easier to implement.

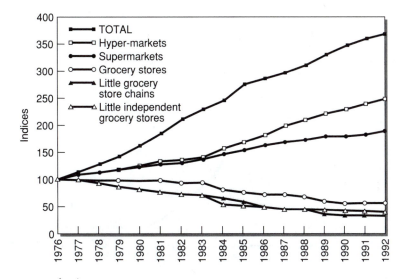

Figure 6–4 Evolution of retail sales in France. Growth in the use of hypermarkets has been replacing the little grocery stores.

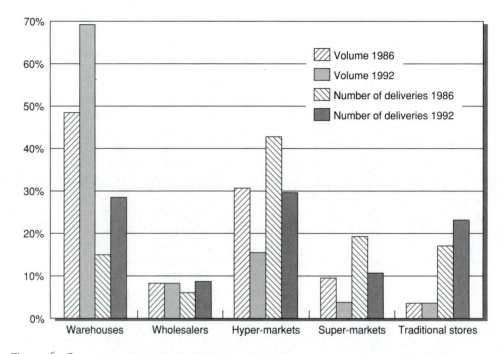

Figure 6–5   Changes in volume and number of deliveries per distribution channel for an European distributor of dry food.

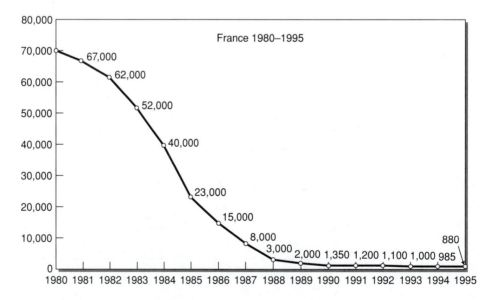

Figure 6–6   Evolution of the number of delivery points

The logistical answers that develop rely entirely on the maturity of the logistics distribution channel, which constrains the options concerning the management of flows. The general trend, however, is toward a growing maturity of these channels. In that sense, there are opportunities for separating the role of logistics—which is mainly to move the products through these mature channels—and the procurement process itself—which requires negotiation of price breaks and quantity discounts. Therefore, we see companies willing to either manage or outsource the pure logistics function and negotiate the purchasing prices. For example, supermarkets impose on many of their suppliers the transportation mode to be used. Some retailers have their own distribution centers or require suppliers to ship directly.

The shift in power toward the retail trade has increased opportunities for partnerships and use of information technology. We discuss logistics information technology at length in chapter 10.

◆ THE ARCHITECTURE OF A PHYSICAL DISTRIBUTION NETWORK IN A GLOBAL OPERATIONS APPROACH

The evolution of the structure of distribution channels requires a similar evolution in suppliers' logistical structures. Reconfiguration of logistical facilities along one distribution channel can only be carried out if the problems posed upstream and downstream are fully comprehended. To illustrate this point, we cite the process followed by a large producer of fresh goods in Europe in a situation where tonnage increased, the number of delivery points decreased, and sales price dropped at the same time (see Figure 6–7).

Logistics operations costs have become critical determinants of profit margins. Moreover, companies are tailoring their industrial strategy based on specializing production to benefit from economies of scales. Paradoxically, such a strategy generates increased logistics costs. In twenty-five years, the firm in Figure 6–7 reduced its number of plants by three and increased the number of items produced at each site by twelve (through expanded range). Today, 95 percent of items have only two possible manufacturing sources. For this company,

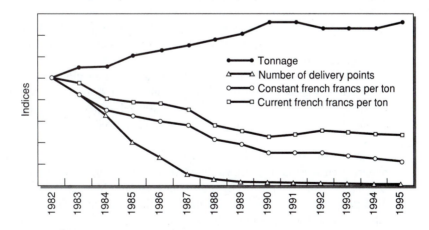

Figure 6–7   Evolution of distribution indicators for a large producer of fresh goods in Europe during the period 1982–1995. The indicators include tonnage (increasing), number of delivery points, and sales price in French Francs, which are decreasing.

physical distribution has undergone profound changes to reflect evolution both upstream and downstream.

- From 1960 to 1975, retailers were delivered from 100 distribution centers managed by the producer. This meant that producers had to set up their own complex logistics operations.
- From 1980 to 1984, the producer started delivering to the distribution center of the supermarkets. Producers' distribution centers were cut to a maximum of one per administrative department in France, including some direct deliveries for big-volume deliveries. Logistics operations consisted, then, of three different parallel organizations. Producers' logistics still included fifty self-managed distribution centers.
- From 1984 to 1986, the whole system was destabilized by two movements, upstream flows and downstream flows. Plants started specializing their activities, and distributors started exploiting the potential of running their own logistics operations, which leads to an increase in the share of products delivered to distributors' warehouses.
- From 1986 to 1992, the logistics organization was transformed with a new set of roles and definitions: Five regional platforms self-managed and three regional platforms subcontracted. The functions of these facilities amounted to flow management, preparation of orders, and dispatching. The wholesaler was responsible for the order-taking and invoicing. The distributor's warehouse was responsible for order consolidation.
- Finally, between 1993 and 1995, the number of sites diminished to four self-managed and two subcontracted facilities. Mixed central logistics facilities were shared between producers and distributors.

This last development of mixed logistics facilities shared by producers and distributors is known as *mutualization,* or the sharing of logistics facilities by two or more supply chain partners. Mutualization is an innovation that stems directly from a global logistics approach. These central logistics facilities function by concentrating flows and preparing the entire order processing according to destination. Their average surface area in Europe is 3,500 square meters with an inventory value of just two days. In this context distributors order every day. An average order includes between forty and sixty listed articles, or 230 cartons, or 800 kilograms.

This transformation is made possible by a concerted global approach with producers, wholesalers, logistics service companies, and retail distributors collaborating closely on logistics matters. Total logistical costs are assessed, depending on the physical distribution scenarios, so that the ensuing profits may be calculated, and ultimately shared, among the actors.

The logistical reconfigurations have far-reaching consequences for the producer— requiring changes in logistics facilities, reduction in force and retraining of personnel, and development of integrated data processing systems. More and more firms are looking to third-party logistics firms to help with these changes. This is one of the reasons behind the rapid growth of logistics outsourcing business.

The case we have just presented is not unique, particularly in the context of several Efficient Consumer Response (ECR) approaches. But the great difficulty of implementing such solutions nevertheless is worth noting.

Specialization of Logistics Facilities

The first change logistics facilities experienced was an extension of the areas they cover. Warehouses, in the same way as manufacturing facilities, tend to specialize. In France, for example, most distributors in the convenience goods market have specialized their warehouses by type of product: dry goods; fresh goods; beverages and seafood. Some warehouses fulfill their function not only at the national but at a European level—for example, one facility will store and manage seafood products for the entire European continent. This same type of consolidated warehouse approach can occur in the world market as well, where a warehouse might store the inventory of C or slow-moving service parts for worldwide distribution.

The physical distribution structure depends entirely on the behavior of the distribution channel and the sales strategy a producer selects. Figure 6–8 shows the evolution of the types of warehouses used by one of the leaders of European food distribution. The type of warehouse used depends on the geographical area covered and the purchasing strategies vis-à-vis their suppliers.

At a time when retail outlets covered a smaller area, direct deliveries were the only reasonable choice in matters of procurement. At a later stage of its development the area the firm covered and its capacity to distribute large volumes led it to use big storage warehouses to make the most of so-called speculative purchases (goods bought in promotion) while at the same time generating inventory.

The next stage saw a diversification of the concept of its stores. Stores' surface areas were cut from 10,000 square meters to a network of outlets whose surface areas were no more than approximately 3,500 square meters. The number of listed articles, around 10,000,

Number of Outlets	8 local	11 regional	53 multiregional	79 national
Inventory automatic reordering				5%
Dispatch warehouse			40%	75%
Speculative warehouse		10%	10%	10%
Direct shipment	100%	90%	50%	10%
	1971/1988	1989/1994	1995/1997	1997

Figure 6–8   Evolution of the type of storage used by one of the leading European food distributors. The type of storage and number of outlets depends on the geographical area covered and the purchasing strategies of their suppliers.

remained the same, however. The entire floor space of each store was dedicated to selling. The "back room" storage area was eliminated. This set-up brought with it the need for a new type of warehouse—warehouses that specialized in cross-docking. In this kind of a network, store orders are consolidated and sent as a block every day to suppliers. Suppliers, in turn, deliver to the flow-through warehouse, which puts together each store's orders as soon as they are delivered from the supplier. The distributors' warehouse delivers to the final destination.

Finally, another form has been developing, that of the automatic reordering. Although it will not affect the latter warehouse concept in its layout, it influences the way orders are made because the check-out counters will, in part, automatically trigger orders.

The Evolution in Freight Resources

An important element of the architecture of physical distribution is the role played by freight providers. The whole freight market has undergone much deregulation over a period of several years. Deregulation, in turn, has facilitated the emergence of new networks and solutions to meet shippers' requirements. As early as 1977, the Airline Deregulation Act in the United States and the 1984 Canadian deregulation allowed airlines to set up hub-and-spoke systems. A host of mergers ensued. Similar changes occurred in both the rail and trucking sectors in the United States, under the Staggers Rail Act and the Motor Carrier Act of 1980.

Reacting to these changes, companies like IBM appointed a logistics vice-president and four area logistics managers with operational responsibility. Tenders for freight services were made worldwide, contrary to previous practice, whereby each country had the autonomy to negotiate deals as it saw fit.

Because goods in transit use different means of transport, which combine railroad, air, highway, sea, and river transport, companies must develop transferable logistical units—specialized pallets, containers or mobile crates that make the transported goods homogeneous to a degree and that allow rapid transfer from one mode to another. This is why we can talk about the growing diffusion of a modality of freight, which characterizes the use of several rather than one mode of transport (i.e., intermodal).

Globalization of physical distribution can lead to the judicious mass treatment in economic terms, but can also jeopardize the need for a degree of service called *proximity service*. Proximity distribution should enable the customer to get deliveries in the afternoon when an order is placed on the morning of the same day, and in the morning when the order has been placed on the afternoon of the day before. It favors the local wholesaler, which may well go against the sales strategy of the producer. This type of demand is typical of the spare-parts market, for example, and illustrates how global and local logistics are complementary. The question is all the more difficult to resolve when it comes up in densely populated urban areas. Then, the question of management of traffic congestion arises along with the possibility that it will cause the flow of goods to be slowed down.

The first question is to find out how far the system of proximity distribution has been properly conceived to satisfy the manufacturer's sales strategy. What is needed, therefore, are solutions that allow the local logistic level to be respected. Oriented toward short-term service, these solutions could be:

- Possible use of the manufacturer's sales network if it exists (e.g., opticians' retail outlet, tire manufacturers, etc.)
- Setting up proximity distribution centers (PDCs) (typical PDC has a surface area of 1,000 square meters storage space and 100 square meters office space)

- Setting up inventory of class A products with a storage operator, a distributor, or an agent
- Relying on express services and dispatch orders from a central place

It is necessary to carefully measure the financial consequences of the solutions just noted—that is, cost of floor space, personnel, inventory express dispatch services. These solutions complement the global physical distribution approach that we outlined earlier.

◆ LOGISTICS SERVICE FIRMS AND THIRD-PARTY LOGISTICS (3PL)

With the increasing recognition of logistics as a source of potential competitive advantage by companies, there has been a rapid growth in the logistics service industry. Many contract logistics companies report annual growth rates of nearly 50 percent. These firms make up a branch business in its own right and offer a wide range of quality services at lower cost compared to the performance of the same services in-house. Outsourcing of freight operations, storage, order preparation, final delivery, and pre- and post-assembly activities fulfills two needs:

1. It improves service levels by improving flexibility and inventory management, thereby leading to greater availability.
2. It reduces costs in many cases.

The services provided by logistics service firms and third-party logistics (3PL) fall into a framework that combines both physical (i.e., warehouse and transportation) and management services. As the complexity and customization requirements of the different companies increase, the integrated nature of the logistics and the specific companies that offer them also increases. Figure 6–9 divides these services into four different types: *basic services,* which do not require major coordination (e.g., typical U-Haul); *physical contract logistics services,* which allow for outsourcing of some of the physical services while the company still maintains control of the management; *management contract logistics services,* which subcontract the management of an existing warehouse or transportation fleet; and *integrated contract logistics,* which incorporate both the physical service and the managerial functions under the logistics provider.

Advantages and Disadvantages of 3PL

In the United Kingdom, distribution costs at the end of the 1980s amounted to between 12 percent and 15 percent of sales. In 1991 this figure had dropped to 5.2 percent. Such savings came from economies of scale and compensation for seasonal effects. Third-party logistics firms in the United States and Europe have enjoyed rapid growth.

Indeed, 3PL business is taking on an increasingly global flavor. Third-party firms more and more are asked to take charge of regular flows internationally, and not just the urgent delivery of packages. That is why firms like TNT have set up their own logistics subsidiaries, TNT Logistics, which recently won the contract to distribute all Fiat parts throughout Europe.

Having access to third-party logistics companies has given rise to an important debate about their value added. Some view them as yet another source of competition, whereas

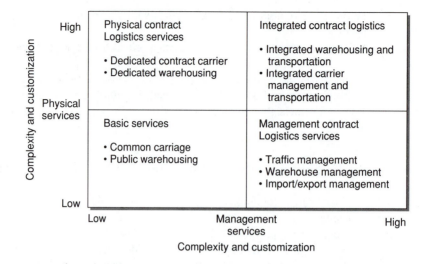

Figure 6–9   Classification of services by Logistic Service Providers
Source: J. M. Africk and C. S. Calkins (*Transportation and Distribution*, 1994).

others assume a loss of control over physical operations. Use of 3PL service providers can allow a company to:

- Penetrate new markets
- Reduce the inherent financial investment risks associated with owning logistics assets like trucks and warehouses
- Coordinate producers and distributors within a global approach
- Access new technologies and innovative solutions—e.g., data and telecommunications technologies, sophisticated warehousing operations, or new delivery options

There are many examples to illustrate the previous points. Marks and Spencer, the U.K.-based retailer, started operations in France from a logistics site built by Exel Logistics. Retailer Laura Ashley gained access to the mail-order and catalog business through an alliance with Federal Express. TNT provided a solution to an automobile parts supplier in the UK with a single point of control, flexibility of loading units, and night trucking. Hewlett-Packard (HP) has been able to handle the return of the disposable cartridges for printers through an arrangement with UPS in which the user simply drops the used cartridge in any UPS mailbox and all the expenses are paid by HP.

Fritz Companies, a successful logistics provider based in the United States, handles the procurement (from Asia) and distribution (including labeling and bar codes) of Christmas ornaments for a big retail chain in the United States. Fritz also established an agreement with General Electric and Lucky Goldstar to support the logistics and order-fulfillment operations for new products, spare parts, and return logistics in the local Hong Kong market. In cooperation with General Motors, Fritz handles warehousing and distribution functions for after-sales parts and accessories in Taiwan. Finally, in cooperation with Apple Computers and several Apple Suppliers, Fritz manages parts and components from different suppliers in Asia for JIT delivery to the manufacturing plants in the United States.

Use of third-party logistics providers is not a risk-free proposition, however. In fact, there are many built-in risks when outsourcing logistics to a third-party firm:

- **Strategic risk.** A producer with a competitive advantage in its internal logistics operations afforded by its ability to deliver to big European cities in less than two hours runs the risk of losing this advantage by working with a 3PL firm. The service firm might offer the same service to the manufacturer's competitor, with the aim of covering investment costs.
- **Commercial risk.** The manufacturer's image will inevitably be linked to that of the service firm.
- **Management risk.** Costs and the real level of service provided must be visible for both the producer and the service provider.

This explains why calling on outside services for logistics requires a company to develop control functions based on data flow (see chapters 10 and 12). Data collected serves to check that the service promised has been carried out as agreed in the contract.

The practice of using logistics providers varies greatly from one country to another. In the United Kingdom we mentioned that it accounted for 70 percent of the distribution market, whereas in Germany and France the figure stands at only 15 percent.

The content of operations subcontracted and the contractual legal frameworks also differ enormously, as the following examples show. For example, in the United States it is possible to arrange for short-term use of public warehouses (30 days) without a contract in a multi-user system. In Europe, the typical storage contract for a producer or a distributor is for a period of two or more years.

By offering increased short-term flexibility at lower cost, logistics service firms are viewed as essential partners. A number of firms, after using third parties, decide against their future use and reintegrate the functions back into their companies.

According to a 1995 survey by Mercer Management Consulting, the most frequently cited benefits from using 3PL services in a sample of the 500 largest American manufacturers include: lower cost (38%), improved expertise/market knowledge and data access (24%), improved operational efficiency (11%), improved customer service (9%), ability to focus on core business (7%), and greater flexibility (5%).

Why and When to Outsource

The main debate about 3PL is deciding when to outsource the logistics service. It is very hard to quantify the medium- or long-term impact of using a 3PL. In most cases the situation reduces to a simple calculation of transportation costs savings. But, as we discussed, the impact goes beyond simple cost reductions.

One of the main prerequisites for a successful "partnership" with a logistics provider is an understanding of the *base case*. The base case is defined as the situation the company presents *before* the arrangement with a 3PL in terms of the metrics it considers relevant for its performance.

Often companies engage in arrangements with 3PL expecting improvements in metrics that were not even clearly defined before any engagement. Deciding when to outsource logistics services is based on four dimensions: company needs (i.e., is logistics a core competence?), tangible values (i.e., are there any measurable advantages?), management commitment, and provider capabilities. Clearly, the first three dimensions involve an understanding by the company as to *why* it should consider outsourcing. This question is probably more important than *when* to outsource, because it involves an overall evaluation of the entire logistics system, including both inbound and outbound implications.

◆ SUMMARY

This chapter shows how the physical distribution system is closely linked to distribution channels chosen by firms. Marketing choices for these channels and the ensuing logistical characteristics of the actors in the distribution channel influence the conception and, ultimately, the network management, which are made up of logistical facilities and means of transport.

Warehouses, in particular, are undergoing major changes due to the increasing specialization, the greater breadth of services demanded by customers, and changes in the geographical areas they cover. At the same time, the means of transport adopted have changed considerably under the influence of deregulation in Europe and the United States. These changes have reconfigured the way physical distribution operates in the United States as well as in the rest of the world. In particular, the level of concentration into big retailers has changed the number of retailer points and the entire dynamic of the outbound logistics process.

Finally, we consider the new trend in companies worldwide to outsource logistics services with what is known as third-party logistics (3PL). Previously regarded as mere subcontractors, they now enjoy the status of full suppliers. Doubtless, using third-party logistics providers offers numerous advantages to companies. Caution is advisable, however, as these companies cannot always provide the level of value expected. Some mechanism for measuring the value added by a 3PL is important before making any decisions.

DISCUSSION QUESTIONS

1. What are the conceptual models used in understanding the structure of distribution channels?
2. What are logistical families? What are the main trade-offs associated with the choice of products that form a logistical family? What criteria would one use in forming a logistical family?
3. Name some of the market trends that affect the structure of logistics networks and the choice of distribution channels.
4. Define the term *third-party logistics* (3PL). What are the advantages and potential disadvantages of using 3PL services by a firm involved in global operations activities?
5. List the main criteria you would use in choosing a 3PL service for some (or all) of your firm's logistics needs.

REFERENCES

Africk, J. M., and C. S. Calkins. 1994. Transportation and distribution.

Angelmar, R. 1988. Conflicts in channels of distribution. INSEAD, Fontainebleau, 1988.

Bence, V. 1995. The evolution of a distribution brand: the case of Exel Logistics. Cranfield University, WP 8/95.

Bence, V. 1995. The changing market for distribution: implications for Exel Logistics, Cranfield University, WP 7/95.

Bowersox, D. J. 1986. Logistical management, 3d ed., New York: Mcmillan Publishing Co.

Council of Logistics Management. 1993. Reconfiguring European logistics systems. Oak Brook.

Harrington, L. H. 1996. Logistics assets; Should you own or manage? *Transportation and Distribution* (March): 51.

Lieb, R. C. 1992. The use of third-party logistics services by large American manufacturers. *Journal of Business Logistics* 13(2): 29–42.

Mallen, B. 1977. Principles of marketing channels management," Interorganizational distribution design and relations, Lexington, Mass:/D. C. Health, Lexington Books, p. 353.

Ploos van Amstel, M. J. 1986. Physical distribution and product characteristics. *International Journal of Physical Distribution and Materials Management* 16: 14–36.

Randall, H. L. 1994. The Logistics Handbook.

Rao, K., and R. Young. 1991. Traffic congestion and JIT. *Journal of Business Logistics* 12(1).

Reve, T., and L.-W. Stern. 1979. Interorganizational relations in marketing channels. *Academy of Management Review* 4: 405–416.

Sheffi, Y. 1990. Third party logistics: Present and future. *Journal of Business Logistics* 11(2): 27–39.

A Survey of Retailing, *The Economist,* March 4, 1995.

Zin, W., and R. E. Grosse. 1990. Barriers to globalization: Is global distribution possible? *International Journal of Logistics Management* 1(1): 13–18.

◆ Case 6−1: Apple Computer's Supplier Hubs: A Tale of Three Cities ◆

In June 1994, Clark Winchester, the director of Apple Computer Incorporated's Sacramento site (the Sacto OPS Center), called a meeting to discuss the need to boost manufacturing capacity at the site in order to meet rapidly growing demand for its desktop PC and server PC products. One major issue to be resolved concerned how to free up at least 60,000 square feet of space for more production lines. As Clark put it, "This is the kind of problem which all manufacturing organizations like to have—the challenge of growth."

It was agreed that the action that would have the least negative impact on daily operations and customer service was a reduction in the volume of raw materials (purchased components) stored at the site. Materials could be stored off-site in bulk, with frequent replenishment of inventory kept on the production line to feed production. Four alternatives for decreasing on-site components inventory were identified:

- Establishing a company-managed warehouse nearby
- Contracting for warehousing with a logistics company
- Having suppliers establish a local source of supply by manufacturing or stocking the components they supply locally and delivering them using a kanban/JIT program
- Contracting with a logistics company to implement a supplier hub

A supplier hub is an arrangement in which multiple suppliers stock material that they have manufactured and that they still own in a shared warehouse close to the customer's site. The warehouse is managed by a logistics service provider, typically a freight forwarder. The supplier hub concept is based on the premise that each supplier is responsible for providing a responsive, local source of supply, and that there are advantages to sharing a facility with other suppliers and to having it managed by a local agent, the freight forwarder. The supplier hub alternative was particularly intriguing because it provided the additional benefit of allowing Apple to decrease the amount of inventory on its books, by negotiating with suppliers to defer payment for incoming materials until the day of use.

As a result of the meeting, Lori Amador, head of Sacto OPS's Supplier Management Organization, was given the task of analyzing the four alternatives and reporting back in early August. Lori assembled a team of people from Apple OPS's supplier management, transportation, and logistics organizations, as well as from the corporate-level supplier management organization, to work on the project. The team would also gather inputs from Apple's existing supplier hubs and from suppliers.

Background on Apple and the Sacramento OPS Center

Apple Computer, Inc. was founded in 1975 in Menlo Park, California. Apple grew rapidly during the 1980s by steadily upgrading its product offering with new PC products incorporating innovative technologies such as icons, menu-driven software, and the mouse. In the late 1980s, competition in the PC market intensified, as IBM and other makers of IBM-compatible PCs entered the market. In the early 1990s, as growth in the U.S. market slowed to about 15% per year, Apple found itself struggling to maintain market share. To continue to compete effectively, Apple focused on two strategies: R & D investment to generate a steady stream of new product introductions and cost reduction to maintain or improve margins while reducing prices. Major R & D investments in its Power PC and Newton products ate into Apple's billion-dollar cash reserve. Apple's sales volume grew to about $8 billion in 1993.

In November 1992, in an effort to decrease distribution and service costs, Apple moved its North American distribution center and service operations from the San Francisco Bay Area to a new site in Sacramento, California. Apple later decided to establish an "OPS Center" in Sacramento, and to move final assembly, test, and packout of its desktop and server PC to the Sacramento site, as well. Co-location of manufacturing and distribution improved response time to customers. Apple opened its manufacturing operations in Sacramento in June 1993. By June 1994, continued sales growth had led to a severe space shortage at the site.

The main challenge for the Sacramento OPS Center, as for all of Apple's manufacturing/distribution operations, was to meet growing, yet uncertain, demand for the various models, while minimizing inventory levels and cost. Key to achieving this goal was excellence in ramping up production of new products and managing the discontinuance of obsolete products. Due to the uncertain demand, the site also spent a fair amount of effort reconfiguring dealer inventory when stocking levels of various models became unbalanced.

Apple used four performance measures to track effectiveness with respect to inventory: inventory turns, dollars of inventory as a percentage of cost of goods sold, number of days of inventory on Apple's books, and obsolescence costs.

Apple's First Supplier Hub—the Cork Facility

Apple implemented its first supplier hub in 1991 near its manufacturing facility in Cork, Ireland. The hub stocked component parts used in the assembly of PCs for the European market. PCs made and configured in Cork were then shipped either directly to customers or to Apple's European distribution center in Apeldoon, Holland. The logistics service provider that Apple used was Irish Express Company, a local freight forwarder. Before the implementation of the hub, Apple stocked component parts on-site. Apple paid its suppliers for components upon receipt by its warehouse. Thus, Apple owned the four weeks of supply of inventory stocked at its site.

Once the hub was implemented, Apple did not take title of component parts until they were pulled from the hub for delivery to Apple Cork's production line. This shifted inventory ownership from Apple to suppliers. Apple was able to defer payment for component parts until the day of use, under a system that Apple called the "Apple Computer JIT Supply Program." Since the supplier hub was a bonded warehouse, duties on parts coming into the European Community were also deferred until the day the material was used. Materials were delivered to the supplier hub under the classification "Delivery Duty Unpaid" (DDU). Duties ran as much as 6% of material cost, depending on the component type.

Apple Cork realized three major benefits from the Cork hub. First, by deferring purchase of component parts, Apple shifted the carrying cost of raw materials inventory to suppliers. Second, by deferring payment of duties, Apple saved an amount equal to the interest on the duties for the period of deferment. Last, by deferring purchase of component parts, Apple paid lower prices for component parts. This resulted from the fact that prices of computer parts decreased steadily over time, sometimes by as much as 10% per quarter, depending on the component type. (Apple negotiated pricing on an ongoing basis with its suppliers.) Through these three benefits, Apple was able to reduce its cost of goods sold by 2–3%.

Apple Cork required suppliers to set up a "local source of supply." Apple Cork *recommended* the Irish Express hub, but didn't *require* suppliers to use that company. (The majority of suppliers did choose Irish Express.) Shipment through the hub was an arrangement between the supplier and Irish Express; the contract was between these two parties and did not involve Apple. Suppliers paid for freight into the hub and for storage and material handling at the hub. Irish Express provided an information system that allowed suppliers to track material through the international shipment process. Apple Cork asked and received permission from Irish Express and from suppliers to access the computer system and the particular screens that showed information on parts destined for Apple Cork.

Some suppliers later used the fact that they had a local source of supply in Ireland as a selling point for doing business with other computer and electronics companies who had plants in Ireland. For example, one supplier eventually set up shipment of parts from the hub to six local customers. Since the hub was viewed as a supplier warehouse, customers were not concerned about having their parts stocked in the same warehouse as those destined for competitors.

Most of Apple's suppliers did not have sales or manufacturing operations in Ireland, so did not pay income tax in Ireland. One concern in setting up a local source of supply was to avoid setting up a sales operation, as defined by Irish tax law. Suppliers were able to do this by listing Apple as the consignee (ultimate recipient of the goods) for the shipment. In this way, the parts stored at the hub were viewed by tax authorities as goods in transit and not as goods owned by suppliers to be sold in Ireland.

Apple Cork steadily increased the number of components that flowed through the hub. By June 1994, about 30% of all component parts (in dollar terms) flowed through the hub.

Apple's Second Supplier Hub— the Fountain, Colorado, Facility

Apple opened a manufacturing facility in Fountain, Colorado, in mid-1992 to manufacture its new Powerbook line of laptop computers. The Powerbook line was extremely successful—*Newsweek* named it Product of the Year. With rapid demand growth came a rapid growth in inventory levels, and the Fountain site soon found itself short on space. Fountain began to store trailer-loads of material in its yard, an expensive proposition.

In January 1993, Apple decided to build some of its desktop PCs in Fountain, as well. In conjunction with this decision, Apple notified the company that was assembling literature kits for Apple on-site using 1500 square feet of space that it would have to find its own space elsewhere. Apple started to reexamine its space utilization.

Shaun Connolly, a senior logistics analyst, was aware of the supplier hub that had recently been implemented in Cork. In mid-March, Shaun presented a one-page *white paper* to the plant manager and his staff, suggesting that Fountain implement a hub. The plant manager authorized Shaun and a buyer to spend a week in Cork reviewing the Cork process, organization and contractual issues. When they returned, Shaun organized a project team including finance, receiving, warehousing and procurement. The project had three goals:

1. Free up space at the Fountain site by developing a local supply base with deliveries to the Fountain site every shift
2. Reduce inventory on Apple's books
3. Defer payment to suppliers until material was pulled for use by production

The team developed a Request-For-Proposal (RFP) and sent it out to thirteen logistics service providers. The RFP was a "vanilla" RFP, intentionally vague. The RFP asked providers to propose a creative solution that would potentially include management of all incoming international freight and customs for the Fountain facility, as well as some type of local off-site warehousing. Apple was hoping to find a provider that had already developed and implemented the processes Apple required.

Apple did not find such a provider—the supplier hub concept was too new. Apple eliminated several providers as either noninternational, too expensive, or "promising the world" without having the necessary capabilities or commitment. In late April, Apple chose Fritz Companies, Inc., an international freight forwarder based in San Francisco. Although Fritz had not implemented anything like a supplier hub, Fritz was investing heavily in information systems and had a team of industry specialists who understood computer industry logistics needs. Apple was currently using Fritz as one of several freight forwarders for freight coming in from the Far East. Irish Express was Apple's second choice. (Apple's main concern about Irish Express was that it did not own and operate in the United States.)

Fritz's Background

Fritz Companies, Inc. got its start in 1933 when Arthur J. Fritz founded a customs brokerage business in San Francisco. Over the years the company grew to provide a broad range of services worldwide. The 1993 annual report describes Fritz as follows:

. . . *Fritz Companies, Inc. is a leader in Global Integrated Transportation Logistics services and related information services for importers and exporters worldwide. The Company's principal services include international air and ocean freight forwarding, warehousing and distribution, customs brokerage and other value-added-services for the international movement of goods.*

Fritz in 1993 served 20,000 clients through a dedicated staff of 3,140 and a worldwide network of 121 offices and affiliates. Fritz also had 500 dedicated partners around the world. Revenues in 1993 rose 37% to $342 million, while net income rose 33% to $14 million. Revenues came from four types of services: customs brokerage (21%), ocean freight forwarding (37%), airfreight forwarding (34%), and warehousing and distributing (8%).

Fritz went public in 1992, and listed its stock on the NASDAQ exchange. Although Fritz was a public company, Lynn C. Fritz, the son of the founder, the chairman and CEO of the company, was very much still in charge. Lynn was known in the industry as a charismatic leader and as an innovator who believed that the company's mission was to become the primary or exclusive supplier of worldwide logistics to a growing customer base. In his 1993 letter to the stockholders he emphasized the company's commitment to invest heavily in its infrastructure of information systems, personnel, and facilities.

The Hub Process at Fountain

In early June, Apple identified four part numbers of one commodity type to flow through the Fountain hub. Moving inventory of these four part numbers to the hub would free up enough floor space to allow installation of two additional production lines at Apple's site. Based on Apple's estimated purchase volumes, Fritz leased 30,000 square feet of warehouse space at a site 25 minutes from Apple's site.

Component parts flowing through the supplier hub under the new "JIT Supply Program" were known as "hub materials." Most hub materials were purchased from suppliers in Asia. Hub materials were generally shipped by ocean, to reduce freight costs, but were shipped by air if there was an urgent need for the parts. Apple specified a default shipment mode (i.e., ocean, air, or some split of the two) for each commodity and supplier. Apple buyers then advised Fritz of changes in shipment mode, as needed. The transit time by ocean and by air were typically four weeks and one week, respectively.

Under the hub process, Fritz coordinated both material flows and information flows and acted as the customs broker. For international shipments, three Fritz entities were involved—one at the port of origin, one at the port of entry, and one at the Sacramento hub. Fritz arranged transportation using as many as four carriers over the various shipment legs. Thus, including Apple and the supplier, as many as nine organizations were involved in making a single shipment (Exhibit 1). Since Fritz coordinated the efforts of the nine organizations, from Apple's point of view there were only three entities involved: Apple, the supplier, and Fritz.

Fritz invested heavily in upgrades to its information systems in support of the supplier hub project. The result was FLEX, an innovative system that was used to track hub material as it flowed through the process. The process started when a buyer at Apple placed a purchase order (P.O.) on the supplier. A copy of the P.O. was faxed to the Fountain hub, who then entered the P.O. into the FLEX system. The quantity ordered then showed up on the summary screen for that part number under the status "On Order." The FLEX system tracked the status of hub material through seven categories (Exhibit 2):

- On Order: P.O. entered
- Booked: Units of transportation capacity reserved, not yet shipped
- In-Transit: Shipped from supplier, customs entry not yet filed
- At Customs: En route, customs entry filed
- Inland transit: Picked up at port of entry, en route to Fountain
- At the Warehouse: Received by the warehouse, in stock
- Released from the Warehouse: Pulled for delivery, en route to Apple's manufacturing site

FLEX had an additional category for defective material. Inventory held in this status could not be pulled for production. This inventory was also physically segregated.

Customs clearance was done electronically using information available in FLEX. For ocean shipments, the customs entry was filed five days before arrival at the destination. For air shipments, the entry was filed after take-off on the last leg of the flight.

Fritz personnel updated the information in FLEX as hub material flowed through the process. Since Apple's buyers had access to FLEX via terminals on their desks, they had full visibility of all material in the pipeline. This "womb-to-tomb" tracking was a breakthrough for Apple Fountain—previously, material that had been shipped from Asia was tracked by hand and did not show up on Apple's system until receipt by Apple in Fountain. It was as though the ship sailed off the end of the earth and reappeared four weeks later. The system became especially valuable when a problem arose somewhere in the pipeline and shipment was delayed. Apple and Fritz always knew which entity had possession of the material and so could avoid a time-consuming tracing process.

In order to simplify the process, shipments through the hub (both inbound and outbound) were made in full pallet quantities. This worked well, except occasionally when a quality issue arose. For example, if a supplier had a quality problem and sorted good material from bad, removal of bad units could leave pallets that were not fully loaded. This could cause an inventory discrepancy. These discrepancies had to be tracked manually.

Financial flows were as complex as information flows (Exhibit 3). Apple paid for all freight, freight management and brokerage costs, while suppliers paid for warehousing and material handling fees at the hub. If material was held in the hub for more than 14 calendar days, suppliers paid for additional warehousing. Exceptions occurred when supplier-caused problems resulted in emergency air shipments or when close-in reductions in the Apple build plan caused excess inventory to be held at the hub. These exceptions usually required some negotiations. While Fritz paid for basic insurance at the hub, suppliers paid for supplemental insurance. Fritz performed "standard" inventory management functions such as weekly cycle counts and inventory reconciliation, and sent inventory reports to suppliers regularly. As the warehouse operator, Fritz was liable for pilferage.

Contract Issues—the Supplier Hub Services Agreement

Implementation of the supplier hub required the amendment of existing contracts between Apple and each supplier. This amendment took the form of a three-way contract titled the "Supplier Hub Services Agreement," which was signed by Apple, Fritz, and the supplier. As stated in the agreement, the purpose of the agreement was

. . . to clarify the respective rights and responsibilities of Supplier, Apple and Fritz with respect to the application of

Exhibit 1a

Material and Information Flows for a Shipment from a Supplier in Penang to the Supplier Hub in Fountain

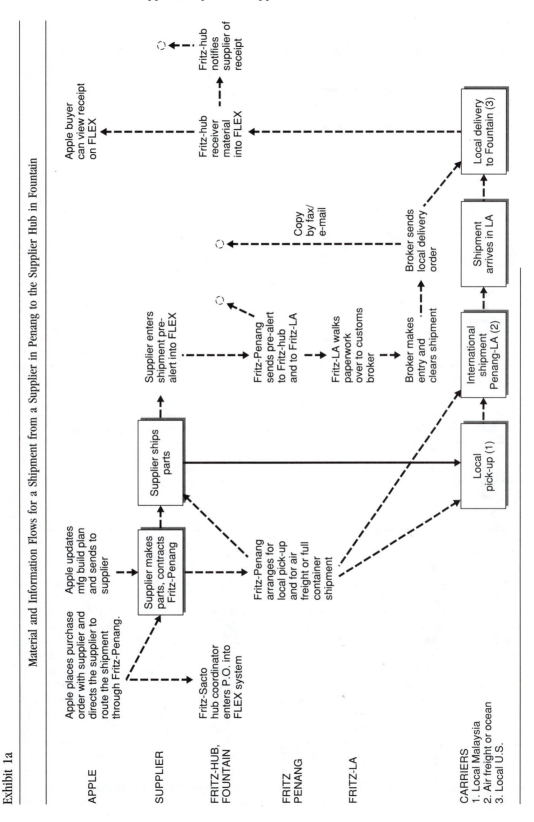

Exhibit 1b

Material and Information Flows for a Shipment from the Supplier Hub in Fountain to the Apple Production Line

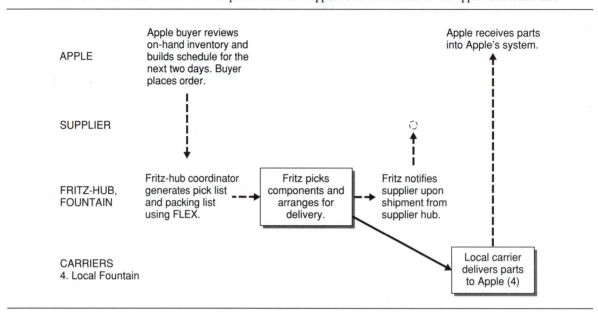

Exhibit 2

FLEX Inventory Tracking System—Sample Screen for Tracking Material Status for a Given Part Number

Client Part: 69A7		Description: 400 Meg Hard Drive	
Vendor Part: 7227		Description: HDSK 400 Mg.	

On Order	Booked	In Transit	At Customs	Inland Transit	At Warehouse	Rlsed from W/H
25,551	20,000	875	1,000	125	500	1,000

---

the Apple Computer JTT Supply Program to Apple's operations at its Fountain, Colorado site and to clarify certain procedures by which Apple will procure various goods it purchases in connection with its operation. . . . The purpose of the program is to facilitate JIT deliveries from Suppliers to Apple at its Fountain Site.

The base agreement included amendments to the terms of sale, payment and delivery, transfer of title, insurance and liability. It specified Fritz as the transportation agent and detailed the services that Fritz would perform related to operation of the hub and delivery of material to the Apple site. It specified the responsibilities of the supplier and of Apple regarding inventory levels at the hub. Last, it specified documentation and invoicing procedures.

Negotiating an agreement with a supplier took about three months. Since it was an amendment to an existing two-way supplier contract, Apple Fountain's Procurement Specialist for the particular commodity took the lead. Once a particular supplier and commodity were targeted, Apple Fountain's Procurement Specialist, Fritz's National Account Executive for the Apple account and the manager of the supplier hub visited the U.S. representative of the supplier. At the initial meeting, they presented the hub concept and the base agreement. Apple and Fritz then worked through the supplier representative to negotiate customization of specific contract terms with the supplier. As part of the negotiation process, representatives from the supplier visited the hub to inspect and qualify the hub's physical processes and information processes.

There were several issues that might require extensive discussion. First, suppliers were concerned about the legality of the purchasing and import terms, with regards to U.S. Customs law. Under existing contracts, Apple purchased

Exhibit 3

	Billings Associated with Hub Material Flows		
Trigger Event	*Parties Involved*	*Nature of Billing*	*Basis for Rate*
Delivery to port of origin	Local carrier bills Fritz	Local drayage	
Customs clearance	Fritz bills Apple	Brokerage fees	Per customs entry
		Freight management fees	Number of containers, with a cap at 10 containers
Customs clearance (ocean carrier under Apple service contract)	Ocean carrier bills Apple	International freight	Number of containers
Customs clearance (air)	Air carrier bills Fritz	International freight	Cubic feet of freight
Customs clearance (air)	Fritz bills Apple	International freight	Cubic feet of freight
Receipt at hub	Local carrier bills Fritz	U.S. drayage fees	
Receipt at Apple's dock	Local carrier bills Fritz	Local drayage fees	
Receipt at Apple's dock	Suppliers bill Apple	Materials	Units of material
Monthly	Fritz bills suppliers	Warehousing and material handling fees	Number of pallets of flowthrough
Periodically	Insurance co bills suppliers	Supplemental insurance fees	Dollar value of goods insured
Special Cases:			
1. Emergency air freight due to supplier problem	Apple bills suppliers	Additional freight cost	
2. Supplier material in hub more than 14 days	Fritz bills supplier	Additional warehousing cost	Per pallet-day
3. Supplier material in hub more than 14 days due to a close-in decrease in Apple's build plan	Supplier bills Apple	Additional warehousing cost	Per pallet-day

product at the origin, took title, and acted as the importer of record. This was standard in the industry. Under the new agreement, Apple purchased the product and took title upon shipment from the supplier hub to the Apple site. Although the supplier still owned the material during customs clearance, Apple acted as the importer of record. (Apple did so because Apple was the party that employed Fritz to manage transportation and customs clearance.) As in the process used by Apple Cork, goods were delivered under a "DDU" status. In contrast to Ireland, however, under U.S. Customs law creation of a bonded warehouse was not necessary for deferral of duties. Although the Fountain hub process was legal under U.S. Customs law, it was not the standard operating procedure, and suppliers were initially uncomfortable with it. One or two suppliers insisted on being the importer of record.

Second, some suppliers customized their products at their U.S. manufacturing sites. In these cases, the product flowed through the hub as hub material, but Apple purchased the product with a U.S. port of origin. The disadvantage of this was that Apple had no visibility of the material during the international shipment.

Third, some suppliers had a close relationship with their existing transportation provider. One of three types of transportation arrangements for hub material might eventually be used:

1. Apple purchases the transportation, and uses Fritz as the provider.
2. The supplier purchases the transportation, and uses Fritz as the provider.
3. The supplier purchases the transportation, and uses another provider.

Last, suppliers balked at paying for supplementary insurance for product in-transit and in the hub. Eventually, most suppliers agreed to pick up these costs.

Crisis Point at the Fountain Hub

In developing the hub concept, Fritz set a pricing strategy that was designed to run the hub at break-even and to make a profit from management of inbound air freight and customs clearance for components Apple sourced in the Far East. Investments in information systems and travel were considered to be investments in Fritz's capabilities and in the relationship with Apple, and so were not included as costs in the break-even calculation.

Based on Apple's forecast of material purchases, Fritz did a rough 12-month profit-loss analysis for the hub, assuming that suppliers would be charged $25 per pallet for handling and storage. The projected flowthrough of hub material started at 200 pallets per month in August, and ramped up to

800 pallets per month by November. The hub capacity was estimated to be about 1200 pallets of flowthrough per month, assuming 14 days of storage. Per Fritz's analysis, the hub would become profitable by the fourth month and would break even at the end of the seventh month. Fritz estimated that in the fourth month of operation, revenues from the supplier hub, and from air freight/customs clearance would be about $20,000 and $300,000, respectively.

Most of the implementation went fairly smoothly. Fritz had the building outfitted and available by mid-August. The freight management rates were finalized in early September. The information systems became available in two phases, with completion in September and October. This actually took more effort and more time than Fritz had originally projected. Fritz estimated the MIS development costs at about $50,000 and travel costs at about $50,000.

One activity that took much longer than expected was the negotiation of the three-way "Supplier Hub Services Agreement" between Apple, Fritz, and each supplier. One problem was that at first only two of the original four targeted suppliers agreed to ship through the hub. Two Japanese suppliers had long-standing relationships with a Japanese freight forwarder, which they wished to maintain. Two smaller volume suppliers were substituted. The first agreement was signed in early autumn.

By mid-November, less than 200 pallets per month were flowing through the hub. Since most of the costs were fixed costs, the hub was losing more than $15,000 per month. Thus, the corporate organization put pressure on the Denver office (which included the hub) to take some action to make the hub break even. This happened in spite of the fact that Apple had placed the bulk of the management of its Far East freight with Fritz. The revenue and profit for the international freight was allocated to the two Fritz offices involved in making the international shipment, and not to the hub. (Apple had benefited financially from a 5% reduction in freight costs and from the ability to track materials via FLEX.)

Fritz's Denver office worked with Apple Fountain to come up with a solution that would allow the hub to break even. Apple at that time was storing inventory in about 40 rented trailers at its site. This was costly, and presented security issues and quality issues (i.e., exposure to the hot sun). Apple transferred the storage of ten trailers worth of materials to the supplier hub. These were not hub materials—Apple paid for storage on a per month basis, and ownership of the material remained with Apple. This arrangement allowed the hub to break even.

Demand Management—the Planning Process at Apple Fountain

Like all PC manufacturers, Apple applied a lot of resources to demand management. Both total sales volume and product mix were highly variable and unpredictable. Factors that led to this instability included new product introductions by the various competitors, pricing and promotions and relative product availability of Apple's products vis à vis those of competitors. In addition, sales were subject to the "hockey stick" effect, ramping up during the quarter, as salespeople closed deals to meet their quarterly quota targets. Sales were least predictable for a given model at product introduction and at discontinuance. Costs associated with inaccurate forecasting were also highest at these times.

This variability and unpredictability in demand affected Apple in several ways. In oversupply situations, dealers who had too much inventory or the wrong mix of inventory were allowed to return product to Apple for a small restocking fee. If Apple had an excess of purchased components in inventory or an order, Apple negotiated with suppliers to return parts or delay shipment of outstanding orders. For unique parts, Apple was generally liable for parts due to arrive within lead time (manufacturing lead time plus transit time). In undersupply situations, Apple negotiated with suppliers to expedite outstanding orders or to accept new orders within lead time. When total industry demand for a particular commodity exceeded supply, suppliers would allocate a portion of their output to each PC manufacturer.

Apple Fountain shared demand information with suppliers and with the supplier hub on a regular basis. Each week, Apple provided a forecast of the demand by week for the next year to key suppliers and to Fritz. As the build date approached, Apple placed purchase orders (POs) with suppliers. Close-in, Apple modified its projected daily build plan and notified suppliers and Fritz weekly.

Per the supplier hub agreement, suppliers were required to maintain ten days of inventory (DOI), where DOI was determined based on Apple Fountain's projected daily build plan. Suppliers delivered material to the hub on a weekly basis. The actual inventory level in the hub varied for several reasons, including close-in changes in the build plan, quality problems with parts, and time since delivery of a shipment of parts (cycle stock level). Suppliers were responsible for having stock somewhere in the pipeline to cover potential upswings in demand. This might include stock at the port of origin or in-transit stock which could be freed up by changing the transportation mode from ocean to air shipment.

It was difficult to estimate the real costs of excess inventory. Apple's estimates of the inventory carrying cost for purchased components was 25% to 40%, including about 10% related to obsolescence risk. The costs of inventory shortage were even harder to estimate.

The Fountain Hub in June 1994

Between November 1993 and June 1994 Apple and Fritz focused on negotiating documents of understanding with additional suppliers, in order to increase the ratio of hub material to non-hub material flowing through the hub. By June, five suppliers had signed up for the program, and the ratio had increased from about 20%/80% to about 40%/60%. They planned to continue their efforts in this direction.

Apple had solved its space problem at the Fountain site. Fritz chose to maintain the hub at 30,000 square feet, though there was some potential to store additional non-hub materials for Apple in the hub on an ongoing basis. (One exception was during periods when Apple put an engineering hold on production, temporarily halting outflow. During these periods, Apple might ask Fritz or local third-party warehouses to store the excess material which was still flowing in.)

One issue with which Apple was wrestling was congestion caused by the large numbers of receipts per day of incoming parts. For example, the supplier of plastic enclosures had opened a plant in Colorado Springs to supply Apple and other local customers. Since enclosures were large components, several large deliveries were made each day. For smaller parts this was not an issue, since only a few pallet-loads of material were used each day.

Although many personnel at the five suppliers and at Apple had been trained by the FLEX system, only about 20% of the people who had been trained actually used the system directly. The remaining 80% would use weekly reports generated by FLEX or work through the first 20% of the people to get information. The extent of usage was related to the likelihood of changes in the purchase plan or of supply interruptions, and on the degree to which the design of the part was likely to change. One reason that suppliers didn't use the FLEX system more was that they found that since Fritz was managing the inventory, they didn't have to track it as closely.

Overall, Apple was satisfied with the partnership, having solved its space problem, reduced its freight rates, reduced its inventory levels and gained some advantage from the FLEX system and from having Fritz manage some of the inventory. Fritz was also satisfied with the increase in business and the opportunity to work with a client to develop the hub process, which it could then market to other clients.

Back to Sacramento

The Sacto OPS Center differed from Apple Fountain in several ways. Sacto OPS built a much higher volume of products than did Apple Fountain. Since Sacto OPS built desktops instead of laptops, its component parts and products were bulkier. These two factors led to much higher space requirements for both component storage and production lines. Since Sacto OPS would decide which components to flow through the supplier hub based on their characteristics (Exhibit 4), Sacto OPS might choose different components than did Apple Fountain.

Another difference lay in several factors related to location. First, weather conditions were better in Sacramento, allowing for more reliable local transportation. Supplier lead times were two days shorter due to its location close to California ports and to airports, and to better weather conditions. Second, since Sacramento was close to the Bay Area, suppliers could easily arrange for KANBAN/JIT deliveries from manufacturing sites or distribution centers located in the Bay Area. Many suppliers had established "local sources of supply" in the Bay Area. Apple Fountain did not have this opportunity. (Of course, Apple could, alternatively, encourage suppliers to set up their own warehouses in the Sacramento area, to provide more rapid response.) Last, there were several PC manufacturers around the Sacramento area, including Hewlett-Packard, Packard Bell, and Intel. None of these manufacturers had yet implemented a supplier hub. There was a possibility for a logistics service provider to establish one or two hubs in the area to service multiple PC manufacturers. This possibility did not exist in Fountain.

Exhibit 4

Characteristics of Major Commodity Groups Used in Final Assembly of Desktop PCs

	Plastic Enclosures	Monitors	Packaging	PC Assemblies	Power Supplies	Mass Storage
Country of origin	U.S.	Asia	Local CA	U.S./Asia	Asia	Asia
Freight mode	Truck	Ocean	Truck	Air	Ocean	Ocean
Lead time (weeks)[a]	8	16	2	12/16	16	16
Number of parts per pallet[b]	8	8	100	144	144	300
$ Value per unit	$75	$250	$40	$175	$30	$250
U.S. duty rate (% of value)	0%	6%	0%	8%	4%	0%
Quantity used per month	60,000	60,000	60,000	120,000	60,000	120,000
Number of active suppliers	1	2	2	3	3	3

[a]Lead time includes manufacturing lead time and transit time.

[b]A pallet measures 42 inches by 48 inches. Pallets are typically stacked two high.

Tough Issues

As Lori saw it, there were three major items the team needed to address. First, the team needed to evaluate the supplier hub option in detail. This included understanding the cost and benefits for each type of supply chain entity—the suppliers, carriers, Apple, and Fritz. The team had decided to include in the analysis an estimate of the value of moving inventory offsite, the value of deferral of payment to suppliers and the value of having access to a pipeline inventory tracking system such as FLEX. One encouraging sign was some rough information that she had recently obtained on the approximate cost to of ten days of storage and processing of material for the various entities. This was about $28 at the Sacto OPS site and $25 at the Fountain hub. Japanese suppliers typically paid about $40 at their Japanese warehouses and $30 at their warehouses in the Bay Area.

In doing this first analysis, the team needed to define the specifics of the proposed supplier hub process to be implemented. Were there opportunities to enhance the process used at Fountain? Should the process be changed to reflect differences between the Fountain site and the Sacramento site? Was Fritz the appropriate provider? Which components should be stocked at the hub? Finally, what performance measures should be used?

Second, in parallel with the analysis of the supplier hub option, the team would analyze the other options and the possibility of combining options. One issue to be dealt with was the congestion that could occur at the receiving dock at the Sacto OPS site due to multiple deliveries from various sources. Last, the team wanted to make sure that its recommendations were in line with Apple's business goals.

Lori settled down in front of her Apple Quadra and started drawing up an agenda for the first meeting of the project team.

◆ Case 6–2: Laura Ashley and Federal Express Strategic Alliance ◆

On March 20, 1992, Laura Ashley ("LA"), a global clothing and furnishings retailer based in the United Kingdom, and logistics leader Federal Express' Business Logistics Service ("BLS") announced a strategic alliance that would result in BLS taking over LA's worldwide distribution. The arrangement was preceded by a letter to the LA board of directors by newly arrived Chief Executive Jim Maxmin in December of 1991 that described "the gross inadequacies of our current distribution and warehousing operations . . . (including inadequate) systems to control our stock outs, stock levels, margins, stock replenishment requirements, etc." The objective of the alliance was to transform LA customer service

Research Associate Robert Anthony, under the supervision of Professor Gary Loveman, adapted this case from Laura Ashley: The Strategic Alliance with Federal Express, *HBS No. 493-018, written by Dr. Gloria Schuck, with Professor Shoshana Zuboff, as the basis for class discussion rather than to illustrate either effective or ineffective handling of an administrative situation. Copyright © 1992 by the President and Fellows of Harvard College. To order copies, call (617) 495-6117 or write the Publishing Division, Harvard Business School, Boston, MA 02163. No part of this publication may be reproduced, stored in a retrieval system, used in a spreadsheet, or transmitted in any form or by any means—electronic, mechanical, photocopying, recording, or otherwise—without the permission of Harvard Business School.*

levels by offering improved reliability, speed, and frequency of deliveries. An aggressive implementation schedule would result in the integration of warehouse systems by September 1992, integration of shop systems by February 1993, and an expanded mail-order business offering delivery within 48 hours to any destination by September 1993.

The prospective alliance held exciting potential, as well as risks, for both parties. For LA the alliance promised more effective, lower cost distribution, which would enhance its competitiveness in the market as well as facilitate a transformation of the way in which it did business at the retail level. For BLS the alliance represented an opportunity to effectively utilize all of its capabilities on a global basis, thereby refining its skills and opening up large new potential markets for the future. On the other hand, a failure of the alliance could mean continuing distribution ineffectiveness for LA, and, for BLS, a tremendous set-back for the idea of "partnership," which possibly could be a large part of the future of BLS. The alliance would be visible, and any difficulties would be highly embarrassing for both companies.

Even as the alliance was announced, managers participating in its development on both sides wondered what its eventual impact on LA and BLS would be, and, if it succeeded, in what creative directions it might evolve.

Laura Ashley

Overview

Laura Ashley, founded in 1953 by Bernard and Laura Ashley when they began printing textiles on the kitchen table of their London attic flat, was a specialty retailer, primarily of upscale women's fashions, fabrics, and home furnishing products. The company was known for products that typified the tradition of English rural life. As Jim Maxmin observed:

Few great brands have been created in the last 50 years and fewer still have achieved global renown. Laura Ashley is quintessentially English, and therein lies its timeless appeal. It is synonymous with English Romanticism.

LA segmented its market in terms of customer lifestyles. As opposed to many of its competitors who targeted specific demographic or age groups, LA offered styles that would be appropriate for a customer from an early age to an older age. This customer tended to be an upscale consumer who was "fashion conscious but not fashion forward." Market research concluded in 1991 revealed similarities in the company's customer base, as described in the FY 1992 Annual Report:

The typical Laura Ashley customer is a well-educated, relatively affluent woman. She is confident, concerned, and interested in ideas, travel, and natural beauty, as well as fashion. She cares about family, health, home, the country-side, relationships, and responsibilities. Generous but not extravagant, the Laura Ashley customer believes in quality, service, value, and things that last. Her loyalty to Laura Ashley is based on her perception that we share those values.

A high level of in-store personal service was important to Laura Ashley's customer base and integral to maintaining the image of the brand. The company encouraged interpersonal interplay between customers and its store employees, although it avoided "hard-sell" approaches. In general, shops were staffed with women who shared the tastes and interests of the LA customer base and had the ability to develop a personal rapport with customers.

The Late 1980s and the Arrival of Jim Maxmin

IN 1990 LA operated 481 retail stores throughout the world, up from 231 in 1986 (Exhibits 1 and 2). However, despite the continuing success of LA branded products in the market, financial performance during the late 1980s was disastrous (Exhibit 3). Andrew Higginson, financial director appointed in 1990, summarized: "Sales went up, profits were flat, and capital employed rose out of control. All of our problems were internal."

Exhibit 1

1990 LA Shop Statistics
(retail space in thousands of square feet)

	1986	1987	1988	1989	1990
Number of shops	231	292	365	439	481
Net retail space	357	492	630	738	816

Source: 1990 Annual Report

Exhibit 2

1989/1990 Geographical Analysis
(retail space in square feet)

	Number of Shops	Retail Space
United Kingdom	184	393,700
North America	185	255,600
Europe	65	99,000
Australia	23	34,800
Japan	24	33,300

Source: 1990 Annual Report

As early as 1986, "at the height of the stores euphoria," an LA report identified fundamental weaknesses in the company. These included an overdependence on in-house manufacturing, significant currency exposure, working capital intensity, excessive short-term debt, and rapid cash outflow. Still, growth continued to strain the management of the business, and by the end of the 1980s, LA had developed an expensive hierarchy with an inappropriate structure. Information technology investments lagged growth and, where systems did exist, they were totally inadequate.

Also by 1990, specific changes in the LA supply chain had added to the complexity of the company. In an effort to reduce dependency on in-house manufacturing, an extensive, worldwide network of third-party product sources was developed, limiting company-owned factories to 42% of sales by 1990, from 100% in 1986. However, systems and management practices were not aligned to optimize the transition. The result was a hodgepodge of logistics relationships and arrangements that were difficult to manage and were often ineffective.

Explained Maxmin:

The organization was overcomplicated. Each operating region (Continental Europe, the United Kingdom, and the United States) had its vertical hierarchy, so functions and systems were triplicated and communications were erratic.

Exhibit 3

Laura Ashley Financial Overview (in millions of English pounds)					
For the 52 Weeks Ended January 25					
	1992	*1991*	*1990*	*1989*	*1988*
Sales					
Sales	260.7	327.5	296.6	252.4	201.5
Operating profit	1.1	5.3	6.1	23.6	23.8
Profit/(loss) from associates	3.6	0.1	(0.2)	—	—
Royalty income	0.3	0.3	1.1	1.6	1.7
Net interest payable	(2.3)	(12.4)	(8.6)	(4.9)	(2.4)
Profit/(loss) before exceptional items	2.7	(6.7)	(1.6)	20.3	23.1
Exceptional items[a]	(11.8)	(4.8)	(6.7)	—	—
Profit/(loss) before taxation	(9.1)	(11.5)	(8.3)	—	—

Source: 1992 Annual Report
[a]Includes charges for restructuring costs, systems costs, inventory writedowns, and other one-time events.

Overhead levels were not supported by gross margins or sales. Despite the brand's global appeal, less than 5% of our range was common to all stores and operations worldwide. In all this we had lost sight of our customers' real wishes and lifestyle, as well as our heritage.

In September 1991 Bernard Ashley handed chief executive responsibilities to Maxmin, who was former chief executive of Thorn EMI Home Electronic International. Maxmin immediately introduced strategic and organizational initiatives aimed at building the LA brand and restoring the company to profitability. They included an aggressive campaign to streamline the business and decentralize decision making, which was called "Simplify, Focus, and Act" (SFA), and a three-pronged strategic focus on branding, distribution, and systems development. Maxmin's goal for LA was to become "strategically led, competitively focused, market oriented, employee driven, and operationally excellent."

A first step in the revitalization process was a restructuring of the company to emphasize its global coordination. A Global Operations Executive team ("GOE") consisting of managers from across the business was formed to oversee global interrelationships, and two layers of field management in the United Kingdom and one layer in the United States were removed. In total, 100 senior- and support-level managers departed. In addition, bonuses were linked to global performance, common merchandising was developed, and uniform financial systems were implemented. The pyramidal reporting structure in the stores was flattened to two levels in the United Kingdom and one in the United States.

The SFA initiative involved empowerment of frontline service providers, enhanced training at all levels, and the integration of information technology to simplify and improve service. A Profit Improvement Program ("PIP") scheme was implemented in ten trial stores, wherein store employees came up with a number of new ideas to increase sales, from special events such as fashion shows and decorating demonstrations to special window displays that reflected the local customer mix. The PIP shops were 62% to 70% over sales forecast for the trial period. Training involved in-store training for frontline personnel, as well as time spent in the store for others throughout the organization. Technology would be focused on providing stores with the capabilities to make decisions with timely, accurate information. Maxmin noted:

I've told everybody that you must challenge complexity. . . . We need to simplify our approach to business and all our operations. . . . (With the PIP Program) we let the staff have more say about how they do things by letting them come up with ideas to attract customers into the store. I only asked four things of them: (1) Love the customer absolutely and keep seeing the problems through the eyes of the customer. If something we do doesn't contribute to our service, we have to get rid of it. (2) Use your common sense. If you get instructions that are dumb, then you should point it out to the people concerned and suggest a better way of doing it. (3) Bring forward your ideas. (4) Each of us must create an open, honest, and trusting structure. In that way we can reduce costs.

The strategic focus on brand management was designed to rectify weaknesses in the brand that had developed, as well as expand its prominence globally. While LA appealed to a 6% to 7% share of local markets, it was felt that the brand had not grown with its traditional customer base. There was too much repetition in the product line (e.g., floral dresses), which also lacked sufficient breadth to reflect customers' career and leisure-based lifestyles. As a result, Maxmin decided to extend coverage of the LA brand in existing clothing and furnishing categories, as well as to identify licensing opportunities in such areas as tableware, bridal wear, and china, which would be sold outside of LA's own retail distribution structure.

The strategic focus on systems development was designed to provide retail shops with information flows and to make the business more "transparent." It was felt that transparency, when coupled with empowerment, would be the key to superior customer service.

Historically, LA systems had been designed to provide information to independent business units. Duplicate systems designed to serve independent business units caused LA to spend twice the industry average on systems in 1990. Over the next two years significant efforts would be undertaken to implement common systems across the business. Major software systems to be introduced in 1992–93 included a merchandise planning system, a group finance/executive information system, an electronic point-of-sale ("EPOS") system, a global purchase ordering system, and a manufacturing and U.K. distribution system. PC-based POS registers would be installed in every shop, which would make the data in the company accessible by everyone. LA expected to make a large investment to convert to common systems, but it expected annual systems costs to reduce greatly thereafter.

The strategic focus on distribution aimed at overhauling warehousing, replenishment, and delivery operations, which were, in the words of Maxmin, "a disaster, out of control." A global team headed by Phil Baker, Special Projects Director in Global Finance, was formed to evaluate options for fixing the problems. The objectives of the team were to develop a system capable of providing 99% availability, 24- to 48-hour delivery, and a 50% reduction of working capital. Currently, availability was roughly 80%, and the company maintained an extended, working capital-intensive supply chain, which housed an average of 18 months' worth of inventory from product design through store sale. The strategic alliance with BLS resulted from LA's distribution initiative.

Federal Express and Business Logistics Services

Federal Express ("FedEx") was incorporated in 1971 by Frederick W. Smith, Jr. He designed a nationwide air service network to resemble the spokes of a wheel, with Memphis, Tennessee, as hub. Utilizing the hub as a central processing center for all packages, FedEx pioneered next-day delivery, and by 1991 the company had become the premier carrier in the overnight delivery business.

FedEx was renowned for its logistics expertise and tracking systems. It employed 90,000 people worldwide, operated 444 aircraft and 30,000 collection and delivery vehicles, with more than 1,300 facilities serving 176 countries. FedEx created the American overnight delivery market and was expanding overseas, mostly in the Far East, with a smaller portion of its business in Europe, where its operations were unprofitable in 1991. FedEx posted operating income in 1991 of $280 million on sales of $7.7 billion, with operating margins down significantly from the prior year. While FedEx had been hurt by recessionary business conditions, it was also dissatisfied with the underlying performance of its business, and, in fiscal year 1992, it undertook several initiatives to reduce overhead and control expenses.

FedEx created the Business Logistics Services Division in December 1987 to provide specialized logistics services to businesses throughout the world. It had operations in the United States, Europe, and the Far East. BLS had earned a reputation for providing quality services, and its long-term strategy was "one of synergy with FedEx's other mainstream operations: to develop pan-European business logistics services that enhance the total range of FedEx services available, and enhance those business logistics services by making maximum use of FedEx global networks." As one BLS manager explained, "BLS is the boutique, the custom shop. We're the people who do it your way in the big contractual context as opposed to doing it in the totally standard way, one package at a time." BLS employed 4,000 people worldwide (940 in the United Kingdom), and its European operations included 1,100 road vehicles and 1,750,000 square feet of warehouse space, made up of 75 contract locations and distribution centers. BLS worldwide revenues were approximately 6% to 7% of Federal Express revenues.

BLS U.K. had three major operations. Through its "Systemline" service, BLS planned, implemented, and operated sophisticated information technology-based inventory management systems under contract. Systemline services tailored to the needs of individual clients included warehouse location and specification, inventory systems, vehicles, routing, and scheduling, as well as provision of a highly trained work force. Markets for the service included automotive, consumer electronics, computers, and toys, with clients including industry leaders in each category.

The "Partsbank" service provided global, low risk, and rapid start-up distribution for high value products by operating pay-as-you-go distribution centers shared by approximately 200 users. Clients, including leading international high-tech manufacturers, purchased services from a menu that included collection, storage, inventory control, customs/administration, customer service support, international forwarding and air freight, and delivery. BLS's

"Systemcare" service provided home delivery of large, bulky, and heavy items such as furniture and household appliances. Systemcare offered both dedicated delivery operations and shared facility operations for smaller clients.

BLS provided three elements where logistics expertise offered a competitive advantage: transportation, primarily through the FedEx network, warehousing, and information systems. International Business Development Director Bill Parsons identified warehousing and information systems as the "real value-added":

Quite often warehousing is at the back end of the client organization. Since it's at the front end of what we do we developed systems and productivity that the client can't match. But where we really score, what puts us ahead of the competition, is systems. There's no question that information is vitally important, as important as product flows. Information flows should go before product flows, then you can get your physical operation as sophisticated as possible and optimize it.

BLS Vice President for Europe Charles Kirk explained that BLS offered clients umbrella information systems that would "take care of the inventory system end-to-end":

We have systems for managing inventories. We have systems for running warehouses which are like shop floor control. Mainly, and most importantly, we have this ubiquitous network that lets you know where parcels are as they flow through the system, ... (can) tell you where every single item is every day.... We have it all.

Sometimes a customer comes and says he's already narrowly predetermined what he wants from BLS. He says he wants "transportation." There's plenty of good transportation providers out there, and given how soft the market is right now there are some extremely low prices. If he just wants computer systems, there's other people who might be able to do that, too. If he just wants warehousing services, there's other people. But if he wants somebody to put all three of those things together and to hook them to an international transportation network that FedEx represents, there's nobody out there to do that except BLS! If he wants all three services and he wants us to manage it for him, too—that's the very best scenario. We end up acting like a general contractor, drawing first upon the resources of BLS worldwide, and next upon the resources that FedEx has all over the world.

The Laura Ashley Opportunity

As 1991 came to a close it was apparent to all in Laura Ashley that its distribution performance was abysmal. Its distribution structure and systems were excessively complicated, and its operations and logistics track record was horrible. Problems LA had with its distribution system included inefficient goods flows, outdated inventory order-ing practices, long lead times, and broken promises to customers. Anecdotes of distribution nightmares abounded. As distribution team coordinator Phil Baker stated at the outset of the project, "Right now we're the opposite of service maximization and cost minimization."

LA maintained eight warehouses. The largest was in Newtown (the United Kingdom), and others were in Milton Keynes (the United Kingdom), Veldhoven (Holland), Mah-wah (New Jersey), California, Canada, Paris, and Australia. The company had been geographically organized and re-gional Strategic Business Units ("SBUs") in the United States, United Kingdom, and Continental Europe operated as stand-alone businesses, with independent inventory, systems, and merchandising. This resulted in a number of problems in the distribution system. First, SBUs' parochial perspectives led to inventory turns of less than two and an out-of-control working capital situation. SBUs maintained, as an objective, filling up their allocations of the ware-houses with inventory.

Second, because BSUs independently managed logistics, the transportation system was suboptimal. Maxmin characterized as "dumb" distribution product flows that, for instance, would involve "manufacturing a T-shirt in Hong Kong, moving it to Newtown, and sending it back to Japan to be sold!" Notwithstanding the fact that LA had inventory throughout the supply chain, its out-of-stock position neared 20% on average. Commented Baker:

All the routes have different transporters. We have numerous distribution contractors and different suppliers. Trying to control this is a nightmare. We're continually renegotiating so that we get the best price. Individual markets don't understand global supply and demand.

We have locations all over the world, and we have numerous echelons of stock for different markets. The supply chain has stock, the market has stock, and the factory has stock.

Maxmin offered an anecdote related to this kind of distribution ineffectiveness, which he had heard from a shop employee in California:

A customer waited a year for a fabric pattern called "cornflower," and she still thought that we were the greatest people in the world for getting it for her! That shop had been out of stock and had faxed the home office 17 times and never got a reply. The shop rang around and finally located the fabric in San Diego. When I returned to the United Kingdom the factory manager told me that he had 27,000 meters of the fabric, and he'd had it for a year.

Baker discovered that the replenishment system was based on ineffective historic practice and outdated priorities:
The replenishment system was based on what happened when the company was a lot smaller. It was based on

custom and practice and the belief that you could only know the demand and merchandise of a shop by looking individually at that shop from headquarters and telling them the products that they needed. If a shop was given 10 of an item last year, when one sold it would automatically be replaced. It could have taken a whole year to sell only one, but it would be replenished! They ignored the rate of sale in their algorithm.

At the Oxford Circus shop they're selling 25 items a week and they've got 100 in stock; they'll place an order for 25 more each week. At the Cardiff shop they may have five in stock and sell them all, and place an order for five more. The warehouse has only 20 items, and the current priority says ship it to Oxford Circus because that's the fastest selling shop.

Delivery problems also multiplied. Delivery pallets often looked like "leaning towers of Pisa," garments could be wrinkled and soiled, and shops would receive deliveries at times when they were not staffed to handle them, or when there was not room for them in storerooms. The result would be shops that were a mess. Perhaps the most disturbing aspect for LA of distribution ineffectiveness was the fact that it often resulted in broken promises to customers. Baker observed that "people thought that 80% on time was good; they never challenged it, standards were nonexistent. The customer was an inconvenience, their needs and concerns were a source of irritation." An Operations Update for the week ending October 11, 1991, summed up this mentality for LA at the time:

Can all managers please ensure that when furniture orders are taken, customers are told that the delivery date given is only approximate and not the guaranteed delivery date, the customer should be told that the delivery arrangements will be confirmed nearer the time. This is very important as many customers think that the date given is the date on which the furniture will arrive, thus causing a considerable amount of bad feeling when a different date is given.

SFA, new structures which provided an enhanced focus on global coordination, and the strategic distribution initiative all were LA responses to its costly and ineffective distribution system.

The Strategic Alliance

Between October 1991 and March 1992, when implementation would commence, LA and BLS reached a comprehensive agreement that would result in BLS taking over LA's Newtown, Wales warehouse and all of LA's distribution activities. The process was initiated by Jim Maxmin, who quickly turned the project over to the Global Operations Executive team to implement. The GOE worked with a BLS team led by Business Development Director Bill Parsons to produce initial solutions, and in December 1991

a joint operating and systems team was formed to detail the solutions and prepare them for planned March 1992 implementation.

Solutions would include the formation of a new company that would be owned and managed by BLS, the creation of new management systems and the integration of existing systems, and ongoing evaluation of the arrangement. The alliance was purposefully created with a loose structure, which would allow it to evolve in appropriate directions as a baseline of experience was garnered, and which was intended to keep both companies focused on the strategic nature of their "partnership." The anticipated timetable of the integration activities was:

- September 1992: completion of global reorganization of warehousing
- February 1993: integration of BLS/LA information technology systems
- September 1993: 24- or 48-hour delivery of LA products throughout the world
- September 1993: development of global mail order capability

LA expected that the alliance would result in significant working capital savings, lower cost distribution, and improved customer service levels. BLS anticipated that the alliance would help define its business in an area with tremendous future growth potential.

Initiation of the Alliance

Upon his arrival at LA, Jim Maxmin sorted out his options for fixing the distribution mess at the company. They boiled down to reorganizing existing operations and writing new integrated distribution systems, or withdrawing from warehousing and distribution altogether and handing them to a third-party expert. Feeling that "it would take 100 years" to write the necessary systems from scratch, and recognizing that distribution was not a "core competence" of the company, Maxmin decided to go outside of LA for help. In October 1991 he approached FedEx to explore pooling the two companies' resources:

I got the idea of a "strategic alliance" between LA and FedEx. I had met [FedEx Senior Vice President] Tom Oliver and was hugely impressed by him. As you go through your business life you meet certain people and you just register that these people are extraordinary. I picked up the phone and told him my idea. He was interested and said we should form the alliance. That was the essence of our conversation; the rest of it has been left to our organizations.

Maxmin then met with the GOE and explained his concept of the "strategic alliance." LA would not solicit competitive bids for distribution, but instead it would form a "win/win business partnership" with BLS. The partnership would have no defined end point, lasting a minimum of 10 years. Maxmin described the reaction of the GOE to his idea:

There was huge skepticism to start with.... Their expectation was that within a few weeks they needed to get a contract with FedEx and have every "i" dotted and "t" crossed. I told them I wanted to do it differently and that I didn't want to be bothered with lawyers, contracts, and all kinds of complications. The partnership was to be an open book—no secrets, no surprises. I kept saying that you have got to have faith and embrace a new way of doing business . . . a different way to compete.... Look out to the twenty-first century, not back to the nineteenth.

In November 1991, BLS vice president for Europe Kirk had a meeting at LA to pursue a deal. Kirk was pleasantly surprised by the attitudes he found at LA:

We try very hard to have strategic alliances, but typically you go to a company and it turns into "traffic manager court." The traffic manager says he wants the cheapest price per kilogram to ship, and then you don't have a deal. Traffic managers don't buy value added. But in LA I never met a traffic manager.... They had already decided that they were going to make drastic changes in their distribution and the way they served the customer before we ever met them.... They just wanted us to get on with it. This was a real marriage made in heaven. These guys really want us to do what we're good at doing.

By November 29, LA distribution team leader Baker and BLS's Parsons produced a presentation of "first-look" solutions for the GOE and a gross schedule of activities, responsibilities, and deadlines. The companies would work toward signing a "global contract" by March 1992, at which time implementation would commence. Prior to the presentation LA and BLS participants agreed to a policy for sharing information in the development of the final deal. The intent was to build trust and to keep the parties focused on areas of mutual interest. Then, on December 3, 1991, LA sent a letter acknowledging its intent to develop with BLS a "worldwide logistics partnership," subject to board approval and completion of a definitive agreement.

Solutions

Forming the alliance involved stipulating the means by which the LA distribution system would be organized, planning implementation of the transition to BLS, and creating the integrated systems that would be the core of the new distribution enterprise. This would be the work of a joint, cross-functional project team, comprised of key managers from both companies. The team organized into subcommittees, under the auspices of a steering committee, with Baker and Parsons leading the work of developing the final arrangement.

In order to achieve the goals, a new company, LA Distribution Ltd., would be formed and "sold" to BLS, which would then manage all aspects of LA distribution. LA would then close the Mahwah and Veldhoven warehouses. The Newtown facility was designated central "processing center" for all product flows, with a satellite processing center for the U.S. market being established in Memphis. Shipments to shops could be through the warehouse system, or, if it made sense, directly from manufacturers to shops (Exhibit 4). As Parsons explained, "You can have a single warehouse worldwide if you've got the links. FedEx has the links, the airplanes. We've also got the logistics and inventory accounting systems to back it up."

LA distribution employees would be transferred to the new company. Both BLS and LA resolved to make the transition as painless as possible for them. Jim Maxmin personally got involved in assuring employees that they would be taken care of, and BLS made its complete program of induction and training available to them. While there was some skepticism and disappointment among former LA employees, many also recognized that they would be joining an excellent company that had managing distribution as its core business.

Two BLS systems would be central to the operation of the new company. BLAST prepared invoices and tracked cartons for dispatch, and Federal Express's COSMOS tracking system provided information on package location through a bar coding system. These would be linked with LA's Shop Stock and Warehouse Inventory System, to provide for complete information on inventory from order through delivery. The integration was slated to occur by the end of 1992. At the same time BLS was developing a Warehouse Management System ("WMS"), which would "dynamically" manage labor scheduling and control, storage management, quality of performance, and product protection. By February of 1993, WMS would be integrated with the LA Merchandise Planning System, Purchase Order Management System, and core retail system (used for shop inventory, replenishment, and shop financial management) to provide for decision making related to inventory, and inventory management. Baker explained:

The shops and warehouses will be linked by BLAST and COSMOS. The movements between those will be goods in transit movements, and we'll have the ability to actually track where something is at any point in time. I call it "GIT," Goods in Transit Control. What we've actually got is a closed loop. These movements then update the shop stock. Then by looking at linking in the warehouse inventory, the shop inventory, and the GIT inventory, what you've actually got is "global inventory."

Once the system was complete (completion was planned for 1993), LA would be able to resupply its shops throughout the world within 24 to 48 hours. Each shop would be

Exhibit 4

Laura Ashley Product Flows

Before Alliance:

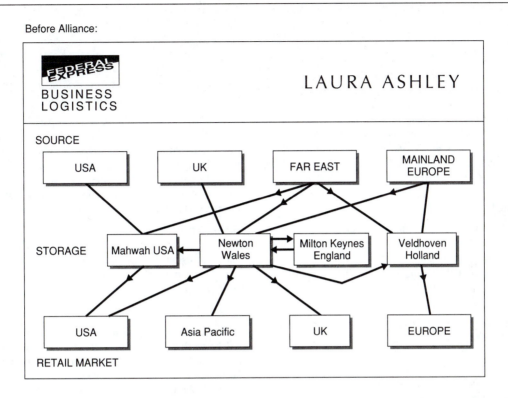

After Alliance:

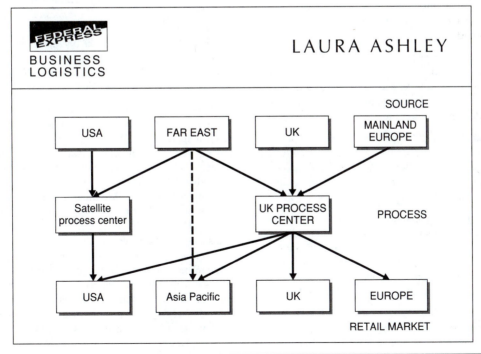

on-line to the global inventory control system, by which it would have total visibility of goods in the supply chain. It was anticipated that simplification of the supply chain would lead to a reduction of 10% to 12% in distribution costs. Baker explained the significance:

With the BLS and Federal Express systems we'll have transparency. At the moment we are looking at our business through a fog. The fog is our own internal organization. We're using the FedEx systems as one of the mechanisms to make the fog clear. We have a multitude of suppliers and distribution contracts all over the world. . . . We are willing to pay a premium to get the clarity and the simplicity that the technology will give us.

Coming to Terms

While BLS and LA reached rough agreement on the mechanics of the alliance, the process of forming the partnership was challenging for both. Specific challenges included structuring the incentives of the deal and decisions regarding how tightly to define the arrangement.

Kirk elaborated:

There's hardly a price in the whole agreement. It's all relative. Everything is a function of something else, and therefore over time that base factor changes. It's only possible that we got it done this quickly for an agreement of this size because we have dealt with things as generalities. Things that are values in other contracts are variables in this contract. There's no numbers in there; everything is a function of everything else. It doesn't give the answer. It gives the formula because over time the specifics change.

The project team toyed with the idea of defining Service Quality Indicators and attaching penalties in the agreement, but, in the end, it decided only to use the indicators, which would be mutually determined, to measure progress. Baker explained why penalties were rejected:

It does us no good at all to get penalties built-in because what they've done is missed the service. No penalty can satisfy a customer that we've lost. At the end of the day, if we have a penalty structure it is meaningless because we still lost the customer.

Developing the final contract was a challenge due to a lack of consensus among counsel advising both parties on how tightly the arrangement should be defined. Throughout the process lawyers on both sides grappled with how to define issues without obscuring the mutual interests on which the success of the alliance would depend. Said one attorney:

At the start we had two different approaches, ours and theirs. I believe that they thought it would be much more straightforward and simple, perhaps because of talk of cooperation and working together. However, I've been present at the start of many marriages and also at the end! A partnership is a marriage. No matter how positive, cooperative, and helpful the partners are at the start, it is essential that they see their relationship in the cold light of the practicalities. They have to look at it as if it doesn't work and walk through the consequences.

BLS and LA agreed on a "transparent, cooperative venture" to last a minimum of ten years. Each had a right to inspect the other parties' business, and there were mechanisms built in to deal with matters that could not be agreed upon. In essence, the companies had "agreed to agree" on issues that would arise in the course of doing business. LA Financial Director Higginson stated:

We hope that the contract is just a fall back position. The intention is to put the contract in the drawer and never get it out again, because the day you get it out again you have to admit that there is a problem with the relationship.

Said Maxmin:

Problems will come up, and people will say, "I told you so." I'll be totally sympathetic to the problems and do everything I can, but I'll just turn my mind off of the negativism, because I know this alliance is going to work.

We lifted this above just distribution and logistics and formed a strategic alliance. It's a systems partnership. It's a business partnership. We're affecting in an integral way the processes of LA, and, therefore, it doesn't have a time scale to it. It doesn't have a time span to it and nobody is worried. You set standards of operations that have to be achieved, but it's not about having a contract and going back and saying that you violated line 82. It's not the spirit in which it was conceived.

Given the loose nature of the alliance, development of a high level of trust among the parties involved was the critical ingredient. "We have all gone through the trust hoop," said one LA manager, "but at the end of the day you have to believe that you're all working for the same end objective." Said another, "You need to trust, not in a naive sort of way, but in an open-minded sort of way—you trust, but skeptically. You know what could go wrong and you work all the more to make sure that trust is maintained." This was not always easy.

At times, project team progress became bogged down in disagreement over the details of the arrangement. At such times leaders from both companies stepped in to refocus the project on the "win/win" aspects of the partnership. Maxmin recalled one day in January (1992) when he met with the team to keep them focused on the strategic aspects of the alliance:

I stayed away other than to attend one meeting. Basically I've watched it evolve with the vacillations and vicissitudes of management inside the business. Everyone is coming up with all of their reservations. In January they started worrying about the size of boxes for delivery and got bogged down. I had to sit down with the team and get them to focus on the real issues. I asked them if there were any systems, political, business process, or commercial issues which say we shouldn't proceed with the alliance? Do you see anything that would actually inhibit our operation? And I asked them to be sure that we can get the rundown on incremental costs. Those were the only things I was interested in.

Other reasons for skepticism existed. Managers from both companies at times wondered if they were being taken advantage of in the negotiation process, and, if they were, when and how they would know it. Jim Maxmin began to receive what he called "defense documents" from some LA managers who were keen to point out all of the risks in the deal. One LA team member described the reaction to the "defense documents":

Jim has refused to listen to any other argument. We all got bogged down in the trucks and sheds issues, but Jim ignored all of it and said that the alliance was going to happen. He's driven it through. Jim takes risk and he takes our blinders off so we can see new possibilities.

On the basis of this support, project team members would return to acknowledging the possibilities for both parties that might accrue from joint efforts, ignoring many of the detailed allocations of risks and rewards. Nonetheless, some project team members had lingering doubts down to the signing of the agreement. "Is this too good to be true?" they thought.

Still, at the end of the process managers on both sides lauded the concept of "strategic alliance" as a means of gaining a competitive advantage in the market, and felt confident that their alliance would succeed. Said one LA team member:

The concept of a strategic alliance is that we both work together to get a competitive edge. But the outcomes aren't really defined, because to define them suggests an endpoint. . . . Jim's view is that we don't know how good we can be and we don't know where that's actually going to take us. Where we're going specifically isn't as important as figuring out how we'll work together to get a competitive advantage.

BLS President Robert May, who was responsible for BLS worldwide operations, summarized:

(This) was just the sort of program that BLS had been striving for—an alliance where both parties worked together to develop each other's business. It represented a step forward for both companies, each recognizing the other's skills and harnessing them to move forward on a truly global level. BLS has always been highly successful in its individual economic markets around the world. With LA we had the opportunity to demonstrate to the global community that FedEx/BLS was the only company worldwide that was capable of providing a tailored global solution. LA had the vision to see that capability and want to use it to their competitive advantage.*

LA and FedEx considered the specifics of its deal to be confidential. They viewed the alliance as a unique opportunity for both parties, and, accordingly, the structure of the highly complicated arrangement was unique in their experience. Basically, LA would pay the direct costs that BLS incurred in managing LA's global logistics requirements and a management fee to BLS as a percentage of cost. LA would pay BLS for freight, with some discount to the market price offered in consideration of LA's large volume. Formulas were then determined to provide incentives for BLS to improve operations. After two years during which BLS would stabilize the logistics operation, if LA agreed to pick up the capital costs of an improvement project, the benefits, for the most part, would be split by the two parties. Longer term, a larger proportion of the benefits, growing to 100%, would begin to accrue to LA in consideration of its funding. In addition, the deal specified certain safety nets for LA in case the alliance failed, which would ease its transition to another option.

Conclusion

Both LA and BLS expected to realize "substantial and real" benefits from the alliance. For LA these included access to new systems in a compressed time frame, new ways of doing business, improved performance, and ability to focus resources on activities where it could add the most value. Also, LA had come to be seen as somewhat of a turnaround story in England, and the positive momentum gained from the alliance could help it consolidate investor confidence. For BLS the alliance would be trend setting, provide entry into the clothing business, provide entry into Europe, utilize existing international loading capacity, establish the global nature of its business, and align it with a well-respected consumer franchise.

On the other hand, the failure of either business, together or separately, would result in dramatically poor consequences for both. At risk for FedEx was the value of its reputation for reliability, which supported an $8 billion business. LA risked its entire operations infrastructure.

In addition to the opportunities and risks, there was the potential for the alliance to evolve in creative directions. For instance, LA had planned to utilize its new distribution capabilities by greatly expanding its mail order business in

1993. Also, the new capabilities would support the empowerment of frontline service providers and lead to improved levels of customer service, as well as make it possible to simultaneously reduce inventories and expand the LA product lines. Clearly, the idea of "global partnership" could be leveraged by BLS with other customers in other industries. As the potential of the deal was assessed, it was left open by both parties that there were other unique forms of competitive advantage that could be gained by LA, and that could be sold in the future by BLS to other customers.

◆ Case 6–3: R. Mer ◆

At the beginning of January 1993, Renault and Renault Véhicules Industriels received a proposal from the management of Aérobus that seemed of particular interest. The airline was expressing its readiness to apply a 30% reduction to current tariffs for Africa, if the two companies would provide them with a total of at least 50 tons of freight per month shared between the two destinations of Abidjan (Ivory Coast) and Douala (Cameroon) where they have installations.

Naturally the task of considering this proposal in a general way was given to the CAT (Compagnie d'Affrètement et de Transport/Freight and Transport Company), which is a subsidiary of both Renault and Renault Véhicules Industriels (RVI), and more specifically to Aircat, the "airways" branch of CAT.

CAT is responsible for transport commissioning, and a very large part of its services are carried out on behalf of the Renault group. In particular it organizes the sales transport, that is to say transport of:

- Finished vehicles ready to be sold
- The collection of vehicles in pre-packed parts, to be put together in the assembly factories owned by Renault abroad (supplied as CKD—Completely Knocked Down)
- Spare or replacement parts

Renault closed down its assembly plants in Africa some years ago and now only has a presence there through the intermediary of its branches or importers. Therefore it is CAT that organizes the transport of spare parts to these two destinations—Douala and Abidjan, mostly by sea. Renault Abidjan covers Renault and RVI activities, whereas Renault Douala covers RVI activities only.

Air routes are only used at present as a contingency measure to alleviate deficiencies in maritime transport. Aircat therefore sends goods in two ways:

This case was written by Professor Philippe-Pierre Dornier, and research assistant Francois Gandon with the help of Jacques Petetin (Aircat) and Jean-Paul Pechmezac (CAT)

- absolutely urgent cases needed within 48 hours (PVI = immobilized vehicle parts)
- urgent stock (where there is nothing in stock)

Aircat would like to develop a regular air carriage service, operating as more than just a palliative measure, for use by the main Renault firm and its other clients. It would like to operate on the principle of "intelligent air transport." This proposal that Aérobus has made to Renault would seem to offer a good opportunity for a renewed consideration of this subject.

During the whole of 1992, the total number of dispatches of parts to Africa was 993 (538 to Douala and 455 to Abidjan), if Renault (tourist and utility vehicles) and RVI (industrial vehicles and buses) are counted together. Detailed figures are provided in the appended information. This information includes:

- Statistical tables of the whole traffic flow to Renault Abidjan and Renault Douala for the period concerned (air) (Appendix 1)
- Statistical sheets for Renault Abidjan of the 50 sea voyages as well as the breakdown of air traffic costs (Appendix 2)
- Statistical sheets for Renault Douala of the 25 sea voyages as well as the breakdown of air traffic (Appendix 3)
- Detailed dispatch files for four air consignments: two to Abidjan, two to Douala (Appendix 4)

The range of parts that are dispatched to Africa cover 20,000 items from the Renault catalog (of 80,000) and about 30,000 from the RVI catalog (of about 100,000 items).

These parts vary a great deal in type, and therefore there are also great variations in their price and in how often they need to be sent. Their value per kilo, price ex works, can be anywhere between 50 centimes and slightly under 4,000 French Francs.

Supply is assured by five MPRs (spare parts stores) in France:

- Douai, Cergy and Flins for Renault
- Blainville and Lyon for RVI

Renault estimates that 70% of the items are organized by the Cergy MPR, and the remaining 30% equally by Flins and Douai, the two latter firms above all dealing with bodywork sections and other large items. In terms of volume and of the price of each item, the share provided by each MPR is as follows:

	Volume (% of total)	PDU (price ex works) (% of total)
Flins	58%	31%
Douai	29%	18%
Cergy	13%	51%
TOTAL	100%	100%

CAT has numerous vessels on the Abidjan and Douala routes, which make it possible to provide one or two departures each week, either from the port of Le Havre for Renault parts or from the port of Marseilles for RVI parts.

As far as air transport is concerned, Aircat has the use of 17 weekly flights departing from Paris, with Aérobus serving both Douala and the Ivory Coast capital. These 17 flights represent a total freight capacity of about 300 tons, given that there are two flights by 747 Combination (each holding 35 tons of freight), and the other fifteen flights use DC-10s, Airbuses, or mixed 747s, with a capacity of between 12 and 14 tons each (see Appendix 5).

The method used by the Africa branch of Renault or RVI to pass on an order can take two forms:

- A stock order sent by diskette, to which the "batch" system responds in lots, rather than in real time
- An order by special telex (the Spitex system), which can authorize the dispatch of a maximum of 20 order lines. This information is dealt with directly by the management information system of the Central MPR. If the item is not available, the system reports it and sends on the order either to the other MPRs or directly to the suppliers. This system is used almost exclusively for orders for repairs.

Stock orders are passed on once a fortnight. Urgent orders (urgent stock or absolute urgency) can by definition be passed on at any time and will be sent by air.

The MPR is responsible for packing the parts. To cover packaging, it charges a fixed rate of 5% of the value of each part for both sea and air carriage. It is not able to improve on this rate given the weights and volume and the methods of carriage (sea or air).

This can be explained by the very large part played by mechanization, whose obvious advantage of great speed in carrying out the supply of orders is counteracted by its limited capacity for adaptation.

However, Aérobus has suggested that the MPRs should deliver the parts in their original packaging to them at their Roissy depot. Aircat teams who specialize in air freight would then be able to carry out tailor-made repackaging on the spot: special palleting, the use of dome-shaped storage containers, and of nets; boxes of 4 to 12 m^3, etc. The whole process could be carried out at a cost of about 2.5% of the value of the items when they leave the factory.

At present, once packaging of the order is complete, the items which have come from different places are regrouped for dispatch:

- By air: to the MPR Cergy (Renault); to the MPR Lyon (RVI)
- By sea: to the MPR nearest to the departure port

The various dispatch documents (notably air waybills and customs documents) are sent with the merchandise when it is freighted by air. However, in the case of sea transport the documents are sent separately, often after the ship has left port for its final destination. It can even arise through negligence that the documents arrive after the ship has reached its destination, which can cause delays in processing through customs and in unloading the merchandise and delivering it to its destination, in this case either Renault Abidjan or Douala.

The goods are transported from the MPR Central Orders department to the port or airport of departure, where they are loaded on to the ship or aircraft. Handling practices vary significantly according to the mode of transport:

- By air, carriage is essentially horizontal and vertical
- By sea, in addition to these handling principles, sloping surfaces are used, and particularly hoists (cranes)

One of the problems that arises when goods are transported by sea is clearly the length of the transportation itself, as well as the conditions. There is therefore some risk of damage to the merchandise en route.

On arrival at the port or airport of destination, the merchandise must be processed through customs, then unloaded and handled on site, before being transported to the place where it is to be used. These are transit costs. There are spoliation risks during this stage of the journey.

On arrival, airport customs procedures take around 24 hours, as opposed to one week (five working days) at sea ports.

When it arrives at the stock depot of the local Renault or RVI subsidiary, the item is finally put into the correct place.

The point when the order is issued to the moment when the required items are stocked in the correct place on site is known as the "supply time." Using a sea route, this supply time is about 90 days (we can simplify given that this time is the same for Abidjan as for Douala, despite the difference in distance). The air route supply time is about a fortnight.

The real money rate is about 14% for Abidjan as for Douala. The full set of costs involved in operating with this stock increases the value of the financial assets by about 8%.

The stocking costs are therefore around 22% in relation to the value of the items.

On the other hand, Renault estimates that the average rate of stock turnaround (in kg) is about a fortnight, whether by air or by sea.

Finally, it should be pointed out that a buffer level of stock has been defined in order to alleviate overrunning the supply time by a third (assuming more or less constant consumption).

Questions

You are asked to consider the Aérobus proposal and prepare a summary of your conclusions. To help you in this task, here are some questions that may be useful to answer:

- What are the parameters to be considered in any calculation of the complete cost of a consignment? What is their nature and their value for the destinations under consideration (taking average costs)?
- Using the examples given by the four air carriage documents and the data sheet of the maritime transport

given in the appendices, on what basis do you think the taxable weight can be defined?

Exercise:

Calculate the taxable weight for the set of maritime voyages when their journeys are simulated by air.

- Is the 30% reduction in freight costs sufficient to justify sending all dispatches by air?
- At what stage of freight volume does it become advantageous to use air rather than maritime transport?
- Which option would it be best to prioritize?:

"Air transport of expensive items with a slow turnover"
or
"Air transport of cheap items with a rapid turnover"?

- Calculate the balanced costs of air freighting consignment no. 18 Renault Abidjan and RVI Abidjan numbers 11, 23, and 8.

In conclusion:

- Can we accept the Aérobus proposal, or should we insert some conditions and renegotiate? If so, in what terms?

The statistics from an average consignment may be used when working on this problem, even though they represent an approximation.

Appendix 1
Total Aerobus Flow North/South and South/North. Abidjan and Douala

ABIDJAN	Annual tonnage carried	
	North/South	South/North
1990	6,523	12,700
1991	6,158	11,146
1992	6,676	9,376

DOUALA	Annual tonnage carried	
	North/South	South/North
1990	3,544	1,059
1991	2,809	788
1992	2,938	618
Note:	Average value of goods North/South: 26F/kg	Average value of goods South/North: 4F/kg (97% perishables)

Appendix 2 Sea Voyages to Abidjan

	Volume (dm3)	Net weight kg	Density (m3/T)	Departure price F	FOB F	Transport F	Insurance F	Duties, taxes	Transit
RENAULT	25,000	5,034	4.97	354,969	3,029	24,352	1,800	295,529	4,965
	65,491	11,674	5.61	1,057,183	6,193	48,952	5,225	832,494	38,479
	30,000	5,848	5.13	483,137	3,031	24,149	2,403	392,143	4,904
	2,440	713	3.42	22,139	1,015	3,525	141	22,347	2,614
	25,000	4,437	5.63	395,894	2,902	24,102	1,991	315,812	10,820
	23,983	4,184	5.73	281,868	2,816	23,885	1,453	235,135	7,045
	25,000	4,563	5.48	331,724	3,197	23,852	1,689	54,427	3,781
	24,779	4,975	4.98	518,376	2,998	24,102	2,567	408,616	10,634
	27,577	5,323	5.18	405,398	2,914	24,178	2,036	344,272	8,565
	27,025	6,578	4.11	574,416	3,228	24,716	2,835	458,805	4,884
	26,431	4,675	5.65	353,322	2,996	24,102	1,791	284,610	3,933
	25,458	4,037	6.31	325,747	2,956	23,977	1,660	260,594	3,929
	26,203	5,021	5.22	454,828	3,037	24,007	2,268	351,107	4,362
	25,425	4,415	5.76	416,190	3,037	23,475	2,084	314,833	4,193
	66,000	10,882	6.07	661,325	8,044	69,549	3,482	550,211	9,937
	27,650	5,598	4.94	533,813	3,093	23,600	2,638	411,727	4,762
	23,604	3,902	6.05	299,202	2,984	22,759	1,529	237,435	3,846
	27,275	6,922	3.94	716,788	3,289	23,757	3,500	552,737	5,355
	20,337	3,467	5.87	325,915	2,971	22,637	1,655	252,179	3,891
	45,709	8,974	5.09	761,503	5,904	45,611	3,827	602,735	6,592
	51,853	9,067	5.72	519,790	5,917	45,550	2,688	427,707	6,856
	25,989	4,549	5.71	420,461	3,677	22,587	2,104	301,287	4,316
	25,458	5,359	4.75	419,562	3,093	22,674	2,135	341,120	4,397
	28,137	4,591	6.13	236,670	3,030	22,487	1,234	201,812	3,420
TOTAL 1	721,824	134,788		10,870,220	85,351	662,585	54,735	8,449,674	166,480
RVI	14,000	2,364	5.92	260,597	1,416	13,199	1,066	216,669	12,423
	30,000	5,136	5.84	771,929	5,324	22,610	2,847	593,060	21,577
	36,682	11,006	3.33	1,034,325	17,010	49,158	4,016	801,514	31,375
	18,890	4,183	4.52	508,357	10,268	29,961	2,013	325,088	15,524
	26,450	9,602	2.75	1,107,021	12,785	49,738	4,383	913,871	14,905
	15,168	3,090	4.91	463,520	3,879	16,053	1,835	300,260	7,620
	12,956	850	15.24	88,045	1,911	5,468	349	58,300	3,101
	48,842	4,700	10.39	107,781	9,165	26,226	427	120,613	7,249
	30,591	9,476	3.23	569,081	12,149	37,076	2,279	558,827	14,056
	3,779	667	5.67	65,190	1,037	3,114	252	51,731	2,854
	16,227	590	27.50	5,266	1,380	3,293	21	15,372	1,593
	11,950	3,664	3.26	394,329	4,573	15,916	1,624	313,317	7,739
	33,146	9,072	3.65	894,312	11,674	41,853	3,713	714,775	15,327
	14,544	2,646	5.50	434,849	4,922	19,340	1,797	337,979	11,419
	6,964	1,537	4.53	247,015	2,423	8,579	1,021	193,905	8,807
	11,766	3,037	3.87	483,441	4,169	13,448	1,985	383,423	12,594
	12,985	3,255	3.99	606,360	4,281	18,092	2,490	460,626	14,065
	33,668	7,324	4.60	979,216	13,389	38,900	4,080	761,217	26,035
	14,873	3,335	4.46	534,371	5,479	16,329	2,201	407,195	14,909
	17,250	4,018	4.29	703,864	5,252	22,423	2,896	544,380	16,967
	26,954	8,866	3.04	1,114,173	13,499	33,892	4,600	853,158	33,968
	6,746	1,864	3.62	358,681	2,385	9,249	1,466	273,019	15,176
	748	302	2.48	65,682	383	1,145	266	46,140	3,007
	10,435	3,236	3.22	599,433	5,142	16,985	2,460	458,361	17,561
	12,902	2,355	5.48	484,334	4,538	12,437	1,985	314,959	16,163
	17,303	2,298	7.53	326,825	3,307	9,703	1,346	245,501	7,027
TOTAL 2	485,819	108,473		13,207,997	161,740	534,187	53,418	10,263,260	353,041
TOTAL 1+2	1,207,643	243,261		24,078,217	247,091	1,196,772	108,153	18,712,934	519,521

Appendix 2 (continued)
Total for Air Journeys Renault Abidjan 1992

	Air
	405 exp.
Price ex works (FF)	8,138,898
Volume (dm3)	537,681
Net weight (kg)	89,345
Taxable weight (kg)	106,321
FOB (FF)	50,029
Freight (FF)	2,255,506
Insurance (FF)	14,860
CIF value (FF)	10,459,293
Duties and taxes (FF)	7,445,672
Transit (FF)	243,016
Total delivery price (FF)	18,430,802

Appendix 3
Douala Breakdown of Operating Costs

	Volume (dm3)	Net weight kg	Density (m3/T)	Departure price F	FOB F	Transport F	Insurance F	Duties, taxes F	Transit F
RENAULT	107,000	17,562	6.09	1,193,014	23,860	308,752	58,276	853,053	21,834
	25,000	11,869	2.11	722,973	5,835	25,395	15,808	419,086	21,280
	38,925	7,097	5.48	568,794	11,670	50,230	12,431	343,980	11,310
	20,000	3,431	5.83	247,317	5,835	24,186	5,391	152,473	7,879
	50,000	13,510	3.70	788,146	11,670	50,790	17,870	472,540	13,950
	87,000	14,260	6.10	1,089,699	21,793	285,502	53,557	771,551	16,858
	130,000	42,220	3.08	1,507,532	30,151	394,973	53,557	1,098,820	34,971
	60,000	13,269	4.52	411,130	17,505	74,217	8,988	283,409	17,286
	40,000	10,818	3.70	359,788	11,670	50,790	7,778	237,138	14,007
	42,000	7,053	5.95	538,453	11,670	50,790	11,758	334,594	11,173
	23,500	4,420	5.32	219,547	5,835	25,395	4,805	139,506	8,906
	75,000	18,611	4.03	321,083	17,505	76,185	6,376	256,778	19,674
	62,844	12,783	4.92	929,826	17,705	76,185	20,315	556,902	15,128
	41,541	9,181	4.52	606,665	11,670	50,790	13,218	369,692	12,054
	25,000	5,000	5.00	409,858	5,988	25,052	8,961	237,398	11,004
	25,000	10,242	2.44	115,106	5,988	24,559	2,524	87,826	12,463
	42,000	7,109	5.91	511,876	11,976	50,104	11,188	316,211	13,254
	50,000	10,895	4.59	449,788	11,976	49,118	9,832	288,392	13,315
	75,000	14,149	5.30	593,067	17,964	73,677	12,961	385,236	20,873
	75,000	12,614	5.95	489,875	17,964	73,383	10,708	331,323	18,617
	75,000	11,566	6.48	738,603	17,964	71,196	16,135	458,123	18,731
	46,000	8,371	5.50	595,165	116,70	50,230	13,007	362,231	11,773
	28,137	4,591	6.13	208,878	3,030	22,487	1,234	201,512	3,720
	24,000	4,714	5.09	255,372	5,835	24,739	5,587	158,420	8,255
	50,000	10,779	4.64	848,314	11,670	48,372	18,535	496,672	15,653
TOTAL	1,317,947	286,114		14,719,869	326,399	2,057,097	400,800	9,612,866	373,968

Appendix 3 (continued)
Total for Air Journeys Renault Douala 1992

	AIR
	513 exp.
Price ex works (FF)	16,305,361
Volume (dm3)	595,861
New weight (kg)	136,019
Taxable weight (kg)	147,901
FOB (FF)	76,173
Freight (FF)	3,697,114
Insurance (FF)	28,600
CIF Value (FF)	20,107,248
Duties, taxes (FF)	11,270,095
Transit (FF)	197,218
Total delivery price	32,077,764

Appendix 4

AIR DISPATCH FROM 18/02/92	ABIDJAN
Volume in dm3	1,307
Net weight in kg	217
Density	6.02
Taxable weight in kg	217.8
Price ex works (FF)	39,858
FOB	122
Transport	6,632
Insurance	66
CIF value	46,678
Value in customs	46,678
Duties and taxes	33,740
Transit through customs	590
Delivery price	81,008

AIR DISPATCH FROM 23/10/92	ABIDJAN
Volume in dm3	380
Net weight in kg	95
Density	4
Taxable weight in kg	95
Price ex works (FF)	18,428
FOB	53
Transport	2,726
Insurance	30
CIF value	21,237
Value in customs	21,237
Duties and taxes	15,394
Transit through customs	258
Delivery price	36,889

AIR DISPATCH FROM 11/04/92	DOUALA
Volume in dm3	1,145
Net weight in kg	97
Density	11.8
Taxable weight in kg	190.8
Price ex works (FF)	6,123
FOB	54
Transport	4,408
Insurance	15
CIF value	10,600
Value in customs	10,600
Duties and taxes	5,941
Transit thorugh customs	141
Delivery price	16,682

AIR DISPATCH FROM 07/08/92	DOUALA
Volume in dm3	36
Net weight in kg	6
Density	6
Taxable weight in kg	6
Price ex works (FF)	332
FOB	3
Transport	270
Insurance	1
CIF value	606
Value in customs	606
Duties and taxes	340
Transit through customs	9
Delivery price	955

Appendix 5
Regular Lines

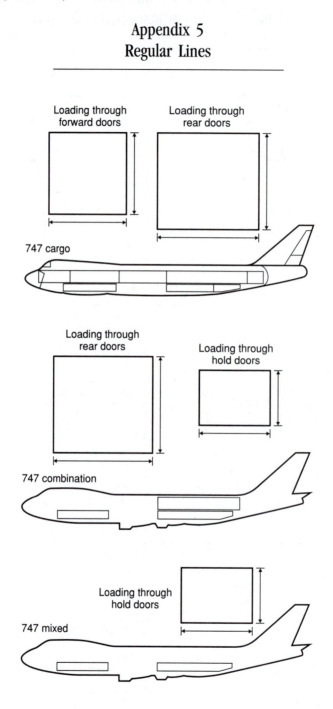

Loading through forward doors

Loading through rear doors

747 cargo

Loading through rear doors

Loading through hold doors

747 combination

Loading through hold doors

747 mixed

Appendix 5
Special Charter

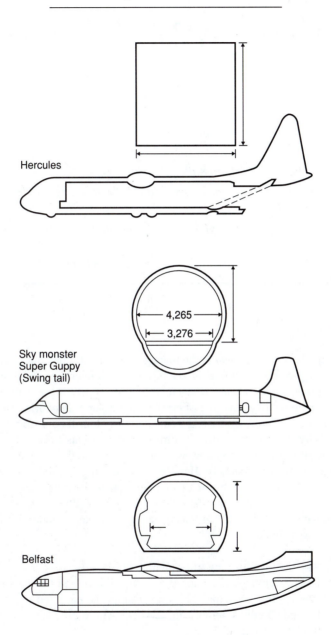

Hercules

Sky monster
Super Guppy
(Swing tail)

4,265
3,276

Belfast

Global Supply Chain Management

♦ ♦ ♦

This chapter will discuss the following topics:

♦ *Demand volatility, information distortion, and the bullwhip effect in supply chains*

♦ *From domestic to global supply chains: Added complexities and uncertainties*

♦ *Vertical integration issues in global supply chains*

♦ INTRODUCTION

Supply chain management is the management of activities that transform raw materials into intermediate goods and final products, and that deliver those final products to customers. For most firms, supply chain management requires operating a network of manufacturing and distribution facilities that are often scattered around the world. The activities of the supply chain involve from purchasing, manufacturing, logistics, distribution, and transportation to marketing. Frequently, different firms own the various links in the supply chain.

For purposes of illustration, we will describe a rather typical global supply chain in the computer industry—namely, Hewlett-Packard (HP) and its Deskjet printer supply chain of the early 1990s. The network of suppliers, manufacturing sites, distribution centers (DCs), dealers, and customers for the Deskjet printer are illustrated in Figure 7–1. The printers were manufactured by HP in Vancouver in a two-stage production process that involved the following activities:

1. Assembly and testing of printed circuit boards
2. Final assembly and testing (FAT), which involved the assembly of other subassemblies (motor, cables, keypad, gears, etc.) and printed circuit boards from Printed Circuit Assembly and Test (PCAT) to produce a working printer, including the final testing of the printer

The components needed for PCAT and FAT were sourced from other HP divisions, as well as from external suppliers worldwide. The printers for different countries had to be customized to meet the language and power supply requirements of the country of sale. This customization process involved assembling the appropriate power supply module and plug for the correct voltage requirements (110V or 220V), and packaging it with the working printer and a manual written in the appropriate language.

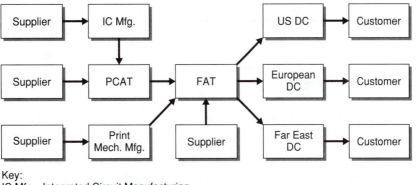

Key:
IC Mfg—Integrated Circuit Manufacturing
PCAT—Printed Circuit Assembly and Test
FAT—Final Assembly and Test
Print Mech Mfg—Print Mechanism Manufacturing

Figure 7–1   The Hewlett-Packard (HP) Deskjet Printer Supply Chain

Source: See original reference of Kopczak, Laura R. and Hau L. Lee (1994) "Hewlett-Packard: Deskjet Printer Supply Chain (A)," Stanford University, Department of Industrial Engineering and Engineering Management.

The finished products of the factory consisted of printers destined for different countries. These products were then sorted into three groups bound for the three distribution centers: North America, Europe, and Asia-Pacific. Outgoing products were shipped to three distribution centers by ocean. The total factory cycle time through the PCAT and FAT stages was about a week. The transportation time from Vancouver to the distribution center in San Jose, California, was about a day, whereas it took four to five weeks to ship the printers to Europe and Asia.

For simplicity of discussion, we frequently discuss supply chain management concepts and issues in the context of the most straightforward form of a supply chain—that of a linear flow process as shown in Figure 7–2. According to this arrangement, suppliers provide raw materials to manufacturers, which deliver finished goods to wholesalers, which combine the products of many manufacturers into bundles of goods for sale to retailers. Retailers, in turn, sell to the consumer of the product. In our discussion we refer to this process as a *linear supply chain*.

This chapter focuses on three main aspects of supply chain management:

1. *Supply chain as a cross-functional entity.* Most supply chain management difficulties stem from an uncoordinated and fragmented allocation of responsibility of the various supply chain activities to different functional areas.
2. *Supply chain as a strategic user of inventory and other production resources.* The supply chain can be used as a potentially effective tool in balancing demand needs and capacity requirements, and in providing operational hedges against uncertainties.
3. *Supply chain as the integrator and coordinator of production and logistics activities.* This approach is the essence of supply chain management, and is the only way to achieve operational efficiency with regard to cost, lead times, and customer service.

Before we discuss the challenges of global supply chain management, we must highlight the most important aspects of how these complex systems behave in response to environmental uncertainties. We will shortly look at the *bullwhip* phenomenon in supply chains. This concept captures the fundamental insights behind the dynamic behavior of supply chains. Later we study the added challenges and differentiating factors in supply chain management

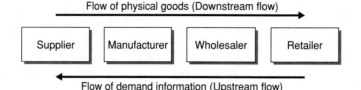

Figure 7-2   Goods and Information Flows in a Linear Supply Chain

as we move from mostly domestic chains (i.e., all activities contained within a country) to global ones. Among the many factors considered are:

1. Substantial geographic distances
2. Foreign market forecasting difficulties
3. Exchange rates fluctuations and other macroeconomic uncertainties
4. Infrastructural inadequacies (worker skill, supply availability, supplier quality, lack of local process equipment and technologies, inadequate transportation and telecommunication systems, etc.)
5. Explosion in product variety in global markets.

Finally, we evaluate backward and forward integration alternatives as a way to better control supply chains in environments of substantial market and supply uncertainty. We discuss the types of environments in which such alternatives are appropriate.

◆ DEMAND VOLATILITY, INFORMATION DISTORTION, AND THE BULLWHIP EFFECT IN SUPPLY CHAINS

Consider the simple linear supply chain—a series of companies, each of which orders from its immediate upstream member. Within this environment, end users (those furthest "downstream") generate the demand for the last company in the supply chain. However, for companies further upstream in the channel, demand is a compilation of orders from the companies downstream. Distortions in demand information can and do occur as we move further away from the end customer along the supply chain. Both the perceived demand seasonality and forecast error can increase as we proceed upstream in the supply chain. This phenomenon is referred to as the *bullwhip* or *whiplash* effect. A small variance or seasonal fluctuation in actual consumer demand can "crack the whip" for upstream suppliers, causing them to alternate between overproduction and downtime situations. Consequently, the bullwhip (whiplash) effect refers to the phenomenon where:

- Orders to the upstream member in a supply chain exhibit greater variance than actual orders at the point of retail sale (demand distortion), and
- The variance of orders increases as one moves upstream (variance propagation).

Figure 7-3 illustrates this phenomenon by depicting a retail store's sales of a product as compared to the retailer's orders issued to the manufacturer.

A simple example illustrates this effect. A company that services a consumer market produces 100 units monthly of a particular product to meet an apparently steady demand.

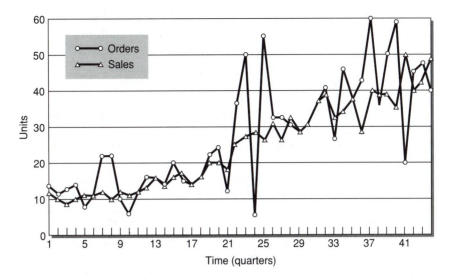

Figure 7–3   The Bullwhip Effect: Orders Versus Sales

Each unit contains three identical components, which the company purchases from an outside supplier. To avoid the possibility of missing a delivery to its consumers due to internal production problems or supplier delivery delays, the manufacturing firm inventories one month's supply of the finished item and two weeks' supply of components. The firm adjusts its production and supplier ordering rates monthly to maintain the desired inventory levels in the face of demand fluctuations. The supplier is able to make deliveries within one week of receiving an order.

Given this scenario, what happens if consumer demand drops by 10 percent? Table 7–1 describes a highly probable reaction. Even though ultimate demand dropped only 10 percent, the manufacturer had to reduce its production rate 20 percent to work down its inventory to the new target inventory level. The manufacturer won't regain its equilibrium with the market until Month 4.

Table 7–1:   *Possible Impact of Demand Change on a Single Manufacturer and Supplier*

| | | Beginning of Month Finished Goods Inventory | | | End of Month | | |
| | During Month Consumer Demand | | | During Month Production Rate | Parts Inventory | | Parts Order to Supplier |
Month		Actual	Desired		Actual	Desired	
0	100	100	100	100	150	150	300
1	90	100	100	100	150	150	300
2	90	110	90	80	210	120	150
3	90	100	90	80	120	120	240
4	90	90	90	90	90	135	315
5	90	90	90	90	135	135	270

This example adapted from Hayes and Wheelwright, *Restoring Our Competitive Edge* (New York: John Wiley & Sons), Ch. 9, pg. 280.

The impact on the manufacturer's supplier is even more dramatic. The supplier's order rate plummets 50 percent in Month 2, then rises rapidly to a rate greater than its initial rate. It takes until Month 5 before the supplier regains equilibrium with the market.

The bullwhip effect is a common occurrence in many industries. Procter & Gamble (P & G) observed it in the distribution of one of its best-selling products—Pampers disposable diapers. While the consumers—in this case, babies—consumed diapers at a steady rate, the demand order variabilities in the supply chain were amplified as they moved up the supply chain. Sales variability at the retailers was not excessive, but distributors' orders and orders of P & G to its suppliers fluctuated wildly. HP encountered a similar amplification pattern in its printer supply chain.

A simple but extremely effective experiential game, the so-called *beer game,* is taught in many business schools and industrial engineering departments as part of modules on supply chain management to demonstrate the bullwhip effect. The game, played on a large board, simulates the flow of material and information in a simplified channel of production and distribution. Locations on the board represent the four stages of the beer supply chain: the factory, the distributor, the wholesaler, and the retailer (see Figure 7–4 for a graphic depiction of the flow of material and information in the beer game). Orders placed by each of the stage managers, as well as the inventory in transit and at each stage, are represented by markers and pennies that are placed at the appropriate locations on the board. External demand is represented by a stack of cards.

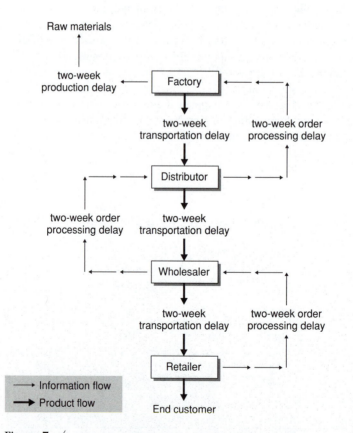

Figure 7–4   Flows of Product Information in Beer Game

Each player manages one stage of the supply chain. Each week, the retail manager observes external demand (by drawing the next demand card), fills as much of this demand as possible, records backorders to be filled, and places an order with the wholesaler. The wholesaler, in term, observes demand from the retailer, fills as much of this demand as possible, records backorders, and places an order with the distributor. The distributor repeats this process by ordering from the factory. Finally, the factory manager, after observing demand and backorders, begins production.

From each position in the supply chain to the next downstream stage, there is a two-week transportation delay—that is, goods shipped this week arrive two weeks later. Similarly, there is an order processing delay from each stage to the immediate "upstream" stage. The factory schedules production by generating a *production request*. Kegs of beer produced to satisfy that request arrive two weeks after an order is placed.

The rules of the game require that all backorders be filled as soon as possible. At each stage of the supply chain, the manager has only local information. Communication between players is not allowed. Only the retail manager knows the customer demand.

The objective of the game is to minimize total supply chain inventory and backorder costs. The costs are calculated weekly and include $0.50 for each keg of beer that remains in inventory at the end of the week and $1.00 for each keg of beer that is backordered by the end of the week.

A typical game is played for thirty to fifty weeks. Inventory (and backorder levels) as well as placed orders are recorded by each player every week. These levels tend to vary dramatically. In Figure 7–5 we illustrate a typical pattern of inventory, backorder, and order levels at each stage of the supply chain in the beer game. At the end of the game, the players are asked to estimate customer demand. Except for the retail manager, who knows the demand, all other players estimate that demand varied wildly. All of them are subsequently surprised when they discover that demand actually followed a stable, almost constant, pattern. The players' immediate reaction is to blame other players in the supply chain for following inappropriate strategies.

Bullwhip Effect and Its Behavioral Causes

The patterns observed in the beer game clearly demonstrate the two main aspects of the bullwhip phenomenon: demand distortion and variance propagation. Distorted information from one end of the supply chain to the other can lead to tremendous inefficiencies, excessive inventory, dissatisfied customers, lost revenues, and ineffective production schedules. The beer game makes apparent to all participants that amplified variability is at least partially driven by the players' irrational decision making. In the following paragraphs we discuss several aspects of managerial behavior that cause the bullwhip phenomenon.

Individual Decisions

Failure to understand the impact of individual (or isolated functional) decisions on the supply chain as a whole is one cause of the bullwhip effect. An upswing in demand produces shortages somewhere in the chain. Typically, when managers perceive a threat of product shortage caused by perceived volatile demand, they react by increasing safety stocks, thus increasing orders from their suppliers upstream. This over-ordering is interpreted by the upstream supply-chain players as a large upswing in demand, which, in turn, leads to a "demand growth psychosis effect" throughout the supply chain. That is, the entire supply chain now believes that demand has increased dramatically. In such a perceived period of

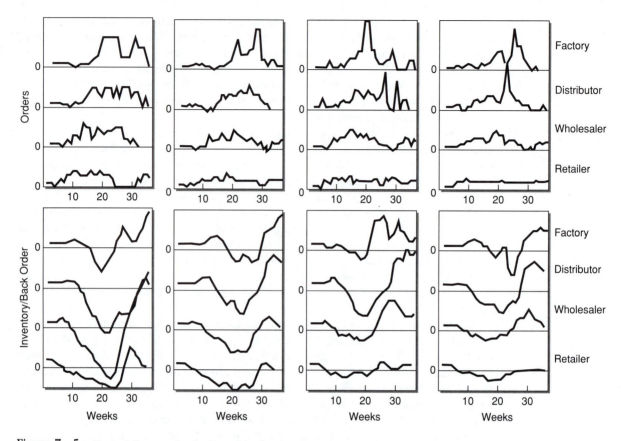

Figure 7–5   Typical Patterns in the Beer Distribution Game

growth, future demands forecasts are adjusted and safety stocks added to ensure protection from stockouts.

In a system of long lead times, safety stocks typically consist of sufficient product to supply a few weeks of future demand. However, the perceived demand growth, when combined with the long lead times, generates a drastic increase in orders and inventories. The miscalculated ordering decision of a single supply chain link can create this chaotic effect.

Types of Incentives

Inappropriate functional incentives contribute to the erratic behavior in the supply chain. In the described beer game, the incentives (the fact that shortages cost twice as much per unit as inventory cost per unit) create an exaggerated "shortages fear," which, in turn, encourages over-ordering. It is a fact of business life that the objectives of marketing, sales, manufacturing and distribution frequently clash. The imbalances resulting from such conflicts are due, in large part, to inappropriate functional performance measures. These outdated functional performance measures are so entrenched that they have become almost structural in nature—bridged only by excess inventory and capacity that attempts to compensate for the isolated functioning of the various departments.

Many companies tend to resist the idea that a better balance can indeed be achieved through better coordination of decision making and appropriate alignment of functional objectives to those of the overall system. It is common for companies to fail to articulate their objectives at the level of the overall supply chain. In so doing, they subsequently fail to understand how the specified performance measures, which are established arbitrarily and with a myopic functional view, affect the overall supply chain's performance.

The beer game teaches the valuable lesson that even rational decisions made by individual players within an ill-structured supply chain can cause the bullwhip effect.

Research indicates there are four major causes of the bullwhip effect:

- Demand forecast updating
- Order batching
- Price fluctuations
- Rationing and shortage gaming

We will comment on each one of these causes, and discuss strategies to effectively counter them.

Major Non-behavioral Causes of Bullwhip Effect

Demand Forecast Updating

Demand signal processing is a major contributor to the bullwhip effect. When a downstream operation places an order, the upstream manager processes that piece of information as a signal about future product demand. Using standard forecasting techniques, such as exponential smoothing, the upstream manager updates forecasts for future demands and safety stock requirements based on updated forecasts of future demand. Many of the forecasting techniques used place substantial weight on recently observed demand realizations, which leads to propagation downstream of any sudden peaks in realized orders at some link in the supply chain. The effect is amplified due to the magnitude of safety stocks covering demand over long lead-time periods as we move downstream in the supply chain. At the same time, the longer the lead time the more inaccurate the forecasted demand, a situation that further contributes to demand variance and higher safety stocks. The lead-time effects are extremely important for global supply chains, as we will demonstrate later in this chapter.

The remedies to this cause of bullwhip effect are (at least conceptually) straightforward. Companies must avoid the demand-signaling behavior via orders and must reduce lead times. Every link in the supply chain must have an accurate picture of the actual market demand and must share this information with all supply chain partners so they can appropriately configure their demand forecasts. If available and possible, point of sale data from the retailers' stores should be passed along to the upstream links of the supply chain. Electronic Data Interchange (EDI) technology can be used to share such information. To avoid unnecessary fluctuations in the order data placed within the supply chain, downstream at times relinquish full control of forecasting and inventory functions to upstream partners. In the consumer products industry, such practices are known as Vendor Managed Inventory (VMI) or Continuous Replenishment (CR). Examples of such practices can be found at Campbell Soup, Nestlé, Nabisco, and P & G.

Lead-time reduction is an obvious recommendation. However, it is also the most difficult to achieve in global supply chains. Lead times often are determined by geographical distances from qualified suppliers. Some companies convince suppliers to follow the company to new foreign locations in order to provide JIT supply. For example, Japanese and

German car manufacturers in the United States have successfully convinced their vital suppliers to locate their production facilities nearby the automakers' assembly plants.

Order Batching

Economies of scale, mostly reflected in expensive order placing procedures to simplify production setup and reduce such setup costs, prompt companies to accumulate demand before issuing an order. Transportation costs cause similar ordering build-ups. As a result, companies order less frequently, quite often on a regular cyclical basis of significant cycle duration (i.e., weekly, biweekly, or even monthly). The farther upstream you move from the retailers, the more erratic the batch ordering pattern becomes. Even smooth demand patterns at the retailer level can be translated via batch ordering into highly erratic order patterns at the supplier level. Any other irrational managerial behavior, such as *hockey stick* phenomenon ordering (i.e., increased orders at the end of the quarter so that sales/production people meet quarterly to set target measures), disturbs the demand or ordering pattern even more and further exacerbates the bullwhip effect.

The remedy for this problem is conceptually simple: devise strategies that reduce batch sizes and promote more frequent ordering. However, this approach can only be realized if the systemic reasons that determined economies of scale in ordering are eliminated, or at least are diminished in importance. For example, the use of information technology can cut the cost of order processing substantially by eliminating paperwork and feedback or checkup points. Using EDI, companies can supplement Computer Assisted Ordering (CAO), cut the cost of purchase orders by tenfold, and provide incentives to customers to order more frequently.

Similar changes in transportation management can help smooth out the demand chain's ordering patterns. Certainly, transportation economies are of extreme importance in the management of global supply chains. Consolidation of shipments is a standard practice. In many cases, consolidated shipments account for a month or more of order supply. Consolidation practices for the purpose of transportation economies contribute to the infrequent ordering and lumped demand patterns observed upstream in the supply chain, and further aggravate the "bullwhip" phenomenon. The remedial strategies for such causes depend on the cooperative attitude of production/distribution and transportation companies. Among the most innovative solutions is the use of third-party logistics companies, which permit economies of scale in transportation/distribution that were not feasible in single supplier-customer relationship. Third-party logistic companies can consolidate loads from multiple suppliers located near each other, or deliver to multiple customers, some of them even direct competitors, in close geographical proximity.

Price Fluctuation

As a result of special trade deals and consumer promotions—that is, price and quantity discounts, rebates—companies often end up buying needed supplies well in advance of demand. Such promotions can be extremely costly to the supply chain. When a product's price is low, a customer buys in larger quantities than needed. However, as soon as the price returns to normal, customers overcompensate for their previous aggressive buying behavior by delaying their buying until they have depleted accumulated inventories. They gamble that the next trade promotion will come along before their inventory stocks are depleted. The resulting buying pattern differs substantially, and is drastically more erratic, than the realized market demand pattern.

The simplest remedial strategy is to reduce the frequency and magnitude of special trade deals and consumer promotions. In the grocery industry, major manufacturers such as P & G and Kraft have moved to an everyday low price (EDLP) in an effort to stabilize prices and smooth demand patterns across the supply chain. Continuous Replenishment Programs (CRP) with rationalized wholesale pricing policies have similar effects.

Rationing and Shortage Gaming

When product demand exceeds supply, manufacturers often ration their products to customers, typically by allocating the amount delivered in proportion to the amount ordered. Customers, aware of this practice, purposely exaggerate their orders in periods of short supply and cancel or reduce exaggerated orders in periods of ample supply. This customer practice, which we call *gaming* of orders, gives little reliable information to suppliers on the product's real demand. Here again, the impact of such behavior is a misperception of market demand patterns as being highly erratic. This misperception typically leads to more erratic ordering patterns upstream.

According to *Business Week,* Motorola faced serious problems in meeting consumer demand for handsets and cellular phones during the end-of-year shopping seasons in both 1992 and 1993. Motorola used a rationing scheme to allocate product to its distributors. As expected, these distributors over-ordered at the end of next year. Unfortunately, however, market demand had cooled down, leaving dealers swamped with inventory. Reacting to this series of events, the financial market penalized Motorola with a 10 percent decline in its stock price.

Many companies correct for gaming behavior in the ordering process during short-supply periods by using clever product allocation/rationing rules. General Motors and Texas Instruments, for instance, allocated products to dealers in proportion to past sales records.

Table 7–2 outlines the various causes of the bullwhip phenomenon and suggests a variety of possible remedies.

Table 7–2: *Bullwhip Effects and Remedial Strategies*

Causes of Bullwhip	*Remedial Strategies*
I. Forecast demand updating	• Access to market demand information (use of Point of Sale (POs) data) • Information sharing across supply chain links (use of Electronic Data Interchange (EDI)) • Vendor managed inventory (VMI) • Lead time reduction and JIT supply
II. Order batching	• Reduction of processing costs (Computer Assisted Ordering (CAO)). • New ways of achieving economies of scale in transportation/distribution (third-party logistics)
III. Price fluctuations	• Reduce frequency and magnitude of special trade deals and consumer promotions (Everyday Low Price—EDLP) • Continuous Replenishment Programs (CRP)
IV. Rationing and shortage gaming	• Better product allocation policies in short supply periods (allocation based on past sales) • Penalties on order cancellations

◆ FROM DOMESTIC TO GLOBAL SUPPLY CHAINS: ADDED COMPLEXITIES AND UNCERTAINTIES

As activities of the supply chain locate all over the world and product flows start crossing national boundaries, supply chain managers face the uncertainties and complexities of the globalized logistics network. From a management perspective, several characteristics differentiate global from national supply chains. They are discussed here.

Substantial Geographic Distances

Increased distances imply longer transportation lead times. Companies compensate for this with higher pipeline inventories. However, longer transportation times do not simply add to the mean length of the supply lead times. They also add variability to lead times. Shipment of goods that cross national boundaries are subject to unpredictable complications and delays due to bureaucratic customs procedures. This added uncertainty is handled by increased buffer inventories, which contributes to the erratic behavior of the bullwhip effect. The resulting stock-level volatility can lead to costly stockout situations, unresponsiveness to consumer needs, and high administrative costs.

Firms managing a global network of production plants face the challenges of implementing JIT production with geographically distant suppliers. Some firms find it almost impossible to achieve the required tight schedule coordination and frequent information feedback with a far-flung suppliers base. For example, a large computer company's global sourcing strategy for finished computer systems was so complex that it was impossible to implement JIT delivery to the country of final sale. Although goods usually cleared customs in two or three days, documentation problems could hold a shipment up for two to three weeks. Such hold-ups occurred once or twice a year for each product.

Added Forecasting Difficulties and Inaccuracies

Increased response times due to greater geographical distances always complicate the forecasting tasks. But distance is only one factor that complicates the forecasting task. Geographically distant locations in most cases imply that companies operate in different cultural environments, use different languages, and observe different operating practices. These differences add substantially to communication difficulties, creating different outlooks and assumptions on which to base scenarios for future market evolution. Add these complexities to the well-known phenomenon of forecasting discrepancies between different functional areas, and companies find themselves with an acute problem of highly distorted, inaccurate information used for planning purposes.

Traditional inventory theory specifies that the needed safety stocks to cover demand uncertainty vary with the size of the forecast error. Therefore, in the global supply chain both manufacturers and retailers end up carrying higher inventory levels and must deal, due to the exacerbated bullwhip effect, with higher volatility in their stocking levels. These effects are aggravated by the typical inability to coordinate the marketing campaign and promotion activities of an expanded network of distantly located international retail outlets.

Exchange Rates and Other Macroeconomic Uncertainties

Exchange rates and inflation are two of the complicating macroeconomic factors in the global supply chain environment. Exposure to exchange rates affects the underlying economics of any firm dealing with foreign buyers, suppliers, or competitors through its impact on input costs, sales prices and sales volume. The topic of exchange rate exposure is covered in more detail in chapter 9. However, we will discuss briefly here supply chain practices the global firm can use to mitigate some of these risks.

Firms can use flexibility in the structure of their global supply chain to counteract unfavorable exchange rate movements. One frequently used tactic is for a firm to shift its purchases to those suppliers who, by virtue of their location, can provide inputs at the lowest cost in the local currency. Under this tactic, firms establish relationships with vendors in a variety of countries so they can best use their global supply experience in implementing such a strategy. Sometimes it may even help to go so far as to establish an international supplier where one does not yet exist. The value of this strategy is high for supplier-country environments that exhibit chronically undervalued currencies.

Global supply chains with both multiple production sources for the same product and some excess capacity can develop an operational hedge against exchange rate fluctuations. They achieve this by using the excess capacity in the network and by reallocating production among different countries in the network.

Within inflationary environments, especially hyperinflationary situations in developing countries, effective supply chain practices are essential. The key to success in such environments is prompt implementation by companies of price increases and minimal delay in collections from customers. The company must emphasize distribution channels that are simple to service and pay promptly. For many country environments and industries this means heavier use of wholesalers and national supermarket chains. Sales coverage should be thorough to assure prompt and complete communication with customers. Such communication facilitates the announcement and implementation of price increases and changes. Finally, lead times in the supply chain have to be shortened to the extent possible to ensure fast and accurate distribution. This allows firms to minimize pipeline inventories and to avoid payment delays due to invoice/merchandise-received discrepancies.

Infrastructural Inadequacies

As firms start operating parts of their global supply chains in developing countries, they encounter substantial deficiencies in infrastructural resources (transportation networks, telecommunication capabilities, worker skill, material/supplier quality, equipment, etc.). We will briefly comment on some of these factors and their implications for global supply chain management.

Worker Skill

Lack of certain worker skills can limit or alter the technological choices a firm might make in a new environment. For example, numerically controlled machine tasks greatly reduce the skill content in that machinists are replaced by more easily trained machine setters and programmers. The growing use of this technology in South American countries stems from difficulties in finding an adequate supply of trained machinists.

Supply Availability and Supplier Quality

Material scarcity can cause serious problems for global supply chains, forcing firms to redesign their process equipment technology or even their product to minimize the use of scarce materials. Imported raw materials are often scarce because of import restrictions caused by foreign-exchange shortages. In other cases supply problems stem from an underdeveloped cadre of input suppliers or from the transportation system.

Companies undertake a variety of creative approaches and actions to overcome such supply problems. A Swedish company designed equipment to produce paper packaging containers that allowed sterilized milk to be kept unrefrigerated for up to three months, thereby overcoming the lack of refrigeration in developing countries. McDonald's faced substantial problems in developing high-quality reliable Russian suppliers in its restaurant operations in Russia. The fast-food chain successfully employed a vertical integration strategy through the development of its own plant and distribution facility for processing meat patties, producing french fries, preparing dairy products, and baking buns and apple pies. They even grew their own potatoes in the early stages of their Russian operations. A Brazilian steel producer developed technology to substitute charcoal for the special metal-grade cooking coal that was unavailable locally.

Supply shortages and irregular schedules can create chaos in the global supply chain planning process. The typical reaction of keeping higher levels of inventories of raw materials or work-in-process exacerbates the perverse dynamics of the bullwhip effect. At the same time, it makes it impossible to reinforce in certain factory networks the principles of JIT supply and production. Sometimes it may even lead companies to modify normally continuous production processes to large batch processes.

Lack of Local Process Equipment and Technologies

A lack of process equipment and technologies in certain countries can also seriously handicap certain product development and production processes. In such cases, firms are forced to carry out R & D locally and develop local process equipment and technologies. The problem becomes serious when such things as import restrictions necessitate the development and use of local equipment and technologies.

Inadequacies in Transportation and Telecommunications Infrastructure

Serious weaknesses in transportation infrastructure can increase distribution lead times. In many cases distribution channels in developing countries are quite long and fragmented. It is not unusual, in these countries, for a product to change hands four to eight times before reaching the final consumer. As a result, supply uncertainty, distribution costs, and inability to control the distribution channel increase. The principal cause of food shortages in Russia has less to do with production than with distribution. The McDonald's venture there organized its own distribution system with its own trucks.

Communications deficiencies create serious market imperfections that can competitively handicap the unprepared global firm. Lack of reliable phone service often means that supply and demand of data are not readily available, thus necessitating substantial investments in the development of effective information systems by the firm.

Explosive Dimensions of Product Variety in Global Markets

The global competitive environment forces the firm to supply highly customized products and services to multiple national markets. This situation leads to explosive proliferation of product models and service options offered by the firm. Usually, manufacturing a product that is suitable for different markets requires the company to produce a basic product that contains most of the features and components of the finished product, and then add on those last-minute components that make the product market-specific. For example, computer products for various countries are manufactured with different, country-specific power-supply modules to accommodate local voltage, frequency, and plug conventions. Furthermore, keyboards and manuals also must match the local language. Such seemingly minor localized variations can cause the firm to produce more than a hundred variations of a seemingly identical computer product.

Product proliferation carries with it a significant supply chain impact. In poorly planned global supply chains, predicting the demands for thousands of items is a forecasting nightmare. Demand uncertainties, in turn, lead to erratic inventory buildups and backorders. The provided service level to customers, both in terms of goods availability and lead times, drastically deteriorates. Many firms end up maintaining extremely high levels of safety stocks in order to assure a reasonable fill rate. If they are inventorying large amounts of highly seasonal or short-lived products, they end up with substantial write-offs due to product obsolescence.

◆ VERTICAL INTEGRATION ISSUES IN GLOBAL SUPPLY CHAINS

Because of the various complexities in global supply chains, companies must make trade-off decisions to develop workable operating and logistics strategy worldwide. We explore some of these trade-offs—particularly as they relate to a firm's decisions on the extent of its vertical integration in its global supply chain.

Vertical Integration to Address Supplier Infrastructure Inadequacies

Many variables can affect the extent of vertical integration of global supply chains in different country or market environments. Table 7–3 presents a summary of these variables. For each variable, and for the different levels of intensity of these variables, Table 7–3 identifies the preferred practice as it relates either to developing a higher level of backward vertical integration (VI) or intensifying the effort to develop local suppliers (LS). Here we offer arguments supporting a variety of approaches. Doubtless, these are general guidelines and each particular case requires a detailed analysis.

Country Environment

Market Size and Growth: The larger the market and the higher its rate of growth, the more likely the firm will be able to justify any decision to invest in integrating into supplier activities.

Labor Cost: Lower labor-cost environments help the long-term economic viability of vertical integration investments.

Labor Skill: Lack of skilled workers substantially complicates the task of expanding into supply activities for the global firm.

Local Managerial Capacity: Management time and resources is a vital asset for most global firms. Unfortunately, in many cases, it is in short supply. The lack of local managerial capacity substantially complicates the task of vertical integration. At the same time, it increases the demand on current management as far as their ability to implement a global strategy goes.

Political Risk: Vertical integration increases the firm's capital asset exposure in environments of political risk, thus making VI less desirable.

Table 7-3: *Backward Vertical Integration (VI) versus Development of Local Suppliers (LS)*

Types of Variables	Condition of Variables	
	Low $\longleftarrow\longrightarrow$ High	
Country Environment		
Market size and growth	LS	VI
Labor cost	VI	LS
Labor skill	LS	VI
Local managerial capacity	VI	LS
Political risk	VI	LS
FG import controls (RM imports controls)	LS (VI)	VI (LS)
Cultural compatibility	LS	VI
Competitive Situation		
Industry concentration	LS	VI
Relative competitive strength	LS	VI
Company Characteristics		
Product		
Maturity	VI	LS
Brand differentiation	LS	VI
Line diversity	VI	LS
Service intensity	LS	VI
Technology		
Maturity	VI	LS
Stability	LS	VI
Complexity	LS	VI
Resources		
Capital	LS	VI
Management	LS	VI
Previous experience	LS	VI
Extent of globalization	LS	VI

Import Controls: Import controls in terms of the finished product sold by the firm in the market favor a VI alternative. Such controls create a protected market in which the firm can easily justify its vertical integration investment. However, if the import controls apply to raw materials and other critical production imports, then the likelihood of operations control problems increases. Capital investment in such situations becomes far more risky.

Cultural Compatibility: The greater the level of cultural compatibility, the simpler the management task of vertically integrating activities. Cultural compatibility also reduces cultural risk and transaction costs with headquarters.

Competitive Situation

Industry Concentration: In oligopolistic environments, firms prefer strong competitive moves that give them more control of their own environments.

Relative Competitive Strength: Stronger firms prefer actions of higher control over their operations and competitive position. As resources tend not to be significant constraints for such firms, VI is typically a preferred option.

Company Characteristics

Product

Maturity: Mature products nearing the end of their product life cycle generate revenue streams that do not usually justify new investment in vertical integration. The development of local supplies becomes a necessity in an effort to extend the product's life in a new market.

Brand Differentiation: For firms with highly differentiated and easily recognizable brands, it becomes a necessity to preserve the quality and service image. Such firms strive for control of operations, and VI serves them well.

Line Diversity: For firms with highly diverse product lines it is a managerial nightmare to try to produce millions of different components themselves. For these firms, the speed and depth of market penetration are of higher priority, and that strategy can be supported by using local suppliers.

Service Intensity: Firms whose products require substantial after-sales service tend to prefer VI. Their customers appreciate fast, high-quality responses to problems in the field. Consequently, an alternative that allows for reduced distances and better communication is preferable.

Technology

Maturity: In the early stages of an industry or in countries with lower levels of technological development, scarcity of qualified suppliers is typical. Thus, firms are forced in the short run to be their own suppliers.

Stability: When the product/process technologies undergo rapid transformation, investing in VI is avoided.

Complexity: The more complex the technology, the higher the required level of control over the production process to guarantee consistent quality levels. Low-tech firms typically prefer local suppliers.

Resources

Capital: For the capital-constrained firm, VI is a hard alternative to justify in the long run.

Management: The more constrained the firm is in terms of managerial talent and time, the less likely it is to invest in a managerial–resource-hungry alternative such as VI.

Previous Experience in Similar Activities: Inexperience in the considered activities for VI is a strong inertia builder against VI.

Extent of Globalization: Firms pursuing global strategies that require them to offer uniform product quality and consistent service to a variety of local markets require very high levels of production control and coordination. VI offers such control and coordination. Product reliability, efficiency, and logistical coordination are essential to preserving the integrity and competitive advantage of a company-owned and -controlled supplier network.

However, in many environments the scarcity of qualified suppliers, even in the presence of all favorable conditions for emphasizing local supply, forces global firms to pursue active supplier development programs. Such programs have to effectively progress from a diagnosis of the supplier's weaknesses, to an effective capability building of the supplier network. The typical deficiencies of local suppliers are in:

- **Technological know-how**—Development programs can transfer technology either from the firm or from some of its existing suppliers (via licensing practices). Know-how can also be built via factory visits of highly qualified suppliers and training.
- **Financial resources**—Local suppliers often lack the financial wherewithal to make needed investment in their product and processes. Financing initiatives, therefore, can be the most effective in upgrading the supplier's equipment, facilities, transportation, and storage infrastructure.
- **Lack of quality and continuous improvement culture**—The introduction and performance monitoring and quality training programs can significantly upgrade the quality of a local supplier. Such continuous improvement efforts should be combined with a clearly communicated and fairly appraised supplier incentive system with positive and negative rewards.

Vertical Integration for Better Control of Distribution Channels

Weaknesses in transportation infrastructure and information services in certain countries make the control of distribution channels in a diverse global environment extremely difficult for the firm. As a result, the firm is forced to contemplate forward vertical integration as an operating alternative for certain county/market environments. Analysis of such a decision will involve multiple trade-offs and variables, and can be done along the lines of the conceptual matrix (see Table 7–3) we used earlier. We will not delve into these details here. However, it should be apparent that the main trade-offs of increased capital exposure and organizational complexity must be weighed against the benefits of a better controlled, coordinated and efficient system.

Forward integration activities, in many cases, cause the company to engage in business activities that are substantially different from their core business—for example, running a proprietary fleet of refrigerated trucks, providing credit extension services, and operating its own retail outlets. Sometimes the firm might have to introduce modern distribution systems to displace traditional ones in developing countries.

◆ Summary

In this chapter we have introduced the concept of supply chain management within the complexities of a global environment. We start by understanding the drivers that make the management of the supply chains so complicated, such as demand volatility and information distortion. The bullwhip effect is the definition used to capture the insights behind the dynamic behavior of supply chains. Demand originating at the customer level starts the overall process. The fact that there are many members in the supply chain (e.g., factories, distributors, wholesalers, and retailers) through which the process has to pass before getting to customers, implies that the information process and coordination should be enforced as a means to reduce the resulting variability. Examples are provided, and the beer game is presented in detail to illustrate the different points.

We then get into the fundamental differences between local and global supply chains. More than the trivial geographical distances involved, we discuss and illustrate approaches used by global companies to deal with the complexities of exchange rates and some infrastructure inadequacies. Finally, we provide a framework for approaching the problem of backward vertical integration versus the alternative of finding local suppliers as a function of the potential country environment, the competitive situation and the company characteristics.

DISCUSSION QUESTIONS

1. What is the *bullwhip* or *whiplash* effect in supply chains? Provide an explanation for the above-used name for this phenomenon. Describe a simple example that clearly illustrates this effect.

2. Why is cross-functional management important in effectively managing supply chains?

3. Within the beer game setting, explain how the performance measurement scheme affects the managerial behavior within the supply chain.

4. What performance metrics would you consider more effective in better coordinating the supply chain? Explain your answer, using as an example the *linear supply chain* with four stages, as in the beer game.

5. What are the major causes of the bullwhip effect?

6. What are suggested practices for firms to follow in order to mitigate the causes of the bullwhip effect?

7. What are Vendor Managed Inventory practices? Why do firms use them?

8. What effects do the use of third-party logistics providers have on the bullwhip effect of the supply chain?

9. What are the advantages and potential drawbacks of everyday low price practices?

10. What are the implications of the use of Continuous Replenishment Programs (CRP) on the bullwhip effect of the supply chain?

11. From a management perspective, how do global supply chains differ from their domestic counterparts? Explain the implications of each one of these differences on the bullwhip effects in the supply chain.

12. Why might companies increase the amount of vertical integration in their global supply chains? In what environments would you expect this approach to be adopted?

13. What are the benefits of backward integration in the supply chain for manufacturers operating in developing country environments?

14. What are the benefits of forward integration in the supply chain for firms operating in developing country environments?

15. What are the advantages and potential disadvantages in investing resources to develop qualified local suppliers when entering new foreign markets?

REFERENCES

Buzzell, R. D., J. A. Quelch, and W. J. Salmon. (1990). The costly bargain of trade promotion. *Harvard Business Review* 68 (March–April): 141–48.

Kelly, K. 1995. Burned by busy signals: Why Motorola ramped up production way past demand. *Business Week* (6 March): 36.

Kopczak, L. R., and Hau L. Lee. 1994. Hewlett-Packard: Deskjet Printer Supply Chain (A). Stanford University, Department of Industrial Engineering and Engineering Management, case study draft of April 1994.

Lee, H. L., V. Padmanabhan, and S. Whang. 1997. The bullwhip effect in supply chains. *Sloan Management Review* (Spring): 93–102.

Sterman, J. 1989. Modeling managerial behavior: Misperception of feedback in a dynamic decision-making experiment. *Management Science* 35 (3): 321–39.

◆ CASE 7–1: Eurofood ◆

In 1975, Mr. Vigneau, a young restaurateur, relocated to Hong Kong and quickly discovered the following:

- Asia is a continent that in the upcoming years will experience an economic boom, of which the British colony of Hong Kong will be one of the principal pillars.
- Certain countries in the region, which includes China and Vietnam, are going to sooner or later open their borders in order to profit from the manna of tourism, and Hong Kong will become a virtually obligatory hub of transit.

If these two hypotheses were true, Hong Kong would rapidly experience a significant influx of businessmen, tourists and expatriates, which would engender new distribution chains of specialty foods, important world-class hotel complexes, and new restaurants serving French cuisine!

Mr. Vigneau therefore decided to create a company specializing in the import, stock, and distribution of food products originating from Europe, and he named it Eurofood. For 15 years, these hypotheses have proven correct, and his company has experienced rapid growth.

But Mr. Vigneau decided to sell his company in order to return to France and to dedicate himself to his primary passion: the restaurant business.

The Olivier Company, specializing in food distribution in Asia, is thinking of extending its network by acquiring Eurofood.

Before making its offer, the firm proceeds with a financial and commercial audit of which the principal elements are summarized here:

- **Commercially,** the company is high-performing. The range of products is very wide and complete as Eurofood distributes the following:
  - wines and spirits
  - dry goods (jams/jellies, chocolate . . .)
  - dairy products (cream, butter, extended life cheeses)
  - frozen foods (fruits and vegetables)
  - perishable goods (fish, cheese, poultry, fruits and vegetables . . .)

Eurofood's clientele breaks down as follows:

- 35% of their business comes from international-class hotels (the Furama, the Hilton, the Meridian, the Oriental Mandarin)
- 30% comes from the purchasing centers of supermarket chains (Park'n'Shop, Welcome, 7 Eleven)
- 25% comes from restaurants that serve Western cuisine

Written by Professor Philippe-Pierre Dornier and Frederic Noyere.

- 10% comes from other clients

Thanks to its undeniable commercial success, Eurofood represents 40% of the luxury foods market.

- **Financially,** the picture is more complicated. Of course, the company makes money, but a certain number of extended expenses are significant.

Upon closer analysis, Olivier Company notices that Eurofood possesses inventory worth 11 million Hong Kong dollars, whereas Olivier Singapore, for an equivalent volume of business, has only 1.3 million Singapore dollars in inventory (or 4 million Hong Kong dollars). This inventory explains in large part the financial expenses that weigh heavy on Eurofood's accounts.

The Olivier Company can only consider acquiring Eurofood if it is possible to reduce inventory in the near future.

You are the new financial director of the Olivier Company and your general director asks that you propose in the next 15 days an inventory reduction plan comprised of:

- the objectives
- the actions to take
- the justifications for the decisions made

upon which the company's offer to acquire Eurofood will largely depend.

All of the products that Eurofood markets arrive from Europe either by airplane or by cargo boat.

Those that arrive by airplane are exclusively perishable products of which the company keeps no inventory. In effect, these products (poultry, fresh cheese, fruits and vegetables) have very short preservation periods and Eurofood must bring them in by airplane and deliver them immediately. The order is only passed on to the supplier in France when a definite order is received from the client. One week's time is required from the time of the client's order to the time of the product's delivery. The only negative point: an elevated price, since cargo costs are 10 Hong Kong dollars per kilogram.

Among the products that arrive by boat, two types must be distinguished:

- those that arrive by complete container
- those that arrive by consolidated container

A container is said to be complete when the total of the products inside are from the same supplier. Thus, inside of a complete "Besnier" container, one would only find "Besnier" products. For example:

- 5,000 packs of UHT cream, 1 liter
- 300 cartons of butter, 10 g portions
- 100 cartons of butter, 25 kg

When Eurofood imports products by complete container, freight costs are 0.5 Hong Kong dollars per kilogram. Four suppliers use complete containers:

- Bel and Besnier, which export dairy products
- George Duboeuf, which exports wine
- Andros, which exports jams/jellies

For more information, consult Appendix 1.

For the importation of small quantities, the complete container is no longer viable. The company must therefore use the consolidated container. This method is based on the idea that one rents only the space that one needs inside of the container. The rest of the container is rented to another supplier, who is also subject to the consolidated container method. For reasons due to bulking, this method is not only more expensive (3 Hong Kong dollars per kilogram) but also more time-consuming: 30 days from the time that the supplier dispatches the order to when the products arrive in Hong Kong.

In order to obtain attractive buying and cargo conditions for those products imported by consolidated container, Eurofood is forced to order them in certain quantities. The company has estimated that, as a standard reference, the optimal duration between the arrival of two containers is 60 days.

To obtain more precise information, you ask Mr. Vigneau to grant you an interview. During the course of this interview, Mr. Vigneau gives you a list that indicates, by product, the annual business sales, the profit margin and average inventory, all three in Hong Kong $. Note that Eurofood has a profit margin of approximately 30%. It equally indicates the retail price in Hong Kong $, unit of measurement and method of transport (refer to Appendix 2):

- consolidated indicates that the product is imported by consolidated container
- complete "Besnier" indicates that it is a Besnier product imported by complete container (same for Bel, Andros, and George Duboeuf)
- airplane indicates that it is a product imported by airplane

When you ask Mr. Vigneau about the reasons for maintaining such a large quantity of inventory, he answers:

"*Certainly, there exists in our inventory products which do not sell much and which have a slow rotation. But commercially, these products are very attractive: we sell them mainly to our best clients, and whereas we are the only ones to import them to Hong Kong, they consider what we do for them a great service. These products are a masterpiece of the commercial success of Eurofood.*

But there exists another explanation: customs duties. In Hong Kong when you import taxable goods (wines and spirits), you have two solutions:
1) Pay the customs duties immediately and stock the products in our warehouse;
2) Place the goods in a bond-store for which the cost is 3 Hong Kong dollars per month and per case of 12 bottles. Then when you desire, you remove the goods from the bond store and pay the taxes at the same time. But note that 4 days are required from the time that you make a decision and the time when you can retrieve these products.

Eurofood has chosen the first solution since we do not have any wines or spirits under customs. In effect, do not forget that our warehouse is already amortized, that bond stores are expensive, and that finance charges in Hong Kong are expensive (12% per year). Additionally, don't forget that if we have part of our inventory under customs and the other part in our warehouse, we must constantly keep track of the latter so as to never experience a break in inventory. The client will receive delivery the day following his order. If we ask him to wait, he will cancel his order and go over to the competition. That would be a total disaster."

You decide to research the issue of customs duties. You obtain the following numbers:

- the cost of the bond store is 3 Hong Kong dollars per month and per case of 12 bottles;
- the taxes are two-tiered: one is a fixed tax of 10 Hong Kong dollars per bottle and the other is a variable 50% tax of the CIF (Cost Insurance Free) price of the product imported.

Appendix 1
Arrivals of Complete Containers over the Last Six Months

Departure Date	Arrival Date	Suppliers	Boat	Freight Forwarder
1/3	1/24	Besnier	Tour du Monde	Clasquin
1/6	1/25	Andros	Ile du Levant	Sagatrans
1/6	1/25	Bel	Ile du Levant	Sagatrans
1/12	2/2	George DeBoeuf	Naissance	Kunehäge

Departure Date	Arrival Date	Suppliers	Boat	Freight Forwarder
1/25	2/15	Besnier	Soleil Levant	SCAC
1/25	2/15	Bel	Soleil Levant	SCAC
2/2	2/24	George DeBoeuf	Diable au Corps	Sagatrans
2/14	3/5	Besnier	Aller et Retour	Andelström
2/18	3/11	Bel	Tour du Monde	Clasquin
2/25	3/15	George DeBoeuf	Bretagne	Kunehäge
3/1	3/21	Andros	Naissance	SCAC
3/5	3/25	Besnier	lle du Levant	Sagatrans
3/5	3/25	Bel	lle du Levant	Sagatrans
3/15	4/7	George DeBoeuf	Normandie	Andelström
3/27	4/19	Besnier	Aller et Retour	Kunehäge
3/29	4/21	Bel	Soleil Levant	SCAC
3/29	4/21	George DeBoeuf	Soleil Levant	SCAC
4/19	5/10	Besnier	Diable au Corps	Sagatrans
4/21	5/12	Bel	Tour du Monde	Clasquin
4/25	5/18	George DeBoeuf	Naissance	Kunehäge
5/4	5/25	Andros	Bretagne	Sagatrans
5/10	5/30	Bel	lle du Levant	Sagatrans
5/10	5/30	Besnier	lle du Levant	Sagatrans
5/18	6/10	George DeBoeuf	Aller et Retour	Andelström
5/29	6/21	Bel	Normandie	Kunehäge
5/31	6/23	Besnier	Diable au Corps	SCAC
6/9	6/30	George DeBoeuf	Tour du Monde	Clasquin

Appendix 2
Products Carried by Eurofood

Name (of product)	Average Annual Business Sales (HK $)	Profit (HK $)	Inventory (HK $)	Hong Kong $	Units	Comments
UHT Whipping Cream 1 Liter	10,181,948	2,138,209	1,980,598	20	L	Complete "Besnier"
Portion Butter Unsalted 10 Grs	6,919,080	2,075,724	1,421,729	180	Case	Complete "Besnier"
Minibabybel Catering 96X22,6	3,641,929	1,092,579	648,563	280	Case	Complete "Bel"
Butter Unsalted Block 25 Kg	2,542,946	686,595	543,424	120		Complete "Besnier"
Apple Tea 125 Grs	1,478,886	443,666	486,209	42		Consolidated
Party Cube Nature 120 Grs	943,670	283,101	180,978	7		Complete "Bel"
UHT Whipping Cream 20 Cl	716,036	214,811	186,366	6		Complete "Besnier"
Cuvee Gd Red 75 Cl	634,565	177,678	130,390	42		Complete "George DeBoeuf"
Cuve Gd White 75 Cl	610,629	170,976	113,761	42		Complete "George DeBoeuf"
Jambon Cru De Bayonne 4–6 Kg	551,455	165,437	135,975	220	Kg	Complete "Bel"
Rolled Mousse of Goose Liver 320 Grs	530,053	159,016	145,220	231		Consolidated
Laughing Cow 8 Portions 140 Gr	509,055	152,717	82,286	7		Complete "Bel"
Party Cube Red 120 Gr	478,589	143,577	255,685	7		Complete "Bel"
Dried Morels France Extra	459,265	137,780	119,535	1,000		Consolidated
Rauw Goose Liver	457,470	137,241	0	1,200	Kg	Airplane
Soles 450–500 Gr	405,760	162,304	0	180	Kg	Airplane

Name (of product)	Average Annual Business Sales (HK $)	Profit (HK $)	Inventory (HK $)	Hong Kong $	Units	Comments
Salmon Gutted Fresh 3–4 Kg	385,012	154,005	0	250	Kg	Airplane
Pouilly Fuisse 1987 75 Cl	364,258	109,277	109,776	75		Complete "George DeBoeuf"
Air Dried Beef	345,259	138,104	0	540	Kg	Airplane
Emmenthal Block	335,692	100,708	94,730	210	Kg	Complete "Besnier"
Laughing Cow 12 Portions	325,698	97,709	74,063	12		Complete "Bel"
Apple Tea 250 Gr	314,526	94,358	90,480	80		Consolidated
Camembert in Tin	310,256	93,077	129,202	25		Complete "Besnier"
Fresh Duck Fillet	305,125	106,794	0	240	Kg	Airplane
Boursin Pepper	298,521	89,556	0	21		Airplane
Minibabybel	289,652	72,413	138,874	12		Complete "Bel"
Orange Marmalade 50 Gr	280,124	84,037	69,072	2,5		Complete "Andros"
Camembert President	275,412	82,624	47,537	18		Complete "Besnier"
Endive	274,256	109,702	0	50	Kg	Airplane
Scottish Smoked Salmon	268,541	80,562	0	240	Kg	Airplane
Belon 000	265,485	92,920	0	270	Kg	Airplane
Norway Smoked Salmon	264,521	79,356	0	310	Kg	Airplane
Roquefort Portion 100 Gr	262,485	78,746	73,352	18		Complete "Bel"
Raw Duck Liver	261,458	91,510	0	270	Kg	Airplane
Fleurie 1987	260,198	72,855	89,109	120		Complete "George DeBoeuf"
Turbot 3–4 Kg	258,413	103,365	0	220	Kg	Airplane
Red Chiroky Italy	257,164	90,007	0	51	Kg	Airplane
Rect Turkey Ballotine	256,983	77,095	278,105	210		Consolidated
Turbot + 4 KG	256,469	89,764	0	200	Kg	Airplane
Beaujolais Village 1987	255,961	71,669	122,721	78		Complete "George DeBoeuf"
Darjeeling Tea 125 Gr	255,120	76,536	134,899	42		Consolidated
Strawberry Jam 50 Gr	254,763	76,429	62,818	2,5		Complete "Andros"
Honey Jam 50 Gr	254,156	76,247	205,414	2,5		Complete "Andros"
Boursin Garlic & Herbs	253,968	76,190	0	270	Kg	Airplane
Cerneaux Noix Extra	253,641	76,092	87,558	270		Consolidated
Carlton Peach	253,248	68,377	437,113	75		Consolidated
Vegetable Terrine	253,120	75,936	55,478	128		Consolidated
Butter Unsalted 1 Kg	252,989	75,897	59,608	10		Complete "Besnier"
Turffle Brushes 1st Choice	252,754	75,826	55,398	1,050		Consolidated
Goose Liver v. Truffles 3%	252,563	75,769	0	1,080		Airplane
Portion Butter Salted 10 Gr	252,436	75,731	82,993	180	Case	Complete "Besnier"
Androuet Cheese 15 Pcs	252,387	80,764	0	260		Airplane
Beluga Caviar 1 Kg	252,358	100,943	0	780		Airplane
Butter Unsalted 227 Gr	252,312	75,694	66,362	4		Complete "Besnier"
Babybel Red Waxed 200 Gr	251,862	75,559	97,985	12		Complete "Bel"
Red Lettuce	251,126	87,894	0	50	Kg	Airplane
Veiga Madeira "Fine Rich" 75 Cl	250,962	75,289	85,946	125		Consolidated
Chablis 1er Cru 1987	250,123	75,037	75,380	210		Consolidated
Darjeeling Tea 250 Gr	246,126	73,838	64,060	80		Consolidated
Scallop Heart with Roe On	245,632	73,690	0	175	Kg	Airplane
Brie in Tin	241,365	72,410	48,273	18		Complete "Besnier"
Snails 6 Doz in Tin	239,462	71,836	114,806	65		Consolidated
Chef Block Goose Liver	230,452	73,745	56,824	1,018		Consolidated
Normandie Calvados 70 Cl	229,541	68,862	75,466	250		Consolidated
Kiri Portions 6	241,365	68,590	41,342	12		Complete "Bel"

Name (of product)	Average Annual Business Sales (HK $)	Profit (HK $)	Inventory (HK $)	Hong Kong $	Units	Comments
Fleurie 1988	245,632	68,224	52,959	79		Complete "George DeBoeuf"
Pouilly Fume 1987	246,126	67,924	68,234	125		Complete "George DeBoeuf"
Morning Tea 125 Gr	250,123	67,689	52,544	42		Consolidated
Sancerre Blanc 1987	250,962	66,317	54,507	178		Consolidated
Soles 300–340 Gr	251,126	88,146	0	250	Kg	Airplane
Fine de Claire	215,896	75,564	0	248	Kg	Airplane
Brie President 1 Kg	212,369	63,711	55,274	120		Complete "Besnier"
B. de Cremant Rose	210,596	63,179	63,467	210		Consolidated
Potatoes Parisiennes 1 Kg	200,365	60,110	68,618	54		Consolidated
Sea Bass 1–2 Kg	189,821	66,332	0	289	Kg	Airplane
Casador Red	187,452	56,236	102,713	58		Consolidated
Kirschco 75 Cl	185,632	55,690	48,315	215		Consolidated
Vin Rouge Cuisine	185,421	51,918	55,880	40		Complete "George DeBoeuf"
Fromage De L'Averne	184,732	55,420	0	80		Airplane
Ronele Garlic & Herbs	162,085	48,656	79,044	17		Complete "Besnier"
Fresh Truffles	154,269	58,622	0	1,080	Kg	Airplane
Yvon Rouge 75 Cl	145,214	43,564	29,838	49		Consolidated
Girolles 560 Gr	124,685	37,406	27,328	740		Consolidated
Laughing Cow Barquette	112,030	330,609	29,158	18		Complete "Bel"
Moulin a Vent 1987	110,854	33,256	21,260	125		Complete "George DeBoeuf"
Bresse Chicken	109,521	32,856	0	215	Kg	Airplane
Apricot Jam 50 Gr	102,584	30,775	29,510	2,5		Complete "Andros"
Beluga Caviar 200 Gr	99,521	39,808	0	250		Airplane
Casador White	97,541	27,311	26,189	48		Consolidated
Calvados Pays D'Auge 1933	96,254	28,876	21,097	215		Consolidated
Chablis 1987	91,256	27,377	25,002	191		Consolidated
Minipic	85,210	25,563	0	18		Airplane
Haricots Verts	82,365	28,828	0	50	Kg	Airplane
Special Butter 49 Gr Unsalted	80,125	24,038	9,878	10		Complete "Besnier"
Passion Fruits Puree 6 Kg	78,541	23,562	20,442	315		Consolidated
Fraise 5 Kg	78,123	23,437	23,544	60		Consolidated
Olive Oil 1 L	77,985	23,396	29,485	27		Consolidated
Beaujolais Village 1988	76,985	23,096	9,491	110		Complete "George DeBoeuf"
Baby Chicken 400–500 Gr	76,125	24,360	0	170	Kg	Airplane
Camembert Terroir Normand 250 Gr	75,845	22,754	0	27		Airplane
Frisee	75,412	24,132	0	50	Kg	Airplane
Framboise 5 Kg	75,125	22,538	20,582	65		Consolidated
Champignon Paris	75,012	22,504	0	115	Kg	Airplane
Lobster Norway	74,963	23,239	0	760	Kg	Airplane
Caprice Des Dieux 135 Gr	72,561	21,768	0	27		Airplane
Pommery Mustard 500 Gr	65,413	19,624	19,714	49		Consolidated
Raspberry Jam 50 Gr	61,023	18,307	15,883	2,5		Complete "Andros"
Chateauneuf du Pape Red 1986	58,632	17,590	28,593	180		Consolidated
Chrande Cuvee Gd Blanc	54,123	15,154	7,562	51		Complete "George DeBoeuf"
Uht Whipping Cream 50 Cl	50,874	15,262	12,962	12		Complete "Besnier"

Name (of product)	Average Annual Business Sales (HK $)	Profit (HK $)	Inventory (HK $)	Hong Kong $	Units	Comments
Cotes du Rhone Red 1987	48,632	14,590	10,393	191		Complete "George DeBoeuf"
Fine de Claire 1	46,512	16,279	0	460	Kg	Airplane
Rambol Walnut	42,831	12,849	16,663	18		Complete "Besnier"
Chanterelles Mushrooms in Tin 460 Gr	39,621	11,886	11,398	540		Consolidated
Dried Morels 1st Choice	33,165	9,950	10,722	1,100	Kg	Consolidated
Asperge	30,895	10,813	0	75	Kg	Airplane
Frozen Cepes No. 0	25,621	7,686	8,494	540	Kg	Consolidated
Dried Cepes	20,785	6,236	6,264	775	Kg	Consolidated
Blue Cheese 30 Gr	18,631	5,589	0	12		Airplane
Pike	16,384	4,915	0	18		Airplane
Bloc of Duck Liver 1 Kg	14,698	4,409	0	1,075		Airplane
Brouilly 1987	11,695	3,509	3,044	211		Complete "George DeBoeuf"
Beluga Caviar 100 Gr	9,321	3,728	0	195		Airplane
Brie Portion 180 Gr	8,691	2,607	2,286	41		Complete "Besnier"
Earl Grey Tea 125 Gr	7,963	2,389	3,818	42		Consolidated
Mangoes Puree 6 Kg	7,269	2,181	4,182	318		Consolidated
Extra Fine Peas Sweet 1 Kg	6,987	2,096	6,317	75		Consolidated
Saint Paulin 30 Gr	6,589	1,977	6,950	12		Complete "Besnier"
Cheateauneuf du Pape White 1987	6,125	1,838	1,846	181		Consolidated
Chablis 1er Cru 1987 37,5 Cl	6,012	1,804	4,908	53		Consolidated
Poire Williams Brandy	5,869	1,761	1,624	215		Consolidated
Special Butter 49 Gr Demi-Sel	5,421	1,518	2,347	10		Complete "Besnier"
Yvon Blanc	5,237	1,571	2,597	48		Consolidated
Myrtilles 5 Kg	5,012	1,504	1,510	318		Consolidated
Terrine of Fish	5,001	1,500	1,535	175		Consolidated
Chabis Round White Goat 100 Gr	4,765	1,430	0	31		Airplane
Parma Ham	4,652	1,396	1,083	318	Kg	Complete "Bel"
Sancerre Blanc 1988	4,215	1,265	2,425	218		Consolidated
Frozen Forestiere	3,986	1,196	2,403	115	Kg	Consolidated
Ravioli Plaque	3,745	1,124	0	91	Kg	Airplane
Brill 800 Gr+	3,429	1,200	0	151	Kg	Airplane
Carrots Parisiennes 1 Kg	3,145	944	2,999	78		Consolidated
Bergerac Red 1985	3,028	908	2,895	211		Consolidated
Chassagne Montrachet 1985	2,965	890	1,706	561		Consolidated
Cherry Jam 50 Gr	2,756	827	740	2,5		Complete "Andros"
Port Salut Baby Round 200 Gr	2,415	725	298	18		Complete "Besnier"
Soles 500–600 Gr	2,346	821	0	240	Kg	Airplane
Cotes du Rhone Red 1988	2,106	632	1,142	175		Complete "George DeBoeuf"
Chevre Cheese	2,059	618	0	41		Airplane
Lobster Norway 11–15	2,018	706	0	318	Kg	Airplane
Airelles 5 Kg	1,985	596	625	315		Consolidated
Petit Chablis 1986	1,856	557	702	213		Consolidated
Butter Unsalted 227 Gr	1,745	524	904	4		Complete "Besnier"
Peach Jam 340 Gr	1,702	511	1,072	51		Complete "Andros"
Present Collection	1,698	509	977	518		Consolidated
Fraise Des Bois 2 Kg	1,621	486	866	110		Consolidated
Norway Smoked Salmon Presliced	1,602	481	0	215		Airplane
Xeres Vinegar Red 50 Cl	1,542	463	1,681	27		Consolidated

Name (of product)	Average Annual Business Sales (HK $)	Profit (HK $)	Inventory (HK $)	Hong Kong $	Units	Comments
Banana Tea 125 Gr	1,530	459	734	42		Consolidated
Chambolle Musigny 1983	1,459	438	839	741		Consolidated
Bourgogne Rouge 1986	1,426	428	1,293	218		Complete "George DeBoeuf"
Bonbel Portion 150 Gr	1,407	422	378	45		Complete "Bel"
Sable Chocolate Cookies 152 Gr	1,389	417	373	18		Consolidated
B de B Cremant Blanc	1,389	407	427	215		Consolidated
Vieux Pane	1,356	398	0	175	Kg	Airplane
Sea Bream Pink	1,327	395	0	418	Kg	Airplane
Hazelnut Oil 50 Cl	1,318	386	415	59		Consolidated
Laitue	1,285	407	0	41	Kg	Airplane
Slices Croque Monsieur	1,272	378	2,173	18		Complete "Besnier"
Ch Beausejour 1985	1,259	371	2,032	789		Consolidated
Vieille Prune	1,236	368	1,403	218		Consolidated
Swiss Gruyer Tiger Cheese	1,225	363	0	218	Kg	Airplane
Chablis 1987 37,5 Cl	1,211	360	658	175		Consolidated
Citron Tea 125 Gr	1,200	355	567	42		Consolidated
Apricot Puree 6 Kg	1,183	344	894	327		Consolidated
Ch. Montrose 1980	1,121	336	863	1,018		Consolidated
Henkell Trocken Reg. 20 Cl	1,083	325	326	210		Consolidated
Ch Yquem 1981	1,056	317	1,094	1,025		Consolidated
Coulommiers S/Paille	1,029	309	0	52		Airplane
Darjeeling Tea 25 Gr	1,012	304	269	20		Consolidated
Fleurie 1988 37,5 Cl	1,003	301	324	41		Complete "George DeBoeuf"
Collavini Pinot Grigio 1987	968	290	1,056	180		Consolidated
Brouilly 1988	923	277	1,037	190		Complete "George DeBoeuf"
Ch. Lagrange 1983	910	273	1,421	741		Consolidated
Crozes Hermitage 1988	859	258	1,318	448		Consolidated
Macon Village 1989	847	254	545	152		Complete "George DeBoeuf"
Rabbit Saddles	823	247	0	218	Kg	Airplane
Tomatoes Beef BB	811	243	0	51	Kg	Airplane
Cassis Puree 6 Kg	756	227	238	318		Consolidated
Griottines	712	214	605	518		Consolidated
Slices Hamburger	698	209	1,195	18		Complete "Besnier"
Pinot Blanc 1987	654	196	385	121		Consolidated
Cotes de Beaune Village 1983	621	186	541	198		Complete "George DeBoeuf"
Oscietra Caviar 30 Gr	546	218	0	121		Airplane
Sweet Butter Cookies 125 Gr	418	125	364	18		Consolidated
Orange Sweet Tea 125 Gr	356	107	206	42		Consolidated
Ch La Fleur Becade 1985	298	89	283	782		Consolidated
Salmon Eggs 30 Gr	219	66	0	75		Airplane
Crozes Hermitage 1987	158	47	2,045	289		Complete "George DeBoeuf"
Chiroubles 1986 37,5 Cl	102	31	145	341		Consolidated
Jasmin Tea 125 Gr	85	26	730	42		Consolidated
Total	5,059E+7	1,47E+7	1,09E+7	4E+4		

◆　CASE 7–2: Phytosante　◆

Phytosante's stocking policy has known highs and lows. Until just recently, the mean inventory was able to cover approximately one month of sales, and up to five months for certain products. Alarmed by a report from the financial directors and the administrative auditors, management has launched the imperative "zero inventory for all products."

This new policy has been marred by frequent breaks in inventory and, therefore, by a deterioration of Phytosante's brand image in the eyes of large-scale distributors and retail and hospital pharmacies. It is to remedy this situation that you have been asked to conduct a study of safety stock inventory.

A certain amount of data has been collected concerning Lanfando, a mild anti-anxiety medication. This product has been essentially designated for the study because of the high volume of units sold; a "small" product would effectively not have been conducive to the collection of significant data.

Theoretically, your study is limited to calculating the value to give to the "safety stock inventory" parameter for Lanfando and to estimate the mean inventory that would result. But you do not want to lose the opportunity to make yourself valuable to the organization by proposing solutions to decrease the inventory levels without increasing the risk of breaks in inventory.

1. General Information

1.1 Organization of Distribution

Phytosante's clients are large-scale distributors (who supply drugstores) and hospital pharmacies. We are only concerned with the former here, even though Lanfando exists equally in hospitals, a situation for which you do not have the figures at your disposal.

Order processing is guaranteed by two regional stores. A daily shuttle service is guaranteed to distribute the available stock to them. To offset errors in permanent inventory, the stores' directors will only release a product if the remaining stock will allow them to guarantee two additional days' worth of orders.

1.2 Permanent Inventory

Products are accounted for in a computerized inventory once a lot is accepted by the pharmacist responsible. Three days maximum are then required before the product becomes available in the two distribution stores.

A product that leaves the store is withdrawn from the inventory in real time (it is counted as gone the moment that the order is verified).

1.3 Production Planning

The planning program calculates inventory projections based on sales accomplished and the estimates of business contacts. The latter are revised every month. The system determines a need date that corresponds to the date at which the inventory reaches a level defined as safety stock (this is the value that you should study).

The factories' planning is determined on the basis of the inventory projections. The start date for production is determined in relation to the need date, hand in hand with the production lead time determined for the particular product. In general, production scheduling should be considered definitive one month in advance.

2. Information Pertaining to Lanfando

2.1 Stocking

The per-unit stocking cost has been evaluated at 0.1 Francs/year for a product valued at 12.00/Francs per unit. We estimate, furthermore, that lost and damaged products (handling accidents or expiration) represent 1.5% of the mean inventory each year.

2.2 Commercial Estimates and Actuals

Table 1 shows the volume of estimated and actual sales over a period of three years. The estimates are established one month in advance (in January for February, etc.).

2.3 Production

Law requires that pharmaceutical products be manufactured in lots: the lots must be numbered and the lot number must be indicated on each unit. For Lanfando, the size of the lots is 75,000 units. However, in order to avoid too frequent format changes on the packaging assembly lines, the company links together 4 production lots (or 300,000 units) at a time.

Table 2 shows the delay in production in relation to the targeted date for 50 production series (or 200 lots), the duration of the production cycle (the delay in the marked parameter in the system is 11 days), and the number of units actually produced.

Outside of the difficulties relating to supply, the most frequent problems involve packaging: packaging is performed on a particularly efficient assembly line, but one that has an often-delicate regulation, which allows it to treat the packaging for Lanfando and other products at the same time.

Written by Professor Philippe-Pierre Dornier and Marc Lamotte.

Table 1

	1987		1988		1989	
	Estimated	Actual	Estimated	Actual	Estimated	Actual
January	1,100,000	1,122,000	1,150,000	1,085,600	1,200,000	1,202,400
February	1,100,000	1,238,600	1,100,000	1,201,200	1,100,000	972,400
March	1,150,000	956,800	1,000,000	974,000	1,150,000	1,071,800
April	1,100,000	1,089,000	1,200,000	1,250,400	1,150,000	1,182,200
May	1,100,000	985,600	1,150,000	993,600	1,100,000	1,128,600
June	1,100,000	1,155,000	1,000,000	1,066,000	1,000,000	918,000
July	900,000	887,400	950,000	908,200	1,000,000	1,058,400
August	900,000	1,065,600	900,000	912,600	950,000	1,052,600
September	1,000,000	926,000	1,050,000	1,045,800	1,000,000	1,008,000
October	1,200,000	1,300,800	1,150,000	1,315,600	1,100,000	1,117,600
November	1,150,000	1,200,600	1,150,000	1,113,200	1,150,000	1,090,200
December	1,100,000	1,058,200	1,100,000	998,800	1,100,000	1,181,400
TOTAL	12,900,000	12,985,600	12,900,000	12,865,000	13,000,000	12,983,600

Estimated and Actual Sales

Table 2

Delay in Production

Number	Delay	Duration	Size	Number	Delay	Duration	Size
1		11	294,292	26		11	290,300
2		12	292,700	27	4	10	302,800
3		12	301,400	28		11	293,900
4		10	302,700	29		11	228,800
5		10	297,000	30	−1	11	302,400
6		13	302,300	31		11	299,900
7		11	301,100	32		13	300,600
8		11	293,200	33		13	302,200
9		11	300,500	34		15	293,900
10		13	299,500	35		16	300,700
11		12	305,200	36	1	13	303,300
12	2	15	302,800	37		10	299,900
13		10	301,800	38		10	301,700
14		12	299,900	39		14	304,100
15		14	304,800	40		16	297,900
16		11	301,700	41		16	306,300
17	5	9	301,100	42		14	296,200
18		14	298,300	43	5	11	299,800
19		12	300,100	44		13	300,600
20		14	299,400	45		20	303,600
21		11	305,500	46		13	301,500
22	2	11	298,700	47	3	10	298,700
23	3	12	297,800	48		14	288,000
24		10	299,500	49		10	301,400
25		15	298,700	50		13	291,500

No. 12 and 36: Delay in another product packaged on the same assembly line

No. 17: Break in inventory of packaging materials (cardboard boxes)

No. 22, 23, 27 and 43: Delay of delivery of raw materials

No. 30: Series of lots ahead of schedule

No. 47: Series of lots changed to fulfill an export order

No. 29: Lot refused by quality control

◆ CASE 7-3: Marmitou ◆

Marmitou manufactures and distributes a range of food seasoning products: tomato sauces, mustards, condiments, spices, mayonnaises, etc.

These products are aimed at clients ranging from major distribution stores (hypermarkets and supermarkets) to distribution by convenience stores (mini-markets). A considerable volume of sales is destined for fast-food clients.

At the end of a survey on the organization and physical distribution of its finished products, the management decided to adopt a two-tiered structure.

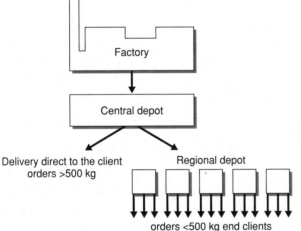

The first level comprises a central warehouse, and the second, regional depots. The draft designs drawn up have located the central warehouse in Angers, in an area where the company has purchased a vast plot of land. The warehouse is to be designed from scratch.

All the products manufactured by the company's single factory in Nantes will pass through this central depot. The

Written by Professors Philippe-Pierre Dornier and Michel Fender with the assistance of Patrick Ploix (Tailleur Industrie) and Joël David (Tailleur Industrie)

products are delivered on standard pallets measuring 800 × 1200 by 1800 cm high. These products will be stored and distributed in either of two means:

- directly to end clients for large orders weighing in excess of 500 kg
- to regional depots for smaller orders with an average weight in 1990 of 250 kg

The factory in Nantes is equipped with an automatic palletizer. The products pass along individually, are packed in boxes, and are placed on a pallet.

Demand is very seasonal, and the overall volume of sales has been increasing for three years.

At the beginning of this year, 1991, the management has assigned you the task of calculating the ideal size of the warehouse looking ahead to 1996. All you have at your disposal is the information relating to 1990. To carry out this project, you have a five-point plan comprising the following elements:

- calculate the dimensions of the warehouse
- calculate the surface area required
- analyze product movement
- calculate human and material resources requirements
- estimate of costs for the different alternatives

You should treat each of these points in an integral way to submit the proposal expected by your manager. The following are guidelines for each of the points mentioned.

1. Calculation of the Dimensions of the Warehouse

To calculate the dimensions of the warehouse designed to contain the finished products arriving from the factory, you will first have to calculate the volume of activity with respect to all the warehouse functions:

- incoming and outgoing flow
- stock levels

The following documents are available:

- List of products stocked
- 1990 sales statistics per product
- Monthly sales figures for 1990
- Monthly stock figures for 1990
- Stock level targets
- Sales forecasts: annual variations per product

List of Products

Marmitou markets essentially three families of products: Family A is the largest and comprises nine products set out in the following list:

	Net weight/ box (kg)	Number of boxes/ pallet	Net weight/ pallet (kg)	Gross weight/ pallet (kg)
Family A				
Product A1	12.0	34	408	460
A2	6.0	68	408	460
A3	12.0	30	360	400
A4	8.0	56	448	510
A5	6.5	64	416	470
A6	6.0	76	456	525
A7	4.8	96	460.8	510
A8	12.0	34	408	465
A9	10.0	44	440	500
Family B	Average 56 kg		550	620
Family C	Average 56 kg		250	280
Others	Average 56 kg		475	540

1990 Sales Statistics per Product

The sales statistics relate to 1990 and show the annual tonnage and number of boxes.

	Net tonnage (in tons)	Boxes (number)
Family A		
A1	8,198	683,000
A2	2,829	471,000
A3	1,218	101,000
A4	483	60,000
A5	44	7,000
A6	8,699	1,450,000
A7	433	90,000
A8	541	45,000
A9	428	43,000
Sub-total	22,873	2,290,000
Family B	2,413	241,000
Family C	912	91,000
Others	78	8,000
TOTAL	26,776	3,290,000

Monthly Sales Figures for 1990 and Monthly Stock Figures for 1990

Stocks for all product families combined are calculated at the end of the month. The management would like to see their volume in the central warehouse brought to the level of average monthly consumption equivalent to the amount that will be consumed in 0.6 of a month. Those products together representing over 50% of the storage requirement shall be stockpiled; the others shall be stored according to traditional procedures (see appendix 1).

Month	12/89	01/90	02/90	03/90	04/90	05/90	06/90	07/90	08/90	09/90	10/90	11/90	12/90	Aver.
Sales (net ton.)	—	1,730	1,970	2,501	2,155	2,113	2,255	1,731	2,320	2,320	2,597	2,446	2,637	2,190
Stocks (net ton.)	1,240	1,492	1,603	1,527	1,802	2,010	2,482	1,416	1,273	1,470	1,385	1,602	1,316	1,615

Sales Forecasts: Annual Variations

Growth for the next five years is stated by the forecasting department as a constant for each component of family A, for family B, and for family C.

	△ year
Family A	
A1	+3%
A2	+8%
A3	+15%
A4	+15%
A5	+6%
A6	+10%
A7	+10%
A8	+10%
A9	+15%
Family B	+5%
Family C	−2%
Others	+10%

No major introduction of new products is planned. The packaging should remain identical and seasonality will not change.

2. Calculation of Surface Area Required

After discussion with the management, it became apparent that the objectives regarding stock level would be quite difficult to achieve and that marketing forecasts were rather optimistic.

Therefore, the discussions led to the adoption of the following conclusions:

Total capacity	7,500 pallets
where pallets are of	
P × L = 800 × 1,200 cm	
• stockpiling	4,500 pallets
• traditional	3,500 pallets
Max. No. arrivals	420 pallets/day
Max. No. departures	420 pallets/day

These figures will enable you at this stage to compare them to the results you have obtained and to judge the relevance of your initial work.

The average warehouse filling rate is quite low:

$$\frac{4.500}{7.500} = 60\%$$

A target of 80% would have been more economical, but the substantial seasonal factor affecting demand is causing this additional capacity requirement.

In a slack period, it would be desirable that Marmitou use its excess capacity by storing the products of others who have a reverse seasonal weighting. But this matter is not on the agenda at the moment.

Your current task is to calculate the surface areas required for warehouse storage. It is therefore necessary to:

- calculate the necessary surface areas for
  - arrivals
  - shipments
  - stockpiling
  - traditional storage
- calculate the total surface area needed, including not only the previous surface areas but additional ones (e.g., technical areas or offices) that you must list and evaluate.

Summarize your evaluations using the following framework:

Type of surface area	Calculation	Surface area needed

For the part of the warehouse used for traditional storage, the management requests that you compare three different options:

- option one: storage by means of front, retractable trolley (the height of the building will be about 9 meters)
- option two: a three-way trolley (the height of the building will be about 13 meters)
- option three: high-level storage (22 meters) and automated storage transfer system

Stockpiling can be achieved by stacking 5 levels high and 4 pallets deep.

The method of calculating the surface area is as follows:

Traditional Storage

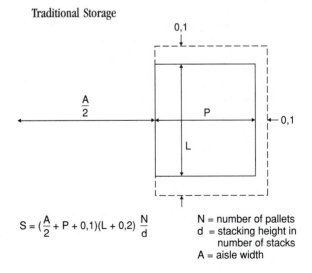

$$S = \left(\frac{A}{2} + P + 0,1\right)(L + 0,2)\,\frac{N}{d}$$

N = number of pallets
d = stacking height in number of stacks
A = aisle width

The aisle width used should be 2.80 m.

Stockpiling

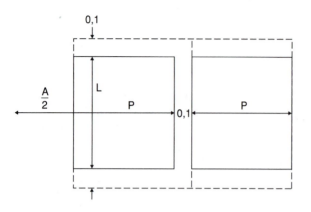

Note that aisle width reduces in this option.

The incoming traffic is of the order of 19 vehicles a day arriving at regular intervals (traffic leaving the factory). Supplies to the warehouse shall be by truck only. Acceptance will be carried out by the carrier completely randomly throughout the year.

Dispatch shall be of the order of 25 vehicles a day, intervals between them will depend on the carriers (all outside).

It should be possible to dispatch consignments by rail and road.

3. Product Movement

You should now turn your thoughts to the movement of products inside the warehouse with the aim of calculating the measurements and resources to be employed (human and equipment).

Your first task will be to define the movement of products in the warehouse by identifying all the different types of activities:

- operation
- transport or handling
- control
- waiting
- storage

Prepared orders are either to be sent to the regional depots or shipped directly to the end customers. In the fourth quarter of 1990, the order processing operations were divided up as follows, expressed as daily averages.

	Depot orders	Client orders	TOTAL
Tonnage	76.4	45.5	121.9
Total pallets	177.0	105.5	282.0
No. orders	22.0	82.0	104.0
No. complete pallets			214
No. boxes	88.0	82.0	
No. boxes/order	4.0	1.0	
No. units	44.0	1,066.0	
No. units/order	2.0	13.0	
No. retail lines/order	4.0	14.0	

Looking forward to 1996, it is planned to have the same number of clients and the same order structure. However, the number of direct client orders should increase in a manner identical to the tonnage divided up as follows:

1991	300 orders	Between	0 to 500 kg
1996	300 orders	Between	0 & 714 kg
	of which 210	Between	0 & 500 kg
	and 90	Between	500 & 714 kg

The number of deliveries to regional depots should not change.

4. Human and Material Resources Requirements

To accomplish this task, an estimate must be made of the personnel and equipment needed to operate the warehouse.

In appendix 2 you will find an evaluation of the basic operations previously mentioned. This evaluation was carried out on the basis of handling time and motion standards, drawn up by IFTIM (Institute for Training in Installation and Handling Techniques).

To assess the personnel required you should take the following into account:

- Working week = 38 hours
  - either 2,280 minutes/person/week
  - or 456 minutes/person/day
- Commitment target of personnel 80%
  - i.e., $456 \times 0.8 = 365$ minutes/person/day

Your interim results should be set out in a table of the following type:

Operation	Type of operator	Type of equipment	No. homogenous units/day (Pallet/day Order/day)	Unit time (in cm per man. unit)	Total time	No. operators

5. Estimate of Costs

a) Building

The building will be constructed on land owned by the company. Thus, there is no land investment to be taken into account. The overall cost of construction, including additional developments, is estimated at 2,00 F/m2 for traditional buildings and 3000 F/m2 for high stockpiling buildings. All the surface areas to be constructed shall be based on this cost.

b) Equipment

The stacking operations plan has enabled the necessary resources in terms of labor to be defined, thereby providing an evaluation of the number of handling machines according to type. The following is a list of items of equipment and their purchasing cost:

- Retractable fork-lift truck   200,000 F
- Electric pallet handler   35,000 F
- Manual pallet handler   3,000 F
- Balanced loading ramp   50,000 F
- Link plate   6,000 F
- Storage rack   160 F/location

c) Personnel

The cost of each employee shall be valued at 150 kF/year.

6. Comparison of Options—Conclusion

You are asked to compare the different options you are examining on a financial and quality basis.

The financial evaluation should indicate the cost of initial investment and corresponding depreciation. These details should be provided in the operating budget section of each option. Your financial analysis shall consider both:

- financial depreciation, repayment of capital and
- interest, calculated on the sum still outstanding

The annuity constant a is:

$$a = Vo \times \frac{i}{1 - (1 + i)} - n$$

where:

Vo = purchase price

n = number of years for repayment

The various assets shall have depreciation periods of:

- building   20 years
- equipment   7 years
- racks   10 years

Only operating costs should be taken into account in the budgets, which will vary from one scenario to another. Modernization over 20 years should also be taken into account.

Appendix 1
Stockpiling and Traditional Storage

The use of consoles and rails on the ladders enables stockpiling to be performed. This procedure makes maxi- mum use of the available storage area, allowing two handling machines to travel in each aisle.

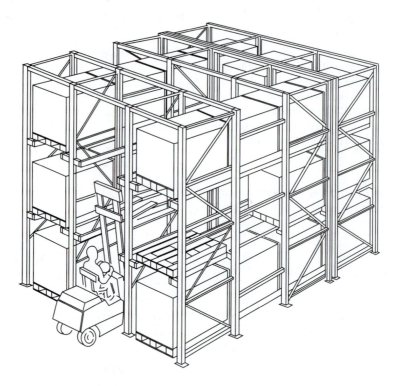

Appendix 2
IFTIM Time and Motion Standards

Operation	Operator	Equipment	Description	Time (in cmn)	Frequency	Total Time
UNLOADING OF A VEHICLE	1 handler	1 manual pallet handler	Collection and removal of a pallet	40.00		
			Journey with change of direction 18 + (3.2 × 60 m)	210.00		
			TOTAL (per pallet)	250.00		
ACCEPTANCE INSPECTION	1 handler		Transfer from 1 pallet to the other	5.00		

Operation	Operator	Equipment	Description	Time (in cmn)	Frequency	Total Time
			Reading of label	1.50		
			Quantity check	25.00		
			Search for card	15.00		
			Noter sur fiche	6.12		
			• Identity	3.24		
			• Quantity	4.32		
			• Date	4.68		
			• Storage location	5.68		
			Marking on pallet of storage location	70.54		
			TOTAL	10.57		
			Contingencies/rest 15%	81.11		
			TIME ALLOCATED (per pallet)			
STOCK ADMISSION	1 handler	1 electric pallet handler	Collection and pallet removal	40.00		
			Journey with change of direction	164.00		
			18 + (0.73 × 200 m)			
			TOTAL (per pallet)	204.00		
STORAGE	1 fork-lift truck	1 fork-lift truck	Lifting pallet from ground	30.00		
			Taking to empty compartment	14.60		
			Placing on 3rd level	65.00		
			Return to another pallet	14.60		
			TOTAL (per pallet)	124.20		
REMOVAL FROM STOCK	1 truck driver	1 fork-lift truck	IDEM Storage	124.20		
			TOTAL (per pallet)			
PLACING DIRECTLY ONTO PALLET AWAITING DISPATCH	1 handler	1 electric pallet handler	Collection and pallet removal	95.00		
			Journey with change of direction	91.00		
			18 + (0.73 × 100 m)			
			TOTAL (per pallet)	186.00		
SUPPLY OF RETAIL AREA	1 truck driver	1 fork-lift truck	Collection and pallet removal (search)	115.00		
			Run 0.73 × 60	44.00		
			TOTAL (per pallet)	159.00		
PREPARATION OF DEPOTS ORDERS	1 commissioner	1 electric pallet	Collection of empty pallet	20.00	1	20.00
			Approach 1st compartment position	40.00	1	40.00
			Collection and setting down of box	21.00	4	84.00
			Tick correctly, read next line	2.00	4	8.00

Operation	Operator	Equipment	Description	Time (in cmn)	Frequency	Total Time
			Go to next compartment	50.00	4	200.00
			Collect unit in box	18.00	2	36.00
			Tick correctly, read next line	2.00	2	4.00
			Bring pallet to end of storage structure	30.00	1	30.00
			Fetch order form	50.00	1	50.00
			Go to empty pallet storage area	50.00	1	50.00
			TOTAL			522.00
			Rest and contingencies 20%			104.00
			TIME ALLOCATED (per order)			626.00
PREPARATION OF CLIENTS' ORDERS	1 commissioner	1 electric pallet	Collection of empty pallet	20.00	1	20.00
			Approach 1st compartment position	40.00	1	40.00
			Collection and setting down of box	21.00	1	21.00
			Tick correctly, read next line	2.00	1	2.00
			Go to next compartment	50.00	14	280.00
			Collect unit in box	18.00	13	234.00
			Tick correctly, read next line	2.00	13	26.00
			Bring pallet to end of storage structure	30.00	1	30.00
			Fetch order form	50.00	1	50.00
			Go to empty pallet storage area	50.00	1	50.00
			TOTAL			753.00
			Rest and contingencies 20%			150.00
			TIME ALLOCATED (per order)			903.00
MISE PALETTES PREPAREES EN ATTENTE EXPEDITION	1 manutentionnaire	1 transpalette électrique	Collection and setting down	95.00		
			Travel	91.00		
			TOTAL (per pallet)	186.00		
CHARGEMENT D'UN VEHICULE	1 manutentionnaire	1 transpalette électrique	Collecting and setting down	95.00		
			Travel	62.00		
			Depalletizing	675.00		
			TOTAL (per pallet)	832.00		

Appendix 3
Receipt of Products from the Factory and Dispatch of Products

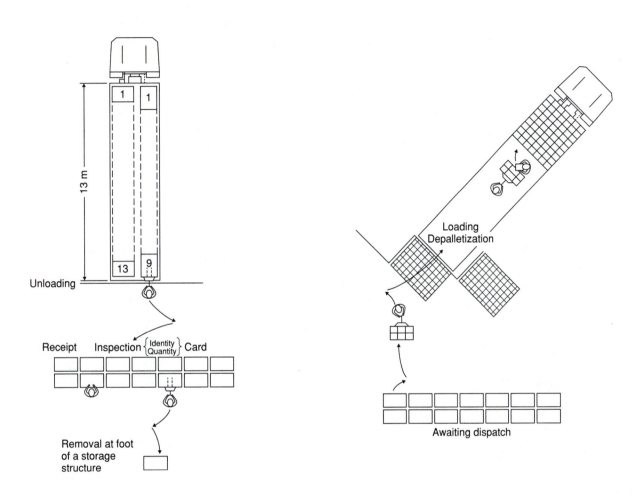

Appendix 4
The Layout Plan Is as Follows:

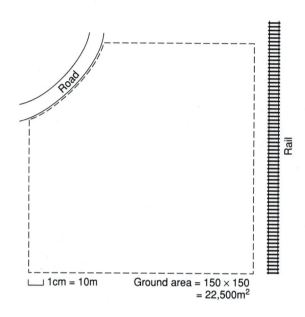

1cm = 10m   Ground area = 150 × 150
                              = 22,500m^2

Chapter 8

Logistics Network Design for Global Operations

◆ ◆ ◆

This chapter will cover the following topics:

◆ *Configuring a global logistics network*
◆ *Orienting international facilities by market, by product, and by process*
◆ *Different approaches to facility location*
◆ *Addressing capacity expansion issues and new product allocation*

Logistics efficiency has become as important to strategic planning as improvements in manufacturing and marketing. As companies have globalized their operations, however, logistics planning and decision factors have become even more complex. This chapter addresses three logistics questions that firms with international value chains must answer:

1. How should we configure our logistics network for global operations?
2. How should we orient our international facilities: by market? by product? by process?
3. What facilities should we use for capacity expansion when dealing with new products?

To help answer the first question, the chapter discusses two key characteristics of logistic network configurations—modularization and postponement. It then presents a framework that categorizes different configurations by their degree of modularization and postponement. The framework, which includes four configuration models (rigid, postponed, modularized, and flexible), represents different approaches companies can take to supply chain management. The discussion includes consideration of the trade-offs involved in using each model and presents corporate examples.

To address question 2, the chapter assesses the advantages and disadvantages of locating facilities abroad. It then analyzes the implications of orienting international facilities networks by market, product, or process focus, and looks at different hybrid schemes. The product dimensions of manufacturing complexity and marketing requirements underlie a framework to assist in analysis and decision making.

Once companies have an international logistics network in place, question 3 may arise. The chapter concludes by reviewing the logistics issues involved in capacity expansion and

251

new product allocation to an existing logistics network. A key consideration is the need for an operational "hedging scheme" to deal with the uncertainties of operating in an international environment.

◆ GLOBAL LOGISTICS NETWORK CONFIGURATION

As a result of global competition and new business improvement approaches, companies today are taking an integrated, holistic approach to supply chain management. Decisions or changes in one aspect of a logistics network now require changes throughout the chain to maximize competitive advantages. Companies with global operations face special challenges in designing and modifying logistics networks. However, focusing on key characteristics of these networks provides valuable perspective and can assist in decision making.

Modularization and Postponement: Key Characteristics of Logistics Networks

Modularization and *postponement,* concepts used in product and process design, should also influence supply chain structure and logistics network configurations. The fundamental principle of these two concepts is essentially the same—marrying the two advantages of scale and scope. *Economies of scale* relates to the cost savings derived from manufacturing many of the same products. *Economies of scope* relates to the cost savings derived from manufacturing a variety of products. While modularization crafts this marriage from the standpoint of product design, postponement does so from a process design point of view. An integrated product–process approach, therefore, can take advantage of both scale and scope benefits, and thereby offers increased potential for obtaining greater strategic advantage.

Modularization is a product design approach in which the product is assembled from a set of standardized constituent units. Different assembly combinations from a given set of standardized units give rise to different end-product models and variations. Thus, modular design effectively weds flexibility of the end product with standardization of constituent parts. It provides opportunities for exploiting economies of scope and scale from a product design approach. The key element is to design for efficient linkage mechanisms in the constituent units so that any required combination can be conveniently assembled. Modularization is associated with inbound logistics, because the combination of different components allows the assembly of the final product. It is closely linked to the capability of *outsourcing*—that is, any step of the manufacturing process that could be subcontracted or outsourced.

Postponement is a value-addition process for a set of end products that maximizes the common processing requirements shared by those products. The customization of the product is delayed (or postponed) as late as possible in the value-addition process. This approach allows companies to exploit scale advantages without compromising on their ultimate product variety (scope advantages). It also exploits the benefits of consolidation, reduces the complexity in manufacturing, and helps make demand patterns more predictable. Postponement is associated with outbound logistics—that is, satisfying end-customer demand.

How the Two Concepts Are Interrelated

A product's manufacturing cost (i.e., inbound logistics) is largely determined by the design of the product. For example, design determines 80 percent of the final production costs of

2,000 parts in the making of a Rolls Royce, and 70 percent of the cost of manufacturing truck transmissions at General Motors.

Concepts such as *design for manufacturability* directly address the importance of considering manufacturing limitations and input during the design process. Companies can extend this concept beyond manufacturing and incorporate issues about order fulfillment (i.e., outbound logistics) and supply chain management.

Consumers are demanding that companies increase product diversity; in order to remain competitive, companies respond with many specialized versions of a product. At the same time, however, the life cycles of existing products are growing shorter all the time. This creates a need for more flexible manufacturing systems, which then limits potential improvements in productivity.

Because consumer requirements are increasing both in the number of details and in diversity, anticipating demand is very difficult. Demand forecasting involves issues such as finding the best place for postponed inventory in a marketing channel and linking inventory management to other parts of the supply chain. Specific relationships of demand, target service levels, substitutability, and lead times also are important factors.

Modularization and postponement are connected in the relationship between product and process design. Products must be designed to maximize the number of common standardized constituent units among a set of end products. The process, at the same time, must allow a flow of discrete steps in the supply chain that enable postponement to take place. The ideal situation is to have both economies of scale and scope.

Unfortunately, it is not possible in every case to maximize modularization and postponement. Technological restrictions may impede modularization, and organizational structures can constrain coordination (e.g., decentralized organizational structures that constrain integration). However, the companies that best implement these two concepts can obtain sustainable competitive advantage along the supply chain. The framework presented in this chapter helps evaluate the trade-offs that exist for both.

Advantages of Modularization and Postponement

The implications and benefits of these accrue to the full logistics function (inbound and outbound), including plant layout, capacity planning, new-product development, outsourcing, reduction in inventory, and distribution of products to different market segments.

Inbound Logistics Examples

On the inbound logistics side, there are a number of examples in which modularization and postponement have been used effectively in designing plant layouts. Magneto-Marelli, an international automotive component manufacturing giant, has reorganized its manufacturing facilities' layouts in France into two broad sections: basic products and model-specific lines. The basic-product section manufactures component modules (basic products) that are subsequently used in multiple (model-specific) end-product lines. This layout pattern simplifies material flow and control and further amplifies the benefits of low inventory in a just-in-time environment.

The capacity-planning approach of Texas Instruments (TI) illustrates another potential benefit. The two broad semiconductor categories of TI are low-cost DRAM memory chips and expensive customized microprocessors and other integrated circuits. Quick delivery and service are very important in this business, and TI has stretched its capacity to accommodate manufacturing of high-end customized microprocessors. A specialized product and process design makes 90 percent of the production process identical for the two product categories; customization through expensive refinement is *postponed* until the end of the process.

With this setup, TI always operates its plant at full capacity by using production of memory chips as buffer—adjusting its volumes to the demand for the customized chips. Thus in 1992, it increased its output of customized chips from 10 percent to 60 percent of the capacity. This capability gives TI a strategic competitive edge in all customer segments. The company effectively and efficiently caters to its customers of specialized products without affecting the market segment for DRAM, a commodity item sold by thirteen other competing manufacturers.

Modularization in product design can help speed up the new product development process. Orienting the basic design of new products to maximize the use of existing standardized component units allows economy in resource usage (financial and human) and reduces time requirements. It also creates savings (time and money) in development of corresponding processes.

Companies that have successfully exploited the benefits of modular design and consequent standardization of parts include the Japanese car maker Suzuki, which has led the industry in standardizing auto parts and reducing variations. Two of its latest product models, the Wagon R minivan and the Alto, share 70 percent of their parts with other Suzuki models. This approach of "frugal" design is ideally suited for periods of economic downturns when companies are strapped for resources but are still unable to scale down their innovative efforts. Other examples of companies using this approach successfully include Dell Computers, Nike, IBM and General Motors.

Many companies have reaped the strategic benefits of modularization in outsourcing. One such example is the U.S. automobile maker Chrysler, which designs its cars to be built in modules. In its highly successful LH series, the interior comprises four easy-to-install units delivered ready-built by separate suppliers. This approach facilitates "consolidated" outsourcing activities such as system purchases and black-box design, which, in turn, exploits advantages of low production costs and advanced technology.

Outbound Logistics Examples

A classic example of the outbound logistics advantages of modularization and postponement is Benetton, which uses a very convenient combination of contract manufacturing in its operations strategy. For Benetton, 90 percent of sales are standardized items with a seven-month advanced committed order; they can be conveniently contracted out, based on known, stable plans. The demand pattern of the other 10 percent is unpredictable and, hence, is postponed under in-house manufacturing until just five weeks before delivery, a practice that provides strategic operational flexibility.

Applying postponement to innovative packaging design and production can increase efficiency in material handling, storage, and transportation; give the customer a better-looking package; and continue service by maintaining the high fill rate targets. For its DeskJet 500 printers, Hewlett-Packard "localized" the packaging of market-specific manuals, software, and other accessories (which resulted in twenty-six versions of two basic models) by using the basic principle of *substitutability* between generic models (i.e., modularization). The benefits included a 187 percent jump in material-handling productivity and a 47 percent decrease in storage space requirements.

In the distribution of HP printers, standardized products may be rolled out from a centralized facility and then routed to destination markets, where market-specific value addition takes place. This practice generates substantial inventory savings for HP.

Framework: Categorizing Logistics Networks by Degree of Modularization and Postponement

The framework that follows captures the degree of modularization and postponement in order to compare and contrast clearly differentiated supply chain structures. In the framework, inbound logistics and outbound logistics represent the degree of modularization and postponement. Thus, inbound outsourcing is the dimension that captures the degree of modularization and usage of subcontractors for making the components. A low inbound outsourcing represents a supply chain with a high degree of vertical integration that might be constrained either by product design specifications or by industry structure. A high inbound outsourced is a highly decentralized supply chain that outsources many components.

Outbound logistics involves a space transformation—it moves products from the plant to the customer. Outbound postponement captures the degree of customization the supply chain offers. A high level of outbound postponement is a supply chain that is organized around a make-to-order environment in which customer demand triggers the completion of the final product. A low degree of outbound postponement is more characteristic of a make-to-stock environment, in which a company maintains an inventory of finished products to satisfy customer demand.

Different levels of postponement can occur according to where in the supply chain the product is differentiated or customized, allowing either *time* or *form* postponement. The first refers to delaying the differentiation tasks (e.g., manufacturing, packaging, labeling), while the second means delaying the actual making of the product (i.e., standardizing the production steps).

Although a supply chain can have many discrete operations, in our model we simplify the logistics flow pattern into three steps: making, assembling, and packing. *Making* involves the manufacture of the component parts. *Assembling* involves putting the different components together to create the finished product. *Packing* involves the actual packaging and labeling of the final product to satisfy customer demands.

Based on the two dimensions of outbound and inbound logistics, the framework contains four categories of supply chain structures: rigid, flexible, postponed, and modularized (see Figure 8–1). The *rigid* structure represents the classic vertically integrated supply chain. Its objective is to exploit economies of scale in production of large runs by maintaining large inventories of finished products. At the other end of the spectrum is the *flexible* structure, which uses many subcontractors to make the different components. Known demand triggers the assembly of the final product. The final product is assembled as a response to this demand (i.e., postponed) and not to stock in inventory. No inventory of final products is maintained. Commonality creates inventory economies.

In between these two extremes lies the *modularized* structure, which has multiple sources for components, but the output of the assembly process is the finished product. Final products are assembled *before* knowing the actual demand (like in the rigid). Inventory of the different final products is maintained in stock. Most industries use this structure. Another intermediate choice, the *postponed* structure, exploits economies of scale in making components, but like the flexible structure, it customizes the finished product to satisfy specific customer demand.

Trade-Offs in the Framework

It is not intuitively clear which supply chain structure is best for a company. Very rigid companies, such as the truck manufacturer Kamaz, are vertically integrated in virtually all

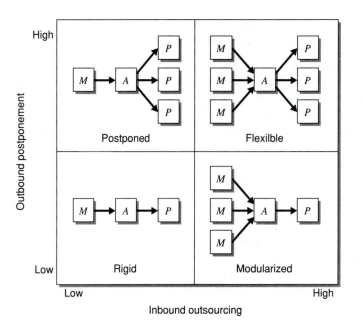

Figure 8−1   Framework for Supply Chain Structures

the raw materials used in the production of trucks. Other companies are more flexible, such as BMW, which buys 80 percent of every car's components.

In the computer industry, Apple, IBM, and Dell contract component making from companies such as SCI Systems, Solectron, or Jabil Circuit. Compaq, on the other hand, manufactures all of its computers in-house.

In the auto industry, GM is the most vertically integrated of the three car companies, producing 70 percent of its components in-house. Chrysler buys 70 percent of the materials in each car from suppliers.

Which supply chain structure is the most appropriate? To answer that question, companies must assess the trade-offs in cost and service. When companies increase the level of modularization by doing more inbound outsourcing, they can significantly reduce their fixed costs. Dell, for example, supports $2.9 billion in annual revenues with $60 million of fixed assets. It takes in $35 of sales for every dollar of fixed assets, while for Compaq, the figure is $3. The trade-off is in the variable cost (i.e., the per-unit cost is higher), since some margin to the subcontractors has to be included.

For the postponement structure, the situation is reversed. By allowing a higher outbound postponement, companies incur the extra fixed cost of maintaining multiple equipment for packaging and labeling (e.g., warehouse facilities with machines to label). However, the variable cost is reduced because of centralized inventories, less risk associated with lower finished goods inventories, and/or bulk shipping from the plants.

Illustration of the Framework

Table 8−1 illustrates the framework for network design with corporate examples.

Rolls Royce customizes production and does not assemble or distribute a car until a customer's order is received. Retail paint stores reduce finished goods inventory by mixing colors upon customer requests. Likewise, Sunoco and other gas stations mix gasoline octane

Table 8-1: *Illustration of Conceptual Framework for Network Design*

		Inbound Outsourcing	
		Low	High
Outbound Postponement	High	POSTPONED	FLEXIBLE
		Texas Instruments	Dell Computers
		Retail Paint Stores	Benetton
		Gas Stations	Mail Order Firms
		Rolls Royce	Burger King
	Low	RIGID	MODULARIZED
		Compaq	IBM
		Apparel Industry	Nike
		Adidas	McDonald's
		General Motors	Chrysler

grades at the retail pump. These are all examples of high outbound postponement with a low inbound outsourcing. Mail-order firms keep inventories at a few centralized locations and only send them when they receive orders, which illustrates a high outbound postponement combined with a high level of inbound outsourcing.

McDonald's uses many suppliers for most of its products (which are assembled in the stores) and follows a make-to-stock inventory policy. Burger King uses similar inbound logistics, but prefers the "make-it-your way" (i.e., make-to-order) policy. Thus, McDonald's is modularized, while Burger King is flexible.

Empirical evidence suggests that vertical integration along the supply chain, modeled earlier by General Motors and Compaq, is not desirable. More and more companies are replacing vertical integration with vertical coordination and developing long-term arrangements with outside suppliers.

◆ ORIENTING INTERNATIONAL FACILITIES: CONSIDERATIONS AND FRAMEWORK

Strategic planning for global facilities network orientation is complex, involving decisions about where to locate factories, how to allocate production activities to the various facilities, how to develop suppliers for the plants, how to manage the distribution of products (e.g., centralized or decentralized warehousing), and how to organize the interfaces along the supply chain. The "givens" that frame these decisions are the company's particular set of markets; products to produce and sell; demand projections for the different markets; and information about future macroeconomic conditions, transportation costs, and production economics (e.g., cost curves as a function of production volumes for each individual process step or component that goes into the product). This section looks at key elements of orientation decisions: the advantages and disadvantages of locating facilities globally, and how to focus facilities and facility networks.

Locating Facilities Globally

For years, U.S. firms have built production facilities overseas. That trend is accelerating; furthermore, foreign businesses are building facilities in this country also.

Global manufacturing is a competitive response to the increasing integration of international markets. Moving production facilities offshore through foreign direct investment, outsourcing, joint ventures with foreign producers, or other mechanisms has clear short-term advantages in foreign market penetration and labor cost containment.

The myth is that by locating in a foreign country, a firm can make its product where it is sold, and the local presence can increase sales or decrease the threat of import quotas. The reality, however, is that long-term repercussions of offshore production strategies are not clear. In some industries, firms must move constantly in search of even lower wage rates; in others, host countries insist on domestic content, technology transfer, and domestic equity positions that lead to independent, competitive production capabilities.

The low-wage, offshore labor strategy has complex pluses and minuses. Industries with assembly operations in which labor remains a high proportion of cost may be candidates for subcontracting or moving to low-wage countries. However, the potential savings from low labor rates abroad must be balanced against the costs of coordinating demand, production, and delivery. Timely production and delivery is important in avoiding loss of orders and inventory costs that competitors may not face. These factors require significant planning capabilities to align production with demand. Advanced technologies can help manufacturers handle data to reduce the disadvantages of offshore operations, but this gain may not be sufficient to offset transportation costs, delays, and the relative isolation of distant production facilities.

In many industries, indications already suggest that large multinational corporations are becoming disenchanted with a low-wage strategy. The need to move facilities continually as wages inevitably rise in developing countries, the increased viability of automating domestic facilities as an alternative to siting plants in low-wage countries, and the pursuit of long-term production strategies have underscored the costs of a low-wage strategy. Other developments have undermined the benefits.

Taiwan, for example, had been a preferred site for offshore assembly in the semi-conductor and other assembly-required industries because of cheap labor. However, following local currency (NT) appreciation, labor was no longer so cheap, and start-up costs became much greater. As a result, industries moved the assembly function offshore (often to Malaysia and Thailand), while Taiwan moved toward high-tech industries.

Factors vary across industries, and some firms in labor-intensive industries may have no choice but to move production offshore or purchase components or products from abroad. As technological developments yield effective alternatives to offshore production and conditions for foreign direct investment become more stringent, companies need a better understanding about the effects of offshore production strategies on the long-term interests of individual firms and the domestic industrial base.

In addition, worldwide manufacturing should not be the only strategy a company uses to meet the challenge of global competition. Although offshore sourcing and world-scale plants may be cost-effective, a better test of competitive effectiveness is the ability to retaliate in competitors' key markets. The framework presented in this section assumes that competitors are not battling simply for world volume but also for the cash flow to support new-product development, investment in core technologies, and world distribution (i.e., competitors with global distribution coverage and wide product lines are best able to justify investments in new core technologies).

Five categories of factors determine whether locating abroad will increase the competitive strength of the manufacturing function. They include: (1) access to low production input factors, (2) proximity to market, (3) use of local technological resources, (4) control and amortization of technological assets, and (5) preemption of competition.

Successfully locating offshore also requires a commitment to strategic planning. With diverse and sometimes conflicting forces driving global expansion, the absence of a clear strategic map for the role of each factory within the firm's international manufacturing network can have dire consequences. Establishing a plant is a binding and generally irreversible decision, locking a firm into long-term constraints. There is no guarantee that a series of such decisions made incrementally will yield an optimal network. Moreover, once a company opens a factory, the firm must guide its development strategically, even though the operational considerations may seem overwhelming.

Orientation of Facility Networks

The objectives of facility orientation are to meet the competitive priorities of the various products at the various markets. These priorities include the cost, quality, service, and flexibility options discussed in chapter 2. Because the global environment is dynamic, another criterion is the ability to react to changes (i.e., hedge against uncertainties of the global environment). In general, companies have three options for focusing their facility networks. These include focusing by market, by product, and by process.

1. **Market focus**—In this approach, the company locates plants in different markets. The driving force behind location decisions is proximity to markets where products are to be sold. In such a scenario, the manufacturing organization is decentralized and each plant produces the entire product line for its respective market. The marketing organization also is decentralized, as each market is treated separately.
2. **Product family focus**—Under this scheme, the company locates plants in different parts of the world driven by economies of scale (i.e., easy new-product development within the specific family). Every plant specializes in a specific product family. The manufacturing organization is mainly centralized because the company has to manage the allocation of the different products to the different markets from the same set of plants. The organization can also be decentralized if some product families belong in specific markets because of structural constraints such as import barriers. The marketing organization may also be either centralized (with sales offices placing orders to the various plants in the network to meet the needs of their markets) or decentralized (by operating sales offices at the various markets).
3. **Process focus**—Using a process focus, a company locates plants in different parts of the world, but each plant specializes in specific steps of the manufacturing process (e.g., metal components, assembly plants, plastic molding, etc.). The driving force behind this strategy is economies of scale in the production of components. Therefore, the manufacturing organization is centralized to coordinate the assembly of the different components. The marketing organization also is centralized to coordinate the final assembly requirements of the different markets. Table 8–2 summarizes the different approaches.

Table 8–2:   *Summary of Approaches for the Orientation of Facility Networks*

	Manufacturing Organization	Marketing Organization
Market Focus	Decentralized	Decentralized
Product Family Focus	Centralized/Decentralized	Centralized/Decentralized
Process Focus	Centralized	Centralized

Trade-Offs Associated with each Approach

Each approach has advantages, disadvantages, and key management tasks that must be performed.

Market Focus

Main Advantages

- Proximity to market
- Transportation economies (speedy delivery)
- Market organization, in which country managers have control over both manufacturing and marketing
- Manufacturing organization at every plant, with production responsibilities over the whole product, resulting in a higher control over the quality of the product
- Product well-adjusted to the market needs

Main Disadvantages

- De-focused production facilities due to processing many different product families
- Economies of scale not exploited (unless market very large for every plant)
- Significant exposure to exchange rate risk (if plants are not allowed to shift production to plants serving other markets)
- Significant duplication of process equipment
- Difficulty in new product introduction (if there exists a centralized R & D department, then production ramp up has to occur at multiple plants)
- High level of final product inventory

Key Management Tasks

- Allocation of markets to plants to determine the level of utilization of various facilities
- Management of multiproduct, de-focused individual facilities
- Hedging against risk factors such as exchange rate, political risks

Product Family Focus

Main Advantages

- Economies of scale where the volume of a product family builds up as the plant serves all markets
- Better serving of competitive priorities of products, which could backfire if similar products at different markets have different competitive priorities
- Reduced duplication of process equipment
- High level of product learning within a family
- Easy introduction of new products (within existing families)
- Well-controlled inventories
- More standardized quality (all products come from the same source)

Main Disadvantages

- Lack of significant local presence
- Significant exchange rate exposure (impact can be very serious, since if one facility gets affected, multiple products and markets are affected)
- Difficulty in coordinating the interaction between manufacturing organization and country marketing organizations (e.g., pricing of products for various markets, allocation of production costs across products, scheduling production of the different markets)
- Transportation diseconomies

Key Management Tasks

- Difficulty coordinating production (production scheduling to meet priorities of different markets)
- Transfer pricing scheme development
- Finding right location of product family plants (extremely important)
- Grouping of products into product families (determines the level of efficiency of each facility)
- Hedging against risk factors

Process Focus

Main Advantages

- Economies of scale (accumulated volume for the various process steps)
- Significant process learning
- If economies of scale allow decentralized assembly, there is significant local presence
- Potential to transform process learning into process improvements and process innovation
- A well-controlled manufacturing organization
- Every country organization has some production responsibilities (i.e., postponement strategy can be easily applied in this environment for every market)
- Avoids almost completely the duplication of process equipment

Main Disadvantages

- Somewhat de-focused production facilities (multiple products with different priorities go through the same processes)
- Significant exchange rate exposure at the component level (some flexibility could be gained at the assembly level if shifting production among assembly facilities)
- Significant transportation diseconomies
- Tremendous difficulty in production scheduling at component facilities and difficulty of scheduling the assembly facilities
- High level of component inventory
- Difficult to control the quality of the final product

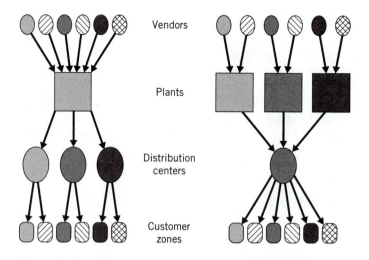

Figure 8–2   Two Extremes of Logistics Networks

- Difficult to coordinate the interaction between the manufacturing organization and the country marketing organizations
- Difficulty in new-product development (due to the spreading out of process knowledge)

Key Management Tasks

- Production scheduling at component facilities to ensure adequate supply at assembly facilities
- Control of component inventories and scheduling of assembly activities
- Location of process focused plants
- Transfer pricing scheme for the components
- Hedging against risk factors

In reality, it is difficult to find a company that follows any of the approaches here presented exactly. However, by analyzing these three approaches it is possible to understand some of the trade-offs inherent in centralizing versus decentralizing the logistics network. Figure 8–2 presents the extremes.

Mapping the Different Approaches

The following framework conceptualizes the different approaches for facilities orientation as a function of two dimensions of product characteristics: manufacturing complexity and marketing requirements. The interaction between marketing and manufacturing cannot be avoided.

Manufacturing complexity refers to the difficulty of the manufacturing process. Comparing the hand tools industry with the computer industry, for example, we see that the complexity for the first is lower than for the second. Complexity can be based on a variety of factors, such as the number of manufacturing steps required, product physical characteristics, and environmental requirements.

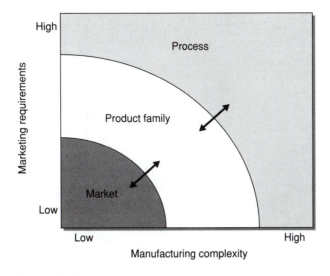

Figure 8–3   Orientation of Facility Networks

Marketing requirements captures the specifications and complexities that the marketing function has in delivering the product. The apparel industry, where fashion is the critical driver, has significantly more marketing requirements (e.g., advertising, sales effort, changes and variability of sizes and colors) than the electronics components industry, where customers are more educated about their requirements and the element of fashion does not exist. (The marketing dimension can be extended to include issues such as duration of the product life cycle [PLC]; products with a shorter PLC have higher marketing requirements than products with longer PLC.)

Figure 8–3 captures the different approaches as a function of the dimensions discussed. When the product has a low manufacturing complexity and low marketing requirements, the market focus fits better. In this environment it is easier to serve customers when one facility or network is responsible for the entire product and the main drivers for customers are service and quality (as opposed to cost). As manufacturing complexity increases, companies must specialize manufacturing facilities into specific tasks, because quality becomes a critical element (i.e., process focus). When combined with economies of scale, quality will give a company a competitive advantage.

If marketing requirements are high, then the driver for going into the process focus is economies of scale. When the marketing requirements are low, such as in the apparel industry for some models of jeans where the PLC is long, companies may decide to automate the manufacturing process and move back to the market focus.

Illustrations of the Mapping

Figure 8–4 places four industries along the manufacturing complexity and marketing requirement axes. Apparel and computers belong to the consumer products category, while electronics and tools fall to the industrial products category.

Figure 8–4 shows that, in general, industrial products have fewer marketing requirements than consumer products. However, the framework captures the difference between apparel and computers, even though they follow the same process focus approach. The framework

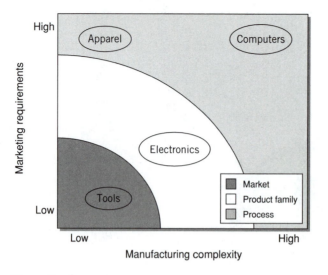

Figure 8–4   Illustration of Orientation for Facility Networks

also validates that, out of the four performance measures (cost, quality, service, and flexibility), the drivers for the computer and apparel industries were first cost for both, and then quality for computers (manufacturing complexity high) and flexibility for apparel (marketing requirements high). For electronics and tools, the key driver was service (to consumers), with an emphasis in flexibility for electronics and in quality for tools.

◆   CAPACITY EXPANSION ISSUES

Companies with a large existing global network of manufacturing facilities may want to expand their capacities for reasons such as the introduction of a new product, an increase in demand for the existing products, or consolidation of operations. They must approach capacity expansion decisions carefully, however, since the easiest solution—physically expanding operations by either buying a new line or enlarging warehouses—might not be the best one. In addition, *capacity* is not a fixed number and must therefore be treated managerially.

Alternatives for increasing the capacity of an existing network include the management of: product mix, production rates, quality control, and yield. Product mix refers to the capability of a company to change the products it currently makes. A particular product may use more set-up and processing time than another. By changing the order and composition of products that a company plans to make, the existing capacity changes without investing in new equipment. The production rate is also a variable very much under the control of management since you could accelerate the pace (i.e., production rate) for a period of time without significantly changing the operation, and allowing for an increase in demand. Quality control is a critical managerial resource where by checking carefully the input quality for example, the amount of scrap could be reduced. Finally, yield is the amount of good products resulting out of a normal operations process. It is directly linked to the type of technology involved and by selecting the appropriate equipment for the different products, the resulting yield could increase.

It is also important to take into account: (1) the reliability of the forecast; (2) the status of the competition; and (3) the speed of technology development. Many times decisions are made regarding capacity expansion based on a forecast that has not been carefully developed. It is very important to evaluate the credibility of the forecast in order to make rational decisions. The other critical element is the status of competition. By allowing capacity decisions to be based solely on the analysis of one company's perception, the process ignores very relevant issues about the splitting of the markets among the potential competitors. Finally, when technology changes rapidly, it might be wise to increase the capacity expansion in steps to allow for adjustments to the new technologies. Jumping to new technologies too early might make the investment obsolete.

New Product Allocation

Two considerations are key decision points for new product allocation: *site competence* and *process technology competence*. The first is considered location-specific, since each facility will have strengths and weaknesses that define its competence independently of the product characteristics. The second is considered product-specific, since each product will be defined by specifications that require *specific* manufacturing operations. These dimensions are difficult to measure, but proxies can help capture their intensity.

Site Competence

Site competence (SC) is defined as the ability of the manufacturing facility to manage the current operation and absorb a new product related to existing products. The intuition is that the higher the competence, the more capable the facility is of managing economies of scope (as opposed to scale) by efficiently managing variety rather than volume. Indicative measures of SC include the following:

1. *Ratio of engineers to blue collar workers.* This measure captures the human dimension of the location in terms of the number of people dedicated to the different application functions relative to the execution of that function (e.g., quality control, R & D, relative to line workers). The assumption is that the higher the ratio, the easier it will be for the facility to adjust to a new product—and therefore, the faster the intermediate manufacturing operation can start. At the same time, facilities with more dedicated departments (e.g., quality control and quality assurance labs) will be better able to correct and/or improve specific steps of the operation.
2. *Age of the facility, average age of the machines, and ratio of machines to engineers.* This measure captures the state of the technology at the location. The assumption is that the older the facility, the further along it is in the learning curve. On the other hand, the older the machines, the lower the ability to innovate on a complicated process (or product) in an efficient way. Finally, the assumption is that the higher the ratio of machines to engineers, the more advanced the technology at the location.
3. *Flexibility.* Flexibility is defined as the ability of a location to respond effectively to changing circumstances. The higher the flexibility, the easier it will be for a location to introduce new products and to implement changes to existing products.

Process Technology Complexity

Process technology complexity (PTC) is the difficulty (e.g., number of steps, amount of detail, etc.) required for the successful completion of a particular operation. Complexity is the enemy of consistency, and process consistency is essential for high-quality production. The intuition is that the higher the complexity, the harder it will be to imitate the product; therefore, the facility that satisfies the requirements will have a technology-driven innovation advantage. Indicative measures of process technology complexity include the following:

1. *Number of steps.* This measure is a proxy for the complexity of the product. The higher the number of separable operations, the higher the process complexity for this product.
2. *Product physical characteristics and environmental requirements.* The size of the product is related to the complexity by assuming that the smaller the product, the more difficult it will be to perform a specific operation. Some operations require certain environmental specifications (e.g., air cleanliness) that complicate the operational conditions.
3. *Engineering change orders.* Engineering change orders typically specify a change in either the materials to be used in producing the product, the manufacturing process employed, or the specification of the product itself. By definition, the higher the number of change orders, the higher the product complexity.

Matrix for New Product Allocation

Companies are not opening and closing plants on a regular basis. However, companies are in fact introducing new products all the time. Each company using a global strategy should have a specific "map" locating all the relevant facilities. The problem for company X is to find the right facility (i.e., with the right site competence) within the existing network to make the new product with its own specifications (defined by the process technology complexity). These two dimensions are represented in Figure 8–5.

The matrix is the framework used to understand the trade-offs involved in the decision. A good example comes from the semiconductor industry. The main competitors in the industry have manufacturing facilities throughout much of the world, including the United States, Asia, and Europe. Advances in semiconductor technology and mass production have dramatically reduced average unit costs and broadened the potential market. The high degree of competition forces companies to rationalize the allocation of resources among different facilities.

From a normative point of view, companies that are ahead should have their facilities in the diagonal of the matrix. A facility with a low site competence should handle products with a low process technology complexity, and vice versa. The lower-left corner of the diagonal corresponds to a *filler of needs* factory where the main objectives are to exploit economies of scale and to imitate rather than to innovate. At the other extreme, we have the *leader in technology* factory, where economies of scope and innovation are the competitive advantages.

In Figure 8–5, the position above the diagonal is the *averse* facility, because it is operating with low PTC products, when it actually has the capability (or competence) to operate with high PTC products.

The position below the diagonal is the *prone* facility, because it is operating with high PTC products when it only has the capability to operate with low PTC products.

The main trade-off of the intermediate manufacturing matrix is *operating costs* versus *opportunity costs*. In general, when moving from low to high PTC, facilities will increase their

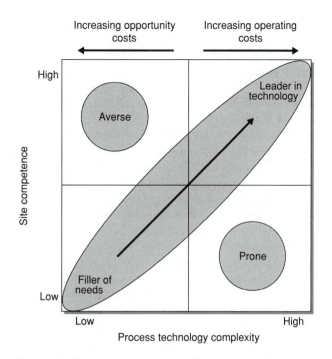

Figure 8–5 New Product Allocation Matrix. The trade-off between Site Competence (facility oriented) and the Process Technology Complexity (product oriented) facilitates the decision of allocating production of a new product to an existing network of facilities.

operating costs, which include the setup and the costs of learning a "more" complicated process (i.e., innovation costs). When moving in the other direction, facilities will have operating savings because the operation is supposed to be "known" or dominated (i.e., imitation costs).

The opportunity cost affects averse and prone facilities differently. When an averse facility moves from low to high PTC, it is decreasing the opportunity cost by better matching its capabilities to the process technology requirements. The same is true when a prone facility moves from a high to a low PTC. When a prone facility moves from a low to a high PTC, it increases not only the operating costs, but also its opportunity cost, since it is matching low capabilities with complicated requirements, increasing the uncertainty.

The same is true for an averse facility, but the opposite happens with the opportunity cost (i.e., it reduces the opportunity cost). The "intensity" of the opportunity and the operating costs are inverse for averse and prone facilities. The higher the SC, the higher the opportunity cost for being away from the diagonal, but the operating costs are smaller because the facility is supposed to have the resources for a more "complicated" process. The opposite happens for a lower SC facility.

In the site competence dimension, to move from low to high implies that facilities are investing in resources to upgrade the operating capabilities. To move from high to low SC implies that facilities are saving in resources (e.g., reduction in white-collar personnel).

Normative Implications of the Matrix

When confronted with the problem of deciding what facility will better respond to the requirements of a new product, the new product allocation matrix can be used to determine the optimal option. Given the current configuration, it would be simplistic to assume that facilities can easily change. In fact, to change a facility into a different position in the matrix is a slow process. On the other hand, the need to find an optimal facility cannot be delayed because of competitive pressures.

What we suggest is to use the trade-offs defined before as follows. We start by mapping the network of facilities in the matrix according to their matched site competence and process technology complexity. That is, relative to the products each facility is currently making, there will be a single point identifying the facilities. The new product can then be represented in the PTC dimension of the matrix. Note that the representation of the product is *not* limited to a single point in the matrix since the process technology complexity is independent of the site competence and is directly related to the characteristics of the new product.

In theory, it is possible to make the new product from any of the existing facilities in the network. However, we have to determine the best option. There are multiple alternatives (represented by vectors) for the different locations currently in the network to satisfy the requirements of the new product. The size of the vectors represents the "effort" that different facilities have to make to satisfy the requirements of the "new" product. Not all facilities will necessarily move toward the diagonal, even though this should be the ideal situation. Then, from each of the existing facilities we can measure and evaluate the alternative options (or vectors) that will result from approaching the facility to the product. To move a facility toward a particular product implies to either increase the site competence (e.g., new technologies) or modifying the existing product mix (e.g., release products with a complex process and dedicate to simple products).

Figure 8–6 illustrates the basic ideas. We are faced with a network of four facilities. Facilities *A* and *B* are prone while facilities *C* and *D* are averse. We assume (for convenience) that the SC for facilities *A* and *B* is the same and the SC for facilities *C* and *D* is the same. That assumption implies that facilities *A* and *B* (and facilities *C* and *D*) are

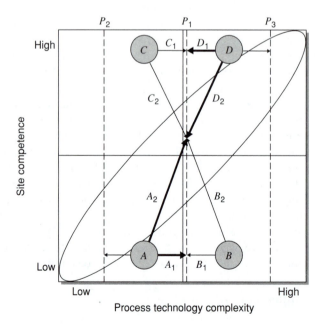

Figure 8–6   Illustration of alternatives for a network of four facilities (A,B,C, and D) when deciding which one should produce product P1.

Table 8–3: *Comparison of Options Within the New Product Allocation Matrix*

B2 to P1	C2 to P1
Reduce Operating Costs	Increase Operating Costs
Increase Investments	Reduce Investment
Reduce Opportunity Cost	Reduce Opportunity Cost
Imitation Strategy	Innovation Strategy
Economies of Scale	Economies of Scope

placed at the same level on the vertical axis in the framework. When a new product (P_1) is introduced, there are (in theory) two options for any of the four facilities to satisfy its requirements (denoted by X_1 and X_2 where $X = A, B, C,$ or D). These options are shown in Figure 8–6.

If facility A is going to produce P_1 by moving horizontally, the required change is measured by A_1 and it involves an increase in operating costs that is not offset by anything else since the opportunity cost is also going up (i.e., it is moving away from the diagonal). If the approach is A_2, the facility is investing in resources to get closer to the diagonal but at the same time is increasing its operating costs. If facility B produces P_1, the change measured by B_1 captures a reduction in the operating costs while reducing the opportunity cost. Therefore B dominates A for P_1 in all cases. By similar arguments C dominates D.

After evaluating the different alternatives (i.e., the direction and measure of each vector), the problem reduces to comparing vector B_2 to vector C_2. If the approach is B_2, facility B will invest in resources to approach the diagonal and at the same time have a reduction in operating costs. If the alternative is facility C, according to C_2 the facility will approach the diagonal by increasing the operating costs but with some savings in resources. Table 8–3 summarizes the trade-offs of B_2 versus C_2. By measuring the impact of "moving" each facility we can determine the optimal decision.

If the new product is P_2 then it is trivial that facility A dominates since it will have a reduction in both operating costs and opportunity costs (i.e., it is getting closer to the diagonal), while facility C would reduce the operating cost but increase the opportunity cost. By similar arguments, if the new product is P_3 then it is trivial that facility D dominates.

◆ SUMMARY

In this chapter, we discussed the issues involved in designing a logistics network for global operations. The competitive pressures of the business environment have forced companies to look at the entire supply chain in an integrative manner. It is no longer enough to optimize the manufacturing function without linking it to the distribution function, or vice versa. Consumers are more informed, more demanding, and less loyal. The concepts of modularization and postponement underlie a framework for configuring the logistics network into four categories: flexible, rigid, modularized, and postponed.

Each of these logistics network designs may have a different orientation, driven by factors such as the competitive environment, the existing manufacturing capabilities, and the strategic objectives. Manufacturing complexity and marketing requirements are the basis for a framework that addresses the possible focus of a logistics network; options include market focus, product family focus, or process focus.

Finally, the chapter reviews the complex issues involved in capacity expansions decisions, which are especially complicated for worldwide firms. An allocation matrix provides parameters for evaluating the capabilities of facilities in an existing logistics network to handle a new product.

DISCUSSION QUESTIONS

1. What is *modularization?* What are the implications of the modularization concept for logistics network design?

2. What is *postponement?* What are the implications of the postponement concept for logistics network design?

3. What are the four different types of supply chain structures? Provide company examples for each type.

4. What are the three different approaches in structuring global facility networks? What are the main trade-offs and key management tasks associated with each one of them?

5. What are the ideal environments to apply a market focus approach for facility network design? A product focus approach? A process focus approach?

6. Provide industry examples for which product, process, or market focus approaches have been used for structuring the global facility network.

7. Describe a conceptual tool to be used in supporting product allocation to manufacturing facilities for a global firm.

8. What is meant by *site competence?* What is meant by *process technology complexity?*

9. What is meant by an *averse* facility? What is meant by a *prone* facility? How are these concepts used within the new product allocation matrix to help with the product allocation to facilities for a global firm?

REFERENCES

Baker, K. R., M. J. Magazine, and H. L. W. Nuttle. 1986. The effect of commonality on safety stock in a simple inventory model. *Management Science* 32 (8) (August): 982–88.

Benetton. 1985. *Harvard Business Review.* Case No. 685-020.

Bowersox, D. J. 1986. *Logistical management.* New York: Macmillan Publishing Co. Inc.

Bowersox, D. J., and E. A. Morash. 1989. The integration of marketing flows in channels of distribution. *European Journal of Marketing* 23 (2): 58–67.

Child, P., R. Diederichs, F. Sanders, and S. Wisioniwski. 1991. The management of complexity. *Sloan Management Review* (Fall): 73–80.

Corbett, J. 1986. Design for economic manufacture. *Annals of C.I.R.P.* 35 (1): 93.

Davis, T. 1993. Effective supply chain management. *Sloan Management Review* (Summer): 35–46.

Dean, J. W. Jr., and G. I. Susman. 1989. Organizing for manufacturable design. *Harvard Business Review* (January–February): 81–104.

DuBois, F. L., B. Toyne, and M. D. Oliff. 1993. International manufacturing strategies of U.S. multinationals: A conceptual framework based on a four-industry study. Symposium on Globalization of Operations Management, Georgetown University School of Business.

Ernst, R., and B. Ramrad. (1997). "Evaluation of Supply Chain Structures through Outsourcing and Postponement," Georgetown University School of Business, Writing Paper.

Ferdows, K. 1993. Leveraging America's foreign production assets. Symposium on Globalization of Operations Management, Georgetown University School of Business.

Friedland, J. 1994. Car industry: Mini miracle. *Far Eastern Economic Review* (April 28): 76.

Howard, K. A. 1991. Packaging postponement lowers logistical costs. In *Logistical Packaging Innovation Symposium Proceedings,* Council of Logistics Management.

Lee, H. L., and C. Billington. 1992. Pitfalls and opportunities in supply chain inventory management. *Sloan Management Review* 33 (Spring): 65–73.

Lee, H. L., and C. Billington. 1992. Managing supply chain inventory: Pitfalls and opportunities, *Sloan Management Review* 33 (3) (Spring): 65–73.

Lee H. L., G. Billington, and B. Carter. 1993. Hewlett-Packard gains control of inventory and service through design for localization. *Interfaces* 23 (4) (July–August): 1–11.

Shapiro, R. D., and J. L. Heskett. 1985. *Logistics Strategy: Cases and Concepts.* St. Paul, Minn.: West Publishing Company.

Silver, E. A., and R. Peterson. 1985. *Decision systems for inventory management and production planning.* New York: John Wiley & Sons, Inc.

Taguchi, G., and D. Clausing. 1990. A robust quality. *Harvard Business Review* (January–February): 65–75.

Takeuchi, H., and I. Nonaka. 1986. The new new product development game. *Harvard Business Review* (January–February): 137–46.

Tarondeau, J. C. 1993. *Strategie Industrielle.* Vuibert Gestion, Paris.

Tully, S. 1993. The modular corporation. *Fortune* (February 8): 52–56.

Tully, S. 1995. Purchasing's new muscle. *Fortune,* (February 20): 75–83.

Wheelwright, S. C., and W. E. Sasser. 1989. The new product development map. *Harvard Business Review* (May–June): 1112–25.

Whitney, D. E. 1988. Manufacturing by design. *Harvard Business Review* (July–August): 83–91.

Zarley, C. 1995. Manufacturers race to install full build-to-order capabilities. *Computer Reseller News* (March 6): 3.

Zinn, W. 1990. Should you assemble products before an order is received? *Business Horizons* 33: 70–73.

Zinn, W., and D. J. Bowersox. 1988. A planning physical distribution with the principle of postponement. *Journal of Business Logistics* 9: 117–36.

Zinn, W., and M. Levy. 1988. A speculative inventory management: A total channel perspective. *International Journal of Physical Distribution & Materials Management* 18 (5): 34–39.

◆ CASE 8–1: General Appliance Company ◆

"What manufacturing strategy makes the most sense for this company?" mused Jerry Peshel, vice president of operations for General Appliance Company (GAC). GAC is a leading producer of major appliances with a moderately wide line of high-quality products. The major appliance industry, marked by several large competitors and relatively slim margins, was expecting strong unit shipments in the coming year. Rising consumer confidence and falling interest rates had stimulated demand for durable goods and new homes, promising increased sales in both the replacement and first purchase markets.

GAC was currently enjoying strong profitability, but there were clouds on the horizon. Process and product innovations by aggressive domestic competitors threatened to leave GAC with obsolete products and cost disadvantages. One rival had recently signaled a push into GAC's high-quality, high-price market segment by sharp increases in advertising and promotions that emphasized quality and reliability. The same company had recently purchased the industry's leading producer of top-quality dishwashers. Foreign concerns were currently small players in the U.S. major appliance market, but many industry observers expected Japanese and European companies to make bids for increased market share within the next five years.

Prepared by Professor Morris A. Cohen and Thomas F. Kendall, the Wharton School, University of Pennsylvania and Professor Ricardo Ernst, Georgetown University with partial funding by the IBM MOIS Program. Copyright 1991 Morris A. Cohen, Ricardo Ernst, and Thomas F. Kendall.

Manufacturing performance plays an important role in maintaining viability in the major appliance business, due to the competitive requirement for responding to consumer demands for higher quality while addressing competitive cost pressures. Although GAC had continuously invested in maintaining and modernizing its manufacturing and distribution facilities over the last few years, many competitors had done likewise.

Peshel felt that there was a need to coordinate the company's piecemeal approach to reducing costs and planning production in the context of an overall manufacturing and distribution strategy. An integrated approach would help him resolve the myriad of trade-offs that confronted him on a daily basis.

Recent discussions with the company's sales and manufacturing managers had forcefully reminded him of many of these issues. Managers at some plants were urgently requesting funds for expansion, while others were plagued with overcapacity. Some of the newer and more efficient plants and distribution centers were underutilized, while older facilities were approaching capacity limits.

Several specific questions formed in Peshel's mind:

- Was the current configuration of manufacturing and distribution facilities desirable? Should new facilities be purchased or built, should capacity be expanded or reduced at existing facilities, or should some facilities be shut down?
- Should each plant produce a wide range of finished products or should they specialize in just a few product

lines? Should some plants specialize in the fabrication of components and subassemblies while others are devoted to assembly?

- Is the existing network of distribution centers and warehouses appropriate? How should it respond to changes in the manufacturing system?
- How should distribution centers be sourced by manufacturing plants, and which customer market zones should be assigned to each of the distribution centers?
- How should overall market production requirements for each product, component, and subassembly be assigned to various plants? How should these production outputs be distributed to other plants, distribution centers, and warehouses? How should these quantities be determined on a regular basis?
- Which production processes are appropriate for the various components and assemblies used in the appliance industry? How should process choices be made, given estimated volumes, product mixes, and costs for each of GAC's plants?
- How will changes in demand patterns, competitor actions, and external costs affect the answers to these questions?

Jerry Peshel grew increasingly uncertain as he contemplated the possible options and their ramifications. He knew that the answer to any one question impacted the answers to the others, and that choices of a manufacturing/distribution policy would have significant impact on GAC's future competitive position. He also knew, though, that his boss, GAC President Bill Clark, was counting on him to come up with a review of the operating function for the next board meeting, which was scheduled in four weeks.

The firm had recently hired a management consulting firm to evaluate GAC's competitive potential. In their report the consultants concluded that there was poor integration between corporate objectives and the manufacturing side of the business. One of their recommendations was to consolidate manufacturing into few plants. They also documented several instances where delivery problems had led to lost sales in key markets. These service problems were traced to excessive production lead times which were brought about by component shortages. Their key finding, however, was that GAC must move to introduce new product designs and expand its market penetration if it hopes to grow in the future.

Company History

General Appliance Company was founded as the Cleveland Washing Machine Company in 1939 by two brothers in Cleveland, Ohio. Fred and William Sherman built their first automatic clothes washer in an abandoned warehouse on Cleveland's south side. The Shermans made improvements on newly introduced automatic washer technology, and demand outstripped their ability to produce the machines almost immediately.

By 1950 unit sales had reached 70,000 and ground was broken for the construction of an additional plant to handle skyrocketing postwar demand. Production of clothes dryers was added in 1953 with the completion of the new manufacturing facility. In 1958, the product line was broadened to include electric and gas ranges and ovens with the acquisition of the Newton Range Company of St. Joseph, Michigan. Two years later, the company officially changed its name to the General Appliance Company and went public, with a listing on the New York Stock Exchange.

A small manufacturer of clothes washers and dryers, located in Fort Smith, Arkansas, was acquired in 1961. When a full line of portable and built-in dishwashers was introduced in 1969, GAC manufactured them in Fort Smith as well as in Cleveland.

In 1975 GAC built a production facility in Dalton, Georgia, to provide southern manufacturing capacity for ranges and a newly introduced food waste disposer line. By 1983 the plant had been expanded twice, and production lines for washers, dryers, and dishwashers had been installed.

A manufacturing facility located near Los Angeles was purchased from another appliance producer in late 1978 and converted to the manufacture of GAC washers, dryers, and dishwashers.

General Appliance consistently enjoyed the largest margins in the major appliance industry, mainly due to its emphasis on quality, product reliability and excellent after-market service. The company had never experienced an unprofitable year and, by 1985, had achieved earnings of $74 million on sales of $685 million.

Product Line

GAC's product line consisted primarily of electric and gas ranges and ovens, clothes washers and dryers, and dishwashers. GAC also produced food waste disposers, but these supplied a relatively insignificant portion of revenue. GAC products enjoyed a high-quality image that was maintained by outstanding product and process engineering, thorough testing, a motivated production work force, and by advertising that stressed reliability. The high prices that GAC products commanded allowed GAC to maintain a high level of R & D and capital spending.

GAC's products required components and assembly procedures that were basically similar. Each had a cabinet composed of a sheet metal exterior and several plastic or metal interior parts, an electrical or electronic control unit and a motor and drive mechanism (or in the case of the ranges and ovens, heating elements).[1] There were also

---

[1]*Smaller heating elements of various kinds were also required for dishwashers and dryers.*

various handles, knobs and trim pieces made of glass, metal, and plastic.

The major steps in manufacturing the products were:

1. Raw material and component purchasing
2. Cabinet manufacturing
3. Component manufacturing
4. Final assembly

GAC had developed methods and systems that, in management's view, accomplished these tasks efficiently and effectively. Each step is described below.

Purchasing

GAC purchased relatively few components, preferring instead to manufacture many of the parts that other appliance producers bought. For instance, GAC produced its own pumps, heating elements, transmissions (drive mechanisms), hoses, wire harnesses, and many molded plastic parts. This was done to maintain high quality levels, lower production costs and lower transportation costs (several GAC plants were not close to qualified parts suppliers). Continuous review of make-versus-buy decisions determined if components currently manufactured in-house should be purchased. For many parts the answer in terms of both cost and quality continued to be to produce them in GAC plants.

Raw materials such as steel, plastic, porcelain ingredients, and cement[2] were purchased by the plants on an individual basis, although there were corporate guidelines for material and supplier selection. Critical purchased components like motors, timers, and assembled circuit boards were obtained only from a limited number of corporate-specified, qualified vendors.

The manufacturing plants currently purchased relatively few parts from each other, although such internal intermediate product sourcing was not prohibited by the corporate office. The Fort Smith and St. Joseph plants were required to buy the major components that they did not manufacture, including pumps, transmissions and heating elements, from one of the other plants.

The volume of plant-to-plant transfers was increasing, and disputes between the plants, mainly over transfer prices, were becoming more frequent. GAC used a "cost-plus" method to set transfer prices because they did not sell their intermediate products externally and no objective market price could be set. Although the "cost-plus" method seemed straightforward, it resulted in disagreements about how costs were calculated and about what the mark-up should be. In particular, Fort Smith plant manager Mike Sloane felt that the prices he paid the Cleveland plant for

components were too high. An analysis performed by his Industrial Engineering department showed that, with the proper capital investment, the parts could be manufactured for a lower cost in Fort Smith. Jerry Peshel was well aware of the problems with the transfer pricing scheme, and was weighing the advantages and disadvantages of alternatives that would promote equity among the plants.

Cabinet Manufacturing

The creation of cabinets from rolls of sheet metal required the following steps:

1. Slitting, sheeting, and stretching of the steel to form blanks
2. Drawing and pressing to form tubs, top panels, and side panels
3. Welding of subassemblies
4. "Pickling" of subassemblies
5. Application of paint or porcelain
6. Assembly

Large presses, from 30 to 1250 tons of capacity, were used for the first two operations. Many of them were loaded and unloaded automatically, allowing one operator to run several machines. All of the welding was done automatically, by robots or automatic welders.

"Pickling" is a process that prepares metal parts for the application of porcelain enamel. It involves removing foreign materials and oil, etching the metal surface with an acid solution, and depositing a nickel film on the surface of the part to promote adherence of the enamel during the firing process.

Cabinet manufacturing consumed a large part of GAC's resources, in terms of people, equipment, and floor space, and accounted for a large part of the appliance manufacturing cost. It also represented a significant portion of GAC's in-process inventory investment. Enough cabinet parts for four hours of production were maintained in front of the paint and porcelain operation, while eight hours' worth were held in front of the assembly department.

For these reasons, GAC paid close attention to innovations in materials and processes that were used to produce appliance cabinets. For instance, Jerry Peshel knew that at least one of GAC's competitors molded clothes washer and dishwasher tubs out of plastic. GAC used porcelain-coated steel for both parts. (Stainless steel was also an alternative for these parts. Although it did not rust and did not require expensive coating processes, it was expensive and difficult to form.) Over the last few years developments in materials and molding technology had increased the viability of using plastic for these parts.

From a production standpoint, the replacement of steel-and-porcelain with plastic was attractive for several reasons. Although plastic cost more than steel on a per unit

---

[2]Cement was used to balance and add weight to washer tubs.

basis, additional material cost was more than offset by labor and quality advantages. Also, molding processes generate very little scrap.

An injection molding and milling process reduces labor costs by eliminating numerous stamping and assembly operations. Elimination of stamping dies and presses and abbreviation of the assembly line significantly reduce the cost of design, engineering, and tooling for new models.

Models may be redesigned almost every year since the costs of retooling decline. Also, the time and direct labor required to setup production lines for each model run are reduced.

Tubs can be designed that reduce the number of parts needed in assembly. The elimination of parts means that raw and in-process inventories are reduced and that manufacturing cycle times are speeded up as assembly is simplified.

Problems encountered by consumers, including cracked and chipped porcelain and the resulting rust, are eliminated. Plastic also makes quieter parts, a characteristic demanded by consumers, especially in dishwashers.

For General Appliance, plastic had its drawbacks, too. For one thing, GAC production personnel had no experience in the molding of such large parts. The major disadvantage, though, was that plastic components required a cure time after molding. While steel parts could be produced in one or two seconds, plastic parts needed to cool for one or two minutes. Thus, if throughput was to be maintained, many expensive injection molders had to be purchased. Consequently, adoption of this innovation would require substantial capital investment and floor space, and could only be justified by a relatively high volume of production.

The industry's largest company, General Electric, had taken advantage of plastic's favorable characteristics by spending four years and $38 million to redesign both its dishwasher product line and manufacturing facilities. Most of the product's steel parts were replaced with a one-piece plastic tub. The well-publicized results included higher product quality, inventory turns, and market share, along with lower production costs, transportation costs and number of parts and assemblies (reduced from 5600 to 850) (*Purchasing,* March 29, 1984, p. 113). An analysis of potential advantages for GAC in carrying out a similar dishwasher product and manufacturing system redesign for the Cleveland plant had been prepared for Jerry Peshel and is shown in Exhibit 1. Exhibit 2 shows the cost/volume trade-offs of dishwasher process and product alternatives, each of which is indicated by the material to be used for the dishwasher tub.

In addition to product and material changes, investment in various production processes also offers reduced cabinet manufacturing costs. For example, some companies have installed steel slitting systems that are used to reduce

Exhibit 1

Cost/Benefit Analysis of Redesigning Dishwasher Products and Manufacturing Systems for Plastic (Millions of Dollars)

Required Investment

Capital investment (4 molding machines)	$17.60
Capital investment (other manufacturing equipment)	6.30
Manufacturing system redesign	1.50
Product redesign	1.10
Consolidation costs (Note 6)	0.90
	$27.40

Annual Cost Savings

Reduced direct labor in assembly	$ 6.50
Reduced indirect labor	0.39
Savings from inventory reduction	0.05
Scrap reduction	0.16
Reduced shipping costs (Note 7)	0.01
Increased material cost	(1.75)
Increased maintenance costs	(0.40)
	$ 4.96

Notes

1. GAC's cost of capital was estimated to be 11%.
2. Annual cost savings were based on an estimated volume of 250,000 units/year.
3. The two-shift capacity of the injection molding machine being considered was 65,000 parts/year.
4. The molding machines and other manufacturing equipment proposed for the project had estimated lives of seven years, but were classified in the five-year recovery class under the ACRS. It was expected that the molding machines would have a salvage value of approximately 10% of the original cost after seven years. Other equipment had no expected salvage value.
5. All of the proposed equipment was eligible for a 10% ITC (although legislation that would eliminate this credit has been proposed).
6. To obtain all of the cost savings indicated, dishwasher manufacturing operations would have to be consolidated into one facility. This was the estimated cost to physically relocate the affected equipment. The effects on other factors, like inbound and outbound transportation costs, administrative costs, customer service, and quality levels had not yet been quantified. Plastic parts reduced the dishwasher weight by 15 to 22 pounds, reducing some shipping costs.

Exhibit 2

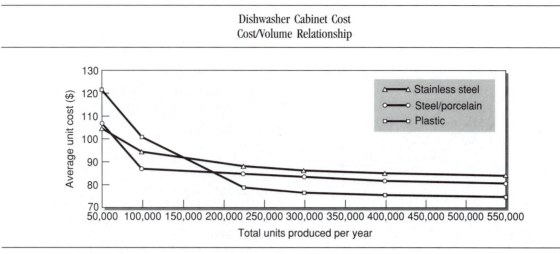

Dishwasher Cabinet Cost
Cost/Volume Relationship

standard-width steel coils to the proper widths for cabinet parts. The alternative to performing this step in-house is to contract with a third party for the service or to pay extra for custom-width steel. Slitting systems require substantial floor space and installation costs (including the digging of a 25-foot deep "looping pit" to maintain proper tension), but allow the appliance manufacturer to reduce steel costs and inventory through the purchase of standard-width coils. Most of these systems require a capital investment of between $0.4 and $2 million.

Some of GAC's competitors had invested heavily in factory automation and flexible manufacturing systems (FMS) to produce sheet metal parts for appliance cabinets. The FMS approach promised reduced direct labor, floor space, and inventory requirements, along with improved quality. The promised advantage of an FMS is its flexibility in producing a large number of part types, over a wide range of production volumes, at a competitive manufacturing cost. However, the fixed and investment costs of such systems were extremely high.

Magic Chef had recently spent $2.7 million for an FMS to produce sheet metal parts and realized a 50% increase in direct labor productivity. Panels for several different appliances were manufactured on the same line. The system required a coil of steel at the beginning of the line and only two operators—one to enter part numbers in the system computer and another to remove finished panels. The FMS had been installed in conjunction with consolidations of their facilities and product lines so that high system utilization was assured. It was anticipated that panels produced at the FMS plant would be shipped to other Magic Chef facilities for assembly (*Appliance Manufacturer,* October 1985, p. 31).

Peshel felt that GAC's product line was not varied enough, and its production runs were too long, to justify a large investment in FMS. There were those in the Manu-

facturing Engineering department who strongly disagreed with Peshel on this point.

Component Manufacturing

Pumps, heating elements, and transmissions were produced in only three of GAC's five plants (Cleveland, Dalton, and Los Angeles). Substantial investments had been made in machinery and automation to ensure low costs and consistently good parts. GAC used robots and employed dedicated automation in the fabrication of many parts and subassemblies. For example, the die casting operation used to make parts for washer transmissions had been automated (at an expense of $1.5 million) so that virtually no direct labor was required. An automatic ladle poured molten metal into the form, a computer controlled the pressure, and a robot removed the finished part.

Powdered (sintered) metal technology is an alternative process that can be employed for the production of some transmission and pump parts. Sintered metal parts are formed by introducing blended, powdered metals into a die under tremendous pressure and then heating to bond the particles. First used commercially ten years ago, the sintered metal process has several advantages. Resulting parts are stronger, more uniform and require little added trimming or machining. Sintered metal forging is said to produce products of higher quality at lower manufacturing costs than other methods. Although an investment of $2.5 to $4 million per plant is required, the potential payoffs are large. Exhibits 3 and 4 show the cost/volume relationship among the possible forging processes for both pump parts and drive unit parts.

Components were assembled in a variety of ways. Control panels for all of GAC's appliances were assembled at individual work stations. Direct labor costs were higher

Exhibit 3

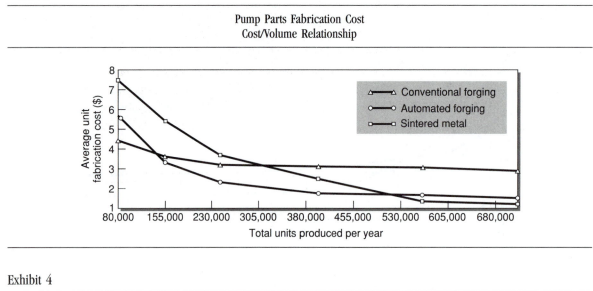

Pump Parts Fabrication Cost
Cost/Volume Relationship

Exhibit 4

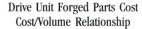

Drive Unit Forged Parts Cost
Cost/Volume Relationship

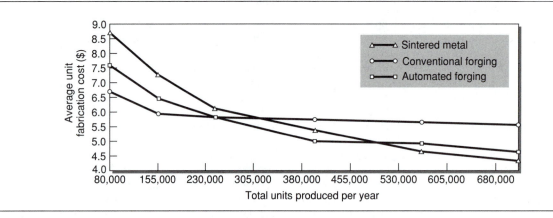

for this method than for an assembly line or automated assembly, but quality was high and it contributed to "job enrichment."

Currently, top-of-the-line dishwashers were the only GAC products that contained electronic control panels (all others used electromechanical timers and conventional switches). GAC purchased fully assembled circuit boards, along with membrane switches and other components, for these control panels. Assembly time was reduced because wiring and component mounting was greatly simplified, but the parts purchased for an electronic panel cost almost $50 more than those for a standard panel. Also, 100% testing of the incoming circuit boards offset assembly labor savings. GAC Marketing and Engineering personnel

were watching competitive products closely and contemplating the introduction of electronic controls on other products. So far, though, consumer resistance to electronics on major appliances and engineering hurdles (including temperature problems during "self-cleaning" oven cycles and washer vibration difficulties) had to be overcome.

Other major components, including pumps and transmissions, were built on machine-paced assembly lines in Cleveland and Los Angeles and on worker-paced (nonsynchronous) lines in Dalton. The Dalton assembly lines produced parts at a slower rate, but component quality was higher. Lower rework costs more than covered the higher direct labor assembly costs.

Final Assembly

Most of GAC's plants used machine-paced final assembly lines, although many subassembly operations were performed individually or on worker-paced lines.

In the Cleveland plant, the Industrial Engineering department had designed a high-speed machine-paced assembly line. The decomposition of final assembly operations in multiple individual jobs, coupled with careful line balancing and the judicious use of automation, allowed for a line cycle time that was several seconds faster than those in other plants. In contrast, the St. Joseph plant used worker-paced final assembly lines to produce ranges and ovens. Each worker completed a number of assembly operations before passing the unit to the next worker.

Machine-paced lines produced at a faster and more steady rate than the worker-paced lines but quality sometimes suffered. Higher capital and maintenance requirements for the machine-paced lines made them cost-effective only if they could be fully utilized for high volume production (generally considered to be at least two full shifts).

The investment required for a typical machine-paced line was $200,000 to $800,000, while the high-speed lines cost $650,000 to $1,200,000. Maintenance costs for the machine-paced lines often ran 20% to 50% higher than for worker-paced lines, due mainly to the complexity of the equipment and the need for skilled technicians to maintain them. The delays and costs associated with retooling such lines for model changes were also considerable.

Automated assembly, in the form of dedicated "pick-and-place" units or robots, could be utilized on the assembly lines to reduce errors and maintain a constant pace. If a suitable application was found, these units (costing between $40,000 and $200,000) could be placed on a machine-paced line to eliminate workers or improve quality.

Manufacturing Facilities

Exhibit 5 is an organizational chart of GAC's manufacturing and distribution operations and Exhibit 6 is a map showing the location of each facility. A description of each manufacturing plant follows.

Cleveland, Ohio

GAC's Cleveland manufacturing plant was the largest and oldest of its facilities. It consisted of the original GAC manufacturing plant and a large addition, which was built in the early 1950s. Several smaller expansions had been made during the past three decades and the entire facility now had floor space of almost 3 million square feet. General Appliance headquarters was located adjacent to the plant, with the Research and Development building directly across the street.

The smaller, original GAC plant produced pumps, transmissions, heating elements, hoses, wire harnesses, small plastic parts and other components. The main plant fabricated sheet metal cabinets and housed assembly lines for all of GAC products.

Building maintenance costs were extremely high. Inefficient material handing, due to the outdated factory design and lack of a modern conveyor system, pushed up unit costs. Labor costs were also higher in this region. Despite recent concessions, the union maintained many work rules that management considered to be inefficient. There was no more room to expand on the current Cleveland site, and facilities were currently utilized at more than 90% of capacity.

Fort Smith, Arkansas

The Fort Smith plant was the sole manufacturing facility of a troubled laundry products manufacturer that GAC acquired in 1961. The plant was quickly converted to the production of General Appliance products and, mainly through the efforts of a GAC manufacturing team (of which Jerry Peshel had been the junior member), operating losses were stemmed within six months. In addition to washers and dryers, GAC manufactured portable and built-in dishwashers in Fort Smith. Fort Smith purchased several major components from Cleveland, including pumps and transmissions.

Although labor costs were low and the union was relatively cooperative, unit costs suffered because of outdated equipment that required much maintenance and that resulted in frequent downtime. Fort Smith was a prime candidate for a large capital outlay to update its manufacturing facilities. The plant manager, Mike Sloane, had submitted project requests in each of the last two years and had been turned down both times. He was becoming increasingly vocal about the potential his plant had for low-cost production if corporate would approve his capital requests. Fort Smith was currently producing at less than full capacity.

St. Joseph, Michigan

The St. Joseph plant, formerly the Newton Range Company, manufactured only gas and electric ranges and ovens. GAC had not invested heavily in the St. Joseph plant over the last few years because of the plant's limited size and product line.

Although St. Joseph was currently producing at capacity, it was questionable whether the fixed cost of the small plant was worth the incremental capacity for ranges and ovens. Little automation had been installed in either the fabrication or assembly areas, but the plant was surprisingly

Exhibit 5

Manufacturing Organization

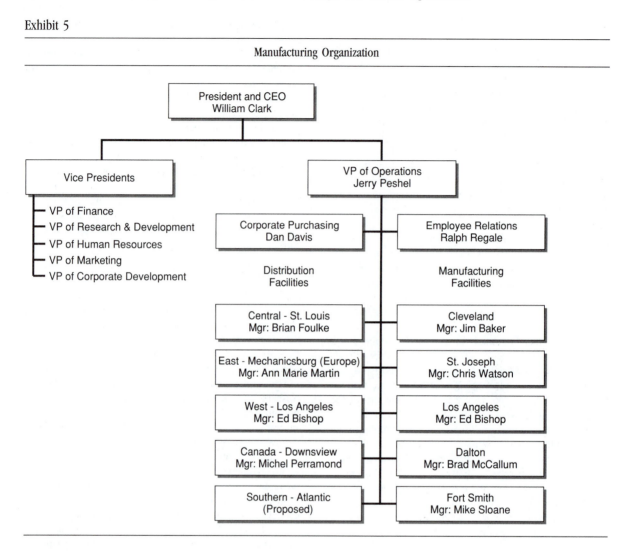

President and CEO
William Clark

Vice Presidents

- VP of Finance
- VP of Research & Development
- VP of Human Resources
- VP of Marketing
- VP of Corporate Development

VP of Operations
Jerry Peshel

Corporate Purchasing
Dan Davis

Employee Relations
Ralph Regale

Distribution
Facilities

Manufacturing
Facilities

Distribution Facilities	Manufacturing Facilities
Central - St. Louis Mgr: Brian Foulke	Cleveland Mgr: Jim Baker
East - Mechanicsburg (Europe) Mgr: Ann Marie Martin	St. Joseph Mgr: Chris Watson
West - Los Angeles Mgr: Ed Bishop	Los Angeles Mgr: Ed Bishop
Canada - Downsview Mgr: Michel Perramond	Dalton Mgr: Brad McCallum
Southern - Atlantic (Proposed)	Fort Smith Mgr: Mike Sloane

---

efficient in terms of labor hours per unit produced. This was attributed mostly to an older, experienced work force that generated little scrap and worked well together. Assembly was performed on an operator-paced assembly line. Each worker performed several operations on the product before rolling it along the line to the next operator. St. Joseph employed only about 200 people. Heating elements were purchased from the Cleveland plant, but all other parts were either manufactured in-house or purchased from approved vendors.

Dalton, Georgia

The Dalton plant was the newest and most efficient of GAC's manufacturing facilities. Although it was almost ten years old, GAC had invested heavily over the last decade to expand and update the plant and its equipment. Several

miles of overhead conveyors provided efficient transport of material from sheet metal, paint, and porcelain departments to the assembly lines. Robots had been installed in several locations, mainly to perform tedious or difficult punch press and painting operations. Machine-paced final assembly lines were used to obtain high-volume production of all of GAC's products, including food waste disposers. Dalton had the same capacity as the Cleveland plant with twenty percent less floor space. Facilities to manufacture all components including pumps, heating elements and transmissions, had been installed.

Union relations were very good and employees were generally more hard-working and cooperative than in the other GAC plants. Wage rates were lower than at any other GAC location.

Exhibit 6

Product Network

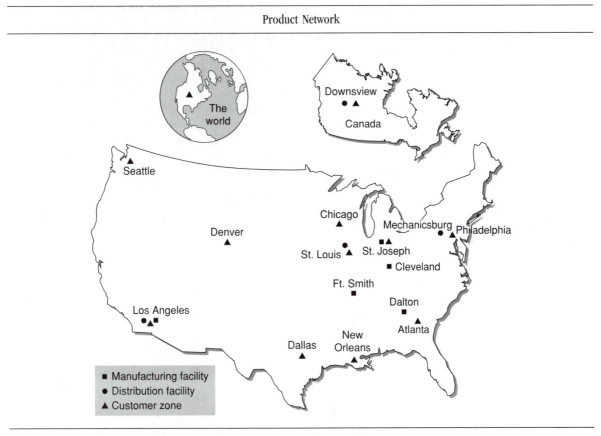

- ■ Manufacturing facility
- ● Distribution facility
- ▲ Customer zone

One disturbing change Jerry Peshel had recently spotted, though, was a significant increase in the unit cost of several products. The change had appeared fifteen months ago, shortly after production of dishwashers was initiated in Dalton (making Dalton the only production facility that manufactured all of GAC's products). These cost increases seemed to be exacerbated by changes in product mix and volume requirements. Dalton plant manager Brad McCallum had assured Peshel that Dalton would remain GAC's most efficient facility.

Los Angeles, California

The Los Angeles plant was a large facility that GAC had purchased in 1978 from another appliance manufacturer to provide West Coast capacity. The transportation of bulky and heavy appliances to the West Coast was expensive and time-consuming. Before the Los Angeles plant purchase, at any given time large amounts of inventory were on trains and trucks between GAC plants and the West Coast. The

Los Angeles plant had been converted to the manufacture of GAC washers, dryers and dishwashers.

Since 1979, however, results had been disappointing. Labor costs were high and quality was the lowest of any GAC plant. Rapid employee turnover was attributed to both problems. Pumps and transmissions were currently produced in the Los Angeles plant, but the rework and scrap rates were high. Attempts by GAC engineering and production people to improve component quality had resulted in little improvement after two years of effort. Jerry Peshel knew that the Dalton and Cleveland plants had sufficient capacity to ship pumps and transmissions to the West Coast if the Los Angeles plant did not get its act together soon.

Many large and expensive presses, automatic cabinet lines and automatic coating lines had been installed to provide high volume capability, but the capacity was underutilized. Likewise, machine-paced assembly lines were used at less than their two-shift capacity because of slack demand. Although it had been unthinkable just two years before, one option being considered was the closing of the Los Angeles plant. The fixed cost savings and lower unit costs at Fort Smith, St. Joseph and Dalton would possibly outweigh the higher transportation and inventory costs. It was anticipated that higher utilization of these other plants would generate cost savings due to scale economies, but this was uncertain.

Exhibit 7 summarizes refixed and variable cost for the different manufacturing plants.

Distribution

General Appliance maintained four distribution centers (DCs) to serve twelve customer market zones. East, Central and West DC's supplied ten domestic customer zones. The East DC served the foreign (mainly European) markets and Canada was served by a DC located in Downsview, which is a suburb of Toronto. Exhibit 8 presents the cost and capacities for the different distribution centers.

The Eastern DC, located outside of Philadelphia in Mechanicsburg, was the newest and most efficient distribution facility; it was also the smallest. It was currently operating at capacity and Manager Ann Marie Martin was already requesting funds for expansion. The Central DC, located in St. Louis, was the largest distribution facility.

The Western DC, in Los Angeles, had the highest handling and fixed costs due to high labor rates and building maintenance expenses. All goods shipped to Europe went through the Mechanicsburg DC, while Canadian shipments went through the Downsview facility.

All products were shipped from the manufacturing plants to the distribution centers where they were inventoried with varying degrees of automation and efficiency. Customer zone orders were generally filled by the nearest DC, but sometimes it was necessary to ship products from other DCs. All DCs maintained a 90% fill rate service target.

The customer zones comprised many wholesale appliance distributors who in turn sold to a total of approximately 10,000 retail outlets. Distribution exclusively through retail stores had allowed GAC to avoid the sales declines associated with housing industry downturns and the price-cutting of mass merchandisers. Most of GAC's appliances went to the relatively stable replacement market.

Peshel was contemplating opening a Southern DC. Fixed and operating costs for a proposed Atlanta facility had been estimated by a team that Peshel had appointed (see Exhibit 8), but the impact of such a facility on overall costs was not yet clear. Transportation costs from existing DCs to many rapidly growing Southern markets were high, but it

Exhibit 7

Manufacturing Costs
Variable Production Costs ($ per units)

Plant	Fixed Cost	Drive Unit	Heating Element	Pump	Control Unit	Cabinet	Washer Assembly	Dryer Assembly	Dishwasher Assembly	Oven/Range Assembly
Cleveland	$30,397,500	24.96	10.88	16.00	12.16	84.48	42.24	14.08	21.76	86.40
St. Joseph	$ 6,037,200	0	0	0	11.52	81.47	0	0	0	82.56
Los Angeles	$19,392,300	26.24	12.16	18.05	12.80	84.48	43.71	15.42	21.70	0
Dalton	$24,420,600	24.00	10.88	15.68	10.24	79.74	40.06	12.42	21.50	83.20
Fort Smith	$14,289,300	0	0	0	11.65	85.50	41.60	12.80	21.12	0

Exhibit 8

Distribution Center Costs and Capacities

	Fixed Cost	Max Thrupt.	Handling Costs ($/Unit)			
			Washer	Dryer	Dishwasher	Range
Mechanicsburg	$1,256,450	590,000	3.32	3.32	3.32	3.32
L.A.	3,279,951	770,000	6.87	6.87	6.87	6.87
St. Louis	2,531,394	1,600,000	4.42	4.42	4.42	4.42
Downsview	615,500	92,000	4.50	4.50	4.50	4.50
Atlanta*	1,250,000	600,000	3.29	3.29	3.29	3.29

*proposed

was difficult to determine if reduced shipping charges would offset the costs associated with operating another DC.

The manager of the St. Louis DC, Brian Foulke, was against such an addition, arguing that his facility could cost-effectively serve the South if GAC would invest in the improved inventory control systems and the state-of-the-art storage and retrieval system that he proposed. The St. Louis facility was not currently operating at maximum capacity.

Manufacturing Strategy Options

Although GAC had its share of manufacturing problems, Peshel knew that his costs were currently competitive, given GAC's quality and service performance. Even though GAC's products commanded high prices, the company could not have enjoyed margins almost double the industry average without a competitive cost structure. He was concerned, though, that changing market demands, foreign and domestic competitors and new product and process technologies could erode those margins quickly.

To maintain a competitive cost position, he wanted to ensure that the configuration of GAC processes, plants and distribution centers was rational and consistent with the company's overall corporate strategy of market segmentation and differentiation. However, the trade-offs to be evaluated were complex. If GAC continued manufacturing the same products at several different locations, scale economies that could be realized by centralizing production would be sacrificed. Also, consistency and quality are enhanced by manufacturing each product at only one location. Recent experience with the Dalton plant suggested that there may be costs associated with overloading a plant with a production mission that is too complex. On the other hand, transportation charges for major appliances were significant and some economies of scope were obtained by manufacturing several similar products at the same location.

Peshel had instructed his new assistant, recent MBA graduate Skip Clark, to pull together relevant distribution and manufacturing cost information as the first step in a comprehensive analysis (see exhibits 9 to 15). With this information and Mr. Clark's assistance, Jerry Peshel hoped to draw some conclusions about the most effective manufacturing strategy for GAC.

Exhibit 9

Transportation Costs ($ per 100 units)

DRYERS, RANGES

	Distribution Centers				
Plant	Mechanicsburg	Los Angeles	St. Louis	Downsview	Atlanta*
Cleveland	964	3955	1288	2924	1805
St. Joseph	1288	3991	1179	3208	1926
Los Angeles	4025	440	2569	6324	3392
Dalton	1439	4297	1163	4894	665
Fort Smith	1984	2626	833	5096	1225

	Distribution Centers				
Customer Zone	Mechanicsburg	Los Angeles	St. Louis	Downsview	Atlanta*
Atlanta	1252	3808	940	4314	316
Chicago	1298	3395	889	5060	1237
Dallas	1753	2033	1129	5167	1237
Denver	2974	1392	1555	5167	2761
Detroit	1018	2801	1133	2650	1633
Los Angeles	3986	411	2303	6072	3497
New Orleans	1655	2263	1128	5039	766
Philadelphia	311	2965	1023	2916	1259
St. Louis	994	2298	257	3783	940
Seattle	4444	1277	2389	6278	4057
Canada				727	
Foreign	4706				

*proposed

Exhibit 10

Inter-Plant and Plant-DC Transportation Cost ($ per 100 units)					

From:	To Plant →	Cleveland	St. Joseph	L.A.	Dalton	Ft. Smith
Cleveland	Drive units	0.00	1.59	3.89	2.11	2.44
	Heating elements	0.00	0.98	2.99	2.00	2.40
	Pumps	0.00	1.05	3.70	2.21	2.50
	Control units	0.00	2.25	8.90	4.70	5.05
	Cabinets	0.00	6.90	22.10	9.37	11.07
	To DC →	Mechburg	L.A.	St. Louis	Downw	Atlanta
	Washers	10.60	43.51	14.17	32.16	19.86
	Dryers	9.64	39.55	12.88	29.24	18.05
	Dishwashers	10.60	43.51	14.17	32.16	19.86
	Ranges	9.64	39.55	12.88	29.24	18.05

From:	To Plant →	Cleveland	St. Joseph	L.A.	Dalton	Ft. Smith
St. Joseph	Drive units	—	—	—	—	—
	Heating elements	—	—	—	—	—
	Pumps	—	—	—	—	—
	Control units	2.25	0.00	8.46	4.84	4.95
	Cabinets	6.90	0.00	21.00	9.65	10.90
	To DC →	Mechburg	L.A.	St. Louis	Downw	Atlanta
	Washers	—	—	—	—	—
	Dryers	—	—	—	—	—
	Dishwashers	—	—	—	—	—
	Ranges	12.88	39.91	11.79	32.08	19.26

From:	To Plant →	Cleveland	St. Joseph	L.A.	Dalton	Ft. Smith
L.A.	Drive units	3.89	3.50	0.00	3.75	2.55
	Heating elements	2.99	2.60	0.00	2.72	1.79
	Pumps	3.70	3.61	0.00	3.90	2.25
	Control units	8.90	8.46	0.00	9.00	4.23
	Cabinets	22.10	21.00	0.00	24.20	13.10
	To DC →	Mechburg	L.A.	St. Louis	Downw	Atlanta
	Washers	44.28	4.84	28.26	69.56	37.31
	Dryers	40.25	4.40	25.69	63.24	33.92
	Dishwashers	44.28	4.84	28.26	69.56	37.31
	Ranges	—	—	—	—	—

From:	To Plant →	Cleveland	St. Joseph	L.A.	Dalton	Ft. Smith
Dalton	Drive units	2.11	2.11	3.75	0.00	1.23
	Heating elements	2.00	2.05	2.72	0.00	1.25
	Pumps	2.21	2.22	3.90	0.00	1.30
	Control units	4.70	4.84	9.00	0.00	2.77
	Cabinets	9.37	9.65	24.20	0.00	6.06
	To DC →	Mechburg	L.A.	St. Louis	Downw	Atlanta
	Washers	15.83	47.27	12.79	53.83	7.32
	Dryers	14.39	42.97	11.63	48.94	6.65
	Dishwashers	15.83	47.27	12.79	53.83	7.32
	Ranges	14.39	42.97	11.63	48.94	6.65

From:	To Plant →	Cleveland	St. Joseph	L.A.	Dalton	Ft. Smith
Ft. Smith	Drive units	—	—	—	—	—
	Heating elements	—	—	—	—	—
	Pumps	—	—	—	—	—
	Control units	5.05	4.95	4.23	2.77	0.00
	Cabinets	11.07	10.90	13.10	6.06	0.00
	To DC →	Mechburg	L.A.	St. Louis	Downw	Atlanta
	Washers	21.82	28.89	9.16	56.06	13.48
	Dryers	19.84	26.26	8.33	50.96	12.25
	Dishwashers	21.82	28.89	9.16	56.06	13.48
	Ranges	—	—	—	—	—

Exhibit 11

Raw Material and Intermediate Product Usage

	Washer	Dryer	Dishwasher	Oven/Range
Raw Materials				
Steel	✔	✔	✔	✔
Motor	✔	✔	✔	
Components				
Drive unit	✔	✔	✔	
Heating element				✔
Pump	✔		✔	
Control unit	✔	✔	✔	✔
Cabinet	✔	✔	✔	✔

Exhibit 12

Raw Material Cost
Average Production Costs—Raw Materials

	($/Unit)				
	Cleveland	St. Joseph	Los Angeles	Dalton	Fort Smith
Steel V1	33	39	67	42	43
Steel V2	37	36	58	38	35
Steel V3	65	51	37	53	44
Motor V4	31	32	31	31	32
Motor V5	30	31	33	31	32

Exhibit 13

Customer Zone Demand Forecast (1988)

Customer Zone	Washer	Dryer	Dishwasher	Oven/Range	TOTAL	DC Assigned
Atlanta	108,000	81,000	33,000	49,000	271,000	St. Louis
Chicago	120,000	61,000	26,000	39,000	246,000	St. Louis
Dallas	69,000	43,000	19,000	25,000	156,000	St. Louis
Denver	55,000	44,000	18,000	23,000	140,000	St. Louis
Detroit	82,000	45,000	22,000	40,000	189,000	St. Louis
L.A.	73,000	58,000	17,000	27,000	175,000	L.A.
New Orleans	54,000	56,000	26,000	42,000	178,000	St. Louis
Philadelphia	85,000	57,000	21,000	41,000	204,000	Mechanicsbg
St. Louis	71,000	72,000	21,000	48,000	212,000	St. Louis
Seattle	54,000	31,000	18,000	25,000	128,000	St. Louis
Canada	25,000	22,000	9,000	15,000	71,000	Downsview
Foreign	6,000	8,000	11,000	12,000	37,000	Mechanicsbg
Total	802,000	578,000	241,000	386,000	2,007,000	

Estimated Demand Growth Rates

	Region				
Product	U.S. West	U.S. Central	U.S. East	Canada	Foreign
Washer	4%	3%	2%	3%	4%
Dryer	4%	3%	2%	3%	3%
Dishwasher	5%	4%	4%	6%	5%
Oven/Range	3%	2%	2%	2%	3%

Current Selling Price

Product	Prices ($/Unit)
Washer	$440
Dryer	360
Dishwasher	320
Range	480

Exhibit 14

Current Configuration Decisions

Plants	ID #	Open?	DCs	ID #	Open?
Cleveland	1	Yes	Mechncsbg	1	Yes
St. Joseph	2	Yes	L.A.	2	Yes
L.A.	3	Yes	St. Louis	3	Yes
Dalton	4	Yes	Downsview	4	Yes
Fort Smith	5	Yes	Atlanta	5	No

Customer Zone	Distribution Center		Customer Zone	Distribution Center		Customer Zone	Distribution Center	
Atlanta	(St. Louis)	3	Detroit	(St. Louis)	3	St. Louis	(St. Louis)	3
Chicago	(St. Louis)	3	L.A.	(L.A.)	2	Seattle	(St. Louis)	3
Dallas	(St. Louis)	3	New Orl.	(St. Louis)	3	Canada	(Downsview)	4
Denver	(St. Louis)	3	Phila.	(Mechbrg)	1	Foreign	(Mechbrg)	1

Final Product Plant Mix   (Actual/Max)

	Cap.Utl. Weight	Cleveland	St. Joseph	Los Angeles	Dalton	Fort Smith	Demand Reqmt.	% Prod
Washer	0.35	230,000	0	128,000	285,000	159,000	802,000	100%
		750,000	0	450,000	550,000	390,000		
Dryer	0.35	212,000	0	103,000	218,000	45,000	578,000	100%
		750,000	0	450,000	555,000	390,000		
Dishwasher	0.35	84,000	0	35,000	80,000	42,000	241,000	100%
		750,000	0	420,000	500,000	230,000		
Range	0.35	145,000	150,000	0	91,000	0	386,000	100%
		520,000	175,000	0	370,000	0		

Intermediate Product Plant Mix   (Actual/Max)

	Cap.Utl. Weight	Cleveland	St. Joseph	Los Angeles	Dalton	Fort Smith	Demand Reqmt.	% Prod
Drive Unit	0.04	772,000	0	266,000	583,000	0	1,621,000	100%
		900,000	0	730,000	900,000	0		
Heatg. Elem.	0.04	295,000	0	0	91,000	0	386,000	100%
		400,000	0	345,000	222,000	0		
Pump	0.1	515,000	0	163,000	365,000	0	1,043,000	100%
		750,000	0	580,000	610,000	0		
Control Unit	0.1	671,000	150,000	266,000	674,000	246,000	2,007,000	100%
		820,000	190,000	650,000	733,000	470,000		
Cabinet	0.45	671,000	150,000	266,000	674,000	246,000	2,007,000	100%
		900,000	200,000	800,000	850,000	470,000		

Exhibit 15

Total Cost Summary

	Item Cost (in $1,000)	% of Total Cost
Inbound Cost		
Raw Material	121,578.0	19.90%
Transshipment	1,249.7	0.20%
	122,827.7	20.11%
Production Cost		
Plant Fixed	94,536.9	15.48%
Variable	329,437.8	53.93%
	423,974.7	69.41%
Outbound Cost		
DC Fixed	7,683.3	1.26%
DC Hndlg. & Transp.	29,991.0	4.91%
Plant Hndlg. & Transp.	26,358.7	4.32%
	64,033.0	10.48%
TOTAL P&D COST:	610,835.4	100.00%

Profit & Losses (In $Millions)

Total Sales (Year 0)	$823.360
Cost of Material, Production, & Distrib.	$610.835
Cost of Marketing, R & D, & Other Overhead	$125.000
Income Before Taxes	$ 87.525
Sales Margin (Year 0)	10.63%

◆ CASE 8–2: The Logistics Impact of the Channel Tunnel ◆

Abstract

The tunnel linking England and France is remarkable in its impact. As the global logistics network grows, the tunnel improves travel for people and goods moving between the UK and the continent. Although many speculated about the financial implications of the tunnel, no one had done a serious study regarding the logistics implications of this new rail infrastructure. This study was motivated by the French train company dedicated to freight (Fret SNCF) in their need to explore commercial opportunities through the tunnel. We started by performing a survey (in cooperation with Coopers & Lybrand) with European exporting and transportation companies as to expectations and strategic evaluation for the channel tunnel as a logistics alternative. We then developed some analytical models to offer guidelines for defining the range of values that would make one transportation alternative superior. In the study we worked with data provided by Fret SNCF, as well as with consultation with many European companies to validate the models and present specific solutions from different areas in the continent to the UK. In particular, we examined nine feasible scenarios for going to London from seven different areas in the European continent.

Introduction

The channel tunnel (Chunnel) linking England and France, which opened in 1994, greatly improves travel for both people and goods moving between the UK and the continent. The tunnel connects the rail systems of the UK and France and, indirectly, their road systems. It adds an

By Philippe-Pierre Dornier and Ricardo Ernst. 1997, in Interfaces 27:3 (May–June): 39–59. Copyright 1997, Institute for Operations and the Management Sciences.

important component to the economic integration of Europe, which (unlike the U.S., which has not built a railroad in decades) is building a network of tunnels, bridges, and high-speed railroads [Sloan 1991]. The Chunnel is important for linking the European continent, not just France and England. It consists of two rail-only tunnels and one service tunnel running the 50 km between the terminals located at Folkestone in the United Kingdom and Sangatte in northern France. The respective ports of entry are Dover and Calais. Each of the twin rail tunnels is used exclusively for trains (capable of moving cars and their passengers, trucks, freight, and just passengers) which operate in one direction only. There are some cross-over sections between the main tunnels to allow for repair of the rail lines. The smaller service tunnel lies between the two rail tunnels and provides access for routine maintenance, ventilation, and safe refuge in the event of an emergency [Merchant, Knowles, and Acheson 1991].

The Chunnel will affect European businesses in three major areas. First, it will change travel patterns for business and leisure purposes, particularly between the South of England and the North of France and Belgium, since the travel time between London and Paris is no more than three hours. Second, it will affect the location of new business and commercial centers as traffic increases. Third, it will alter the organization, management, and control of logistics in companies that move goods, since the Chunnel offers shuttle services for freight trains and trucks.

The Chunnel offers an interesting new option to be considered in evaluating logistics alternatives in Europe. It has advantages that go beyond any advantage in cost. It offers continuity in service; that is, transport service will not be affected by stormy weather or ship timetables. The Chunnel will always be open (365 days a year), with three trains departing per hour in each direction during heavy activity and at least one departure per hour otherwise. The quality of transport has also improved with the reduction in transfers among modes of transport, since it is now possible to load freight on a train in a location at the south of France and unload it in the northern UK without the exchange from train to ferry and back at the channel (Figure 1). These conveniences have to be considered in comparing the Chunnel to other alternatives, instead of using only simple transportation cost calculations based on distance.

From a financial point of view, the Chunnel has not been a successful project. Eurotunnel (the publicly traded British-French company that manages the tunnel) has spent more than double its $7.5 billion projection to build the tunnel, and only in the summer of 1995 was it able to cover its operating costs and capital expenditures out of its cash flow for the first time. It is still far from able to meet interest charges on its $12 billion debt, which are accumulating at a rate of $90 million a month. The company expects to have sufficient revenues in six to ten years to pay its interest bill. By the end of 1995, it had captured 41% of the cross-channel market for cars, 45% of the coach market, and 47% of the freight market.

The Channel Tunnel as a Logistics Alternative

The tunnel links Calais in France to Folkestone in the United Kingdom, joining the European railway of 240,000 km to the British railway network of 15,000 km. The tunnel is 50 km long: 38 km are under the sea, 3 km are in France, and 9 km are in the UK. The freight traffic crossing the channel at the beginning of the twenty-first century is expected to be 122.6 million tons each year, of which 21.1 will be through the Chunnel (Table 1).

The tunnel system is designed to accommodate shuttles that can transport 180 cars every 15 minutes during peak periods, giving it the capacity to transport 10,080 car passengers in each direction per day. There are also 40 high-speed passenger trains (no cars) per day in each direction. It is also expected to transport up to 28 trucks traveling each way daily. In addition, trains carrying freight accommodate 35 shuttles that are allocated as follows: 22 for combined transportation, that is, carrying containers of merchandise that are transferred from trucks to the train and at the other end of the Chunnel transferred back to trucks (about 4 million tons during the first year); five for conventional freight (about 2 million tons during the first year); and eight for new cars, that is, trains moving new cars, such as Renaults (about 0.5 million tons during the first year). There are separate loading platforms for freight and passenger traffic, and separate custom facilities to expedite the processes.

Since Britain joined the common market in 1973, its exports to the continent have grown from $6 billion in 1973 to $42 billion in 1986 [Project Cost-CEE 1993]. Currently exports to the continent account for approximately 65% of Britain's foreign trade in services and goods, excluding petroleum products [Merchant, Knowles, and Acheson 1991]. According to customs data for 1992, the total flow of merchandise, including petroleum products, is 56,363,000 tons from the continent to the UK and 79,962,400 tons from the UK to the continent. Excluding petroleum products (which are generally moved by pipe), the numbers change to 47,016,200 and 35,671,800, respectively (Figure 2).

For almost all the exchanges between the largest continental countries and the UK, the balance favors the continent. This balance depends on several factors:

- It depends on the nature of the product. For example, the flow of agriculture and food products from the continent is twice that from the UK. For cars, chemicals, and health care products, the ratio goes down to 1.5.
- It depends on the country, with France exporting 40% more than it imports from the UK, the Netherlands 80%, Germany 30%, and Spain 20%.

Figure 1   The Chunnel offers a new alternative for linking the continent and the UK. Should a Spanish company shipping goods to the UK use its current existing Route 3, or the Chunnel with the combination Route 1 and Route 2? The same question applies to a German company going to the North of the UK. Should it use its current Route 3' or the Chunnel with the combination Route 1' + Route 2'?

Table 1   *The 1993 Eurotunnel forecast for channel traffic predicts an increase for passengers and freight between 1994 and 2013.*

Channel Traffic	Opening 94/95	2003	2013
Passenger cars:			
Million cars/year	67.1	93.6	118.7
Chunnel share	29.7	39.5	46.6
Freight: Million tons/year	84.4	122.6	170.4
Chunnel share	14.8	21.1	27.8

- It depends on the country and the product. The ratio between exports from and imports to for France in agricultural and food products is 4.6, while for Germany it is only 2.2.

- It also depends on the mode of transportation. Forty-six percent of the products coming into the UK are in containers, while 38% of those leaving the UK going to the continent are in containers.

These figures explain why transportation prices and commercial conditions differ between the UK and each country in the continent. Today, for example, the prices are 40% higher from France to the UK than from the UK to France. This study was motivated by the French train company dedicated to freight (Fret SNCF) in their need to explore commercial opportunities through the channel tunnel. We worked with data provided by Fret SNCF and in consultation with many of the logistic providers in Europe to validate our ideas. We started the study with a survey of expectations for the Chunnel with exporting and transportation companies. The survey was performed in cooperation with Coopers and Lybrand Europe during the period July 1993 to March 1994.

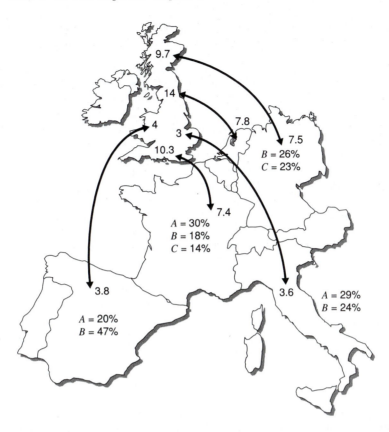

Figure 2   The figures at the head of the arrows show the merchandise that flows between the continent and the UK in millions of tons (excluding petroleum products). The percentages refer to types of products: A indicates agriculture and food, B indicates intermediate goods, and C indicates chemicals (Customs data from 1992).

Logistics Opportunities of the Chunnel

Using the tunnel has advantages and disadvantages: In terms of service, measured as the time it takes to go from the continent to the UK or vice versa, the tunnel crossing is fast and reliable (London to Paris in three hours), 35 minutes from Calais to Folkestone (versus two hours by ferry), and 80 minutes from the French highways to the British highways. For passenger traffic (those traveling by train through the Chunnel without cars), the time advantage is even greater since the train goes to train stations situated inside the cities (the train station in France is in Paris). For freight, a difference of less than 1.5 hours makes little difference except in special cases. The disadvantages are mainly the problems of monopoly in case of a strike (highly unlikely) and the transit time, which does not allow truck drivers much rest time, thereby requiring a second driver.

For truck drivers, the Chunnel's quicker transit gives no significant advantage over the ferry. Ferry companies offer services on board, such as restaurants and private cabins. Therefore, price is the factor available to obtain the truck drivers' business.

In terms of quality, the Chunnel requires fewer changes of modes of transportation (relative to the ferry) for merchandise traveling directly by train from factories on the continent to final clients in the UK. That is, with the ferry the merchandise might need to be transferred from the train or truck to the ferry and then, at the other end, to the train or the truck (each mode of transportation is called a *platform*). With the Chunnel the intermediate exchange of platforms for crossing the channel is avoided, and therefore, there is less manipulation of the merchandise, which reduces the opportunities for accidents. In addition, orders could be consolidated at different points on the train network. In fact, the Transport Development Group (TDG) has invested more than $10 million in the construction of the UK's first distribution center (250,000 square feet) dedicated to rail and road transport and located next to the Chunnel rail terminal to offer customers direct access throughout the UK and Europe.

In terms of cost, experts foresee a price war between the tunnel and the ferry. The cost of ferries from the north of Europe to the south of the UK has decreased by 20% between January 1994 and July 1996. The Chunnel competes with the ferry, especially in the Calais-Folkestone area [*Journal de la Marine Marchande* 1994]. Even if enough market exists to support the two modes, a price war for market share is expected. In fact, the current figures on market share for the Chunnel are below expectations because of delays in the delivery of trains, railway strikes in France and Belgium in December of 1995, and aggressive fare cutting by ferry companies.

The tunnel can serve the following potential markets [Coton 1994]:

- Companies that currently ship by train will find it attractive to continue into the UK without having to break their trains down to get them into the ferry. This is particularly important for companies that ship bulk products in big volumes (for example, sand, cement, steel, and paper). The Chunnel permits complete trains to pass at specified times (mid-day or nights).
- Companies that currently ship full containers to the harbor by train, transfer them to ships to cross the channel, and then transfer them again to train or truck to get them to their final destinations (such products as whiskey and beer from north England, Scotland, and Ireland, or wine from France). Companies, such as Bell Lines, currently run freight ferries twice a day. Trains running from source to final destination may provide advantages of time, quality, and service.

The Chunnel train can also serve companies that move small volumes in trailers (containers with wheels that can be connected to trucks), carrying just the trailer across the channel. Other markets for the Chunnel are companies that use isolated freight cars for long distances (for example, from Italy to England), those who ship small and high-value parcels to be delivered quickly or automobiles or fresh products in refrigerated wagons. For example, the rail service operator European Passenger Services (EPS) introduced four-hour parcel delivery services from London to Paris and Brussels using the Chunnel trains.

Container Movement: Now an Improved Alternative

The Chunnel makes the container movement with a combination of modes of transport an improved alternative. That is one of its most important contributions. Trucks (or

trains) can load containers on any location linked to the train system in the continent (not necessarily at the channel crossing point), and cross (through the tunnel) to the UK where the container can be delivered closer to a final destination and picked up by another truck (or linked to another train system). The UK train system has invested in underslung coaches, that is, flat cars that carry containers and are low enough to pass through the existing tunnels in the UK, to increase the scope of accessible cities.

Before the Chunnel opened, moving containers was not very efficient: it required five handling steps on average and three modes of transport (truck, train, and boat or ferry). For instance, a container traveling from the south of France by a combination of modes (truck and/or train) might be transferred in Ostende or Zeebrugge from a train (or truck) to a boat and then reloaded on a truck (or train) for the final destination.

In our study we found that combining modes of transport is a competitive alternative (relative to the other options to be discussed later) for freight coming from Italy, eastern and central Spain, the majority of France, and eastern Germany and Austria.

Reduction in Exchange of Platforms

A boat or a ferry used to be necessary for all but air transport between the continent and the UK. Transferring freight from train or truck to ship adds cost and affects quality without any value added. Direct linkage by train or combination of modes may change the logistics network for many companies.

Renault, for example, sells between 80,000 and 120,000 automobiles per year in the UK. Their distribution is affected by such issues as seasonality (25% of sales take place during June and July), the high value of the product, and the high risk of damage during transportation. Renault transports the cars in several steps. First they ship the cars by boat or train to the port of Le Havre in France. Then, "jockeys" drive the cars onto roll-on, roll-off ferries, which carry them to Southampton for delivery in the south of the UK or to Goole for delivery in the north. In each of those ports, Renault maintains a distribution center that handles deliveries to dealers.

The trip from the plant in France to the UK distribution centers takes 10 days and involves a high risk of damage and other problems associated with changing modes of transport. With the Chunnel, Renault could ship directly to its distribution centers, which it could relocate closer to its customers. The Chunnel would reduce the transportation time to two days, requiring less inventory in the pipeline.

Electrolux/Distrilux in Italy exports approximately 850,000 appliances per year from five plants in Italy to five distribution centers in the UK. This represents about 10 freight cars a day. Currently, 90% of the freight goes to

Le Havre by train where it is off-loaded into a company warehouse, from which it is shipped by ferry or boat to the different distribution centers in the UK. The company is considering shipping directly to its customer markets in the UK via the Chunnel, which will mean changes in costs, quality, and speed of delivery.

This is the type of analysis that Fret SNCF was interested in quantifying in their need to offer logistics solutions to different companies. Working in collaboration with a team from the French company, we developed the models presented in this paper as a tool for evaluating alternatives. Before we did this study, many ideas existed about the financial implications of the tunnel. However, no one had made a serious attempt to study the logistics implications of this new rail infrastructure.

European Companies' Perceptions of the Chunnel

As part of our research project, we collaborated with Coopers and Lybrand Consultants to survey companies in France, England, and the Netherlands. The objective was to gather information about how these companies perceived the Chunnel and what they expected from it. For each country, Coopers & Lybrand divided the sample into exporting companies and transportation companies to discover any differences between companies that sell products and the companies that deliver them. They obtained 83 responses from transporters (17 French and 66 English, 39% of the sample) and 136 responses from exporters (59 French, 56 English, and 21 Netherlands, 18% of the sample).

The results of the survey revealed that the transportation companies or carriers are more directly involved with the Chunnel than the exporters. The majority of those sending goods from the continent to the UK subcontract their shipping and have no interest in its route. The exporters, then, have no realistic view of the current problems or future opportunities. Even more, transportation companies are usually free to select routes (66%), and those answering the survey questions recognized twice as many ports in Europe as those representing the exporters. With respect to informants' awareness about the Chunnel, we found that 88% of the French exporters and 63% of the French transporters were not aware of the services offered by Eurotunnel, as opposed to 27% of British exporters and 9% for the British transporters.

As a consequence, exporters do not consider the opportunities available with the Chunnel in evaluating their logistics alternatives. As might be expected, the transporters better understand the current problems with the ferry than do exporters. When asked how satisfied they are with current transportation methods (excluding the Chunnel), 63% of the French exporters answer they are satisfied versus only 53% of the transporters. The figure for British exporters is 69% versus 58% for the

transporters, and for Dutch exporters, it is 95% versus 81% for the transporters.

We considered the most important factors related to the use of the Chunnel to be cost, delivery time, weather dependence, labor conflicts, fixed schedules, frequency of service, speed of service, and exchange of platforms. We charted the results for exporters and transporters in France and the UK (Figure 3). Based on Figure 3 we obtain the following general results:

- Cost is an important factor for both transporters and exporters. Because the ferry has had a monopoly crossing the channel, people believe its prices are high.
- The issue of frequency of service and delivery time was classified as intermediate in importance.
- Weather is more important to transporters than to exporters.
- Labor conflicts are important to French companies in particular. This might be because the French ports have had labor problems over the last four years in response to government attempts to implement new laws and regulations.
- Changing modes of transport is not considered a problem by the British since they do it for all their exports. The French are used to shipping directly to other markets on the continent. The opportunity to ship direct thanks to the Chunnel seems to be extremely important to the French, British, and Dutch transporters, but not to exporters.

Sixty-one percent of the British exporters and 41% of the French exporters think that the tunnel gives them an opportunity to modify their logistics networks. For French transporters, the response is 88% versus 40% for the British. Here are some of the reasons that might explain this:

- The tunnel alters the competitive situation and will attract new transporters and third-party companies [Vicherman and Craven 1986]. Seventeen percent of the French exporters, 28% of the British, and 14% of the Dutch believe that they will use new transportation companies or third-party logistics companies by the time the Chunnel is fully operational. They expect to reallocate freight to different modes, particularly the British (22% of the exporters and 32% of the transporters). This change should benefit train companies.
- Suppliers will increasingly send goods just in time. Exporters (77% of the French, 87% of the British, and 48% of the Dutch) expect to increase the frequency of their deliveries. Transporters expect this increase in demand and therefore are planning to increase the number of trips they make (74% of the French, 90% of the British, and 71% of the Dutch).

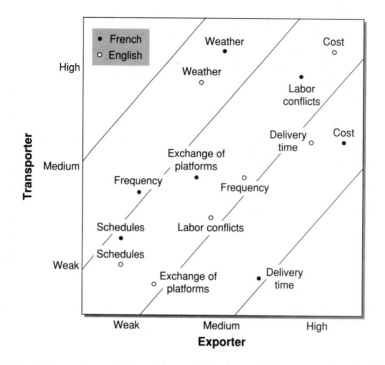

Figure 3   French and English exporters and transporters differ in their perceptions of the Chunnel concerning cost, delivery time, weather dependence, labor conflicts, fixed schedules, frequency of service, speed of service, and exchange of platforms. On the horizontal axis we present the perceptions of the exporters and on the vertical axis the perceptions of the transporters. When both observations are on the diagonal, the perceptions of exporters and transporters coincide.

Finally the most interesting contrast in responses between British and French participants was to the question: Do you think about the logistics impact of the Chunnel in your organization? Seventy-seven percent of the French exporters and 63% of the French transporters answered "no" while 88% of the British exporters and 80% of the British transporters answered "yes." Given the current flows of freight between the continent and the UK, and among the countries on the continent, the British have a more urgent need to include the Chunnel in evaluating their logistics since the continent is their main market.

Optimal Selection of Transportation Alternatives

We constructed a model to permit companies to determine the optimal transportation alternative for moving a defined quantity of products between the continent and the UK. We assumed that the company ships its products by either train or truck and therefore must choose between a ferry or the tunnel. To capture the different possibilities available, the model allows for changing modes of transportation (from train to truck or vice versa) before and after crossing the channel. This generates four possible intervals (two for each side) plus the one crossing the sea, resulting in 32

combinations or alternatives. Some of these alternatives are very inefficient a priori.

We compare, in particular, the option of using a short route that includes a ship or ferry (the current alternative) with a longer route that includes the tunnel. Then, for example, a company in Spain that currently loads its freight on a ship in a nearby harbor might benefit from a longer route that includes the tunnel. The main trade-offs for that company would be greater expenditure for land transportation (possibly including the cost of extra drivers) versus the savings from avoiding changes in logistics platforms (to use the ferry, shippers must transfer their goods from either truck or train to the ferry, and back to truck or train on shore). When the ferry used is close to the Chunnel, the distance over land may be the same. The model quantifies the different options available and selects the option that minimizes total transportation cost while satisfying a predetermined level of service measured as the required time to deliver the predefined freight quantity. We made the following general assumptions:

1. The shipper can move the predefined freight quantity by either train or truck; that is, in each interval, it will use only one mode of transportation.

2. Every time the shipment changes mode of transport (from truck to train or vice versa), the company pays a fixed cost and a variable cost for changing platforms.
3. If the company uses a ship or ferry, it will always pay a fixed cost for changing from either the train or truck to the ferry and then back. If it uses the tunnel without changing mode of transport, it pays no such cost.

We formulated the problem as a mixed-integer problem that minimizes total transportation cost. The model incorporates no charge for transit time. In theory, the time in transit is inventory being kept in the logistics pipeline and therefore should be part of the decision process. However, we assumed that the difference in time among the transportation alternatives (for the type of products to be moved) would not result in significant inventory costs.

Companies can use the model to discover which way is the cheapest, using a ferry or the Chunnel, train or truck, and to examine sensitivity on price increases. The results

can be used as a benchmark for comparison purposes. The model's application is limited, given its specific assumptions. For example, in addition to the two alternatives, train or truck, a company could use the combined mode. Modeling this alternative is complicated because the stations that accommodate change of platforms for combined mode may not necessarily be those at which changes of regular transport mode are made. Also, in the model we assume that the routes by train and truck are of the same length, which might not be the case.

To study the hypothetical implications of the different alternatives, we performed a sensitivity analysis on two different scenarios (Figures 4 and 5). One scenario is for a company in Spain moving products to the UK with two possible routes, a short one using the boat and a long one using the Chunnel. The other scenario is for a company in Germany moving products to the UK with the same two possible routes. We started the analysis with a base case for each scenario (Tables 2 and 3). Our objective was to find out

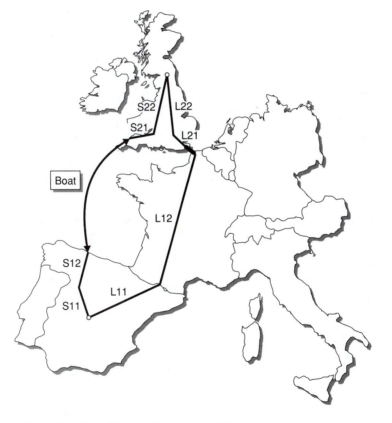

Figure 4   We used the analytical model to perform a sensitivity analysis and compare two transportation alternatives for a company in Spain moving products to the UK. One alternative is using a short route combined with the boat, and the other is to use a long route crossing the channel. L11 and L12 are the two segments of the long route on the continent, and L21 and L22 are the two segments in the UK. The intersection point in each case allows (if necessary) a change in mode of transport. The same applies to the short route (S11, S12, S21, S22).

Figure 5   For goods coming from the north, we use the analytical model to perform a sensitivity analysis and compare two transportation alternatives for a company in Germany moving products to the UK. One alternative is using a short route combined with the ferry and the other is using a long route crossing the channel. L11 and L12 are the two segments of the long route in the continent, and L21 and L22 are the two segments in the UK. The intersection point in each case allows (if necessary) a change in mode of transport. The same applies to the short route (S11, S12, S21, S22).

Table 2

In evaluating the analytical model, we used this base case of parameters for the scenario for freight coming from the south of Spain and going to the north of the UK.

Continent		Crossing	UK	
Interval 1	Interval 2		Interval 3	Interval 4
Truck	Truck	Ferry	Truck	Truck
$F_{k1} = 10$	$F_{K2} = 10$	$F_F = 5$	$F_{K3} = 10$	$F_{K4} = 10$
$V_{KQ1} = 1.0$	$V_{KQ2} = 1.0$	$V_{FQ} = 1.0$	$V_{KQ3} = 1.0$	$V_{KQ4} = 1.0$
$V_{KD1} = 1.1$	$V_{KD2} = 1.1$	$V_{FD} = 1.25$	$V_{KD3} = 1.0$	$V_{KD4} = 1.0$
$F_{PK1} = 10$	$F_{PK2} = 10$	$F_{PF} = 10$	$F_{PK3} = 10$	$F_{PK4} = 10$
$S_{11} = 250$	$S_{12} = 250$	$D_F = 1{,}000$	$S_{21} = 100$	$S_{22} = 600$
$L_{11} = 750$	$L_{12} = 900$		$L_{21} = 150$	$L_{22} = 800$
Train	Train	Chunnel	Train	Train
$F_{T1} = 6$	$F_{T2} = 6$	$F_C = 7$	$F_{T3} = 6$	$F_{T4} = 6$
$V_{TQ1} = 1.0$	$V_{TQ2} = 1.0$	$V_{CQ} = 1.0$	$V_{TQ3} = 1.0$	$V_{TQ4} = 1.0$
$V_{TD1} = 1.0$	$V_{TD2} = 1.0$	$V_{DC} = 1.0$	$V_{TD3} = 1.05$	$V_{TD4} = 1.05$
$F_{PT1} = 10$	$F_{PT2} = 10$	$F_{PC} = 10$	$F_{PT3} = 10$	$F_{PT4} = 10$
		$D_C = 50$		

Table 3

In evaluating the analytical model, we used this base case of parameters for the scenario of freight coming from the north in Germany and going to the north in the UK.

Continent		Crossing	UK	
Interval 1	Interval 2		Interval 3	Interval 4
Truck	Truck	Ferry	Truck	Truck
$F_{K1} = 10$	$F_{K2} = 10$	$F_F = 5$	$F_{K3} = 10$	$F_{K4} = 10$
$V_{KQ1} = 1.0$	$V_{KQ2} = 1.0$	$V_{FQ} = 1.0$	$V_{KQ3} = 1.0$	$V_{KQ4} = 1.0$
$V_{KD1} = 1.1$	$V_{KD2} = 1.1$	$V_{FD} = 1.25$	$V_{KD3} = 1.0$	$V_{KD4} = 1.0$
$F_{PK1} = 10$	$F_{PK2} = 10$	$F_{PT} = 10$	$F_{PK3} = 10$	$F_{PK4} = 10$
$S_{11} = 250$	$S_{12} = 250$	$D_F = 900$	$S_{21} = 100$	$S_{22} = 300$
$L_{11} = 650$	$L_{12} = 500$		$L_{21} = 150$	$L_{22} = 800$
Train	Train	Chunnel	Train	Train
$F_{T1} = 6$	$F_{T2} = 6$	$F_C = 7$	$F_{T3} = 6$	$F_{T4} = 6$
$V_{TQ1} = 1.0$	$V_{TQ2} = 1.0$	$V_{CQ} = 1.0$	$V_{TQ3} = 1.0$	$V_{TQ4} = 1.0$
$V_{TD1} = 1.0$	$V_{TD2} = 1.0$	$V_{DC} = 1.0$	$V_{TD3} = 1.05$	$V_{TD4} = 1.05$
$F_{PT1} = 10$	$F_{PT2} = 10$	$F_{PC} = 10$	$F_{PT3} = 10$	$F_{PT4} = 10$
		$D_C = 50$		

how changes in the different parameters would change the solution. In particular, we wanted to know what increase or decrease in the fixed and variable costs for the Chunnel versus the ferry would make it optimal for shippers to switch between alternatives. We performed the same kind of analysis for train and truck options. We didn't include a sensitivity analysis for the service level constraint.

Coming from the South

For the first scenario, we obtained the following results (Table 2). The company currently ships goods from Spain to the UK by train on the continent, boat across the channel, and truck in the UK. Train service in the UK is not as good as that in France. For the company to switch to using trucks for the entire route, the truck company in Spain must reduce its variable cost to just 4% over the variable cost of the train.

To obtain the business of this company, the UK train company must reduce its variable cost to just 2% over the truck cost in the UK. The company could then use train transport for the entire route. These results are based on the assumption that the variable cost for the boat is 25% higher than the variable cost of the Chunnel.

We next explored what happens when the variable cost of the boat increases. It has to be 50% higher than that of the Chunnel for the company to switch from the boat to the Chunnel for the channel crossing. If the variable cost of the boat is just 20% over that of the Chunnel, the company is better off using the boat. It will, however, use the train for the first three intervals (the first two in the continent and one in the UK) and change to the truck only for the last one;

that saves the additional charge for changing modes of transport at the crossing point (there is an incremental cost for changing from train to truck before crossing). The company will use the Chunnel instead of the boat if the variable cost of the train is reduced to just 2% over the variable cost of the truck. If, on the contrary, the variable cost of the truck on the continent is reduced to just 1% over the variable cost of the train, the company will ship its goods by truck and Chunnel for the entire route. As expected, the cost of the train or truck affects the choice of train or boat since companies look at total transportation costs.

Coming from the North

Under this scenario, currently the company uses the train for the entire route with the ferry for the channel crossing (Table 3). If the truck reduces its variable cost to just 4% over that of the train on the continent, the company will switch to using the truck for the entire route. The UK train should then reduce its variable cost to 3% over that of the truck to make it attractive for the company to switch again and use the train through the entire route.

If we keep the costs of the base case (Table 3) and change the variable cost of the ferry, the company will switch to the tunnel when the variable cost of using the ferry is 35% higher than the variable cost of the Chunnel. In this case the optimal combination for the company is to use the train for three intervals and change in the last interval to the truck.

If the variable cost of the ferry is 35% greater than that of the tunnel and the variable cost of the truck on the continent is reduced to 2% above that of the train, the company will switch and use the ferry and the truck for the entire route. The variable cost of the ferry has to be 40% over that of the Chunnel for the company to use the tunnel instead.

If the train reduces its variable cost to 4% over the variable cost of the truck in the UK, the company will use the train over the entire route and the ferry. Again, the variable cost of the ferry has to be 40% over that of the Chunnel for the company to use the tunnel, but if the trucking company makes an additional reduction in its variable cost to just 2% over that of the truck, the company will use the train over the entire route.

As we can see, the options for freight coming from the north are highly sensitive to changes in the variable cost of the ferry relative to the Chunnel. For all the scenarios examined, we changed the variable costs as a function of distance while keeping other costs fixed. More than to obtain normative results, our objective in the sensitivity analysis was to determine the potential outcomes for different possibilities. We didn't explore a scenario for shipments coming from Italy, because in that case, the short and long routes coincide, and the comparison is simply between fixed and variable costs for the different transportation modes, that is, given the fixed costs for the ferry and the Chunnel, the variable cost for the ferry has to be at most 4% over the variable cost of the Chunnel for it to be attractive.

The model was very useful in helping us to understand the trade-offs among the different transportation alternatives. We could analyze different scenarios with the model, but the base cases require detailed validation. Although it doesn't provide exact results, the analytical model offers guidelines for defining the range of values that would make one alternative superior. In making a decision, companies would consider additional variables not included in the model formulation.

Empirical Approach

We could extend the analytical model to include many realistic restrictions. However, to obtain specific and precise results, we compiled a database of actual costs related to distance, exchange of transportation modes, and physical locations for different alternatives, including conventional train, truck, or combined transport (that is, when the container is transferred from one mode to another) and a ferry or boat, or the Chunnel. In each case, we obtained data for nine different scenarios (combinations of transportation modes). The database consists of 41 possible departure cities in the continent and three destinations in the UK (London, Manchester, and Glasgow). We chose the departure cities for their importance in Europe. The entire database is presented in the IHEL report [1994].

For each linkage (one continental city to one UK city), we examined nine scenarios:

1. Truck–Ferry 1 (departing from the most often used port)–Truck.
2. Truck–Ferry 2 (departing from the second most used port)–Truck.
3. Train–Ferry–Truck: The continental train transfers the goods to a truck at the ferry port; the truck crosses by ferry and makes the delivery in the UK.
4. Train–Shuttle–Truck: As in scenario 3, but the truck crosses the channel on the Chunnel shuttle.
5. Train–Boat–Truck: The continental train transfers the goods to a boat at the most popular port. A truck picks them up at the UK for final transport.
6. Truck–Boat–Truck.
7. Train–Chunnel–Train.
8. Combined: Containers travel from the departure city to the closest combined platform station by truck, travel

Table 4

We compared different transportation modes for freight coming from Milan, Italy and going to London, England.

MODE			Transportation Cost (in FF)	Delay	Total Cost for 20FF/Kg (in FF)	Total Cost for 150FF/Kg (in FF)
Continent	Channel	UK				
Truck	Ferry 1 (Zeebrugge)	Truck	10,189	3	10,456	12,162
Truck	Ferry 2 (Calais)	Truck	10,189	3	10,456	12,162
Train	Ferry	Truck	9,958	3.5	10,370	12,259
Train	Shuttle	Truck	11,416	3.5	11,728	13,717
Train	Boat	Truck	22,452	9	23,253	28,370
Truck	Boat	Truck	20,288	9	21,039	26,206
Train	Chunnel	Train	10,204	2	10,383	11,549
	Combined (Milan)		9,776	2	9,954	11,091
Truck	Shuttle	Truck	11,700	3	11,962	13,673

by train through the Chunnel to the combined platform nearest the final destination, and then by truck.

9. Truck–Shuttle–Truck: The truck travels through the Chunnel on a special car.

For two scenarios, from Milan, Italy, to London, UK, and from Porto, Portugal, to London, UK, we calculated the transportation costs as the aggregation of all the logistics costs (transportation, handling costs when necessary, exchange of platforms, and so forth) (Tables 4 and 5). Then we calculated a global cost by adding the inventory pipeline costs. We adjusted the inventory pipeline cost for the delay incurred in each case (the opportunity cost of the inventory in the pipeline).

We obtained data on costs from transportation companies (train, trucks, boat, ferry, combination), industrial companies with international activities, and specialized consulting companies. We hoped to obtain realistic costs by taking into account the commercial conditions. For each of the nine scenarios, we used a combination of transportation and handling costs. We obtained empirical results for the entire sample and can draw some general conclusions as to the best alternative:

- For western Spain and Portugal, transporting freight to the UK by ship is the cheapest option. Truck or combined modes cost 40 to 50% more. For areas east of a North/South axis going through Madrid, the various options are in close competition; the worst solution is only 15% more expensive than the best.
- For the Atlantic and areas bordering the channel between Nantes, France and the Netherlands, truck is the best option. The further north the final destination is in the UK, the more attractive the combined option becomes.
- For Italy, all modes are competitive, but shipping by train is usually cheapest. Companies must weigh the

cost advantage carefully, because the train offers poor service in the UK.

- For East Germany, Austria, and the rest of France, truck and the combined mode compete closely.
- For most of Germany, truck offers an advantage. However, for final destinations in the north of the UK, sending freight by ship is more attractive. The state-owned train company in Germany and the harbor in the north of Germany provide combined low-cost service.

For shipments to London, we identified seven areas in the continent (Figure 6). For area 1, boat and truck (scenario 6) and less often boat and train (scenario 5) are the cheapest options. For area 2, boat with truck or train is usually most competitive. For area 3, all options are competitive. For area 4, the only competitive option is ferry-truck (scenarios 1 and 2). For area 5, the combined option dominates. For area 6, truck/ferry/truck, all train, and combined are all competitive. For area 7, the best solution is truck/ferry/truck (scenarios 1 and 2), but the combined option (scenario 8) is also competitive.

Conclusions

There are no generic solutions to the logistic implications of the Chunnel. Each industry and each company within an industry will have its own limitations and constraints. In some companies, distribution costs are high and significant (relative to sales) and in others, they are not. However, by developing general frameworks for the issues and analytical models for specific cases, we offer a tool that will allow companies to evaluate and understand the advantages and disadvantages of the Chunnel. The analytical models supported with empirical data allow companies to quantify the impact.

One company heavily affected by this study is the French train company in charge of freight (Fret SCNF). The

Table 5 *We compared different transportation modes for freight coming from Porto, Portugal and going to London, England.*

Continent	Channel	UK	Transportation Cost (in FF)	Delay	Total Cost for 20 FF/Kg (in FF)	Total Cost for 150FF/Kg (in FF)
Truck	Ferry 1 (Cherbourg)	Truck	13,424	4	13,780	16,054
Truck	Ferry 2 (Calais)	Truck	14,202	4	14,558	16,832
Train	Ferry	Truck	15,169	4.5	15,570	18,127
Train	Shuttle	Truck	15,367	4.5	15,767	18,326
Train	Boat	Truck	10,702	7	11,325	13,304
Truck	Boat	Truck	8,072	7	8,695	12,675
Train	Chunnel	Train	17,082	3	17,349	19,055
	Combined (Bordeaux)		12,090	3	12,357	14,063
Truck	Shuttle	Truck	15,729	4	16,085	18,359

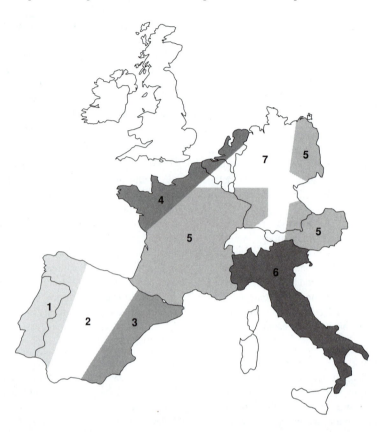

Figure 6   Transportation alternatives vary for goods going to London from different locations in the Continent. Each area indicates the transportation alternative that minimizes total cost. For Area 1, the boat and truck combination dominates. In Area 2, the best option is boat with either truck or train. In Area 3 all options are competitive. For Area 4, the ferry-truck combination dominates. In Area 5, the combined (Chunnel) option is the best. In Area 6, the combinations truck/ferry/truck, all train, or combined mode are competitive. Finally, in Area 7, the best option is truck/ferry/truck.

head of its international department recognized that our results are very useful for its strategic thinking and permit it to refine some of its marketing and commercial decisions.

The opening of the channel tunnel offers an alternative that can improve freight distribution in Europe. Transportation solutions are not better or worse in isolation but in the context of the overall logistics function. Our research summarizes the issues that are relevant from a global logistics point of view.

Appendix

The general analytical model requires the following notation.
Define:

i = subscript that indicates the intervals, i = 1, 2, 3, 4.

j = subscript to indicate the mode of transportation where t is for train and k is for truck.

l = subscript to indicate the linkage between the UK and the continent, that is, f for the ferry and c for the Chunnel.

Q = predefined quantity to be shipped between the Continent and the UK.

Q_{ji} = quantity of shipment with the mode j for interval i.

Q_l = quantity of shipment through the linkage.

D_{ji} = distance on mode j for interval i.

D_l = distance on the linkage, that is, ferry or Chunnel.

F_{ji} = fixed cost for using mode j in interval i.

F_f = fixed cost for using the linkage l.

V_{jqi} = variable cost for using mode j as a function of the quantity Q in interval i.

V_{jdi} = variable cost for using mode j as a function of the distance d in interval i.

S_{11}, S_{12} = are the two short intervals in the Continent.

S_{21}, S_{22} = are the two short intervals in the UK.

L_{11}, L_{12} = are the two long intervals in the Continent.

L_{21}, L_{22} = are the two long intervals in the UK.

δ_j = binary variable equal to 1 if the company uses mode j of transportation, 0 otherwise.

δ_f = binary variable equal to 1 if the company uses the ferry, 0 otherwise.

γ_{tki} = binary variable equal to 1 if there is a change of platform from train to truck at the end of interval i, 0 otherwise.

γ_{kti} = binary variable equal to 1 if there is a change of platform from truck to train at the end of interval i, 0 otherwise.

F_{pji} = fixed cost for changing platforms using mode j at the end of interval i.

ω_{ji} = speed of mode j in interval i.

T_l = time it takes to cross between the UK and the continent by linkage l.

Minimize

$$F_{k1}\delta_k T + t\sum_{i=2}^{3}(F_{ki} + F_{pki})\gamma_{tki} + \sum_{i=1}^{4} V_{kqi}Q_{ki}$$

$$+\sum_{i=1}^{4} V_{kdi}D_{ki} + F_{t1}\delta_t + \sum_{i=2}^{3} (F_{ti} + F_{pti})\gamma_{kti}$$

$$+\sum_{i=1}^{4} V_{tqi}Q_{ti} + \sum_{i=1}^{4} V_{tdi}D_{ti}$$

$$+(F_f + V_{fd}D_f)\delta_f + V_{fq}Q_f$$

$$+(F_c + V_{cd}D_c)(1 - \delta_f) + V_{cq}Q_c$$

$$+F_{pf}\delta_f + F_{pc}\gamma_{tk2} + F_{pc}\gamma_{kt2}$$

Subject to

$$\left.\begin{array}{l} Q_{f1} \le Q\delta_{tf}, \\ Q_{k1} \le Q\delta_k, \\ Q_f = Q\delta_f \end{array}\right\} \quad (1)$$

$$\left.\begin{array}{l} Q_{t1} + Q_{k1} \ge Q, \\ Q_{f2} + Q_{k2} \ge Q, \\ Q_f + Q_c \ge Q, \\ Q_{t3} + Q_{k3} \ge Q, \\ Q_{t4} + Q_{k4} \ge Q. \end{array}\right\} \quad (2)$$

$$\left.\begin{array}{l} Q_{t1} - Q_{t2} \le Q\gamma_{tk1}, \\ Q_{k1} - Q_{k2} \le Q\gamma_{kt1}, \\ Q_{t2} - Q_{t3} \le Q\gamma_{tk2}, \\ Q_{k2} - Q_{k3} \le Q\gamma_{kt2}, \\ Q_{t3} - Q_{t4} \le Q\gamma_{tk3}, \\ Q_{k3} - Q_{k4} \le Q\gamma_{kt3}. \end{array}\right\} \quad (3)$$

$$\left.\begin{array}{l} D_{t1} + D_{k1} \ge S_{11}\delta_{ft}, \\ D_{t12} + D_{k2} \ge S_{12}\delta_{ft}, \\ D_{t1} + D_{k1} \ge L_{11}(1 - \delta_f), \end{array}\right\} \quad (4)$$

$$\left.\begin{array}{l} D_{t2} + D_{k2} \ge L_{12}(1 - \delta_f), \\ D_{t3} + D_{k3} \ge S_{21}\delta_f, \\ D_{t4} + D_{k4} \ge S_{22}\delta_f, \\ D_{t3} + D_{k3} \ge L_{21}(1 - \delta_f), \\ D_{t4} + D_{k4} \ge L_{22}(1 - \delta_f), \end{array}\right\} \quad (4)$$

$$\left.\begin{array}{l} \dfrac{Q_{ji}}{Q} - \dfrac{D_{ji}}{L} \ge 0 \\[2mm] \forall i, j \wedge m = 11, 12, 21, 22 \\[2mm] \dfrac{D_{jl}}{S_m} - \dfrac{Q_{ji}}{Q} \ge 0. \end{array}\right\} \quad (5)$$

$$\left.\sum_{i=1}^{4}\sum_{j=t,k} \dfrac{D_{ji}}{\omega_{ji}} + \delta_f T_f + (1-\delta_f)T_c \le \text{Required Time.}\right\} \quad (6)$$

$$\left.\begin{array}{l} \delta_f \wedge \delta_j \in \{0, 1\} \; \forall j \\ \gamma_{tjl} \in \{0, 1\} \; \forall i = 1, 2, 3, \wedge \; \forall j. \end{array}\right\} \quad (7)$$

The first part in the objective function captures the fixed and variable costs of using the truck in each of the intervals. When the truck is used for any two consecutive intervals, no extra fixed costs are incurred (only the variable costs). This condition is captured by the binary variable δ_t and γ_{tkl}. The same is true for the train in the second part of the objective function. The third term in the objective function captures the cost of using either the ferry ($\delta_f = 1$) or the tunnel ($\delta_f = 0$). The remaining terms in the objective function capture the costs incurred for changing the logistics platforms at the crossing.

Constraints (1) and (2) make sure that the predetermined quantity Q will be delivered by any of the possible alternatives. Constraint (3) captures the changing of platforms and constraint (4) determines the distances by mode of transportation according to the predefined short or long distances. It is assumed that $S..$ is smaller than $L..$ for any subinterval. Constraint (5) makes sure that if quantity Q is going to be delivered by train (or by truck) in interval i then the corresponding distance will be traveled by train (or truck). Constraint (6) is a service constraint for the minimum lead time required. Finally, constraint (7) is the binary constraint.

References

Journal de la Marine Marchande 1994, "ADPF: Les liaisons transmanche," No 393 (February).

Bonnaud, L. 1994, *Le Tunnel sous la Manche: Duex Siecles de Passion,* Hachete, Paris.

Coton, M. 1994, "La manche," FRET Magazine, No. Special Tunnel, No. 60 (May), pp. 38–47.

Institut des Hautes Etudes Logistiques 1994, "Logistics impact of the Chunnel," cahier de IHEL, No. 2 (November), ESSEC, Cergy-Pontoise, France.

Merchant, J. E.; Knowles, J. B.; and Acheson, J. M. 1991, "The Channel and the changing face of a U\unified European market," *Proceedings of the Seventh International Logistics Congress,* Society of Logistics Engineers, French Chapter, Paris, pp. 198–208.

Project Cost-CEE 1993, "Rapport final d'action: Evaluation des effects du tunnel sous la manche sur le flux de trafic," Office of Official Publications, European Community, Luxembourg.

Sloan, A. K. 1991, "Eurotunnel vision: The new focus on site selection, shipping routes, and business travel," *Journal of European Business,* Vol. 2, No. 3 (January–February), pp. 8–12.

Vicherman, R. W. and Graven, J. 1986, "The fixed channel link: Consequences for regional growth and development," Regional Studies Association Conference, London, March 21.

◆   CASE 8–3: ISOL +   ◆

A. Presentation of ISOL +

The ISOL + Group makes and sells a range of insulating products for the building industry, rigid boards blanket insulation, and sheathing for pipes.

Its subsidiary ISOL + FRANCE is an autonomous unit run as a profit center covering France, Italy, and Spain.

It has its own manufacturing plant and adds to its own production capacity by buying from another of the Group's plants those products it cannot make on its own because of technical reasons or at times when its plant is working at full capacity.

Sales in 1992 reached 2,854,000 cubic meters (m^3). The breakdown by country was:

France	2,635,000 m^3
Spain	125,000 m^3
Italy	94,000 m^3

The organization structure at ISOL + is rather traditional.

The general management, headed by Mr. Dupont, coordinates the three main departments, namely production, sales, and marketing.

The production department is headed by Mr. Lenoir, who enjoys dual responsibility for manufacturing on the one hand and for logistics and end-product distribution on the other. Mr. Martin is in charge of logistics at ISOL +.

The sales department is run by Mr. Faure and is organized into three parts according to a geographical division by country. The three main areas covered are France, Spain, and Italy.

At a management committee meeting, Mr. Dupont initiated a thorough rethinking of logistics matters in the Group. The idea was to assess the situation for business in 1992 and put forward a logistics organization geared to the evolution in products and markets.

During the meeting Mr. Faure, sales director, gave the sales results for 1992 and expressed great satisfaction at the results achieved by his salespeople.

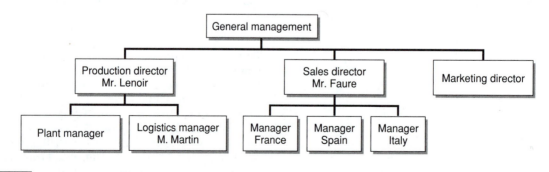

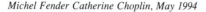

Michel Fender Catherine Choplin, May 1994

Regarding ISOL +, he recalled that the biggest market was clearly in France, but pointed out that the Spanish and Italian markets were developing quickly. Nevertheless, he talked about development prospects in southern European countries.

Sales per product type and per country are set out in Table 1 (in thousands of m^3).

The products made and sold by ISOL + are grouped into five product types depending on their use (see appendix 1).

He also recalled the main obstacle to service quality, namely, the need to palletize those products that fall into the first product type for the French market (2,056,000 m^3). The products in the remaining product types are delivered in bulk to French customers, whereas all products are sent in bulk in Spain and Italy.

Mr. Lenoir then spoke and gave a rundown on production. The French plant (UF), located in the Puy-de-Dôme, covers 85% of production for France and all production for the Spanish and Italian markets. It cannot make all products, though, which are manufactured by another of the Group's plants in The Netherlands (UNL). These products are intended for the French market only.

Table 2 shows production volume in 1992 for each plant and for each product type. Information concerning the possibility of manufacturing different products in a given plant is specified.

Maximum output capacity at the French plant is 3,000,000 m^3.

There are five shifts. In fact, the manufacturing process is similar to that of the glass-making industry and is only interrupted two or three times a year to allow for maintenance of the production tools.

The production process contains successive operations carried out in sequence. The surfacing process may then be started, according to needs, before shaping and packaging, which includes a process of laying a film.

Production management follows the pattern of the arrival orders, which means that manufacturing can be managed from an order portfolio.

Planning and production control are carried out according to a weekly basis. Manufacturing of an order in week W will be delivered to the customer in W + 1.

Lastly, Mr. Lenoir recalls that only the French factory is equipped to palletize and that Spain and Italy are served preferentially from the French plant rather than the one in the Netherlands. In fact, since ISOL + is a profit center, it is better to manufacture in France (see appendix 2B).

Mr. Martin, responsible for logistics and distribution, describes to the members of the committee his side of the business:

- Order-taking is centralized at headquarters. The minimum unit for an order is a *crate,* that is to say a volume of 60 m^3 corresponding to half a truckload. Actually, 98% of customers throughout the countries make orders for at least a full truckload, which represents the equivalent of two crates (truck and trailer).

  The customer is notified of delivery time when he puts in an order, which may be by telephone, or sent by fax or mail. It varies between one and two weeks. Usually by the beginning of the following week, a fixed day for delivery can be given.

- Consignments to customers are direct from the plant. No other premises exist for purposes of stocking

Table 1

Sales per product type and country

	France	Spain	Italy
Type 1: Traditional building	2,056	80	29
Type 2: Waterproofing	320	20	19
Type 3: Manufacturing industry	56	15	45
Type 4: Heating	72	0	0
Type 5: Decoration	131	10	1
TOTAL	**2,625**	**125**	**94**

Table 2

1992 Production by Plant (in millions of m^3)

	Production 1992		Feasibility of Manufacturing	
	French plant (UF)	Dutch plant (UNL)	UF	UNL
Product type 1	2,165	—	YES	YES but products in bulk and French market requires palletization
Product type 2	48	311	YES	YES
Product type 3	116	—	YES	YES
Product type 4	—	72	YES	YES
Product type 5	98	44	In current mix	
TOTAL	**2,427**	**427**		

finished articles, because as soon as an order has been done, it is sent to the customer.

- Transportation planning is based on production planning. ISOL + subcontracts to carriers with large-volume vehicles (see appendix 2A).

B. The Logistics Problem

After going over the 1992 situation, Mr. Dupont goes on to talk about the firm's strategy for the following five years.

Two important developments are being considered as far as sales volume and service quality are concerned.

1. Increase in Sales Volume

For the following five years (up until the 1997/98 financial year), forecasts are as shown in Table 3.

For each country the sales growth is the same for all product types.

Mr. Lenoir interrupts at this point to draw attention to the fact that production capacity at the French plant would not be sufficient to cover such needs. The following solutions could be conceived:

- Call on the Dutch plant, and have them invest in a palletizer.
- Set up a new production line in the French plant, which would lead to an increase of 1,000,000 m^3 per annum (one line equals 1,000,000 m^3 a year).
- Build a new manufacturing facility with one production line in France close to the firm's southern European markets.

2. Service Quality

Mr. Dupont stressed ISOL + determination to directly target some "small" customers who purchase materials at whole-salers. Two changes in the present logistics set-up are required to accomplish this:

- Cut delivery time to 48 hours. There would have to be an increase in inventory, as production-per-order would no longer be possible, given the manufacturing times required.
- Cut the minimum order possible to the equivalent of four pallets for a given customer.

The impact on the allocation of delivery volumes of such a change is shown in the histogram concerning deliveries in Table 4.

To sum up, Mr. Lenoir asks three questions about the choices they have:

- What solution can be found to the problems of increasing production capacity? Possible solutions are investing in palletization equipment for UNL, setting up a new production line at the existing facility in France, or building a new plant somewhere else in France.

A preliminary study has been carried out and shows that the best place to build one would be in the southwest France at Pau (UP).
- What impact will reducing the minimum quantities that a customer can order have on logistics costs?
- Does cutting delivery times to 48 hours require reorganization of the present logistics distribution?

C. Questions

Faced with this strategic problem, Mr. Lenoir has suggested to Mr. Dupont that they should agree to a suitable way of going about studying the target structure that ISOL + must move toward in the coming years, both in organization of production and physical distribution.

You are asked to put forward a structured plan to general management that will achieve the following:

- Keep the logistics budget at its present level.
- Extrapolate this budget in the current set-up, taking into account the announced prospects for growth and using the French facility working to full capacity.
- Recommend an efficient organization in terms of costs and service for needs in 1998 with the French facility working to full capacity.

Table 3

Sales forecasts	
FRANCE	2,767,000 m^3 (+5% compared to 1992)
SPAIN	463,000 m^3 (+270% compared to 1992)
ITALY	330,000 m^3 (+250% compared to 1992)

Table 4

Foreseeable development				
Volume range and number of pallets	< 30 m^3 4 pallets	30 to 60 m^3 6 pallets	60 to 120 m^3 12 pallets	120 m^3 24 pallets
France	17%	30%	30%	23%
Spain	0	0	50%	50%
Italy	0	0	61%	39%

Mr. Dupont asks you to summarize the results of your study and distinguish between the main budget items for logistics costs as well as the profitability of possible investment. To make it easier to understand the results of the study, general management at ISOL + suggests using the table that you will find in appendix 3.

Appendix 1
ISOL +'s Products

ISOL + makes high-performance products. Their characteristics are the following.

- A high degree of thermal and sound insulation
- Low sensitivity to damp and humidity
- Almost uninflammable
- Easy to install

Their applications are in the building industry and in manufacturing.

There are five product types, depending on the characteristics of the products and their packaging.

1. A range of products for the traditional building sector contains rigid boards and blanket insulation for walls and roofs.
2. A range for waterproofing in the building industry, essentially for purposes of roofing. They are similar to the first type, but have been tarred.
3. A range of products for manufacturing. This range includes boards for which the finishing (cutting, etc.) is done by the manufacturer.
4. Heating. Mainly small units in the form of hollow tubes, shells, etc. They are used in pipes and water tanks.

5. Decorative. Applications in the home and in office buildings are standard boards with a decorative layer (for example, slabs for ceilings).

The main characteristic of all of these products is that they have a low density, which means they are large but light.

The cubic meter is, therefore, the best physical unit as the difficulties of stocking and transportation are related to their volume and not to their weight.

The following table shows average density by product category:

	kg/m^3
Category 1	27
Category 2	150
Category 3	74
Category 4	82
Category 5	87

Appendix 2
The Basic Data

A. Transport Cost

The following prices correspond to a linear model (F = Francs):

$F/m^3 = a + b \ m^3$

The model, which is definitely limited, allows us to report the real prices charged by transportation companies for a given distance.

Full truckload (24 pallets)

French plant (UF)	$\rightarrow$	France: 6.4F/m^3 + 0.031F/km m^3
UF	$\rightarrow$	Spain: 19.2F/m^3 + 0.053F/km m^3
UF	$\rightarrow$	Italy: 17.4F/m^3 + 0.049F/km m^3
Dutch plant (NL)	$\rightarrow$	France, Spain, Italy: 7.5F/m^3 + 0.082F/km m^3

Crate (half a truckload = 12 pallets)

UF	$\rightarrow$	France : $10.8F/m^3 + 0.093F/km\ m^3$
UF	$\rightarrow$	Spain : $22.8F/m^3 + 0.068F/km\ m^3$
UF	$\rightarrow$	Italy : $20.3F/m^3 + 0.064F/km\ m^3$

Loads of four and six pallets:

Concerning France only:

6 pallets: $12.33F/m^3 + 0.093\ F/km\ m^3$
4 pallets: $15.4F/m^3 + 0.093\ F/km\ m^3$

Average Delivery Distances

from	present		with palletizer at UNL		with new line at UF		with new plant		
to	UF	UNL	UF	UNL	UF	UNL	UF	UP	UNL
France	419	690	390	254	430	831	390	334	831
Spain	1103	—	1103	—	1103	—	1103	713	—
Italy	815	—	815	—	815	—	815	—	—

B. Production Cost in francs per ton

Product category/Plant of origin	UF or UP	UNL
1	2,500	3,500
2	2,500	3,000
3	5,000	5,900
4	2,200	2,700
5	8,000	10,000

C. Stocking

- Plant warehouse
- Fixed cost

  = 5,565 kF per year at UF
  = 2,800 kF per year at UP (light structure)

- Loading

  On pallets   = 2 F/m³
  Wholesale   = 6 F/m³
- Inventory

  Average level   = 1.6 weeks
  0.4 m² for each cubic meter of stocked product.
  surface area cost = 0 for UF and 150F/m² for UP

D. Financial Data

Financial cost of stocking rate	15% ± 12%
Tax rate	34%
Inflation rate	3%

The amount needed for investment is the following:

- Palletization machine: 30 million francs (period of linear depreciation over 10 years)
- Assembly line: 150 million francs (depreciation over 20 years)
- Plant (excluding machines): 100 million francs (depreciation over 20 years).

Appendix 3
Summary of Results

	Current Cost 1992	Time Scale 1997–1998		
		Scenario 1	Scenario 2	Other Scenarios
TRANSPORTATION Deliveries from French plant Dutch plant Pau plant				
Subtotal				
WAREHOUSING In French plant In Pau plant				
Subtotal				
INVENTORY French				
Subtotal				
If savings for ISOL +				
ANNUAL NET COST				
INVESTMENTS Net Pay Back Internal Rate of Return				

Chapter 9

Risk Managment in Global Operations

◆ ◆ ◆

This chapter will cover the following topics:

◆ *The concept of operating exposure to exchange rate risk*

◆ *Factors that complicate the assessment of true operating exposure*

◆ *General options for managing operating exposure risk*

◆ *Price strategies for exporting firms*

◆ *Using operational flexibility to minimize risk*

◆ *The impact of exchange rates and hedging strategies in global sourcing strategies*

◆ *How foreign exchange markets function*

◆ *Micro-level and macro-level strategies for managing exchange rate risk*

◆ **OPERATING EXPOSURE TO EXCHANGE RATE: RISK AND ITS MANAGEMENT—INTRODUCTION**

In 1944, the United Nations held a monetary conference in Bretton Woods, New Hampshire. Out of that conference came the Bretton Woods Agreement, which established the International Monetary Fund and set fixed exchange rates between currencies. In 1976, however, the IMF revised its policy and based exchange rates on the supply and demand of currencies in international markets. These changes took effect in 1978. Member countries were charged with encouraging economic growth and currency stability, but the end result was a much more volatile currency market. Since that time, exchange rate volatility has become an important element in the operations decisions of multinational firms. A company's degree of exposure to exchange rate volatility is determined by the following:

- Source of the firm's inputs, including financing
- Location of the firm's final markets
- Location of production

Because firm structure is unique, no one statement can be made as to how all firms will choose to deal with the risks introduced by exchange rates.

Companies have different ways of coping with the uncertainty posed by exchange rate swings. The typical one is to use financial markets to hedge against exchange rate risks. Alternatively, firms may choose to adjust prices in export markets in response to exchange rate changes and in order to protect their market share. A last and sometimes overlooked option is for the firm to use operational strategies as long-term hedges against volatile exchange rates. Such strategies include the use of excess capacity in facility networks, the switching of production between production facilities in response to exchange rate movements, the use of global sourcing portfolios with suppliers located in various countries, and the appropriate structuring of global sourcing contracts that effectively take advantage of flexibility in the timing and quantity of purchased components. Finally, firms may choose to exit or enter export markets in response to exchange rate swings. In most cases, a firm's response to ongoing exchange rate uncertainty involves one or more of the alternatives.

In this chapter, our goal is to answer the following questions:

- Why does an operations manager need to worry about exchange rate fluctuations?
- Are financial instruments adequate to hedge against operational risks from volatile exchange rates? If not, what operations strategies can be used to complement them and enhance the firm's long-term competitiveness?

The chapter proceeds to explicitly define the concept of *operating exposure to exchange rates,* which is of utmost importance for the operations manager. The operations manager controls many decisions that affect the *operating exposure* of the firm. Hence, his or her decisions will impact the corporation's future operating cash flows and competitive position. Thus, the operations manager should be equally well informed and held responsible for effectively accounting for exchange rate fluctuation in his/her decisions.

To that point, we outline a number of approaches to effectively managing operating exposure to real exchange rate shocks. In particular, we emphasize understanding pricing strategies of exporting firms and entry/exit and production switching strategies in supplying foreign markets.

◆ THE CONCEPT OF OPERATING EXPOSURE

There are three main ways in which foreign exchange fluctuations affect a company's financial performance. These are:

1. *Transaction exposure:* by changing the expected results of transactions denominated in nondomestic currencies
2. *Translation exposure* by changing the domestic currency value of net assets held in foreign currency
3. *Operating exposure* by changing the domestic currency value of future cash flows to be earned in foreign currencies or by changing a firm's future competitive position

Each of these exposures, results from different corporate activities, is determined in a different way, and must be managed through alternative means. The exposure most important to operations managers is the operating exposure because, as we said, it is the exposure that is largely under their control. Nevertheless, it is important for operations/ logistics managers to understand the differences between the drivers of the three different types of exposures.

The *transaction exposure,* as its name implies, denotes the exposure of contracts denominated in a foreign currency; for example, firms may have cash deposits or debt obligations that carry a specified foreign currency denomination. The risk associated with the exposure is that the exchange rate will fluctuate before the transaction specified by the contract is completed and the currency exchange occurs, thereby changing the amount of domestic currency paid or received. This type of risk is relatively easy to calculate and is driven by fluctuation of the *nominal exchange rates*. It is also easy to hedge this type of contractual exposure with the use of financial instruments.

Translation exposure, in contrast, denotes the changes in a firm's reported results and financial statements brought about, again, by fluctuating *nominal exchange rates*. It occurs because of the need to translate the financial statements of foreign subsidiaries and affiliates into the currency of the parent company in order for consolidated financial statements to be prepared. As exchange of cash or other assets occurs, this exposure is solely the result of the financial accounting and reporting process. Obviously the particular rules adopted for effecting this translation play an important role in determining its magnitude. Again financial instruments can be used effectively to hedge against this type of exposure as soon as its magnitude is estimated.

By definition, *operating exposure* is a significantly different kind of exposure from the two other types of foreign exchange exposures. It pertains to expected future operating cash flows, and explicitly deals with the effects of exchange rate fluctuations on the overall competitive position of the firm. Second, it is different because the contemplated change in the exchange rate has to constitute a "real" shock (i.e., it is driven by *real exchange rate changes* rather than nominal ones). The differences among exchange rate exposures are summarized in Table 9–1. However, in order to fully understand the *operating exposure concept,* we need to first fully understand the differences in nominal and real exchange rates.

The *nominal* foreign exchange rate is the nominal price of one nation's money in terms of another; for example, the number of U.S. dollars it takes to buy each French franc (FF). The price of one currency in terms of another can be quoted either directly or indirectly. A *direct quote* expresses the foreign exchange rate in terms of the number of units of home currency it takes to buy each unit of foreign currency. From the U.S. perspective, a direct quote would be written $/FF. An *indirect quote* is the reverse—the number of units of foreign currency it

Table 9–1

Differences in Various Types of Foreign Exchange Exposure

	Exposure	
Characteristics	*Transactions/Translational*	*Operating*
Nature of exposure	Contractual/Accounting	Future operating cash flows and competitive
Financial items considered	Contractual and asset valuation: debt, payables, receivables	Noncontractual: revenues, cost and profit (margin and volume effects)
Inputs to measure exposure	Accounting statements/Contracts	Future cash flows and competitive position
Exchange rates that affect profit	Nominal	Real

takes to buy each unit of home currency, which could be written FF/$. In our further discussion, we will use the direct quote definition, and denote by e the nominal exchange rate. Using the direct quote, a currency is said to depreciate when there is an increase in e, and appreciate when there is a decrease in e. To repeat:

> e increases *imply* home currency depreciation
> e decreases *imply* home currency appreciation

A *real* change in exchange rates is one that changes the relative prices of the goods and services consumed and produced by firms. If a change in a given exchange rate only reflects the difference in inflation rates associated with two currencies, then relative prices do not change and the change in the exchange rate is said to be nominal rather than real.

To the extent that changes in exchange rates reflect only the differences in inflation rates among currencies, they are consistent with the purchasing power parity (PPP) theory. There are two well-known versions of this theory, the absolute version and the relative version.

The *absolute PPP* relationship says that

$$P = eP* \qquad\qquad (9.1)$$

where P is the domestic price level, $P*$ is the foreign price level, and e is the exchange rate. A less stringent definition of PPP is called *relative PPP*, which expresses the relationship in terms of price levels and exchange rates today (time 0) relative to our expectation for some future point in time (time 1). This relationship is illustrated in Equation 9–2.

$$\frac{P_1}{P_0} = \frac{e_1}{e_0}\frac{P_1*}{P_0*} \qquad\qquad (9.2)$$

where P, $P*$, and e are as in Equation 9.1, and the subscripts 1 and 0 refer to the two different points in time. The relative PPP can be expressed approximately also as

$$\Delta e \approx \Delta P - \Delta P* \qquad\qquad (9.3)$$

where
> Δe = expected percentage change in exchange rates
> ΔP = expected percentage change in domestic prices
>   (i.e., domestic inflation rates)
and $\Delta P*$ = expected percentage change in foreign prices
>   (i.e., foreign inflation rates)

Thus, from Equation 9.3 we can say that PPP implies that the rate of change of an exchange rate should be equal to the difference between inflation rates for the two currencies. If PPP always held, changes in real exchange rates would always be nominal rather than real and would not give rise to operating exposure. However, empirical evidence indicates that PPP is not a good explanation of exchange rate movements, except in the very long run, and it has done especially poorly during the 1980s and early 1990s.

When PPP fails to hold, changes in exchange rates may be associated with changes in relative prices. When this happens, cost and profit structures of the firms change, and firms may change their pricing, sourcing and production decisions; as a result, expected future cash flows and the competitive position of a firm may change, and according to our definition, operating exposure occurs. For such environments we define real exchange rate changes as

$$\Delta s \approx \Delta e + \Delta P^* - \Delta P \qquad (9.4)$$

where Δs refers to percentage change in the real exchange rate. Using absolute PPP, the real exchange rate s is

$$s = \frac{eP^*}{P} \qquad (9.5)$$

Example 1:   If the deutsche mark (DM) strengthens by 4 percent, inflation in Germany is 1 percent, and inflation in the United States is 4 percent, the real exchange rate change is

$$\Delta s \approx 4\% + 1\% - 4\% = 1\%$$

Example 2:   If the Japanese yen appreciates by 40 percent, the inflation rate in Japan is 30 percent, and inflation in the United States is 5 percent, the real exchange rate change is

$$\Delta s \approx 40\% + 30\% - 5\% = 65\%$$

Now that we understand the concepts of operating exposure and real exchange rates, we can proceed to understand the effects on the magnitude, and sign of change, of the operating exposure of a firm by changes in real exchange rates. The typical story about such a relationship found in international business textbooks goes as follows.

Let us consider a U.S. firm whose primary activity is manufacturing a product in the United States for sale in the United States and Germany. The company imports none of its inputs, a large percentage of which is labor, and it exports roughly half of its output. Suppose, now, that the dollar appreciates unexpectedly against the mark and that this change is real. What happens to the expected future cash flows of the U.S. firm?

The typical answer to this question proceeds by picking one of two extreme scenarios. One scenario leaves the prices in deutsche marks constant; the other scenario adjusts prices in Germany (in DM) to fully account for the depreciation of the U.S. dollar. In the first scenario, German consumers continue to purchase the product as if nothing had happened, and sales volume and revenue in DM remain the same. But the firm's shareholders measure their returns in U.S. dollars, and the same revenue in DM represents a lower U.S.$ revenue, and, because U.S.$ costs are unchanged, lower U.S.$ cash flow.

In the second scenario, the firm raises DM prices to keep U.S.$ equivalent prices the same as before, the German consumers reduce their consumption of the products, and this drop in sales volume might finally result in a drop of the firm's revenue in U.S. dollars. In either scenario, an appreciation of the U.S. dollar for an exporting U.S. firm results, according to this story, in an increased operating exposure (also referred to as *negative* operating exposure).

In a similar way, we can reverse the argument and say that a depreciation of the U.S. dollar helps an exporting U.S. firm increase its revenues and thus leads to a positive operating exposure. The story needs slight modification if the firm is only sourcing from foreign suppliers (and not exporting). Then appreciation of the U.S. dollar leads to positive operating exposure for the U.S. firm and depreciation of the U.S. dollar leads to negative operating exposure.

The above discussion is instrumental in understanding the fundamental concept of operating exposure and its relationship to real changes in exchange rates. However, it is important to also realize that this story is quite simplistic and therefore might be misleading. Our next section emphasizes complicating factors that affect the magnitude of operating exposure and, in many cases, might invalidate the simplistic story thus far described.

◆ FACTORS THAT COMPLICATE THE ESTIMATION OF OPERATING EXPOSURE

Looking beyond the traditional view of operating exposure for an exporting firm, where a home currency appreciation leads to decreased revenues and a negative exposure, and a home currency depreciation implies increased revenues and a positive exposure, there are at least four complicating factors the firm needs to consider in assessing its operating exposure to real exchange rate shocks. These factors are:

1. Customer reactions
2. Competitor reactions
3. Supplier reactions
4. Government reactions

We will discuss relevant points of each in terms of the example of the U.S. firm exporting to Germany. The emphasis is on how each factor contributes to the assessment of operating exposure. Although each is discussed separately, the factors are often interrelated.

Customer Reactions

Customer reactions are reflected in the elasticity of demand for the product. If the elasticity of demand is high, firms will be able to raise prices and thus face a relatively small decrease in sales volume, and a relatively insignificant revenue decrease in the presence of an appreciating U.S. dollar. On the other hand, if elasticity of demand is low, customer reactions to any price increases will be more severe.

Although we explicitly discussed the German customer reactions, we should not forget the reactions of U.S. consumers. The U.S.$ appreciation translates to an increase in the purchasing power of the U.S. consumer. As imports become less expensive, U.S. consumers have more discretionary income to spend on other goods, and thus local demand for the U.S. firm's product may rise, offsetting any losses in demand in Germany. The net effect of the changes in the purchasing power of the consumers is unclear.

Competitor Reactions

Just as consumers respond to exchange rate changes, so do competitors. If all of a company's competitors are German firms (i.e., sourcing components, producing, and selling only in Germany), they might decide to pursue one of two strategies. The first strategy will attempt to translate the favorable currency situation into market share advantages through reduced prices. This will imply substantial sales volume losses and negative operating exposure for the U.S. exporter. However, they might decide to use the current business situation for short-term profit maximization. Then they might use the exporting firm's price increases as an opportunity to increase their own prices and profit margins. This second scenario will probably lead to a positive operating exposure for the U.S. exporter.

If all of the firm's competitors are similarly structured U.S. exporters, then none of them has a cost advantage over the others and the real exchange rate change will have minimal operating exposure implications.

Supplier Reactions

Factored into this equation is the element of flexibility in reaction. How agile are the firm and its competitors in adjusting their sourcing structures? For instance, the German competitors may be sourcing most of their components locally. But as the German suppliers, and workers, realize diminishing purchasing power, due to the DM depreciation, they might also react. The workers might demand higher wages and the suppliers might charge higher prices, thus forcing the German competitors to follow suit in increasing their prices and subsequently reducing the operating exposure of the U.S. exporting firm. Similarly, if the suppliers of the U.S. firm import their own raw material from Germany, then they will benefit from the U.S.$ appreciation, and thus might pass cost savings to their customer, the U.S. exporter, and reduce its operating exposure.

Clearly, these examples demonstrate that whether a firm realizes an advantage from an exchange rate change depends on how the firm's suppliers react to the exchange rate change.

The nature of competition among suppliers also must be examined. For example, suppliers competing on price will respond differently to an exchange rate change than if they competed on quality, service, or flexibility. In general, the location of suppliers, their cost structures, and the types of demand they face will affect their customers' exposures.

Government Reactions

Government intervention can play a large role in determining the operating exposure. First, a government may intervene in the capital markets to stabilize the currency if it perceives that it is beneficial to the home country economy as a whole, or if it believes the currency appreciation is irrational or temporary. In addition, the government might take measures to support firms affected seriously by the exchange rate shock. The U.S. government might provide subsidies to exporting firms; it may cap the amount of foreign imports or assess tariffs to foreign imports to shelter the U.S. firms' operations, and thus reduce their operating exposure.

To summarize our discussion thus far, we have delivered two main points:

1. *Traditional operating exposure story:* All other things equal, a real appreciation of the "home" currency makes exports from the home country more expensive for consumers abroad, and makes goods from abroad cheaper for consumers in the home country.
2. *Complicating factors:* Assessing operating exposure requires a detailed knowledge of how consumers, competitors, suppliers, and the government will react to the real exchange rate shock. Therefore, understanding operating exposure requires a thorough understanding of how a specific business works, and this makes it very difficult to accurately estimate. As a result, it is extremely difficult to hedge against operating exposure through financial measures, and as we will see later in this section, flexible global operations strategies can help minimize the exposure.

We would like now to demonstrate the concepts with the use of illustrative situations typical to those encountered by companies in various industries.

Situation 1: Ford General, a U.S. company that manufactures small cars domestically, sells exclusively in the home market, and has no foreign debt. Can we say that it has no exposure to changes in exchange rates?

Unfortunately, the answer is no. The company competes in the home market with Japanese manufacturers. As a result, it is exposed to real changes in the yen–dollar exchange rate. A depreciation of the yen will strengthen the competitive position of the Japanese competitors. This is a situation that many U.S. companies faced in the early 1980s in industries as diverse as automobile manufacturing and consumer electronics.

Situation 2: Home Computers, the Canadian subsidiary of a U.S. company, distributes microcomputers to the Canadian market produced by its parent company in the United States. It has no debt, and its exposure to nominal exchange rate fluctuations is due to receivables in Canadian dollars. But what is its operating exposure to real changes in the Canadian–American dollar exchange rate?

To answer the question we must have information on the firm's competitors. Let us say that all of its competitors are also importing from parent companies in the United States. Then all of the firms will have similar cost and price structures, and with appropriate price adjustments, will be able to minimize their exposure to unfavorable situations such as a weakening of the Canadian dollar. This situation is typical in the computer and aircraft industries.

Situation 3: Uneven Care Products, the Mexican subsidiary of a U.S. company, sources its products from its parent company and then distributes them exclusively to the Mexican market. However, all of its competitors have manufacturing facilities in Mexico. What will be the firm's operating exposure to a real devaluation of the peso against the U.S. dollar?

Its exposure is negative and could be of a substantial magnitude. The firm's cost of sourcing the product will rise, and in the presence of a competitive market that forces the firm to be a price cutter, it is logical to expect that the firm's profit margins will decline. Its competitors will be in a stronger position that the firm will only be able to match by counteracting and building facilities in Mexico. This situation is typical of firms in the consumer goods industry such as Procter & Gamble, Unilever, and Colgate-Palmolive.

From these scenarios, the following features of operating exposure should be clear:

1. Operating exposure has no necessary relation to transaction (contractual) or translation (accounting) exposures.
2. The structure of the marketplace in which the company and its competitors source labor, raw materials, and components, and distribute and sell products, determines operating exposure.
3. A firm might be facing operating exposure to real changes of a lot of different currency exchange rates even though it contacts no business in many of them. Operating exposure has no necessary relation to the country in which goods are sold and inputs are sourced, and is not linked to the currency in which prices and/or profits are quoted. Ford General was exposed to real changes in the yen/U.S.$ exchange rate even though it did not source anything from Japan and sold nothing to the Japanese markets. A U.S. firm might be exposed to real changes in the Taiwanese $/U.S.$ real exchange rate just because one of the main suppliers of one of its major competitors sources heavily from a Taiwanese vendor.
4. Expected future cash flows and the firm's competitive position are affected by real changes in the exchange rates and not necessarily by changes in nominal exchange rates.

5. Operating exposure is peculiar to a particular firm. Firms in different industries are expected to have different operating exposures to the same real change in exchange rates, but even firms in the same industry might end up having different operating exposures, and sometimes not just a magnitude difference but a sign difference (positive versus negative). This is a consequence of differences in sourcing structure, use of automation in process technology, and/or location of manufacturing facilities.

◆ MANAGING OPERATING EXPOSURE

The operations manager, in order to effectively structure his or her options in effectively handling operating exposure, needs to

• Adequately conceptualize the implications of a specific situation for operating exposure
• Estimate the magnitude of operating exposure as accurately as possible
• Use a combination of financial and operational options in effectively managing operating exposure

We will list some helpful tools and suggestions for handling all three steps of the managerial process required to manage operating exposure.

A simple conceptual tool in structuring the thinking process for understanding the implications of a specific situation for operating exposure is the so-called *operating exposure matrix* (see Figure 9–1). The two dimensions of the matrix capture the effect of the real exchange rate shock.

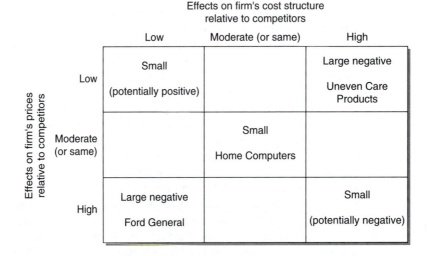

Figure 9–1   Operating Exposure Matrix and Illustrative Situations

The two undesirable cells of the matrix, which imply large negative operating exposure, are the ones for which the firm experiences either of the following:

1. Substantial increases in its cost structure with small control over prices in the marketplace (Uneven Care Products situation, upper-right hand corner of the matrix)
2. Substantial price pressures in the marketplace with limited effects on its cost structure (Ford General situation, lower left-hand corner of the matrix)

For most of the other cells of the matrix, the firm can exercise simultaneous control over prices and cost structure to alleviate negative effects of real exchange rate shocks, as, for example, in Home Computer's situation, where the increases in sourcing cost were counteracted with increases in prices by all firms in the marketplace. The operating exposure matrix is not suggested as an overall comprehensive tool in structuring a difficult concept like operating exposure, but is definitely a starting point in that thinking process.

Measuring operating exposure is a challenge in itself. Estimating the magnitude of operating exposure is substantially more difficult than transaction or translation exposure and the reason is that operating exposure is long term and the risks are not associated with known events or timing. The measurement of operating exposure requires an understanding of both the markets in which the company and its competitors obtain labor and materials and sell their products and also the degree of the firm's flexibility to adjust to market changes, sourcing cost increases, product mix changes, and technological advancements.

The only viable tool in estimating operating exposure is the so-called operating exposure audit, whereby a team of experienced managers brainstorms answers to the following questions in anticipation of a real exchange rate shock:

- Who are the main competitors in various markets? Who are low-cost producers? Who are price leaders? What is their expected reaction to the real exchange rate shock?
- What is the firm's operating flexibility? How can we adjust the product mix? Can we change production methods, reallocate production among facilities and/or improve our sourcing cost structure? What is the operating flexibility of our competitors?
- What happened to operating profits in the past when real exchange rates shifted?

With respect to the last question, a statistical approach can be used if past data are available. For example, regression analysis explaining changes in the firm's operating profits by changes in past real exchange rates can be used to project estimates for future operating exposures to real exchange rate shocks of different magnitudes. However, operations managers should accept the fact that these estimates are going to be inaccurate and substantially less precise than corresponding estimates of accounting or contractual exposures.

In managing operating exposure the firm may choose among various financial or operational options. For a long-term competitive exposure, which an operating exposure is, operational options of a strategic rather than tactical nature are most effective. And since changes in real, rather than nominal, exchange rates drive operating exposure, the traditional financial instruments (futures, forward contracts, options, etc.) used to manage the accurate and easy-to-estimate contractual exposure are not very effective. We will discuss the specifics of these instruments later. For the time being, we will concentrate on the more strategic operational options.

As will be discussed, the operational options in managing operating exposure to real exchange rate shocks involve *appropriate configuration of the business* (i.e., manufacturing site selection, sourcing arrangement, ownership structure of production facilities, choice of distribution channels, and product mix) and *exploitation of operational flexibility* built into the operating network of facilities and operational policies.

Development of a Global Network of Production Facilities with Excess Capacity

The firm exploits exchange rate volatility by selecting manufacturing locations and configuring its facility network in a way that allows it the flexibility to increase production in countries where currencies become strongly undervalued in real terms. The trade-offs associated with such a flexible global facility location/capacity strategy include the cost of switching production locations for various products, product mix adjustment costs in specific facilities, and building/maintaining excess capacity. On the other hand, such a strategy can seriously reduce operating costs across a spectrum of exchange rates.

Development of a Portfolio of Global Suppliers

The firm exploits sourcing flexibility in various ways. The most obvious ways are by switching the sourcing of raw materials and components among global suppliers, and by emphasizing sourcing from countries whose currencies are undervalued in real terms. Flexibility in global sourcing is relatively easy to build into innovative global supply contracts. For example, flexibility in purchase timing and quantities of various components over the planning horizon can be exploited by making earlier and larger purchases in response to appreciation of the firm's home country currency. Additionally, firms can benefit by keeping an appropriately balanced mix of local and global outsourcing for any market in which they operate. In environments of dual exchange rates (i.e., a lower government-controlled rate and a higher market rate), particularly in periods of strong devaluation of the local currency, the mix of local and global sourcing can be used advantageously to reduce the firm's tax obligations to the local government through aggressive outsourcing at the government exchange rate and through creative transfer pricing from the parent company. Such policies can also be used to effectively repatriate profits.

Design of Flexible, Creative, and Fast Product Development Processes That Result in New and Substantially Differentiated Products

The ability of the firm to increase its prices with minimal market share losses is substantially enhanced by effective new-product development processes that introduce new products or enhance existing products in a way that maximizes the firm's product demand elasticity. A company may enhance the features of an existing product to customize it for various market segments, and thus reduce its operating exposure relative to a standardized (commodity) product offered by a competitor. When a company introduces a new product class, the operating exposure starts out small and then grows as competing products enter the market. The ability to introduce many new products quickly can, in many cases, reduce operating exposure in high-technology, hypercompetitive markets.

Ability to Select and Expand Product Line for Various Markets

From the earlier discussion, it is apparent that mature products tend to be more exposed to real exchange rate shocks. Similarly, in hyperinflation, devaluated-currency country environments, the government often imposes strict price controls on various product categories. Thus, ability of a firm to carefully and dynamically adjust its product line in response to the specifics of the macroeconomic environment in a specific country/market can substantially reduce its operating exposure. The company should be able to offer a balanced mix of products in various stages of the product life cycle (both growth and mature products), and products in price-controlled and nonprice-controlled product categories in hyperinflation environments.

Development of Flexibly Structured Supplier and the Distribution Channel Selection for Fast, Efficient Product Delivery

Supplier and distribution channel flexibility is important in a competitive environment, but even more so in unstable, hyperinflation, currency-devaluated country environments where wasted time creates higher exposure risks. Although suppliers must be selected on a variety of criteria, companies must consider suppliers' flexibility in terms of credit terms and payment times. Similarly, the use of fewer, better-controlled distribution channels becomes crucial. The distribution channels should be updated frequently on pricing changes, and should be able to clear their payables in short credit periods. Thus, appropriate supply chain structure from supplier to distribution channel selection can add operating flexibility. Such flexibility, in turn, can help a firm reduce its operating exposure to macroeconomic shocks.

Larger firms have the option of reducing their overall operating exposure by selecting a portfolio of individual businesses that minimizes operating exposure for the parent company. In other words, they can establish a portfolio of businesses that have offsetting exposures to real exchange rate shocks, thereby reducing the overall corporate exposure. This approach, though intuitive and straightforward, is difficult to implement because of the difficulty in estimating operating exposure of the various operating units, and the continuous adjustments of these exposures over time.

◆ PRICING STRATEGIES FOR EXPORTING FIRMS

The most straightforward way for an exporting firm to respond to exchange rate fluctuations is through responsive pricing policies. We provide a brief treatment of this topic based on recent research results.

Exchange Rate Pass-Through Pricing Policies

The simplest pricing analysis involves a foreign producer who completes all manufacturing processes abroad in his own country. The final product is then exported for sale in the United States. In this example, the foreign producer incurs all costs in his home currency. (We momentarily ignore sales costs and assume that no costs are incurred in other currencies.)

The simplest pricing policy involves the complete pass-through of all exchange rate changes to the consumer. The foreign firm achieves this objective by charging a price in the United States that is equal to its foreign sales price, multiplied by the current exchange rate.

$$P_{us} = e\,P_r \tag{9.6}$$

where

P_{us} = the dollar price of the foreign good (sold in the United States)
P_r = the foreign currency price of the foreign good (sold in the foreign country)
e = the exchange rate, the number of dollars per unit of foreign currency
(# of dollars/1 unit of foreign currency)

In Equation 9.6, all exchange rate movements are passed through completely. The pricing formula implies that a 50 percent dollar depreciation (represented by a 50 percent increase in e) results in a 50 percent increase in the dollar price of foreign output sold in the United States. Note, however, that if the foreign firm immediately repatriates its U.S. earnings at the current exchange rate, it will receive P_r units of foreign currency for each sale it makes in the U.S. regardless of the current value of the dollar.

Although the simple price formula guarantees the foreign exporter a fixed amount of foreign currency per sale in the United States, it does not guarantee that the foreign exporter will generate the same revenue every quarter that it operates in the United States. The formula implies that dollar prices charged to U.S. consumers will increase and decrease with depreciation and appreciation of the dollar, respectively. Unless the exporter operates in a market that is completely price-insensitive, the fluctuation of the retail price will affect the level of their purchases. Market share will be lost every time the foreign exporter increases the retail price charged in the United States.

Pricing Adjustments to Preserve Market Share

There are a number of reasons why firms may choose a more sophisticated pricing response to exchange rate movements. First, if exchange rates are volatile, the firm may prefer to maintain a stable price in U.S. markets and absorb the shocks caused by temporary fluctuations. This is especially true in cases where the firm establishes ongoing supply relationships. Second, full pass-through of exchange rates will, at times, imply the loss of market share. The firm may choose to reduce its current profit margins rather than permanently lose market share. Price stability will be most important in cases where the firm is involved in a long-term supply relationship, or in markets characterized by a high degree of consumer brand loyalty. For many companies, today's prices have long-run implications for future demand levels and profits.

The circumstances facing the firm determine the extent to which it passes exchange-rate–induced price movements on to the consumer. Firms typically charge their customers a price that is a certain percentage markup over their costs. In this vein, we now consider pricing that is responsive to characteristics of the U.S. market, as well as to the dollar exchange rate.

Following the economic arguments as they are presented in Hooper and Mann (1989), the foreign price of output is some markup λ over foreign production costs C_f. Equation 9.7 represents the amount of foreign currency that the foreign producer collects for each unit sold in the United States.

$$P_f = \lambda C_f \tag{9.7}$$

where

P_f = foreign markup price
λ = markup
C_f = foreign production costs

The ultimate price charged to U.S. consumers, P_{us}, is the foreign *markup* price multiplied by the exchange rate.

$$P_{us} = eP_f = e\lambda C_f \qquad (9.8)$$

where

P_{us} = price charged to U.S. consumers
e = the exchange rate

The actual level of markup varies from industry to industry, based on competitive and cost circumstances. The markup also varies with the level of the exchange rate. The determination of the markup is shown in Equation 9.9.

$$\lambda = f(P_i, \alpha, e, C_f CU) \qquad (9.9)$$

where

P_i = the average U.S. price of goods in industry i
α = degree of competition in industry i ($0 < \alpha < 1$; $\alpha = 1$ implies perfect competition)
CU = capacity utilization

The following conditions will cause the value of λ to increase:

1. An increase in the average U.S. price of goods in industry i
2. An increase in the foreign firm's market power; or a reduction in the value of α
3. And increase in the capacity utilization of the foreign firm

On the other hand, increases in either foreign costs or the exchange rate will result in a reduced markup. Note, however, that foreign costs and the exchange rate appear in both Equations 9.8 and 9.9. As a result, the full impact of changes in either requires that one accounts for both effects simultaneously.

Although the specifics of the formula are not of particular interest for the arguments, we will provide them here for interested readers. Hooper and Mann (1989) use the following formula:

$$\lambda = \left[\frac{P_i}{eC_f} \right]^{\alpha} [CU]^{\beta} \qquad (9.10)$$

where β is an empirically determined constant.

To make the arguments more tangible, the discussion is couched in terms of foreign supply to the U.S. market. The arguments apply equally well to any firm selling its output in a market besides its home. In order to gauge the effect of each variable in isolation, each argument is made assuming that all other factors remain constant.

Average U.S. Price

If the average U.S. price for goods is high in an industry, then the foreign firm can increase its price with less fear of eroding its own market share. Hence, it will pass more of the exchange rate fluctuation on to the consumer. If the average U.S. price is relatively low, then passing a price increase on to consumers will cause the firm to lose significant market share. At a lower average U.S. price, the firm will choose a lower markup and maintain market share, rather than pursuing higher profits per unit sold in periods of dollar depreciation.

Competitiveness of Markets

α represents the level of competition in the market. If α is equal to 1, this implies that the market is characterized by perfect competition. If the market is perfectly competitive, we assume the U.S. price for output sold in the United States is constant at the competitive price. The foreign firm has the choice of selling at the competitive price or exiting the market. As long as the firm continues to sell to the U.S. market, the foreign firm will sell at the U.S. price. This means that it cannot pass on the effects of exchange rate fluctuations, and will have to absorb the full impact of the exchange rate movement. In other words, increases or decreases in the exchange rate e have no effect on the markup λ.

α may range in value from 0 to 1. As the value of α falls, we know that the market is becoming increasingly concentrated. Lower values of α reflect a market in which there are only a few competitors, and in which the foreign firm has less concern about the possibility of losing market share to other firms. Hence, the firm will pass more of the exchange rate effects on to the consumer than it would at higher values of α. Because firms in less competitive circumstances are less concerned with the loss of market share, they will shift the exchange rate movements on to the consumer. The result is that the markup λ is larger for firms with stronger monopoly or oligopoly power.

Exchange Rate

The value of the exchange rate e also influences the degree of markup of foreign goods sold in the U.S. market. If e is large, this means the dollar is relatively weak. The firm's markup will be lower when the dollar is weak, because the firm will lose a large portion of its U.S. demand if it were to choose a large markup. If, instead, the dollar is strong (small e), the firm will choose a larger markup. When the dollar is strong, the firm's prices are relatively competitive, and it can charge a larger markup without fearing a big loss in overall sales.

Foreign Costs

Foreign costs affect the degree of markup similar to the way in which the exchange rate affected the markup. A foreign firm with high costs C_f is not particularly competitive. As a result, that firm can only afford to charge a low markup if it is to meet the domestic competition in the U.S. market. On the other hand, if foreign costs are low, the firm can afford to charge a larger markup and still remain competitive. Hence the markup will increase as foreign costs decline.

Capacity Utilization

Finally, the rate of firm capacity utilization influences the foreign firm's choice of markup. If the firm is running close to capacity, it will charge a high markup. A firm with a lower rate of capacity utilization would choose a lower markup. The difference in choice reflects the firm's ability to service demand. If the dollar appreciates (e decreases), the foreign firm has the choice of reducing the dollar prices it charges to U.S. consumers and expanding sales to the United States, or the foreign firm can choose to maintain its U.S. prices. Maintaining its U.S. prices at a constant level will increase the firm's profit margin. (Because dollar appreciation has decreased the value of e, the foreign firm receives more foreign currency per sale $P_f = P_{us}/e$.) Because the firm running close to full capacity can't immediately expand output, it will choose a high markup and will enjoy high profit margins. On the other hand, the firm with low capacity utilization can benefit from an expansion of output and will reduce its U.S. prices in response to the appreciation. This firm is selecting output expansion rather than enhanced profits on each unit sold.

Combined Effects

As was mentioned, both the exchange rate and underlying foreign costs have direct effects in Equation 9.8, as well as indirect effects through their influence on the level of the markup λ. Hooper and Mann's formula for the markup is given in Equation 9.10. If this formula is taken in conjunction with the price-setting equation, and logarithms are taken on the two sides of the equation, we find the following pricing relationship in Equation 9.11. Changes in the exchange rate or foreign costs change the price charged to U.S. customers, but by a smaller percentage than the change in the value of e or C_f. The exact amount relates to the level of market power, as the changes are multiplied by $(1-\alpha)$.

$$P_{us} = (1-\alpha)e + \alpha P_i + (1-\alpha)C_f + \beta CU \qquad (9.11)$$

Suppose that the exchange rate depreciates by 50 percent. This means that the value of the dollar has fallen, and as a result, the foreign exporter's goods are now less competitive in U.S. markets. As long as the foreign firm has at least a small amount of market power, it will respond by reducing its dollar prices charged to U.S. customers. The amount by which the foreign firm changes its prices will be $(1-\alpha)$ 50 percent. In other words, the prices will be reduced, but by an amount less than 50 percent.

The following issues are not addressed in the markup formula, but they are important to full understanding of firm decisions on the level of markup.

1. The rate of exchange rate pass-through will depend on firm expectations regarding the permanence of exchange rate fluctuations. If the exchange rate movement is believed to be temporary, the firm is less likely to pass the price changes on to U.S. consumers. On the other hand, if the exchange rate movement is assumed to be permanent, the firm will readjust its prices, or possibly alter its level of operations in the United States.
2. Firms are rarely all domestic, or all foreign. They have costs that are incurred in their foreign currency and costs that are incurred in their export market. The true markup will depend on the cost structure of the specific firm, and the location in which it incurs costs.
3. Equation 9.11 assumes that foreign costs C_f and the exchange rate e enter the markup formula identically. In most circumstances, though, the exchange rate will be much more variable than costs. As a result, the firm will be more likely to pass cost increases through to consumers at a higher rate than exchange-rate–induced movements. Because the exchange rate movement may in fact be temporary, the firm is more willing to absorb the variability in its profit margins. Cost increases will more generally reflect ongoing changes in the cost of operations, and hence, will be passed on to consumers more completely.

◆ USE OF OPERATIONAL FLEXIBILITY TO MINIMIZE OPERATING EXPOSURE

Recent research in international operations has emphasized the value of operational flexibility in global manufacturing and distribution networks. The value of this network derives from the opportunity to benefit from uncertainty in competitor reactions, future technologies, macroeconomic uncertainties, and, for our discussion purposes in exchange rates, through the coordination of subsidiaries that are geographically dispersed. In addition to adjusting markups or profit margins, firms may choose to enter or exit a market, switch production of various products from one country production facility to another, or adjust purchased quantities from a portfolio of global suppliers when faced with large swings in the value of the exchange rate. Such decisions will involve considerations surrounding current performance, as well as their expectations regarding the future. For simplicity, in our further discussion we will refer to such decisions as *entry/exit* decisions.

Many possible entry and exit scenarios exist. It could mean the entry and exit of sales operations or distribution networks. Alternatively, it could mean the entry and exit of production facilities. This example investigates the entry/exit decisions of sales and logistics operations in the context of fixed set-up and departure costs and ongoing exchange rate uncertainty. However, the same ideas support the switching from exporting strategies to foreign-owned production facilities or the reallocation of production of products among factories in global production facility networks with excess capacity.

Production is assumed to occur in the foreign country. Before the foreign firm can sell its output in the United States, it must establish a logistics and dealership network in the United States. The network has fixed start-up costs. Expansion of the network also requires the expenditure of additional funds. The decision to abandon or contract the U.S. market also incurs fixed shut-down costs. As long as the firm maintains its current level of sales, there are no fixed costs, only the variable costs associated with the level of production destined for the U.S. market. Firm expansion/contraction decisions will involve the following elements:

1. *Exchange rate expectations:* The company makes decisions based on its predictions regarding the exchange rate. This prediction is based on (1) the expected future exchange rate $E(e)$, and (2) the standard error of the exchange rate estimate.
2. *Profit expectations:* The firm will generate expected profit forecasts that are based on operation at current capacity.
3. *Costs:* The firm will consider the cost associated with expansion or contraction of its sales and logistics network in the United States.

If the firm could make changes at no cost, it would always choose the profit-maximizing choice of sales and logistics network in the United States. As the firm's products became more or less competitive in U.S. markets, the company would instantly expand or contract its network.

Adjustment costs alter the firm's choice, however. Even if the firm is certain about current and future profit opportunities and the exact path of exchange rates, it still may not choose the profit-maximizing level of sales and logistics structure. Why? The firm will compare the costs of adjustment with the expected change in profits. If the change in profits associated with the change in sales and logistics structure is less than the costs of adjusting the sales network, it will choose not to change its current level of operations.

Suppose that a firm starts out at a profit-maximizing size. Dollar depreciation causes its product to become less competitive in U.S. markets. It could choose to incur the costs and contract out its U.S. sales and logistics network. If the exchange rate moved only a little, however, it is very likely that the company would want to return to its previous position, and bring its sales network back in-house in a year's time. Rather than dismantling the network, it will keep the excess capacity as an option.

If the dollar depreciation were really large, the effect on profits could be substantial. In this alternative case, a small reversal of the exchange rate's value would not alter its decision to contract U.S. operations. In this case, the firm will spend the money to shrink its U.S. sales and logistics network.

a: No adjustment costs in contracting/expanding the sales/logistics network

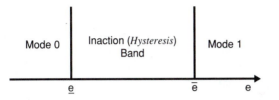

b: Significant adjustment costs in contracting/expanding the sales/logistics network

Figure 9-2   Hysteresis Policies in Switching Between Operational Strategies

The larger the uncertainty regarding the exchange rate, the greater the force required to get firms to change their plans.

Let us now summarize the main observations of this discussion. For simplicity's sake, let us say the firm has to choose between two operational modes of sales and logistics network. Mode 0 involves the operation by the foreign firm of a fully developed sales and logistics network in the United States, and Mode 1 is a downsized logistics and sales network that operates with a minimal level of resource commitment by the foreign firm.

The optimal operational strategies for the firm are summarized in Figure 9-2. In the absence of adjustment costs in switching between operational modes, there exists a threshold real exchange rate e_{st} such that for values larger than it, Mode 1 is the optimal choice for the firm. For values less than e_{st} the optimal mode is Mode 0.

In the presence of positive adjustment costs in switching between operational modes, we can identify two threshold levels of exchange rates $\underline{e}$ and $\bar{e}$, which we use to describe the optimal operational policies. If the exchange rate is less than $\underline{e}$ (i.e., highly appreciated U.S.$), then the firm chooses as optimal mode the fully expanded sales/logistics network of Mode 0. For values of the exchange rate higher than $\bar{e}$ (i.e., highly depreciated U.S.$), the firm employs as optimal Mode 1, and incurs all necessary costs for shrinking its sales/logistics network. For values of exchange rate between the two thresholds the firm prefers to keep operating in whatever is its current mode. In the presence of positive adjustment costs in switching between operational modes, it is optimal to stay longer with the current mode, reflected by the use of a higher exchange rate $\bar{e}$ ($\bar{e} > e_{st}$) before switching from Mode 0 to Mode 1 and a lower exchange rate $\underline{e}$ ($\underline{e} < e_{st}$) before switching from Mode 1 to Mode 0. We refer to the positive quantity $\bar{e} - \underline{e}$ as the *Hysteresis Band* (or inaction band), which captures the inertia associated with an operational mode switching decision.

We could use the same modeling paradigm, and results, to discuss the choice of production strategies (i.e., exporting (EXP), joint ventures with local partners (JV), or wholly owned production facilities (WOS)) in supplying the demand of a foreign market. When considering the selection between a strategy that involves investment in foreign production facilities (i.e., JV or WOS), and an exporting strategy, the simple rules to remember are:

1. Strongly depreciated home currency favors an exporting policy for the firm.
2. Strongly appreciated home currency favors investment in production facilities in the foreign market (i.e., a JV or a WOS).
3. The switchover costs between strategies and the uncertainty in exchange rates force a period of inaction (*hysteresis band*) during which the firm will continue to use its current production strategy even though the immediate operating profits favor switching strategies.

The magnitude of the hysteresis band is a measure of both organizational inertia and volatility of the macroeconomic environment. The larger the band gets, the more persistent the firm is in maintaining its current strategies. The following are the most important factors, and their corresponding influences, on the hysteresis band:

1. Switchover costs between strategies are measures of organizational inertia, and any increase in them leads to an increased hysteresis band.
2. Production cost advantages (due either to supplier infrastructure, work force skills, or product/process know-how) in the home country favor exporting strategies (reflected in decrease of critical numbers $\underline{e}$ and $\bar{e}$), while cost advantages in the foreign market favor direct investment in production facilities there (reflected in increase of the critical numbers).
3. The higher the market power of the firm in the foreign market, the more the foreign direct investment strategies are favored (reflected in increase of the critical numbers $\underline{e}$ and $\bar{e}$).
4. The volatility of the exchange rates is a major contributing factor to the hysteresis phenomenon, and increased volatility leads to an increased hysteresis band.
5. An increased foreign market demand provides favorable conditions for earlier switching to an exporting strategy in the case of a depreciated home currency (as reflected in a decrease in $\bar{e}$) while favoring the longer duration of foreign direct investment strategies for relatively appreciated home currencies (as reflected in an increase of $\underline{e}$).

There is adequate anecdotal evidence to justify these results. From early 1980 to the end of 1984, the real value of the U.S. dollar increased by about 50 percent. As a result, the ability of foreign firms (Japanese, for example) to compete in the U.S. market through exporting soared. But the volume of U.S. imports did not begin to rise substantially until the beginning of 1983 (i.e., an indication of the presence of an inaction period), when the stronger dollar was already well established.

The Plaza Agreement, enacted in 1985, changed the whole picture. Such an abrupt change in the exchange rate value—for the yen, a 30 percent drop in just a year, compounded to 46 percent in three years—made it unprofitable for Japanese manufacturers to hang on to mere domestic production. However, their reaction was not immediate. Any noticeable change in Japanese exports was observed four years later (in 1989 the Japanese manufacturing sector experienced an export decline from 26 percent to 20 percent). Finally in the 1990s, with the yen at its peak values, came the announcements that Japanese manufacturers (particularly in automobile, household appliances, and electronics industries) planned to expand into U.S. production facilities. Once established in the U.S. market, the Japanese companies were slow to scale back their exporting operations and switch into development of U.S.-based production facilities when the exchange rate moved unfavorably, thus providing another indication of the hysteresis phenomenon.

◆ GLOBAL SOURCING STRATEGIES UNDER EXCHANGE RATE UNCERTAINTY

Firms competing in the global marketplace must take into account the comparative advantages of various countries in forming their manufacturing and sourcing strategies. Developing countries, for instance, have advantages in many cases over developed nations in terms of low labor and raw material costs. Such cost advantages offer strong motivation for multinational firms to seek offshore sourcing arrangements in developing countries.

In other cases, critical technological components and/or process equipment are available only from a handful of select foreign sources, which are in many cases located in technologically advanced countries other than the firm's home country. In such cases the firm has no choice but to look to these foreign suppliers for its sourcing needs. For these reasons, global sourcing is emerging as a key strategy for companies seeking competitive advantage, and now represents a more strategic activity at multinational firms. Nearly 10 percent of Chrysler's $8.6 billion outsourcing budget is spent on global purchases. Westinghouse spends more than 7 percent of its total purchasing dollars on international procurement.

The greatest risk in global sourcing contracts is that of the currency exchange rate. Exchange rates affect the price paid for imported material or components when payment is in the supplier's currency. Because there is a lag between the time the contract is signed and payment is made, exchange rates may change such that the buyer may end up paying substantially more or less than the original contract price. The problem becomes even more complex when two or more foreign suppliers from countries utilizing different currencies are under consideration for a contract. Each potential supplier's currency would typically fluctuate differently in relation to the U.S. dollar. Thus, two equally capable suppliers from different countries who quote the same U.S. dollar equivalent price at a given point in time can end up generating significantly different costs for the buyer over the life of the contract.

A study by consulting firm McKinsey & Co. found that the unpredictability of currency fluctuations makes strategies based on single-supplier sourcing and on forecasting currency swings ineffective. On the other hand, volatile exchange rates allow the buyer an opportunity to exploit favorable price changes or avoid unfavorable price differentials through supplier selection in multisourcing arrangements, adjustment in procured quantities, and the careful timing of purchase.

Because the impact of currency fluctuations is so large (fluctuations of 1 percent in a day or 20 percent in a year are not uncommon), recent research suggests that companies should consider selecting suppliers on the basis of their contribution to balancing currency flows, rather than price and performance. In this way, firms can operationally hedge against currency risk by establishing a portfolio of suppliers in different countries and exploiting the sourcing flexibility inherent in such a portfolio.

If there is one point on which the literature agrees, however, it is that the majority of operations and purchasing managers lack a broad-based understanding of the importance of using exchange rate information in a supplier selection decision and in structuring global sourcing contracts. The goal of this section, then, is to put forth some basic tools that operations managers can use to minimize currency exposure risk in global sourcing situations. Our emphasis here is on understanding the intuition, benefits, and disadvantages of these various available tools.

We start by illustrating the significant impact of exchange rates on the valuation of global sourcing contracts. Then we will look at currently practiced strategies of minimizing currency risk exposure in global sourcing, breaking them into two categories of micro- and macro-level strategies. We devote separate subsections to analyzing each class of currency management strategies in global sourcing. At the end of this chapter, we present the most effective exchange rate management strategies so that the operations manager can understand the distinction of financial- and operations-based hedging strategies in global sourcing, and, we hope, can appreciate the importance of using exchange rate information in supplier selection.

◆ IMPACT OF EXCHANGE RATES AND CLASSIFICATION OF HEDGING STRATEGIES IN GLOBAL SOURCING

To demonstrate the impact that exchange rates can have on the value of a global sourcing contract, we use a simple example. The data of the example is summarized in Table 9–2. A U.S. firm has a sourcing contract with a Japanese supplier. The contract involves twelve equal shipments from Japan to the United States, and for each shipment the U.S. firm is obligated to pay the amount of 20.248 million yen. When the contract was signed (we make the convention that this is period 1), the currency rate was 202.48 yen to the dollar. Evaluated at that exchange rate, each payment was equivalent to $100,000. Unfortunately, the yen appreciated during the contract term, and in Table 9–2 we see the actual amount in dollars the firm ends up paying for each shipment. A contract that was estimated to cost U.S.$1.2 million at the signing of the agreement ends up costing U.S.$1.43 million—a 20 percent sourcing cost increase.

This simple example illustrates an important point. Exchange rates have a significant impact on sourcing costs. In fact, exchange rate fluctuations are among the most difficult costs to account for in global sourcing. It is thus important for the operations manager to be well versed in the various tools that can be used to effectively hedge against currency fluctuation risks. A few months of currency shifts can wipe out hard-won gains made through technology investment or productivity improvement programs.

Table 9–2

Example Data to Illustrate Impact of Exchange Rates on Global Sourcing Contracts

Period	Yen Expenditure	Exchange Rate (¥/US$)	Actual Payment in US$
1	20.248M	202.48	100,000.0
2	20.248M	192.30	105,293.8
3	20.248M	180.15	112,395.2
4	20.248M	180.45	112,220.8
5	20.248M	169.63	119,365.6
6	20.248M	174.10	116,300.9
7	20.248M	161.10	125,685.9
8	20.248M	153.65	131,780.0
9	20.248M	155.50	130,212.2
10	20.248M	154.30	131,224.8
11	20.248M	163.50	123,840.9
12	20.248M	162.10	124,910.5
			Total $1,433,230.6

Table 9–3

Classification of Currency Risk Management Strategies in Global Sourcing	
Micro-Level Strategies	
	*Proportion of Use**
1. Payment in U.S. dollars (Risk avoidance)	85%
2. Buying foreign currency forward (Risk avoidance)	20%
3. Buying foreign currency futures (or options) (Risk minimization)	35%
4. Risk-sharing contract agreement (Risk minimization)	55%
5. Payment in supplier currency	5%
Macro-Level Strategies	
	*Proportion of Use**
1. Supplier selection through exchange rate forecasts	20%
2. Flexible sourcing contracts on volume/timing of purchases	10%
3. Develop a portfolio of global suppliers/supplier switching	N/A

*Percentage of surveyed firms using the strategy (Carter and Vickery (1989).

In our presentation of the various hedging tools we will use the classification scheme introduced by Carter and Vickery in 1989. In their conceptual framework, currency management strategies are divided into two major categories:

- *Macro-level strategies:* These affect the sourcing decision itself (for example, supplier selection, structure of a global sourcing portfolio), or pertain to the structure of the sourcing contract (e.g., flexibility in volume-timing of purchases).
- *Micro-level strategies:* These are employed after the source selection has been made, and constitute short-term protection for the buyer from the risk of exchange rate fluctuations.

Table 9–3 presents the various currency management strategies in global sourcing that we will discuss. The micro-level strategies are financially based strategies, while the macro-level strategies are primarily operations based. Effective global sourcing management requires the use of an appropriate combination of macro- and micro-level strategies.

◆ BASIC FUNCTION OF FOREIGN EXCHANGE MARKETS

To understand our discussion, we first need to grasp the basic function of foreign exchange markets. Foreign exchange markets exist only for convertible currencies. For these currencies, the exchange rates generally are determined by market forces, without substantial government interventions. The currencies of all established industrialized and some newly industrialized countries are convertible.

Trading in the foreign exchange markets proceeds through contracts made between buyers and sellers of foreign currency. Three types of exchange markets exist, each distinguished by the type of contract involved. These are the *spot, forward,* and *futures* markets. In a spot market, the parties agree to exchange one currency for another at a fixed ratio to be delivered immediately, but more likely in one to two business days. Typically, individuals and companies exchange at the spot rate through banks. The spot exchange rate is set based on trading among banks for immediate exchange (i.e., allowing one or two days for clearing).

In the *forward* market, the buyer and seller agree to exchange currency at a fixed ratio at some specified future date. Nothing happens until that date, at which time the exchange is made at the agreed upon exchange rate. In general, forward contracts exist between a bank and a buyer and/or seller. Each of these contracts is designed by the bank to meet the specific needs of the other party with regard to amounts and timing of the transaction. Traditionally, forward contracts are negotiated for delivery in one, two, three, six, and twelve months, although for major currencies (e.g., U.S. dollar, Japanese yen, British pound, German mark, Swiss franc, French franc, and Canadian dollar), future delivery dates of up to three years are possible.

Futures markets are organized markets for trading contracts for the future delivery of currency. They differ from the forward markets in that the contracts are standardized in terms of time of delivery and size of contract. For example, each futures contract on the German mark traded on the International Monetary Market (IMM) in Chicago has a standardized size of DM125,000. The contracts available for trading have different expiration dates, depending on the time of year. For example, on September 25, 1997, the available contract expiration dates on the German mark were December 1997 and March 1998. An additional feature of futures contracts is that they may require the exchange of cash before the delivery date. The disadvantage of futures contracts over forward contracts is that the standardized features may not exactly match a company's requirements. Forward contracts can be designed to match those requirements. On the other hand, the standardization of futures contracts can make them less costly.

Table 9–4 reports quotes for spot, forward, and futures markets for British pounds and German marks. The first quote for British pounds is the spot rate of 1.6285 dollars per pound. The subsequent quotes are forward rates for 30, 90, and 180 days from the current date. Futures prices are reported in the second half of the table. The first line for each currency specifies the size of the contract and below that are listed the contracts that are available for trading and the most recent exchange rates at which the contracts were traded.

The spot rates are the prevailing market rates determined by the supply and demand for a particular currency relative to another currency. Forward and futures rates differ from spot rates in that they are rates for exchange at future dates, and usually are quoted at a premium or discount to spot rates. The size of a currency's premium or discount depends on the financial communities' assessment of the future of the relative strength of that currency. This assessment is based on such factors as the country's balance of payments, trade figures, international reserves, GNP, money supply, rate of inflation, difference in interest rates, and other domestic and international economic indicators.

Quite often, especially outside the United States, forward and futures exchange rates are expressed in terms of an annualized percentage deviation from the spot rate. This is the case in the *Financial Times*. The following equation is used:

$$\frac{FR - SR}{SR} \times \frac{12}{N} \times 100\% = \text{Discount (or premium) in percentage terms}$$

where

FR = forward or future rate (local currency per unit of foreign currency)
SR = spot rate (local currency per unit of foreign currency)
N = months to maturity

Table 9–4 *Example of Spot, Forward and Futures Rates*

Exchange Rates Thursday, September 25, 1997

The New York foreign exchange selling rates below apply to trading among banks in amounts of $1 million and more, as quoted at 4 P.M. Eastern time by Dow Jones and other sources. Retail transactions provide fewer units of foreign currency per dollar.

Country	US $ equiv.		Currency per U.S.$	
	Thurs.	*Wed.*	*Thurs.*	*Wed.*
Britain (pound)	1.6285	1.6138	.6141	.6197
30 days forward	1.6266	1.6119	.6148	.6204
90 days forward	1.6224	1.6075	.6164	.6221
180 days forward	1.6165	1.6016	.6186	.6244
Germany (mark)	.5683	.5642	1.7595	1.7725
30 days forward	.5695	.5653	1.7559	1.7690
90 days forward	.5717	.5675	1.7491	1.7620
180 days forward	.5749	.5706	1.7395	1.7524

Futures

	Open	High	Low	Settle	Change
British Pound					
(IMM)[1] – 62,500 pds.; $ per pound					
December 97	1.6088	1.6250	1.6064	1.6228	+.0144
March 98	1.6150	1.6190	1.6150	1.6164	+.0144
German Mark					
(IMM) – 125,000 marks; $ per mark					
December 97	.5273	.5710	.5656	.5709	+.0035
March 98	.5696	.5735	.5696	.5740	+.0035

[1]IMM is International Monetary Market at the Chicago Mercantile Exchange.

For example, a U.S. purchaser of a 90-day forward contract in British pounds would be buying at a 1.50 percent discount.

$$\frac{1.6224 - 1.6285}{1.6285} \times \frac{12}{3} \times 100\% = -1.50\%$$

On the other hand, a 90-day forward contract for the German mark would be purchased with a 2.40 percent premium.

$$\frac{.5717 - .5683}{.5683} \times \frac{12}{3} \times 100\% = 2.40\%$$

The spot market serves immediate currency needs, whereas the forward and futures markets provide the means of dealing with foreign exchange risks.

◆ ## MICRO-LEVEL STRATEGIES FOR MANAGING EXCHANGE RATE RISK

In the case of a U.S. buyer, the simplest way to avoid the risk of volatile exchange rates in a sourcing contract is to pay in U.S. dollars. This strategy transfers all the risk of an adverse currency fluctuation from the buyer to the supplier, if the supplier is willing to accept it. The drawback of such a strategy is that the purchasing firm is not able to take advantage of a favorable movement of the exchange rate.

Financial hedging tools dominate the methods used by current operations managers in risk management associated with global sourcing contracts. Three different financial products are available to the operations manager—forward contracts, futures contracts, and options. We will discuss each of these tools separately and the ways they are used to hedge currency exposure.

Forward Contracts

A forward contract is an agreement between a firm and a financial institution to buy or sell a certain amount of a foreign currency at a specified price at a specified future date in time. The worldwide foreign exchange forward market is well developed. It consists mostly of banks that trade the forward contracts electronically. Its main advantages are that forward contracts can be tailored to meet the needs of any firm, and it is a relatively easy process to implement.

Since a forward contact is an individually negotiated agreement between buyer and seller, it is very flexible. A forward contract can be written on any currency as long as the counter party to the agreement is willing to accept the risk associated with the currency. Most banks will accept the extra risk of highly unstable currencies, but the price for accepting greater risk will be high. Also, the forward contract can be for any amount of currency, and it can be for a very precise amount. For instance, if a firm needs to hedge exactly $3,562,488 into German marks (DM) it can do so. Also, the length of the contract is flexible. It can be from one day to many years in length.

The downside of forward contracts is that they are more expensive than futures contracts. The higher price reflects the greater flexibility. They have a thin secondary market, as well. That is, they cannot be sold, once owned, as easily as futures contracts. Another negative for forward contracts is that there is counter party credit risk involved. That is, if a contract moves strongly against the issuing bank, the bank may suffer substantial losses and may not be financially able to honor the forward contract.

In the following discussion we will use a simple example. A U.S. automaker, USAuto, buys windshields from a German supplier. If the supplier is paid in German marks, USAuto has a transaction exposure that is an *outflow* of German marks. On the other hand, if USAuto sells its cars in Germany, USAuto will be paid by its German dealers in marks and, in this case, the currency risk represents an *inflow* of German marks. Both types of risk can be effectively hedged via financial markets, particularly by using forward contracts.

As an example of how USAuto would use a forward contract, assume that it wants to hedge both windshield purchases and cash inflows from sales of its cars in Germany. Assume the current exchange rate is $.69:1DM. It knows that it will buy $1,000,000 (1,449,275 DM) worth of windshields from the German supplier and it will sell $2,000,000 (2,898,550 DM) worth of cars in Germany over the next three months. Say the 180 day bid/offer forward rate is .68/.70 dollars per DM. To hedge the windshields, USAuto needs to purchase forward 1,449,275 DM for 180 days. It will pay U.S.$.70 per DM, or $1,014,492 for the German marks. Now, no matter what the German mark does in relation to the U.S. dollar, USAuto will pay exactly $1,014,492 for the windshields.

To hedge the $2,000,000 in car sales, USAuto needs to sell a DM forward contract. It needs to sell forward 2,898,550 DM for 180 days, which would be converted into

$2,000,000 after 180 days. However, because of the bid/offer spread, it can only sell forward the DMs at U.S.$.69 per DM or $1.971,014. The firm's higher costs are a result of paying a premium ($.70) when buying the contract and getting a discount ($.68) when selling a contract. This bid/offer spread is the price of locking in a fixed rate of exchange. It is also how the bank makes its commission on the transaction. This transaction could have been undertaken in any currency as long as the bank agreed to accept the risk. This is not true for futures contracts.

If, after 180 days, the DM depreciated to $.75, the windshields would have cost $1,086,956 instead of $1,014,492 if USAuto had not purchased the forward contract. The car sales revenue would have been $2,173,912 instead of $2,000,000. Net, the firm would have benefited from the DM move. However, if the DM appreciated to $.65 the windshields would have cost only $942,028 and the car revenue would have been only $1,884,057 without the forward contract.

Thus, forward contracting removes the risk of an unfavorable currency fluctuation by providing the buyer with a firm future price. The forward contract is bought by paying a substantial commission to the bank handling the transaction, and this is set by the difference between the bank's buy and sell price. To engage in forward buying, the firm must have a line of credit with the bank. Because the expense of individual contracting is significant, the forward market is limited to large customers dealing in foreign trade.

Futures Contracts

Futures contracts are a useful tool for hedging currency risk as well. They are very easy to buy and sell, and are extremely liquid. Most brokers can buy and sell futures contracts by making a telephone call. Futures contracts are much more structured than forward contracts. They always expire at a fixed date, usually the third Friday of March, June, September, and December. This time inflexibility can reduce the effectiveness of the hedge. Also, futures contracts can be traded only on the Japanese yen, German mark, Canadian dollar, British pound, Swiss franc, Australian dollar, and Mexican peso. However, other currency futures contracts exist in other countries' trading exchanges. This limited availability can hinder hedging effectiveness as well. Finally, the futures contracts are written for a prespecified amount of currency and are not flexible. All firms have to trade futures contracts in whole numbers. This also hinders the futures' hedging effectiveness.

The trade-off against all of these negatives is that futures contract trading is inexpensive and easy. Using the same USAuto example, we can calculate how to hedge against most of this currency risk. Assume the same bid/offer of U.S.$.68/.70 per DM. The DM futures contract trades in 125,000 DM lots, and one contract expires every 90 days.

For a 180-day hedge the firm has two options. First, it can buy the nearby contract and roll it over to the next contract after 90 days. Or the firm can buy the 180-day futures contract. The first strategy will create an unhedged exposure if after 90 days the DM has moved substantially, but the bid/offer spread will be very narrow (i.e., U.S.$.68/.70), for each futures contract. The second strategy will remove currency movement risk, but the bid offer spread will be wider (e.g., U.S.$.67/.71) causing the strategy to be slightly more expensive.

We will assume the first strategy for this example. To hedge the windshield purchase we need to hedge a 1,449,275 DM outflow. We also need to hedge a 2,898,550 DM inflow from the car sales. To hedge, we need to determine if we should buy or sell the futures contract. *A mistake in this determination will double a firm's currency risk exposure.* If operations managers are trying to hedge a cash outflow at a future date, they need to buy futures contracts. If a cash inflow is to be hedged, a sale of futures contracts should be made. Next, the manager needs to calculate how many contracts to buy or sell. The DM futures contract is for 125,000 DM each. So the manager would divide the DM amount to be hedged by 125,000. To overhedge, round up (this creates a small exposure); to underhedge, round down (this also creates a small exposure). The windshield purchase is a dollar cash outflow so the manager would buy DM futures contracts. The goal is to only pay $1,000,000 for the windshields. 1,449,275 DM times the current rate of $.69 equals $1,000,000. The hedger will pay $.70 for each DM to be hedged, although no cash changes hands in a futures contract transaction. (A margin account needs to be established, but it can be in Treasury bills so no opportunity cost is created.)

To calculate the number of contracts to buy to hedge the 1,449,275 DM, we need to divide by 125,000. This will give us 11.6 contracts. We can use DM forecasts to determine if we need to overhedge or underhedge. For this example, we will round up, or buy twelve contracts. We would agree to buy at $.70 per DM on twelve contracts, or 1,500,000 DM. That is a total of $1,050,000 worth of DMs.

After 90 days, if the exchange rate moves to $.80 per DM, we would pay out $1,159,420 for our windshields [1,449,275 (.8) = $1,159,420]. But we would make $150,000 on the futures contract. We buy 1,500,000 DM (.7) = $1,050,000, and sell 1,500,000 DM (.8) = $1,200,000. Our net outlay for the windshields would be $1,159,420 less $150,000, or $1,009,420.

If, after 90 days, the DM rate moved to $.60 per DM, we would be protected as well. We would pay out only $869,565 for the windshields (1,449.275 (.6) = $869,565), but we would lose $150,000 on the futures contract. We buy (−) $1,050,000 worth of DM (1,500,000 DM (.7) = $1,050,000) and sell back only (+) $900,000 worth of DM (1,500,000 DM (.6) = $900,000). So our net price paid for the windshields would be $1,019,565. The difference between the two examples is caused by the over/underhedge created by the inability to buy fractional contracts and by the bid/offer spread the market makers collect. The operations manager needs to be able to explain that the loss of $150,000 is part of the hedging strategy. Derivatives draw attention from shareholders and the press because they are misunderstood. It's not really a *loss,* but rather, the cost of locking in the $1,000,000 price for the windshields.

In the case of the incoming car sales revenue, USAuto can hedge just as effectively by selling futures contracts immediately. At the spot rate of $.69 per DM they need to lock in the $2,000,000 or 2,898,550 DM. To do this, USAuto should sell 23 DM futures contracts (2,898,550/125,000 = 23.2). As in the case of the windshields, this strategy will lock in an exchange rate 90 days before the cash actually changes hands. Again, due to the inability to buy fractional contracts and the bid/offer spread, the actual revenue received will vary slightly. Also, a futures loss in a hedge position needs to be explainable to management.

Some authors in the international operations area suggest that when a currency is expected to move against a firm's exposure, the firm should hedge. And, when a currency is expected to move in the firm's favor or is not expected to move, the firm should not hedge. *This idea is very dangerous.* It is similar to the idea that one should buy car insurance if one expects to be involved in an accident and not buy car insurance if one expects not to be involved in an accident. Speculative strategies on exchange rate movements should be avoided.

Another dangerous misunderstanding for international operations managers is based on the argument that exchange rate forecasts can predict what currencies will do over the long-term. This may be true, but foreign exchange markets don't just move in the long-term, they move in the very short-term. We would cite the Mexican peso as an example. In late 1994 the peso was appreciating fairly steadily. Wall Street expected it to continue its appreciation. However, in early 1995 the Mexican central bank unexpectedly devalued the peso by more than 20 percent. This shock caught most expert Wall Street forecasters completely off guard.

Firms should realize that they are not in the business of speculating on foreign currency movements. Not hedging a currency exposure is the same as speculating in the foreign exchange markets. Firms should stick to their core businesses (e.g., making cars), and not speculate on currency moves. That means always hedging away currency risk and not trying to "outsmart" the foreign exchange markets.

From our discussion so far, we can conceptualize the difference between a forward contract and a futures contract as follows: The forward contract avoids currency risk by locking a fixed exchange rate at a future date, while the future contract minimizes the currency risk by exploiting the movement of the exchange rate. If the buyer's selected currency of payment goes up in value in the interim, the buyer sells the futures contract for a profit and uses it to make up the difference when making sourcing payments. If, on the other hand, the buyer's selected currency falls in value, the buyer loses value when selling the futures contract but makes up most of the differential from the sourcing contract.

Options

An option is an insurance policy against adverse currency movements. Any firm can buy rights to sell or buy currencies at set prices. These hedging tools are structured like the futures contracts. The distinct advantage of an option is that if the currency moves in the buyer's favor, the buyer need not execute the option. The buyer will then make a profit on the currency move. If the currency moves against the firm, the option will be exercised and will protect the firm from exchange losses. An option, then, protects the buyer with zero downside potential. The chief disadvantage is that these instruments can be very expensive.

In the windshield example, when the currency moved to $.80 per DM the option would have given USAuto a $150,000 gain to negate the currency loss. If the exchange rate had instead moved to $.60 per DM the $150,000 loss would *not* have been incurred. However, the firm may have had to pay $20,000 for the option contract. Firms can easily adjust the amount of insurance they wish to buy. For instance if a firm bought a contract that only hedged half of the risk, it should have made $75,000 but paid only $10,000. Also a firm can adjust the rate at which insurance begins to cover the loss. USAuto could have bought an option that covered losses past $.65 per DM. This lower level of protection would have also cost USAuto less in insurance premiums.

Apart from these methods of reducing exchange rate risks, involved parties also use various forms of risk-sharing contracts. One common type of risk-sharing contract stipulates that exchange rate losses, or gains, are to be shared equally (or by a prespecified percentage) by both parties (buyer and supplier). Thus, if the buying power of the U.S. dollar declines, the loss incurred by the buyer computed with respect to the original contract price (expressed in U.S.$) is divided equally (or by a prespecified percentage) and subtracted from the current (higher) cost of the needed quantity of foreign currency. If the buying power of the U.S. dollar increases, the gain experienced by the buyer is divided equally and added to the current (lower) cost of the needed quantity of foreign currency.

Another type of risk-sharing contract employs an *exchange rate window*. The window is defined as plus or minus a given percentage movement in the exchange rate. As long as the exchange rate varies within the window, no adjustments to price are made. If the exchange rate moves outside the window, the price is adjusted. The adjustment process might require renegotiation of the contract price, or it might involve the use of a risk-sharing formula.

◆ MACRO-LEVEL STRATEGIES

Even though operations managers are trained to thoroughly screen potential foreign suppliers by considering a myriad of factors such as quality, delivery service, technical support, price, and managerial capability, it is still rare to find operations managers that accurately and consistently use exchange rate information in the supplier selection decision. The firm survey of Carter and Vickery found that only 20 percent of the surveyed firms used exchange rate information as an input to the source selection decision, and only 10 percent used exchange rate information in the volume-timing of purchases decision.

The simplest way to demonstrate the importance of the use of exchange rate information in the supplier selection decision is through an example. A U.S. electronics firm is considering entering into a sourcing contract for electronics components with one of two equally qualified suppliers, one Japanese and one Korean. The proposed contract with the Japanese supplier calls for the payment of yen in twenty-two biweekly installments of 15.365 million yen (exchange rate of 153.65 yen/U.S.$ at the date of the decision), while the contract with the Korean supplier calls for the payment of won in an equal number of biweekly installments of 88.41 million won (exchange rate of 884.1 won/U.S.$ at the date of the decision). Both contracts evaluated at the exchange rate of the date of the decision involve twenty-two payments of $100,000, thus an undiscounted value of $2.2 million.

In Table 9–5, we present the naturally required payments based on realized exchange rates. The Korean won rather consistently depreciated over the contract period, while the Japanese yen depreciated in the early parts of the contract but appreciated later. Clearly, from the results in Table 9–5, expected exchange rate movements seriously affect supplier selection in this situation.

It is straightforward to conclude that global supplier selection should be based on forecast information about exchange rate movements. However, the difficulty lies in the implementation—that is, in developing forecasts that are relatively accurate. In practice, it has been found that the accurate forecasting of exchange rates is extremely difficult. While a number of professional forecasting services exist, their mediocre track records attest to the challenge accurate forecasting presents. The point, however, should not be misunderstood. Regardless of the difficulty in estimating exchange rate movements, it is still to the advantage of the global firm to consider exchange rate information during supplier selection rather than ignore it.

Flexibility in the structure of global sourcing contracts in terms of the timing or purchases and volume adjustments allowed is misunderstood and inadequately practiced by operations managers in volatile exchange rate environments. Unstable exchange rate environments provide the buyer with an opportunity to either exploit favorable price changes or avoid unfavorable price differentials through the timing of and volume adjustments in the purchased amount. The intuition behind this strategy is simple. If the price of a particular item (i.e., foreign currency appreciates) is expected to increase, the buyer could purchase in a quantity larger than the usual and store the inventory until needed. If the prices are expected to decrease (i.e., depreciation of foreign currency) the firm should delay to the extent possible its purchases, depleting previous built-up inventory.

In many situations firms might have a limited control over the price specified on the sourcing contract, but through careful and innovative structuring of the supply contract, they can influence substantially the actual price they pay, and thus improve their overall competitiveness.

Returning to our supplier selection example, we demonstrate how flexibility in timing/ volume of purchase can be advantageously used. A suggested buying policy is presented in

Table 9–5

	Example Data to Illustrate Use of Exchange Rate Information on Supplier Selection			
Payment#	Exch. Rate ¥/$	US$ Needed	Exch. Rate W/$	US$ Needed
1	153.65	100,000	884.1	100,000
2	153.87	99,857.02	884.8	99,920.89
3	153.80	99,902.47	880.7	100,386.06
4	155.25	98,969.40	879.3	100,545.89
5	154.30	99,578.74	879.1	100,568.76
6	154.40	99,514.25	860.0	102,802.33
7	161.40	95,198.27	874.0	101,155.61
8	163.50	93,975.54	874.0	101,155.61
9	164.00	93,689.02	868.9	101,749.34
10	162.10	94,787.17	867.5	101,913.54
11	163.10	94,206.01	867.3	101,937.05
12	158.10	97,185.33	861.4	102,635.24
13	153.40	100,162.97	858.1	103,029.95
14	153.50	100,097.72	857.9	103,053.97
15	153.60	100,032.55	856.3	103,246.53
16	153.66	99,993.49	855.8	103,306.86
17	152.20	100,886.41	855.0	103,403.51
18	147.20	104,381.79	851.8	103,791.97
19	142.80	107,598.04	844.3	104,713.96
20	139.75	109,946.33	844.3	104,713.96
21	139.55	110,103.91	835.2	105,854.89
22	140.67	109,227.27	831.1	106,377.09
		TOTAL 2,209,293.70$		2,256,263.00$

Japanese Yen Contract 15.365M¥/payment
Korean Won Contract 88.41MW/payment

Table 9–6. As one can see, buying forward when the yen appreciates results in an improved overall cost of the sourcing contract (savings of $2,209,293.70–2,174,698.40 = $34,595.30). In deciding the timing of the increased purchased quantities, one has to trade off expected savings in the purchasing price with increased inventory holding costs.

Recent research literature points out the benefits of operational hedging against currency risks by establishing a portfolio of suppliers in different countries and exploiting the sourcing flexibility in response to exchange rate movements. The firm's ability to adapt its sourcing strategy in response to altered macroeconomic conditions increases its value (or decreases its sourcing costs) by improving its upside profit potential while limiting downside losses. For example, if a firm sources from two foreign suppliers, and the cost of one of them increases due to its currency appreciation, the firm has the option to switch some or all of the sourced quantity, depending on the nature of the contract, to the other supplier with the more favorable cost structure. The irreversible nature of supplier switching due to switchover costs (examples of such costs are contract termination penalties, loss of transportation economies due to lower sourced volumes from a specific country, cost of finding and developing new suppliers, developing needed infrastructure such as local freight forwarders and hiring

Table 9–6

Example Data to Illustrate Advantages of Flexibility in Timing/Volume of Purchase in Global Sourcing Contracts

Period#	Purchase in Yen (in weeks of demand)		Exch. Rate ¥/$	U.S.$ Needed
1	15.365 million (2 weeks)		153.65	100,000
2	15.365 million (2 weeks)		153.87	99,857.02
3	15.365 million (2 weeks)		153.80	99,902.47
4	15.365 million (2 weeks)		155.25	98,964.40
5	15.365 million (2 weeks)		154.30	99,578.74
6	15.365 million (2 weeks)		154.40	99,514.25
7	15.365 million (2 weeks)		161.40	95,198.27
8	15.365 million (2 weeks)		163.50	93,975.54
9	15.365 million (2 weeks)		164.00	93,689.02
10	15.365 million (2 weeks)		162.10	94,787.17
11	15.365 million (2 weeks)		163.10	94,206.01
12	92.190 million (12 weeks)		158.10	583,111.95
13	0	0		0
14	0	0		0
15	0	0		0
16	0	0		0
17	0	0		0
18	76.825 million (10 weeks)		147.20	521,908.96
19	0	0		0
20	0	0		0
21	0	0		0
22	0	0		0
				Total 2,174,698.40$

administrative personnel for locally handling sourcing details), and the future uncertainty in exchange rates make the choice of timing in switching of suppliers a critical issue.

From what we discussed in this chapter, the optimal operating policy in switching between suppliers in a global sourcing arrangement resembles entry/exit decisions in foreign markets under exchange rate uncertainty. We will try to draw insights on the nature of supplier switching decisions by drawing a parallel to entry/exit decisions and what we know about such decisions so far.

In the global sourcing context, the entry into and exit from foreign markets can be thought of as switching between two suppliers in different countries, with one of them being the home country (market where the final product is sold). The option to enter a foreign market (i.e., source from a foreign supplier) is similar to a financial call option where the exercise price is the cost of the investment required to enter the market (i.e., set up the foreign supplying arrangement). The option to enter (foreign source) is not exercised unless expected operating profits (purchasing cost savings) are at least sufficient to provide the required rate of return on committed capital. The option to exit (use home country supplier) is not exercised until operating profits (purchasing cost savings) are insufficient to provide the required rate of return on the salvageable capital. The gap between the expected profits that trigger entry and exit (switching from home to foreign supplier and vice versa) induces a hysteresis (inaction, inertia) in the firm's investment (foreign sourcing) behavior. An increase in exchange rate volatility widens the gap, thus increasing hysteresis.

Before we conclude this chapter, we will provide one more example to demonstrate the effectiveness of the various hedging strategies in an illustrative global sourcing situation. The main objective of this illustration is to indicate the benefits of operationally hedging through a global supplier portfolio in sourcing environments with currency risks.

Consider a U.S. firm that can source from two foreign suppliers, one in Canada and the other in Japan. The current date is January 1, and the goods are needed on January 1, April 1, July 1, October 1 of the current year, and January 1 and April 1 of the following year. The current price quoted by both suppliers for each shipment is U.S.$100,000. Both suppliers have agreed to freeze their price at the current rate (in U.S. dollars) for the next six quarters. Assume that payment is made on the date of purchase.

The spot, forward, and futures rates for the two currencies are given in Table 9–7a. The spot rate is the actual realized exchange rate between the currencies of the two countries; the forward rate is the rate at which a financial institution will sell forward currency contracts, and the futures rate is the rate at which currency futures are traded in the currency futures market.

Now consider the effect of various hedging strategies on sourcing from the Canadian supplier. Referring to the situation just described, if the firm pays throughout the six quarters in U.S. dollars (called *base case strategy,* henceforth), the net present value (NPV) of its payment stream for the next six quarters is $479,078.68, irrespective of the realized exchange rates throughout the time period. All results related to this example are tabulated in Table 9–7b. All the reported costs in this table are in U.S. dollars, and the discount rate used for NPV calculations is 0.1 per quarter. If the firm pays throughout in Canadian dollars without any hedging, the NPV of its costs will be $449,546.64, making a net gain of $29,532.04 compared to the previous case. If it were to get into a risk-sharing agreement with its suppliers (sharing 50 percent of loss or gain because of the exchange rate movement) while paying in Canadian dollars, its NPV would be $464,312.66. The gain is less than the previous case because of the sharing of gains with the supplier.

If the firm decides to pay the Canadian supplier in Canadian dollars and hedge its risk by buying forward contracts from a financial institution, it can buy contracts at the forward rates and use these to settle its accounts. The NPV of its payments in this case is $456,986.90. Suppose the firm decides to hedge its risk by buying currency futures instead of forward contracts. To keep the exposition simple, assume that one futures contract for the Canadian dollar is for the delivery of U.S.$100,000 and the delivery dates are the same as the dates the firm needs to make the payments. The firm therefore buys long on futures contract at the beginning of each quarter and uses this to hedge against the exchange rate risk for its payment that is due at the end of the quarter. In this case, the NPV of the firm's payment is $459,354.38. Table 9–7 also reports the respective costs associated with sourcing from the Japanese supplier using these hedging strategies.

Using any of these strategies, the firm could have kept its sourcing costs close to the NPV of a stable currency (i.e., $100,000 every quarter for the next six quarters), which we describe as the base case strategy. Now consider the situation where the firm switched between suppliers to take advantage of favorable exchange rates. Table 9–7c shows the optimal sourcing strategy for any given starting supplier. If the firm chooses to start with the Canadian firm, it will make four switches in six quarters. It would have to make five switches if it started sourcing from the Japanese supplier. The NPV of the payments is $441,465.37.

The numerical example, though simple, clearly illustrates that maintaining a portfolio of suppliers and switching among them in order to take advantage of the exchange rate

Table 9-7   *Illustrative Example on Effectiveness of Various Strategies in Global Sourcing*

Table 9-7a

Assumed Information on Spot, Forward, and Futures Rates for Canada and Japan

| Date | Canada | | | Japan | | |
	Spot	Forward	Futures	Spot	Forward	Futures
1-Jan	1.168	1.180	1.182	158.856	158.813	158.721
1-Apr	1.283	1.299	1.297	150.202	151.576	150.998
1-Jul	1.297	1.160	1.163	177.986	166.243	166.565
1-Oct	1.294	1.311	1.301	148.896	147.966	147.786
1-Jan	1.129	1.290	1.299	171.786	171.967	171.567
1-Apr	1.342	1.313	1.315	146.976	146.786	146.896

Table 9-7b

Total Sourcing Costs on Various Sourcing Strategies

	Canada	Japan
U.S. dollars	$479,078.68	$479,078.68
Foreign currency	$449,546.64	$480,336.10
For. curr.-risk sharing	$464,312.66	$479,707.39
Forward contracts	$456,986.90	$480,026.54
Futures	$459,354.38	$474,229.50
Switching to cheapest supplier	$441,465.37	$441,465.37
Combination of futures and supplier switching	$451,273.11	$435,358.77

Table 9-7c

Optimal Sourcing Strategy and Timing of Supplier Switches

Date	Sourcing Strategy	
1-Jan	Starting-Canada	Starting-Japan
1-Apr	Canada	Japan
1-Jul	Canada	Canada
1-Oct	Japan	Japan
1-Jan	Canada	Canada
1-Apr	Japan	Japan
	Canada	Canada
	4 Switches	5 Switches

fluctuations can be used as an alternative to "financial" as well as "contractual" (risk-sharing) hedging. Because the currencies of the two countries move in opposite directions during the six quarters of the sourcing arrangement, the buyer can take advantage of the fluctuations of the exchange rates by always choosing the cheapest source. These calculations do not take into account the transaction costs associated with implementing each of the hedging strategies (i.e., costs of purchasing the futures or forward contracts, switchover costs between suppliers). It can be argued that the transaction costs for financial instruments may be lower than the costs of switching between suppliers, but given the big difference in the NPV of the switching option and the other hedging mechanisms, the use of this strategy should not be ruled out. In particular, if the operational hedging is combined with appropriate financial hedging to avoid short-term risks of macroeconomic shocks, the firm can obtain substantial long-term profitability benefits. In our example, the combination of a "futures" contract and a supplier switching strategy leads to the lowest overall sourcing cost of $435,358.77 from the Japanese supplier.

Summary

Clearly the operations/logistics manager must be thoroughly versed in the workings of the world currency markets in order to minimize the company's risk both in operations and in sourcing strategies. In this chapter we have elaborated in detail the concepts of operating exposure when dealing with the exchange rate risk. In particular we have defined the three types of exposure that companies face in front of exchange rate fluctuations: Transaction, Translation and Operations exposure. More than the traditional financial hedging strategies, we have presented new alternatives to manage the risk and hedge the company in a more complete way. This is accomplished by operational hedging and its implementation is linked to the additional factors that complicate the assessment of the true operating risk such as customer reactions, competitor reactions, supplier reactions and government reactions.

The examples outlined in this chapter can assist operations/logistics managers in understanding the options and making choices that benefit the corporation over the long run. In addition to presenting general options for managing the operating exposure risk, we have developed specific price strategies for exporting firms and detailed micro- and macro-level strategies for managing that risk.

DISCUSSION QUESTIONS

1. Why does an operations and logistics manager need to worry about exchange rate fluctuations in managing a global firm?

2. What are the three different types of exposure to exchange rate fluctuations? How do you differentiate one from the other? Which exposure is the most important, and which one can an operations and logistics manager affect?

3. What is *real exchange rate,* and how does it differ from *nominal exchange rate?*

4. What is Purchasing Power Parity?

5. Provide examples of positive and negative operating exposure to fluctuations of a foreign currency real exchange rate.

6. What are the complicating factors that a firm needs to consider in assessing its operating exposure to real

exchange rate shocks? Provide examples of situations in which each one of these factors might play an important role in affecting the firm's operating exposure to an exchange rate shock.

7. Use the simple construct of an operating exposure matrix to discuss illustrative situations of operating exposure to exchange rate shocks.

8. Explain why firms in the same industry might end up having different operating exposures to the same exchange rate shock.

9. How would you estimate a firm's operating exposure to an anticipated future exchange rate shock?

10. How can an operations and logistics manager help in managing the firm's operating exposure?

11. What is operational hedging of operating exposure to exchange rate risks? How is it different from financial

hedging? What are the advantages and shortcomings of operational hedging versus financial hedging?

12. Describe some pricing strategies that a firm can use to respond to fluctuations of exchange rates.

13. How can a firm use operational flexibility in its global manufacturing and distribution network to respond effectively to exchange rate fluctuations? Provide examples of ways to use operational flexibility for operational hedging purposes.

14. Explain the notion of *hysteresis* in firm behavior in switching between operating strategies in the presence of switch-over costs and uncertainty in the operating environment.

15. Differentiate between macro-level and micro-level currency management strategies. Provide examples of each.

16. Define spot, forward, and futures markets.

17. What are the advantages and disadvantages of using forward contracts to hedge exchange rate risks in sourcing contracts?

18. What are the advantages and disadvantages of using futures contracts to hedge exchange rate risks in sourcing contracts?

19. What are the advantages and disadvantages of using options to hedge exchange rate risks in sourcing contracts?

20. What are aspects of flexibility in the structure of global sourcing contracts that firms can advantageously use to operationally hedge exchange rate risks?

21. What are the advantages and disadvantages of using multi-supplier arrangements in sourcing environments with exchange rate uncertainty?

22. Why do you think firms might have to use both financial and operational hedging tools simultaneously to more effectively hedge against exchange rate risks in sourcing situations?

REFERENCES

Carter, J. R., and S. K. Vickery. 1988. Managing volatile exchange rates in international purchasing. *Journal of Purchasing and Materials Management* (Winter): 13–20.

Carter, J. R., and S. K. Vickery. 1989. Currency exchange rates: Their impact on global sourcing. *Journal of Purchasing and Materials Management* (Fall): 19–25.

Carter, J. R., and R. Narasimhan. 1990. Purchasing in the international marketplace: Implications for operations. *Journal of Purchasing and Materials Management* (Summer): 2–11.

Dixit, A. K. 1989. Entry and exit decisions under uncertainty. *Journal of Political Economy* 97 (3): 620–38.

Hertzell, S., and C. Casper. 1988. Rethinking financial strategies: Coping with unpredictable exchange rates. *The McKinsey Quarterly* (Summer): 12–24.

Hooper, Peter, and Catherine L. Mann. 1989. Exchange rate pass-through in the 1980s: The case of the U.S. imports of manufacturers. *Brookings Papers on Economic Activity* (1): 297–329.

Huchzermeier A., and M. A. Cohen. Valuing Operational Flexibility Under Exchange Rate Risk. Operations Research 44(1): 100–113.

Hull, J. C. 1993. *Options, futures and other derivative securities*. Englewood Cliffs, N.J.: Prentice Hall.

Kogut, B., and N. Kulatilaka. 1994. Operating flexibility, global manufacturing, and the option value of a multinational network. *Management Science* 40 (1): 123–39.

Kouvelis, P., and V. Sinha. 1995. Exchange rates and the choice of production strategies in supplying foreign markets. Working paper, The Fuqua School of Business, Duke University.

Kouvelis, P., and V. Sinha. 1996. Exchange rates and the choice of production strategies in supplying foreign markets. Working paper, The Fuqua School of Business, Duke University.

Lessard, D. R., and J. B. Lightstone. 1986. Volatile exchange rates can put operations at risk. *Harvard Business Review*, No. 86405 (July–August): 107–14.

◆ Case 9–1: BMW: Globalizing Manufacturing Operations ◆

BMW's new plant at Spartanburg, South Carolina, was a source of pride. In a record-breaking 24 months, BMW had put together a state-of-the-art facility. By September 1995, only a year after the first vehicle (a model) had rolled off its assembly line, BMW management was considering expanding the plant's capacity ahead of schedule. This was to accommodate a faster ramp-up of production of the Z3—a brand-new roadster produced only at Spartanburg (see Exhibit 13). Eberhard Von Kuenheim, chairman of the BMW Supervisory Board and former CEO, took pride in this accomplishment:

The United States is the largest, most competitive and dynamic consumer market in the world. If BMW cannot thrive in the U.S. market, it will ultimately suffer the same fate in Europe.

I do not think the Japanese have anything to teach BMW. We plan to produce a brand new model at our American plant. The Japanese would consider that too risky in a new factory with a new work force. Their transplants began by making models already produced in Japan to make it easier to develop factory skills and establish high quality practices before they dared to introduce a new model.

For Spartanburg, the challenge of producing a brand new model had become even more arduous by an unexpected surge in the demand for the Z3. An astute advertising campaign for the Z3 as James Bond's car in the movie *Golden Eye,* favorable reviews in trade journals, and the car's relatively low price had created high demand for the car. In September 1995, as the first Z3s were being produced, Al Kinzer, president of BMW Manufacturing Corp. (BMW MC), was under pressure to formulate a strategy for dealing with this unexpected demand. He

was proud of what had already been accomplished at Spartanburg and wanted to be sure that this short-term pressure would not cause a long-term setback for BMW MC.

The History of BMW

Traces of BMW's origin may be found in its logo: a rotating propeller in blue and white, the colors of Bavaria. In 1913, Karl Rapp opened an aircraft engine design shop near Munich and called it RAPP-Motorenwerke. It became Bayerische Motoren Werke in 1917. After WWI, the Treaty of Versailles prohibited German firms from producing aircraft and aircraft engines. BMW sought other engine-making opportunities, and in 1922 began producing a small engine for the Victoria motorcycle. One year later BMW began production of the R 32 motorcycle.

In late 1928, BMW acquired the struggling Eisenach Vehicle Factory, just north of Munich. Eisenach had been making cars since 1899. When BMW took over, the factory was producing a single model, a licensed version of England's Austin Seven. This car would become the first BMW automobile, known as the 3/15 or "Dixi." In the years that followed, BMW moved quickly, introducing several new models and enlarging its engines from 1.2 liters to 3.5 liters. During the 1930s, BMW established its reputation as a maker of high-quality, sporting motor vehicles. By winning famous races—such as Italy's Mille Miglia in 1939—BMW's fame spread. When WWII broke out, BMW was forced to build engines for the German Luftwaffe, and ceased all auto and motorcycle production. Its factories were dismantled after the war, but BMW survived by making kitchen and garden equipment. The Eisenach plant, where all BMW cars had been produced, was in the eastern zone, which later became East Germany.

Shortly thereafter, BMW rebuilt its bombed-out Munich plant and began producing motorcycles again. In 1948, the company introduced a one-cylinder motorcycle, which sold well as cheap transportation in postwar Germany. But that did not pull BMW out of trouble. BMW cars produced in the 1950s were too large and expensive for the postwar economy, and sales were disappointing. As motorcycle sales began to decline, BMW was again on the verge of bankruptcy. In 1959, Herbert Quandt bought control of BMW for $1 million. Quandt was a visionary who set a new direction for BMW, concentrating on sport sedans. He was determined to build a car for the driver, as opposed to the rider. The first of the "new range" of BMWs was

---

This case was prepared by Sibel Berzeg, Michael Maier and Juan Carlos Páez, Georgetown MBA '96, under the guidance of Professor Kasra Ferdows, Georgetown University School of Business, as a basis for class discussion rather than to illustrate either effective or ineffective handling of an administrative situation.

launched in 1961. This niche strategy proved successful, and in 1966 BMW expanded by purchasing the ailing auto-manufacturing company Hans Glas.

Over the next two decades, BMW grew considerably. It climbed from 69th to 11th place among Germany's top industrial corporations, and its market value reached almost $9 billion. Still, BMW was small compared to the big U.S. auto makers: it was one-third the size of Ford, and one-fourth the size of GM. The Quandt family still owned 60% of BMW, and many believed that this allowed the company to accept moderate short-term returns in exchange for long-run profit potential. BMW was one of only two auto manufacturers that had continuously shown a profit for thirty years. From 1984 through 1994, sales grew almost 8% annually, while profits grew approximately 1.5% annually. Although the overall trend was upward, in 1990 and 1993 BMW's profits declined. In 1994, sales and profits increased substantially. This was partly due to the acquisition of the Rover Group (UK), but even after adjusting for that, sales and profits grew at a healthy rate throughout 1994 (see Exhibit 1).

BMW 1995

BMW had 34 wholly owned subsidiaries—14 in Germany and 20 dispersed around the world. It also had more than 130 foreign sales operations. Before the Spartanburg plant, BMW's manufacturing activities were essentially concentrated in seven plants in Germany. These included a motor-cycle plant in Berlin, a tooling plant in Eisenach (now a part of re-unified Germany) and a plant in Steyr, Austria (three hours south of Munich by car). The plant in Austria was BMW's largest facility for production of its 4- and 6-cylinder engines. BMW also operated various so-called "kit factories" outside Europe. Kit factories assembled either complete knockdown kits (CKDs) or semi-knockdown kits (SKDs). BMW's oldest and most sophisticated SKD plant was located in Rosslyn, South Africa (near Pretoria). In Thailand, Indonesia, and Malaysia, local partners assembled BMW cars under joint manufacturing agreements (see Exhibit 2). In 1994, two new assembly plants were established, one in the Philippines and another in Vietnam avoiding high tariffs, taxes and trade restrictions. The kits supplied from Germany were exempt from these restrictions because they were augmented with locally purchased components and complied with local content and value added regulations.

BMW's market share in Germany had increased in recent years to 6.69%; but the figure for the United States was a disappointing 0.94% (see Exhibit 3). The German market was served by 800 exclusive dealerships, while the much larger U.S. market was served by only 354 dealers, only 30% of them exclusive.

BMW in the United States

BMW of North America, Inc. (BMW NA) was established in 1975. The "yuppie" generation's preference for imported

Exhibit 1

BMW Group in Figures						
		1990	1991	1992	1993	1994
Sales	DM million	27,178	29,839	31,241	29,016	42,125
Rover Group contribution to sales	DM million	–	–	–	–	10,173
Percent change in sales	%	2.5	9.8	4.7	-7.1	45.2
BMW automobile sales	units	525,866	552,660	594,895	535,492	568,733
Rover Group automobile sales	units	–	–	–	–	391,700
BMW motorcycle sales	units	29,701	32,187	35,675	35,031	44,203
Work force		70,984	74,385	73,562	71,034	109,362
Investment	DM million	2,066	2,123	1,975	2,214	3,543
Investment as a percent of sales	%	7.6	7.1	6.3	7.6	8.4
Cash flow		2,780	2,831	2,880	2,567	3,569
Fixed assets	DM million	6,707	6,748	6,834	7,151	11,748
Total assets	DM million	22,501	25,405	27,504	30,295	38,693
Shareholders' equity	DM million	5,860	6,392	6,718	7,025	7,922
Material cost	DM million	15,749	17,472	18,542	17,368	24,694
Personnel cost	DM million	5,314	5,823	5,387	6,245	8,425
Net income	DM million	696	783	726	516	697

Source: BMW Annual Report 1994.

Exhibit 2

	Work force	Production Capability	Capacity (per day)	Plant Area (in sq.m.)
		BMW Plants		
Munich, Germany	11,700	3-series, 6.8 and 12 cylinder engines	850 cars, 950 engines	450,000
Dingolfing, Germany	17,528	5-series, 7 and 8-series, axles and central part supply	900 cars	1,500,000
Regensburg, Germany	7,420	3-series sedan, coupe, and convertible, components	700 cars	1,420,000
Landshut, Germany	3,056	components and parts	n/a	320,000
Eisenach, Germany	212	tooling	n/a	85,000
Berlin, Germany	511	R and K series motorcycles, motorcycle engines	150 engines	195,000
Steyr, Austria	2,116	4 and 6 cylinder engines	1600 engines	206,000
Rosslyn, South Africa	2,920	parts and electronics, kit assembly	n/a	n/a
Spartanburg, U.S.	591	3-series, Z3 roadster	120 cars	135,000

December 1994.

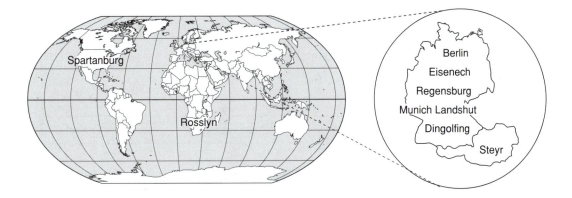

cars in the early 1980s made the United States the fastest growing market for BMW. By 1994, the United States was BMW's largest export market. BMW exported 84,500 units, 14.7% of its total automobile production, to the United States that year. Accordingly, the trends in the U.S. market in the late 1980s and early 1990s had a huge impact on BMW. Between 1986 and 1991 the United States automobile industry experienced a 24% decline in sales (20% between 1986 and 1989). The stock market crash of 1987 and the Tax Reform Act of the same year (which directly affected deductions and depreciation on luxury vehicles), made owning a luxury car less affordable. Also, a "luxury tax" of 10% was levied on cars selling for more than $30,000, and the "gas guzzler" tax was doubled. By 1989, total BMW sales in the United States had fallen to 65% of the 1986 level. By 1991, BMW realized that there were serious limitations to its export strategy in the U.S. market (see Exhibit 4).

Meanwhile, Japanese automobile manufacturers had started to introduce a new group of lower-end luxury cars. In 1986, Honda introduced the Acura, and in 1989, Nissan introduced the Infiniti and Toyota introduced the Lexus. These strong models were favorably reviewed, and quickly established a reputation for quality, service, and reliability among the U.S. consumers. The Japanese undertook an aggressive strategy to gain market share and drastically undercut BMW's prices with similar product offerings. While BMW's least expensive 3 series in 1990 was $25,000 to $35,000, Acura's most affordable model was $22,000 to $29,000. Both Lexus and Infiniti offered a range of models priced from the low $20,000s to the upper $30,000s. The Japanese manufacturers were also overspending BMW in advertising (Lexus's 1991 advertising budget was double that of BMW). Although these luxury models were imported from Japan, Japanese manufacturers had set up impressive factories in the United States and were rapidly

Exhibit 3

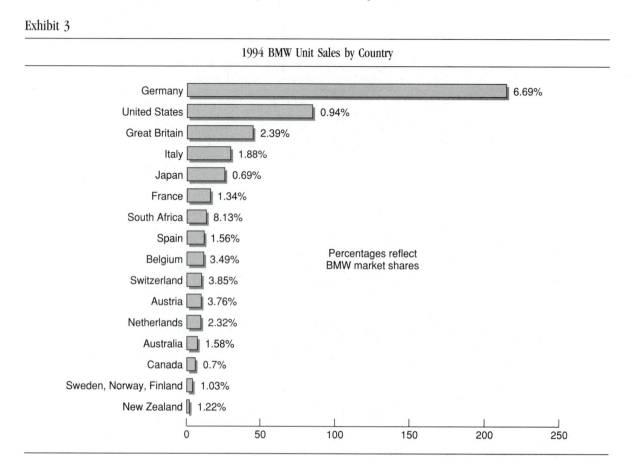

1994 BMW Unit Sales by Country

Country	Market Share
Germany	6.69%
United States	0.94%
Great Britain	2.39%
Italy	1.88%
Japan	0.69%
France	1.34%
South Africa	8.13%
Spain	1.56%
Belgium	3.49%
Switzerland	3.85%
Austria	3.76%
Netherlands	2.32%
Australia	1.58%
Canada	0.7%
Sweden, Norway, Finland	1.03%
New Zealand	1.22%

Percentages reflect
BMW market shares

Exhibit 4

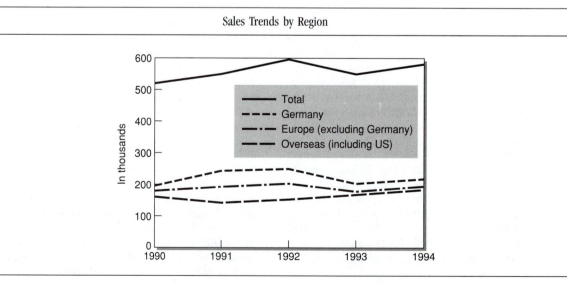

Sales Trends by Region

Exhibit 5

		Transplant Car Factories in the United States			
	Production Launch	Location	Products	Employment	1994 Capacity (cars only)	Ownership
Auto Alliance Intern. Inc.	1987	Flat Rock, MI	Mazda MX-6, 626 Ford Probe	3,800	240,000	Ford 50%, Mazda 50%
Diamond Star Motores Corp.	1988	Normal, IL	Mitsubishi Eclips and Galant, Chrysler Sebring, Dodge Avenger, Eagle Talon	3,900	240,000	Mitsubishi 100%
Honda of America Mfg. Inc.	1979 1982 (cars)	Marysville, OH East Liberty, OH Anna, OH	Accord sedan, coupe, motorcycles, TRX utility vehicle, Civic sedan and coupe car and motorcycle engines	10,100	380,000 220,000 575,000 engines	Honda 100%
New United Motor Mfg. Inc. (NUMMI)	1984	Fermont, CA	Toyota Corolla, Tacoma pick up, Geo Prizm	4,600	370,000	GM 50%, Toyota 50%
Nissan Motor Manufacturing Corp. USA	1983	Smyma, TN	Altima, Sentra, 200SX coupe, compact pickups, engines and components	6,000	450,000	Nissan 100%
Subaru-Isuzu Automotive Inc.	1989	Lafayette, IN	Isuzu pickup, Rodeo, Honda Passport, Subaru Legacy	2,220	170,000	Fuji 51%, Isuzu 49%
Toyota Motor Mfg. USA Inc.	1988	Georgetown, KY	Camry, Avalon, engines and axles	6,000	400,000 cars, 500,000 engines	Toyota 100%
Mercedes Benz US Intern. Inc.	1997 (planned)	Vance, AL	sport utility vehicle	n/a	60,000 to 80,000	Daimler-Benz 100%
BMW Manufacturing Corporation	1994	Spartanburg, SC	3 series, Z3 Roadster	2,000 (by 1997)	90,000 (by 1997)	BMW 100%

Source: Ward's Automotive Yearbook 1994/1995

expanding production in these factories (see Exhibit 5 and Exhibit 6).

At the same time, a soaring German mark and high labor costs in Germany were putting more pressure on BMW. The mark had appreciated against the dollar over the previous ten years (see Exhibit 7). With most of its costs denominated in marks and virtually all of its manufacturing activities concentrated in Germany, BMW had no operational hedge, and currency fluctuations were eating into its profit margins. With an average of $22.32 per hour, wage rates in Germany were 45% higher than those in the United States ($15.38). Also, Germans worked an average of 1,647 hours per year, 16% fewer hours than workers in the United States. Higher fringe benefits, longer vacations and higher absenteeism further contributed to elevate labor cost in Germany—making it among the highest in the world.

Direct labor constituted about 15% of BMW's total production cost. It was estimated that BMW's production cost in Germany exceeded U.S. production cost by 30% due to Germany's more expensive labor, materials, and overhead functions.

All this pointed to the need for more aggressive measures to maintain and increase market share in the United States. In 1991 BMW's German plants were operating at capacity—550,000 units per year. Any significant increase in output would require further investment in production facilities. As Eberhard Von Kuenheim, BMW's soft-spoken, aristocratic chairman at that time, put it, "An American factory is a logical next step for BMW because, among other things, it would reduce our exposure to exchange-rate fluctuations." Thus, plans for establishment of a U.S. factory went into high gear. In the interim, BMW

Exhibit 6

Production Data of Japanese Transplants in the United States

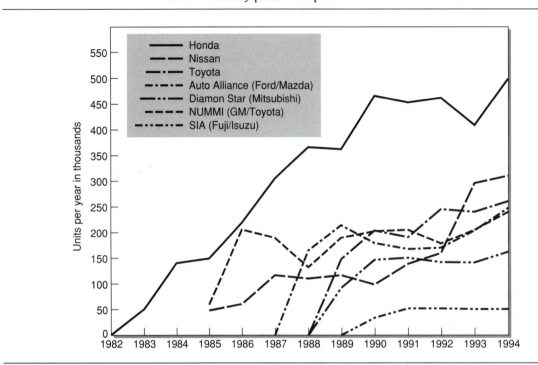

Exhibit 7

Exchange Rate Index

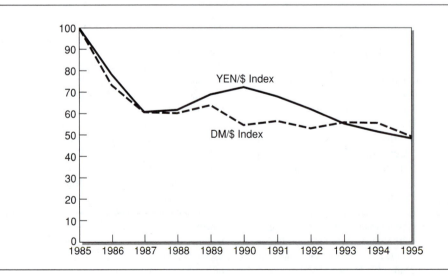

repositioned its 5- and 7-series luxury models by cutting prices. Although this reduced profitability for these models, it allowed the company to maintain its market share in the early 1990s (see Exhibit 8 and Exhibit 9). In 1994, BMW began to import its 3-series coupe (or "compact") to the United States. With a sticker price of $20,000, this car was the least expensive BMW on the market. It was BMW's first attempt to appeal to a more price-sensitive consumer, which meant that BMW had to sacrifice its usual high profit margins.

Manufacturing in the United States

Von Kuenheim's objectives for the U.S. plant went beyond reduction of short-term costs and exposure to currency fluctuations. He stated that expanding production to the United States would help BMW "maintain, secure, and build up its position in the United States luxury-car market, the world's biggest." To achieve this position, Von Kuenheim believed that BMW should develop a flexible and technologically advanced plant and take full advantage of being close to the demanding American consumer.

On June 22, 1992, BMW announced that it would set up a manufacturing plant in Spartanburg, South Carolina. This announcement was the result of a long process during which BMW narrowed its choice from 215 possible locations to 4. Spartanburg triumphed over competing sites partly due to an attractive incentive package from the South Carolina state government, which included reduced building and infrastructure costs. Furthermore, the BMW plant was granted free-trade status as a part of the Greenville-Spartanburg airport's free-trade zone. This meant that BMW would not pay U.S. duties on parts imported from Germany or elsewhere unless the final product was sold in the United States. The free-trade zone status would provide considerable savings on duties, which would only be paid at the vehicle's final destination—be it the United States or another country. Financing charges would also be reduced, as duties would be paid only after the completed car had left the factory.

The South Carolina site also provided other advantages: it offered easy access to highways and rail, it was close to the big port of Charleston, and was only ten minutes from an international airport. Also, the cost of living in the region was considerably lower than many other areas in the United States.

In 1994, BMW AG (Germany) established the BMW Manufacturing Corporation as a wholly owned subsidiary with headquarters in Spartanburg, SC. BMW MC was in charge of manufacturing operations and various corporate functions such as human resources, finance, and purchasing for North America. This did not affect BMW NA (headquartered in New Jersey), which was still responsible for marketing and sales in the United States.

Building a Plant in the United States

Press releases, a vision statement, and interviews by several BMW officials all indicated an ambitious goal for the newly created BMW MC:

To quickly develop a flexible, technologically-advanced plant which satisfies BMW's stringent quality standards. Using a single assembly line, this plant would be capable of producing different models—including a brand new one.

Exhibit 8

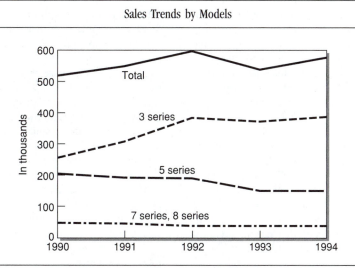

Sales Trends by Models

Exhibit 9

Competition in 1994			
Make	*Model*	*Manufacturing Location*	*Price Range*
BMW	3 series	Spartanburg, US, Munich and Regensburg, Germany	$25,125–39,250
	5 series	Dingolfing, Germany	$38,875–47,950
	7 series	Dingolfing, Germany	$56,400–84,400
	8 series	Dingolfing, Germany	$68,550–98,500
	Z3 Roadster (1995)	Spartanburg, South Carolina, US	$28,000
Cadillac	De Ville	Hamtramek, Michigan, US	$33,615–38,615
	Seville	Hamtramek, Michigan, US	$42,055–45,955
Honda	Acura Legend	Sayama, Japan	$34,185–41,885
Jaguar	XJ6, Vanden Plas	Coventry, UK	$52,330–59,980
	XJ12	Coventry, UK	$72,330–73,780
Mercedes	C-Class	Sindelfingen and Bremen, Germany	$30,375–35,375
	E-Class	Sindelfingen and Bremen, Germany	$40,475–81,275
	S-Class	Sindelfingen, Germany	$71,075–133,775
	SL-Class	Bremen, Germany	$85,675–120,575
Nissan	Infiniti G20	Oppama, Japan	$19,950–20,850
	Infiniti J30	Tochogo, Japan	$37,400
	Infiniti Q45	Oppama, Japan	$50,900–57,500
Toyota	Lexus ES 400	Tsutsumi, Japan	$31,670
	Lexus SC 300	Motochi, Japan	$38,470–39,370
	Lexus SC 400	Motochi, Japan	$45,570
	Lexus LS 400	Tahara, Japan	$51,670

Source: Wards Automotive Yearbook 1994/1995

Quick

With only twenty-four months between the laying of the groundwork for the plant and the start of production, the Spartanburg plant was built in record time (see Exhibit 10). BMW initially invested $400 million in Spartanburg, which included construction of a 1.2 million-square-foot plant. This was followed by an additional $200 million investment in tooling, bringing the total investment to $600 million. The Spartanburg plant was designed to produce 300 cars a day, with future expansion to 400 cars per day. Plans called for the production of the 3-series models 318 and 328. Assembly of the 4-cylinder 318i sedan was scheduled for September 1994, and production of the second model—the 6-cylinder 328 sedan—was scheduled for the fall of 1995. BMW planned gradual expansion of the plant from 100 vehicles per day at the end of 1995, to 300 vehicles by the first quarter of 1997 and 400 vehicles per day in 1998. This was still considerably smaller than a production rate in a typical auto assembly plant which was over 1,000 vehicles per day (see Exhibit 5).

Flexible

Although most automobile plants, including BMW's German plants, were built with a high degree of hard automation, Spartanburg focused on manufacturing flexibility. The layout was designed to support a flexible-team working environment rather than transfer-line automation. In a radical departure from tradition, the body shop, the paint shop, and the assembly line were all located under one roof. The plant layout was L-shaped to allow for a higher degree of integration between the production line, quality control and supporting functions. Also, to facilitate communication, the assembly line was in the form of a lower-case "e" (instead of the typical "s" or "u" shapes), meaning that the final part of the assembly line curved back to the middle of the shop. Testing operations were located in the middle leg of this "e" (see Exhibit 11). In addition to bringing the assembly line workers closer to each other, the "e"-shaped layout reduced required space by 40% and sharply reduced construction costs.

The Spartanburg plant had only a limited number of robots. Fewer than 25 robots were installed in the plant: one

Exhibit 10

Chronology of Events	
June 1992	BMW AG of Germany announced the intention to build an assembly plant in Spartanburg, South Carolina.
September 1992	Groundwork for the plant began.
April 1993	Construction work on buildings began, followed by production facilities and interior.
January 1994	First production associate hired.
June 1994	First imported BMW arrived at port in Charleston and was prepared at the plant for delivery to U.S. dealers.
September 1994	The first 3-series BMW (3181 Sedan) built in the United States rolled off the assembly line.
November 1994	Official plant opening ceremony took place.
March 1995	First cars are shipped to U.S. dealers.
September 1995	First Z3 roadster comes off the assembly line.

Exhibit 11

Spartanburg Plant Layout

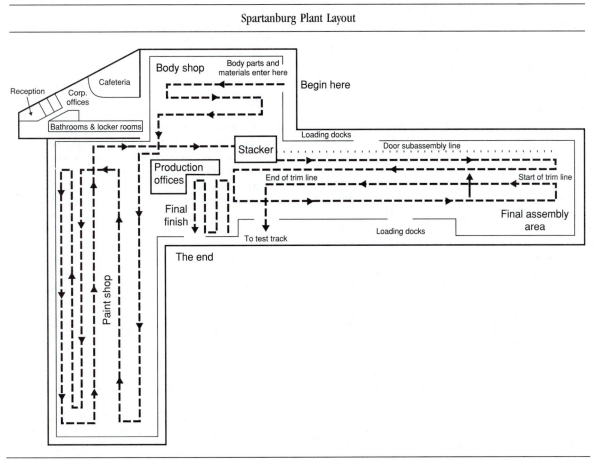

in the assembly line (used for windshield adhesive application), a few in those welding operations that needed a high degree of speed and accuracy (much of the welding was still done manually), and the rest in the paint shop.

Technologically Advanced

The new facility in Spartanburg was state-of-the-art. It integrated all the concepts BMW had learned from auto makers around the world. The U.S. plant's fully automated paint shop had a water-borne system, which was used in BMW's Regensburg plant in Germany, and an experimental line to test new innovations. BMW was the first car manufacturer that used water-based paint on four of the five paint layers. Only the clear top coat was solvent-based.

Forty percent of the total initial investment in Spartanburg was for the paint shop. The water-borne system was environmentally safer but trickier to launch and operate. First, the car body had to be thoroughly cleaned to remove all residues. Next, a special coat was applied by lowering the entire body into a water-diluted paint in a giant cathode dip bath. This layer was baked onto the automobile, and after cooling, the underbody protection was applied, followed by a base coat. High-speed atomizers were used to create an ultra-fine mist that was drawn to the body of the car by high-tension electrostatic charge. The final top coat was then applied and hardened in a drying oven. All paint layers were applied by robots to maintain consistent thickness. In all, BMW used 18 colors of primer and 32 base coat colors, all of which were water-based. This was a color spectrum unheard of in auto assembly plants.

BMW had studied Harley-Davidson's success with powder coating and GM's ground-breaking acrylic powder system. The paint shop in Spartanburg was designed with provisions to allow powder coat equipment to be added later.

Scheduling the daily production at the paint shop also posed a challenge. Painting was done in batches based on colors. Operations before painting (in the body shop) and after painting (final assembly) were done in series based on orders. Synchronizing painting with these operations was not easy. The master production schedule at Spartanburg was based on sales orders, and suppliers delivered parts in the exact sequence in which they were used both in the body shop and the assembly line. There was a stacker or "post office," which was located between the paint shop and the assembly line. The post office had four levels which each held six rows of four cars for a total of 96 vehicles. The post office could reshuffle the cars into the desired sequence necessary for either painting or assembly line production. All this required sophisticated material handling and scheduling systems.

Besides the paint shop, the rest of the Spartanburg plant was also designed to be friendly to the environment. It recycled corrugated cardboard, office paper, aluminum cans, scrap metal, glass bottles, plastic bottles, solvents, rags, and used oil. The total amount of recycled materials was 180 tons in 1994. It also used a cogeneration system to produce some of its own energy. The gas turbines were equipped with nitrogen oxide reduction technology which reduced emissions to less than 10% of the Federal standard for stationary gas turbines. The plant operated an on-site wastewater pre-treatment plant that cleaned the wastewater before releasing it into the community waste- water treatment.

BMW Quality

"Production ramp-up will be deliberately slow to absolutely ensure first-time quality." Al Kinzer, President of BMW MC.

Everyone at BMW was conscious that an important asset of BMW was its quality image. Part of this image, historically, was built on the German reputation for high quality work. The Spartanburg plant had paid careful attention to this concern and had developed several systems for quality control. For example, suppliers were screened carefully and were held responsible for meeting strict quality standards (Spartanburg did not perform incoming inspection).

Within the plant, team members checked each other's work throughout the production process and final quality checks were performed at the end of the assembly line by workers from each shop. Production errors were referred back to the person (or the "associate," as everyone was called in BMW MC) who installed the system or part; he or she was solely responsible for the rework. This system distinguished between person-based and system-based errors, and identified major system-wide quality problems.

Spartanburg had a separate "Import Car Processing" (ICP) line that served as a final check for all imported BMWs from Germany destined for dealers in the southern United States. (BMW also had two other ICPs in the United States.) In addition to extensive checks, installation of custom items such as radios, compact disc players and computer equipment was performed in the ICP. When this operation started in Spartanburg in July of 1994, the line prepped approximately 20 vehicles per week. This rate increased rapidly to 60 vehicles per day, and reached 100 vehicles per day by February 1995.

Single Line, Different Models

In July 1994, BMW R & D chief, Dr. Reitzle, announced the introduction of a new sports car for the model year 1996. Named Z3, the two-seat roadster was unveiled at the Detroit Auto Show in January 1995. Code-named E36/7, the two-seater was based on a 3-series platform. The original model was made of steel and had a canvas top, with a hardtop option to follow. Though the car's striking body matched no other BMW, key pieces of Z3—engine, transmission, suspension, seats, steering—were taken from parts used in other BMW models. The Z3 used the same underbody and wheel base as the 3 Series coupe. The car was powered by a 1.8 or 1.9 liter, 4-cylinder engine with 115 HPs—the same as in the 318 sedan. Even the planned 6-cylinder version of the Z3 was to use an existing engine—the one used in the 328 sedan.

Through the development of the Z3, BMW officials tried to remove costs from the design and manufacturing processes. "This car will be a big step forward for us in design for manufacturability and assembly," stressed Reitzle. Aware of the need to catch up with the world's leaders in overall efficiency—Toyota, Honda and Ford—Reitzle said the Z3 program would spearhead BMW's drive to lower design cost, shorten the development cycle and increase production efficiency. "We can't afford to wait until the cost pressure from the market gets worse," he stated. "Germany's auto industry cannot expect to keep up with Japan's in productivity unless we act now."

One example of this improved design for manufacturability was the reduction in the "hits" that body panels required at Spartanburg. "Hits" refers to the number of times a die (or press) must stamp a panel before it assumes its final shape. At BMW, major body panels generally required seven hits; for the Z3, the average was only four hits—which meant that the final shape was achieved using four dies instead of seven. Dies were expensive, and reducing their numbers generated large savings—especially in a small-scale operation such as Spartanburg.

BMW estimated the world market for all roadsters to be 150,000 to 160,000 units per year, of which the Z3 was expected to capture 20%. This small market implied that the location chosen for production of the new model would have to supply the world market of 100 countries. Because of its flexible assembly process and lower expected costs, Spartanburg was the prime candidate. But, if selected for the Z3, Spartanburg would have to produce the 318 sedan, the 328 sedan, and the Z3 roadster simultaneously. In addition, the Z3 had to be produced in 74 country-specific variations to accommodate the differences in exhaust systems, safety features, lights, steering, and other requirements. All this would demand enormous flexibility from the single assembly line at Spartanburg.

There were also the usual concerns about the risks of producing a brand new model in a brand new plant—especially a plant outside the "home base." Would there be enough time for Spartanburg to develop the necessary engineering competence to support the introduction of a new model—particularly one that encompassed many innovations for BMW? It was argued that since Regensburg

produced all the 3-series models—including the Coupe—it was a logical place to introduce the new Z3. Regensburg could solve the inevitable problems of introducing a new model while Spartanburg focused on the standard 318 and 328 models. The Z3 could then be relocated to Spartanburg to take advantage of cost differences. But eventually this argument was not accepted, and BMW decided to introduce the Z3 at Spartanburg.

Globalizing BMW's Manufacturing Network

There were many within BMW who felt that the repercussions of creating a U.S. plant went beyond Spartanburg and the U.S. market; this move had far-reaching consequences for BMW's entire manufacturing network. BMW had to reconfigure its global supplier network, create a unique and effective work culture, and design mechanisms for necessary knowledge transfer.

Building a Global Supplier Network

NAFTA granted tariff exemption within North America for all goods manufactured with a local content of at least 65%. That provided BMW with a strong incentive to develop local suppliers in the United States. Many high quality parts and components could be found in the United States at lower prices than in many other countries: stampings, frames, seats, fasteners, glass, and interior and exterior trim could all be purchased in the United States for less than in Europe. Eventually, BMW planned to import only engines and transmissions from Germany. "We are looking to develop an adequate U.S. supplier base: it is inefficient to use suppliers halfway around the world because it drives costs up," said one BMW MC executive.

Developing a local supplier base was no easy task. Although Spartanburg wanted to choose suppliers that were also supplying BMW's other plants, it could not simply favor German-based suppliers with U.S. operations or global suppliers with a German base. It wanted to identify the best supplier and, when appropriate, encouraged U.S. suppliers to form joint-ventures with German firms. Spartanburg also wanted to work closely with its suppliers. In late 1994, it held an unprecedented 2½-day seminar for over 100 suppliers' quality control managers, and another seminar for suppliers' account managers (to handle operational details such as details of BMW's payment system). Supplier representatives were often invited to the new plant to show assembly-line workers the best way to handle their parts and systems, and plant employees often visited the suppliers plants.

The procurement office in Spartanburg had the responsibility for all North American procurement activities. Although this office interacted directly with its German counterpart, it had no reporting relationship with Germany and was managed separately. Nevertheless, in 1995 a group of German engineers was still in Spartanburg to assist in the development of the supplier network and to ensure global coordination.

Spartanburg's attempt to enlist local suppliers ran counter to a very strong industry trend to rationalize the network of suppliers. Like other car manufacturers, BMW faced the issue of choosing suppliers who could deliver parts and components to the company on a global basis—thus providing more consistent quality as well as an improved bargaining position for the company. The so-called "tier-one" suppliers provided more complete subassemblies and helped in product development. Chrysler's LH program used 230 parts and materials vendors and the Ford Mustang was targeting 180. BMW was aiming for 100 tier-one suppliers. More than 60 tier-one suppliers were already committed to Spartanburg, and nearly half planned to set up facilities close to Spartanburg. Of the sixty, only a few (eight) were based in Germany. Some, like Robert Bosch Corp., were large multinationals that had operated in the United States for a long time.

High on the priority list for BMW was a drastically enhanced role for the suppliers in the design and manufacture of its models. This included buying more completed subassemblies from top-tier suppliers. To enhance the supplier's role in design, cross-functional procurement teams had been formed with designers, engineers, manufacturers, and purchasers. An important objective was to build in more quality control and to work on friendlier terms with the 100 systems suppliers. The teams involved the suppliers at the concept stage of new models, and enlisted them to look for ways to reduce costs and improve manufacturability. They also helped to change the traditional cost orientation of the purchasing function. In fact, somewhat unlike other auto makers, BMW did not mandate extreme and continuous cost-cutting by the suppliers. There were only clauses in the contracts for "negotiating cost adjustments."

Tier-one suppliers were expected to assume responsibility for more complete subassemblies. Eventually, twenty of them were expected to provide 80% of all BMW's purchased parts. A sun roof, for example, which used to be assembled by BMW from sixty different purchased parts, now came semi-assembled from one supplier, with only three sub-assembled pieces. This integrated approach was estimated to yield a cost reduction of at least 20% and perhaps as much as 40% in some cases. "Non-systems suppliers ultimately run the risk of becoming sub-suppliers" said Dr. Reitzle, BMW's head of R & D.

Creating a New Culture

One of the most important objectives for Spartanburg was to develop a new atmosphere in which employees could be creative and productive. This work atmosphere would be different from the traditional one found in Germany. In a sense, Spartanburg presented BMW with a unique opportunity to experiment with a new format combining the best of German and American traditions. The results were extraordinary.

The entrance to the Spartanburg plant—spacious, impeccable, and very organized—reminded a visitor of a German setting. To the left, two assistants diligently and efficiently took in visitor information and provided name tags. To the right, a series of pictures showed the history of the development of Spartanburg, from groundbreaking to the present. Straight ahead was a huge, inviting corridor that led to the production area. At the end of the corridor, a BMW Z3 roadster prototype hung from a movable wall.

To the left, another wide corridor led to the open area that housed all BMW MC corporate offices. There were three small conference rooms on this corridor, which were the only closed rooms throughout the Spartanburg plant. The corporate office layout resembled that of a Japanese corporation—eighty desks were tightly packed across a large open room creating small clusters of barely discernible work units. Somewhere within each cluster, a small signpost indicated the appropriate corporate function—finance, public relations, human resources, etc. There were no cubicles, walls, or separations of any kind.

At the corner closest to the window, at a desk slightly slanted with a view of the whole room, sat Al Kinzer, president of BMW MC. Mr. Kinzer dressed exactly the same as everyone else in the office and the plant. At Spartanburg, BMW tried to erase the difference between office and manufacturing employees by having all employees—including managers—wear a white uniform with a BMW emblem. Only those employees whose specific duties required special gear departed from this common uniform.

There was no division between this large area and the rest of the plant. Sitting at their desks, managers and office workers could see part of the paint shop, some of the assembly shop, and the impressive Z3 prototype hanging from the movable platform. The hanging car stood in front of another set of offices, which housed plant operations, including plant procurement and manufacturing support functions. Interestingly, these offices were located in the geographic center of the plant, surrounded by the body shop, the paint shop and the assembly line. Initially, they were supposed to be completely open, but due to noise problems glass walls had been erected to surround the office area. The very layout of the building conveyed the message that there should be no difference between office and production workers.

This philosophy of equality and a shared environment extended to all facets of life at Spartanburg. All employees lunched at the same cafeteria—an enormous hall seating close to 1,200 people. Three lunch shifts were necessary due to capacity constraints, but, in general, office workers lunched with production workers and corporate staff. Also, workers from all areas shared the same rest rooms and locker rooms.

All employees were organized into teams. A typical team had twenty members and was composed of smaller teams of four to five people. Teams had rotating leaders who were democratically selected by the team members. Each team worked on a section of the car and put an identifying signature on its work. Teams were also responsible for their own quality control. Teammates always checked each other's work systematically, and corrected their own mistakes. If the error had originated outside of the team, they called on the team that had signed the part to correct the mistake. As Bobby Hitt, Spartanburg's manager of Community Relations, said: "We all have bad days. Teams allow us to tell the difference between someone having a bad day and a recurring mistake which might be happening due to larger, system-wide problems."

At Spartanburg, BMW recruited workers who were new to auto production and trained them from scratch—not only in manufacturing cars, but also in team-building and conflict resolution. It also instituted a carefully designed compensation program. Benefits were the same for production, staff, and managerial positions. For example, a perfect attendance bonus of $100 was given for every twenty consecutive work days. All other bonuses depended on overall plant performance regardless of the employee's rank.

Transferring Knowledge Between German and American Operations

To provide sufficient engineering support in the ramp-up phase of the plant, BMW formed an engineering group of forty German engineers. They were linked to Germany and to suppliers by a CATIA system—an on-line CAD system. The engineers served in the United States on a rotating basis. They were responsible for design, quality and reliability tests, export homologation, Reitzle explained.

Each management position in production was filled with two persons: a U.S. manager and a German manager. German managers provided expertise as well as assistance during the startup process. Meanwhile, they also learned the innovations which were introduced in Spartanburg and eventually, upon return to Germany, would transfer this knowledge to other BMW plants. All these German managers were expected to return after two years, leaving the U.S. manager in charge.

Reitzle planned to expand BMW MC's design engineering group from 40 to 150 in a few years. All would be networked via CATIA with engineering headquarters in Munich. This, Reitzle explained, would allow virtual real-time engineering between the United States and Germany. BMW also had a small design studio in California, which would be on-line with this system.

In general, transfer of knowledge and systems between the United States and Germany posed a cultural challenge. BMW in Germany was highly hierarchical, whereas the new culture at Spartanburg emphasized a flat organization (see Exhibit 12). According to Bobby Hitt, to ensure better communication, BMW tried to standardize managerial positions across BMW's plants and administrative offices. In this way, everyone could easily identify his or her counterparts in the other BMW operations. But since Spartanburg's organization and culture were markedly different, it was difficult to match the positions between Germany and the United States. This presented a trade-off: imposing a hierarchy in Spartanburg would improve communication with Germany, but it would also inhibit its unique culture.

The Dilemma

By September 1995, as the first Z3s were leaving the assembly line, the huge success of the new car had already created a new challenge. The original manufacturing plan for Spartanburg called for a gradual ramp-up of production of the Z3, continuation of production of the 318 model, and later production of the 328. But the strong demand for the Z3 was forcing major changes to this plan. Already, instead of the 328, Spartanburg was to focus on producing more Z3s. However, due to larger differences between the Z3 and the 318 (than between the 328 and the 318), this ramp-up would have to be slower than for the 328 model. Spartanburg's production for 1995 would therefore not reach the planned 20,000 units. Instead it would be under 16,000 units, of which only 6,000 were Z3s. Plans called for expansion of Z3 production to 35,000 units in 1996, but even that would not satisfy all the demand. The entire production planned for 1996 had already been sold by BMW's dealers.

There were also other reasons to expand production at Spartanburg. In September 1995, Bernd Pischestrieder, the newly appointed CEO of BMW AG, had made an announcement that due to pressures on margins, volume levels would have to increase to maintain profitability. Especially troublesome was the Z3 situation: "It's a question of capacity more than anything else, and the capacity [at Spartanburg] is limited." Not meeting the demand was troubling, especially since 1996 was the only year in which the Z3 would have only one competitor, the Mazda Miata. Mercedes, Porsche and Audi were all planning to introduce roadsters in 1997.

But how should Spartanburg respond to the pressure to expand the Z3's production? Al Kinzer knew that he had to formulate a response quickly. This was the main topic of

Exhibit 12

BMW Manufacturing Corporation Organization Chart

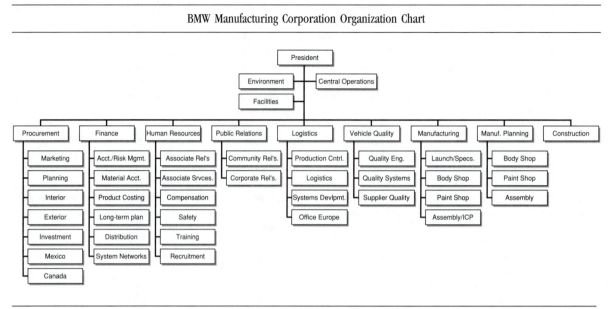

Exhibit 13

The Z3

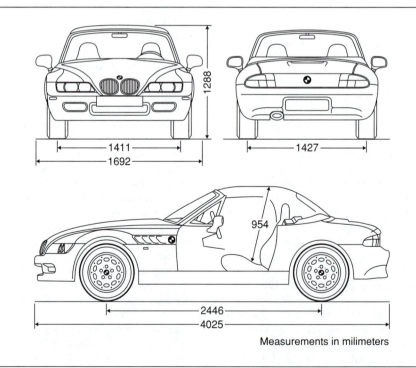

Measurements in milimeters

discussion in the board meeting that was to be held the following week in Munich.

Kinzer narrowed his options to three: one was to gear up for higher production of both the Z3 and the 3-series models. This required an additional investment of $200 million, bringing the total at Spartanburg to $800 million. This rate of growth was phenomenal and demanded careful management attention. New construction would add about 300,000 square feet of manufacturing space to the 1.2 million square foot plant. The expansion would increase the daily capacity of the body and assembly areas from 300 units to 400. The plant's paint shop was already rated at 400 units per day. This investment would allow BMW to expand the body and assembly departments while maintaining the plant's single line production concept. Furthermore, Spartanburg would have to move to two shifts by November of 1995, instead of the originally planned February of 1996.

Another option was to send the 318 back to Germany's Regensburg plant. Regensburg had recently cut back work

hours and had excess capacity. By concentrating all its energy on the Z3, Spartanburg would become a specialized plant for the roadster. Meanwhile, Regensburg could easily supplement production of the 318, albeit at a somewhat higher cost.

The third option was to resist market pressure. Kinzer understood that quality was the most important element of BMW's strategy. For eighty-five years BMW had been able to rely on a carefully constructed base of German engineers and had gained a leading reputation for technical excellence and quality. The risk of capitulating to market pressure and increasing production levels was the possibility that quality problems would develop. Even the smallest failure in Spartanburg's quality would have far-reaching consequences—corporate headquarters might lose confidence in the plant's capacity to supply BMW-quality vehicles. Worse, the public might decide that U.S.-made BMWs did not deserve the premium price tag or might demand only German-made BMWs.

PART III

♦ ♦ ♦

Effective Management of Global Operations and Logistics

Chapters 10 – 12

We conclude the text with an examination of the structure and coordination of international manufacturing and distribution networks and the challenges encountered by management for the effective operation of these networks. This part of the book also addresses the coordination issues of international supply networks, since the manner in which information, experience, and management planning and control systems are used to control the provision of customer service is critical to the way an operations and logistics network functions. To this end, we discuss vertical supplier relations and horizontal relations among different country subsidiaries of multinational corporations. The specific requirements of information and the available technologies are discussed in relation to the definition and measurement of customer service. Effective management within the global supply chain network is proven to require a close coordination between a global approach and a local understanding of preferences (i.e., glocal logistics). Detailed analyses of appropriate metrics for organizational structures in global logistics networks and typical forms of managerial control in global logistics organizations are also provided in these chapters. The cases in this part highlight interesting issues, including the problem of international service operations, evaluating the role and the performance of the various facilities in global networks, and coordinating manufacturing activities within the network. ♦

Chapter 10

Information Management for Global Logistics

◆ ◆ ◆

This chapter will cover the following topics:

◆ *Describe and define the global logistics information system*

◆ *Discuss the logistics systems' capabilities and limitations, including today's technologies and in particular Electronic Data Interchange (EDI)*

◆ *Describe the characteristics of a logistics information and telecommunications system (LITS)*

◆ *Discuss logistics organization and it's relationship to LITS*

◆ *Discuss the functional and geographic dimensions of LITS*

◆ *Describe how to develop a sectorial LITS and the role of information systems*

◆ INTRODUCTION

Physical flow of information is becoming an increasingly important logistics management tool. The obvious complexity of today's flow management systems places heavy demands on information systems. Materials, semi-finished goods, finished goods, or spare parts all bear a financial and storage cost, but the successive generations of data processing equipment have brought with them vast improvements in processing speed and capacity at continually decreasing costs. Thus, being in essence a deflationary resource, information is replacing physical material, which has become an inflationary resource. The trend in logistics and operations management for several years has been to invest in data processing, information systems, and telecommunications resources in order to better manage physical flows.

Moreover, customers expect suppliers to be able to provide up-to-date logistics information such as product position and order status. Two critical factors in increasing customer satisfaction are *information about the physical distribution or supply operations* and the *ability to transmit that information*. Lastly, outsourcing some functions has made it necessary to closely follow the operations of these outside organizations. Consequently, logistics experts find themselves increasingly relieved of daily management of physical operations and freed up to spend their time developing and exploiting information systems that allow them to monitor operations better, and to adapt the logistics system to respond in real time to strategic objectives and to the operating constraints.

The logistics information system (LIS), consequently, has become a key success factor in logistics strategy. LIS encompasses flow monitoring across the full chain of logistics activity. It performs the following functions:

- Captures the basic data
- Transfers data to handling and processing centers
- Stores the basic data as necessary
- Processes the data into usable information
- Stores the information as necessary
- Transfers the information to users

The information captured by LIS satisfies the objectives of logistics monitoring and can be used to:

- Forecast, anticipate, and plan
- Ensure that operations can be traced in time, and products can be located
- Control and report operations completed

Although monitoring these subsystems has traditionally been a logistics responsibility, with the help of new information technologies it is now possible to reposition or even reshape these functionalities in a global logistics approach.

The logistics information and telecommunication system (LITS) is the centerpiece of the logistics information system for global operations. Telecommunications plays a decisive part in disseminating logistics information across multiple geographical sites (in separate countries), different functions (marketing, sales, production, etc.), and various sectors (orders, logistics information transfer between suppliers, manufacturers, distributors, and logistics service providers).

In global operations and logistics management, the efficiency of the logistics organization, the quality of production, and the quality of logistics services all depend on an effective LITS.

The main issues at stake involved in setting up an LITS are the following:

- Contribute to cost reduction in the management of the material flows cycle. The LITS looks after all the processing steps needed for an efficient flow of products within the constraints of service level and costs (order preparation forms, delivery sheets, shipping notes, delivery receipts, etc.).
- Optimize the physical resources put in place all along the logistics chain. In this way the LITS makes up the required database and implements decision support tools to manage resources and use them to maximum efficiency.
- Follow up operational performances. The LITS provides useful information feedback to logistics performance control and thus to logistics indicators.
- Provide decision-making tools for management.

In a global operations and logistics management approach, LITS must have more features than a traditional system. Features allowing the following must be included:

- Management of interfaces between different functions in the form of pooling databases or interfunctional information transfer
- Information transfer between different players in the logistics chain (manufacturers, distributors, customers, logistics service providers, and carriers)
- Compatibility of LITS, often developed on the scale of a national subsidiary, and which now must be harmonized among the different countries (e.g., accounting practices)

In summary, LITS appears as a critical factor for the internal efficiency of the operations and logistics organization and for the overall services provided by logistics. This chapter deals with the specific aspects of logistics information management systems. It looks at the links between the organizational dimension and the information systems architecture, and the underlying logic of an information system that satisfies global operations and logistics objectives from the functional, sectorial, and geographic viewpoints.

It also outlines the capabilities and limitations of logistics information systems for global logistics operations. It then discusses two factors that are critical to maximizing capabilities and potential strategic advantages: developing a system that meets diverse user needs, and designing the system to address the geographic, functional, and sectorial requirements of global integration.

◆ THE GLOBAL LIS/LITS: CAPABILITIES AND LIMITATIONS

Global operations and logistics present some characteristics that make information important for maintaining coherence of physical flows. The integration of the three dimensions—functional, sectorial, and geographical—generates new constraints for the LITS. Chapter 12, for example, illustrates how logistics can be structured around new types of professional expertise in order to better satisfy sales and marketing needs in the sectorial cooperation that ensues. Regarding information, functional integration requires a significant increase in transfers between functions on operations and logistics matters. Introduction of new products is an example of the constant updating of information between operations and marketing.

Sectorial integration means sharing information to improve the overall performance of the logistics system. The availability of products by manufacturers to be sold by distributors is one example. Placing orders by means of electronic data interchange (EDI) has also allowed both manufacturers' and distributors' telecommunications and information systems to develop significantly.

Geographical integration requires that all entities spread out over very large areas and involved in the logistics process be linked by networks. Use of satellite communications or global positioning systems (GPS) allows for better control over logistics on a global or continental scale.

In a similar fashion, the increasing use of third-party logistics service providers heightens the need for more extensive monitoring and control capabilities. In some cases, logistics providers may assume responsibility for the entire physical flow of the product. However, producers and distributors still need to control and monitor the flows.

The emphasis on monitoring makes the reliance on LITS by manufacturer or distributor even stronger. Service providers have understood this point very well. Indeed, one of the differentiation elements in the positioning of logistics providers is based on their information systems capabilities. Logistics service providers have developed their own systems in information technology and data processing. Different systems and their compatibility with the customer company's existing systems constitutes an important selection criterion for logistics providers.

◆ CAPABILITIES OF TODAY'S TECHNOLOGIES

New information technologies can help to meet the integration challenges of globalization. They can be particularly useful in adapting three aspects of LITS:

- Listing and storing basic information
- Transferring information
- Transforming data into information

Technologies such as code bars, CD-ROMS, GPS, or EDI help make global logistics information more reliable, industrialize their processing, and speed up information transfer. Electronic data interchange enables the transfer of structured data from one computer system to another, according to preestablished standard messages and using telecommunications networks. This type of information transfer is so pivotal that, in some fields, a firm can stay in business only if it controls the transfer. For example, companies cannot operate in the automobile industry in France (and, in fact, throughout Europe) if they cannot transfer information through the Galia system in France and the European system to which it is connected, Odette.

EDI not only makes it possible to transfer information from one country to another, but it also enables transfer between actors in the same sector or between economic sectors. Companies most often use it to transfer information between *subsidiaries* (forecasting, inventory, delivery) *or the logistics sites of the same firm* (shipping note, order details, etc.), and between *suppliers and their customers,* either between manufacturers and distributors in the field of mass market goods or between parts manufacturers and manufacturers in the automobile and aeronautics industries.

It must be stressed that these technologies do facilitate operations but that they are not sufficient to set up a global logistics organization. There are major limitations, including technical constraints, to the cooperative approach required with EDI. Introducing these new information systems technologies, without taking into consideration important internal and external organizational factors, can lead to failure. In particular, the issue of asymmetry between manufacturers and distributors in both size and expertise relative to the information requirements creates a problem.

Overall, we draw the following general conclusions about logistics information systems:

- Information systems can become specific assets, which lend greater control to operators who develop them (reward and penalty attribution or accountability). Innovative technologies alter the attribution of power.
- The benefits of setting up EDI are not equally shared between the partners involved in the relationship. Empirical studies seem to demonstrate that the originator of the cooperative approach gets the most out of the cooperation. For most suppliers in the study mentioned, EDI does not lead to significant competitive advantage. On the other hand, EDI does preclude being at a competitive disadvantage.
- By separating physical and logic flows more clearly, new technologies change the distribution of functions and responsibilities among actors in the supply chain. But it is difficult to say whether this change weakens supply chain relationships (fostering impersonal and routine data processing relations) or strengthens the relationship (disposing of monitoring information with resulting transparency and reactivity).
- In a system influenced by downstream factors, point-of-sale information becomes the leading element driving logistics activities. And whoever defines the EDI communication standards holds the most power in the supply chain.

EDI relationships carry with them numerous limitations. Information and communication technologies are only capable of totally or partially automating relatively simple, routine decision processes. They are suitable in cases of repetitive processes (to make investment profitable), stable ones (the system is not designed to manage diversity and variations), and perfectly defined data that neither actor deems to be confidential.

Only by taking into account all this information can the implementation costs (operational dimension) become justifiable and effective in the global logistics context. As illustrated in Figure 10–1, EDI makes it possible to globally optimize the supply chain and to create competitive advantage through better customer service, while respecting the information systems of the actors in the cooperative relationship.

This figure helps us to understand why, irrespective of technical factors, EDI remains seldom used as a tool compared to the number of transactions it can actually handle. Nevertheless, EDI does generate some positive results, which include:

- Knowing a lot more about the business: Accurate knowledge of sales at the checkout counter; awareness of the impact of advertising, sales promotions, and merchandising; improved supply management; adapting the production tool to demand
- Getting rid of costly errors such as differences arising from data entry errors (item code, wrong quantities), articles missing; damage during transportation and pricing errors; systematic price reductions; return of goods
- Reduction of delivery times by knowing in advance about changes in item codes or palletization rules, for example
- Improved service levels as a result of more timely, synchronized, and reliable information

Regardless of the multiple advantages, sectorial integration requires transfer of confidential information. Producing and transmitting confidential sales information in real time is only possible if systems of the EDI type are used.

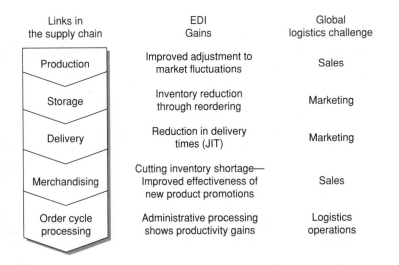

Links in the supply chain	EDI Gains	Global logistics challenge
Production	Improved adjustment to market fluctuations	Sales
Storage	Inventory reduction through reordering	Marketing
Delivery	Reduction in delivery times (JIT)	Marketing
Merchandising	Cutting inventory shortage— Improved effectiveness of new product promotions	Sales
Order cycle processing	Administrative processing shows productivity gains	Logistics operations

Figure 10–1   Position and Challenge of EDI in Supply Chains

Although it appears a relatively easy task to install EDI systems in distribution channels that are managed vertically (such as franchising operations), installing them in more complex relationships between manufacturers and distributors (in which each party maintains autonomy of decision) is a different matter altogether. The difficulties encountered are:

- No critical mass or volume to justify the investment in technology
- Defining a common standard between distributors
- The nature of the information to be transferred

The behavior of distributors varies a great deal regarding how information from the checkout counter is made available to manufacturers. Three likely attitudes are:

1. Sell the data, which is what the French chain Carrefour does to consumer groups. This attitude reflects the will to exert a degree of power and places limits on the cooperative relationship in logistics and operations.
2. Give the data to selected manufacturers with whom the distributor develops a partnership and expect, in return, improved shelf sales of the articles. This attitude serves to strengthen the differentiation of the chain and the dual nature of the cooperative relationship, while creating the opportunity of taking the relationship to the logistic-commercial stage, or even logistic-commercial in administered channels.
3. Give the data to as many manufacturers as possible, without any real follow-up and without asking for anything in exchange.

Figure 10–2 shows the information sequence of EDI technology used by Bernard Faure (French manufacturer of automobile seats) in their just-in-time operation. EDI makes it possible to manage delivery of inventory not yet allocated when the truck sets off and to transmit delivery instructions and invoices. In this company, where production and delivery are organized in just-in-time, the automaker sends in orders every fifty seconds, and the lapse of time between the order arriving and fitting the seats in the vehicles is ten minutes. Transportation is integrated into the process, and the trucks are connected at the loading bays to the seat supplier's and the automaker's LITS.

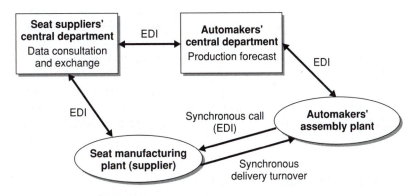

Figure 10–2   Information Flow for Just-in-Time Delivery and the Role of EDI for a French Manufacturer of Automobile Seats

◆ CHARACTERISTICS OF A LOGISTICS INFORMATION AND TELECOMMUNICATIONS SYSTEM

LITS also can play an important part in a global firm's sales and production strategy. It strongly influences the firm's ability to react quickly to changing events and developments (and consequently its capacity to satisfy demand quickly), its ability to identify problems, and even its capacity to set up barriers to protect its markets against existing competitors and potential competitors.

Seita, the company that monopolizes cigarette production in France, illustrates these points. Seita proposed to distribute its own brands, as well as the brands of its competitors' as they entered the French market, to some 28,000 tobacco sales outlets. To avoid a competitor's setting up a rival distribution network, Seita came up with a scheme to equip tobacco products outlets with a system to manage inventory on hand. The system also manages the reorder/restocking process by directly connecting Seita to its customers' point of sale/cash register systems. Each day the Seita system proposes replenishment orders for its connected customers. If these orders are confirmed manually by the sales outlets, the system transmits the orders directly to Seita's order processing system. Because the outlet is freed from the day-to-day management of inventory and replenishment, it has much to gain from such an arrangement. As a result, Seita's competitors find themselves partly dependent on the French company's physical distribution system. The existence of this system also encourages Seita's manufacturers to continue to work with the company rather than seeking alternative relationships. This competitive advantage is likely to be long-term, since once tobacconists install the system, it is difficult to imagine their substituting or adding additional systems that makers of other brands may propose.

Each information system is designed for one or several functional uses, without excluding the use by others. However, the goal of the main users is to set the system's standards. LITS should be designed with certain basic characteristics in mind to make it a complex, yet an open system. These characteristics are discussed in the following paragraphs.

A Vision for the Customers

LITS should focus on the firm's customers. Because logistics' main objective is to contribute to offering a service to the customer, the information system should be developed with this end in mind. LITS are too often designed in order to optimize costs. They neglect considerations of customer expectations in logistics matters.

LITS, therefore, may provide all the indicators needed to know precisely how the logistics process works per customer, delivery site, order, and listed article. It is also important to develop a system that reports differentiated performance evaluations at different levels, such as distribution chains by supplier (sectorial integration) and by location, which makes it possible to take into account promotion management in time and by product.

Accuracy of Data, Information and Systems

LITS gives an accurate picture at a given moment in time of the state and status of all physical flows. The coherence sought in the monitoring of the entire logistics system can only be achieved if the relevant data are entered and transmitted free of errors and consolidated with all the other elements noted in the same period. In order to achieve this, the nature of the data chosen to describe a physical flow must be done so as to best capture reality.

Distinguishing between the notions of data and information is of the utmost importance in this respect. Logistics data multiply very quickly because they concern hundreds of customers, thousands of delivery points, and hundreds of listed articles and transportation entities. Data are the elementary constituents, and the input process must be reliable. However, it is the structuring and initial processing of the data requirements that transforms them into useful information to be exploited in a more direct fashion.

Relevance of Data over Time

The most complete synchronization possible must exist between physical and information flows so that decision making may correspond to the real way operations happen. Information flow is the reliable reflection of physical flow. The time frames from which basic data are taken may prove to be very different in manufacturing of products versus JIT distribution.

Adapted to the Diversity of Physical Flows

LITS must be capable of introducing different solutions for different customers, products, and/or markets. The particularities of a customer, a new product, and a new distribution channel for a new product must be taken into consideration by the logistics information system. It must be capable of evolving in order to keep up with market changes.

Capability for Mobility

LITS must be migratory. The very nature of logistics solutions is to adapt to the strategic objectives and tactical constraints at any given moment. This being true, physical responses change so as to be able to put forward service offers expected at an acceptable cost. Obstacles to logistics flexibility are not so much that infrastructure has to be moved (warehouse relocating) or that logistics must change (inventory), but that information systems must be changeable. The logistics expert, as manager of the corporation's operational information system, must pay careful attention to this feature of LITS.

LITS often represents the least flexible element in the evolution of logistics systems. Moving from one warehouse to another takes a few days and causes disturbance for a few weeks. Modifying the information systems requires developing new programs that takes many months and considerable investment in means and training. For manufacturers and distributors, outsourcing to logistics service providers gets logistics experts concentrated on design and monitoring tools. As a result, they are asked to spend an increasing part of the time on the design and development of telecommunication and information systems. In general, the development of an LITS, as for all information systems projects, consists of a ten-stage process, as illustrated in Figure 10–3.

In the context of global logistics, Figure 10–3 presents a particular difficulty in that it will more often than not concern several countries, several functions, and several organizations. Improving the development processes requires, therefore, a growing standardization of procedures.

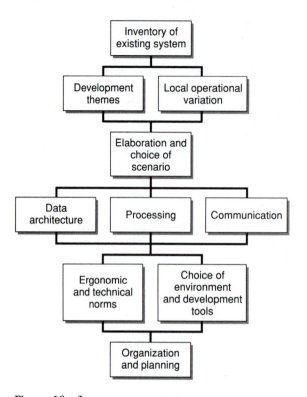

Figure 10–3   Design of a Logistics Information and Telecommunications System

◆ LOGISTICS ORGANIZATION AND ITS RELATIONSHIP TO LITS

LITS users are positioned at a functional level (plants, sales organization, logistics, marketing), a geographical level (central and local logistics, central and local sales, subsidiaries), and a sectorial level (manufacturer, distributor, wholesaler, logistics service provider). The LITS is instrumental for the logistics activity in the sense of flow monitoring. It mainly covers the following functions:

- Capture the basic data
- Transfer the data to handling and processing centers
- Store as necessary the basic data
- Transform the data into exploitable information after processing
- Store the information as necessary
- Transfer the information to users

In order to understand the architecture of the logistics telecommunications and information systems, we have to identify the users. The different system functions previously described are used coherently at chosen levels of the general organization of the corporation and, in particular, within the logistics function. In chapter 12 we stress the coherence between organizational and logistics information system.

The LITS is destined to satisfy multiple user needs. These users may be internal to the organization or external. The former are not necessarily involved in logistics activities.

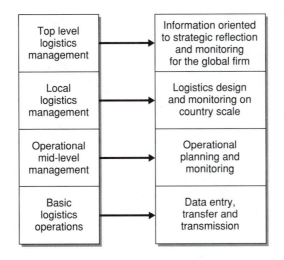

Figure 10−4 The Nature of Logistics Information Necessary for the Different Logistics Users Inside the Firm

Functions such as finance, sales, or marketing use logistics data or information (e.g., status of customer orders for sales, or inventory levels for the finance department or management controller). Also, internal users have different information at their disposal, depending on their level of responsibility. As is the case with all management information systems, the needs are diversified according to whether the user is top management or at a lower operative level. Then, four main logistics users may be identified (see Figure 10−4): top logistics level, local logistics level, operational mid-level management, and those who perform basic logistics operations.

Data and information intended for *top logistics-level management* are oriented to strategy and monitoring. Aggregate data will suit these requirements, because top management does not need to be aware of details concerning delivery volumes for a given client on the smallest geographical scale possible. In the same way, the time frame needed to monitor logistics at this level is relatively long term. Aggregate data should be included that allow top managers to test scenarios based on different hypotheses and constraints, particularly regarding internal and external logistics interfaces.

Operational mid-level management is responsible for specific logistics activities. Middle managers work through small teams to carry out the tasks successfully. The information system must offer the means to do short-term planning and operational control of activities.

At the *local logistics level,* responsibilities correspond to a medium-term monitoring prospect (up to 18 months). At this level work on flows entails exploring, simulating, measuring, approving, and deciding on actions that are within the scope of the manager's logistics responsibilities. For example, planning logistics activities on the basis of a yearly budget per country is a basic function of the information system intended for this level of responsibility.

Those who carry out *basic logistics operations* need the most detailed basic data to follow all elementary logistic operations and, of course, react to them. Needs at this level require a lot of data entry throughout the logistics information system.

Outside actors in the logistics chain might also want to get or give logistics data or information. Suppliers will supply the physical characteristics of logistics entities in which sold products are delivered. Customers will want access to inventory levels to put in their orders or to know what stage order preparation has reached. Lastly, carriers and logistics service providers will need a lot of information to serve customers.

The LITS at SKF, the world's leading manufacturer of ball bearings, is an example of a global information system that meets diverse user needs. It contains three parts:

- **The domestic customer service system,** which enables customers to consult a data base in real time to find out when the products they need will be available. If the date suits them, customers can use the system to put in an order.
- **The internal customer service system,** used to monitor national replenishment inventory mainly from specialized plants' production.
- **The manufacturing planning service system,** which manages one of the interfaces between the inventory of products available ex-works and production scheduling.

The components of this LITS illustrate the underlying logic of global logistics, namely:

- The customer dimension is addressed before and after sales, which puts logistics at the interface with the sales and marketing, as well as with manufacturing and distribution planning. This approach optimizes product availability.
- The geographical dimension is reflected in the links between central and local management, which allows the sales and logistics specificities of countries to be respected.
- The LITS manages sales terms specificities.

◆ FUNCTIONAL AND GEOGRAPHIC DIMENSIONS OF THE LITS

The order-processing system is the hard core around which the logistics information system is often built. However, the definition for an order-processing system has widened and today it takes in the internal product replenishment system as well.

To understand the operation of a logistics information system, it is absolutely necessary to comprehend the dual logic around which it is built. In firms that operate in several countries using local subsidiaries, each country is geared to sales, on the one hand, and to the operation and management of logistics on the other. The process is a double loop. The upstream loop works like a push system from the sales forecasts of the different sales subsidiaries. The forecasts serve to replenish inventory made available to the sales forces in each one of the countries. A second loop downstream processes orders coming from the subsidiaries or directly from customers and organizes the product distribution process (see Figure 10–5). This second loop, which works like a pull system (pulled by the demand of the subsidiary or the customer), is the one that corresponds most closely to the order-processing system.

Push Flow Functionalities

The logistics information system manages the operations involved in the double flow. The functionalities associated with the upstream loop in the push flow are sales forecasts and production planning.

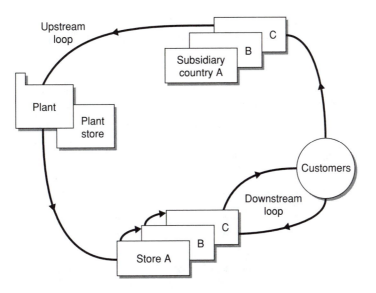

Figure 10–5   Double Loop of the Logistics Process

Sales Forecasts

Sales forecasts are important information elements because they initiate all physical flows upstream. Factors that may bias sales forecasts include:

- Forecasting based on annual sales targets rather than on factors that give an accurate reflection of market trends.
- Forecasting based on consumption by the end user rather than on supply of distribution channels. This is the phenomenon of sell-in/sell-out. A market may well show an increase in purchases without there being any impact on the firm's sales to distributors. This is often explained by a phenomenon of inventory disinvestment of the distribution channel. The sell-in is low (manufacturer's sales to the distributor), while the sell-out is high (sales by the distribution channel to the end user). The contrary phenomenon can be explained by speculative purchases on the part of the distributor, who anticipates a price rise.
- Overestimating needs in times of severe shortage. The aim in such cases is to try to obtain maximum quantity in the allocation of final quantities available.

To enhance accuracy, the forecast process requires data from several sources. Sales records, marketing information (price change impact, new products, etc.), and sales plans (special promotions) are some examples.

Production Planning

Production planning creates production schedules for different time frames. In the short term and the medium term, planners determine actual product manufacturing needs. They begin with gross needs, a consolidation of different forecasts about the consumption of a product adjusted for two types of hazards, sales and logistics. To determine the net product manufacturing needs, they subtract the product inventory available for distribution, as well as factory inventory not yet allocated. They aim for the latest possible withdrawal from production site and the sharing of risks associated with sales and distribution logistics hazards.

Pull Flow Functionalities

The functionalities of the information system related to the end consumer ordering from the subsidiary are situated the farthest upstream and illustrated in Figure 10–6. These functionalities include the following.

Replenishing Subsidiaries' Inventory

Companies replenish inventory according to subsidiaries' demands. However, an automatic control must check that orders correspond in quantity (article by article) to the subsidiaries' sales forecasts. When big discrepancies appear, shortages may occur, penalizing other subsidiaries. Processing replenishment requests is one of the most sensitive areas of the logistics process. It is at this juncture that forecast-pushed flow meets subsidiaries' order-pulled replenishment flow. Achieving the ideal balance between push and pull flows is difficult and rare. Arbitration and adjustments usually are necessary when the flows do not converge. As a result, sales, marketing, and logistics interaction is very intense at this stage.

Managing Replenishment Transportation

Replenishment generates transportation flows. The choice of means, the choice of carrier, and the loading means are important aspects of the LITS.

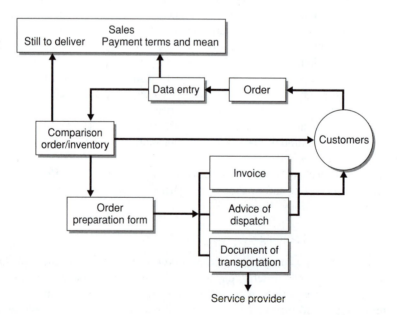

Figure 10–6   Data Requirements from the Information System for Order Processing

Handling Customers' Orders

The last stage of the process, handling the customer's order, is another source of data that initiates part of the logistics process, including the load schedule of the warehouses in their pick-up and preparation activities and the transportation plan.

The quality of order handling is one aspect of customers' satisfaction. It depends on:

- The combination of the means of reception (telephone, mail, EDI, fax), which give a range of possibilities of exchange with the customer and different options for speed delivery.
- The process of order handling, whether it be batch, with or without priority rules or exploitation constraints, such as multipacks, in which one order filler prepares several similar orders.

Both order handling (data entry, preparation) and dispatch management need constantly updated databases.

◆ SECTORIAL DIMENSION OF LITS

Shared replenishment flow management is a key challenge in sectorial logistics integration, and supporting coordination is a prime function of logistics information systems. Sharing sales forecast information and checkout counter information are important roles.

Upstream of the order cycle, the sales forecast role is of the utmost importance. It is the entry point of hierarchical scheduling systems, which allocate spare production resources. Two principles enable needed flexibility in items and quantity at point of sale or warehouse: *mutualization* or "pooling effect" (consolidating forecasts from all points of sale, which makes it possible to keep safety inventory as low as possible) and *delocalization* or *postponement* (by applying the concept of delayed differentiation to optimize product physical distribution).

Following these principles, three solutions for monitoring inventory are possible. From the simplest to the most complex, they include:

- The distributor does the forecasting for the shelf products for each store, which requires automated communication (level 1 in Figure 10–7). The monitoring system includes retroactive information, which sets the physical distribution process in motion.
- The unit of forecasting is the distributor's warehouse, which supplies products by consolidating orders from stores that the warehouse services. The outlet does not manage inventory, but follows it; the warehouse guarantees mutualization of needs for the stores it serves (see level 2 in Figure 10–7). Real needs, rather than forecasts, prompt product deliveries. Under this scenario, the manufacturer proposes continuous replenishment which takes into account different variables such as sales history, warehouse inventory level, promotion schedules, and potential beginning date of operations. The warehouse approves the proposal after modifications and transforms it into an order. Finally, the manufacturer delivers to the warehouse.
- In a more integrated version of this approach, the manufacturer manages shelf inventory for the distributor. The latter takes care of inventory in his stores and

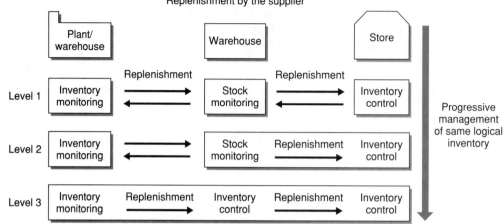

Figure 10-7   Shared Replenishment Modes

warehouse. While achieving optimum mutualization effects, this system requires advanced cooperation between the actors (level 3 in Figure 10-7). The manufacturer deals with consumption forecasting for warehouses and outlets, using checkout counter printouts, and looks after inventory replenishment on the shelves. This approach affects decision decoupling to local sites (e.g., the store level for distribution of mass consumption products, the country level for tire manufacturers) and group level departments (central group logistics).

Figure 10-8 illustrates the progression for a shared replenishment management within the sectorial integration when automated replenishment is available.

In sectorial integration, the manufacturer must be able to forecast sales to the consumer, which requires close collaboration between manufacturer and distributor. This forecasting capability is critical, because it affects performance level in terms of fee rate on shelves and overall gains (increasing turnover rate, maximizing margins per square feet).

Checkout counter data collection devices are a key source of useful information. The information they collect is transferred every day from the points of consumption to the warehouses (large stores like Auchan in Europe), to a central logistics group (as is the case for the large Carrefour stores), or directly to the manufacturer. The latter occurs infrequently, with the exception of franchised vertical marketing systems like Benetton or chain outlets. In Great Britain, Tesco makes all information from its checkout counters available to all its suppliers.

The use of point-of-sale scanning data offers numerous advantages, including:

• The ability to analyze inventory shortages at the end of the day and make delivery adjustments
• Time saved in information processing
• Improved promotion management—sales forecasts are purified adjusted from the temporary effects of promotions, and inventory needs of promotions are better anticipated
• The ability to forecast based on real consumption information rather than on information from the distributor's warehouse

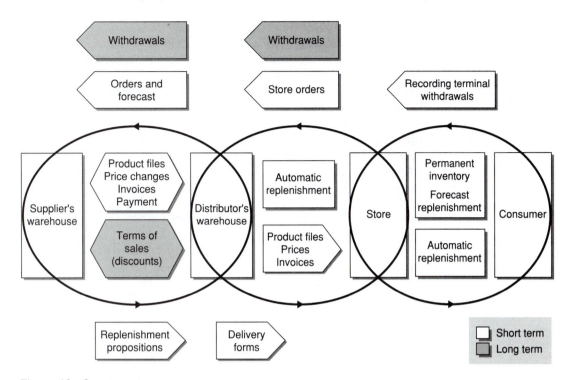

Figure 10–8   Optimizing Flow of Goods Under Automatic Replenishment

This capability of this last advantage allows companies to avoid relying on the biased information that results from the speculative purchasing practices of some distributors. Checkout counter information helps manufacturers spot such practices and work with distributors to change them.

◆ DEVELOPING A SECTORIAL LITS: THE ROLE OF INFORMATION SYSTEMS

Within the global operations and logistics framework used in this book, we have distinguished the dimensions of functional, sectorial, and geographical as a way of understanding the different angles that allow a better analysis of the logistics system. In any situation, the logistics system will be responsible for linking producers, distributors, and customers. Regardless of the nature of ownership in a particular company (vertically integrated or formed by multiple owners), there are important issues with respect to the relationship between manufacturers and distributors, when designing the logistics information and telecommunication system. We outline these issues here.

Information for Shared Planning

Information must be communicated so that each actor in the logistics chain may translate downstream demand into internal operations tasks. For example, distributors convert local sales into store replenishment requirements, which are consolidated to indicate demand for intermediate warehouses belonging to the manufacturer, distributor, or service provider. The manufacturer then converts the new demand into production terms. Upward demand planning of this type (from distributor to manufacturer) is concomitant to downward distribution planning (from manufacturer to distributor).

At the distributor's level the planning process for the logistics chain at the distributor's or service provider's level includes:

- Forecast demand for finished products
- Flow management in the stores
- Planning of warehouse-to-store transportation
- Warehouse flow management

At the manufacturer's level, the planning process includes:

- Forecast of demand for finished products converted into delivery forecasts to intermediate warehouses
- Planning of delivery transportation
- Product flow management
- Production planning
- In-process inventory control
- Supply management

The planning processes of the different actors are closely linked. The distributor's planning approach, based on the consumer's demand, affects the manufacturer's planning process, guaranteeing that manufacturing will meet the known product need. In the same way, downward planning, starting with the manufacturer, partly determines the distributor's plans for making products available to the customer.

Sales campaigns shared between manufacturer and distributor and/or distributor's outlets is a typical form of collaboration. These operations are carried out at the national level (an important event run by the firm's national marketing and national purchaser), regional level (an operation run by the regional marketing level, purchaser, and store), and store level (run directly by the store manager or department manager). The chain's marketing department and product managers define pulled promotions (under the chain's responsibility) and negotiate with stores and manufacturers.

Information to Reduce Shortages

Coordination and shared planning between partners has pluses and minuses. For example, tight planning schedules may result in shortages if the capacity of the logistics system is not sufficient to satisfy such demand. On the other hand, a firm can expect a reduction in storage costs that result from reduced lead times and production linked to improved planning.

Production-driven shortages can be explained by two main reasons. First, forecasts sent to production units are unreliable, which leads to badly adjusted production schedules. Second, production units do not respect the forecasts.

To reduce shortages, information transfer is the key success factor. In particular, manufacturers and distributors must cooperate in developing forecasting information. The chain approach will enable each chain corespondent and customer manager to work hand in hand with the retailer in deciding forecasts. The contribution of the retailer, who knows market characteristics, also would be extremely helpful.

Distributors must communicate sales information. The aim is to compare sales forecasts with the real situation of sales achieved. This information enables production facilities to change production schedules early enough to avoid shortages. One of the major problems in plants today is that they make adjustments only at the last moment—when it is too late to narrow much of the gap between predicted and actual sales.

Succeeding in reducing shortages means making supply more suited to demand (supply of goods from plant). Scanning data that provides sales information is the key to tailoring supply to demand.

Information to Speed the Availability of New Products and Promotions

Knowing distributor inventory levels is essential to speeding the process of stocking shelves with new items or during promotions. The aim is to make sure that inventory levels at the distributor's warehouse are as low as possible when the operation is launched, so that unsold older products do not take up the shelf space new products need. It is not worth designing new products and new formulas ahead of the competition if they are stalled at the warehouse for one or more weeks.

Information for Product Range Optimization

Thanks to the detailed analysis of product turnover on the shelves that data scanning makes feasible, manufacturers and distributors can detect product performance in terms of turnover per outlet. By seeing which products sell badly, the chain will be ideally placed to maintain high product turnover on its stores' shelves. The number of items sold will not diminish, but products will be suited to each chain's needs.

Evaluation Information

Data scanning allows a firm to evaluate the success of a new product launch or new advertising campaign. Rapid measurement allows immediate redesign of advertising messages if needed, optimizing the manufacturer's advertising budget. Similarly, a company can learn quickly which products are failing and halt production, avoiding an inventory glut that hinders the efficient flow of other goods.

Information Systems to Enable Easy Electronic Promotions

When an information system of the level 3 type (see Figure 10–7) is installed throughout a supply chain, the manufacturer and the distributor can launch promotional campaigns at the touch of a button. The logic is as follows:

1. The manufacturer and distributor define promotion campaigns and agree on a way of launching them.
2. At the moment the distributor learns about the sales of a store (targeted approach by outlet and data scanning) and the type of customer (analysis of store traffic times and loyalty schemes making customer type identification possible), the distributor conveys the information to the manufacturer.

3. The distributor uses communication tools that make it possible to advertise promotions limited in time (an hour). The campaigns concern specific products, determined through surveys that are carried out in some chains.
4. Electronic price marking on shelves gives customers confirmation of the reductions the promotion affords.
5. Updating of the price, done automatically, enables the correct price to be registered at the store's checkout counters.

The stakes are important for these forms of virtual promotion, including improving sales for products on shelves and reducing costs through product standardization. However, the pertinence of such promotional methods has to be approved by marketing departments as far as suitability to customers' needs. In addition, organizational sectors must share sales and marketing information and accept their respective roles to achieve the common goal.

◆ SUMMARY

To summarize, the LITS is a critical piece of the total logistics channel. It performs a host of vital functions, including:

- Helping companies optimize their material flow cycles. The LITS manages all the processing required for effective circulation of products within the constraints set by service levels and costs.
- Optimizing the physical resources put in place all along the logistics chain. In this way, then, the LITS makes up the required database and puts into operation decision support tools to allocate resources and use them to maximum efficiency.

Additionally, the LITS provides a means for monitoring operational performance. It allows useful information feedback to logistics performance control and, thus, to logistics indicators. Finally, the LITS supplies valuable decision-support information for management to manage the global supply chain.

DISCUSSION QUESTIONS

1. What are the effects of the need for functional, sectorial, and geographic integration on the requirements for an effective logistics information and telecommunication system (LITS)?

2. What are the most prominent information technologies that substantially impacted the development of LITSs?

3. What is electronic data interchange (EDI)? What are the advantages and potential drawbacks in EDI implementation? What are the major challenges in implementing EDI?

4. What are the contributions of EDI in the implementation of JIT manufacturing systems? Provide examples.

5. What are some important issues to consider in the design of a logistics information system?

6. Outline a structured approach to follow in designing an LITS.

7. What are the different user levels of an LITS? What are the main requirements at each level?

8. What are the needed functional and geographic integration dimensions of the LITS?

9. How do you achieve shared replenishment management required by sectional integration with the LITS?

REFERENCES

Bensaou, M., and N. Venkatraman. 1992. Configurations of interorganizational relationships: A comparison between U.S. and Japanese automakers. INSEAD, Working Paper 81.

Bensaou, M., and N. Venkatraman. 1995. Vertical relationships and the role of information technology: An empirical study of U.S. and Japanese supplier relationship in the auto industry. INSLAD, Working Paper.

Brousseau, F. 1993. L'e'conomie des contrats, Technologies de l'information et coordination interentreprises. Paris: PUF.

Christopher, M. 1985. The Strategy of Distribution Management. England: Gower Publishing 1985

Dawe, R. L. 1993. The impact of information technology on materials logistics in the 1990's, Transportation and distribution. Penton Publishing.

Carets d'Ars des, V. 1991. Implantation et impacts des nouvelles technologies dans l'entreprise de distribution: approche methodologique et pratique, These en sciences de gestion, Montpellier II (December).

Carets d'Ars des, V., and M. Filser. 1993. Organization of the marketing channel and implementation of new technologies: The case of French mass retailing, December, IAF Dijon Crego, France, 9397, Working Paper.

Lambert, D., and J. Stock. 1993. Strategic logistics management. Boston: Irwin.

Lemoine, P. 1993. Le commerce dans la societe' informatisee, Rapport ICC, *Economica*.

Marcussen, C. 1996. The effects of EDI on industrial buyer-seller relationships: A network perspective. *International Journal of Purchasing and Materials Management* (August): 20–26.

Peters, T. Information technology and distribution, in J. C. Cooper (ed.), Logistics and Distribution Planning: Strategies for Management (revised ed.). London.

Powers, R. 1989. Optimization models for logistics decision. *Journal of Business Logistics*. 10 (1):106–21.

Skjott–Larsen T. 1977. Integrated information systems for materials management. *International Journal of Physical Distribution and Materials Management* 8 (2).

Zinn, W., and D. J. Bowersox. 1988. PLanning physical distribution with the principle of postponement. *Journal of Business Logistics* 9 (2):117–36.

◆ Case 10–1: Manugistics ◆

Sandra Curtis, head of Manugistics's support services, shut her eyes in disbelief as she tried to ignore the ringing telephone. This was the third time this week she had been called in the middle of the night. It was Mr. Chen again, calling from Beijing.

Mr. Chen, apologetic but obviously irritated, described in broken English Downing's latest problem with Manugistics's manufacturing planning software. It was late in the afternoon in Beijing, and even though he had tried all day, he could not generate the production schedule he needed for tomorrow. This was an urgent problem because if he did

not come up with a schedule, not only would he lose face, but the factory would also be producing the wrong products and they would be in a greater mess.

Thirty minutes into the conversation, Sandra decided that she was unable to diagnose the problem without seeing the data for herself. She had to replicate Mr. Chen's problem by importing the data into Manugistics's testing lab at the headquarters in Rockville, Maryland (near Washington, DC). Sandra promised to call Mr. Chen back in 45 minutes.

As Sandra put on a pair of jeans and a T-shirt, she dreaded making the next call. She knew that she could not complete Downing's data replication at the lab without the technical assistance of a product support analyst. Joyce Liptak was the analyst most familiar with the Downing configuration, but she was in Germany this week solving a crisis for a different client. Sandra decided to call Eric Newman because he was still new to the company and willing to put in extra effort. Luckily, Eric answered the phone on the first ring and agreed to meet Sandra in 30 minutes.

As Sandra drove through the empty streets, she thought about her five-year tenure with the company. She had joined Manugistics after receiving her bachelor's degree in logistics management at Pennsylvania State University and at a young age had been promoted to the position of manager in charge of support services. Manugistics had been growing rapidly in these years, and with over 50 TBHs (to be hired) on the organizational chart, everyone had to stretch.

When Sandra arrived at the lab at 3:15 A.M. Eric was already there. She contacted Mr. Chen and downloaded the data from the Chinese operation. After three hours they were able to write a temporary fix to get Downing through the next few days. But the root of the problem was still unknown. This same problem had plagued Downing in Beijing two other nights this week. Sandra knew that Downing needed someone to visit Beijing to diagnose and fix the problem.

However, no one was available. She was the only consultant familiar with the project, but she had pressing responsibilities related to her new promotion. "This is going to get worse before it gets better!" she thought to herself, as she was driving home to change and return to the office again. And it was not clear to her how it would get better.

Company Background

Manugistics, or Scientific Time Sharing Corporation (STSC) as it was named at the time, began operations in 1969 as a lessor of mainframe computing time. STSC leased computer power to run statistical analysis and data manipulations. After many years of comfortable margins, the bottom dropped out of the time-share market. Many of its previous clients were looking for new PC-based statistical software applications, and STSC decided to focus on that specialty.

STSC first developed a series of statistical packages that catered to the engineering professionals who required programs capable of crunching large volumes of data. But that niche did not seem to be promising. Plagued by software bugs and a very limited consumer base, STSC shifted its focus from scientific statistical packages to the broader and rapidly growing arena of supply chain management. The packages aimed to help manage the flow of goods and information from procurement, through manufacturing and distribution, to delivery to consumers. In 1992, the company changed its name to Manugistics, a combination of the two words *manufacturing* and *logistics.*

The company grew rapidly in the early 1990s. (See Exhibits 1 and 2 for a balance sheet and income statement.) By 1995, Manugistics offered software and services to integrate planning activities for product demand, distribution, manufacturing, and transportation. Its clients were Fortune 1000 companies in the retail, consumer goods, chemical and pharmaceutical, consumer electronics, food distribution, and transportation industries. (See Exhibit 3.) They included major companies that were market leaders in consumer products, grocery retail operations, and fast food chains. Client firms used Manugistics' software "solutions" to re-engineer their supply chains. Manugistics typically charged from $100,000 to $1,000,000 for its package—about half of which was for the software and half for services. Most companies recouped this cost in less than two years.

One-fourth of Manugistics clients operated internationally. All used Manugistics systems in their American operations, but many extended it to their international divisions quickly. To serve the foreign markets, Manugistics opened an office in London in 1989 and later, in 1993, purchased a division of Marketing Systems. Marketing Systems was based in Germany and supplied business operations software and services for retail, manufacturing and distribution industries in several European countries. After a training period of several weeks, the former Marketing Systems employees were able to service some of Manugistics' clients in Germany.

Sales & Service

A typical project involved sending a team of consultants to analyze the client's needs, design a customized solution, install the software, and train the employee "users." This "Implement Solutions" process took three to six months. It was often customary for the consulting team to revisit the client site six months after implementation to fine-tune the process and break bad habits before they stuck. When a client reached significant cost savings and was comfortable with using the software, Manugistics referred to it as "referenceable." Nearly all prospective clients interviewed referenceable clients extensively before making a purchase decision.

Once they had installed a Manugistics system, clients remained as Manugistics' customers. Almost all (96%) would make additional purchases, and even the remaining 4% would not necessarily switch to competitors' systems. Manugistics promoted a "partnership" with its clients and aimed at continuous improvement of their operations. Clients received from three to six software updates per year (at some cost), plus special "patch" fixes to correct problems, which were mostly due to customization of the package to fit their needs.

For service and support, U.S. and European clients paid an annual maintenance fee equal to approximately 15% of the system's initial purchase price. This fee entitled them to purchase new software enhancements and have access to unlimited English language telephone support during normal working hours at the Rockville head-

Exhibit 1

Balance Sheet at Fiscal Year End, Four-Year Summary ($000)

ASSETS:	2/28/95	2/28/94	2/28/93	2/28/92
Cash	4,599	1,997	1,259	2,035
Marketable securities	20,366	15,566	na	na
Receivables	14,900	10,793	8,004	5,976
Inventories	600	496	683	813
Other current assets	1,063	1,108	745	996
Net property, plant and equipment	2,672	1,870	6,314	4,487
Accumulated depreciation	na	na	3,031	2,090
Deferred charges	3,268	2,782	na	na
Intangibles	1,531	na	na	na
Deposits and other assets	140	53	61	75
TOTAL ASSETS	49,139	34,665	14,046	12,273
LIABILITIES				
Accounts payable	2,231	1,587	2,711	1,654
Current portion of long-term debt	188	247	859	743
Accrued expenses	3,092	2,398	523	1,397
Income taxes	309	117	22	460
Other current liabilities	5,844	4,337	6,347	3,715
Deferred charges	626	552	416	350
Long-term debt	337	526	795	840
TOTAL LIABILITIES	12,627	9,766	11,672	9,159
STOCKHOLDERS' EQUITY				
Preferred stock	na	na	1000	1000
Common stock net	21	20	12	12
Capital surplus	30,311	21,920	554	1,020
Retained earnings	6,180	2,959	807	1,082
TOTAL STOCKHOLDERS' EQUITY	36,512	24,899	2,374	3,114
TOTAL LIABILITIES AND NET WORTH	49,139	34,665	14,046	12,273
Number of employees	372	280	179	121

Source: Company Annual Reports

quarters or the London support center. Thus, clients had access to support centers 17 hours per day, Monday through Friday.

Several international clients split support for their operations between the two locations. For example, one firm serviced its European operations through the UK office and its domestic operations out of Rockville. In such cases, Manugistics maintained a support team assigned to the parent company to provide consistent communications and make sure nothing would fall through the cracks of the two service centers.

Clients paid for unlimited free access to Manugistics's telephone help line as a component of their annual maintenance fee. A person in the client organization (who would be most familiar with the system) was usually designated as the "contact," and would handle the minor problems without calling Manugistics. Nevertheless, the help line at Manugistics was generally swamped with calls. At Rockville, two call-routing operators directed these calls to fifteen product analysts. The analysts were either specialized in Manugistics' products for a mainframe or for a client/server system. Although no client was guaranteed a dedicated analyst, the same analyst usually worked with each client to ensure consistency. A typical call could last from fifteen minutes to three hours. Some problems required continuous attention of an analyst over several weeks. The number of service calls could be charted as a bell shaped curve following each released upgrade of software, with its peak around two to three months after the release.

Exhibit 2

Income Statement, Four-Year Summary ($000)				
Fiscal Year Ended	*2/28/95*	*2/28/94*	*2/23/93*	*2/23/92*
Net sales	49,410	37,961	28,284	30,005
Cost of goods sold	15,832	12,396	10,207	8,125
Gross margin	33,578	25,565	18,078	21,880
R & D expenditures	7,550	5,011	4,097	3,978
Selling, general and administrative expenses	21,710	17,088	13,976	14,041
Interest expense	59	83	187	316
Income before taxes	4,961	3,612	−87	3,721
Provision for income taxes	1,740	1,460	188	1,357
Net income	3,221	2,152	−275	2,384
Outstanding shares	10,127	9,448	5,778	5,794

Source: Company Annual Reports

Exhibit 3

Typical Customers				
Type of Company	*Number of Employees*	*Number of Locations*	*Company's Annual Revenue (000)*	*Fees to Date to Manugistics**
Pharmaceutical company	74,000	45	$ 9,000,000	$2,250,000
Consumer products company	32,800	28	7,500,000	1,675,000
Grocery chain	98,000	630	14,000,000	3,800,000
Confections manufacturer	23,000	16	7,400,000	1,600,000
Trucking company	15,500	11	3,200,000	950,000
Software development firm	6,800	34	42,000,000	2,200,000
Discount retail chain	528,000	2,200	70,000,000	5,500,000
Animal food manufacturer	12,500	16	2,200,000	800,000

Source: Company Documents

*Numbers in *Fees to Date to Manugistics* have been disguised.

Calls to the help line were rated on a scale from one to four in their urgency. One signified that the client's system was down. All available Manugistics resources would be mobilized to get the client's system up and running. A rating of four was only a request for a more convenient feature. (If applicable, these were added to a wish list to be incorporated into future software versions.) Issues in the middle of the scale received a diligent but not urgent effort by the product analysts.

The specific problems also varied considerably and were classified into three "tiers." In tier one were minor problems usually related to local language releases and other questions that could be answered easily by an analyst who had broad and general knowledge about the specific application. In tier two were those issues that required more complicated diagnosis (and possibly duplication of the client's situation in

Manugistics' service laboratory). Tier three problems involved fixing a bug in the application package itself, which was considerably more complicated and required a good knowledge of the software and the codes.

Progress in resolution of each issue was tracked on an internal logging system by client, severity, and analyst responsible. Performance data from this system, such as average resolution time by severity code, was tracked carefully and used to measure individual and departmental performance. The average resolution time in 1995 was 62 hours for class one issues and 41 days for class three issues. Some class three issues had remained open for over two years.

Product analysts, like all new consultants, were required to complete a rigorous three-month training program called the "Manugistics University." Besides short modules on Manugistics "Proper Business Etiquette," and "Dress for

Success," the focus of this program was on teaching complex software packages and different computer platforms and databases. The analyst would learn, for instance, how to handle a client's system, which might operate a UNIX platform accessing an Oracle database, while another might use a client/server configuration running on OS-2's within an SAP R-3 system. Product analysts needed the hands-on skills to replicate client problems in a sophisticated testing lab. They also played a significant role in testing new software releases for bugs before they were installed on client systems.

Access to the help line was limited to domestic and European clients only. Manugistics did not have the resources to offer help line support to its Asian or Latin American clients. Instead, these clients usually maintained working relationships with the members of the consulting team who had implemented their package. Manugistics charged for the services of these employees at consulting rates ranging from $150 to $200 per hour, per consultant.

Of the total annual maintenance fees collected, around three-fourths were plowed back into software development for further improvement of the product. The remaining quarter was used to sustain the fifteen-person telephone support staff at the Rockville headquarters. There was a delicate balance involved in the allocation of resources between software development and product support. In the short term, product support needed resources to walk clients through the minefields of bugs and limitations in the software. But in the long run, software development needed resources to fight the continuous battle against faulty codes and to improve the software's facility. Moreover, Manugistics wanted to be a front runner in ten years, when they predicted client/server technology would offer miraculous applications. This goal required a steady stream of resources dedicated to improving Manugistics' software. The two departments in charge of development and service often struggled to live up to the company's motto "Working as One."

Finding qualified employees for either software development or support services was not easy. In addition to requiring an undergraduate degree, preferably in logistics management, Manugistics sought candidates who were academically at the top of their class, with excellent interpersonal skills, and willing to travel up to 90% of the time. Once hired, the candidate had to complete the three-month "Manugistics University" and spend several years on a team to develop adequate expertise.

Downing

Downing, Inc., established in 1921, was a leading producer of household products with a large market share in the United States and growing international share. In 1992 Downing purchased Manugistics' Manufacturing Planning module for its three U.S. manufacturing plants. In 1994, when it entered into a joint venture to manufacture in China, Manugistics was asked to extend the application for the Chinese operation. Sandra Curtis was put in charge, and a team of four under her supervision started to work on the project.

Downing's China implementation proved to be a particularly tough project. Sandra and her team had underestimated the task by a wide margin and were simply not prepared for the challenges of this international assignment. Sandra's own preparation had been to read a 1990 HBS case entitled, "China, The Great Awakening," which she received from an MBA intern the morning of her first trip to China!

Implementing Manugistics software into a new plant and then integrating that plant into the company's existing centralized system created problems at many different levels. There were problems at the local level due to system incompatibility, training, and organizational processes. Then the plant had to be "plugged in" to the company's centrally controlled integrated system. The central system had to anticipate problems from the new plant's extra volume and imperfect data.

Manugistics had scheduled eight weeks for implementing the system in the Beijing plant. It was dragged out to sixteen. Hardware problems, construction delays, and language barriers all contributed to its difficulties. Interpreters, always in short supply, had to help the consulting team instruct every training class.

The sixteen weeks had been especially hard on Sandra. She was under pressure, constantly traveling back and forth between Beijing and Rockville, and she was often frustrated. Even when the local implementation was supposedly complete, she knew that she would have to be back soon. She had not felt the "connection" with her "students" and doubted their understanding of the more complex issues. She hoped that employees from Downing's plants in the United States would step in and help in the future, but so far that had either not happened or was not effective.

Options for Globalizing Support Services

Manugistics's easiest sales were when an existing client opened a new operation in a different geographic location. Often the client would return to Manugistics and ask for help. Even though the new location might be half way around the globe, Manugistics had to follow and provide its services if it wanted to keep the client satisfied. By 1995, international sales accounted for 20% of total sales and were estimated to increase to 60% by the end of the decade. With domestic sales growing at an annual rate of 30%–40%, the increasing number of international projects was putting pressure on the company. Manugistics could not hire enough qualified employees to fill the positions available, and bilingual and internationally experienced consultants were the hardest to find.

Living with the Chinese project had convinced Sandra that it was time for Manugistics to establish a strategy to meet this growing challenge. As manager of support services she knew that she had to take the initiative to formulate this strategy. After some discussion with colleagues, she narrowed the options to three:

1. Use Services of Third-Party Consulting Companies.

Several of the big international consulting firms specialized in providing assistance with computer-aided management systems. They provided the service not only for their own systems but sometimes also for other vendors. Manugistics had experimented with this option via a pilot program in Spain. This experiment involved offering the "Manugistics University" to a handful of consultants from the Spanish office of a well-known international consulting firm. This would form a core group to act as a self-sufficient sales and support operation in Spain. However, after two years of operations, Manugistics was disappointed by lower than projected sales figures.

Manugistics had extended this concept also to consultants from a few other companies in what they called "channels and alliances." By paying the "tuition," these consultants were admitted to the "Manugistics University." The cost to Manugistics was low and there was a potential for a profitable external training operation, especially since there was demand for expertise in specific software packages. There was little risk of losing proprietary technology to those "partners" who could become competitors because Manugistics packages were complex and changed continuously. One of the largest software companies, German-based SAP America, had capitalized on this strategy and ran a full-time training facility in Dallas, Texas, to train consultants from other companies to implement and support SAP systems.

2. Train Clients to Help Themselves.

One of Manugistics's clients, Myers and Fischer, a large international chemical company, had employed this strategy. Manugistics trained one Myers and Fischer employee as the "trainer" who then returned to the company to train nine more employees. The team traveled around the globe and implemented the new system in each location.

Both Myers and Fischer and Manugistics seemed to be satisfied with this arrangement. But it was difficult to assess if this practice could be extended to other clients. In Downing's case, three other factories were successfully running using Manugistics' software. If Downing's current users could help Manugistics implement new solutions to other divisions within their own company, Manugistics could share the burden of support. Additionally, Downing could eliminate a large amount of consulting fees due to Manugistics.

On the down side, the Downings of the world were usually too busy to complete the work within their own divisions, let alone have excess employees available to spend three to six months helping other divisions. Training even ten extra people

during the initial implementation added very little cost to the overall project. But they would have to be made available for training and later for trouble-shooting.

This option was risky because it might give the unfavorable impression that Manugistics was unable to service its own client base. In an industry where the perception of service quality played a big part in the purchase decision, this was not a reputation that Manugistics wanted to have. On the other hand, this practice not only provided significant savings for the client in consulting fees, but, more importantly, resulted in smoother and improved manufacturing and logistics operations.

3. Provide Direct Service from Central Location.

In 1996, Manugistics set up a bulletin board system on the World Wide Web. Located outside the company's "firewall," the bulletin board was monitored hourly by product analysts in Rockville during normal working hours. Manugistics clients were given a password to access the system. Clients deposited written questions on the system and a product analyst would reply with assistance within a few hours. Clients worldwide could easily use this system to access the Rockville office directly.

This option offered a low-cost solution to answer basic questions. More complex questions would still require a telephone conversation which could also be handled directly from Rockville. It was too early to judge the efficacy of this system, but Eric Newman, one of the product analysts who had been working with this system for a few weeks, felt that this option could prove to be very useful in servicing international clients. Perhaps a strategy based on more sophisticated use of the internet could be adopted by Manugistics to service its international clients.

Formulating a Strategy

Finding a solution to the problem of servicing the international clients was more than a passing interest to Sandra. She was spending too much time and energy on these clients and, if she did not come up with a new idea, would have to spend even more. Another trip to China in the next few weeks—as she was afraid was inevitable—was exhausting and took her further away from her current responsibilities.

She was determined to make a presentation to Bill Ryan, president and CEO of Manugistics, and suggest what should be done for servicing the international clients. She recalled that in a recent address, Bill Ryan had expressed a concern over growing too quickly. He feared that sustained growth at 30–50% would require Manugistics to lower its hiring standards and jeopardize its strong corporate culture. Yet if Manugistics planned to achieve its goal to be the global leader in supply chain management software, it had to find a way to grow its international business at even a higher rate.

Chapter 11

Performance Measurement and Evaluation in Global Logistics

◆ ◆ ◆

This chapter discusses the following topics:

◆ *Why performance measurement is important in global logistics*

◆ *Different types of available metrics*

◆ *How to determine which set of metrics to use*

◆ *Measuring performance in an integrated company*

◆ *Measuring performance of third-party logistics service providers*

◆ INTRODUCTION

The integration and globalization of logistics has major implications for the design and use of logistics performance measurements. Developing approaches and metrics that are tailored to current logistics realities is critical, because effective cost and operations management control demand appropriate information on logistics performance. Most companies entering the global marketplace will need new metrics and databases with which to manage their logistics, because existing systems (e.g., general accounting) will not provide the needed information.

This chapter outlines key activities involved in operations and logistics control and describes the types of performance information they require. It then discusses how to measure performance effectively from two common global corporate scenarios: functional (intrafirm) integration and sectorial (interfirm) integration.

◆ OPERATIONS AND LOGISTICS CONTROL: KEY ACTIVITIES NEED PERFORMANCE INFORMATION

The major tasks in managing operations and logistics are similar to those of managing other functions. However, the types of information that managers need to monitor and adjust performance in these areas vary according to logistics activities and specific logistics designs. Level of detail is also important. Companies should monitor the service level quality by product, distribution channel, customer, operational unit, and so on. These measures must be set up to ensure that the logistics service accomplishes the desired objectives.

Primary management functions fall into two categories: planning and control.

Planning

The planning process is dynamic by nature, because it allows a firm to identify strategies to achieve desired goals. Goals are usually formalized through budget forecasts and through operational investment and strategic plans. Like other managers, those in charge of operations and logistics need information to determine whether any gaps exist between the desired objective (what the firm wants to do) and the result that would be achieved with no change in resources (a simple extrapolation using past information). Figure 11–1 illustrates this process.

Planning requires both quantitative and qualitative information. The following factors are important in elaborating budgets, investment plans, and operations and logistics strategy plans in line activities. They reflect the current competitive positions affected by planning decisions.

- **Quality.** The key issue is customer satisfaction and whether operations are geared to and capable of producing it.
- **Timeliness.** Many aspects of logistics have deadlines, and logistics activities also affect the ability of other parts of the process to meet their time-related goals.
- **Productivity.** The productivity of resources used, whose performance level is traditionally measured in costs, remains an unavoidable challenge.

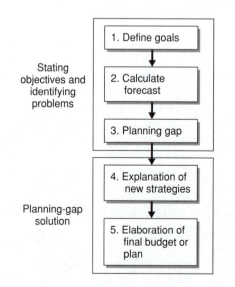

Figure 11–1   The Flow of Management Control

Control

Control activities, which may occur yearly, half-yearly, quarterly, or monthly, look for any differences between planning goals and actual results. Analysis of the differences leads to corrective action (Figure 11–2).

Cost Management: The Relationship Between Desired Level of Service and Minimization of Logistics Costs

In chapter 1, we emphasized the importance of logistics costs as part of the overall cost structure of companies. In some cases, they represent as much as 20 percent of the sales dollar. Because costs are a key competitive factor, cost management is integral to the logistics function.

The logistics orientation is basically one of optimization—that is, either to minimize cost subject to a predefined level of service or to maximize service subject to a budget constraint. Many factors affect cost management in logistics and operations management—for example, setting up a JIT flow management organization, differentiating service by product, or differentiating other elements by market.

Considering flow management in a more integrated fashion across functions, sectors, or geographical areas requires a new approach to performance measurement. Where hierarchical organizations set and monitor individual function-specific goals, in an integrated supply chain, all the actors in the system are encouraged to work toward the goals of integration and global optimization of activities. For example, improved integration between production and distribution may result in production's storing more semi-finished goods to reduce the number of finished goods stored in the distributor's warehouses (postponement). Differentiation to satisfy market changes also may require postponement. Traditional inventory-level objectives and performance metrics will no longer apply in such scenarios.

To optimize global operations and logistics functions, managers need to monitor the following cost elements:

- Procurement costs for raw materials, components, and subunits (the financial and physical aspects of freight, maintenance, and storage)
- Purchase cost for raw materials, components, and subunits (orders, taking into account quantitative discounts)
- Production costs (labor, work-in-process inventory)
- Distribution costs (freight, order preparation, maintenance, finished goods inventory, and spare parts)
- Sales price of finished goods (customer account management, calculation of reductions on quantities due to promotions)

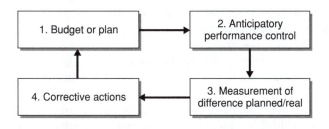

Figure 11–2   Dynamic Nature of Control

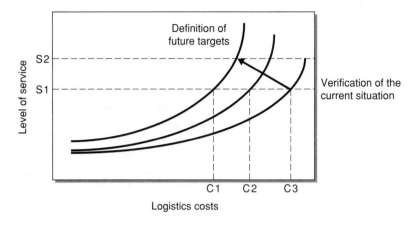

Figure 11–3   Objectives of Controlling the Logistics Activity

Doubtless, managers must consider the effects of all cost decisions on service and customer satisfaction. As illustrated in Figure 11–3, the main objective of logistics performance measurement is, on the one hand, to verify the operational accuracy of the curves and, on the other hand, to explore alternatives to obtain higher levels of service at a lower cost.

Many of the strategic choices that global companies and logistics managers must make have a major impact on logistics costs, quality, and performance measurement. They include the following:

- Sourcing raw materials, including components and subunits, nationally or internationally
- Relocating manufacturing
- Developing new geographical markets or consolidating national ones
- Investing in production process technologies, such as JIT, or staying with inflexible processes
- Using JIT or speculative purchasing
- Incorporating logistics parameters (such as freight costs) in pricing schemes or maintaining one price
- Launching promotions several times a year or adopting an every day low price (EDLP) strategy
- Developing a comprehensive product range or concentrating on a narrow product mix
- Using a wide or limited choice of marketing channels
- Adopting means of transport for bulk, using rapid means of transport, or building a local distribution network
- Determining the size of packaging facilities
- Opting for outsourcing logistics operations, such as procurement and distribution

All of these options should be put through economic simulations based on costs and service impact for the firm's profitability. To create meaningful simulations and to monitor the impact of changes, managers must have access to reliable, appropriate cost data. However, compartmentalized structures (see chapter 12) and traditional information systems (see chapter 10) do not provide the types of cost information global logistics managers need to make the best decisions. Determining what information to gather and designing new databases are critical to measuring performance as companies integrate functions.

Type of Logistics Responsibility Center

Businesses create different types of cost management entities for different cost goals. Known as responsibility centers, these cost-related management structures have defined missions, constraints, and resources that affect their performance. Performance measurement systems for logistics must reflect the types of responsibility centers involved.

Traditionally, five types of responsibility centers exist:

1. *Production cost center.* Its goal is to achieve a given level of productivity while minimizing the costs. This cost center often applies to workshops, warehouses, or corporate truck fleets.
2. *Discretionary cost center.* This type of center works within an operating budget. Its traditional approach—typical of financial and data processing departments—does not allow continuous performance improvement.
3. *Income center.* The principal goal here is to obtain a given return on investment, corresponding to a desired market share in relation to a sales budget. Companies in these cases spin off their logistics operations to a subsidiary, with the goal of better identifying costs and turning the operation into an income center.
4. *Investment center.* The objective is for minimum production and logistics costs to maximize the productivity of the given economic asset.
5. *Profit center.* In this structure, the global operations function or even the logistics function is completely open to the market and offers service to customers from both inside and outside the organization. This very dynamic arrangement often prepares for and precedes outsourcing of the activity or function.

Cost Accounting Methods in Logistics

The issue of cost accounting methods is at the heart of performance measurement and logistics control. Logistics costs frequently are split across several functions and, thus, are difficult to identify. Many existing accounting methods do not provide appropriate information on total logistics costs.

The total cost method causes particular problems for performance measurement. This method endeavors to charge, in an arbitrary fashion, indirect costs to products or customers. These costs originate from financial accounting (natural costs) and do not correspond to functional costs measurement. Although this system measures profits by each product family or customer, focusing on the activity costs that create overall profit and loss (usually indirect costs) would be more appropriate for measuring performance. Thus, companies must add a logistics system structure for economic indicators (total cost covering everything from materials procurement to distribution to the end-user), and qualitative indicators (lead-time, dependability, product quality, and efficient utilization of scarce resources).

Other accounting methods include the *direct cost* and the *standard cost* method. The *direct method* breaks costs down into two categories: fixed and variable. This approach is very useful for break-even analysis (calculation of necessary investments and preliminary economic profitability evaluation). However, it must be appropriate to the volume strategy pursued.

Using *cost/service standard* indicators in logistics allows operational managers to set objectives and to measure the difference relative to a standard—that is, between what should have happened and the actual situation. This method is particularly suited to logistics operations because they are repetitive by nature. Compared to the manufacturing environment, the greatest difficulty lies in the choice of common units of measurement. For example, for preparing orders should the common unit be the order, the order line, the number of packets prepared, or even the number of deliveries? One advantage is the potential to use this information in statistical process control (SPC). However, frequent information collection and updating are needed for SPC. Information gathering and measurement that are driven by the budget process and its objectives may not meet these needs or be appropriate for improvement efforts.

◆ MEASURING PERFORMANCE IN FUNCTIONAL INTEGRATION

As firms integrate functions for business improvement and globalization, objectives and ways of doing business change. A key element of successful integration is to develop performance measurement systems that reflect these changes and allow evaluation of their progress and impact on competitiveness. Changes that result from integrating marketing, production, and logistics affect both what is measured and who solves identified problems.

For example, marketing may now affect logistics by establishing the servicing limits within which the system must work. So marketing must accept substantial responsibility for the design and operating costs of the logistic system. The performance measuring system for logistics must thus report the effectiveness of some decisions of a marketing nature.

Promotional campaigns that a manufacturer's marketing department sets up regarding distributors illustrate the issues involved in an integrated approach to performance measurement. Such campaigns or special offers usually generate limited quantities or quotas, and managers must closely monitor sales. Two types of results must be measured: Has the quota been reached? What conclusions can be drawn about the interaction with the distribution chain?

Answering these questions means checking the two initial objectives—that is, maximizing turnover and sales quantities at a given date. It is important to measure two types of quantities:

Q_b = total quantity of the product reserved for the chain considered
at the beginning of the promotion (i.e.,original quota)

Qf = total quantity of the product reserved for the chain considered after
reallocation of the quota (at the end of the promotion)

In addition, it is important to monitor:

- Length of the operation (i.e., promotion)
- The sum of quantities ordered
- The number consumed
- The number broken, creating loss
- The number left over, generating extra logistics costs
- The quality of the quota in quantity: deviation compared to forecast quantities, and in lead times: number of days blocked or extra compared to length initially forecast
- The number of days blocked
- The number of extra days necessary for selling excess inventory (planned from final consumption)

By putting the results on graphs, managers can compare global performance and can compare one campaign to another to determine progress made in quota management. In a similar manner, we can measure global flexibility of the company in quota management by charting the distribution of the products included in the promotion as a group. Figures 11–4 and 11–5 illustrate comparative analysis.

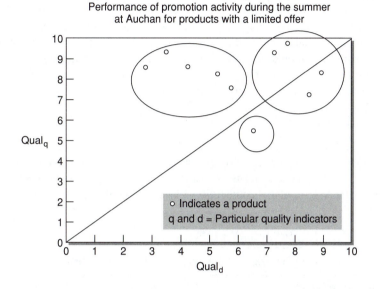

Figure 11–4 Example of Distribution Chain Performance for a Particular Promotion

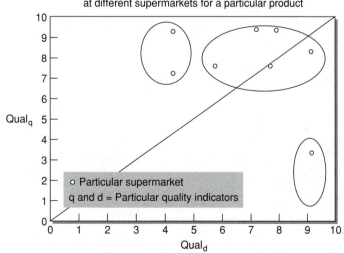

Figure 11–5 Example of Performance of a Particular Product in Different Distribution Chains

Packaging is another example of the logistics performance control system taking into account marketing elements. Packaging involves two considerations: the marketing component (the packaging itself) and the logistics component (e.g., the container, cardboard box, pallet). Packaging influences the product's cost, price, logistics productivity, and product sales results.

The integration of logistics and manufacturing functions has a similar impact on performance measurement. In particular, implementing pull systems like JIT, new manufacturing technologies, or flexible manufacturing units requires a complete rethinking of the management control systems and the indicators used. Indeed, the objectives assigned to a JIT unit are very different from those assigned to a traditional one, and include satisfying demand, total quality, reduced inventory, shorter lead-times, and cooperation with suppliers. Companies also should introduce new performance measurement tools intended for measuring flows. Table 11–1 briefly demonstrates the different types of performance indicators companies can use to measure progress toward different types of goals.

Metrics for Measuring Performance

The relevant metrics or logistics indicators are the key tools of the control system, enabling coherent, strategy-driven actions and decisions (Figure 11–6). The basis of effective metrics is an analysis of success factors for a product or process step. Appropriate metrics for today's global competition measure more than traditional productivity indicators

Table 11–1

Sample of Performance Measures in a JIT Environment

Goals	Inventory reduction	Flow performance	Partnership with suppliers
Performance measurement	materials, current and finished goods inventory value and turnover quality of forecast	lead times/dispatch times cycle efficiency = total operating time/lead time rate of breakdown idle time, set-up time and inspection time batch size number of breakdowns	delivery frequency delivery times percentage of deliveries of ready-to-use packaging number of exceptional trips number and percentage of suppliers in quality assurance

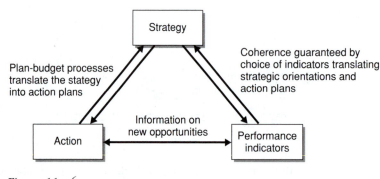

Figure 11–6   Relationship between Metrics and Strategy

(ratio of real output to real input) and include utilization and performance indicators. Utilization indicators concentrate on the frequency with which means are made available to logistics. Performance indicators measure activities compared to goals or set standards.

Overall, metrics can measure the level of:

- Efficiency of the managerial functions involved—in particular, quality, organization, and costs
- Adaptability to customer requirements, which involves organizations' measuring performance in dealing with unpredictable customer demand
- Adaptability to market requirements, or performance relative to uncertainties in the market

Table 11–2 suggests possible criteria for evaluating the level of service for a commercial logistics dispatch department. It illustrates the necessary relationship between performance criteria, customer satisfaction, and competitive positioning.

Table 11–2

Internal and External Performance in a Benchmark Perspective for a Commercial Logistics Dispatch Department

Customer Requirements			Criteria for Evaluating Level of Service	Position Vis-à-Vis Competitors			Trend		
of little importance	*important*	*very important*		+	=	–	+	=	–
			Order time delivery						
			Respecting delivery times						
			Delivery frequency						
			Adaptability of vehicles						
			Drivers' competence						
			Product conformity						
			Qualitative defaults in picking						
			Quantitative defaults in picking						
			Inventory break made known at time of order						
			Inventory break stated on delivery						
			Product presentation						
			Product identification						
			Pallet identification						
			Quality of telephone contact						
			Answering complaints						
			Swift response when problems arise						
			Shipping documents clear and readable						
			Quality of nomenclature documents						
			Global quality rating						

The Objectives of Metrics

Collecting information on performance indicators gives managers the ability to monitor and control many aspects of logistics performance. These include:

- Measuring the activity (volume) and the logistics performance. The metrics should be suited to guiding future investment and new restructuring, and analyzing different types of organizations for foreign subsidiaries. Determining the strengths of some subsidiaries and the weaknesses of others will encourage managers to bring all these subsidiaries up to standard (internal benchmarking).
- Setting goals and comparing the actual situation at all times.
- Following a market plan (gap analysis related to goals). Through extrapolation of past trends and by gap analysis, performance data enables forecasting and reduces uncertainty.
- Determining the levers that will help achieve goals and single out the priority actions to be implemented.
- Revealing the degree of flexibility of the organization and how variable its costs are. The set of indicators is a dynamic tool, which must reflect the organization's behavior.
- Leading, mobilizing, and managing personnel.

Principles of Metrics Design

Speed, reliability, and simplicity are the three main criteria for efficient metrics. Following key design principles can help logistics and other managers develop efficient, useful metrics. These principles include

- Arranging indicators by priority
- Segmenting the metrics
- Visualizing the function content
- Clarifying objectives of the function or team
- Selecting indicators that deal with quality
- Formatting the metrics effectively

Figure 11–7 examines how to arrange indicators by priority based on performance and importance, using as an example the transportation metrics for a particular company. The principle to segment the metrics involves to classify according to constraints, product types, and market types in relation to logistical families (see chapter 6). Table 11–3 illustrates logistical family groupings for after-sales service. Table 11–4 shows how metrics related to calculation of order-picking costs have been thought out according to service by type of store.

Metrics are indicators designed for a given manager, with a given set of responsibilities. The point in describing and visualizing the function content is to determine the degree of responsibility for each person and to identify the means that managers have at their disposal to measure performance in these responsibility areas. Objectives must be clearly expressed, and quality indicators must be selected. These indicators require the choice of appropriate common units of measurement and a global economic unit of measurement (e.g., currency).

Metrics must be presented in an understandable format. Tables, diagrams, and similar visual aids are effective formats for establishing and tracking indicators. They communicate results clearly. As an example, Figure 11–8 illustrates the metrics used to indicate delivery problems as deviation from target.

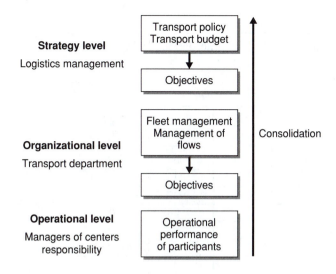

Figure 11 – 7   Example for Transportation Indicators

Table 11 – 3

Logistics Families for Parts in the After-Sales Service

Logistics Family	Rank Typology	Class and Content
1	Technical	• By function: e.g., electric, body
2	Captive or competing parts	• Captive parts for which manufacturers have a monopoly of distribution, since they hold the patent rights
3	Rank according to original equipment	• Original parts • Adaptable parts • Approved spare parts
4	Whether brand parts or not	• Brand new parts • Second-hand parts • Reworked parts
5	Rank according to parts' physical characteristics	• Size • Weight • Volume • Fragility
6	Rank according to unit value	• Expensive parts • Low-value parts
7	Rank according to sales volume or value	• High volume parts • Medium volume parts • Low volume parts
8	Degree of standardization parts	• Number of listed parts needed to cover one or several models
9	Level of technical difficulty of parts and their assembly	• Accessories and technical parts • Easy or difficult assembly

Table 11–4

	Units	$/U	Warehouse 5 tons # of Units	Warehouse 5 tons $	Outlet 1 1 ton # of Units	Outlet 1 1 ton $	Outlet 2 0.5 ton # of Units	Outlet 2 0.5 ton $
Pallets arrived	pallet	9	10	90	1.2	10.8	5	45
Pallets processed	pallet	12	2	24		0		0
Packs type 1	pack	1	1100	1100		0		0
Other cartons	pack	1.5		0	500	750	300	450
Preparation	sales units	0.5		0	100	50	30	15
Labeling	sales units	0.05		0		0	30	1,5
Third party	ton	300		0		0		0
Fixed costs	ton	70	5	350		70	0,5	35
			Total 1564			880.80		546.50
			$/T 312.8			880.80		1093

Calculation of Costs in Order Picking by Type of Store

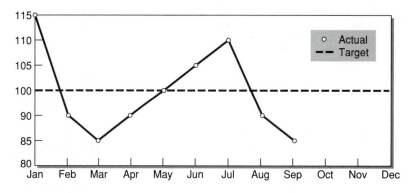

Figure 11–8   Target versus Actual for Interruption in Distribution

The form metrics take and the way they are used are specific to each organization and should express the individuality of its structure. Although different users may personalize some aspects of tracking, it is important to retain the same type of overall presentation across the organization, despite the specificity of each user's indicators.

Metrics information should be readily available. It is better to move ahead with approximate, yet rapidly obtainable information, than to delay taking corrective actions by waiting for more exact information. It is also important to remember that in the search for continuous performance improvement, the priorities may change as some problems are solved and new ones, with new performance indicators, are addressed. Thus, the metrics system should remain flexible.

Table 11–5

	Choice of Indicators for Intra-Firm Integration		
	Manufacturing	*Marketing*	*Finance*
Quality	Of Forecasting and production	Of Deliveries	Of Data
Organization		Volume, quality, and situation of stocks	
Costs	Production runs	Distribution centers	Information systems

Table 11–6

	Illustration of Transportation Information and Metrics	
	Indicators	*Objectives*
Quality	Deadline, punctuality	Analysis of competitors breakages, losses (benchmarking)

Organization	Flow-mapping
	Determining segments
	  • plant to warehouse
	  • plant to channel
	  • Distribution
	Nature of fleet
	  • Own fleet
	  • Public transport
	Optimizing inventory/freight ratio (load factor)
		Quest for best organization in terms of economic viability by using:
		Operational research models (e.g., simulation)
		Close involvement with logistics service companies

Costs	Market segment or distribution channel Geographic area Type of fleet Unit transported	Separate fixed from variable costs Reduce freight cost to minimum

Key management decisions involved in metrics design include determining the:

- Presentation models
- Frequency of updating—to be based on the frequency of production or execution of operations
- Deadlines for updating at the end of each period
- Responsibility for updating

The choice of indicators and metrics is one of the most critical steps for measuring performance. Table 11–5 shows a matrix that illustrates how looking for indicators provides the opportunity for cooperation and collaboration between the functions within the company or intra-firm integration.

Selection of indicators and metrics must be validated according to the objectives being pursued. This is clear from Table 11–6, which contains transport information for the logistics manager.

Characteristics of Effective Metrics

The purpose of metrics is to be able to act upon causes. For example, companies can only manage costs by controlling the activities that generate costs and produce results. Thus, a performance measurement system should track the cost-generators. Characteristics of indicators that enable decision-making and action include the following:

- *Independence:* each indicator should measure a given aspect of the logistics activity.
- *Linkage with other indicators:* each indicator adds to the picture provided by the others, reducing the likelihood that problems will be missed or masked.
- *Appropriateness:* the indicators must be representative of the phenomena they set out to measure.
- *Objectivity:* useful indicators do not judge, but define quantitatively the extent and direction of the problem.
- *Regularity:* when the same control is carried out in exactly the same conditions, the result observed is strictly the same. This should be the case no matter how long the time period between measurements might be.
- *Coherence:* the definition of an indicator should not vary. It must always be the same:
  - In space, for firms with several sites, and in particular those with overseas affiliates.
  - In time, the parameters chosen must be as independent as possible from every factor, internal and external to the company to avoid a definition change.
- *Simplicity:* overcomplicated reasoning compromises utility. The best indicators allow key measurements to be understood immediately.
- *Cumulative:* this characteristic enables successive aggregates of data.

◆ MEASURING PERFORMANCE IN SECTORIAL INTEGRATION

The basic principles of designing performance measurement systems and the characteristics of effective metrics are the same for measuring performance in sectorial integration as they were for measuring functional integration. However, measuring performance in sectorial integration has unique considerations, such as interfirm dynamics, potentially differing levels of intrafirm integration, and differing, possibly competing, firm-specific goals.

In evaluating the process and outcomes of interfirm cooperation, a good example of which is the efficient consumer response (ECR) discussed in chapter 4, some of the indicators must be designed to measure the cooperation itself. Why? Because of the following:

1. Logistics cooperation projects (introduction of promotions, improved use of shelf space, adapting packaging facilities, etc.) often lead to productivity gains and higher levels of service. These need to be measured to assess their value and to work out the rules for sharing the gains. In addition, other indicators must measure the timeliness of project steps and the advantages achieved for each partner.
2. Data on specific indicators for cooperative projects can help convince top management of the advantages of the cooperative approach to logistics.

3. Data on cooperation are a source of stimulation and emulation for the people involved in logistics. In this way they improve their own performances.

The fundamental goal of a logistics partnership is the improvement of all the members in the logistics system. A good example would be in cosmetics, where the improved value through logistics partnerships for the manufacturer could be the creation of new products, optimization of promotions management, advertising, use of shelf space and logistics in terms of the continuous availability of products (no shortages in stock). For the distributor the advantages could be selling as much as possible, making the highest margins per square meter. The partnership could create a competitive advantage.

To develop metrics for this situation requires equal consideration of the manufacturer's logistical means and the distributor's logistical demands. Table 11–7 outlines different logistics subfunctions for which the partners should develop objectives and related indicators of results and means necessary to achieve the objectives.

Case Example: Performance Measurement for Inventory Control

In the cosmetics business in Europe, a major goal is to increase the average number of purchases a customer makes. When companies do not reach their targets, one root cause could be shortages in inventory. To solve this problem, managers need information on the causes of these shortages. The metrics should measure factors related to both the producer and the distributor.

Producer Factors

For the producer, measurable potential causes of shortages in supply are:

- *Inventory level.* Holding too much inventory can have the effect of a lot of shortages in inventory because of the high number of references (the difficulty to get the right amount of inventory) and low level of inventory renewal (nonselling inventory and slow turnover). Moreover, even when production facilities know the inventory situation globally, the sheer mass of articles may prevent them from modifying their production planning in order to respond to changes in demand.

Table 11–7

	Sample of Information for Inter-Firm Integration				
	Logistics Subfunction				
Indicators	*Customer function*	*Credit function*	*Inventory function*	*Portfolio function*	*Logistics distribution center*
Indicator 1					
Indicator 2					
Indicator 3					
Indicator 4 . . .					
Indicator n					

- *Promotion management.* Management wants to avoid inventory shortages for a promotion. However, when a promotional campaign works better than was forecasted, plants alter their production planning to meet this extra demand, which may disturb other flows. What often happens is that overproduction leads to inventory jams, which cause new substitutions.
- *The lack of reliable forecasting.* Estimates may prove inaccurate, and the process of forecasting (e.g., inputs from both partners, timing of estimates, expertise of forecasters) may need to be improved.
- *The unreliability of suppliers.* Evaluating a supplier's performance may show, for example, that their artificially low prices also come with low-quality service levels.
- *Inadequate coordination* between the logistics function (distribution to the stores), manufacturing (production) and sales/marketing (innovation, promotions) can also create shortages.
- *Using too many outside logistics service providers.* While this practice may save money, it also complicates flow management.
- *High level of logistics costs,* which may be related to substitutions and supplementary orders.

In some cases, the distributor is not told about a shortage in inventory. The producer simply substitutes another product and hopes the distributor—and the customers—will accept it. Such substitutions are all the more frequent when the producer has former promotion articles to offload, which may "add value" (e.g., 10% more in a package). Although such practices may in some instances satisfy the distributor, they often generate a high number of returned goods. For example, to deliver whole lots, the producer rounds up the order to the higher level and sends 400 rather than 300. The risk that the distributor will refuse the substitutions and disagree over invoicing is real. Extra costs result because of more freight, order picking, putting the orders back into inventory, administrative work with credit slips to make out, and above all, myriad disagreements that disrupt the logistical and sales procedures.

Extra costs can also stem from supplementary orders. Here, the costs incurred are very high because of the cost of the store having to input the data again, repeat order picking and handling, and the supplementary cost of freight (several shipments for one order rather than optimization of truck utilization).

Distributor Factors

Distributor factors that may explain the inventory shortages are:

- *The practice of speculative purchasing.* Producer price incentives may encourage this potential problem for inventory flow.
- *Uncoordinated management of shelf space* (merchandising) pushes the sale of some items to the detriment of others.

Correcting the Problems

To eliminate shortages in inventory, the manufacturer will need to improve internal functioning and possibly integration. Some solutions require shared corrective action from the manufacturer and distributor. Possible corrective steps that can be measured using performance indicators include:

- *Making promotions logistically efficient;* in other words, measuring the impact on logistics operations of inventory shortages when promotions are inadequately managed.
- *Coordinating the dates* of passing and handling orders (piloting data flows), so that delivery times are limited and information contained in orders is reliable. This coordination will produce the standard of quality expected by the customer.
- *Coordinating data flows,* which means:

1. Disseminating information about the inventory levels of the partners (distributor and producer).
2. Relaying data captured at the checkout counters to the production plants through the warehouses of the middlemen.
3. Practicing data exchange to enable plants to attain improved performances and meet shifts in demand from the market more quickly and more efficiently. The manufacturer and the distributor should, on this subject, share their forecasts. The distributor's contribution is particularly relevant, because distributors tend to know market characteristics well.
4. Sharing information about the distributor's sales. The important thing in this case is to be able to compare actual sales with forecast sales, which have already, in this approach, been made reliable.

These actions may require specialized tools, such as electronic data interchange (EDI) and the use of bar codes. In addition, the companies must ensure a system for measuring the progress of the logistics partnership. Performance indicators may include the following:

- The percentage of canceled or supplementary orders by store
- The number of orders and sales turnover for the direct and indirect flows
- The breakdown of the number of order lines by store, i.e., orders executed, substituted, supplemented, and canceled
- The breakdown of the number of order lines having undergone a change:
  - substituted
  - supplementary
  - canceled
- Shipments refused (as a percentage of the number of lines delivered and expressed in dollars)
- Returned goods (as a percentage of the number of order lines and expressed in dollars)

Performance Measurement of Logistics Service Companies and Third-Party Logistics

Taking on an outside operator to run logistics operations does not mean abandoning all interest and responsibility in logistics. The opposite is true. The company outsourcing the functions must develop and monitor indicators of performance (e.g., the quality of the service, the quantity of operations when payment is based on a common unit of measure, and the cost of the operation). Ideally, data collection occurs each day and the company collects it by week, month, and year for each service provider. Table 11–8 presents an illustration of the type of data to be collected.

Table 11−8

Sample of Metrics for Third-Party Logistics Evaluation

	Logistics family 1	Logistics family 2	Logistics family 3
Number of delivery forms			
Anomalies upstream			
Returned documents			
Missing			
Breakages			
On time delivery and reliability			
Information concerning delivery problems			
Service rate upstream			
Service rate third party			
Real service rate			

The goal of performance measurement in this situation is the constant improvement of the service company's performance. The third-party logistics company and the company requiring the services should design incentives to generate synergy. Most problems that arise between third-party providers and their customers derive from a lack of communication or conflict between the objectives, which result in failures. The critical point is to be able to define metrics that will capture the value added by the logistics provider and therefore eliminate the source of friction.

◆ SUMMARY

In this chapter we have described performance metrics that give companies better control of their operations and logistics in the global environment. In particular, we distinguish the approaches for dealing with inter-firm integration and intra-firm integration. The geographic dimension of global operation does not require a separate treatment because it is an integral part of the other dimensions for performance evaluation.

Key principles of metrics design in both types of integration include the following:

- It is important to develop a common language across the participants of the logistics system.
- Accurate data is necessary.
- Coherence among the various metrics is critical. Different metrics should not lead to different objectives.
- Metrics are there to be used. If the number of metrics is large, it is very difficult to keep track of the indicators in a usable manner.
- Different members of the logistics system should participate in the definition of logistics indicators. Those who fulfill the function can best determine performance measures. By taking part, they also will understand the performance objectives the indicators are designed to track and be able to contribute to problem solving based on the information.

DISCUSSION QUESTIONS

1. What are the different types of logistics responsibility centers?

2. What performance measurement scheme are you going to introduce to understand the effects of a promotion campaign on your distribution system?

3. What is the ideal relationship between performance indicators and strategy?

4. What do you consider as an adequate sample of performance measure to monitor the performance of a JIT manufacturing environment?

5. Why is it important to use both internal and external performance measures, and to benchmark them against competitor performance?

6. What are appropriate criteria to segment parts in the after-sales service into logistical families? What is the importance of such segmentation for logistics performance measurement?

7. Provide examples of performance indicators for functional integration purpose and how they can be used to provide opportunities for cooperation between functions.

8. What performance indicators and metrics are you going to use to evaluate third-party logistics activities?

REFERENCES

Barton, M., S. Agrawal, and Mason Rockwell L. 1988. Meeting the challenge of Japanese management concepts. *Management Accounting* (September):49–53.

Berliner, C., and J. Brimson 1988. Cost management for today's advanced manufacturing. The CAM-I conceptual design. Harvard Business School Press.

Brimson, J. 1986. How advanced manufactured technologies are reshaping cost management. *Management Accounting* (March):25–29.

Bruns, W., and R. Kaplan. 1987. Accounting and management: Field study perspectives. Harvard Business School Press.

Christopher, M. 1985. Effective logistics management. Brookfield, Vt.: Gower.

Dornier, Ph.P. 1991. Plein flux sur l'entreprise. Nathan, Paris.

Foster, G., and C. Horngreen. 1988. Flexible manufacturing systems: Cost management and cost accounting implications. Graduate School of Business, Stanford University Working Paper.

Hiromoto T. 1988. Another hidden edge, Japanese management accounting. *Harvard Business Review,* (July–August):22–26.

Magee, J., W. Copacino, D. Rosenfield. 1985. Modern logistics management. New York: John Wiley and Sons, Inc.

Maskell, B. 1986. Management Accounting and Just in Time. Management Accounting (UK) (September):32–34.

McNair, C., W. Mosconi, and T. Norris. 1988. Meeting the technology challenge: Cost accounting in a JIT Environment. Coopers & Lybrand: National Association of Accountants.

National Association of Accountants (NAA), National Council of Physical Distribution Management (NCPDM). 1985. Warehouse accounting and control: Guidelines for distribution and financial management. Oak Brook, Ill.

Novack, R., S. Dunn, and R. Young. 1993. Logistics optimizing and operational plans and systems and their role in the achievement of corporate goals. *Transportation Journal* 32(4) (Summer):29–40.

◆ Case 11–1: The China Lacquer Product Line ◆

Introduction

Created more than a half century ago, the S.A. Paints Company manufactures and distributes products for the

Written by Professor Michel Fender.

Decoration market, where it realizes annual business figures of 700 million francs. Particularly more present in the "Large Public" sector, of which it is the national leader, it realizes 3.5 percent of its business figures from exports.

Its national market share is between 15 and 18 percent but is tending to increase, despite strong competition, thanks to its policy of innovation and the quality of its

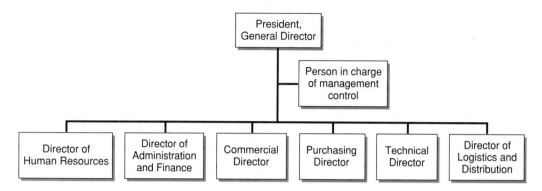

products and services. In parallel, its profitability has tended to improve since its refocus on traditional trades, where it occupies the dominant place in the market.

The last fiscal year shows operating profits of 7.5 percent.

The S.A. Paints Company is run by a president general director, and a Direction Committee of seven members, six directors, as well as a person in charge of management control, who reports directly to the president.

The paints commercialized by the S.A. Paints Company in the Decorations market can be divided into three large families:

glycerin-based, or solvent paints
emulsion, or water-based paints
specialty paints (refinishing paints, for floors, wood, etc.)

For these different product types, we find distinctions in terms of the characteristics and quality of the product. Globally, we can consider that 60 percent of the company's volumes are realized by solvent paints, 30 percent by emulsion paints, and 10 percent by specialty paints.

The "China Lacquer" product line in which we are interested here belongs to the category of glycerin-based paints and constitutes one of the company's oldest product lines. It is a top-of-the-line product whose distribution is reserved for specialized markets such as pottery and customers of traditional chemists.

The shades of this line comprise 44 colors, a portion of which are revised every year in collaboration with a stylist in order to follow the aesthetic trends of the Decorations market.

Marketed at a base price of 50 Francs per kg, China Lacquer achieved a sales volume of 1,400 tons in 1993, for a significant annual business figure of 63 million francs (18% of business figures realized in the Decoration market), up 12 percent the preceding year.

Table 1 allows us to follow the evolution of the line over the course of the last ten fiscal years in volumes sold, market share, and the relation between the product's average sale price and that of the average market price.

The product's evolution over the last ten fiscal years has shown a consistent increase in sales volume with a more accentuated increase in 1988, which is considered to be the direct result of a rejuvenation in packaging (a more modern image, the cover displaying the color of the paint, instructions enhanced with pictures).

The pricing policy adopted for this product line has always positioned it above the average market price but never by more than 10 percent. This policy is only justified by the product's positioning as a top-of-the-line product. The increase in the average sale price over the last three fiscal years, higher than any registered to date, corresponds to the necessary repercussions from an increase in the cost of raw materials, followed by modifications of the formulation introduced in 1991 in order to abide by changes in legislation.

Production Machinery and the Characteristics of the Process

The production line for this product is located at the heart of the company's Decoration production factory. It consists of a specialized homogeneous production line solely dedicated to this product line. Its average production volume is 6 tons per day in 1988, for an average factory production total of 50 tons.

Of a very recent design, this factory allows for the assembly line production of products, without a break in loading, or at the least without a "discontinuous" transfer of the product from one line to another.

Some facts about the manufacture of paints follow:

Composition

The following components are found in all paints:

The binding agent:	Resin or emulsifier, which will give the finished product the vast majority of its physical/chemical characteristics, such as hardness, suppleness, weather resistance, etc. This is always a liquid product, more or less viscous.

Table 1

			Evolution of the China Lacquer Product Line		
Year	Sales in Tons	Average Net Sales Price	Net Business Figures (in million francs)	Estimated Market Share	Average Market Price
1983	850	27 F	22.95	17.70%	25.00 F
1984	1000	28 F	28.00	17.85%	25.50 F
1985	1050	29 F	30.45	18.42%	26.70 F
1986	1100	31 F	34.10	18.50%	28.50 F
1987	1150	32 F	36.80	9.00%	30.40 F
1988	1250	33 F	41.25	20.50%	31.40 F
1989	1260	35 F	44.10	20.00%	31.85 F
1990	1270	36 F	45.72	19.80%	34.20 F
1991	1300	38 F	49.40	20.00%	35.00 F
1992	1340	42 F	56.28	20.30%	37.80 F
1993	1400	45 F	63.00	20.90%	42.75 F

The pigment: Solid, colored particle, of mineral or synthetic origin, which will give the finished product its color and coverage ability.

The coating agents: Less troublesome than the pigments, they give coverage ability to the product.

The solvents: They allow for the regulation of the product's viscosity according to its usage. Generally composed of hydrocarbons for solvent paints, alcohol, ammonia, and water for water-based paints.

The adjuvents: Involves those products introduced during the course of production either to facilitate the process (anti-foaming agents, dispersion agents, etc.), or to improve the final qualities of the paint (anti-skin), or to guarantee its usage (quick drying agents).

The Production Process

All fabrication can be broken down into four distinct phases.

Dispersion: During the course of this operation, we assure the mixture of the solid particles, pigments, and/or the coating agents into one part binding agent and one part solvent, and when the situation calls for it, with several adjuvents as well. Here we utilize dispersers and this phase lasts about 1.5 hours for 6,000 liters of product.

Grinding: Its role is two-fold. On one hand it allows the dispersion process to complete, by assuring a higher or lower degree of fineness in relation to the desired finish (high gloss, matte, or satin) and, on the other hand it will allow the color to develop by increasing the specific surface of the pigment particles. We use continuous, horizontal grinders and this phase lasts between one and two hours depending on the product.

Dilution: This essential phase encompasses all of the operations that produce the product's final characteristics.

In certain cases, this phase will furthermore permit the fixation of the product's color when the color is produced with the help of tinting pastes from an initial solution, which is more or less colorless. The dilution process is accomplished in 6,000-liter, 12,000-liter, or 24,000-liter vats, which are in fact used from the beginning of the dispersion process to the end of the packaging process, encompassing therefore the times for inspection, color fixation, and dilution.

Packaging: Specific to this product line, the packaging line allows for the packaging of cans containing between 0.125 and 5 liters of product.

The production line assigned to this product is composed of a disperser, two grinders, seven dilution vats (1 × 24,000 liters; 2 × 12,000 liters; 4 × 6,000 liters) and one packaging line.

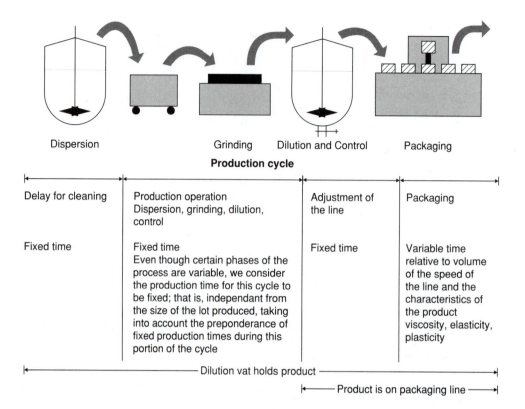

Dispersion   Grinding   Dilution and Control   Packaging

Production cycle

Delay for cleaning	Production operation Dispersion, grinding, dilution, control	Adjustment of the line	Packaging
Fixed time	Fixed time Even though certain phases of the process are variable, we consider the production time for this cycle to be fixed; that is, independant from the size of the lot produced, taking into account the preponderance of fixed production times during this portion of the cycle	Fixed time	Variable time relative to volume of the speed of the line and the characteristics of the product viscosity, elasticity, plasticity

— Dilution vat holds product —

— Product is on packaging line —

This process has been diagrammed across the four production stages: the delay for cleaning of the vats; production time, which covers the total of the process described above with the exception of packaging; the delay for regulating the packaging line; and finally, the packaging. The first three phases correspond to fixed times for each batch; the packaging time is directly related to the size of the batch.

Organization of Production

The products of the Decoration product lines are basically "convenience products," that is, those that are for general usage and which are not perishable. They can be utilized in steps subsequent to the production process or sold right away. As a result, there is always an inventory of these products.

The production administration uses an annual sales forecast for each product line, and within the product line, coefficients for each color, allowing them to determine the demand for each product. From this data, and keeping in mind the constraints of inventory and ability, the production administration defines a standard batch size for each product that will be put in effect according to precise rules of planning.

The available inventory is evaluated in terms of rate of coverage on the basis of sales forecasts. It is compared to the trigger point expressed by the number of days of sales

that are covered by the security inventory and by production delays.

The security inventory on hand has been designated to absorb the gaps between the theoretical data and the reported actuals (gaps in sales forecasts, gaps in the production cycles) and to assure total product availability. The base inventory is three days' worth for whites and five days' worth for colors. Nevertheless, the level is tied directly to the rate of use of the equipment and increased whenever the rate of use of the equipment is less than 85 percent.

Additionally, an analysis of the production cycles over the past two fiscal years has allowed us to characterize each one of the components in the following manner:

	Cleaning the vats	Delay in production	Readjustment time	Speed/rate of packaging
Whites	1 day	2 days		
			2 hours	1.250 liters/hour
Colors	2 days	5 days		

This analysis excludes the impact of disruptions such as a shortage in supplies, machinery breakdown, errors in planning, and so on.

Economic Results

The management and controller have implemented an analytical breakdown by product line. The results of this line over the course of the last ten years are given in the following table.

China Lacquer Financial Results

Year	1983	1984	1985	1986	1987	1988	1989	1990	1991	1992	1993
Inflation Rate	1.00	1.03	1.06	1.11	1.15	1.18	1.25	1.28	1.35	1.42	1.46
Sales volume (units)	850	1000	1 050	1 100	1 150	1 250	1 260	1 270	1 300	1 340	1 400
Business figures (F)	22 950	28 000	30 450	34 100	36 800	41 250	44 100	45 720	49 400	56 280	63 000
Average sales price (Francs/kg)	27.00	28.00	29.00	31.00	32.00	33.00	35.00	36.00	38.00	42.00	45.00
Raw materials and packaging	11 645	14 110	15 527	16 786	18 078	20 238	21 521	22 339	24 011	25 996	28 000
Transport	578	700	756	836	897	1 000	1 071	1 105	1 196	1 286	1 400
Gross markup	10 727	13 190	14 437	16 478	17 825	20 012	21 508	22 276	24 193	28 998	33 600
Operations costs	1 900	1 957	2 016	2 116	2 180	2 245	4 000	4 120	4 244	4 371	4 500
Logistics cost	1 257	1 212	1 375	1 609	1 760	1 011	1 197	1 200	1 359	1 771	2 095
Gross surplus of operating profits	7 570	10 021	11 046	12 753	13 885	16 756	16 311	16 956	18 590	22 856	27 005
Sales and marketing	918	1 120	1 294	1 449	1 656	1 856	2 095	2 286	2 717	3 236	4 095
Advertisement	1 377	1 820	1 979	2 387	2 576	3 094	3 528	3 886	4 323	5 065	6 300
Research and development	459	560	609	1 023	1 104	1 238	1 764	1 829	1 976	2 251	3 150
Other fixed expenses	1 607	1 960	2 132	2 558	2 760	3 094	3 749	3 886	4 199	5 065	6 300
Depreciation	508	488	469	460	453	520	563	593	625	680	700
Total fixed expenses	4 869	5 948	6 483	7 877	8 549	9 802	11 699	12 480	13 840	16 297	20 545
Gross operating profits	2 701	4 073	4 563	4 876	5 336	6 954	4 612	4 476	4 750	6 559	6 460
Requirements for operating profits	7 737	7 904	9 840	9 321	11 132	11 703	12 104	12 709	13 594	15 533	15 647
Inventory	7 049	6 994	8 698	7 957	9 476	9 743	9 788	10 195	10 630	11 734	11 080
Debit account	3 672	4 550	5 024	5 712	6 256	7 116	7 718	8 115	8 892	10 271	11 655
Credit account	2 984	3 640	3 882	4 348	4 600	5 156	5 402	5 601	5 928	6 472	7 088
Variation of operating profits requirement		167	1 936	519	1 811	571	401	605	885	1 939	114
Fixed assets	10 163	9 655	9 172	8 714	8 278	7 864	7 471	7 097	6 742	6 405	6 085
Depreciation	508	483	459	436	414	393	374	355	337	320	304
Invested capital		100	100	250	250	1 500	1 000	750	750	1 000	500
Invested capital (average Francs)		103	106	278	278	1 770	1 250	960	1 013	1 420	730
Cumulative of invested capital		103	209	487	487	2 545	3 795	4 755	5 768	7 188	7 918
Depreciation of invested capital		5	10	24	24	127	190	238	288	359	396
Cumulative of depreciations		5	15	39	39	205	395	633	921	1 280	1 676

China Lacquer Financial Results (cont.)

Year	1983	1984	1985	1986	1987	1988	1989	1990	1991	1992	1993
Fixed assets on invested capital		98	194	448	448	2 340	3 400	4 122	4 847	5 908	6 242
New fixed assets	10 163	9 753	9 366	9 162	9 162	10 204	10 871	11 219	11 589	12 313	12 327
Cash flow before taxes		4 292	2 991	5 557	5 557	5 134	3 524	3 502	3 478	3 880	6 315
Profit		22.91%	24.76%	25.88%	25.88%	33.11%	20.55%	19.09%	19.34%	24.74%	23.15%

Commercial Strategy for the China Lacquer Product Line for the Years 1994 to 2000

The commercial director of the S.A. Paints Company has established four scenarios for the development of this product line. Each scenario is defined by data in terms of the volume and the mix produced, and aims its objectives at a specific segment of the market.

The following pages outline each of the four scenarios presented by the commercial director during the last direction committee meeting.

Scenario #1: Objective 2000 – 1,000 Tons/25% market share

In this hypothesis, we simply envision a progression of the current product line, the evolution of which we will assure by way of an important technical modification of the product, without engendering the launch of a new product line or an extension of the current product line.

Supported by the product's reputation and a modification of the package image, we can use the same line of colors and packaging to introduce significant technical innovations to improve the conditions of product usage. Thanks to the current development of new resins, we can envision the development of a product whose odor has been significantly reduced or even eliminated, as well as the possibility of being able to clean brushes and rollers with only water.

The advantage of such a product is certainly ecological, and in the current context where consumer legal pressures are moving more and more toward hygiene and safety, this benefit is far from negligible and could engender, with a fair-sized marketing push, a new penetration of this market.

Nevertheless, this product is not ready today and with the current state of affairs we cannot realistically expect to have it available before 1996, which leaves us with two years without a sizable opportunity to distinguish ourselves from the competition.

The data for this scenario can be outlined as follows:

Year	Market Volume	China Lacquer Volume	Goal of Market Share	Average Price of Market Sales	Average Price of Company Sales	Net Business Figures in Million Francs
1993	6700 T	1400 T	20.90%	42.75 F	45.00 F	63.00
1994	6800 T	1430 T	21.03%	43.60 F	45.30 F	64.80
1995	6900 T	1450 T	21.01%	44.40 F	45.60 F	66.10
1996	7000 T	1700 T	24.28%	45.30 F	48.50 F	82.45
1997	7200 T	1750 T	24.30%	46.00 F	49.00 F	85.75
1998	7250 T	1780 T	24.55%	47.00 F	49.30 F	87.75
1999	7350 T	1820 T	24.76%	48.00 F	49.60 F	90.30
2000	7400 T	1850 T	25.00%	49.00 F	50.00 F	92.50

If we expect a mean progression equal to the inflation of direct production costs (material and manufacturing), in the year 2000, we should obtain a gross profit of 22.75 francs against 20.79 francs/kg, for a total sales volume of 42.08 million francs.

Scenario #2: Objective 2000 — 2,000 Tons/27% market share

The basis of this scenario maintains the hypothesis of scenario #1. But from 1994 on, we engage an aggressive policy with respect to the white paints by the creation of new packaging targeted at the market of professional products, thereby increasing the sales totals of these products.

In this hypothesis, we estimate that we can obtain a goal of 2,000 tons (+ 150 tons in relation to the preceding hypothesis, or an 8% increase), without too strong a deterioration of our average sales price and of our profits.

Year	Sales Volume of "China Lacquer"			Market Share	Average Sales Price		Business Figures in Million Francs
	Colors	White	Total		Colors	White	
1993	890 T	510 T	1,400 T	20.90%	45.00 F	45.00 F	63.00
1994	910 T	640 T	1,550 T	22.80%	45.30 F	43.00 F	68.70
1995	920 T	780 T	1,700 T	24.60%	45.60 F	43.30 F	75.70
1996	1,080 T	720 T	1,800 T	25.70%	48.50 F	46.00 F	85.50
1997	1,110 T	740 T	1,850 T	25.70%	49.00 F	46.60 F	88.90
1998	1,130 T	770 T	1,900 T	26.20%	49.30 F	46.80 F	91.70
1999	1,155 T	795 T	1,950 T	26.50%	49.60 F	47.10 F	94.50
2000	1,175 T	825 T	2,000 T	27.00%	50.00 F	47.50 F	98.00

If we apply a sale price that is 5 percent less than that of the colored paints, and keeping in mind the average increase in production costs, the increase obtained by this hypothesis would be 21.93 francs/kg or −3.6 percent and would produce for this year's sales 43.85 million francs, or +4.22% in relation to scenario #1.

Scenario #3: Objective 2000—2,100 Tons/28.60% market share

The basis of this hypothesis is to aggressively attack the market beginning in fiscal year 1994. In order to do this, we can offer today a new product for which consumer tests are extremely positive. We will speak of this product henceforth under the code name "PAGODA."

The "PAGODA" project involves a completely new and innovative product line. Without being definitive, we have the idea that this new product line could be called "China Lacquer Cream." This new product will be characterized by its exceptional finish qualities—high gloss, garnishing, coverage ability; but its most important quality resides in its structure, which will give it a property so it will not run during application. Nevertheless, this product could only be applied by brush, and therefore it is uniquely a finishing product.

As a result, we have limited the packaging to a single size of 0.75 liter and we will use a new packaging especially designed for this product. We will come back to this project, after we analyze the impact that we expect from this product.

The product would be considered top of the line and as a result, marketed at a price higher than that of traditional products. We can in effect consider that it will be sold on the basis of 50 francs per 0.75 liter can, or 55.50 francs/kg.

We estimate that 30 colors will make up this line. It will be launched in 1994 with a sales goal of 300 tons the first year, but will have a "bundling" impact on the China Lacquer product line of 100 tons.

Under these conditions, the preceding table becomes:

Market Evolution	Market Volume	Evolution of Sales of "China Lacquer"	Evolution of "Cream"	Total Volume	Market Share (%)	Average Sales Price 1	Average Sales Price 2	Business Figures (net)
1993	6,700 T	1,400 T	—	1,400 T	20.9%	45.00 F	—	63.00
1994	6,800 T	1,300 T	300 T	1,600 T	23.5%	45.50 F	55.00 F	75.65
1995	6,900 T	1,350 T	300 T	1,650 T	23.9%	46.00 F	55.75 F	79.40
1996	7,000 T	1,400 T	350 T	1,750 T	25.0%	47.00 F	60.50 F	87.00
1997	7,200 T	1,500 T	350 T	1,850 T	25.7%	47.50 F	63.50 F	93.50
1998	7,250 T	1,550 T	400 T	1,950 T	26.9%	48.00 F	66.50 F	101.00
1999	7,350 T	1,600 T	450 T	2,050 T	27.9%	49.00 F	69.50 F	109.70
2000	7,400 T	1,600 T	500 T	2,100 T	28.4%	50.00 F	73.00 F	116.50

Keeping in mind an increase of 23.09 francs for the "Lacquer" family, and a 40.27 franc increase for the China Lacquer "Cream" family, in 1995 we can expect for accumulated gross profit of 57.06 million francs or a 35.6% increase in relation to the first scenario.

Scenario #4: Objective 1995 — 2,250 Tons/30% market share

The final scenario that we have envisioned constitutes, in fact, the optimum of the scenarios previously presented, namely:

- Concerning the current "China Lacquer" product line, beginning this year, we plan to launch professional products and to continue, as we have discussed, with a complete re-launch of this line through modifications in both formula and packaging.
- Beginning in 1994 we launch a new line, "China Lacquer Cream," with significant public support.

Under this hypothesis, we believe we can optimize the totality of the product's positioning and optimize our market share with these product lines.

We can outline this hypothesis by way of the following table:

| Year | Volume Evolution | | | | Market Share | Business Figures in Million Francs |
	Colored China Lacquer	White China Lacquer	China Lacquer "Cream"	Total		
1993	890T/45.00F	510T/45.00F	—	1400T	20.90%	63.00
1994	890T/45.30F	615T/43.00F	300T/55.00F	1805T	26.50%	83.30
1995	895T/45.60F	755T/43.30F	315T/57.75F	1965T	28.50%	91.70
1996	975T/48.50F	695T/46.10F	330T/60.50F	2000T	28.60%	99.20
1997	975T/49.00F	715T/46.60F	345T/63.50F	2035T	28.30%	103.0
1998	990T/49.30F	745T/46.80F	360T/66.50F	2095T	28.90%	107.60
1999	990T/49.60F	770T/47.10F	375T/69.50F	2135T	29.00%	111.40
2000	1050T/50.00F	800T/47.50F	400T/73.00F	2250T	30.40%	119.70

On this basis, our strategy will bring us to practically double our annual business figures. According to this increase, if we always calculate the base average sales price in the year 2000 as 26.91 francs for the China Lacquer family and as 32.73 francs for the China Lacquer "Cream" family, our annual business figures would increase to 57.2 million francs, or a 35.9 percent increase in relation to our first hypothesis.

There you have it, esteemed colleagues, said the commercial director, a quick outline of the different hypotheses that we could apply to our solvent and high-gloss paints strategies.

Bearing in mind the data just presented, we have decided, if the president agrees, to develop scenario #4. In effect, it is the one that will allow us to obtain all the advantages of a leader's position and will open up the most future opportunities. With a 30 percent market share and the first steps toward a professional line, we can hope to rapidly develop this line by complementing it with other products in our catalog.

At this point, the direction committee becomes animated and a debate quickly ensues. Let us therefore consider the point of view of each of the protagonists, but first, that of the president general director.

President General Director

Mr. Commercial Director, I thank you for your brilliant intervention. I must admit to being very impressed by the perspectives that you present, especially when I consider that you estimate it is possible for us to double our annual business figures in just several years. You have presented us with what each of your different scenarios would engender, but I assume that all of these will require investments, if even only for advertising, or you have been very discreet about this particular point.

Commercial Director

Mr. President, it is clear that these different hypotheses all support themselves with modified communications policies. In the case of the first two scenarios, we have considered that the advertising and promotional budgets will represent approximately 10 percent of the annual business figures. In effect, there is not much of a change, and our advertising will be designated exclusively to China Lacquer. In the case of scenarios 3 and 4, this investment would represent 12 percent of the annual business figures, dividing itself to give one-third to China Lacquer and two-thirds to China Lacquer "Cream."

President General Director

All of this gives us a vastly different landscape to consider, for our profit margin after advertising becomes with each of these different hypotheses: 32.8 million francs for scenario #1, 1.34 million francs for scenario #2, 43 million francs for scenario #3, and 42.8 million francs for scenario #4, which significantly reduces the profitability gap between each of these different scenarios.

Commercial Director

That's exactly right, Mr. President, but do not lose sight of the fact that we win some 5 percentage points of market share with this strategy, and therefore win a dominant market position, which will guarantee us a higher profitability in the medium term.

President General Director

We will admit that; but how will the competition react? I don't suppose that it will remain without reaction.

Commercial Director

Our strategy in this regard consists in innovating and investing in advertising to force them into a profit loss in the hypothesis that they will attempt to imitate us. In effect, bearing in mind their lower average market price, they will be forced into a smaller range of choices due to the fear of not quickly being able to follow our innovations. In all events, we have counted on the significant investment represented by our adherence to the legislation in order to preserve the technical lead acquired with China Lacquer "Cream" and to break through the market with this product.

President General Director

Yes, but let us not underestimate, colleagues, it can very well be that the competition also has a plan that has already been finalized.

Industrial Director

Well, I must say that I am still a little bit concerned when faced with this presentation. In effect, you are proposing, for a progression in volume of 850 tons, or more than 60 percent, to increase our fiscal year numbers by 60 percent in going from 44 to 74, but without telling us what that means in terms of production; for in any case, we will have to invest in production machinery.

Director of Logistics

And in distribution, for it seems inevitable to me that we will be required to review and come to terms with the problem of inventory space, as much with the increase in volumes as with the number of references to stock, and also on the level of raw materials and packaging as well as finished product.

Management Controller

Yes, I completely share the views of my two colleagues. I fear that the profitability that you have presented will be somewhat compromised by the amount of investments that will be necessary to obtain it, and that, in fact, the final results of each hypothesis are not substantially different from the image that you give us once we factor in the total costs.

Commercial Director

Sirs, I will not deny the fact that it is necessary to invest in order to have adequate abilities at our disposal in order to meet this demand, but I fear that we will not have another avenue if we desire to remain on the market and to strengthen our presence.

Management Controller

Additionally, I must insist that we return to a particularly important point, the weight of inventory on our results. With a volume of close to 19 percent of the business figures, inventory represents a heavier expense to support every year, and which, in time, will compromise not only our results, but our capacity for investment as well. I believe it therefore urgent to implement an inventory reduction plan.

Director of Logistics

To do this we do not have to neglect our capacities and in no case we can work with a base utilization rate greater than 85 percent, which already constitutes a dangerous limit.

Management Controller

I don't understand this last point very well. I have always heard it said that in order to reduce our production costs, we should on the contrary use the production machinery at 100 percent of its capacity.

Director of Logistics

Well, I think that you better resign yourself to that idea. Personally, I share the point of view of those who consider that a factory in which all of the positions are continually occupied at 100 percent of their capacity is a globally inefficient factory.

How can we effectively confront risks such as a sudden variation in sales, materials that are not sufficiently reliable, delays in the delivery from a supplier that halts a production cycle, and finally, a production problem that abnormally elongates the delay in production for the product?

To address this issue, we can adopt the following plan.

Our very simple approach begins with our existing capacity and attempts to saturate it with the shortest possible production series that will allow us to reduce inventory, while satisfying the integrity of the demand.

Our decisions should therefore rest on the respective quantities of each product that must be manufactured. For that, we must find the best balance between the three components of demand, inventory, and production capacity.

President General Director

Sirs, I have listened with great interest to you all, but I must say that in fact, I find myself without any concrete element to position myself in relation to our starting point: to know which of the scenarios we should choose for the years to come, with regard to our high-gloss paints and especially how to obtain the optimal profitability in each case.

How do you therefore think we should respond to this particular problem?

Director of Logistics

I believe that our only possible route is to support ourselves with the forecasts of the commercial director and establish for each scenario the different production policies that can be envisioned. Understandably, it would be in our best interest to determine for each one the profits that we anticipate, but equally the investments that will be necessary, both in production equipment and in inventory, in order to evaluate the real impact on economic profitability. In this fashion, I believe that we will have the best possible understanding and will be able to determine which scenario to adopt.

President General Director

This seems totally reasonable and I propose that we return to this subject as the order of the day at our next direction committee meeting in fifteen days.

Having been seduced by your approach, which is based on economic profitability, and I hope that it will be according to this criterion that you will evaluate the impact of each scenario.

I await your recommendations.

The dossier that follows was given to each of the members of the direction committee. This dossier contains the following elements:

- The technical characteristics of the two product lines
- The policy concerning safety stock inventory
- The actions of type just-in-time, which we can envision in order to increase the flexibility of the factory while reducing the level of inventory in progress
- The different levels of production capacity and the total fixed costs introduced by these different levels
- Investment possibilities to argue for the production capacity
- A presentation of the China Lacquer product line and the percentage of sales represented by each color in the line in relation to the total sales

Policy of Safety Stock Inventory

In "normal" operation—that is to say, with an average maximum production usage rate < 85 percent (capacity of the vats or capacity of the packaging line)—the security inventories are at three days for white paints and five days for colored paints.

Technical Characteristics of the Two Product Lines. Results include various anomalies that can affect the production cycle and generate an additional consumption of production capacity.

	China Lacquer		China Lacquer Cream
	Standard	Average result/1988	Estimated
Delay in production			
White	2 days	3.5 days	2 days
Colors	5 days	6 days	4 days
Delay for cleaning			
White	1 day	1 day	1 day
Colors	2 days	2 days	2 days
Adjustment of packaging line	2 hours	2 hours	4 hours
Speed/rate of packaging	1.250 liters/hour	1.250 liters/hour	1.00 liters/hour

Beyond a production capacity usage rate of 85 percent, each 1 percent of additional capacity translates into a 1/4 day increase in inventory for whites and a half-day increase for colors, and beyond 90 percent an additional half-day for whites and one day for colors.

Additionally, we will consider that in the case of a creation of a new product line, the additional lock-up of stock would be equivalent to five days of safety stock inventory for the whites in the China Lacquer product line.

Finally, with regard to the China Lacquer Cream product line, a maturation delay of five days is considered necessary before the product is put on the market.

Safety Stock Inventory Policy*

| Maximum usage rate/ packaging line or vat | China Lacquer | | | | China Lacquer Cream | |
| | Without professional line | | With professional line | | | |
	White	Colors	White	Colors	White	Colors
<85%	3 days	5 days	8 days	5 days	8 days	10 days
86%	3.25 days	5.5 days	8.25 days	5.5 days	8.25 days	10.5 days
90%	4.25 days	7.5 days	9.25 days	7.5 days	9.25 days	12.5 days
95%	6.75 days	12.5 days	11.75 days	12.5 days	11.75 days	17.5 days
100%	9.25 days	17.5 days	14.25 days	17.5 days	14.25 days	22.5 days

Additionally, we estimate the lock-up for warehoused inventory (at the distribution point) to be the equivalent of twelve days for whites and fifteen days for colors, which are added to the preceding data.

Just-In-Time (JIT) Action

The directors of production and logistics have evaluated a certain number of actions of a JIT approach within the production organization. You will find here the list of the actions considered, their costs, and their anticipated benefits.

Action	Cost	Effect
Increase in control staff + 2 persons/position	+450 KF	One-day reduction in the production cycle for colors
Investment in an automatic vat cleaning system	Investment of 500 KF and operations costs + 75 KF/year	Maximum cleaning delay for whites and colors of 0.0625 day
Increase in maintenance and polyvalence with packaging adjustment personnel + 1 person/position	+ 200 KF	Packaging adjustment time of 0.3 hour for China Lacquer and 0.5 hour for China Lacquer Cream

Production Capacity and Fixed Production Costs

Production capacity is defined by the maximum number of batches that can be produced by production without taking into account packaging. It is therefore possible that for a certain volume, even if the number of produced lots is inferior to the number indicated below, the packaging capacity may be insufficient. Under that assumption we will refer to the table of investments or to the work of a partial team.

Number of positions	1 in production 1 in packaging	2 in production 1 in packaging	3 in production 1 in packaging
Maximum capacity	250 batches	400 batches	550 batches
Fixed production costs	4.500 KF*	8.500 KF*	12.700 KF*
Number of positions	1 in production 1 in packaging	2 in production 2 in packaging	1 in production 3 in packaging
Maximum capacity	250 batches	250 batches	250 batches
Fixed production costs	4.500 KF*	6.790 KF*	8.900 KF*
Number of positions	1 in production 1 in packaging	1 in production 2 in packaging	1 in production 3 in packaging
Maximum capacity	250 batches	250 batches	400 batches
Fixed production costs	4.500 KF*	6.790 KF*	9.700 KF*

*The costs indicated are based on the franc in 1993. We will apply the inflation rate according to the information specified in the financial table to determine the value of this production cost for a given year.

Investment Possibilities

The investments presented here correspond to an increase in the capacity of the production factory. We will consider that all investments made in year *N* will be realized and paid in year *N* but will only translate into an increase in production capacity for year *N* + 1.

All costs are given at the value of the franc in 1993.

Increase in the dilution capacity

Without major equipment, the current platform allows for the receipt of three new dilution vats each with a volume of 6,000 liters. The cost of one vat is 100 KF, and in the hypothetical increase to 10 vats (+3 × 6,000 liters), the repercussions for production costs is 200 KF per production position.

Every additional augmentation in dilution capacity requires:

A platform extension costing 400 KF and pipes costing 150 KF for each section of four vats. The per unit cost for the vats is:

24,000 liters	200 KF
12,000 liters	150 KF
6,000 liters	100 KF

Above and beyond ten vats, we consider that operational costs are increased by 600 KF per production position for the four vats installed.

Additionally, above and beyond fourteen vats, an additional investment would be necessary to assure the dispersion and grinding capacity, at a cost of 1,250 KF to which is added 400 KF per production position.

Increase in packaging capacity

Two options can be envisioned.

1. Traditional packaging line

Packaging only
- Rate for China Lacquer of 1,250 liters/hour, adjustment time two hours, China Lacquer Cream 1,000 liters/hour, adjustment time four hours
- Cost 500 KF
- Operations cost/packaging position 1,000 KF

Packaging plus peripheral equipment, same rate as above
- Cost 2,000 KF
- Operations costs 400 KF

Peripheral equipment of the existing line without modifying the parameters for packaging rate and adjustment would represent a cost of 1,500 KF and an operations gain of 600 KF.

2. Rapid packaging line

Packaging plus peripheral equipment
- Rate for China Lacquer of 2,500 liters/hour, adjustment time four hours, China Lacquer Cream 2,200 liters/hour, adjustment time five hours
- Cost 2,800 KF
- Operations cost 400 KF

China Lacquer Product Line

Colors	% Family	% Family Outside of White and White-on-White	% White and White-on-White
White-on-white	4.09%		11.19%
Raw silk	1.00%	1.58%	
Silver	0.11%	0.17%	
Black	3.68%	5.80%	
Off white	7.04%	11.09%	
Snow white	32.43%		88.81%
Pastel gray	2.52%	3.97%	
Pure gray	2.15%	3.39%	
Ivory	2.20%	3.37%	
Tortoise shell	1.68%	2.65%	
Lemmish gray	0.99%	1.56%	
Pebble	0.99%	1.56%	
Sky blue	1.83%	2.88%	
Radiant blue	1.47%	2.32%	
Marine blue	0.42%	0.66%	
Sand	0.99%	1.56%	
Pastel green	1.20%	1.89%	
Springtime green	0.74%	1.17%	
Lutéce green	0.95%	1.50%	
Lapis lazuli	0.58%	0.91%	
Josephine green	1.47%	2.32%	
Sea green	1.63%	2.57%	
Carriage green	1.52%	2.39%	
Peach	1.05%	1.65%	
Primavera	0.23%	0.36%	
Narcissus	0.23%	0.36%	
Almond	0.21%	0.33%	
Ecru beige	0.95%	1.50%	
Pastel cream	1.58%	2.49%	
Brilliant yellow	1.37%	2.16%	
Eggshell	3.47%	5.47%	
Azalea	0.74%	1.17%	
Water lily	0.22%	0.35%	
Hazelnut	1.62%	2.55%	
Dark chestnut brown	2.84%	4.47%	
Cork	1.37%	2.16%	
Flanders leather	2.04%	3.21%	
Wood tone	3.31%	5.21%	
Van Dyck brown	1.79%	2.82%	
Willow	0.63%	0.99%	
Magnolia	0.95%	1.50%	
Paprika	0.42%	0.66%	
Madras red	1.83%	2.88%	
Basque red	1.47%	2.32%	
44 Products	100.00%	100.00%	100.00%

China Lacquer

Each color is packaged in three or four different packaging types. All of the products were sold in .5 liter and 2.5 liter packages. Certain colors are also available in .125 liter packages.

China Lacquer Cream

This product is packaged in .75 Liter only.

Colors	% Family
Alabaster cream	3.79%
Tradewind cream	1.79%
White-on-white cream	33.44%
Opal cream	2.91%
Tawny beige cream	1.51%
Caramel cream	1.97%
Gallic blue cream	1.92%
Midnite blue cream	2.30%
Black cream	4.20%
Bronze cream	1.26%
Coffee cream	1.73%

Colors	% Family
Hawthorn cream	2.76%
Chestnut cream	2.11%
Poppy cream	1.11%
Seashell cream	3.20%
Sand dune cream	2.12%
Emerald cream	1.44%
Wisteria cream	1.71%
Garnet cream	2.76%
Storm gray cream	2.91%
Havana cream	1.41%
Ivory cream	3.26%
Honey cream	1.23%
Mother of pearl cream	3.60%
Pacific blue cream	2.22%
Spice bread cream	0.85%
Sun cream	2.10%
Forest green cream	1.74%
Hawaiian cream	2.83%
Offwhite cream	3.82%
30 Products	100.00%

◆ Case 11–2: Ciments Antillais Corporation: The Automatic Palletizing Machine ◆

Les Ciments Antillais Corporation has a production plant located at Jarry, Guadeloupe. This plant receives raw materials (clinker and gypsum) from several countries by boat (boats of 12,000 tons). The "pouzzolane" comes from the area of Basse Terre and is supplied by truck. From these raw materials the plant builds only one quality type of finished product, but it is packaged in different ways. The finished product is packaged either in bulk (reservoir) or in bags. When it is packaged in pallets, it is packaged in pallets lost (PP), in pallets lost covered (PPH), or in bags called big bag (1.5 tons).

The production cycle consists of the following operations: unloading of boats, stockage in the halls, put on hopper for dosage, grinding of the raw materials, siloing, bagging and shipping. Two lines of grinding insure the production of the product called half finished by convention, which is then stocked in silos. The teams in charge of the production are divided into three work sites.

The bagging is done by two bagging machines, both manual but of a different composition; thanks to its advanced technological features, the most recent one can be integrated in an automatic bagging process.

The structure of the expedition workshop goes as follows:

- To satisfy the market, three teams work from 7:30 a.m. until 6:30 p.m. The loading of the bags is done manually (the bags are put on the loading tray of the truck or on the pallet of the customer).
  Team: 12 workers
- The afternoon, one team makes sure that the palletizing process of the cement on the pallets called "lost" is completed.
  Team: 4 workers + 1 driver

This palletized cement is stocked in a depot able, in its actual shape, to hold 2,000 tons. This buffer inventory enables the corporation not only to export (Guyane and other islands), but also to supply the area of Basse Terre. It also allows more rapid delivery to the customers who wish to buy cement packaged on PP (pallets lost) or on

Written by Professor Michel Fender July 1993

Exhibit 1

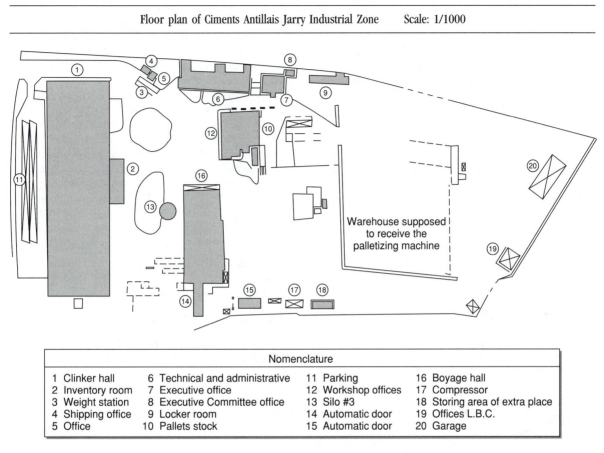

Floor plan of Ciments Antillais Jarry Industrial Zone   Scale: 1/1000

Nomenclature			
1 Clinker hall	6 Technical and administrative	11 Parking	16 Boyage hall
2 Inventory room	7 Executive office	12 Workshop offices	17 Compressor
3 Weight station	8 Executive Committee office	13 Silo #3	18 Storing area of extra place
4 Shipping office	9 Locker room	14 Automatic door	19 Offices L.B.C.
5 Office	10 Pallets stock	15 Automatic door	20 Garage

Warehouse supposed to receive the palletizing machine

PPH (pallets lost covered). However, no preparation of the stock on pallet is possible in case of rain.

The bags are either directly loaded on the loading trays of the trucks or palletized (PP or PPH) and stored in the depot mentioned above. The preparation of the orders and the shipping are also done from the same depot.

Both the work relative to the direct shipping by trucks to the customer and the formation of the pallets for the inventory involve a strong manual labor dependence. In addition, it forces the trucks, which came to load cement, to wait (maximum waiting time: 4 to 5 hours). As a consequence, the streets are overcrowded, which in turn create tension between truck drivers (blocking, etc. . .).

The waiting time can even be greater if the machines are out of order.

The automatic palletizing process might also impede the preventive maintenance that is at present scheduled outside the opening hours. This will involve additional labor costs.

The major inputs of the workshops are as follows:

- work force: 17 workers
- average daily sales: 1,300 tons (assuming 270,000 tons per year)
- sales in bags: 1,000 tons/day (approximately 70% of the sales)
- palletized tonnage/day: 650 tons
- work force needed for the palletizing process: 10 workers (60% of the work force)
- according to the distribution of the pallets (1.5 tons, or 2 tons), the estimated number of pallets loaded per day is 375
- the average internal and external labor cost per hour equivalent to the part-time labor (estimated for one year), is 120 francs. A work day is 8 hours long, which means that the 10 workers in charge of the palletizing process represent a total cost of 9,600 francs per day. Thus, the loading of a pallet costs 25.60 Fr. Currently, an order with palletization increases the marginal revenue by 10 Fr. per ton, which means about 15.00 Fr per pallet (only for customer's pallet).

Exhibit 2

Estimated Evolution of the Market

---

1. Without investment and without evolution with a percentage of pallets (60% of bags tonnage)*

Year	% of Increase	Total Sold (in tonnes)	Palletized Bags (in tonnes)
1992	Base	290,000	121,800
1993	2%	295,800	124,236
1994	2%	301,716	126,721
1995	2%	307,750	129,255
1996	2%	313,905	131,839
1997 and later			

---

2. Evolution of the pallet market after investment

Year	Estimated Tonnage	% Pallets of Bag's Tonnage	Pallet's Tonnage
1992	290,000	60%	121,800
1993	295,800	70%	144,942
1994	301,716	80%	168,960
1995	307,750	90%	193,883
1996 and later	313,905	100%	219,733

*We assumed a 30% sales in bulk

Projection tends to prove that it will become more and more difficult to find workers willing to be *trimmeur*. The tedious and mechanical aspects of the tasks make the position neither interesting nor motivating for the individual.

The depot, which is used to stock the finished products, has a maximal capacity of 2,000 tons of cement on pallets and could be extended.

The Ciments Antillais' goals are to meet customer's expectations while being flexible and increasing their satisfaction. The buffer inventory allows the firm not only to face production hazards, such as the bagging machine downtime, but also unexpected selling changes, such as the selling shocks before the holiday season. On the other hand, the investment in the automatic palletizing machine will succeed only if the market share of the Ciments Antillais increases abroad.

The analysis of the constraints and the objectives mentioned above leads to the proposal of the following investments:

- acquisition of a palletizing machine with nominal capacity of 120 tons per hour (exhibits 3 and 4)
- purchase of a bag applicator with a 2,200 bags/hour capacity
- purchase of a forklift truck of 6 tons

Only 9 of the actual 17 employees of the shipping department will stay. We assume that 40 percent of the bagged market on trucks will be without pallets with a work

Exhibit 3

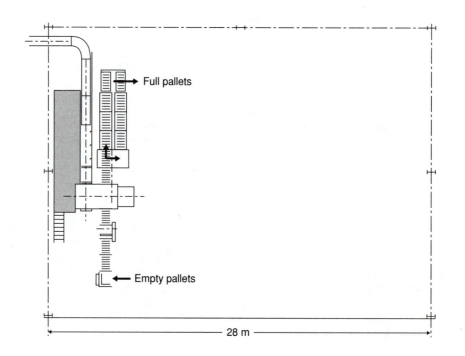

Full pallets

Empty pallets

28 m

Exhibit 4

Automatic Palletization of Batipal Bags
Type 2,500 HP S 1,000 B26
General Characteristics

Maximum Capacity

Empty Pallets	width	:1,000 mm
	length	:1,200 mm
	thickness	:160 mm
Full Pallets	width	:1,100 mm
	length	;1,300 mm
	thickness	:1,400 mm
	(pallet included)	

Automatic Part

Minimal temperature	:+5 degrees C°
Maximum temperature	:+50 degrees C°
Entrance stress	:24 V/DC
Exit stress	:24 V/DC

Energy Consumption

Installed power	:32 kW
Compressed air	:<1 Nm3/h (6 bars)

Notes

Entry level of bags	:4,250 mm mini
Entry level of pallets	:1,000 mm
Exit level of pallets	:1,000 mm
Instantaneous rate	:2,400 bags/hour in 5 bags/layer arrangement

force of 4 workers on a three-nozzle bagging machine. The rest of the market will be palletized.

The other bagging line dedicated to the automatic palletizing machine will be made up of 5 people spread out in the following way:

- 1 worker in charge of the applicator supply
- 2 drivers
- 2 unassigned workers ready, either to constitute an additional team or to reinforce another department

The overcost of fuel will be of 0.17F/ton.

The truck-loading process is currently done by the courtyard service, and will continue to be that way.

The previous work organization allows optimizing utilization of forklift trucks, with the following schedule:

- palletizing process: in normal stage from 2 p.m. to 10 p.m.
- customers' delivering from 7 a.m. to 3 p.m.

The need to satisfy customers will certainly lead to increasing the delivery hours to 6 a.m. until 3 p.m.

The permanent stock on pallets will be around 2,000 tons. The effective palletizing process rhythm is 500 tons per day, which means that it would be useful to have two positions in the palletizing process in the future. This structure allows us to deal easily with the stock composition in silos required for supplying the Guyane market (2000 tons/month).

The palletization creates a problem of pallet control. Different solutions are possible:

- registered pallets
- lost pallets
- pallets sold to subcontractors
- pallets controlled by "important customers"
- pallets sold in depreciation

For this project, the last hypothesis was selected.

The actual charging system of the pallets is very inconvenient (heavy control, theft, etc.) and costs 250,000 francs annually to the company.

On the logistic and commercial levels, installation of the automatic palettiseur will come with the systematic set-up of the system named "lost bought back pallets" for all customers. Its economic size can be studied on two different levels:

1. Cost analysis:
   Pallets' price: the average cost of the pallets is currently 65 francs, to which you need to add a 7 percent cost of property. Hence, the total cost is 69.55 francs.

2. Pallets selling price:
   One pallet will be sold for 75 francs. The cost of packed pallet (2 tons) is:
   - Professional rate
     - If the pallets are sold to customers, the total cost of one ton of sold cement is:
       $$574 * 2 = 1148 + 75 = 1223 \text{ Fr}$$
       $$\text{thus } 1223/2 = 611.50 \text{ Fr/ton}$$
     - If the customer supplies its own pallets, the total cost of one ton of sold cement is:
       $$574 * 2 = 1148 + 20 = 1168 \text{ Fr}$$
       $$\text{thus } 1168/2 = 584.00 \text{ Fr/ton}$$
     - Therefore pallets increase the price by 4.7 percent for the customer.
   - General rate
     - The same operation leads to an increase of 5.58 percent.

3. The buying back of the pallets:
   The company will buy the reusable pallets back for 35 francs per pallet, and for a minimum quantity of 10.

The investment, which for the study should include ten years for fixed assets and five years for the equipment, amounts to:

installed palletizing machine with nominal capacity of 120 tons	3000 KF
bags applicator	700 KF
conveyor (between the bagging area and the *palettiseur*)	1000 KF
contraction and covering up machinery	500 KF
forklift truck 6 T.	450 KF
shipping costs	20% FOB

It is important to precise that the palletizing machine set up will force the company to sell the bagged cement, exclusively on pallets. This change of market habits will take place little by little over a three- to four-year period (exhibit 2).

The additional cost due to investments can be estimated as 26,000 francs/year for the forklift truck (fuel, lubricant, maintenance) and 50,000 francs/year of palletizing machine maintenance, which will be covered by the company.

Besides, the pallets selected by the project will be standardized with a 2 ton capacity.

Using the above information, suggest a study process for the different parameters that will allow you to make a decision on the investment of an *automatic palletizing machine*. These parameters will be not only commercial (influence on the customers), but also technical (for example, on the foreseen control of the pallets), social, and financial (a document in exhibit 5 will allow you to know the work environment used by the Ciments Antillais to financially estimate an investment, as well as the acceptable estimations of these measures by the company).

Exhibit 5

1 - Elements

Investment amount	300
studies amount	0
amortization category	2
rate of inflation	3.5
economical life time for TRI computation	10

Amortization categories

		fiscal amortization mode (for payback)	economic amortization mode (for Rona)
buildings, offices, civil engineering	1	straight line 5%	straight line 5%
technical installations + office furniture	2	straight line 10%	straight line 10%
fixed and mobile equipment	3	accelerated 25% over 10 yrs	straight line 5%
shipping material	4	straight line 25%	straight line 25%
electric material	5	accelerated 37.5% over 8.33 yrs	straight line 5%

payable scaling (%)

yr 1	yr 2	yr 3	yr 4	yr 5
100	0	0	0	

	yr 1	yr 2	yr 3	yr 4	yr 5	yr 6	yr 7	yr 8	yr 9	yr 10	yr 11	yr 12	yr 13	yr 14	yr 15	yr 16	yr 17	yr 18	yr 19	yr 20	yr 21
constant francs of yr 1	134	134	134	134	134	134	134	134	134	134	0	0	0	0	0	0	0	0	0	0	0
savings achieved	134	134	134	134	134	134	134	134	134	134											
new funds needed																					
fiscal amortization rate	10	10	10	10	10	10	10	10	10	10	0	0	0	0	0	0	0	0	0	0	0
economic amortization rate	10	10	10	10	10	10	10	10	10	10	0	0	0	0	0	0	0	0	0	0	0

2 - Payback

	yr 1	yr 2	yr 3	yr 4	yr 5	yr 6	yr 7	yr 8	yr 9	yr 10
annual savings achieved	134	139	144	149	154	159	165	170	176	183
fiscal amortizations	30	30	30	30	30	30	30	30	30	30
net income before tax	104	109	114	119	124	129	135	140	146	153
tax (34%)	35	37	37	39	40	42	44	46	48	50
net income	69	72	77	80	84	87	91	94	98	103
cash-flow	99	102	107	110	114	117	121	124	128	133
funds needed	0	0	0	0	0	0	0	0	0	0
free cash flow	99	102	107	110	114	117	121	124	128	133

SUM OF THE FREE CASH-FLOWS 201 THUS 67% IN THE FIRST TWO YEARS

INITIAL FUNDS/2 150

respected criteria group (recall of the criteria: 50% pay-back of the investment is returned over 24 months)

3 - Return on investment with an economic life of the investment of 10 yrs

	yr 1	yr 2	yr 3	yr 4	yr 5	yr 6	yr 7	yr 8	yr 9	yr 10	yr 11	yr 12	yr 13	yr 14	yr 15	yr 16	yr 17	yr 18	yr 19	yr 20	yr 21
annual savings achieved	134	139	144	149	154	159	165	170	176	183	0	0	0	0	0	0	0	0	0	0	0
fiscal amortizations	30	30	30	30	30	30	30	30	30	0	0	0	0	0	0	0	0	0	0	0	0
net income before tax	104	109	114	119	124	129	135	140	146	153	0	0	0	0	0	0	0	0	0	0	0
tax (34%)	0	35	37	39	40	42	44	46	48	50	52	0	0	0	0	0	0	0	0	0	0
net income	104	74	77	80	84	87	91	94	98	103	-52	0	0	0	0	0	0	0	0	0	0
cash flow	134	104	107	110	114	117	121	124	128	133	-52	0	0	0	0	0	0	0	0	0	0
funds needed	0	0	0	0	0	0	0	0	0	0	0	0	0	0	0	0	0	0	0	0	0
free cash flow	134	104	107	110	114	117	121	124	128	133	-52	0	0	0	0	0	0	0	0	0	0
internal return on investment	38																				

respected criteria group (recall of the criteria: Internal return on investment = or > 18)

4 - RONA

	yr 1	yr 2	yr 3	yr 4	yr 5	yr 6	yr 7	yr 8	yr 9	yr 10
annual savings achieved	134	139	144	149	154	159	165	170	176	183
funds needed	0	0	0	0	0	0	0	0	0	0
cumulative funds needed	0	0	0	0	0	0	0	0	0	0
economical amortizations	30	30	30	30	30	30	30	30	30	30
RONA	36.5	42.7	50.7	61	75.2	95.6	128.6	186.7	324.4	1020
RONA for first three yrs	128.2									

respected criteria group (recall of the criteria: RONA = or > 17 over a period of 36 months)

Exhibit 6 *Financial Statements of the Ciments Antillais Corp. (income statement and balance sheet for 1991)*

Ciments Antillais Corp.   Statement from 01 01 91 to 12 31 91

BALANCE SHEET

Address Industrial Zone of Jarry Mahaultpointe A Pitre Bay

| SIC Code | :1506 | Statement reported over a 12-month period |
| SIRET number | :30309525100011 | Last year's statement also reported over a 12-month period |

ASSETS

	Financial Year			Last Year
	Gross	*Amortization*	*Net*	*Net*
R & D				
Grant, patent				
Commercial budget				
Other intangible properties				
Land properties	3,201,663		3,201,663	3,201,663
Construction	53,083,117	33,419,845	19,663,272	16,289,034
Technical Installation equipment	86,141,261	66,312,795	19,828,466	18,906,181
Other tangible properties	19,970,974	11,384,045	856,928	7,583,659
Current immobilization	26,500		26,500	818,784
Account receivable				
Equivalent participation				
Participation	1,938,600		1,938,600	1,938,600
Account payable				
Other immobilized titles	530,000		530,000	505,000
Lending				
Other financial immobilization	1,028,498		1,028,498	977,208
TOTAL	65,920,615	111,116,686	54,803,928	50,220,131
Raw material inventory	24,182,047		24,182,047	27,811,750
Unfinished goods				
Unfinished services				
Work-in process & finished goods	3,139,606		3,139,606	2,267,133
Merchandise	922,955		922,955	5,966,334
Account receivable	2,807,262		2,807,262	
Clients and related accounts	45,803,327	4,589,509	41,213,818	44,448,976
Other receivables	3,754,951		3,754,951	3,394,062
Paid in capital				
Marketable securities				
Cash	83,641,891		83,641,891	53,637,029
Prepaid expenses	373,260		373,260	189,175
TOTAL	164,625,303	4,589,509	160,035,793	137,714,461
Several financial years				
TOTAL	330,545,918	115,706,196	214,839,722	1,879,345,931

Ciments Antillais Corp.

LIABILITIES AND SHAREHOLDERS' EQUITY

	Current Year	Previous Year
Common stock	21,647,600	21,647,600
Paid in capital		
Reevaluation difference	513,419	513,419
Legal reserves	2,164,760	2,164,760
Contractual and statutory reserves		
Regulated reserves	2,500,634	
Other reserves		
Postponed capital	79,580,342	61,929,320
Statement's total	26,359,661	27,836,657
Investment subvention		
Regulated provision	7,302,462	6,308,025
Total	140,068,881	120,399,782
Income from issuing shares		
Prepaid expense regulated		
Total		
Prepaid expenses for risk	689,633	535,337
Prepaid expenses for charges	6,082,156	4,589,777
Total	6,771,789	5,125,114
Convertible obligatory loan		
Other obligatory loan		
Loan and debt to banks	1,903,732	726,942
Financial loan and debt	6,028,498	4,209,507
Prereceived payments		
Accounts payable	46,627,299	43,545,858
Taxes and salaries payable	11,077,529	10,025,347
Other debt	1,432,619	3,863,918
Guaranteed future profit		
Total	67,069,679	62,371,575
Liabilities conversion gap	929,372	38,121
Grand Total	214,839,722	187,934,593
Total liabilities and shareholder's equity in francs and centimes	214,839,722.49	
From which special reevaluation reserve	513,419	513,419
Debt and sales that have already occurred from less than a year	60,075,272	
From which current bank participation, creditor bank CCP	1,903,732	

Ciments Antillais Corp.   Statement from 01 01 91 to 12 31 91

INCOME STATEMENT

	Current Year			Previous Year
	France	Exportation	Total	
Revenues from merchandise	50,427,653		50,427,653	29,544,699
Goods sold	328,628,635		328,628,635	313,161,379
Service sold				
Total sales	379,056,288		379,056,288	342,706,078
Stored production			872,473	(98,362)
Immobilized production				604,761
Aids for exploitation				
Profits on prepaid items and depreciation			3,948,686	7,859,189
Other products			1,402,477	1,383,047
Total of exploitation product			385,279,926	352,454,715
Purchase of merchandise (tariffs included)			42,061,737	32,085,564
Inventory variation (merchandise)			5,132,929	(4,129,299)
Purchase of raw material—other supplies			198,847,016	210,072,521
Inventory variation (raw material—other supplies)			6,081,533	(11,071,600)
Other purchase and external charge			47,589,327	48,823,850
Taxes, tariffs and like			5,403,779	4,888,779
Salaries and compensation			25,492,873	23,641,407
Social Security			12,345,101	10,533,070
Allotment exploitation/depreciation immobilized			6,278,710	6,183,022
Allotment exploitation/prepaid expense immobilized				
Allotment exploitation/assets attributable to prepaid expense			169,278	1,681,238
Allotment exploitation for risk and charge to prepaid expense			2,932,011	1,768,661
Other charges			45,000	86,000
Total exploitation expense			352,379,299	324,562,887
Exploitation results			32,900,626	27,891,828
Attributed profit or loss transferred				
Loss beared or profit transferred				
Profit from capital participation				
Profit from other property and account receivables				
Other interest income and like			4,739,159	4,355,229
Prepaid expense recovered and expenses transferred				3,704
Positive balance of change			96,766	169,972
Profit from selling property				
Total financial income			4,835,925	4,528,905
Financial dotation on depreciation-prepaid expenses				
Interest expense			1,014,397	650,572
Negative balance of change			351,656	157,124
Loss from selling property				
Total financial expenses			1,366,053	807,696
Financial result			3,469,872	3,721,208
Income before taxes			36,370,498	31,613,037

Ciments Antillais Corp.   Statement from 01 01 91 to 12 31 91

INCOME STATEMENT (end)

	Current Year	Previous Year
Unexpected income from operations on managing	1,210,519	786,171
Unexpected income from operations on capital	13,580	5,64,828
Prepaid expenses recovered and transfer of expenses	108,058	1,307,803
Total of exceptional income	1,332,157	7,778,803
Unexpected expense from operations on managing	36,607	2,461,993
Unexpected expense from operations on capital	36,065	53,900
Unexpected allotment to depreciation and prepaid items	1,752,495	1,734,579
Total unexpected expense	1,825,268	4,250,473
Net income from unexpected operations	(499,011)	3,528,329
Employees participation	2,432,782	2,029,186
Taxes	7,085,042	5,275,522
Total Income	391,448,009	364,762,424
Total expenses	365,088,347	336,925,767
Net income or loss	26,359,661	27,836,657

DETAILS OF EXCEPTIONAL INCOME AND EXPENSES
(See table of exceptional income and expenses)

Chapter 12

Organizational Structures for Global Logistics Excellence

◆ ◆ ◆

Highlights of this final chapter include:

◆ *New organizations related to manufacturing and logistics*

◆ *The organizational implications of sectorial logistics cooperation*

◆ *The international factor in global organizations*

◆ INTRODUCTION

It is impossible to implement the new approaches to global logistics described in the previous chapters without having thought clearly about how they will affect the organizational structures of the companies implementing the changes. Companies will see internal as well as inter-organizational changes appearing in their supply chains.

In this chapter, we outline the appropriate steps needed to change the structure and workings of these organizations. We approach the issue from the standpoint of measures to be introduced, rather than from that of describing types of organizational structures. Thus, we strongly advocate an approach whereby the organization undergoes a gradual learning process—one that would enable the corporation to meet its goals of globalization of logistics operations.

We focus in particular on the question of sectorial integration. We show how creating inter-organizational cooperation figures into making the necessary organizational changes. We also look at the way that key functions such as marketing, sales, management of services and, of course, logistics, are affected.

Our thinking embraces ongoing experiments taking place in large corporations. The solution involves developing flexible organizational structures that allow all parties to deal with the complexity of the task. Creating this dynamic flexibility depends on the corporation's success in restructuring itself, and on the professional expertise and the management tools used to create these changes. With a heavy emphasis on optimal satisfaction of customer demand, the cooperation mode implies sharing of the supply management function. It also implies a shared definition of what is actually supplied by effectively taking into account the needs of customers in the market segment targeted by the producer-distributor partners involved in the cooperation. Achieving this objective may mean that the distributor goes so far as to delegate both point-of-sale product restocking and integrated flow management. The result will be maximization of sales promotions and new product launches. Here, we reach the stage of real integration of the supply chain with the demand chain. Cooperation becomes more than a matter of optimizing flows. Such cooperation between producer and distributor offers a real alternative to vertical integration.

◆ NEW ORGANIZATIONS RELATED TO MANUFACTURING AND LOGISTICS OPERATIONS

Recalling Aspects of Organization Theory

There are numerous different schools of thought on organization theory. In this chapter, we will discuss in general terms a number of these schools of thought and identify how they shed light on global operations and logistics activities. We offer three guidelines with which to define the best structure for a goal of a given performance level:

- Centralization reflects the extent to which decisions are shared within the social system.
- Formalization represents the degree to which activities and relationships are governed by rules, procedures and contracts.
- Specialization/differentiation investigates the degree to which tasks are divided up into separate elements.

Centralization leads to increased efficiency through capacity for decision making in planning, coordination, and control of activities. Therefore, it is important to study the decision-making processes that actors in the organization employ. This proposition concerns logistics as a coordination and planning function in manufacturing and transport. Although the logistics function allows for assuming responsibility at the local level, in cases of arbitration it is the power of centralized decision makers that carries greater weight. Two good examples of such centrally rendered decisions are the allocation of manufacturing in a multisite manufacturing setup on an international level and the location of finished goods stocking points.

Formalization allows for increased efficiency. Procedures are used to industrialize or formalize repetitive actions and recurring transactions. Logistics managers frequently industrialize administrative or physical operations in order to minimize logistics costs for a given service. The manager does this by introducing standardized information communication systems that allow operations to be normalized or even standardized. Cooperation between producer and distributor also leads to normalization and standardization of procedures. With such cooperation, uncertainty decreases and inventory levels stabilize to more cost-effective levels.

Greater *specialization/differentiation* means greater adaptability. Experts understand problems more clearly and are able to adapt themselves to changing conditions more quickly. They discover new ways to do things. The notion of specialization forms the basis for logistics outsourcing—that is, the hiring of a particular type of logistics specialist to perform a set of logistics functions. Because they are specialists in their functions, the customer company stands to gain from this outside expertise through better cost control and improved service quality.

These three propositions are illustrated in a matrix with two axes in Table 12–1. The matrix depicts four types of organizational structures.

From this table we see that the relational form enables long-term contracts with service providers, as well as relations with consultants. Additionally, the transactional form tends toward buying transport or contracting out for capacity where repetitive and nonspecialized operations are involved.

The central issue in performance-based models lies in the relative efficiency among different organizational forms. The objective of elaborating typologies, such as the one presented in Table 12–1, is to classify them. They emphasize a particular explanatory parameter—for example, achieving objectives adapted to uncertain environments, the technological factor of the manufacturing process, the long-term strategy pursued by the corporation, the relationship between the behavior of actors, and the structure appraised as a collection of groups fulfilling functions.

However, this approach is inadequate as soon as it becomes evident that performance level depends more heavily on the interactions in intensive communication with one another than on the accuracy and speed of basic logistics and manufacturing operations. Going beyond this approach becomes necessary, as does the integration of learning processes with innovation processes. This integration enables factors of change to be taken into account, such as those that result from sectorial logistical cooperation or installing JIT, as we will see in the rest of this chapter. The need is no longer solely to measure performance efficiency of the operation as we have seen in chapter 11, but rather, to measure the performance efficiency of inter-operations.

The problem of economic performance raises the issue of the way in which resources are allocated. The organization is viewed as the efficient alternative to the marketplace when the price system becomes deficient. This definition opposes the organization and the market-

Table 12–1

	Typology of Organizational Structures	
	Internal Organization of Activity	*External Organization of Activity*
Centralized Formalized Nonspecialized	**Bureaucratic form**	**Transactional form**
	Appropriate context use • low degree of environmental uncertainty • repetitive tasks	*Appropriate context use* • low degree of environmental uncertainty • repetitive tasks nonspecialist investment
	Performance feature • high efficiency and productivity • less flexible	*Performance features* • the highest efficiency for some tasks • less flexible
Decentralized Nonformalized Specialized	**Organic form**	**Relational form**
	Appropriate context use • high environmental uncertainty • nonrepetitive tasks • specialized investment	*Appropriate context use* • high environmental uncertainty • nonrepetitive tasks • investment not very specialized
	Performance features • high efficiency for nonroutine specialized tasks • high degree of flexibility • less productive	*Performance features* • high efficiency for nonroutine specialized tasks • high degree of flexibility • less productive

From Ruekert, Walker, Roering, 1985.

place. The latter no longer fulfills its fundamental role of regulating as set out in the neoclassical normative approach. In this light, the marketplace becomes a place of noncooperation (spontaneous order, chance results of intentional behavior). The organization is, on the contrary, the place for voluntary real cooperation (order built through intentional articulation of intentional behavior). The organization appears, therefore, as the mechanism of intentional cooperation between individuals.

It is necessary to go beyond this cooperative view. Cooperative logistics projects in distribution channels are illustrations of hybrid inter-organizational structures resulting from intentional cooperative mechanisms.

The environment as a factor influencing the structure of organizations is the contingency theory associated with concepts of differentiation and integration. It is used to show that the organization assumes its shape through the analysis of external conditions. According to that theory, the quality of collaboration between departments must unite their efforts to satisfy the demands of the environment. Consequently, they reveal the importance of the role of coordination and conflict solving. Here we acknowledge a role attributed to the logistics function among the functions that act upon the production of the service related to the product. It is assumed that this integrating of functions possesses power or delegated authority to fulfill this role (see the following model).

This approach has undergone further development with the advent of the *model of resources dependency* associated with the perspective of the context taken as the environment. This model enables the organization to be viewed as a coalition in which performance is an objective, and within which there exists a power phenomenon. This suggests the contingency theory previously described. In this case the organization is seen as a quasi-marketplace in which influence and control are negotiated and allocated according to external agents within a relationship typified by reciprocal dependence. This position is a transitional one, halfway between that of the models that came out of the industrial economy and the models of sociological inspiration described later.

This approach satisfies the logistics experts. On the one hand, it refers to the demands of service provided to an external customer before internal demands are defined. On the other hand, the logistics expert attempts to reduce uncertainties linked to fluctuations in stock with two things in mind—namely, service and cost through managing the environment more effectively (e.g., developing partnerships with customers and suppliers in a JIT approach).

The organization can be defined by its sociological dimension, which is based on the structural-functional concept. This approach defines the roles associated with a function. The organization becomes a system of roles where authority and power come into play. The notions of motivation and adherence to roles help us understand why corporations set up and develop logistics cooperation projects. In particular, the question of the loss of autonomy in decision taking is raised as soon as relations are forged between a manufacturer and a subcontractor, or between a manufacturer and a logistics service firm.

Lastly, a *cognitive research program* has been elaborated based on the notion of the rule or system of rules as collective cognitive arrangements, which is completely different from the procedures described previously. This notion replaces the notion of contract, voluntary agreement between rational individuals, and services as key descriptions of organizations and markets. The rules make collective knowledge possible and the organization makes up an articulation of these rules, oriented to the possibility of an extension or transformation of this collective knowledge. In this way, organizations are dependent on the logic of collective learning, and renewed dynamism is lent to the model of professional expertise and the project-based organization model, which we will apply in cases of sectorial logistics cooperation.

Organizations Oriented to a Manufacturing and Logistics Cooperation

The previous models are essentially oriented to the internal organization of the firm and have adopted an approach that embraces both the technical–economic and sociopolitical aspects of operations. Early on, agreements or cooperation between different firms were considered as secondary organizational solutions adopted only when unforeseen factors made a go-it-alone strategy difficult.

In concentrating on their core businesses, however, corporations now cultivate numerous interfaces with parties both upstream and downstream in the channel. These partnering relationships can engender competitive advantages over those corporations that are not part of the relationship. This is true for both horizontal and vertical relationships. However, we must distinguish between coordination and cooperation. *Coordination* involves establishing rules that govern the production and allocation of outputs. Some rules prove to be more effective than others do.

Cooperation, on the other hand, is completely different. It implies sharing aims and goals. Consequently, choices concerning cooperation need not be regarded as a mere alternative between marketplace and hierarchy, but rather, as a real choice between three possible solutions: marketplace, hierarchy, and cooperation. The third solution does not represent an intermediate form but is a structure existing in its own right. It is characterized by the fact that several separate and independent organizations have reached an agreement whereby their plans are laid together. To a certain extent, these independent organizations mutually guarantee their future conduct. The end motive for organizations entering into such relationships is clearly to achieve results that they would not be able to obtain independently.

With this in mind, it becomes necessary to take into account technical–economic parameters and sociopolitical ones. The second rule, which has general implications, consists in managing cooperation as a process of negotiation and searching for agreements in a context full of uncertainty. The organization is then seen in a dynamic structuring process. The paradoxical dimension of the cooperative organization is that although the outcome of the cooperation itself is uncertain, it seeks to reduce the uncertainty in its environment and that of its partner by sharing information and expertise. Figure 12–1 shows this paradox quite clearly.

The essential feature of cooperation between different firms entails the creation of new resources and new expertise. In logistics sectorial cooperation, one of the most important issues is to decide how benefits from the partnership are to be divided between manufacturer and distributor. As far as creating resources is concerned, those that are specifically shared by both organizations are potential ones and will be the outcome of a collaboration process laid down according to the contribution made by each partner.

In this way, one may use the term *transorganizational* to describe the corporation and marketing coalition. From a marketing point of view, one can distinguish between a corporation engaged in marketing that involves complex operational exchanges and information transfer, and a marketing coalition arrangement that assigns functions through alliances with specialized firms.

Transorganizational systems (transverse organizations) run on the basis of rules and norms rather than by hierarchy and contract systems. In order to work, systems driven by norms must be self-regulating and self-balanced. The process of self-regulation is achievable through an entirely transparent information system (see chapter 10). The relations and the activities will be organized in an interfunctional and interorganizational fashion. The features of these systems are shared, as opposed to being closely guarded from any sharing. Therefore these shared features clash with the current competitive culture and involvement.

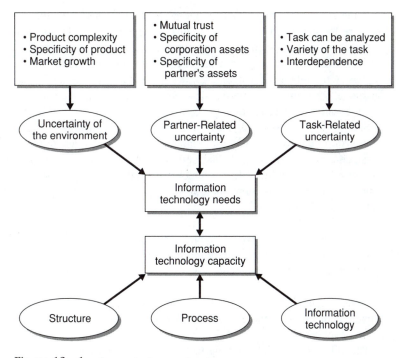

Figure 12–1   Dynamic Structuring Process
Based on Desreumeaux, 1994.

Network organizations reflect the intermediate dynamics between marketplace and hierarchy. The network may be viewed as an organizational form, which leads to a lower global economic cost because it increases the expertise of those involved. It also responds with maximum effect to fast growth, to greater complexity due to scientific and technological innovation, and to the globalization of the market. Different forms of networks have been identified, differentiated by their degree of openness (i.e., the number of outside actors involved in the network organization and the voluntary character of the players). The *dynamic* form put forward is characterized by the interactive processes between its members, the explicit specification of expectations stated by each partner, and the ways of measuring the benefits and performance that are a result of the relationship. These very features enable us to liken this form of cooperation to an interorganizational relationship of the horizontal cooperative type.

The Impact of Just-in-Time Systems on Organizations

Studying the logistics function whose basic task is to provide the service related to a product sheds light on the questions of the transverse nature (transversality) of the organization, strengthens the importance of interfunctional cooperation within the organization, and interorganizational logistics cooperation. This dual dimension, transversality and integration, is a fundamental one in logistics organization models. We have stressed the importance of the logistics function assuming responsibility for those interoperations that occur at the interfaces between organizations. Only this kind of cooperative dynamism produces maximum performance. In the past, whereas the efficiency of operations mattered most, now the efficiency of interoperations is preeminent.

If the corporation's goal is to value customer satisfaction as the overriding performance measure for supply chains, partners must go beyond the traditional and partial performance attributes of measurement for each function and each player in the distribution channel. Moving from productivity as a target to optimizing the service provided to the customer implies a rethinking of the organization. The outcome, quite logically, is to abandon a functional, divisional, or matrix view and respond to the demands of the marketplace in keeping with the reactive model.

Setting up JIT systems has an impact on organizations engaged in this type of relationship. Increased integration among purchasing, conception, manufacturing, stock management, marketing, and distribution is often a prerequisite for a JIT system to be introduced. Some writers have demonstrated the effects of JIT systems on traditional organizational concepts mentioned at the beginning of this chapter. These conclusions are laid out as follows:

- More elaborate control procedures are introduced.
- Degree of normalization through the control system becomes greater.
- Specialization is intensified.

Shared manufacturing programs, complexity related to the increased frequency of shipments of smaller batches, and the need to take up new technologies all lead to a required higher level of expertise.

The JIT-type organization may be understood as a mediator in the relationship between uncertainty and the structure. There are three possible ways of making JIT effective in a buyer–supplier relationship:

- *Apparent JIT:* customers receive shipments in accordance with their needs, but the supplier continues manufacturing large quantities and supplies customers from stock.
- *Organized JIT:* customers still transfer the weight of organizational change to the supplier without directly helping in the supplier's attempts to change. However, customers cooperate by making the project economically acceptable by sharing transport costs, packaging costs, and simplified order management.
- *Integral or total JIT:* this extends the JIT approach to the customer, thereby spreading the total burden of the change in keeping with the new form of exchange between buyer and supplier.

The JIT exchange is a relational type based on long-term relationships. It must go hand-in-hand with effective organizations, with relations capable of managing the complex nature of the links binding partners together and saving management from conflicts that appear between participating members. JIT is characterized by the need for far-reaching cooperation between customer and supplier. The coordination requires an increase in the frequency of communications and a broadening of interorganizational links. In order to reduce the risks of functional interdependence, it is not only necessary to select one's partner with utmost care, but it is also very important to define those internal procedures governing the workings of the relationship with a view to limiting the potential conflicts that could arise in such a relationship.

The main tools for change when setting up a JIT include personalized visits, frequent supplier–customer meetings, frequent communication with suppliers, changes in the forward order system, addressing the supplier, and making all costs clearly available. The four main organizational shifts observed at the end of a change to JIT are:

- An increase in the number of communications with manufacturing and quality functions
- Integration of quality
- Intensification of functional contacts between customer and supplier
- Greater involvement of other functions in the process of choosing new suppliers

This new direction requires that the isolated operation model with the single aim of individual productivity be abandoned and replaced by the horizontal cooperative model, and the vertical cooperative model. As we have already stressed, cooperation in this context does not only mean information transfer. Instead, cooperation creates a specific and distinctive value for the partners engaged. On both the horizontal and vertical cooperative models, this sharing of the common expertise constitutes a shared representation of the situation. In the horizontal model, information is shared between the actors on a horizontal plane within the organization. In a vertical model, organizations cooperate along the line to provide information that will make each step optimal. The outcome of this shared vision is therefore, shared aims and improved performance.

It is shown, then, that integration does not translate as cooperation, and that information transfer is not to be confused with communication transfer. It also follows that innovation is possible inside the framework of relational integration.

◆ THE ORGANIZATIONAL IMPLICATIONS OF SECTORIAL LOGISTICS COOPERATION

General Organizational Implications of Logistics Cooperation

Broadened customer–supplier logistics cooperation requires functions to be involved more heavily with their partners' functions than in traditional relationships. The logistics relationships range from contacts established between the manufacturer's distribution logistics and the distributor's supply logistics, to the involvement of sales and purchasing functions, factory production, and sales at retailer. Figure 12–2 gives an initial idea of the different areas that functional cooperation may cover.

Figure 12–2 points to the importance of the changing nature and content of the relationship where the organizations, manufacturer, and supplier meet. What stands out in type 1 is a small interface—in fact, it is the smallest imaginable. A monofunctional relation exists, focused mostly on price conditions, which frequently are a source of conflict. This behavior is typical of a transactional type of relationship.

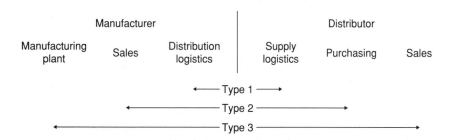

Figure 12–2   Organizational Implications of Different Types of Cooperation

The type 2 stage allows for denser and more broadly based transfers by involving more functions in the operations, both on the supplier's and the distributor's sides. This type of relationship can be called a multifunctional interorganizational one. It brings together logistics, production, and financial aspects of the commercial relationship. This type does not bring into question the partners' internal structural organizations, however. The logistical-marketing cooperation and, to a certain extent, the trickier aspects of the logistical-sales dynamics, for example, require organizational coordination beforehand. Second-stage relationships lead not only to a redefinition of the roles of functions within each organization, but also to the creation of new jobs, expertise, and communication systems capable of transmitting the information necessary to intra- and interorganizational cooperation. Therefore, in type 3 we can consider that functions no longer operate opposite each other in a separate fashion, but rather, that they operate in cooperative teams. Specialized functions such as merchandising, logistics, sourcing, finance, and customer service continue to exist but are to be found in the back office (i.e., essentially affording a support role to the cooperative organization).

The Evolution of Manufacturers' Sales and Logistics

Figure 12–3 depicts the traditional organization chart for a manufacturing organization. The organization relies on functional departments, one of which is the technical department, including all the plants, which work for all the product divisions in the corporation. The product division has different markets, customers, product ranges, and distribution channels.

Figure 12–4 specifies the internal organization of one of the product divisions as it was before any functional integration. The plants are attached to the technical division. Units dealing with logistics, the main warehouses, and order preparation centers are part of an operational division. A particular product's division includes two main elements: marketing—in charge of developing and promoting products—and sales—responsible for meeting market-share targets. There is also an administrative function comprising accounting, information systems, and logistics. The logistics function is therefore completely absorbed into the organization's administration function and, given this logic, is confused with an administrative sales function.

On closer inspection of the logistics function's role, we note that it is assigned three main aims:

- Provide assistance to the sales rep in the field, with samples, advertising, and documentary information on products
- Ensure that products meet quality requirements when they appear on the shelf
- Respect service demands made by distributors—chain by chain, or for a given chain, at the national level

A number of factors in the structural framework and in the environment argue for an evolution of logistics organizations. Some may be due to laws compelling greater clarity in sales conditions, others may result from technological changes (see chapter 10). Such an example would be a cooperative movement in the food distribution chain or the advent of electronic data interchange (EDI). All such factors mean that logistics organizations must specify objectives in detail in each product division, as illustrated in Figure 12–5.

The main objective for sales logistics is to develop cooperative partnerships between manufacturers and distributors. Consequently, the axes that structure the organization should enable partnership structures to be put in place. The two axes encountered most frequently are:

- Bringing together the logistics function, whose main concern is to provide the service demanded by its customer, and the sales function. Such an integration presupposes that the current organizational structure be modified and that a chain-by-chain approach be adopted.
- Project management in the logistics field. Information systems development is an excellent illustration of a transversal project linking different actors concerned with achieving set objectives.

The ideal situation is to obtain a closer cooperation between sales and logistics functions. Figure 12–6 shows the resulting logistics–sales structure.

The origin of this reorganization arises from the demand for more specific services, such as merchandising, commercial arrangements, increasingly specific logistics requirements, as well as for the strategic reasons we have already outlined. The improvement of distribution can best be explained by the need to gain competitive advantage in markets where consumers expect greater and greater degrees of segmentation.

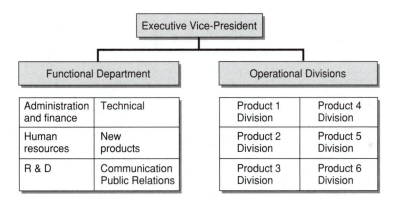

Figure 12–3   Traditional Manufacturer's Organization

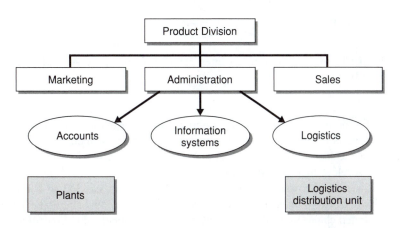

Figure 12–4   Organization of Product Divisions before Any Functional Integration

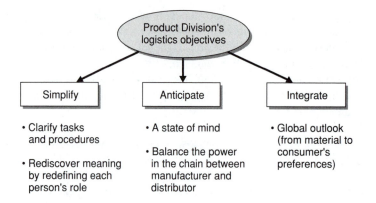

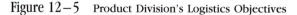

Figure 12–5   Product Division's Logistics Objectives

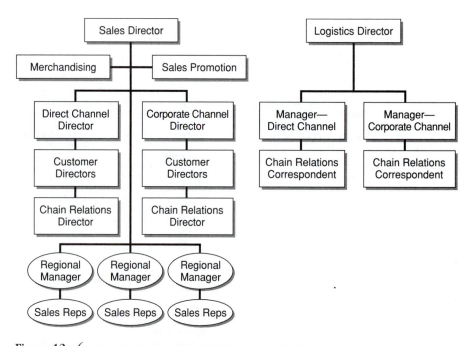

Figure 12–6   Manufacturer's Internal Organization in a Cooperative Relational Mode with a Distributor

Furthermore, some large supermarket and hyper-market chains have gotten to know their customers extremely well by having gained mastery of their information flows. Each chain is able to identify what targets to attack and thus determine accurately the types of products and services that its customers are likely to want.

This trend toward mastery of information flows has led to a reorganization of sales networks. Reps have been organized up until now on a regional basis. Today they are allocated chains divided into two categories or channels: the *direct channel* (for example, 50 percent of sales volume) where the rep must take orders and negotiate directly with each point-of-sale, and the *corporate channel* (the other 50 percent of volume), in which case the central warehouse is targeted by the reps.

At headquarters, customer directors have been placed in charge of several chains. The chains that they oversee belong to one of the two types of channels. Two-channel directors—one for the direct channel, another for the corporate channel—coordinate all the sales activities that customer directors undertake.

The adopted organizational principle stems from the recognition of upstream logistics relative to support of the activity, and of downstream logistics related to action in direct contact with the customer.

The ideal scenario occurs downstream according to a continuous logic comprising successive stages:

- Takeover in catalog of product files
- Eventual replacements
- Stock allocation
- Order preparation
- Delivery to customer

Upstream the support functions work by:

- Product database management
- Transfer to main catalog of product files after customer decision
- Coordination of technical information into the product file so that the main catalog becomes active and serves the purpose of filtering customers' orders

The customer process contains two stages:

- With regard to entry in the product database, the customer is listed in a product file created by the rep. This file contains information taken from the product database, plus a photo or picture. At this stage of the negotiation the customer decides whether to list the product.
- The catalog, which is continuously updated, serves to help the customer come to a decision. When he puts in his order, it is filtered through the catalog and sets into motion the change from downstream to upstream logistics.

The importance attached to the decision taken upstream stands out clearly. The smooth running of the process depends on this stage, particularly thanks to the catalog. In an ideal case, everything is run upstream, the definition and choice of product, negotiation, availability, and so on. Likely problems should be discussed at this point, and solutions should be found before chain correspondents get involved. The latter can thus devote their energies to providing the service to the customer, as the customer will no longer have to be burdened with the task of dealing with last-minute emergencies.

It is of interest to give more detailed information about the role of the chain relations correspondent, whose previous title was customer manager and who reports to logistics. The chain relations correspondents' main role is to extend the sales function by providing improved service to the customer. They assume the role of service provider instead of simply fulfilling a purely administrative one. As such, they have a reactive position, relying on efficient logistic support services. Their position is, therefore, key in the cooperative setup, placed at the interface between manufacturer and supplier.

The chain relations correspondent's job is called to undergo far-reaching changes, with an important role in chain differentiation. This role will mainly consist of:

- Analyzing results achieved with the chain, in logistics terms as well as payment terms
- Working with a sales counterpart to establish a monthly global report on results achieved with the chain
- Putting forward solutions; chain relations correspondents know their chains perfectly and are therefore in an ideal position to pinpoint the causes of problems and the most appropriate solutions to them; they will be the driving force in the move to differentiate the chain through the introduction of constructive solutions for their own chain
- Assuming results achieved; performance measures and salary will be set according to the results achieved, or, in the future according to the service level

To help achieve the objectives, the chain relations correspondent must rely on new tools that information processing offers. These tools can speed up flows and take part in the development of new indicators (e.g., credit per chain, monitoring of special events, monitoring sales, service rate performance obtained). In such a context, acquiring the reflexes for dealing with repetitive tasks that engender no real added value and reinforcing the responsibility of personnel whose role is to provide service to the distributor has become all-important. Figure 12–7 sets out these ideas.

The content of the role in terms of customer service evolves as Table 12–2 shows.

The system just described means that a customer service structure must be in place on different levels: providing direct contact with the customer at the operational level and rendering support functions for the operational level. Then the functions of sales reps (sales) and chain relations correspondents (logistics) are parallel. The latter are in charge of the direct relationship with the customer. They receive the support of the channel director, whose role of managing people diminishes as the chain relations correspondents become more autonomous.

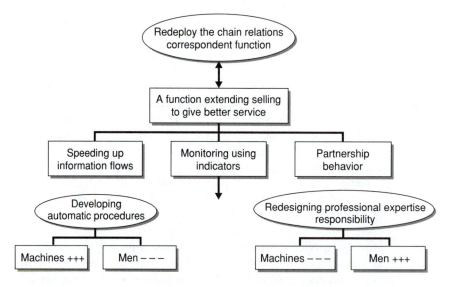

Figure 12–7   Separating Repetitive Activities from Those with a High Added Value for the Chain Relations Correspondent

Table 12–2

Details of Customer Service Role Evolution		
Functions	*Trend*	*Evolution*
• Managing sales transactions	• Decreasing	• Automatic registering orders (catalogs, EDI, standard fax forms, etc.)
• Inventories available, registering	• Decreasing	• Exceptional supplementary information
• Claims on customers	• Increasing	• Carried out in real time
• Customer accounts management	• Increasing	• Integration in cooperation with customer
• Problem solving (customer claims, returns, etc.)	• Increasing	• Integration customer complaints (delivery, out of stock, refusals)
• Information to sales representatives	• Increasing	• New tools and services
• Quantitative indicators		• Service indicators
		• Indicators by chain

The support functions have less to do with the customer. They have more to do with the use of tools that provide service to the operational functions. The credit and product functions provide backup to logistics. They set out the framework of the relationship between the chain relations correspondent and the customer. Further upstream the task remains that of discovering and perfecting new logistics solutions to improve customer service.

In the long run, creating a function to analyze sales per chain should be envisaged, so that a very detailed study of sales per chain, or even sales per outlet, may be carried out. These jobs will be situated at the junction between sales and logistics, since they will serve to identify those products that sell from those that don't by point of sale, as well as by the advertising impact on sales. The people filling these jobs will be in contact with sales staff, with the task of anticipating events, promotions, new product launches, advertising campaigns, and so on. Additionally, they will be responsible for keeping sales and marketing people up-to-date on the results achieved (overall, chain by chain and even for each point of sale).

Alongside these developments, the logistics support function, whose role is to ensure security and mastery of the system, will be strengthened through the development of new transversal projects related to product management and inventory management.

The product function provides information for the product file. The portfolio function pilots the flows between ordering, data forecast, and manufacturing planning. As a consequence, products are made available when there is demand for them. These ideas are captured in Table 12–3.

By using suitable goals, the logistics function can achieve its objective of anticipating customers' needs in this new setup. It is also able to differentiate between chains, outlets, products being routinely restocked, products part of a promotional campaign, and lastly, adjustments between supply and demand.

Organization and Logistics by Project

The approach adopted for implementing this organizational development consists in defining specific logistics projects. Identifying these supposes that a comparison is made of the objectives set for logistics and the functions that logistics has to carry out whether they are taken over by organizational units or whether they are fulfilled by tools used transversally by these units. Table 12–4 illustrates the approach.

Table 12-3

Division of Functions Between Product and Portfolio		
Product	*Procedures and methods*	*Portfolio*
• Procedures for creating and canceling codes and data on products • Quality of product information • Updating main catalog • Management of listed items • Rules governing code definition • Formalization of palletization plans	• Technological watch • Logistics studies • Partnership projects • Knowledge of chains • Information system	• Coherence of overall information system • Putting in place and managing tools • Arbitrating in order choices and management of shortages • Operations management • Coordination of different actors in the distribution channel • Inventory analysis and supply/demand adjustment

Table 12-4

Definition of logistics projects required for implementing organizational development				
	Catalog Project	*Efficiency of Customer Function*	*Setting up EDI Tools*	*Customer Service*
Product function	***	***	PL	**
Portfolio function	PL	***		***
Customer function	***	PL	***	PL
Distribution center	**	**	***	***
Merchandising	***	*	***	**

*degree of involvement of the unit
PL = project leader

How Jobs Have Evolved in Retail Distribution

Category management is one of the latest trends in retail distribution and is an essential part of the Efficient Consumer Response (ECR) project that we introduced in chapter 4. The distributor's organization in terms of the role attributed to the buyer reveals three basic stages:

• The traditional buyer's main target is to make money upstream. The chain's responsibility is to make money downstream.
• The product manager is in charge of a department or a whole range of products. His or her job includes a marketing approach.
• The category manager manages buying according to categories and not in relation to a market.

This management approach for retail distributors, whose aim is to satisfy customer needs as well as possible, is based on vertical responsibility for all the activities that concern product category. The main characteristics of category management are:

• Concentration of distributors' attention on selling rather than purchasing; the distributors no longer sell what they have bought. Rather, they buy from and pay the manufacturer what they have sold.

- The categories' function as strategic business units in which precise objectives are attributed, the main one of which is the consumers' satisfaction.
- Category management implies that links between manufacturer and distributor be established and enriched; they should be seen as a process geared toward satisfying the consumer; for distributors this means that the purchasing, merchandising, price, promotions management, and stock management are fused together into category management for a given product for which sales volume and profit margin objectives should be anticipated.

It is of interest to note a recent development in ECR in Europe, dating from August 1996, where the term *category management* is replaced by *demand management*. This shift in terminology strengthens the idea that category management embraces improvements in sales performances.

Usually the number of categories in a supermarket is about two hundred. Consumer buying serves to define the categories. The Food Marketing Institute recommends four ways of putting products into categories:

- *Destination,* meaning that the retailer gives priority to those categories for which the retailer wants to be recognized as a leader; these products convey an image that reinforces the retailer's distinctiveness
- *Routine nature,* meaning products are classified on the basis of target customers being accustomed to purchasing them at that retailer
- *Occasional and seasonal,* meaning a distributor wants to serve customers at the right time (i.e., when the latter wants to buy them)
- *Convenience,* the notion that covers products that the retailer supplies from a wide and comprehensive range

It is obvious that within one category one must also have subcategories that lend greater nuances to the objectives for the category in question. These subcategories may contribute to increasing the number of some types of consumers coming to the chain and, inside the same chain, encourage customers in impulse buying, generating cash flow through sales of high-margin products or establishing an image of creation through the quality of products in a subcategory.

Some information has to be shared between manufacturers and distributors so that the categories function properly. This information includes definition of category content, consumer needs, or actual sales, and the impact of promotional campaigns including the way shelves are stocked.

This approach cannot be envisaged unless jobs are redefined. The category manager's role covers the following:

- Developing and putting into place strategic plans for given categories
- Developing and maintaining relations with suppliers in charge of specific category plans
- Managing product range in the given categories regarding quality, variety, and so on
- Managing price strategies and margin objectives for each category
- Supervising merchandising for each category and managing shelf space
- Identifying opportunities to increase sales and profitability, cutting costs, and improving output; also, identifying other fields such as distribution, information flow, and financial aspects (payment conditions)

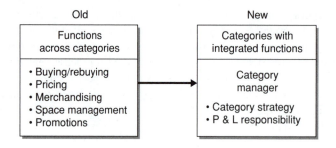

Figure 12-8   Definition of the Category Manager's Role

Most of these functions are not, in fact, new ones, but few people are able to assume all of them. It is recommended that the category manager be assisted by someone whose role is producing and analyzing data. Figure 12-8 summarizes the way the category manager's job will develop.

◆ THE INTERNATIONAL FACTOR IN GLOBAL ORGANIZATIONS

Difficulties Related to Setting Up Global Organizations

The splitting up of logistics missions between business units and the logistics functions creates a number of problems that contribute to a new definition of the way in which the latter intervenes and the way it is actually organized.

The question is, how does one reconcile the objective of optimizing flows at the level of the business unit with the quest for global optimization undertaken by the global logistics management? Production and sales decisions taken by business units have great consequences for logistics. There is dynamic interaction between the people in charge of flows in the business units and top logistics managers. In fact, there is a real risk of a rise in intercontinental flows within business units as a result of arbitration at the manufacturing and sales levels. A business unit may also—solely on the basis of production criteria—choose to specialize its plants and generate flows to make their ranges complete. Product sourcing for a given country will thus be dealt with independently by each business unit. So sourcing in a piecemeal fashion will lead to an even more pressing need for grouping together sourcing, which must come under the responsibility of a centralized logistics function.

How does one ensure the generation and sharing of information intended for the business units? They must receive comprehensive information intended for their logistics activities in such a way as to ensure that, on the one hand, they can assume their share of monitoring operations, and on the other, their service and costs performance can be monitored. A global management structure for logistics must ensure clarity through the information systems, and continuously provide information about inventories in hand. Products available cause no problems at all. However, for product shortages, an allocation or arbitrage by sales will be necessary. Business units need, therefore, to know the state of their orders. Competing information systems frequently confuse efforts to distribute the same information to all logistics parties.

How do business units share benefits with the centralized logistics management (with operational resources at its disposal) for logistics services provided? The centralized logistics department has to develop a cost-monitoring tool suitable for business unit organization to allocate the specific costs related to each unit's logistics activities (e.g., in a problem involving cost allocation for a container with products destined for one country and carrying products from different business units). On the other hand, the cost-monitoring tool must be suitable to give estimates.

Whose responsibility is the delivery or providing of service? Calculating lead times up to delivery is not an easy task, especially when it is uncertain whether the product is available or not. Moreover, the business unit is responsible for the production planning in the plants, and therefore for the availability of products. When a product is delivered, late responsibility for the delay must be established. It is either that of the follow-up service at the business unit or that of the service provided by the centralized logistics department.

Who speaks to the customer? The likelihood of there being several products for some customers suggests that a common approach between the different business units and the different logistics levels is required.

These questions shed light on the type of logistics organization to be set up in a geographically integrated approach to flow management.

Glocal Logistics

The efficiency of geographically integrated logistics depends more and more often on a subtle balance between a global and a local approach. This has led to the term *glocal logistics*. The way logistics systems have been conceived, their design and organizational management require reflection at least at two levels:

- Centralized—whose task is to guarantee across-the-board harmony.
- Field-level operations—where the primary concern is the day-to-day operations management and taking care of the customer.

The breaking up of national organizational structures and the decomposition of manufacturing processes alone justify the creation of a global logistics structure. Increasing globalization or continentalization of business activity has led to business units, in particular, being set up in many fields. Whether in basic manufacturing industries (the chemical industry, for instance) or in transformation industries, or in intermediate products or consumer products, the concepts and structures to support a global logistics approach have been put in place.

Corporations have been broken up into microcompanies. Some business units may, however, have a turnover of several billion dollars and be in total control of their results. To achieve results, business units have their own manufacturing and marketing resources. Sales departments, on the other hand, often keep an organization on the scale of each country, so that the sales approach may be adapted to the specific situations in each one.

In the framework of this organization of worldwide product lines, logistics management is placed in a complex matrix-type organizational position. It is in relation with each business unit that has a flow manager. The flow managers are responsible for plant planning, attribution of products to sales organizations in each country according to forecasts and demand, orders management, and product allocation.

In such a context, logistics is bound to undergo geographical integration. Logistics will function at the local level, close to sales organizations, at one extreme, and at the global level, guiding the overall activity, at the other extreme. In between, other intermediate levels are likely to appear for groups of countries or continents.

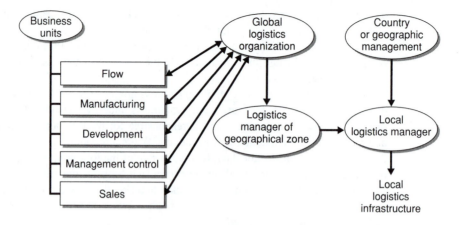

Figure 12−9   Glocal Logistics Organization

Another level where logistics is present is at the level of a group of countries and not at the national level. Setting up business units raises questions about national networks coexisting. Transnational flows or import flows created by specialization in manufacturing plants are strong contributory factors. National warehouses, therefore, tend to become transnational ones (e.g., one for southern Europe and one for northern Europe). Logistics, then, manages intermediate organizations located between the global level (business unit or central logistics structure) and the remaining local level (the sales force).

Lastly, the third level is the level of proximity that the specific nature of local approaches to marketing and sales requires. Such specifics include delivery times, order consolidation prepared on several sites upstream, and operators capable of adapting their services to local needs. Figure 12−9 illustrates the glocal logistics organization.

Glocal logistics management has at its disposal centralized resources that are used to design the global logistics network. Moreover, it also has geographical logistics managers who coordinate activities more closely in each of the geographical zones. At the local level in each country there is a logistics manager who reports in the hierarchy to the country manager but who operates under the central logistics management.

The case of spare parts distribution is particularly revealing of this trend in logistics to adopt organizational structures at several levels. Thus, it is not unusual to find a spare-parts after-sales organization set up as an international profit center for which some infrastructures have an international vocation (expensive parts manufactured in small numbers) and others are destined to local markets of close proximity (emergency stock, under-two-hour delivery). Logistics has to adapt its expertise according to the needs of one of the three levels described. Sales practices are not the same, and physical infrastructure tools and logistics information and telecommunications systems (LITS) tools differ greatly. Logistics organizations have to be structured, therefore, on several levels.

◆ SUMMARY

In this chapter we have discussed the required changes at the organizational level for a successful implementation of the new approaches to global operations and logistics. Doubtless, companies have existing organizational structures that respond to their particular environments. We start with a brief outline of the typology used in organizational theory such as bureaucratic, organic, transnational, and relational forms, and discuss how each of these links to the global logistics issues introduced in the book. Rather than describing organizational structures, we discussed some of the metrics and measures that would allow a better learning process of the implications of globalizing the logistics operations. In particular, we explored in detail the sectorial dimension of our global operations and logistics framework, since vertical integration is disappearing as an organizational structure and the interfaces with other companies require a new type of cooperation that looks beyond the short term. Some of the changes involve a closer relationship and definition of functions in the customer–supplier logistics, which has been accelerated by the use of JIT or the arrival of electronic data interchange (EDI). We conclude by discussing the difficulties of accomplishing efficiency on the geographically disperse organizations. We define glocal logistics as the balance that has to be obtained between the global approach (i.e., geographically integrated logistics) and the local approach (i.e., each area has specific requirements that cannot be ignored). The ideal glocal organization would use centralized resources to rationalize the resources available to the global logistics network, combined with regional or local logistics managers that respond and customize to the particular needs. Different examples are provided to illustrate the previous ideas.

DISCUSSION QUESTIONS

1. What are the dimensions used to categorize organizational structures?
2. Briefly describe each organizational form and the environment it fits best.
3. What is the impact of JIT systems on the organizations engaged in this type of relationship?
4. What are the organizational implications of different types of cooperation between a manufacturer and a distributor in a supply chain?
5. Outline conceptually the manufacturer's internal organization in a cooperative relational mode with a distributor.
6. Outline conceptually the structure of the glocal logistics organization.

REFERENCES

Achrol, R. S. 1991. Evolution of the marketing organization: New forms for turbulent environments. *Journal of Marketing* 55 (October): 77–93.

Bensaou, M. 1994. Interorganizational cooperation: The role of information technology: An empirical study of U.S. and Japanese supplier relations. *Working Paper INSEAD*.

Borys, B., and D. Jemsison. 1989. Hybrid arrangement as strategic alliances: Theoretical issue in organizational combination. *Academy of Management* 14:234–49.

Bowersox, D. J., and P. J. Daugherty. 1987. Emerging patterns of logistical organization. *Journal of Business Logistics* 8(1):46–60.

Brousseau, P. 1993. *L'economie des contrats, Technologies de l'information et coordination interentreprises*. Paris: PUF.

Calvi, R. 1994. *Le "juste a temps dans les approvisionnements: l'étude d'un changement interorganisationnel*. These de Doctorat Université Pierre Mende's France, Grenoble.

Desreumeaux, A. 1994. *Problemes organisationnels de la cooderation interfirmes*. Working Paper IAF Lille, USTL.

Dwyer, R., P. Schurr, and S. Oh. 1987, Developing buyer–seller relationships. *Journal of Marketing* 51(2): 11–27.

Favereau, O. 1989. Organisation et marche. *Revue Francaise d'Economie* IV(1): 65–96.

Germain, R., C. Drogge, and P. Daugherty. 1994. The effect of Just-in-Time selling on organizational structure: An empirical investigation. *Journal of Marketing Research* XXXI (November): 471–83.

Jarillo, J. C. 1988. On strategic networks. *Strategic Management Journal* 9(1): 31–41.

Juffe, M., and J.-P. Schmitt. 1995. *Organiser et communiquer: deux faces du management. Humanisme et Entreprise,* pp. 45–69.

Lamming, R. 1993. *Beyond Partnership: Strategies for innovation and supply.* Englewood Cliffs, N.J.: Prentice Hall.

Lawrence, P. and J. N. Lorsch. 1986. *Adapter les structures de l'entre Drise,* Paris: Ed. d'Organisation.

Mathe, H., and R. D. Shapiro. 1993. *Integrating service strategy in the manufacturing company.* London: Chapman & Hall.

Miles, R. E., and C. C. Snow. 1992. Causes of failure in network organizations. *California Management Review* 34 (Summer): 53–72

Oliver, C. 1990. Determinant of interorganizational relationships: Integration and future directions. *Academy of Management* 15(2).

Quelin, B. 1994. *Cooperation inter-entreprises et creation de ressources. Contribution a l'ouvrage collectif* Les coope rations inter-entreprises, GDR en Economie Industrielle (20), CNRS, Juin.

Ruekert, R.W., O. C. Walker, and K. J. Roering. 1985. The organization of marketing activities: A contingency theory of structure and performance. *Journal of Marketing* 49 (Winter): 13–25.

Thorelli, H. 1986. Networks: Between markets and hierarchies. *Strategic Management Journal* 7: 37–51.

Veltz, P. and P. Zarifian. 1993. Vers de nouveaux mode les d'organisation. *Sociologie du travail* (1) (Dunod): 3–25.

Zarifian, P. 1993. *Ouels mode les d'organisation pour l'industrie europeenne? L'émerence de la firme cooperatrice* Coil. Logiques economiques, L'Harmattan.

Zipkin, P. 1991. Does manufacturing need a JIT revolution? *Harvard Business Review.*

We have reached the end of our long tour through the fascinating, at least to us, world of global operations and logistics. We have provided descriptions of interesting operating systems in a variety of country environments; outlined the basic concepts, ideas, and tools to be used in understanding them; and finally outlined the challenges that lie ahead for operations and logistics for companies competing in increasingly interdependent world markets. We will close our tour by revisiting its major stops and highlighting the most important of the ideas/concepts we encountered.

The three conceptual cornerstones of our global operations and logistics framework, and at the same time the essential elements for the success of the global supply chain, are:

- Sectorial integration
- Functional integration
- Geographical integration

The *sectorial* dimension of interfirm integration refers to the efforts by global supply chain partners to coordinate and manage their activities as a single, unified entity, rather than multiple separate entities. The *functional* dimension of intrafirm integration highlights the cross-functional nature of operations and logistics. The operations and logistics process cuts across all functional areas and enables the creation of interfaces that must be managed collectively. *Geographical* integration requires a network of facilities located worldwide that are managed as a single entity in an effort to supply global demand with uniform standards for offered products and services.

A multiplicity of factors are driving the globalization of operations and logistics activities. We have categorized them into:

- Global market forces
- Technological forces
- Dynamically changing global cost forces
- Turbulent political and macroeconomic forces

The development of successful global operations strategies requires careful consideration of the dynamic nature of the forces that shape the global competitive environment, and careful allocation of their resources in meeting long-term competitive goals.

Outsourcing activities have become fundamental blocks of globalized operations and logistics strategies. A variety of reasons, from strategic (e.g., improved business forces, access to world-class capabilities, shared risks, etc.) to tactical (e.g., cash infusion, resources not available internally, etc.), are behind the prominence of such activities. All firms face the challenge of deciding:

- Which products/components to outsource
- Which criteria to use for selecting suppliers
- How to change the outsourcing mix and suppliers across the life of the product

We provide a powerful, and simple, framework to analyze such issues: the *Strategic Importance and Criticality Matrix*.

With the increasing recognition of global logistics as a source of potential competitive advantage by companies, there has been a rapid growth in the logistics service industry, with *third-party logistics (3PL)* accounting for most of it. We have clearly outlined the debate on the added value of 3PL, its advantages and disadvantages, and how it can be successfully used through the selection of the appropriate logistics partner.

As activities of the supply chain are located all over the world and product flows start crossing national boundaries, *global supply chain management* ends up facing the tremendous uncertainties and complexities of the globalized logistics network. All supply chain managers understand well the paralyzing case of the *bullwhip* phenomenon (i.e., demand distortions and variance propagation in a supply chain). They have to live the nightmarish reality of accentuating factors for it in the global supply chain. These factors are:

- Substantial geographic distances that add forecasting difficulties and inaccuracies
- Exchange rates and other macroeconomic uncertainties
- Serious infrastructual inadequacies (worker skills, supply quality, lack of local process equipment and technologies, transportation and telecommunication network inefficiencies)
- Explosive dimensions of product variety in global markets

Firms respond to the challenges of an effective global supply chain network design in many different ways. In order to categorize different logistics networks or supply chain structures, we used the concepts of *modularization* and *postponement*. Modularization is associated with the inbound logistics, since the combination of different modules (components) allows the assembly of the final product. Postponement implies that products tend to get differentiated as they approach the point of actual purchase (i.e., as they flow down the supply chain). Postponement is associated with the outbound logistics. We end up finally defining four supply chain structures:

- Rigid
- Flexible
- Postponed
- Modularized

The *rigid* structure represents the vertically integrated supply chain where the objective is to exploit economies of scale in production of large runs by maintaining large inventories of finished products. The other extreme is the *flexible* structure, where many subcontractors are used to make the different components and the assembly of the final product is conducted in response to known demand. The *modularized* structure has multiple sources for the components but the output of the assembly process is the finished product. Finally, the *postponed* structure exploits economies of scale in making the components but customizes the finished product to satisfy specific customer demand.

Firms use different approaches and concepts in deciding how to choose factory location, and then allocate the production activities to the various facilities of the network. The three most commonly used approaches are:

- Market focus
- Product family focus
- Process focus

We outlined the trade-offs and managerial challenges associated with each of these approaches. The discussion also clarifies the main issues and trade-offs behind the centralization versus decentralization of the global operations and logistics network debate.

Development of *risk management* strategies to effectively hedge against and counteract catastrophic macroeconomic and other shocks is an important challenge facing firms with global operations. We have explicitly discussed risk management of currency exchange shocks. We outlined the different types of a firm's exposure to such shocks:

- Transaction exposure
- Translation exposure
- Operations exposure

Our discussion emphasized operations exposure. We explained in detail the important complicating factors a firm needs to consider in assessing its operating exposure to real exchange rate shocks. These are: customer, competitor, supplier, and government reactions. We presented a single conceptual tool, the so-called *operating exposure matrix,* to help structure the process of understanding the implications for operating exposure of a specific situation. The operational options in managing operating exposure to real exchange rate shocks involve appropriate configuration of the operations and logistics network and exploiting of any operational flexibility built into the operating network of facilities.

The main risk in global sourcing contracts is the currency exchange rate risk. We categorize hedging strategies to deal with such risks in:

- *Macro-level strategies* (i.e., supplier selection, structure of a global sourcing portfolio, flexibility in volume-timing of purchases in sourcing contracts)
- *Micro-level strategies* (i.e., forward contracts, futures contracts, options, risk-sharing sourcing contracts)

Effective combinations of macro-and-micro level strategies can effectively reduce currency exchange rate risk in global sourcing situations.

Implementation aspects of global operations and logistics strategies always account for a significant part of their success. Logistics information systems is a key factor of implementation success. We have outlined many recent developments in this area, and their successful influence for the management of the global supply chain have outlined the issues and challenges in designing a successful logistics information and telecommunication system. We clearly described the role of *electronic data interchange* (EDI) and important implementation aspects of it.

Another important ingredient for the implementation success of global operations and logistics strategies is the design and administration of an effective performance measurement and evaluation system. Performance metrics are described for functional, sectorial, and geographic integration purposes. We also discuss the challenges for performance measurement of logistics service companies and third-party logistics partners. Finally, as we have seen in this last chapter, the development of an appropriate organizational structure is essential for achieving global operations and logistics excellence.

Index

◆ ◆ ◆